PICTURES, INC.

RNIA

NICATION

4, 1947.

VID O. SELZNICK, a resident of the Coun

ate of California, being of sound and d

and not acting under duress, menace, f

of any person whomsoever, do hereby ma

Will and Testam

---

because we couldn't possibly
ever be apart;

Because eleven is a lucky
number — but so is
twelve, and so too is
many times eleven;

And because, with every
fibre of my being,
I adore you.

David

Hotel Pierre
NEW YORK

Thursday

Sweetheart:

Big confession. Last
should waste your preciou
beach-hours looking for
something that isn't. Di
missed a day in this.
series. Wired you yester
day, but didn't write.
Was upset about it for

---

and for the
know the awful
and I can
my work or

---

smart-alecks w
was put into

July 16, 1941

---

hita:

ugh I ha
so hand
toothpi
a formal
ing is th
ivities —
orties!

It was good to hear your voice again,
that as soon as I resume the Sunday grou
l be very soon, we may count
ce. And I do hope you will
whenever you receive an
pping us the news as to the
nt victim.

most affectionate regards
as always,

Sincerely

serv

perso

expen

---

my trip to the Retreat. I had a nice talk with
sit with Howard as well; and I enjoyed the trip

This Book Belongs To:

Amelia
Peddler

SHOWMAN

Showman

THE LIFE OF DAVID O. SELZNICK

DAVID THOMSON

ALFRED A. KNOPF
NEW YORK 1992

This Is a Borzoi Book Published by Alfred A. Knopf, Inc.

Copyright © 1992 by David Thomson

All rights reserved under International and Pan-American Copyright Conventions. Published in the United States by Alfred A. Knopf, Inc., New York, and simultaneously in Canada by Random House of Canada Limited, Toronto. Distributed by Random House, Inc., New York.

Grateful acknowledgment is made to Alfred A. Knopf, Inc. for permission to reprint excerpts from *A Private View* by Irene Mayer Selznick, copyright © 1983 by Irene Mayer Selznick.

Library of Congress Cataloging-in-Publication Data
Thomson, David.
Showman : the life of David O. Selznick / by David Thomson.—1st ed.
p.   cm.
Filmography: p.
Includes bibliographical references and index.
ISBN 0-394-56833-8
1. Selznick, David O., 1902–1965.   2. Motion picture producers and directors—United States—Biography.   I. Title.
PN1998.3.S395T46   1992
791.43'0232'092—dc20
[B]   91-47886   CIP

Manufactured in the United States of America

First Edition

FOR LUCY

CONTENTS

PROLOGUE

THIS WAS the first weekend of the war and the last of the summer vacation for 1939. On Monday, the kids would be back in school. But, before then, as the newspapers warned on Saturday morning, the Nazis would have entered Warsaw. On Friday, President Roosevelt had proclaimed a national emergency and the Soviet army had mobilized. The Los Angeles *Times* ran pictures of the first air raid in London. That city had few sirens yet, and so there were photographs of a man in a tin hat on a bicycle wearing placards—"Take Cover" and "Raiders Passed." London was still like a village.

"Tonight," said Hal Kern to David O. Selznick early on the morning of Saturday the ninth. "We'll go tonight."

And the boss grinned in that mixture of panic, delight, and sheer mischief typical of D.O.S. The look alarmed Kern, who had been planning a secret operation.

"Don't tell anyone," said Kern.

"Right!" David agreed.

"Go home a little early—"

"Right!"

"Say you're not feeling so good—"

"Terrific!"

"And we'll come by and pick you up."

"Yes!" said David, with only the rest of the day to negotiate.

The studios worked all day Saturdays then, just as they went into overtime whenever they had to. It was only the war and the new union powers that brought five-day weeks and eight-hour days. On that Saturday, the offices of Selznick International were doing business as usual. It was the second day of shooting on Alfred Hitchcock's *Rebecca*—as that picture got under way there was reason for Selznick to be edgy and impatient. But the opening of *Intermezzo* was only a month away, and the detail of its campaign had to be pursued.

The day was warm. By ten in the morning it was 80 degrees in Los Angeles; by noon it was 90 degrees. Everyone was going to the beach. In the early afternoon, the radio news was of fighting on the outskirts of Warsaw; Britain was reckoning on a three-year war, while spokesmen in Vienna expected it would all be over in a week. The Boston Red Sox slugger Jimmie Foxx had had to have an appendectomy. Now it was certain the Yankees would win the pennant. That afternoon they beat the Washington Senators 5–2, and DiMaggio went three for four.

By four o'clock it was 85 degrees. David yawned and said he was going home.

The car drove him north from Culver City, on Club Drive and Motor, across Pico and then by Roxbury across Olympic and Wilshire (past his brother Myron's office building) and on to Sunset, then north by way of Benedict Canyon, and up the twisting Summit Drive to 1050. David's wife, Irene, and his best friend and partner, Jock Whitney, were waiting for him in the elegant house. The Selznick boys, Jeffrey and Danny, seven and three, were in the care of a nanny. They would not get their normal hour with their mother that evening.

Around five o'clock, two black limousines came through the gates of 1050. David, Jock, and Irene got into one car. The other held Hal Kern, Selznick's chief editor, and Bobbie Keon, his script assistant. There were also more than fifty cans of motion picture and sound track. For a film still being edited, the picture and the sound were separate. And if a film ran about four and a half hours, on ten-minute reels, there had to be that many cans.

Kern's car set off in the lead. He had still not said where they were going. He was still not quite sure. For if any arrangements had been risked ahead of time, then the word might have got out. There could have been reporters waiting for the sneak preview. *Gone With the Wind* had been over three years in the making. David had driven himself and the movie world crazy waiting for it and wondering. By September 1939, who could tell whether the public was eager, exhausted, desperate, or angry? Was the picture a white elephant or the key to the kingdom?

The two cars headed east, past Hollywood, past downtown, past Covina and Pomona, toward . . . toward Arizona maybe? While it was evening now, the heat did not abate, for they were driving toward the desert.

In Riverside that day, a suburban town fifty miles from the Pacific, the temperature had reached 104 degrees.

They were looking for a movie theater, the right kind, big enough with the equipment for double-head projection and one with a full house and a movie that was in the same league as their more than fifty cans of work in progress.

It was Kern's decision. Sometime after 7:30 p.m. he pulled up outside the Fox theater in Riverside. The theater was playing a double bill: *Hawaiian Nights* and the big picture, the recently opened *Beau Geste*, starring Gary Cooper.

Kern got out to talk business. But David would not let him do it alone. Kern called for the manager of the Fox.

"Would you run a preview?" he asked the man.

"Tonight? What have you got?"

"It's long. It's over four hours," said Kern.

The manager looked at David, who would have been grinning.

The manager was not an idiot.

"I'm David O. Selznick," said David, just in case.

"Terrific!" said the manager. And David chuckled. He turned around to laugh for Jock and Irene, still in the car. It was going to be all right. *Gone With the Wind* was going to meet its public at last. David's sense of mischief enjoyed the notion of squeezing four and a half hours into the middle of a double bill. Yet both his panic and his delight rose to the occasion, out there at Riverside, getting on for 8:00 p.m. and eighty-five degrees, on what might be the greatest night of his life.

ᎠOP'S BEST BOY

1 · LIVING IN THE FUTURE

ON A MISTY, sunny afternoon in February 1991, the biographer was in an apartment close to Beverly Hills High School, waiting to talk to a man who had known all the Selznicks. Sam Jaffe had been studio manager at Paramount in the late 1920s, then a producer and an agent. Now he was a couple of months shy of ninety. He came into the living room—a room of fine, modern paintings—dressed in a crimson track suit. Not that Jaffe did much jogging, but he had been to take his class at U.C.L.A. As a student.

I asked him about Lewis J., the father of David Selznick.

"Yeah, I knew Lewis J. In the last years of his life, I used to play poker with him. David and Myron, his two sons, they staked him with a little money for the game. This was after L.J. had gone broke, you see. We used to take a room at the Roosevelt Hotel to play—L.J., me, and usually Chico Marx. This was just before L.J. died. Early 1930s."

"How old did L.J. seem to be when he died?"

"Oh, late seventies, I'd say."

"He was only sixty-three."

"Is that right? He seemed a lot older."

"Did he ever talk about his childhood in Russia?"

"Russia? I never knew about that."

The past had gone—maybe that's why Lewis J. seemed so much older than he really was. Starting again that drastically can age you.

Lewis J. Selznick is little known now, even in Hollywood. But he was a big shot once. In the books that do mention him he is referred to as the father of David O. Selznick. It is an epitaph in which he would have rejoiced. For even if he had made, and lost, $10 million once, when $10 million was money, there was nothing in his life to match his feeling for

David. And there were those later on who lived with David, and loved him, who wondered if he had ever recovered from the unsettling estate of big shot to which his father had raised him.

Pioneer big shots must come from nowhere and nothing—that is how Russia could remain unknown to a poker friend. No class of people has ever had such a chance (or such a need) at being big shots as the immigrants who came to America out of the confusions of Eastern Europe in the second half of the nineteenth century. They had much to escape or forget: poverty, another language, a religion, the soldiers of the Tsar, intricate family obligations, perhaps even wives, children, and old promises. They were often brave or reckless people to have come so far, so ready to gamble. But they were sometimes racked with guilt over many kinds of betrayal. So they needed a fresh story that put them in a good light. How providential that the new industry of motion pictures lay waiting for some of these newcomers, all desperate and determined to be good Americans with knockout stories.

Around the year 1920, David's father, Lewis, had a net worth of over $11 million—at least, in prospectuses, he did. He threw that money and its perks around. Yet he was not so generous with the personal history that made the $11 million astounding. So David had only an image of his father materializing out of the hard times of Russia. No doubt the father preferred to stress the present and the future. For he had begun again in America and earned the right of putting his past behind him. David liked to call Lewis J. "the only gentleman in the business." Yet he heard the stories and saw evidence of his father's real wildness. There were rivals to Lewis J. alarmed at his brazen ways; they said he brought disgrace on immigrants, on Jews, and on moving pictures. He flaunted his sudden wealth; he behaved as if America was a gambling casino instead of a paradise for new conservatives.

David was the darling of his father. Pop's influence on him was vast and unquestioned. For as Pop encouraged David, so the boy justified and exaggerated the father. In David's eyes, Pop was not just a great man but a crucial innovator in the picture business. Whereas history would have forgotten Lewis J. but for his sons. Whenever David chose to recollect, there was a hint of vagueness and conflicting strains: "I only remember him as a wonderful man and a wonderful father, a very gentle man, and a man on the other hand of great courage and great foresight, great gambling instincts."

Lewis Selznick did spread his bets around. In his lifetime, he sent information to *The National Cyclopedia of American Biography* saying he had been born in Kiev, Russia, on May 2, 1872. Yet in one of the few documents about him—and signed by him—he said he was born in Poland on May 5, 1871. There are more reliable suggestions of 1869 as the year of his birth, and it seems clear, from the claims of his wife, that he was actually born in or close to Kovno (or Kaunas), in what has been for centuries the troubled state of Lithuania.

David Selznick was never exactly a man's man, and so he may have been daunted by the legend of his father's physical courage—how Pop walked out of Russia when he was twelve, frustrated at an overcrowded home and by every other obstacle and impediment presented to an ambitious young Jew. There was something of David Copperfield in it.

It's a good story, with Joseph the father of Lewis J., a lusty man whose wives wilted from the efforts of giving birth so often and who took on younger women to match his strength. Lewis Joseph, it seems, was the firstborn of the first marriage, the son of a woman named Ida. The twelve-year-old had gumption, courage, and legs to make his escape. This is a boy who gathered up just a few things, denied himself farewells, and walked away into a distance he could not understand. You know this scene from movies: it is Vito Corleone, alone on the ship, watching Liberty slide into view.

This Lewis Joseph would have walked from Kaunas to the sea—to Riga, Danzig, or Hamburg. And from there he went by ship to England where, in the early 1880s, it is said, he worked in a factory earning more money for his greater westward passage. This is so good a story that one can understand Lewis J. being careful with it—even to the point of not mentioning that his father, the mighty Joseph, lived not in Russia in 1900, but in Cleveland, Ohio.

As far as I can discover, David O. Selznick made no written or spoken reference to his grandfather, Joseph Seleznik (this is not a misspelling, but it is not to be taken as gospel either). His first wife, Irene, had never heard of this grandfather, though she did recollect a passing mention of some relative in Cleveland with "many children"—some sort of rogue.

Joseph Seleznik was born in Russia, he claimed, in January 1851, in a village called Amixt. This was in Lithuania, but the family were Russian Jews, and the name suggested that its owners had once dealt in green things—fields, grass, or possibly rare metals. Some stories say Joseph was a forester or a landowner even—though when he became American, in 1893, he said he was a dealer in barrels. This Joseph married: Ida Ringer was the wife's name, and they had six or seven surviving children, all born in Russia. The boys were Lewis (though possibly Louis once), Solomon, and David, and there were at least three girls, Jenny, Sarah, and Lillian. One story has it that Joseph's father had been a rabbi. Yet the point of that story is only to explain why few Selznicks stayed Orthodox.

Lewis's American naturalization papers say he arrived in the country in 1888. Further, it is the firm recollection of Milton Selznick, the son of Lewis's younger brother Solomon, that Solomon was also in America, aged about thirteen, in the year of the Johnstown flood, 1889. Moreover, Milton believes that Lewis and Solomon came to America together.

Lewis J. Seleznick became an American citizen on September 29, 1894, in the Court of Common Pleas for Allegheny County, in Pittsburgh. Six months later, on March 27, 1895, his father, Joseph Seleznik, received the same rights of naturalization in Cuyahoga County, Ohio, in Cleveland. His application was filled out by a clerk and signed in Cyrillic script; it said Joseph had arrived in America on February 20, 1889. By then he was already married to his second wife, Libbie Fine, and that marriage had been made in Russia. It is likely that the first wife, Ida, had died in Russia. But it is not impossible that she was just left there. The second marriage produced children, too, including a son, Hyman, born in Cleveland in 1893. Apparently, Libbie died very shortly thereafter, and the children of that marriage were adopted by their uncle, Louis Fine. Thus Hyman became Hyman Fine, a popular orchestra conductor on stage and radio.

Such an adoption suggests there were those who regarded Joseph as a wayward parent. Such attitudes can only have been added to when, on January 20, 1894, he married for the third time and chose a twenty-three-year-old Austrian, Celia Parness, who had been in America less than a year. This union had four new children, all in Cleveland: Lottie, Rose, Philip, and Leo. By 1900, they lived in Cleveland, at 159 Orange Street. They had been joined by Israel Yochel, aged thirty-eight, a son-in-law—it would be said later that Joseph had twenty-one children, thirteen of whom lived to middle age.

All thirteen children were in America by the time David was born. Joseph and at least six children from his first marriage had ended up in Ohio or Pennsylvania. They may not all have come at once, but it was generally the way that immigrant families traveled in relay, one or two at a time, according to a plan. While Lewis J. would be the most successful of his generation, none of the others did badly. Evidently, the family had some funds, much nerve, and ample ability. If Lewis J. walked, it was with instructions and good shoes, to say nothing of a ticket on the boat (and a younger brother for company). But if he changed the story—especially for his sons—it was because success needs to feel safely out of reach and because a big shot wants greater things yet. So Pop raised David to adore and aim at that great rival to family—the audience.

An audience is made of strangers. Talk to them, and you are talking to yourself. The charm, the heroism, and also the comic folly of David Selznick lay in his habit of hearing what he hoped and believing what he heard—especially when it was him talking. That optimism swept him past barriers of realism as if the urging were wind and reality just a flapping door. And in his work he made worlds that he longed to inhabit. They were movies, without actual substance or comfort, but for David they were houses where he wanted to be. Put like that, it sounds a little crazy. But David had a hunch there was an audience ready to go with him, and humankind took no form that pleased him more than that of audience.

Lewis J. Selznick was a heartfelt dynast who bound his three sons into the business. Yet he did not tell David about his grandfather, and he left the youth to wonder about family ties in Russia. Suppose that Lewis was sent out of Russia ahead of the father, like a pioneer; suppose that he resented later stepmothers and was never sure or happy about what happened to his mother. Suppose Joseph was too uncouth or controlling a man for him. Something made for detachment. It could have been that Flossie Sachs, the wife Lewis found in 1896 or 1897, disapproved of Joseph. David's recollection was that it was his mother who eventually recommended dropping Seleznick for Selznick. In that simple elision, Europeanness was replaced by the promise of Americans who could sell you anything.

The Sachs family were socially acceptable in Pittsburgh. They had come from Lithuania as well. Hyman, the father, was dead, but he had held the role of chicken-killer. His wife, Libbie, lived on with a son and four daughters on Dinwiddie Street. The son, Charles, was a brilliant example of how far a newcomer might go. Forceps had broken his back in the moment of delivery, leaving him a hunchback. But after only six years of formal schooling, he passed the bar at the University of Pittsburgh Law School at the age of nineteen. So young, he had to wait two years before he could practice. This Uncle Charlie was a stooped figure of wisdom and counsel not just for the Sachs family, but for the Selznicks, too.

Flossie, or Florence, had been born on July 5, 1875, near Vilnius, only fifty miles from Kaunas. She was a large, cheerful young woman, practical, down-to-earth, not inclined to fall for nonsense and with a reasonable sense of social superiority toward her husband-to-be. She was a better poker player than he was. Yet she learned to abide by his recklessness, and before long her allegiances were given over to the Selznicks. She would be the first woman in the life of David Selznick, a man not just fond of women, but their disciple. It should have been a crucial relationship. But the father was the far stronger parent, and it is worth noting that, whatever her qualities of perseverance and reliability, Florence was not pretty or seductive. Further, she had learned long before David was able to understand that she could do nothing to control or subdue her restless, inventive, self-destructive hus-

4743 Ben Venue Street, Pittsburgh, in the spring of 1903. Myron, David (in carriage), Howard, and the maid. Flossie sits on the verandah, and Pop is the likely cameraman.

band. Lewis J. spent his money; Florence saved so that there were secret supplies ready for the crashes.

Pittsburgh is only a little over a hundred miles from Cleveland. In the 1890s, that could be another world. It is equally possible that Lewis went back and forth between the two cities until such time as he learned to concentrate on the future. When he took out a license to marry Flossie Sachs, on October 15, 1896, he lived at 1311 Bluff Street in Pittsburgh, and he gave his occupation as Secretary of the Nickel Savings Bank. But by the late 1890s, Lewis J. had several jewelry stores in the Pittsburgh area, the most notable of which, the Keystone, was at Fifth Avenue and Smithfield Street. He called himself a diamond expert.

It was with at least a base in Pittsburgh, experimenting in precious stones and the raising of money, that Lewis and Flossie had their children and had them as Americans. The first was Howard, born in 1897, on November 11, about thirteen months after the marriage license was taken out. Howard was long-lived: he did not die until 1980. Yet there was something wrong with him, and at this distance it is difficult to pinpoint the problem exactly. Most of the Selznicks preferred to remain in doubt over Howard.

Irene Mayer, when she married into the family, saw Howard as an example of his parents' ability to look the other way whenever awkwardness occurred. They "denied reality even when faced with it; they chose escape and optimism. For instance, they finessed Howard, their firstborn; they simply ducked his problem—he had suffered a slight brain damage at birth." It was supposed to have been the result of a forceps delivery. Yet no medical treatment noted this at the time or gave his "retardation" special treatment. Decades later, when Howard was permanently hospitalized, doctors passed no opinion on the family's claim that there had been "cerebral injury at birth." By then, Howard was married with two children. Both those children were to suffer from mental illness. Whatever Howard's condition, he was overlooked until such time as he was an embarrassment, and then he was removed. For David, in later life, Howard was a cause for increasing concern and insoluble guilt. For Lewis and Flossie, in 1897 and 1898, he must have posed so many awkward questions that the unquenchably optimistic Lewis ignored him, while Flossie had to endure an imperfect firstborn.

There is a birth certificate for the next child: Myron Charles was born on October 8, 1898, at 44 Federal Street in Pittsburgh. He was without evident flaw; indeed, he would prove tough, clever, charismatic, and the most competent person the family ever possessed. With relief, the mother heaped her love on this boy so that there would not be enough left for David. In the event, no amount of ability or maternal fondness could keep Myron from self-loathing: if suicidal alcoholism means unstable, then Myron, too, was a disturbed person. He was also, in an odd way, both the oldest and the second son in the family; he would feel responsible for the Selznick name in the way of a firstborn, but he would have a burden to look after, an older liability to take out and about.

A daughter was born, in 1899 or 1900. Her name was Ruth, but there is no record of her and she was dead before the age of two. Irene Mayer was told that Ruth had died from blood poisoning after a minor infection in her foot. There was a hint of neglect, of being caught unawares, though the family now had a maid who lived with them, Lizzie Swilsky, an Austrian.

Then on May 10, 1902, in Pittsburgh, probably at 4743 Ben Venue Street, David was born, once more without documentary records. He was alert, gentle, pretty, and he had a terrific smile—his father's heart opened to him. Something in Lewis J. had gambled on waiting, and with this fourth child he had found someone to treasure. Once David was born, people could see how tough Myron was. There would be no more children. Instead, a year later, as soon as David was able to walk, Pop moved them all farther away to New York.

Just a few years later, in 1908, still in Cleveland, Joseph Seleznik died. That past had fallen away. The only one of his four grandparents that David ever knew was Libbie Sachs, his mother's mother. Misspelled Selznicks were left behind and when, decades later, some of them tried to get reacquainted with lucky David, the smash-hit kid was torn all ways. He clung to the idea of family. He would make up stories about family ties and the resonance of home. He was raised in nepotism, and he would marry into the business and then find an actress for his second wife. Yet he was always ruinously confused over it. "One relative in a place, and the worm is in the apple," he told his mother as late as 1949.

2 · LIBERALITY AND QUICK ACTION

LEWIS J. SELZNICK did not thrust himself into pictures until 1913. In other words, he and his family had ten years in the New York area, a decade of trial and error, of search and disappointment, that helps account for the scorn with which L.J. later regarded the film business. The family was far from poor or pressed. Flossie's greatest problem was in moderating her husband's schemes and in hoping the boys would not take them too seriously.

The Keystone Stores in Pittsburgh were not yet given up. The Lewis Selznick name was kept on them, and brother Sol took over as manager. Lewis led wife and boys to the smart Bay Ridge area of Brooklyn, and it was at 425 Fiftieth Street that David passed his infancy. L.J. had a new jewelry

Howard, David, and Myron in 1907

*Outside 425 Fiftieth
Street, Brooklyn*

store in Manhattan, the Knickerbocker, at Sixth Avenue and Twenty-third Street. But he was out of that business by 1907, looking around for something new with just the gravel of precious stones in his pants pockets to impress others. What next? Patent promoting and wholesale electrical supplies, but L.J. was ready for anything. Between 1908 and 1909, the family name changed from Seleznick to Selznick.

David and Myron both attended P.S. 94 (at 5010 Sixth Avenue in Brooklyn). David was there from May 1907 to June 1910. Howard must have been there, too, but as his younger brothers passed him by, the older brother dropped out of family discussion. Howard learned to read and write, he had a talent for music otherwise absent in the family, and he showed an innocent interest in general knowledge. But he made mistakes, his handwriting was hard to decipher, and he was "slow." There is a picture of the three boys in their Brooklyn era with a pony and cart. Their clothes and rig show how well the father was doing. The boys wear good suits, neckties, and hats.

One teacher at P.S. 94, Miss May Cushing, recalled David as "a little boy with curly hair and a low voice—a diffident, bashful lad." Myron was the exact opposite, a dominant and manipulative young man. Years later, David looked back on their school days and described his brother's perverse prowess:

> His tendency to become a perfectly legal outlaw was early demonstrated at school, where it was his habit to refuse to join the school teams—despite a natural athletic tendency—and to organize rival teams within the school, with no rules for training, for the purpose of challenging and defeating the school teams.

David had no aptitude for sports. Though a large boy for his age—he would tower over Myron by the time he was eighteen—he was soft and ungainly. He was diffident and romantic, whereas Myron was already priding himself on being laconic and to the point. But they were two rapid brains: that and the lumpish Howard were what they shared. Without Howard there as a diversion, Myron might have been more of the bully to David. As it was, Myron got into a lot of fights over being Jewish and defending the gentler David. But just as Myron privately reveled in scathing anti-Semitic remarks, so he needled David at home and "taught" him fisticuffs. There was a bond between them, but not everyone mistook it for absolute sympathy. In so many ways they were opposites, with parents who made it clear where their allegiances lay. This is a reminder that Lewis and Flossie seldom seem like a couple: I have seen no photograph of just the two of them together. Flossie loved the shining hardness of Myron, and Lewis was crazy about the good nature of David.

Myron laughed at David and called him "a chump." But he must have been envious of the time their father lavished on the bookish David. Lewis had had to learn English, and in the process he had come to revere the classics. People said he spoke with an odd accent, half Russian and half English. He told David to read Tolstoy and Dickens—and David claimed to have read *Anna Karenina* and *David Copperfield* at a very tender age so that he could discuss them with his father.

In time, David would make movies of both those books—and one is so good teachers still use it to encourage students daunted by so many pages. Books were a way ahead, and Lewis inspired David over the whole enterprise of being literary. Myron in later life wrote as economically as military orders. For good and ill, David filled his life with memos, to the exclusion of life itself. This, too, was the influence of his father:

> my father was very proud of my "compositions," even when I was extremely young, and this encouraged me to try to improve my vocabulary. So I found myself night after night with a dictionary by my side, laboriously looking up all the words in the classics that I couldn't understand. This process was so slow that naturally the scenes engraved themselves indelibly on my mind. . . . I can to this day tell the exact details of scenes from books that I read when I must have been somewhere between ten and twelve years old.

David's room was a small library and a measure of how his tastes surpassed his brothers'. Howard had thirty-three books in his room, Myron a bare ten, including a history of the Great War. In David's room there were over 200 volumes: *Everybody's Encyclopedia*, the *Encyclopaedia Britannica*, a ten-volume photographic history of the American Civil War, and the collected works of Charles Dickens and Sir Walter Scott.

By the time David was twenty-one, his literary tastes were set on an earlier gilded age. There was no Dreiser, no James, no Edith Wharton or Booth Tarkington. He might seem the bookworm in the household, but David's reading looked back to times and countries he had never known.

As a producer, David loved to rebuild that past. He hardly made a film where the modern world would stand forth stark, urgent, or lovely. As an independent operator, he would take as his headquarters a property that resembled an old manor house. And, like Gustave Flaubert and Emma Bovary, David's most characteristic imaginings dealt with the struggles of ill-starred heroines. He was a regular boy: he watched girls, he chased them, grabbed at warm bodies. Yet he also wrote them poems and other "romances" and felt himself close to the spirit of lovelorn women with worlds to move.

He was not only a reader of books. There is another photograph of the three boys a few years later: David is about thirteen. The three of them are sitting on a brocaded sofa in a salon where net curtains soften the light. The ample figure of Flossie presides over the scene, lounging against the sofa, leaning toward Myron. Howard is in the middle, arms folded, leaning to one side; he could be braced, as if he had some difficulty in sitting up straight. He is not far from twenty, and he has a cheery grin that nearly conceals the slight disparity in direction of his eyes. Myron sits at one end of the sofa, in the gloom, his face sleek, round, and cocky, like a balloon above his collar. He could be a bodyguard to Howard; there is already the panache of a would-be gangster.

David is not attending to the picture. He sits at the other end of the sofa in a suit, tie, and spectacles, eyes demurely down on a newspaper. There is a suggestion that he would just as soon not be a part of this family. A ghostly smile rests on his fleshy face. His mouth is curved and frilled, while Myron's is a blunt, zippered line.

There was tension between David and Myron, but even as boys, they seemed to some people like fast friends and allies. In their later dealings, fondness and respect were cloaked in challenging banter. They had a competition for success, with Myron the early leader and David the eventual winner. Onlookers were impressed with them both, but "David was brighter than Myron—if not as shrewd—he had a creative quality." All of which helped foster the uneasiness central to David's being. He wanted to make himself into a kind of Myron.

How did Lewis J. Selznick get into the motion picture business? Perhaps he was lost at the time. Or, if you prefer, he had been waiting several years for the opportune moment. Do not rule out the possibility of a decision taken casually and on the spur of the moment.

In 1910 or 1911, Pop moved the family to Manhattan, to 445 Riverside Drive, and in the telephone directory he called himself a promoter. It was in 1913, in New York, that he ran into an old acquaintance from Pittsburgh, Mark Dintenfass, who had been in the herring trade before becoming a stockholder in the Universal Film Manufacturing Company. That horizon-testing name was the disguise for an untidy, eager enterprise that had lately emerged victorious in a struggle with the Motion Picture Patents Company. Under its leader, Carl Laemmle, German-born and both a jeweler and a clothier before he turned to pictures, Universal had resisted the monopolistic tendencies of the new film business in its first ten years. That was often a street war, with film cans pillaged, projectors smashed, and nickelodeons requiring protection. As in most fresh and sudden businesses, the pioneers had made their own laws; uninhibited contest determined what would soon be seasoned tradition. We are dealing with the unscrupulous, those gangsters and geniuses who read *Variety*, and whose chief ambition was to secure power for themselves before laying down a new age of law, order, profit, and conservatism.

So what follows could have a glimmering of truth behind it, *or* it just shows the importance of being in a position to tell the stories that will last.

Universal was suffering from an impasse of control in which its two partners, Laemmle and an Irishman, Pat Powers, would not talk to each other. Mark Dintenfass was apparently dismayed by this state of affairs and anxious to sell his shares before confusion stopped all business. He turned to Lewis J. Selznick, a guy who could sell anything. Thus, L.J. walked into the Universal office, on Broadway, to unload the Dintenfass stock. It is said that rather than charm Laemmle or Powers with requests to buy their own paper, he first spilled his pocketful of gems on their desks to catch their attention.

He did a deal, or he didn't; the story varies. It is more important that he got a smell of the business and saw an empty office on the premises. So he sat himself down there and in the lunch hour went out and purchased a "General Manager" sign which he put on his bare desk. In time, attention, interest, and even business gravitated toward this self-appointed functionary. As he became more noticeable and decisive in Universal affairs, Laemmle and Powers asked where he had come from. He told each one that the other had appointed him.

It is as hard to believe this story as it is to exclude it. For without it, there is nothing to be said about Lewis J. and Universal—the records of this early show business have gone, along with most of its product. There is no good documentary evidence for the Selznick-as-manager story. It comes instead from Terry Ramsaye's book, *A Million and One Nights*, a racy romance, and an early instance of the show business book and its need to deliver anecdotes. But the yarn never stops: in 1988 Neal Gabler employed it in *An Empire of Their Own*, a book praised for its historical research.

All of which testifies to Lewis Selznick's acute understanding of how publicity was affecting American discourse. For Terry Ramsaye was well known to L.J. The great story is not one that Powers or Laemmle were likely to repeat. Whereas L.J. is not just its hero and active begetter; he is the raison d'être. If he didn't have the nerve to take over that office, then he had the wit to tell the story of it. And who was most likely to hear the tallest of L.J.'s stories—when they wearied of analyzing Tolstoy? Why David, his favored son, the kid whose lovely face was torn between credulity and disdain.

L.J. did not last at Universal—how boring that post would have been once the joke was revealed. He said that Laemmle and Powers fired him in outrage; they were reunited at last. But something was liberated in L.J.: an innate ability for self-promotion, chutzpah, and flimflam, an energy hitherto thwarted or restrained. He was in his forties, but he was on his way, a short, stocky man whose wavy, fair hair was going gray and whose prim, settled look concealed helpless cunning and a taste for risk.

Even Ramsaye guessed he was being used and taken. It was Ramsaye who would invent the verb "Selznicked" to describe those who discovered their shirts had vanished during a conversation. Ramsaye called L.J. a "jester" who burst in on the banquet of the picture business "to thumb his nose toward the head of the table and make impertinent remarks while he helped himself to the wine and meats."

It was Groucho-like, the way L.J. operated; he was loath to be in a club that would have him, and he was so cocky he would tell Congress in 1917 that "less brains are necessary in the motion picture business than in any other." In ten weeks, he said, he turned capital of $1,000 into $105,000. Such tricks were not uncommon in those days. But there were two types of characters in the business: the adult kids who could not hide their amazement and who spent their money as ostentatiously as possible, and the pillars of rectitude who thought it was giving away the game to talk of money, success, or the crazy, greased ease with which such things came. Discretion would keep others away: the best of the lucky prospectors took vows of silence. There was also that desperate wish in recently impoverished Jewish immigrants—scrap men, herring merchants, rag trade salesmen, costume jewelers—to be taken as American gentlemen. From the very earliest days there was an earnest desire on the part of those upstart hustlers to treat wealth as a private part and to allay any fears that the movies were an immoral sensation visited on sound American minds by the Jews. This is the essential contrast between Lewis J. Selznick and Louis B. Mayer, who would himself employ the term "to Selznick" as a measure of abuse, once he read it in Ramsaye's book.

With some knowledge and some reputation, L.J. was meeting the right people—other leaders in the picture business and those who might put up money for a smart venture. He was present when the future Warner Brothers first organized in 1913. It was in 1914 that Lewis J. attached himself to the emerging World Film Corporation. This was a loose gathering of companies and interests engaged in producing films, with a nationwide system of exchanges and theaters where they could be shown. Lewis got in through legitimate theatrical contacts, for he had been angeling plays in a small way, and one large force in pictures then was the urge to put hit plays on film so that provincial audiences could see them.

David was taken along to some of these plays when he was ten and eleven—there is no suggestion of mother or brothers going, too. He was editing a school newspaper then—all done on the typewriter Lewis had given him—and he may have been taken to the theater as a budding critic. For the father's love took the boy's views very seriously. And at about the same time (he would have been twelve), David was "dragged down to a big Long Island estate where I sat on the porch while my father organized the World Film Company—with my father occasionally directing questions at me."

Twenty and thirty years later, David had weekends of his own on Long Island, with the Whitneys and the Paleys. He reckoned his father was a pioneer in many ways, but above all in going to Wall Street for his funding. Again, that may be just what the father told the boy, but Lewis J. was a special kind of connection in the World arrangement. He knew theater people and bankers, and he was sure he could sell the product. After all, a diamond ring was meant to last a lifetime. But a movie had revolutionary possibilities. For the studio brought out a new one every two or three days!

In the first six months of 1914, World took shape. The directors included Lee Shubert, the theatrical impresario, as vice president; Jules Brulatour, the distributor of Eastman film stock; Van Horn Ely of Wall Street and the National Properties Company was president; Briton Busch was secretary and treasurer; and Lewis J. Selznick was both vice president and the holder of the office he had invented, general manager.

In a year, World had profits of $329,000. L.J. talked to the trade press as if they were his equals: "They tell me I have succeeded in the film business. If I have it is because of two things—liberality and quick action. I have been willing to share profits with others who could contribute to the making of these profits and I have moved fast—I have consummated deals while others were talking about them."

3 * THE STANDARD OF
       SELZNICK PICTURES

BETWEEN THE AGES of about twelve and twenty-one, David
Selznick's view of the world and his place in it was transformed. His father
went from being a scrambling huckster to one of the most paper-rich men
in America. Pop catered to the boy's every wish to be in the business, even
at the expense of schooling. For Lewis J. had made his way by educating
himself. Why did David need any other teacher?

Sometime in 1915, the five Selznicks moved to "a good, solid apartment house" at 590 West End Avenue (close to Eighty-ninth Street).
Howard, by then, had been retired from school, and he was given sinecures
in L.J.'s business. But he was not bound to attend the office, so he began to
explore the city on his own. The others were too busy now to look after
him, and Howard could get by—as events would prove. He was "a nice
doddering fellow," observed a friend of the family, "but he had a distant
look and you couldn't carry on a conversation with him. He shook a bit. I
think Lewis J. Selznick had a slight palsy, too." This is the first warning that
the exuberant L.J., carrying all before him, was himself not quite sound. He
had been suffering from diabetes since about 1906 and doing very little
for it.

For a while, David and Myron attended P.S. 165, on West 109th Street.
But by January 1, 1916, David was a pupil at the Hamilton Institute for Boys,
at 599 West End Avenue, under the guidance of the principal, N. Archibald
Shaw. He was "a fake, an old windbag," said Sam Marx, a fellow student,
"and the school had no substance. . . . It was a dishonest school. I don't
believe their scholastic standards reached above the ground. Their report
cards didn't mean a thing."

There is evidence for this claim: in February 1917, David's weekly
report card shows a 94.3 average, including 100 for Deportment, 98 for
Spelling, 95 for American and English Literature, and 95 for Stenography.
Yet a few years later, when Mr. Shaw was obliged to supply a general
reference for David, he conceded that in the school year of 1917–18 (David's
last—he dropped out in March 1918), his highest mark was 70, and he failed
geometry, physics, and French.

In June 1918, David took the College Entrance Examination Board in
New York, and he scored as follows:

English Literature	60
American and Civil Government	51
French	14
Algebra	47

The same year, he tried the entrance exam for Columbia University with these results:

English	50
Mathematics	66
Algebra	12
Trigonometry	37
French	18
American History	32

Sam Marx took pride in being late for school, but whatever time he arrived David would come in fifteen minutes later. Why did he need to study when he was already forging ahead in the picture business? David was apprentice to a sorcerer, and he was beginning to behave like a man—or like a teenager playing the part. Another childhood friend was Niven Busch, the son of Briton Busch, who became treasurer at World. As Busch recalled it (he was a year younger than David), his father had been installed by "a group of Wall Street risk-money entrepreneurs to watch their investment." Briton Busch was available for this role because he had gone broke on Wall Street and been banned from the stock exchange for five years. But watching L.J. and the money was no easy task, according to Niven Busch:

> It was very hard to track old Lewis J. down. He was an extraordinary man. Had a wizard brain—I think he was much more intelligent than his peers, like Jesse Lasky, Louis B. Mayer, Joe Schenck. But the trouble was he was so smart he met himself coming round the corner.

Niven met David at the office of the World Film Corporation at 130 West Forty-sixth Street. They might eat together at a nearby chicken rotisserie. And David—"He was kind of the gofer and errand boy"—would let the Busch kid sweep out the cutting rooms.

"I *was* rather in awe of David," said Busch, recalling their heady teenage years. "He was precociously mature. He was more sophisticated than I was. He was going to bed with girls when I was buggering off. And he was a very bright fellow."

It was already David's habit as soon as school let out—or as soon as he got out—to make his way downtown to the World offices to absorb all aspects of the business—smelling the celluloid, watching the cutters at work, or chatting with the young actresses. Money was not scarce, and

Pop in his prime

sometimes David would take a taxi over the river to the studios at Fort Lee, New Jersey, where many World films were shot. Then, at the end of the day, he'd ride home with his father, "discussing the picture business, and learning a great deal that was useful to me later on."

The world was telling David his father was a marvel—instead of just an adventurer, a gambler, and an opportunist. Moreover, L.J. was making the Selznick name famous, and as the city's first electric signs went up in the night sky—"Selznick Pictures Make Happy Hours"—so David could rise to the height of those illuminated letters.

World had grown too cramped for L.J.—or he was too bumptious for them. He moved away, into independence, by taking one of World's best properties, the actress Clara Kimball Young. She was twenty-six in 1916, a star and a beauty with long hair, wounded eyes, and languid poses. At World, she had been bait to exhibitors: to get her pictures they must take a quantity of duller films. But L.J. would showcase her, boosting the asking price by isolating the star's material. He formed the Clara Kimball Young Corporation (of which he was president and general manager). To escape World recriminations, he had Flossie take Miss Young to Havana for a rest. On their return, the actress was provided with an apartment across the hall at 590 West End Avenue. One day, Charlie Sachs's daughter Rena was at the West End Avenue apartment for dinner with her mother. They arrived early and caught Clara Kimball Young in the parlor in a sexy clinch with the actor Eugene O'Brien.

There was gossip and a story about Flossie and Clara receiving fine sable coats at about the same time. Was L.J. having an affair with his star? There is only suggestive, scenariolike evidence. But he was behaving in such a way that a fourteen-year-old son, precocious and on the rise, very likely believed he was. And no one ever accused Lewis J. of not taking a chance. Added to which, it was only a short time until L.J. and Clara would be locked in litigation, which is so often the sequel to infatuation in show business.

The question is not minor: David would give up a great deal for an actress. Beautiful women were being chosen from the populace of the world, adorned, bedecked, and taken to 1916's most thrilled anticipation of abandon. They were being lit, posed, and photographed and put up on the wall for millions to speculate over. And a few men—many of them homely, some ugly, and most of them of a race shunned by lovely American girls—were doing the choosing.

Once L.J. was set up on his own, as Lewis J. Selznick Enterprises (a holdall for many other companies) at 729 Seventh Avenue, David became an official employee. By November 1916, he had his own letterhead paper printed for "Reports on Personages" at 590 West End Avenue. And on November 15, he typed out his first extant memo. It is to his father, and it says all we need to know about the pomp and earnestness of a fourteen-year-old and the delicate family situation he enjoyed.

> Dear Sir,
>
> In the future, I would be greatly obliged if you would send your request for reports by mail. The reason for this is that many of your telephone messages, as well as several given to my brothers to be delivered to me, have been delayed in reaching me or have not reached me at all. . . .
>
> Very sincerely yours.

It is a delicious denial of nepotism to address the father as "Dear Sir." But David was often confused over that subject. Nor should we assume that L.J. was simply giving kindly encouragement to his son. David made it his business to see pictures so that he could be up-to-date on the talent available. Even at fourteen, he had a decisive literary style and the confidence to arrive at an opinion on very little evidence. He was asked to report on O. A. C. Lund as a director:

> In response to yours of the 27th inst., asking for a report on O.A.C. Lund and the features, "Just Jim," "Autumn," "Dorian's Divorce," and "The Price of Malice," I would say that while I have not seen any of the above named films, I know enough of Lund's work to say that

he is by no means good enough to produce Selznick Pictures. . . .

Hoping that you will not lower the standard of Selznick Pictures, by adding Lund to your forces, I remain,

Very truly yours,

The actress Mary MacLaren was less fortunate in her treatment. David reported two reasons for doubting she would ever become popular: "first, she has a sad, rather queer face, that will never be liked; second, she cannot act. Whenever I have seen Miss MacLaren on the screen, it has seemed to me that she needed a good sleep. She strolls through the picture with the same, never-changing expression, until you either fall asleep or walk out of the theatre, disgusted."

David wrote up a storm, and by March 1917 he was having to make a request of his father's secretary in which bashfulness was as poignant as the plain paper on which the letter was typed:

Dear Miss Koch,

I have exhausted my supply of "Report" stationery, and I would be greatly obliged if you would ask my father if it is all right for me to order plates for new paper and envelopes. If he says it is O.K. would it be asking too much to have you tell Myron to order the same? He already knows the kind I want.

We know as much about the way L.J. encouraged his employees as we do about his attitude to his sons. But the sons were employees, and L.J.'s energy swept away boundaries between public and private life. And anyone who was *his*, salesman or son, got the same pep talk:

> A sound sleep;
> An early awakening;
> A cold shower;
> A good breakfast;
> A pair of seven league boots . . .
> A clear head;
> An unconquerable soul;
> A determination to win;
> An optimistic mind;
> A supreme self-confidence;
> An intelligent aggressiveness;
> An unbounded ambition;
> Those are the ingredients.
> Mix and shake thoroughly.
> Hotdoggie!
> Lookit that bunch of contracts!

L.J.'s concentration and his ability were fixed on selling the pictures and making contracts for them with the many local exchanges that operated in America—the places where theaters sought new product at a time when travel was too slow, expensive, or difficult to make America a commercial unity. L.J. did deals with stars and directors to take their films for distribution and with exhibitors anywhere and everywhere. He spent most of his time making those deals, driving tough or insane bargains, talking up a project that as yet had no script. He was his own first and best salesman:

> Don't let anyone pull that old wheeze, "Salesmen are born, not made." Reverse it and it's right. Salesmanship comes only through intensified "plugology," and comprises in about equal parts persistence, pep, perseverance, pugnacity and patience.
>   Try that on your saxophone.

Other *p*'s could have been added: publicity, put-ons, promises, and perjury. The smooth and prompt delivery of lies was necessary because of the regularity with which the story changed. Marketing slogans always set up tremors of dissonance whenever they are put side by side. L.J. advocated "Ten Commandments of Selling," and they are crammed with internal contradiction. Thus:

> V. Tell the truth. By the law of averages, honesty gives the greatest profits. If you are working for a concern where you cannot tell the truth, quit and go elsewhere. . . .

> X. Think success. Radiate prosperity. Do not mention calamities, dirges, funerals. Be a Pollyanna.

David was his father's complete accomplice in all of this, and he was under great pressure to do more radiating than thinking. For example, the Clara Kimball Young Corporation did not enjoy smooth sailing for long. The men who made movies came to appreciate that their world was crowded with pretty young women eager for opportunity. As the tycoon aged, magically there were always fresh lines of nineteen-year-olds to choose from. Newcomers were the more appealing when stars of yesteryear, or just last year, were already becoming indignant about getting screwed on the deal. L.J.'s contract with Clara Kimball Young provided her with 50 percent of the income from her films for him. But she and her manager, Harry Garson, were realizing it never was 50 percent of what they'd hoped for. Distributors have expenses, not least of which was Clara's $1,000-a-week spending money. And if L.J. had once given her a sable coat, he had very likely taken its cost out of her share. Further, if—out of fair play and domestic prudence—he had had to give Flossie a matching coat, wasn't that really an expense incurred by Clara, too?

Already in 1917 there was talk on both sides of contract breaking. But it was years before litigation caught up. In 1920, the case of Clara Kimball Young and Equity Pictures (the shelter she had sought) against L.J. came to trial in New York. When it did, Equity simply backed off. By then it was only one of many cases L.J. had on his docket. Lawyers had fallen on the picture business very early, and they have never lacked patience, perseverance, or philosophy.

But here is David, still short of his fifteenth birthday, endeavoring to be a practical and pugnacious Pollyanna in easing his father's advertising director away from the old uninhibited boosting of Clara Kimball Young. This is a fourteen-year-old that some fathers might have sent off to the country for six months to smell the flowers and listen to the birds:

> Dear Mr. Moses,
>
> Acting under instructions from my father, Mr. Lewis J. Selznick, I am following very closely your press matters, mainly to keep myself posted, but also to cause to be corrected any mistakes which may come to my attention.
>
> A few weeks ago, I informed my father that Clara Kimball Young was being favored in the publicity sent out by you. When this was brought to your attention, I understand that you made a denial. I now stand ready to back up this claim. Your reason for this preference is beyond me. I am not aware that we are at present giving Miss Young an extensive publicity and advertising campaign. Certain it is that Miss Young is not in need of one more than the other Select stars. . . .
>
> If I have exceeded my authority in writing this letter, I am sincerely sorry. But it is in the interests of the firm, and can do no harm. I would appreciate an acknowledgement.

L.J. had gone beyond the wishes of most distributors in fostering companies that served the needs of individual stars. The distributors (and in time the major studios they became) were intent on overpowering the stars so that those beauties could be screwed without the noise of complaint. Moreover, in his frantic dealings, L.J. was disturbing the calm exploitation that distributors liked to visit on exchanges and theater owners. He was throwing his weight around, and he was as greedy for personal publicity as he was gratified to have his name up in lights above Manhattan. As rivals saw it, L.J. was behaving like a brash kid. This helps fill in the context in which David was having to sound like a pocket adult.

Lewis J. had successful deals with Constance and Norma Talmadge patterned on the Clara Kimball Young agreement. When the Russian actress Alla Nazimova had a great success on stage in *War Brides*, L.J. signed her to make a film of it and paid her $1,000 a day. The picture grossed $300,000. Thus, there were great rushes of income just as there is evidence of days when L.J. was broke. All through his picture period, Pop was keeping his hand in with jewels and real estate.

But it was the exuberance that offended more than the haphazard mix of humbug and sharp practice. L.J. needled his rivals and boasted of his success, and no one was more irritated than Adolph Zukor, a diminutive Hungarian who would live over 100 years on the juices of power. Zukor was self-effacing. He did not like his own name to wave over the pictures he profited from. Mary Pickford was one of Zukor's greatest assets, and little Mary had learned enough from the example of Clara Kimball Young to force a very good deal for herself. L.J. reacted with gratuitous relish. He sent an open letter to the trade press in August 1916:

> I congratulate you, Mary. You are a pretty shrewd, as well as a pretty *little* girl.
>
> What stronger evidence could there be that the Clara Kimball Young Corporation is organized on the most progressive basis than your adoption in the Mary Pickford Film Corporation of the very idea and ideal that I have originated?
>
> Will you please express to my friend, Mr. Adolph Zukor, my deep sense of obligation? It is indeed delightful to encounter among one's co-workers a man so broad-gauged that neither fake pride nor short-sightedness can deter him from the adoption of an excellent plan, even though conceived by another.

A war broke out between L.J. and Zukor in the trade papers, and Zukor could never surpass or kill the heckling cheek of L.J.'s letters. Thus 1917 is the noisiest year of L.J.'s life, even if it is not quite the height of his prosperity. "L.J.'s gall," said B. P. Schulberg, who ran publicity for Zukor, "couldn't be divided into three parts like Caesar's. That gall was as big and as durable as Gibraltar. The sharpest knives in the industry, including my own, couldn't make a dent in it. . . . Zukor despised him, but I always had a sneaking admiration for him. He wasn't a good gambler because he liked to bluff all the time, in business and at cards, but at least he did it in a big way. And he always laughed when he lost."

L.J.'s greatest laugh came, on a plate, in 1917. He released a cable to the American press and claimed he had sent it to the Tsar in Petrograd. The cable would become one of David's best poetic forms—and maybe David helped draft this one. The reference to Kiev is either a sign of all we do not know about Lewis Joseph's early life or a publicist's use of a place-name the public will recognize:

TO NICHOLAS ROMANOFF

WHEN I WAS POOR BOY IN KIEV SOME OF YOUR POLICEMEN WERE NOT
KIND TO ME AND MY PEOPLE. I CAME TO AMERICA AND PROSPERED. NOW
HEAR WITH REGRET YOU ARE OUT OF JOB OVER THERE. FEEL NO ILLWILL
WHAT YOUR POLICEMEN DID SO IF YOU WILL COME NEW YORK CAN GIVE
YOU FINE POSITION ACTING IN PICTURES. SALARY NO OBJECT. REPLY MY
EXPENSE. REGARDS YOU AND FAMILY.

SELZNICK   NEW YORK

4 · PERPETUAL MOTION

IN AUGUST 1921, Lewis J. Selznick entered into an agreement with the Famous Players–Lasky Corporation and its president, Adolph Zukor. The Selznick legend, as put in print by Terry Ramsaye and generally subscribed to by David, is that Zukor mounted a vicious campaign to humble L.J. and rid New York City of the name "Selznick" in flashing lights. All of which might pass in *Batman* but is too single-minded for real businessmen.

That Zukor and L.J. disliked one another is not in dispute. But why should Lewis J. Selznick have submitted to the famous wiles of Zukor unless he was obliged to, needed money and support, and maybe hoped to become a part of the larger and more illustrious Famous Players–Lasky (soon to go under the name of its distribution company, Paramount)?

The document of agreement (August 6, 1917) makes it clear that L.J. was being bailed out. A new company was to be formed, Select Pictures Corporation, to be owned half by Famous Players and half by Selznick. Selznick could nominate one director, while Famous Players appointed three people to the board. L.J. was to be president of Select (at $1,000 a week) and Morris Kohn (a Zukor man) would be treasurer (at $1,000 a month). Lewis J. was bound to devote himself to Select:

I will enter into a contract with the New Company and agree therein
that during the period of my employment by it I will not be or
become interested or engaged directly or indirectly in any other motion picture or theatrical enterprises and that I will devote my entire
time and attention exclusively to the services of the New Company.
This shall not, however, interfere with my right to continue to retain

my existing interests in other enterprises, as per Exhibit G hereto attached.

That sounds like the fencing in of a notorious maverick, bringing him so totally into the employ of Zukor that he could not find more mischief. In addition, L.J. transferred to Select (and thus to half ownership by Famous Players) the various exchanges he had interests in: this entailed New York, Buffalo, Pennsylvania, Virginia, Pittsburgh, Ohio, Missouri, Minnesota, Georgia, Denver, New Jersey, Chicago, Boston, Detroit, Dallas, San Francisco, Los Angeles, and Seattle, most of which had been totally owned by L.J. Beyond that, he was also assigning half the entire capital stock in Lewis J. Selznick Enterprises to Famous Players.

In return for those large concessions, Select was to receive $250,000 in capital from Famous Players.

L.J. had also to furnish a complete listing of his assets, liabilities, and pending litigation. Those liabilities totaled $274,569.02, consisting of accounts and notes payable, a debt of $38,000 to the Harriman National Bank, $12,500 owed to Universal for the film 20,000 *Leagues Under the Sea*, and notes payable to Jamaica First National Bank and the East River National Bank.

L.J.'s situation was not entirely bleak. He had distribution rights to several movies through his association with Clara Kimball Young, the director Herbert Brenon, the Talmadges, and the actor Robert Warwick. Still, the pain of dried-up cash flow is evident in the deal: L.J. was trading away half of everything for money to keep going. And he was agreeing to limit his own activities to an enterprise that no longer bore his own name.

L.J. had no choice in the matter, which vindicates the opinion of a man who was a Select employee for a few months in 1917, Louis B. Mayer. Mayer at that time was based in Boston, where he had become a leading New England distributor: he had made a killing on the rights there to *The Birth of a Nation*. But he was still behind L.J. in the game, and so he had joined Select as its New England distributor. The appointment didn't last. Mayer was quick to detect the lack of substance in another man. "Watch what I say," he said, in the hearing of his daughters, Edith and Irene, "watch and see what happens to him. There is no firm foundation. Things must be built stone by stone."

But L.J. was not lost. In that Exhibit G in his agreement with Zukor, there appeared the Film Advertising Service Inc., of which L.J. admitted to owning 50 percent. Most of the other half was Myron (then eighteen) and David (fifteen). A special meeting of the directors of Film Advertising Service had been held on July 27, 1917, ten days before the big deal with Famous Players. It was held at the offices F.A.S. (the initials of David's

*Myron and Flossie, a
bond as powerful as that
between David and Pop*

mother) shared with Lewis Selznick Enterprises, and David himself recorded the minutes. The chairman of the subsidiary was John Derham
(comptroller of the parent company), but Myron was the moving force
behind it.

Myron, too, had been enlisted in the business, though not at quite the
early age of David. But Myron was employed in ways that show the different
regard L.J. had for the two sons. "He was broken in to the business," said
David, with a touch of guilt, "via the dirtiest job you could possibly hand
anybody—that of a film inspector in the New York Exchange of the World
Film Corporation." This must have been in 1914 or 1915, when Myron was
sixteen. It was L.J.'s estimate at the time that David was the likely business
genius, the promoter and advertiser, whereas Myron, more practical, should
learn film craft and go into production. Myron was also better able to
handle the unpleasant task of inspection. David winced: "One discovers the
tears in the film by running it through one's fingers."

Myron was not dependent on the $12 a week; his father gave him a
lavish allowance, though not yet at the scale it would rise to. Moreover,
Myron was always expected to make his own way. It was David who was
most protected—and Myron who was left envious and mistrustful. But as
a would-be producer, Myron frequented the local Selznick studios: in the
Bronx first and then at Fort Lee. It was his considered opinion there that
other filmmakers didn't know what they were doing: the family arrogance
given an extra edge with Myron's aggressiveness. David had the charm to go
with his confidence. L.J. marveled at David's superiority. But in Myron it
looked ugly. So Pop threw the older boy out of the studios and told him
"to get out on his own." Thus it was, according to David, that Myron had
created the Film Advertising Service "to devise and produce all sorts of trick

accessories for films, together with a twin company to design ads." Myron called this adjunct the Rembrandt Art and Advertising Service, and he claimed it had an office in Paris.

L.J. appreciated the value of this small family venture when it came time to deal with Zukor. Ten days before that deal, L.J. passed over to F.A.S. electrotyping and printing contracts as well as the Selznick electric advertising signs at 200 West Forty-second Street and 1552–1554 Broadway. And so it was no longer strictly necessary for L.J. to be implicated in the wicked fireworks of these signs. Later on, as Irene Mayer learned the Selznick family history, she guessed it was David, "both poet and promoter," who was "the culprit behind the mammoth electric signs which blanketed Broadway and so outraged the other companies." But it was Myron who had the idea of the signs and hungered to see the Selznick name still shining.

It had been an unwritten part of the agreement with Zukor that Myron's potential as a producer would be encouraged by sending him out to California to work with Cecil B. DeMille, Famous Players's top director. But Myron would have nothing to do with the plan. As David observed, he "was so generally burnt up at the whole Paramount crowd, which he hated, that my father couldn't persuade him to accept the job."

Instead, Myron badgered L.J. to give him $25,000 so he could start on his own. Thus, in the second half of 1917, the nineteen-year-old Myron went to California and virtually kidnapped the beautiful young actress Olive Thomas to be his star. As Oliveretta Duffy, the girl had escaped Pittsburgh (had she known Selznicks there?) to get to New York. She had become a star for the Ziegfeld Follies and then with' Triangle Pictures. But her contract was up for renewal, and Myron was the least likely contender for it. That he won speaks for the kind of impact he had on her, David recalled:

> She was so intrigued with the kid producer that she told Myron that when she had received the highest offer she could get from the other companies, she would sign a contract with him for exactly half—which is precisely what she did.

Myron had Olive for $1,000 a week. He brought her back to New York, and on December 21, 1918, *he* formed Selznick Pictures Corporation to make films with her. Myron was president, David was secretary, and L.J. was treasurer. The directors of the company were Myron, L.J., and Howard—for David was still too young to hold such office.

The lights went back on again, proclaiming Olive Thomas in a Selznick picture. But Myron had become the active force in the family, as determined on his own decisions as David was pledged in loyalty to the father. Zukor was furious. Legend had it that he offered L.J. $5,000 a week,

Olive Thomas

for life, if the irritating Selznick would go off to China and stay there. For a while, David believed the story until Myron cornered him and said no, it was *he* who had had Zukor's offer. Zukor lost interest in Select—perhaps he did not want a new young rival; perhaps he saw that the father was a spent force. He sold the Famous Players's half share back to L.J. for $750,000—a 200 percent profit.

Myron was perfect casting for this moment. He would never be more insolently handsome; he had the belligerence to back his orders; he was in charge and riding a new age. His innate, depressive cynicism looked smart and modish. He could handle his liquor still, though he was pouring great quantities of Scotch into his stocky, restless body.

Myron was inspired by Olive Thomas (no matter that he liked to scorn inspiration). He secured the rights to *Upstairs and Down* for her, and in hiring Cosmo Hamilton as her writer he even outmaneuvered L.J., who sought Hamilton for other ventures. Moreover, Myron moved away physically as much as he could: he opened offices for the Selznick Pictures Corporation at 501 Fifth Avenue, and he began to spend time in California. From its earliest days, upstart urges in the American picture business had been drawn west, not just for sun and another shore, but to escape Eastern monopoly, interference, the law, patents, and parents. More and more, David was expected to look after Pop.

Olive Thomas made three Selznick films—*Everybody's Sweetheart*, *Upstairs and Down*, and *The Flapper*. But in 1920, with her husband, Jack Pickford

(Mary's brother), she went to Paris for a second honeymoon. In the early hours of the morning, in their hotel, the Ritz, Olive swallowed bichloride of mercury. There was talk of a suicide attempt, but it is more likely that under the influence of drugs, she drank from the wrong bottle. She died in the hospital on September 10 after several days of agony.

The blow to David was intense and romantic. He had been infatuated with his brother's star; she was his "Ollie," somewhere between older sister and fantasy. He spoke of "a fragrant rose-bud suddenly crumbled to ashes, a dancing sunbeam snuffed out like a candle."

But the company prospered: *Everybody's Sweetheart* tripled its business, and old Olive pictures were revived. In addition, the Selznicks had a $300,000 life insurance policy on their star. There was a funeral in New York, with Myron as one of the pallbearers. At the sale of her effects, L.J. bought an emerald and diamond ring for $680. As for the $22,000 limousine Olive had ridden in, inlaid in ivory, that was company property, and L.J. passed it on to his brother Sol, in Pittsburgh, who was trying out the automobile business.

There were plenty of other actresses. Myron signed up Elaine Hammerstein, and he already had his eye on Marjorie Daw. He tried to steal Corinne Griffith away from Vitagraph.

David was the junior brother; Myron often called him "chump" because David seemed held back by so many gentler, creative attitudes. But with Myron away, David could be the big shot. The family still lived at 590 West End Avenue. They had several Rolls-Royces for getting around town and a tiny but imposing Japanese butler, Eataro Ishii. The two boys had whatever money they wanted. There is a story that Myron had an allowance of $1,000 a week and David $500, but clearly these were salaries for officers of various Selznick companies. It was money for real work and money the boys rejoiced in spending. L.J. believed people were impressed by lavish gesture: if promoters picked up the tabs they seemed like sound prospects.

They took a three-story summer house, near the water, in Long Beach on Long Island. Rena Sachs spent a summer there—1918—and she loved the grandeur. The Biddle Dukes had a place across the street; Mischa Elman was around the corner. The Selznicks kept a German maid as well as Ishii; the boys told stories about them both being spies. L.J. and Myron went into Manhattan to work every day. But David stayed home: he had a tutor for college, and there was talk of Harvard or Columbia. The boys were fun for Rena. Myron was dating Constance Talmadge. David wasn't good-looking, but with his charm he didn't need to be. And if Howard "didn't have all his marbles," he could play any tune on the piano as soon as he heard it.

One day that summer Myron brought another girl home, a lovely redhead, Bertyce Kennedy. Then he learned that Connie Talmadge was coming by so he passed Bertyce off on Howard. As if in exuberance, Howie sat down and played the piano. Bertyce joined him, and she took out the pins so her hair fell down. At that moment, Pop came in and, as it seemed to Rena, he was bowled over by the girl. She had to have a screen test! A few years later, the redhead married Jules Brulatour, one of L.J.'s partners. It was a family where you had to hold on to your girlfriends.

The family also had an apartment on Park Avenue, at 270, the Marguery Building. This blocklong edifice, between Forty-seventh and Forty-eighth, had been opened in 1918. It is part of Selznick lore that the family went from West End Avenue to Park Avenue as they prospered. Yet there was a period of overlap when they rented both properties. West End Avenue may have been kept as "home" for Howard and even Pop, whereas 270 Park was for show and entertainment. Niven Busch went to parties at 270 and got the impression the Selznicks were often behind with its rent. David ran those parties, and he brought girls in from the studio. "Mother Selznick would be sitting off in some back room, knitting. And David was a ceaseless stream of animal energy. We'd be up all night, and I'd have to go to sleep. But when I woke, there was David ordering in a catered breakfast."

Another outsider was Maurice Rapf, the son of Harry Rapf, who had joined the Selznick ventures as manager to Robert Warwick. Maurice recalls the impact David made:

> This was in 1919 and '20 . . . even then, he was very sharp and to me represented a kind of idol. He was still a boy, because I know that he was seventeen or eighteen. But he dressed like a man. Tie, straw hat. Always very well dressed. And he had a car, a big car.

Myron and David at the beach with Natalie and Norma Talmadge

David had been very ill in January 1919, with that year's terrible influenza. For several days, his life had been in the balance. But nothing else hindered him or slowed that animal energy. In February 1919, he made his own first trip to Los Angeles to visit Myron: it may be revealing of L.J.'s health that having set out with David and Florence, he chose to remain in Pittsburgh while they went all the way out to the coast. In transit, David gave interviews, bursting with the old plugology: "We intend to go into production on a big scale. We are out to get the best stars, stories and directors that are available. We are going to make the name 'Selznick' stand for the highest quality in motion picture production."

David was seeing girls, or gazing on them. He might be boastful enough to persuade Niven Busch that he had picked up racy experience. But he was also shy, unsure of himself, and lavishly romantic. Love as he understood it from great literature was something far higher than Myron's brusque dispatch of dames. Further, Norma Talmadge, the actress wife to Joe Schenck, had warned him to be careful with girls—for they would surely be after the prestigious name and fortune of Selznick.

It was in the summer of 1919 that he succumbed, seventeen years old and recovering from influenza. He was sent to gain strength at the Long Island beach house of a movie executive. There he was set upon by the man's rather younger but more experienced adopted daughter. David was seduced and horrified at his own abuse of hospitality. But this trepidation hardly mattered, he noticed, for he was in love with sex.

As if inspired, or spurred by David's debut, Myron then took the young woman for himself. (He had this habit of stealing David's girls and showing them how little the kid knew.) As time passed, the girl became pregnant, and suspicion fell on Myron. Yet it could just as easily have been David, said Myron, laughing. Still, for David, this had been an occasion of wonder, and then Myron had spoiled things.

As Myron labored over the pictures, David became a spokesman and one worth waiting for. In October 1920, he went to Indianapolis to speak to 600 members of the Federated Women's Clubs of Indiana. Rail delays made him five hours late, but the audience waited and then listened to him for an hour. David made a case he would never give up on—that movies spoke most intimately to the dreams of women. He said that women accounted for 90 percent of the movie audience—not just in their presence, but in their urging men to go and in their choice of what film to see. Charlie Pettijohn, a Selznick employee, was on the same trip, and he had no doubts about David's eloquence:

> David Selznick made the most effective talk to this large group of
> women I ever heard fall from the lips of any man connected with

motion pictures addressing an assemblage on behalf of the industry. It wasn't an oration but a clean cut comprehensive discussion from the producer's viewpoint upon the subject of how the industry can be helped by the women of the country.

This report was offered in *The Brain Exchange*, the weekly journal "of, by and for Selznick employees." This paper may have been L.J.'s original idea, but it was David's baby. *The Exchange* was edited by L. F. Guimond, and Randolph Bartlett was a regular writer. But Bartlett was also David's mentor as the kid tried to write movie treatments. Bartlett's poetic prose style had a huge influence on David in subsequent years, and in 1920 Bartlett wrote impressions of Myron and David that may be gross flattery but which reveal some differences between the two:

David Selznick

A young eagle.
A mountain stream.
Playing truant from school to
    go home and saw wood.
Nothing but the truth.
A steel mushroom.
Sir Galahad.
A machine gun.
A chip of the old block.
Perpetual motion.
Now.

Myron Selznick

Business before pleasure.
—David and a lot of Goliaths.
An island in an ocean of girls
—without a landing place.
Astronomy.
The seven labors of Hercules.
Fun.
A home run with the bases full.
All bluffs called.
The enthusiasm of youth
—with the caution of age.
Speed.

And Howard? The oldest brother was twenty-two in 1919, and he sat on the board of directors of the Selznick Corporation, of Select Pictures, and of Selznick Pictures Corporation. Nevertheless, in a will written in 1919 (it would prove his last), L.J. had ordered that Howard's one-third share of the estate be held for him in trust. The director, said Myron, was recognized as incompetent. Howard had his room at West End Avenue, his car, and some spending money. So it was, sometime in 1919—just a company director on the lam—that Howard met Mildred Schneider in Brooklyn. She was eighteen and lived with her family in a wooden shack on Atlantic Avenue. "I asked Howard how he met Mildred," said Randolph Maller, "and he said he picked her up either through some flirtation on the street or else she was some telephone operator who answered the phone when Howard was calling someone. . . . Howard had a lot of girls—he would go from one to the other."

Maller worked for the Selznicks in the purchasing department. Myron had put him there to keep an eye on the slow brother: "Howard never did anything, no matter what department he was put into—he didn't come to work—they put him in the purchasing department and he never did a thing. If Howie was my brother, I would term him as of no account. . . . he was only looking for good times and girls—no ambition whatsoever." Howard had business cards printed—"Casting Director"—a sure ticket in impressing young ladies. On his marriage certificate, he claimed to be a "Motion Picture Director."

It was Maller's practice to track Howard's social life. He had met Mildred, and he reckoned the girl was only out for what she could get. The couple went to absinthe bars. Maller saw Howie try to kiss her, and Mildred rebuffed him. She was cold, indifferent, and lacked affection. In Maller's eyes, she was just "one of those smart little Brooklyn dames." He warned the Selznicks of what was going on, but he never discovered that, on January 21, 1920, Howard had married Mildred Schneider.

Maller had one conversation with Flossie, also unaware of the marriage, in which the mother said, "Randy, you are a Brooklyn boy—I have heard some bad things about Mildred. I don't expect Howard to not marry a poor girl, as we have been poor, too. But I do expect him to marry a good girl."

To avert the union, Florence and L.J. begged Maller to take Howie away to California so that he might "forget" Mildred. The whole family saw them off at Grand Central Station, and a Selznick star, Owen Moore, was there to lend celebrity moral support. But at the last minute, Mildred appeared and Howie got so excited he fell over and bumped his head. As Howie tried to talk to Mildred, Maller and the family bundled him onto the train.

In Los Angeles, they stayed at the Hollenbeck Hotel, and Maller asked Harry Rapf for $1,000 to show Howie a good time. Rapf wired back to New York and L.J. gave his permission. Properly funded, Maller started scouting starlets to catch Howie's eye. He found a beauty from Salt Lake City and "told her he wanted her to take Howard and interest him in every way possible." But before a date could be arranged, Howard had vanished. Maller called L.J., who "told him to have all the railroads guarded, to check everywhere, and get detectives on Howard's trail, but to keep Howie away from Brooklyn."

The date never came off. Howard went up to San Francisco, where he made wire contact with his wife. But he never acted like a man in love, said Maller: "It was more like a person who was threatened—he was groggy and stupefied."

Later that year Howard and Mildred were reunited. A daughter, Ruth, was born on December 8, 1920. Mildred was given a weekly check for $200 and the new family moved into an apartment at 885 West End Avenue. From the outset, Flossie was deeply suspicious of Mildred's motives and hostile to her existence.

What did the Selznicks think of Howard? Was he safe to let out? Should the chance of marriage have been risked? Or was Howard just one of those company directors with a car who needed a friend? They told stories about Howard and never noticed how much they lied to themselves. When Irene Mayer came along a few years later, a very appealing match for one of their boys, she was told the Howard story as if he were just a lovable simpleton who went about his own life without troubling anyone. As Irene heard it, Howard had made a habit of leaving the dinner table early until someone asked where it was he went. "I go to see my wife," said Howard. "I've been married two years."

The Brain Exchange did its best to run public relations for Howard. A new father, he was made assistant manager at the company's Paragon Studio in Fort Lee. The magazine gave him a barefaced plug:

> It has often been pointed out that personality and ability go hand in hand, and there has been no surer demonstration of this fact than in the case of Howard Selznick. His natural ability has enabled him to succeed at the task, and his winning personality has aided him by making friends of all who come in contact with his office.
>
> There may be another reason why Howard is fast climbing to the top of the ladder. Howard is now a daddy, and it is a safe bet that the paternal instinct has made him buckle on his sword with the determination to win against all odds. And don't forget that the odds are great. The mere fact that he is a son of "L.J." piles up enough obstacles to make the average man think twice. A member of the family has to show twice as much speed as any person else.

5 · A PRACTICALLY CASH BUSINESS

DAVID HAD NO TIME or distance to make a decision about what he would be—this was a characteristic dilemma, and it lasted all his life. But it left him thinking, well—why not?—he might be anything. When Irene Mayer met him a few years later, she found a young man torn between go-getter and dreamer, an academic, a writer perhaps, or an entrepreneur: "He was a mass of conflicting impulses . . . he wanted all ends as well as the middle." He was susceptible to influence and dominated by father and brother. From the earliest age, he had the feeling of being pressurized and somehow deprived of freedom.

He was trying to write ideas for movies—two-page treatments, something a boss could read, or have read to him, while he shaved. One of these was "The Man Who Was Nobody," about Eddie Gibbs, whose sweetheart is killed on their Sunday afternoon drive, with Eddie jailed for five years on a manslaughter charge. When he gets out of prison he is "a human derelict." One night he is ready to throw himself off the Brooklyn Bridge when a bum stops him and tells him to shape up. So Eddie tries again and gets a job as an elevator man in an apartment building. There's a girl in the building he loves from afar, Virginia. A fire threatens the building and Eddie saves the girl from death. In the hospital, as he recovers, "a beautiful love develops between them. But Eddie realizes its hopelessness. 'I'm nobody,' he tells her. 'Some day,' she whispers, 'some day it will be different.' But she leaves."

Randolph Bartlett was as generous as he could be. He thought the outline had intriguing elements. "But there is no story. . . . Something should be planted at the beginning that would bring the hero out on top at the finish." What is most startling about the treatment is the downcast, nearly depressive tone coming from the speaker who could excite 600 ladies in Indianapolis. It reveals the sadness in David that he did so much to mask with laughing activity. More than thirty years later, in the last film David made, *A Farewell to Arms*, the couple also fall in love in the hospital, where the man is incapacitated.

"The Man Who Was Nobody" was never made, and it doesn't show the influence of Tolstoy or Dickens. David wanted to make a show for the public, but he was not a born storyteller. Pop had his moment in the business, yet his movies did not last. Much as he adored Pop, in later life David never referred to or seemed to remember any of Pop's pictures.

The author of "The Man Who Was Nobody" had money, girls, cars, and New York spread out for him. There was nothing to fight against, no unwelcome tasks or discipline. If David came home late at night, L.J. was there to be his manservant. The father would tuck the weary boy into bed—he would have dreamed his dreams for him.

There was little apparent cause for alarm. In May 1921, the audited balance sheet of the Selznick Corporation, certified by Barrow, Wade, Guthrie & Company, reported gross assets of $15,153,178 and net assets of $11,643,505. Such figures must be multiplied by at least ten to come close to their modern meaning. But in 1921, the real question was how far they had been exaggerated.

The Selznick Corporation had been organized in May 1920 "to consolidate all the motion picture interests of Lewis J. Selznick and to bring under one directing group of executives the various subsidiaries making up his complete organization. The business of the corporation is the production and distribution of motion pictures through its subsidiaries. It does a practically cash business, extends its distribution of product throughout the United States into Canada and many foreign countries."

Pictures had depended on cash for most of their life. Exhibitors paid advances to screen pictures, and the advances were used to make the pictures. But in the boom years after the war, the business began to consolidate. Theaters were being built and joined into chains. The leading production-distribution companies were taking control of theaters, and risking Wall Street money to underwrite the necessary building. Motion picture budgets were rising, and some stars—like Chaplin, Mary Pickford, Gloria Swanson, and Douglas Fairbanks—owned enough of their pictures to be fabulously wealthy. As Adolph Zukor made Paramount larger, so he bought theaters and, in 1919, made a stock issue of $10 million. His major rivals were William Fox, Universal, Goldwyn, and the companies that would merge, in 1924, to become Metro-Goldwyn-Mayer. Whereas in the years 1908–18 there had been hundreds of companies in the business, many of which lasted only a short time, by the early 1920s the landscape was dominated by a few "majors"—the names of which survive to this day. Lewis J. Selznick was not small, and he had lasted. But he was not a dominating figure, and the majors did not want to make life easier for him. Men like Zukor were bent on achieving monopoly: a chain of theaters committed to taking all the Paramount product—and nothing else. L.J.'s business was on the cusp: he was bound either to grow or to wither. Despite the huge claims of assets, Pop was still living in rented property and, apparently, struggling to make the monthly check. If anyone became alarmed, he started to spend dramatically to pick up their spirits.

So he sought expansion and grandiose declarations. In 1921, using the
H. V. Greene Company of Boston as brokers, the Selznick Corporation
made an issue of 40,000 shares at $25 each. The promotion was a four-page
brochure: L.J. was president, Myron was vice president, and David was
secretary. Howard was a director, but he was not mentioned in the brochure.

The language of the brochure plainly came from H. V. Greene rather
than David. It saw the rising prosperity of the Selznicks as part of the
independent success of movies. Selznick pictures, it said, had earned gross
rentals as follows:

1917	$2.111 million
1918	$3.269 million
1919	$5.717 million
1920	$8.143 million

American admission receipts for 1920 as a whole were reported as $1 billion,
based on 50 million tickets sold every week. Picture-going had become a
universal pastime, and comfortable, attractive theaters were being built for
the audience. There were already 18,000 theaters in America, and $872
million had been invested in those and in the ones being planned. The chief
goal of the stock offering was a new studio. The premises at Fort Lee had
been leased. But the Selznicks were looking ahead:

> To provide even better facilities and increased efficiency of manage-
> ment, an entire city block in Long Island City has been acquired and
> here it is proposed to build the largest and best-equipped studio in the
> world.

*David, age twenty, as
drawn by Al Hirschfeld*

Even amid such positive thinking, there were signs of cash problems. L.J. was often on the lookout for personal loans. For instance, sometime in 1919 or 1920, Cecelia and Leonard Morris of Pittsburgh were visiting New York. Cecelia was Flossie's sister, and in the course of the family get-together the Morrises loaned the Selznicks $17,000. Shortly thereafter, they offered another loan of $27,000 if their son could have a job with L.J. The young Morris was made an assistant secretary at Select for $100 a week. He worked about six months and was paid for five weeks. By 1921, the Morrises had learned the Selznicks were in difficulties, and so they sought repayment. But they were never paid back more than a few thousand.

The two portraits of L.J. do not fit together. In 1922, he had productions under way on both coasts and two busy floors at 729 Seventh Avenue. The young Al Hirschfeld was hired that year as art director. One of his responsibilities was advertising. Selznick ran more ads than larger outfits—sometimes as many as twenty pages in *The Saturday Evening Post*. L.J. offered the films of Elaine Hammerstein, Conway Tearle, Eugene O'Brien, Norma and Constance Talmadge, Alice Brady, Owen Moore, and even a few Marion Davies films. He had thirty branch offices in the United States, with his brother David J. Selznick manager in Pittsburgh and his half brother Philip Selznick as a roaming field executive. He boasted of offices in London, Paris, and Australia.

In the fall of 1922, Myron was bicoastal, supervising the editing in New York of *One Week of Love* (the latest Hammerstein-Tearle vehicle), going west for the shooting of Owen Moore's *One Dollar Down*, and finalizing details on *Rupert of Hentzau*, which Victor Heerman would direct. L.J. had played a leading part in the formation of the Motion Picture Producers and Distributors of America and in getting Will Hays (postmaster general in the Harding administration) to serve as its first president in January 1922. L.J. and Myron are in the first group portrait of the association, and Myron is the youngest person there.

On the other hand, in October 1922, it was announced that Sam E. Morris was leaving Selznick to join the Warner brothers. Morris had been with L.J. nearly a decade. He was a vice president of the Selznick Corporation and Selznick Pictures Corporation. He had also made the several overseas contacts that L.J. needed. Further, in March 1922, Eugene O'Brien and actor-director Ralph Ince were released from their contracts. In the same month, Selznick failed to renew his lease on the electric sign at 1552 Broadway.

It may be just as indicative that David was thinking of going back to school. Later in life, David claimed that for several years he had attended "all sorts of extension courses" at Columbia, as the university "permitted me

to keep on with my education but never for a day leave the picture business."
He did register there three times in the period 1918–23. He took evening
courses, and he had a B–/C+ average. But there was no design or stamina
in the work and never any prospect of graduation. Still, in March 1921, he
wrote to Yale seeking entrance the following October:

> I am eighteen years of age, but will be nineteen before the opening of
> the next semester. Two years ago an intense desire to enter business
> caused me to give up practically all my studies. I have been successful
> in business, and today am Secretary of the Selznick-Select moving
> picture enterprises.
>
> At eighteen I have under me several hundred persons, yet I long for
> the college training that might have been mine. I trust, and I hope
> most deeply, that the realization of what I have missed has not come
> too late.

That summer David attended the Milford School for cramming, and
in September he sat for the Yale entrance exams, with these results:

English A and B	67
Ancient History	55
American History	93
French A	44
Plane Trigonometry	70

These marks were adequate, but David omitted to send in recommendations from his schools—was he still confused about what to do? He
tried again in his own way, and in 1922 he got the Reverend Orville Petty,
of the Plymouth Church in New Haven, to exercise influence for him. But
the answer was disappointing: "They maintain that your credits are not
sufficient; that your marks were not unusual, and that since 1921 you have
made no efforts with them to secure credits by further examination."

This letter from Petty has one novelty: it is addressed to Mr. D. O.
Selznick. The O. had something of Oliver Twist and Olive Thomas; it was
a way of distancing himself from the uncle David who was working for the
Selznicks, but it was also a measure of rhythm, gravity, and business ambition.

Yale's requirements were too fussy and maybe beyond his reach. On
November 11, 1922, *The Brain Exchange* dropped its big news: "David O.
Selznick, in his new capacity as Eastern Production Manager of the Selznick
Pictures Corporation" had announced his debut film. It was to be Theda
Bara in *The Easiest Way*, a play by Eugene Walton. Bara—the first great vamp
on the screen—was past her prime. She was thirty-two. Her contract with
William Fox had expired, and she had not worked since 1919. Nevertheless,

David was going to have to pay her $5,000 a week. "We are ready to pay ANY price for the right kind of story for Miss Bara," David had said as he searched for material. "Miss Bara's first story must be big enough, dramatically, to measure up to her wonderful emotional ability, and while I'm getting grey-headed trying to find it, I'm going to wait until I get the RIGHT story."

At the Los Angeles office of Selznick Pictures—5341 Melrose Avenue—Edward Montagne, Myron's top writer, offered the hope that Myron would let him work for the kid. Montagne added that the rushes of *Rupert of Hentzau* were good enough to be "our very best picture. We have broken through now," wrote Montagne. "There is not a player out here who would not be proud to work in a Selznick picture."

The Brain Exchange was over the moon about *The Easiest Way*, and it gave the Selznick salesmen its best plug:

> Give you a thrill? Say, brother, if it don't, just grab your skimmer and Benny off the hook as you pass out because there's something wrong with your reflexes and you'll NEVER succeed in the film business.

On the evening of Friday, November 3, 1922, L.J. threw a New York party for the opening of *One Week of Love*. He was famous for such spectacular previews, and this would be his last. It's not clear how many of the 2,000 guests at the Ritz-Carlton Hotel had forebodings. Those present included not just David and his parents (Myron was in California), but Edna Ferber, David Belasco, George M. Cohan, Will Hays, the Hearsts, Ziegfeld and Billie Burke, D. W. Griffith, and Edith Wharton. The party moved on to the Crystal Room, "where they pranced, danced and frolicked to the syncopated strains of a Paul Whiteman aggregation of jazz hounds."

But there was a hint in the *Moving Picture World*'s coverage of wanting to salute L.J. for all he had meant to the business: "the Selznick showing was blazed with a pretentiousness and replete with an atmosphere of sociability that put it in a class all by its lonesome." Reviewer Charles S. Sewell thought the picture was "a big box-office bet," and he especially praised the exciting train crash scene. Written by Montagne and directed by George Archainbaud, *One Week of Love* concerned a "pampered and blasé society belle" who crashes in an air race, meets "Buck Fearmly" in the wilds of Mexico, and then gets caught up in flood and railroad disaster before "the definite realization of their love comes to the happy pair."

In its gossip column, *Moving Picture World* tried to rally support for the melodrama, and here is the suggestion that some in the business knew L.J. needed rescuing:

Lots of conversation after viewing *One Week of Love.* A railroad wreck climax that furnished Saturday's conversation in Film Row. And a general production excellence that has given new strength to Myron Selznick's name. Lots of boosters for Lewis J. Gamest fighter and most picturesque character in the game.

There is no chance of judging these films. They have not survived. Unfortunately, that is true of many films from the silent era, especially those made by a company as close to disaster as Selznick. So we cannot say how good a producer Myron Selznick was or whether his movies were out of date for 1922—the year of Rex Ingram's *The Prisoner of Zenda,* Griffith's *Orphans of the Storm,* von Stroheim's *Foolish Wives,* and Flaherty's *Nanook of the North.*

What counted painfully was that Selznick could no longer secure those stars most in demand. Hammerstein and Tearle, the stars of *One Week of Love,* were not first-rank players. Worse than that, Selznick pictures were not getting sufficient exposure on exhibition circuits increasingly dominated by larger forces. It would become the bitter legend of the Selznicks that L.J.'s product was blackballed by Fox and Zukor, that those giants were out to get him. Sam Jaffe (who worked for Zukor) said it was the other way around: L.J. had tried to defeat Zukor, but was nowhere near good enough. L.J. was paying the price for independence. He had not bought in on any of the major alliances, and he could not finagle the screen time he needed with the stars at his command. More than at any other time in movie history, in the decade after the Great War audiences followed personalities. Stardom built the business. The great pioneers and independent figures were forced to deal with combines and competition. Their world was tamed. In two years' time, von Stroheim's *Greed* would be taken from the director and drastically reduced in size to fit the industrial slots. True independence had flourished very briefly, and it would not come back until the libertine, creative egomania of the 1980s. Getting movies to work—having them made *and* marketed—required a network of distribution and exhibition. Myron may have chosen to believe his father had been victimized and wronged—because Myron looked for grievance. But L.J. had denied reality.

He was a poor businessman who flinched from being organized—the need for independence was so profound it meant not fitting into his own organization. This was another pattern that David would repeat. Pop was also a gambler and a loser. He was part of a poker crowd in which the pots reached as high as $100,000. And in his boyish habit of both borrowing and offending, he ensured that someday the world would foreclose.

The records are very sketchy. But in two years, assets of $11 million

Myron: half producer, half gangster, all alone

came to bankruptcy. In October 1922, L.J. had to borrow $30,000 from a William Rosenfeld. At the same time, he had to assign the rights to a package of his films to the Pacific Southwest Trust & Savings Bank to cover a debt.

The apartment on Park Avenue has grown rather in the telling over the years, but it was intended as an advertisement. As well as the cars, the servants, and the exotic figure of Ishii, the apartment had antique or antique-style furniture, rugs, and carpets from Kurdistan and an "Italian Renaissance gilt and polychrome walnut console with female figure front supports, cupids, etc." There were paintings—a Turkish market in Smyrna by L. Diamant and portraits of L.J. and David by E. Myer Silverberg. There was no painting of Myron or Howard. There was a Flemish tapestry, a full-length Russian sable coat, and a great deal of jewelry. Even when bankruptcy

came, the contents of the apartment were appraised at over $300,000—
which likely means that L.J. paid $1 million for them.

On December 22, 1922, L.J. retired as president of Select and was
replaced by Myron. Maneuvering had begun, but L.J.'s health was too
uncertain to guarantee his grasp of the problem.

In January 1923, David went to California, trying to drum up new
product. He sent a telegram to Nicholas Carter in the New York office
proposing a couple of sea pictures, to be based in Portland, Oregon, and
shot simultaneously with one cast and one boat.

Two days later, Myron wired David, ignoring the two-for-one proposal. Myron rarely put himself down on paper, but when he did he
punched like Dempsey:

> Production activity suspended until present financial problems solved.
> Every dollar needed now for pressing obligations here, therefore elim-
> inate immediately all expenses not absolutely necessary to the very
> existence of the corporation. Montagne return New York. Force
> ninety days contract suspension, and extension. Dispense tomorrow
> with Lane, studio kitchen, Jap cook, readers various secretary. When
> production completed one stenographer should handle office work,
> Sibrans and one assistant, Dent yourself must handle auditing depart-
> ment. Discharge Cronjager, McCord, Bretherton, Cole, Hornbustel,
> eliminate studio car as soon as practical. Although bank advancing
> money it is our interest to keep this to minimum for money must be
> repaid by us. Western Union voluntarily drew attention unnecessary
> length our wires, here-after do not wire if letter will suffice, and David
> cease requesting New York telephone calls. Present circumstances do
> not justify entertainment therefore discontinue allowance immedi-
> ately. These instructions final.

Three days later, at 3:45 in the afternoon, there was a special meeting
of the board of Selznick Pictures Corporation. The three directors were
present—L.J., Myron, and Howard. They proceeded to move, second, and
pass the resignations of L.J. and Howard, followed by the election in their
places of J. E. McDermott and J. S. Frazer. Myron also reported to the
meeting that David had resigned as secretary. He was replaced by E. J.
Doolittle.

As Al Hirschfeld saw it, Doolittle of the Syracuse Bank forced the
crisis. There were two pictures coming up for release, intended as big
first-run movies that might stave off disaster: *The Common Law* and *Rupert of
Hentzau.* Many employees and creditors were ready to back L.J. in waiting
for their release, but Doolittle insisted on pushing them out quickly and
cheaply. Hirschfeld never guessed the full debt, and like everyone else, he

began to be paid at half rate, with the rest in "trade acceptances" that no bank would honor. Still, Hirschfeld believed in L.J.: "a remarkable man with a wild talent for theatre . . . he seemed to guess right; he had a finger in the public's rectum."

Myron next reported on the assignment of several pictures to the Pacific Southwest Trust & Savings Bank "and stated that the Board of Directors had never approved or ratified such action of its officers." (Those miscreant officers were Myron, David, L.J., and Sam Morris.) The new board therefore voted to revoke and rescind the assignment. Shortly thereafter, a new company, Selznick Distributing Corporation, was set up as the new parent company for all the debts and problems.

Two weeks later, David was still in California, but getting ready to return. He received a letter from Nick Carter that warned him:

> Many things have transpired since you left and you will have a great shock when you get back to see the difference in the office. We have only a skeleton staff and the place is dead. . . . Please hurry back. Your Father is not feeling at all well and if you can possibly be spared I wish you could be here to consult with him.

So David went back to New York to face the family's music. He was not quite twenty-one, and the first phase of his career was ending before it could begin. His early hopes were dashed, and he was about to get his first experience of struggle and dismay. Yet Myron had more reason to feel victimized—he was further on in his career, and he would never quite be the same again. Moreover, Myron took disappointment deep inside himself: it only fulfilled the knowledge that Pop scarcely noticed him.

Failure would enrich David. For even at this age, he could be funny with his sorrows, just as he had a rare, ironic view of the picture business. This Selznick would never be an ordinary mogul or a one-note showman. Though picture greatness beckoned David, he had seen through it early on. That was why he smiled so much and wrote in this tone about a "Great American" who contained a bit of Pop, a bit of Zukor or Mayer, and a promise of himself:

> He controls a Chinese valet, seven movie stars and his passions. Re this last, there is not much credit due him, as he is the man who married that beautiful, dumb wife. He made a star out of her and accepts her gratitude nightly: this is remarkable, for he is well past fiddle-age.
>
> His ancestors were not Nordic; no. Neither is he Spanish; no: he is a movie man. He speaks Jewish with an Anglo-Saxon accent, and he plays golf like his forefathers. . . .

He is, in his own crude way, a Robin Hood. That is to say, he gives away thousands and steals millions. Of course this is something of a reversal of the Sherwood forest procedure—but then look at all the trouble Robin got into, whereas our Man is a Distinguished Citizen.

Seventeen publicity men exude his square-shooting doctrines, for he looked at some movie captions and they gave him an Idea; fourteen publicity women are permanently pregnant with the fruit of his gen-'rous salaries. He reads what they all write; he reads it religiously, except on those days when he has it read to him. But he doesn't believe it, and so he goes his way alone.

Yes, yes . . . he is a solitary figure in a wilderness of press sheets—a Distinguished Citizen, a Great Man.

Then and now, Hollywood is a waiting room crowded with solitary, great men, sustained by suspicion and egomania. But not many see the joke of all that loneliness. David had fallen, and his father was finished, yet David was a man to grin if he ever read the press conference Adolph Zukor gave in Paris early in March 1923. Reporters had wanted Zukor to agree with them that Hollywood was a "terrible" place, full of melodrama, scandal, and noise. Not at all, said Zukor, "Hollywood is a very quiet place—no drink-ing—very little smoking. And as for the evenings—they're just as quiet! Why, they're practically inaudible. No sound at all but the popping of California poppies."

Brain Waves and Setbacks

1 • A VERY RUGGED TIME

BANKRUPTCY HELPED FORM DAVID: having survived it once, he resolved never to let it happen again. Yet, having escaped, he began to believe it had not been merited and had not quite happened.

In the picture business, the ferment of doing well is so hard to distinguish from the disorder of doing badly. What counted for Pop was his credit, the cash in hand, or the rosary of small gems in his pocket. If a bankrupt can get a good table and dinner at the best restaurant, he is in business. He knows the worst thing he can do is brood over recent failure or let it show. Bankruptcy is a springboard for inventive entrepreneurs. The creditors may remember. But losers move on with forgetful energy, their sense of adventure renewed.

For decades after L.J.'s failure, David received reminding or brow-beating letters about old loans and sacrifices. He would sometimes refer them to his mother for interpretation and background, just as Flossie was asked to adjudicate on the authenticity of every Selznick or Seleznick who wrote, in flawed English, to the studio. David's own reaction to these requests was never consistent. Sometimes he lied and protested, as if he were his own lawyer; sometimes he said he had been too young, in 1923, to know; yet often he went to exceptional lengths to pay off the past.

There was a further problem, mentioned by David in 1944 while discussing one debt, that helps show us what the uncommonly experienced twenty-year-old actually felt when Pop went bust—that Pop's affairs were so complex, how could anyone understand them, let alone feel culpability? Hadn't that been Pop's policy? As David complained to his uncle Charlie Sachs, there had always been the "unfortunate way in which he mixed up his personal finances with those of his corporations, even when he didn't own these corporations."

In February 1923, the claims against L.J. were more than anyone could deal with. The law firm of Konta & Kirchwey was charged to present a summary "of pending litigation affecting the various Selznick companies." Their seventeen-page letter included the following:

- a claim for $25,000 against Select and L.J. over "false and fraudulent representations" made to secure distribution rights for a package of films from Kempner and Jacobson
- a claim for $38,000 by Herbert Kaufman charging that L.J. had not made and released pictures based on literary material delivered by Kaufman
- a very intricate case in which Jacob Wener and T&T Films had taken on twelve films starring Constance and Norma Talmadge and had paid L.J. $175,000 on the agreement that in three years L.J. would repurchase T&T after Wener had served as manager at $700 a week—a sum L.J. had not paid
- a claim for $18,069 made by the architects hired to design and construct the new Selznick studio in Long Island City; the architects did the plans and were paid $40,000 before the scheme was abandoned; they were suing for the balance of their fee

The lawyers listed twenty-two claims and then laid down the terms on which they would represent L.J. But even while the letter was being typed, seven other claims came to light.

In later years, David presented the disaster rather as if it had befallen Mr. Micawber. "Everything we owned personally was taken away from us," he said, "and we went out to make a living." Two weeks after the crash, David seemed to remember, they had to vacate the apartment at 270 Park Avenue. Instead, "we were living in a three-room flat, and my mother was doing all the housework and cooking."

The truth is less harrowing. The family was obliged to make an inventory and valuation of the contents of the 270 apartment in October 1923. But they were still in occupation as late as May 1924. Money was found somehow for immediate needs. At some point in 1923, L.J. persuaded Hyman Winik to lend $35,000 to Flossie, who had to put up what L.J. said was $200,000 worth of her jewelry as collateral.

On February 1, 1923—only days before disaster struck—L.J. and Flossie also raised another $35,000 from Samuel Falk, when they mortgaged "certain goods and chattels consisting of household furniture, hangings, draperies, objets d'art, etc."

At some time shortly after these transactions, Flossie and L.J. assigned "ownership" of both the collateralized jewels and the mortgage to their son David. Which suggests that rather than wait for something to turn up, this Micawber was making safeguarding plans to avoid it. Whatever the state of his health—and there is a later remark by David that his father had a stroke "after" the failure—L.J. was out and about, raising cash loans wherever he could. One old pal, Joe Toplitzky, remembered L.J. had come to his office with a hard-luck tale about how he couldn't get the leaders of the business to see him. "He then proceeded to break down and cry like a child," said Toplitzky. "When I asked him how much he wanted he said $2,500. I wrote him a check for it. He asked me to write the check to a certain corporation which he owned. He gave me this corporation's note and endorsed it."

In February 1923, a petition for involuntary bankruptcy was filed against Select; then on May 6, notes for $3,000 were used in a similar action against the Selznick Pictures Corporation. Press coverage could not explain the need for $3,000 in an enterprise that had lately estimated assets of $14 million. There were stories that the company was only "film poor" for the moment; reorganization would soon put things straight. That was the silver lining Al Hirschfeld and other employees wanted to believe.

Ever afterward, David asserted that the bankruptcy had been not just involuntary, but a ganging up of enemies in which the free-spirited but unworldly Pop had been trapped. The legend that Zukor and others in the business had plotted against Pop was a way of evading responsibility or the need to explain where all the paper money had gone. There is no evidence of malign conspiracies. Rather, it is clear that Pop (and other Selznicks) had had a business pattern of rapid legal maneuver, bluff, and outright deceit, of throwing money around in the hope of attracting more, and of being unable to compete in the more sophisticated picture business.

There was a committee set up to reorganize Select—it consisted of Hyman Winik, Ralph Ittelson, W. C. J. Doolittle, M. C. Levee, and Charles Pain, many of whom were also L.J.'s creditors.

The reorganization never worked—if anything saved Pop from greater disgrace it was the sheer number of companies, charges, and countersuits. By October 1924, a receiver was appointed and even Myron sued for unpaid salary. In December, there was a sale of assets, as Universal purchased the offices at 729 Seventh Avenue, several film exchanges, and a mass of scripts and story properties. For two more years, the court actions went on until lawyers guessed their fees would never be paid. In July 1925, a judge sustained Pop's refusal to answer whether "he had knowledge of wrongdoing in the management of his old company by members of a reorganization committee." Pop said he was opting for silence so as not to injure himself in other cases.

As for David, he did consider taking a job. But he decided the crisis was too grave for that. Instead he would promote a bankroll for new pictures. The distinction may seem comic, yet promotion was a higher calling to the Selznicks than being employed. As early as February 1923, he had several schemes in case the worst came to the worst. He had approached A. C. Blumenthal, the financier, with a story for a film he had found but not yet purchased. He reckoned it could be made for $100,000, with Ralph Ince directing, Edward Montagne on the continuity, and an ideal cast of Elaine Hammerstein, Conway Tearle, and Lew Cody. The letter that survives does not name the story or describe it beyond proposing "a Long Island society opening, with an opportunity for luxury and clothes." The story was not important. David had the package lined up, and all he asked was a weekly drawing account of $4,000 and half the profits. Yet Blumenthal preferred to think it over.

So David pitched his plans on a grander scale. Five days after talking to Blumenthal, he was dealing with William Connery and a group of investors at the Los Angeles Athletic Club. Now he had a series of four or six pictures in mind over the course of the year. They would cost no more than $125,000 each and were to be made with David "in complete charge of production." He had no hesitation in asking for half the profits again, despite the absence of his own investment. He was offering his vision, his talent, his energy, and his being—"because my entire future in the industry is at stake."

All he asked in the meantime was $150 to $200 a week, cash in hand, "the exact amount to be determined by you." David would have made sprocket holes for spending money.

In 1923, David had the promoter's instinct for what was happening and what people wondered about. After all, for Pop, he had been active in making newsreels, and he had hired Will Rogers as a drawling commentator on current events.

Boxing was a great rage of the early 1920s, in part because it had a new heavyweight champion, not a giant who fought in the slow, grand image of bareknuckle pugilism, but a hustling, aggressive thug. In 1919, in Toledo, Ohio, Jack Dempsey had taken the world heavyweight championship from Jess Willard. For three rounds, Dempsey had battered a man five inches taller and sixty pounds heavier into submission.

Dempsey became a national figure and a promotable force. He was managed by Jack Kearns and promoted by Tex Rickard, and he was known as the "Manassa Mauler." On July 2, 1921, the cheerfully ugly Dempsey was pitted against "Gorgeous" Georges Carpentier—handsome enough for movies. The fight was held in New Jersey in a specially built arena. Rickard made it a social attraction and sold $1.789 million worth of tickets, the first million-dollar take.

In the course of 1922, Dempsey fought only exhibitions: he was too rugged for most fighters, and a big gate needed an opponent with enough reputation. A bout was scheduled for September 1923. It would be Dempsey's return to the New York area, for the fight was set for the Polo Grounds. The opponent was a creation from Argentina, Luis Angel Firpo, otherwise known as "the Wild Bull of the Pampas." That was a label to sell tickets, especially when few boxing fans knew where Argentina was or what Firpo had done.

David spent $15 taking an acquaintance, Phil Rosen, to lunch. Rosen was a director and of Russian birth. In 1922, he had directed Rudolph Valentino in *The Young Rajah*. Rosen would find the modest financing that David needed. It seems likely that Tex Rickard was involved in this venture, for no one would benefit more from a short movie that told the public why they should be afraid of Firpo. But there is no evidence of where the $2,000 came from so that David could make *Will He Conquer Dempsey?*

It was a film shot in one day, sometime in the spring of 1923. Firpo made himself available for $1,000, and with a cameraman named Johnson, David went to work:

> We ran Firpo's tail ragged around Central Park, and wore the big bull
> out boxing on roofs and in other places where I didn't have to pay any
> rentals or pay for any lights.

The two-reeler (not more than thirty minutes long) cost $2,059.71, and it boasts the most meticulous budget of any Selznick picture. One hundred forty dollars went for library footage of the two fighters, and $161.45 covered film stock, but David recouped $32 for negative not exposed. There was $17 for a park permit and $5 for horses and grooms. Among the taxi fares, there was $3.30 for a trip out to Long Island. David made $50.

He did better eventually. The film played as a supporting short in New York area theaters that summer. David was in line for 60 percent of the profits after expenses had been covered—he never got a better deal. The fight took place on September 14, with 90,000 inside the Polo Grounds and another 25,000 outside rioting to be let in. In the first round, Dempsey floored Firpo seven times before Firpo knocked Dempsey clean out of the ring. Fans pushed him back in, and in the excitement the referee forgot to count. But in the second round, Dempsey hit the bull "on the button" and knocked him out. Once again, the take had gone over a million dollars for four minutes' action. (In 1934, in *Manhattan Melodrama*, David remembered the fight: old pals Clark Gable and William Powell meet on the ramp behind the seats, and they talk long enough to miss the show.)

Firpo was not David's only coup. It must have been Phil Rosen who alerted him to doing something with Valentino. *The Young Rajah* had premiered on November 12, 1922. After that, there was nothing, for Valentino was in a contract dispute with his employer, Famous Players–Lasky. The actor went back to New York with his wife, and he issued statements: "I cannot endure the tyranny, the broken promises, the arrogance or the system of production." The studio offered more money ($7,000 a week), but Valentino was courted to "ghost" his memoirs and "author" a book of poetry in which he served as psychic intermediary for Robert Browning and Walt Whitman.

David could not fail to hear the cry of beleaguered independence or miss an opportunity to show up Zukor. The Mineralava Company (in cosmetics) had prevailed on Valentino's spare time to judge a beauty contest, to be held in October 1923 at Madison Square Garden (still the Stanford White building at Madison and Twenty-sixth Street—not the new Garden that Tex Rickard would build for fights). Myron talked Mineralava into a two-reel newsreel it could use for advertising.

This was a larger venture than the Firpo film. With Rosen, Herman Thearman, and George Ullman, Valentino's public relations manager, David formed Beauty Pictures Corporation. In fact, the eighty-eight competing beauties took more screen time than Valentino, but the picture was so successful that David claimed to have made $15,000 on it.

David was not the only Selznick fending for himself. Myron was enamored of the young actress Marjorie Daw, who was still married to, though separated from, the director Eddie Sutherland. In 1923, Myron took Marjorie to England, where she appeared in a picture, *The Passionate Adventure*, produced by the young Michael Balcon and directed by Graham Cutts. Myron had some participation in the project, presumably as provider of talent. But the most significant aspect of the film was that it introduced Myron to a future client, the young art director and coscenarist Alfred Hitchcock.

In New York, L.J. was stirred by thoughts of a new start. In the summer of 1923, Pop Selznick issued a statement—a short essay—in which he decried the drive for bigger and more expensive pictures. Some were fine, he said, but others only spurred the producer toward extravagant expenditure. Further, he said, the small exhibitors throughout the country simply could not afford the terms attached to the big pictures.

He had a scheme that would remedy the situation:

> Based on the experience which I have had and the wealth of literary and dramatic talent which is available in New York City, I propose to produce at the outset one picture a week, not exceeding 4,500 feet in length, and to cost not more than $15,000. Production at this figure

will be made possible by the most rigid economy in production, emphasis upon the entertaining character of the story, the use of undeveloped dramatic talent and unpretentious sets. Such pictures can be turned out in the space of two weeks in studios in New York City, of which there is an abundant supply at insignificant rentals.

Only one film was made according to this scheme, but it was David's debut as a producer of fiction movies. It was a piece called *Roulette*, only fifty minutes long, and financed by William Rosenfeld's Aetna Pictures for distribution by the shell of the Selznick Distributing Corporation. Rosenfeld had loaned money to L.J. in 1922, and he controlled his investment here as closely as possible. The movie was made late in 1923, directed by S. E. V. Taylor, from a script by Gerald C. Duffy, and starring Edith Roberts and Norman Trevor.

David never felt affection for the movie, yet he was aggrieved over what became of it. He had made the picture for $17,500, and then faced marketing obstacles from Rosenfeld. David had taken it upon himself to order advertising for the film beyond the contractual limit of $4,000. Rosenfeld had responded by telling W. C. J. Doolittle, president of the Selznick Distributing Corporation, "that David O. Selznick is not an officer of this company and had and has no authority to make or approve any changes whatsoever in the contract between our company and yours, whether affecting advertising or anything else."

In the spring of 1924, as *Roulette* came to nothing, David was still using 270 Park Avenue as an address. But the era of Lewis J. Selznick was very near its close: *Roulette* was the last movie made by any of his interests. On April 29, L.J. issued a new statement of intentions:

> I am in the radio business—and I am in it with both feet. I believe
> in the tremendous possibilities of Radio, and have every confidence
> that I can accomplish big things in it.

He had organized the General American Radio Manufacturing Corporation—it had taken office space and was "now in full swing." They had acquired the Voceleste machine, a radio made in Cleveland. Several of L.J.'s backers in the venture came from that same city.

By July, General American Radio was consolidating with other "independent" companies and making brave noises about $10 million of preferred stock. L.J. was president of the outfit, and he talked knowledgeably now of vacuum tubes and tungsten filament wire, all covered by patents that were "of the greatest importance in the radio field." But Pop had never had a project that was ordinary or normal—just as David could never make a modest picture.

2 · YOUR FOOLISH KIND OF MAN

IN 1924, David had energy to burn, but no direction to follow. There was not much cash to play with, and living arrangements were uncertain. If ever the teenager raised to the smell of celluloid was to think of another career, this was that moment. And David thought of many other things: to be an author or a publisher, to be in love and write poetry, to be a thrusting newcomer in the radio business, or to seethe with frustration.

The young actress Aileen Pringle knew David then. She was several years older than he was, and he looked on her with adoration as a "lady" who had overcome parental waywardness. Miss Pringle's father was George Bisbee, president of the Pioneer Fruit Company. When he died bust, the daughter—not far short of thirty—went boldly into films and was a hit, playing Elinor Glyn's flapper in *Three Weeks* and *His Hour*, in 1924. "Pringie" remained always a friend, and nearly sixty-five years later she recalled the young David: "He had a great laugh as a young man. He was lots of fun, but a nervous wreck—he must have walked 20 miles if he was saying good-bye to you!"

David was more romantically involved with Mary Giblyn, the daugh-

Mary Giblyn

ter of Charlie Giblyn, who had directed for L.J. Mary, who lived in Yonkers, was a petite, sharply pretty brunette. The two romantics exchanged poetry, David's a version of that cabled impressionism fashioned in *The Brain Exchange* and Mary's somewhat more conventional and worked over.

He sent one to her, "David-O sees Mary," as if the O of his name was a kind of syncopation:

> *Mignonette*
> *On décolleté . . .*
> *A silken silhouette . . .*
> *A crystal vial*
> *Of rare perfume . . .*
> *Youth sitting on the dial . . .*
> *A cameo*
> *On a Princeton desk . . .*
> *The masterpiece in embryo . . .*
> *A rose*
> *Blooming under incandescents . . .*
> *A bit of Cabell prose . . .*
> *Vanity fair*
> *Visits Hellas*
> *Diana tries to dress her hair . . .*
> *Filigree*
> *On a saxophone . . .*
> *The lotus-eater's phantasy . . .*
> *Bill Nye*
> *Dons a petticoat . . .*
> *A young man's sigh.*

We do not have to admire David's verse—but which other movie mogul wrote poetry or took such pains to preserve it? (It is tempting to surmise that David confined his poetry reading to one author—himself. Indeed, he would make a career out of never quite having the time to read. He was the first person to dispatch his own memos without reading them.) Mary Giblyn saw the clashing urges in David—she tried to fend him off. She called him "J. Pierpont Morgan in a Fauntleroy Suit" and "an apology personified," and in July 1924 she placed him as best she could in a poem called "Nice?":

> *I think it must be nice to be—*
> *Your foolish kind of man,*
> *And be so awfully fond of me—*
> *Tho I wonder how you can!*

For the most part, David was still too gentle and pondering at the brink of passion, too inclined to explore motivation. He wrote a brooding poem, called "A Common Riddle":

> I kissed her
> But I don't know why;
> I kissed her
>   And she didn't try
>   To stop me
>
> I kissed her;
>   And before I die
> I'd like to know
>   The reason why
> I kissed her
>   And she didn't try
>   To stop me.

David was also, whether he liked it or not, acting as agent for L.J. and Myron. A friend, Reggie Ford—in Paris with Myron—had written wondering about the French franchise for the Voceleste (the radio sold for $215 complete, but David was ready to offer Ford 55 percent off for cash business). Ford had also enquired about sending French radio valves or tubes that David could sell in the United States. But David said R.C.A. had a monopoly, and "I do not see how we could import tubes through you unless we chose to become boot-leggers."

He added in his letter to Ford that he was "stealthily carrying on propaganda for a little voyage" to France himself. By July, he was ready to sail, on the *Leviathan*, but was put off by the promise of Myron's return. Not long after that, David was required to do a little promoting on behalf of Marjorie Daw. Myron must have guessed that David had more credibility as a salesman. So David wrote to Louella Parsons, columnist at the New York *American*, to say that Marjorie was "appearing now under our guidance, if not our actual management." He sent recent photographs, supplied an update on Miss Daw's work in Europe as well as her next film (*The One-Way Street*, with Anna Q. Nilsson and Ben Lyon), and concluded, "I do wish you could see your way clear to giving her a nice, illustrated write-up. And if you will remember her kindly and often in the future you will be granting the only favor I could ask of you these radio days."

But he had spare time enough for jokes and games. He typed up a private news sheet, "The Idiot's Gazette," rather along the lines of *The Brain Exchange* but meant for his increasing circle of movie people, socialites, flappers, and family. It had jocular stories about Myron, Mary Giblyn, another girlfriend, Wilhelmina Morris, and even Ishii, for no economies had yet deprived the Selznicks of their Japanese butler.

He even did a mock stock report from "Sellsnix and Chump" on M.T.G. Preferred (i.e., Mary Taylor Giblyn). He called the stock a "romantic insecurity," and the point of the joke was to persuade Mary (and himself) that he wanted her to marry him: "Rumors of an impending statement from the M.T.G. headquarters have been rife for several days; its failure to materialize has caused considerable consternation and depression, and old traders are somewhat surprised that there has been no appreciable resultant slump."

David was tall now; he had thick wavy hair with not a trace of gray yet—no matter how hard he searched for it. He could be brilliant when he talked, but too often a little clumsy physically. No one knew anyone half as smart or as Old World romantic. There was no doubting his fascination, for his address book kept data on a bevy of girls, most of them more sophisticated or less worldly than he was. There was no ideal match, yet no one so clever or so naive. But the young women who came closest to being it saw that David was a handful, hard to hold or please, and evidently destined for something grand.

He was also intrigued to date Gentile girls, shiksas. There is no hint in the verse that Mary Giblyn flinched from David because he was Jewish. L.J. had raised the boys without religious training. Yet the movie business was already dubbed the province of Jews. There were those who traced the unscrupulousness of monetary pursuit in pictures to the presence of the Jews.

David and Myron wanted to pass in Gentile society—with men as much as with women. They liked to kid themselves that people did not notice or care about their Jewishness. They believed they had acquired American looks and a show-biz manner. But they were angry about this act, like any people engaged in betrayal. Myron, especially, got into fights if people made Jewish cracks, but then later repeated the jokes himself as a way of seeming superior.

Though David moved through New York in those years like a hurrying taxi, with friends galore and ideas coming out of his ears, still he could not have avoided the prejudice of the time. There had always been those opposed to Pop for a reason best confined to private correspondence. Thus, Lewis J. had seemed to one man, "A little fat, sawed off, undersized, hooknosed Jew simp by the name of Selznick (you don't pronounce it, you sneeze it)." David typed out a mocking litany, "Fifteen Reasons for Hating a Jew." Ten of the reasons are just "Because he is a Jew," and the others are:

3. Because he isn't eligible at the country club. . . .

6. Because he disagrees with you as to whether a certain Jew had a
   father or a Father. . . .

9. Because a couple of thousands of years ago some Jews had
   something to do with the death of a Jew. . . .

12. Because, Jew though he is, he thinks he's as good as you are. . . .

15. Because your friends have fifteen reasons for hating a Jew.

There came to New York at this moment a Jew from Chicago, a newspaperman and a writer-to-be, Ben Hecht. Hecht was nine years older than David, and he was about to become his first significant friend, the best male to talk to beyond Pop and Myron. Hecht lived on West Fourteenth Street, and he saw how a curious Jewish anti-Semitism worked in New York.

In Chicago, Hecht had grown up un-Jewish—he did not feel Jewish, but he did not doubt or discredit it. Yet in New York, he saw many Jews attempting to escape their condition:

> I understood what the trouble was with these colleagues. They were full of pretense missing in me. To become un-Jewish involves no pretense. The pretense lives in the delusion that, having ceased to be a Jew, you have become something else.
>
> Also, my colleagues had become un-Jewish out of fear, rather than out of sacrilege or indifference; and this fear stayed in them. It kept them as vulnerably Jewish as if they attended their First Nights and Croquet Tournaments with talliths around their shoulders. Their pretense that they were something else made my New York un-Jews easy victims for any hostess who chose to stare at their origin rather than their billing.

David responded quietly to such mordant insight in Hecht. Their friendship would be based on David's admiration for Hecht's dark skill with words and on Hecht's pleasure at seeing the furious gaiety of David's great act, "being a success."

It was in the years 1924–26, under the influence of Hecht, that David thought seriously of writing and publishing. For before he even began to be a Hollywood producer, David had formed a low opinion of the mainstream of American films. He was never the heart and soul of the business (no matter how good at it he was). Instead, he was a dissatisfied seeker of alternative ways and of a more literary and distinguished product.

In the mid-1920s, as he attempted to set up a publishing house with Arthur Brentano, David planned a book of his own. It was never written, but part of an outline survives as well as a fragment of the introduction. The reason for the book, David said ingenuously, was "no high purpose: I have no hopes whatever that it will elevate an industry that is, and should be, essentially 'low.'" He was writing just to correct "the erroneous amount of silly rot" that had been written about the movies. In the opening to his introduction, David expected to be "promptly and very properly branded as a traitor." The outline sums up disdain in one paragraph:

> The picture man who says that the movie game has at last reached a normal condition, and is now run on the same business lines as older industries, is either a damned fool or a damned liar. The movie game can never be normal until persons in the production end (and I do not refer to stars) are paid reasonable salaries; until some sort of sane selling method is devised, and the prevailing primitive bartering system is dropped; until a better class of men replace the hacks in production, the cut-throats in distribution, and the illiterates in exhibition.

As he began his introduction, he maintained this aggressive flourish. He pleaded guilty to having been part of an industry that turned out worse junk than the hot dogs of Coney Island. He owned up to being a traitor to what Adolph Zukor and movie magazines called "the Cause of the Silver Screen." In short, he wound himself up for crushing attack with:

> And now, with a conscience that even the Board of Directors of that public-spirited organization whose purpose is to "attain and maintain the highest artistic and moral standards of motion picture production," the Motion Picture Producers and Distributors of America, might envy, I proceed with my story.

But he stopped. The detailed onslaught was more than he had stamina or nerve for. Perhaps he recognized that he could very soon be back in the pit of iniquity. He was young and uncertain—it is fair to say he remained so all his life. So there is some hypocrisy at work here. Still, David never gave up the notion that the business was peopled with hacks, cutthroats, and illiterates.

No one was better suited to fuel this superiority than Ben Hecht, a sardonic wordsmith raised in journalism and pledged to novel writing, yet getting ready to go to Hollywood to write screenplays. As the notes on anti-Semitism may have indicated, there was a self-admiring fraud in Hecht. Like Myron, Hecht was dazzled by and fearful of David's unrelenting idealism: that's what made Myron call David a "chump" and why, in response, David saw his older brother as "a magnificent brute."

But David was used to Myron's bullying and needling. Hecht was a new kind of terror, better read, more artful in his conversation, and a real

Ben Hecht (right) with Arthur Rosson, 1927

friend. But Ben overawed David and in a forty-year friendship never stopped sneering at the movies, reminding David of his own distaste. The sneers were the more pungent in that Hecht had demonstrated how ridiculously quickly he could write a movie. David was impressed with Hecht's black suit and his black ribbon tie: he said the writer looked like something out of *The Cabinet of Dr. Caligari.*

He wrote a prose portrait of Hecht, "Neurasthenia, Muse, and Black Fedora," vibrant with hero worship, though David noted something sour in Ben's insight, something that kept him from the level of a Dreiser. David found him curiously naive about business matters—all borne out in later years when Hecht would do or doctor scripts for cash in hand, but never plan long-term strategies. It was as if, by committing himself, he might have to face selling out. In the 1920s, David saw it as a superb trick:

> His Semitic instincts will cause him to do and to sign what rubbish you will for pictures, the theatre, the magazines—if there's money in it. Tomorrow will never know. But his books! He lives for them, and them alone. Four months extra on those last chapters; but what of it? He'll make up for it with four pot-boilers in a single week.

The plans to publish with Arthur Brentano did not materialize, but not until the early 1930s did David give up all thoughts of being a publisher, and I doubt he ever surrendered the private consolation that he *could* have done it. There were nights of talk and ideas, often at the bridge table, out of which one sure commission was made: for $2,000 Ben Hecht would write him a novel.

Still, David felt trapped in New York. Myron had gone to Los Angeles to play golf and sell radios. Wilhelmina Morris had been in town, but she was on the road again, "leaving one despondent publisher-or-what looking for flappers in a broken, bewildered fashion." So he sat and read his author-to-be:

> Hecht, by the bye, has proven a great mental stimulus to your cor-
> respondent (two R's; though I daresay he might prove a stimulus to
> the one-R variety too). He is eccentric, possibly, and radical; but one
> needn't share his views to appreciate the Brain of the man. Brains and
> humor: these have Hecht, and how many sins one can forgive a
> possessor of the two. . . . And the sentences he weaves are in them-
> selves romances in miniature. . . . More like associations and—I live
> on dreams.

3 • WHERE WINTER SPENDS THE SUMMER

ALWAYS THINK of the future.

Florida happened, or tried to happen. In 1925 and '26 there was a land boom in that state of swamp, mosquito, and sunshine. Florida was as far away from Los Angeles as America could manage. But what it offered—sun, ease, and escape—were not so different from the imaginary vacation shining from the screen. In the years after the Great War, the preponderance of Americans lived with a long, hard winter in the northeast parts of the country. In 1916, the population of the Greater Los Angeles area was only one million; that of Miami was under 20,000.

So many American habits expanded and broke in the 1920s as people began to believe they might catch up with happiness. There was peace and a sense of American empire making the world safe. There was prosperity for many; there were automobiles, suburbs, liberated women, and confident men all getting under way. There were movies as there would never be again: there has never been an age in which Americans went so steadily to the movies or were so shaped by them. Do not underestimate how, in Pitts-burgh, Cleveland, and all the other winter cities of the nation, there was no more potent message on the screen than light. The movies had all kinds of narrative, glamour, and deceit, but they were all radiant, and much of that light was sunshine.

Florida in '25 and '26 was too early. But David Selznick was often premature in his ideas. In Florida, David saw the possibility for grand entertainment for people hitherto snowbound and cabin-fevered. He saw that Palm Beach was a trick, "where winter spends the summer," and he understood the liberty the place might afford. Surely, he felt it himself:

"Democracy overtaken by the Gold Coast: Knickerbockers now are worn here by the Gotham-goniff gentry with walking sticks and no coats." It was in Florida that David formed a lifelong taste for sunny beaches where he could "bake out his problems" or snooze.

It isn't clear which Selznick thought of Florida first. But they all went down there, including Howard, Mildred, and their two children. The calls of publishing and the radio business were set aside; even if Florida didn't work, it would be a family vacation.

When David first went to Florida in the summer of 1925, he kept up his publishing hopes. Hecht and his wife, Rose, had gone with another friend, Charlie MacArthur, to Woodstock, New York, to write at the home of the writer J. P. McEvoy. David hoped Ben was working on "their" book, but Hecht was already trying photoplays, scenarios, or what Western Union scrambled as "sceneries."

Once in the South, David cabled Ben, full of dreams:

> I urge you to keep on the right side of me. Am in Florida with all ambitious Jewish gentlemen and am threatened with shortly becoming a highly important individual. Directly I have gathered sufficient of this loose wealth I will return and personally direct your degradation to an affected scenarist. Anxious for news of you and whole lot more anxious for news of the opus. Write or wire me Pan Coast Hotel Miami Beach.

Ben's reply boasted of "selling scenarios right and left" to Warner Brothers and Famous Players. The opus, he alleged, was "well done but is very lousy." Two weeks later, Hecht was on the wire again—this time to the Ponce de Leon Hotel—to say he was rewriting the book and "its a peach best thing in the ice box." Seeing the jumpiness in David's residences, he predicted, "I bet you skip your hotel bill."

Years later, David admitted all the Selznicks were "flat broke" in Florida. They had only talk and promotion to carry them from one grand hotel to the next: the Royal Daneli in Palm Beach, the Fleetwood in Miami Beach, the Poinciana in Miami.

By November, Hecht was in Miami himself—or offshore. He came down the coast by ship, with McEvoy, trying to write a script on the way for actor Thomas Meighan. He assured McEvoy that "anybody with a good memory for clichés and unafraid to write like a child can bat out a superb movie in a few days."

But off Miami, Hecht sensed new excitement and plunder: "I am about to meet the free-enterprise system in one of its most hooligan hours." Once ashore, Hecht spoke glowingly about Miami—soon he was being paid to write promotional materials. He loved the mania he found, as business-men "looked at rubbish heaps and reeking swamps and visioned the towers of new Babylon." Why not more hotels, apartment buildings, retirement homes—why not the modern Florida?

> Everybody was trying to get rich in a few days. Nobody went swim-ming. Nobody sat under the palm trees. Nobody played horseshoes. Seduction was at a standstill. Everybody was stubbing his toe on real-estate nuggets. People who had been worth only six hundred dollars a few weeks ago were now worth a hundred thousand dol-lars—not in money but in real estate.

As early as July 7, 1925, the Selznicks had made an agreement with a local syndicate, headed by J. Charles Weschler, to buy 8,000 acres in Palm Beach County called the Gomez Grant. For what would the new Florida need but a movie studio? Picture City Studios was planned for this Gomez Grant. By the end of August, David, Myron, and a Claude Mercer were the subsidiary stockholders of Picture City Studios Inc., and they were in the old business of raising money and suing people who said ugly things about them.

It would be the largest picture operation in the world, "a Los Angeles of the East." At the same time, for Charles Apfel, another partner, the studio was a way of promoting real estate. Apfel was giving the Selznicks $750 a week for six months as operating money, as well as $500,000 for buying the land and building the studio. The first sum seems more realistic than the second. But the press coverage apparently helped raise close to $2 million. In that time, Apfel began to detect unsoundness in the Selznicks and tried to buy them out of the deal.

Nothing ever developed; nothing was built; the Gomez Grant empire faltered. There were already creditors appearing and dismayed investors. So the Selznicks sought to hide their name in the formation of the Equitable Finance and Securities Corporation. There were prospects for leasing a theater in Fort Lauderdale and a plot of land available in Tallahassee.

Then there was the notion of a bond and mortgage company in Lake Worth. To this end, Equitable was out to raise $500,000, and it had engaged two extra salesmen (called vice presidents), namely Leroy H. Davis and an old friend, Briton Busch. The latter appointment was the more bizarre in that Busch was one of those rare creatures, someone who owed L.J. money. Pop Selznick had loaned Busch $24,000 in 1920 and secured a court order for repayment in 1924. So, if Busch did well in Florida, then his commission (7½ percent split with Davis) might defray the old debt. However, Busch's son Niven recalled that his father jeopardized all schemes there by hitting up potential investors for personal loans.

Years later, poignant claims were made against David and Myron for Floridian undertakings. In June 1940, a Miss Violet Chapman would write to David, reminding him of 1925 and '26 and saying, "the little Gods of good fortune were not as good to you then as they are today." Miss Chapman's father had put "quite a lot of money" into the Equitable and had then got drunk night after night at the Royal Palm Hotel so that L.J. could take more money at cards. "I don't believe the story," David told his lawyer, "if only because I never knew my father to win in gambling or anything more than I can win."

Far worse, in November 1941, Charles Apfel wrote to David "from the Hospital between lucid intervals." Apfel said he had paid for the Selznicks' trip to Florida and that L.J. had regarded Apfel as his "best pal." Apfel found enough lucidity to claim his original $500,000 investment in Picture City, with interest and subsequent profits based on the later success of the Selznick sons in the picture business. This claim totaled $3,524,602.30. David howled that Florida had had nothing to do with his or Myron's later success. In the end, David was able to settle for $3,500.

David may have known at the time in Florida that these were activities a wise man should not remember or understand. He had other things on his mind: girls in New York, a few movie reviews he was trying to get into *The New Yorker*, how to extricate himself as a publisher, and so on.

Hecht had not delivered, and Myron was nagging David about this foolish venture. So, in February 1926, while David and Ben were in Florida, but somehow avoiding one another, a settlement was made and Hecht's advance was written off. David wrote Ben:

> I am enclosing herewith, the new agreements on "Panini," thereby completing, after a wait of one year, the history of David O. Selznick & Company, publisher. These papers look very impressive, but do not let them throw you. They will make Myron much happier, and this is one of my principal objects in life. You will observe that the paper is so brilliantly drawn that it also includes a receipt for the $2,000.

Myron had already returned to California, and David was back and forth to New York, where he stayed at the Algonquin. Florida had been one more disaster. It would have been easy to believe he was getting nowhere, with only a suntan to show for it. His admiration for Hecht was not diminished. He never said a word against the foolhardiness of his father. But his idealism had to stay youthful to survive such ordeals without becoming hardbitten.

''WE CAN SKIP LIGHTLY over the Florida chapter," David would say years later, adding that—whatever scheme ⁙ ⊦he family had

had—they turned down an offer of $250,000 for it. Whereupon they all made their ways back to New York in the spring of 1926, "just as broke as when we started." But Myron was already fixing himself up on the West Coast, and even Pop searched for resurrection. Mildred, Howard, and the children stayed with Pop and Flossie on Park Avenue still, but higher up, at 1111, a residence that seems to have been leased in David's name. This was not the much smaller place that David remembered, for 1111 was a brand-new building at Ninetieth Street with large apartments that rented for $285 to $600 a month. (A few years later, David and Pop were sued for arrears in rent on 1111 and compelled to pay $1,500.)

When David got back to New York, he learned that Mary Giblyn was engaged to someone else. He told her he was "glad sincerely and almost vigorously" that she sounded so happy. The loss left him feeling more worldly and mature, even if he and Mary had tired of each other sometime before. He needed to gather experience, and he had Myron's caustic urging from California. Ben Hecht was such a ridiculous instant success out there that his sarcasm became all the more outrageous. His first filmed story, for *Underworld*, would win him an Oscar.

In the brief period since L.J.'s failure, the center of picture-making had shifted to the West. Famous Players, under the overall and "modern" name of Paramount, had become larger and more successful. Nineteen twenty-four had seen the merger of the Metro and the Mayer companies and the formation of a true rival for Paramount, Metro-Goldwyn-Mayer, run by the former Bostonian theater owner Louis B. Mayer and his production "genius," brought in from Universal, Irving Thalberg.

David had a world still in New York. There was a base, he had friends, and there were plenty of girls besides Mary. But he was not being appreciated, and he depended on whatever money Flossie could give him as an allowance. His old school friend Sam Marx was writing for *Zit's Weekly*, a gossip sheet. "One day, the editor, Paul Sweinhart, asked if we had friends in the social/theatrical field he could hire as a tipster," Marx recalled. Marx recommended David. There was a lunch at which Sweinhart offered him $75 a week for tips and news—David was even then on the edge of high society, as well as on nodding terms with gangsters: he had Arnold Rothstein's phone number in his address book.

"$75?" said the broke David. "Mr. Sweinhart, I've been looking for work in New York. And you have just given me the best offer I've had. And if that's the best I can get I'm going to California."

In that summer of 1926, Pop gave his name and his promoting zeal to a foundering company, Associated Exhibitors. He became president of the company and, on July 20, there he was on the front page of their house journal, *Manpower* (twin to the old *Brain Exchange*):

> To able independent producing brains I say, "Here is the sole door remaining open to you. I will continue to hold it open." . . .
> My hands are full; my brain is busy. When weeks hence, my plans are completed, I will look at sheets of figures. I will look long and carefully.

David left New York for California by train on July 29, just five days after the Utica Holding Company sued for $349,200, debts from Pop's several movie operations. At first, David was traveling on behalf of Associated Exhibitors, and by early September *Manpower* was announcing "one of the greatest box-office line-ups of action pictures ever offered to exhibitors." There would be sea pictures derived from Jack London and a Western, *The Four Horsemen of America*, all to be personally supervised by David. Yet even *Manpower* said of the Western, "Don't start selling this picture until we have further details. We can't afford to undersell it."

There would be no more details. Associated Exhibitors collapsed and David found himself in L.A., without a job.

He lived with Myron on Yucca Street before they moved to the Villa Carlotta Apartments at 5959 Franklin, up above Hollywood Boulevard.

One thing David had learned from Pop was that a deal could win a cash advance large enough to keep one going—the kind of working cash that might permit a bigger, better deal. In September, on his own, David entered into an agreement with Raymond Bill of the Chester Syndicate to sell off stories owned by the Triangle Liquidation Corporation. (Triangle had had a brief life ten years earlier when it had attracted such large talents as D. W. Griffith, Thomas Ince, Douglas Fairbanks, and Mack Sennett.) David was advanced $25,000, but he made no progress. Very soon, he had a full-time job elsewhere. Pop tried to pick up the task, to no avail. By 1931, David was sued and obliged to pay back $7,200. But the $25,000 had kept the family going and financed the move west.

Myron was making progress. Pathé was running off $25,000 Westerns with a "bohunk cowboy" named Bill Cody. So Myron said he could do them for $15,000 and produced a few pictures until Cody himself learned to economize and fired Myron. Whereupon Myron was given a job by Joe Schenck, chairman of United Artists and one of Pop's poker circle. For $100 a week, Myron was to be assistant to Johnny Considine, a famously handsome and ruthless writer-producer. Conflict was certain because Myron and Considine had both been chasing Constance Talmadge. After six weeks,

*Louis B. Mayer, just
before moving to Los
Angeles*

Considine threw Myron out. It was only then that Myron began to consider some better alternative to production work.

But in that summer of 1926, David was out of work and wondering whether he shouldn't have remained a publisher. So he talked books. He had just read *The Great Gatsby* and he liked it, if not as much as Ben Hecht's novel *Erik Dorn*—"a masterpiece, or I'm a dolt." He did wonder if friendship with the writer was affecting his judgment. But, no, he thought not: "each of a thousand sentences is a symphony in itself."

He was reading Aldous Huxley—"I'll have to try again—and honest, Hux old boy, I will"—and enjoying some of Robert Louis Stevenson's short tales ("Dainty they are, and yet meaty—like Ruth Chatterton"). He passed on gossip, laughing over the marriage the year before of Sam Goldfish (Goldwyn) and Frances Howard—"Beauty and the Beast in films at last." Above all, David was studying himself closely:

> I've developed a strand or two of grey hair: I shall oil each one carefully and murder the barber who touches 'em.

Such avid mirror gazing can't have impressed Myron, who had been paying the rent until he lost his job at United Artists. In addition, another Russian, the director Lewis Milestone ("Milly"), had moved in with them. It was David's turn to do some supporting. Myron pointed out that Harry Rapf was now a production supervisor at MGM, and Rapf had been a Selznick employee only a few years before. He owed the family a favor.

Rapf and David had a meeting and wondered what David could do. David begged for a two-week trial at $75 a week, the rate he had declined at *Zit's Weekly*. The next day, when David reported to MGM for work, Rapf had to tell him there was a problem. Louis B. Mayer had heard about the appointment and lost his famous temper. Mayer despised all Selznicks, and he would tolerate no one of that name at the Culver City studio.

David refused to settle for dismissal. He knew that Nicholas Schenck was in town. Nick, the brother of Joe Schenck, was then vice president and general manager of Loew's Incorporated, the parent company of the old Metro outfit and the distribution arm of MGM.

A year or two earlier, as MGM labored to produce *Ben-Hur*, L.J. had seen a way of making a coup. MGM had had a deal with two men, Klaw and Erlanger, who claimed the rights to the novel. With the aid of his sometime ally Pat Powers, L.J. had a plan to buy up the Klaw/Erlanger rights and then put the screws to MGM. There was a meeting between L.J. and Nick Schenck in an attempt to settle the matter, and David had gone along as company for his father.

Schenck had protested. He said he was being held over a barrel. L.J. replied, "That's all well and good, Nick. But when you did everything possible to break me, and refused to help me since, I see no reason why I should do you a favor."

As David told the story years later, the two men argued, though why is far from clear if L.J. really had rights to sell. But L.J. finally heeded Schenck's claims of foul play and said, "I'll put it up to David. Anything he says, I'll do."

Schenck turned to David. "Well, Davie, my boy," he said. "What's it to be?"

Whereupon David said, "I think you ought to drop out of it, Pop."

This was the concession of which David needed to remind Nick Schenck in the summer of 1926. He waited outside the Ambassador Hotel to catch the great man. He said this vigil lasted two days—which is unusually bashful, since he might have called on the man. Nick was coming out of the barbershop in the hotel when David cornered him.

And Nick Schenck agreed it was a fair plea. He passed the word along, so David was engaged for two weeks at MGM. On October 4 he turned up at the studio to begin. Myron and Milly got up late and went over to the Hollywood Athletic Club to play handball. It would be Myron's twenty-eighth birthday on the eighth and they could celebrate.

4 · WOULD IT NOT BE A GOOD IDEA?

DAVID WANTED to be appreciated at Metro-Goldwyn-Mayer in October 1926. He needed to erase the years of shame and uncertainty, and MGM was the best place to be. The lot was becoming the centerpiece of the drab part of town known as Culver City, named after a developer, Harry H. Culver. Movies had started there in 1916 with Thomas Ince, who sold out to Triangle, which subsequently leased the place to Sam Goldwyn. By the time the Goldwyn Company was merged with Metro and Mayer, in 1924, the lot was forty-three acres.

In 1926, there were six stages, presided over by the most famous sign in town after HOLLYWOODLAND: a lion looking through a wreath, "Metro-Goldwyn-Mayer Studios," and the smaller, but not to be forgotten, "Controlled by Loews Inc." Over a thousand people were employed at the studio to produce fifty films a year to be sold to the world by the Loew's organization. New York was run by Marcus Loew himself and by Nick Schenck. But Loew had been in poor health for several years, and when he died in 1927 Schenck would become president of Loew's. On the West Coast, Louis B. Mayer was head of production with Irving Thalberg as his chief lieutenant. In 1926, Thalberg was only twenty-seven, three years older than David.

It was Thalberg who had drastically reduced Erich von Stroheim's *Greed* while doubling the budget on King Vidor's *The Big Parade.* Together, Mayer and Thalberg had drawn to the studio John Gilbert, Lillian Gish, Marion Davies, Lon Chaney, Buster Keaton, Ramon Novarro, Greta Garbo, and Norma Shearer. Moreover, Thalberg was already paying court to Miss Shearer. Mayer had two daughters of his own, Edith and Irene, who might have been appropriate consorts for Irving. But, quietly, L.B. warned his daughters away: Thalberg was frail—he would not last. Let an actress marry him.

MGM was a factory, with J. J. Cohn as its expert production manager. All the resources of writers, camera crews, stages, back lot, wardrobe, properties, and makeup had to be kept busy. There was a studio cafeteria—so the staff had to eat there. The great stars and ambitious directors were harnessed to this scheme of efficiency. A small team of executives, or producers, carried responsibility for several pictures each. There was no reason for them to be less than creative, but they were intended as brilliant, decisive managers. They numbered Harry Rapf, Hunt Stromberg, Bernie Hyman, and Eddie Mannix, but Irving was their model and their leader.

There had been only one great loser on the recent MGM roll of films, *Ben-Hur*, a picture that had cost close to $4 million finally, but which had been "saved" by the producer's surgery of recasting and bringing the extravagant project home from Italy to be shot at Culver City. *Ben-Hur* lost some $700,000, but it seemed a great success to the crowds who flocked to it, and it was famous for its epic scale, its chariot race, and its literary prestige. Mayer and Thalberg were alike in their hungering after class. It was just that the desire showed so much more nakedly in the rough, uneducated Mayer. There was a bonus to *Ben-Hur*: it was on his trip to Europe to rescue the film that Mayer found Greta Garbo.

But best of all was the great gamble of King Vidor's war movie, *The Big Parade*, with John Gilbert and Renée Adorée: though it had cost $382,000, it made a profit of nearly $3.5 million. It was the picture that brought confidence to the new studio, and it had everything MGM took pride in: spectacle, stars, romance, sentimental ideas, and a vague but strident air of seriousness. *The Big Parade* is to Ford Madox Ford's *No More Parades* as ketchup is to claret. But in 1925 and 1926, popular culture was the call of demagogues and tycoons alike. To stand in the way of the popular was to be unpatriotic, stuffy, stupid, and old-fashioned. "Everybody" saw *The Big Parade* and congratulated themselves on realizing war was wicked and pointless.

Now Mayer was "everybody's" movie mogul. At Culver City, Thalberg was regarded as the "genius." He had taste, he was well read, he was courteous, elegant, and efficient in all he did and said. Thalberg spent hours with writers or in the cutting room, demonstrating how thorough a producer could be without ever putting his name in the credits. For Thalberg did not like to boast, even if he was content when others did it for him. He did not add his name to the credits of his pictures. Nor did Mayer—but L.B.'s name was in the company imprint. And Mayer was as demonstrative as Thalberg was private and controlled.

L.B. was full of the great journey he was making, from Russia and being a junk dealer to becoming the highest paid executive in America. He outdid others in word, gesture, pride, self-denial (and pride at the denial). He was very strong physically; he could be cruel and brutal emotionally; he was as easily moved as dust; and he liked nothing more than to move others. He was the greatest actor on the lot, the one who never rested or sought pay for the acting. He was so much his own hero that he could not think without dramatizing the process. In what he did (running a great studio and balancing the needs and attitudes of East and West coasts) and in the unceasing theatricality of his behavior he was the most influential figure that

Hollywood ever had. And David would never be able to make up his mind whether he despised or worshiped Mr. Mayer.

In October 1926, David wasted one day to look around and feel the un-Selznick-like scheme of things. On his second day at work, October 5, he began to beat on the good-natured Harry Rapf with memoranda, typing them himself:

> I do not know whether the firm has ever had an employees' house organ, or what the policy of the company is on the same; but it is immediately apparent to the newcomer that the organization is so vast, and its departments so varied and unrelated in duties, that contact is practically impossible. Wouldn't it help all around if the Accessories Department back in the Home Office in New York knew the magnitude of certain coming productions; and if the salesman that covers Kansas knew just who was who in *Annie Laurie*; and if people here on the lot knew how exhibitors in Jersey raved about a thrill in this picture while they didn't even notice some expensive effect in that one? . . .
>
> Would it not be a good idea to discuss this with Mr. Mayer and with Mr. Thalberg, and with Mr. Schenck before he leaves town.

Another memo of the same day proposed making occasional pictures in overseas countries: "I know beyond doubt that astonishing almost un-believable grosses can be rolled up in foreign countries on pictures that are both big and local." David harped on Australia, one of those countries Pop had exploited, and he proposed that MGM could easily make a McCoy Western there. McCoy was Colonel Tim McCoy, who had risen from being an adviser on *The Covered Wagon* (in 1923) to the star in a series of B Westerns. "The one picture in question," David suggested, "should gross well over its cost in Australia alone . . . and it would be just as good for the American market as though it were made in Newhall—better perhaps, for here would at last be a cowboy picture that was different."

By October 6, David had found the basis for "a really big picture." It was a story called "Tell Them to Stop," by Bessie Beatty, which reminded David of his father's hit *War Brides*. There had been too many other pictures about "the-girls-who-went-to-war," but David had seen an angle: "The idea of the title . . . the idea of Womanhood, the outraged victim of war—of Womanhood, suffering since the beginning of time the loss of all who are dear to her that man may play at pointless butchery, rising at last with a prayer, with a plea, with a command: *Tell them to stop!* . . . If War is to end, Woman alone can end it: this, I think, is the thesis of a story that might sway the world."

This was more than a memo, it was an address. And it was so

composed in its rhythm and rhetoric it was hardly what a fresh junior could *say* to his boss. It needed to be written. Yet movie companies were not used to such memos. People talked to one another. They had meetings. Harry Rapf was quickly overwhelmed by David's memos. Here was the start of a voice, a personality even, that David exercised only in memos. It amazed people, it displayed his ability better than speech—so he thought.

A few days later, his hot idea was for an MGM in-house newsreel (another Selznick device)—most of David's early lobbying at the studio was toward publicity and promotion. The newsreel could include a few shots from new pictures and "inside stuff"—"perhaps Mr. Mayer or Mr. Thalberg or yourself in conference with author or director."

There was no limit to David's range, however. On the same day, October 15, still within his two-week test period, he proposed that the studio get a firm option on the Saint Bernard being used in an Alpine picture, and he wondered if there might not be a house screening of a picture he had had the privilege of seeing a few months before, *Battleship Potemkin*:

> I shall not here discuss the commercial or political aspects of the picture, but simply say that regardless of what they may be, the film is a superb piece of craftsmanship. . . .
>
> . . . its vivid and realistic reproduction of a bit of history being far more interesting than could any film of fiction; and this simply because of the genius of its production and direction. (The firm might well consider securing the man responsible for it, a young Russian director named Eisenstein.)

David's energy was irresistible. He was hired. His salary was doubled, and he began to take on extra supervising responsibilities in the writers' department, tracking the progress of scripts and trying to ensure that contract writers were kept busy. He rose at 6:30 and took the bus down from Franklin to Culver City, ready to work a fourteen-hour day. The memos—even the most foolish and vainglorious ones—have the drive of a young man who believes in what he is doing. On December 14, he cast in his lot with California: he traded in the return half of the rail ticket he had purchased in July.

But David was now a company man, and sometimes there were assignments of duty and loyalty that frustrated him. Edith and Irene Mayer wanted to go to the New Year's Eve Mayfair dance at the Biltmore ballroom. Rapf was charged with finding two safe young men, and he chose his new assistant to be Irene's partner. Don't worry, Rapf told Mayer, he's not like a Selznick at all, and Mayer reassured Irene, "This one got saved, the old man didn't have time to ruin him. Harry says he's a clean boy, has a good character."

Miss Irene Mayer

David was not a willing escort. He wanted to spend the night with Myron, who knew *real* girls, more approachable than the nineteen-year-old daughter of the boss. To have touched Irene would have been to lose his job and risk a beating up. Dances at the Biltmore were not that relaxed or tempting to David. He had written to Ruth Feld, one of his girlfriends in New York, about "the Biltmore boobery." He could not disguise from Irene his indignation with himself about being there. And he was getting drunk. When she pointed that out to him, he replied, "Not drunk enough."

Irene stammered sometimes. She had a low voice; she was rather withdrawn and very watchful. A drunken, bored young man might easily not have appreciated her—and David the *Potemkin* spokesman would not toady to bosses. Indeed, he saw in this haughty young woman all the handicaps of her class, even if the Mayers had actually experienced a more complete revolution in circumstances than anything achieved by the Bolsheviks. So he turned on her at the end of the tense evening:

"Listen, Miss Mayer, I have something to say to you. Once I was a much bigger prince than you are a princess. I know all about it, and let me tell you, there's nothing to it. Don't take it too seriously."

The put-down had a fateful effect, the opposite of what David had intended. For if the cocksure man could so quickly read this uneasy princess, perhaps there was something to him. By chance, or on the spur of some bored moment, he had seen deep into her—now she would never let him go.

5 · VALKYRIE OF THE KINEMA MILLS

THERE WOULD BE no way of understanding Irene without feeling the force of her father. Long before his death in 1957, some claimed Louis B. Mayer was the most fearful monster of movieland. More than thirty years later, the "awfulness" of L.B. is a given, and it is not put to much test of fact.

Irene had grown up put out of true by her father, like a tree that has to lean away from a prevailing wind. That does not mean she understood the damage or ever lost faith in a father who was supreme in every situation he could dominate and who avoided those he could not. David and Irene were both children of Russian immigrants who had risen from darkness to grandeur, but Irene always believed—with an increasing sense of recrimination, fifty years after Pop Selznick's death—that L.J. had ruined David. Whereas she was not as discerning of the effect L.B. had on her—because her father had told her, in word and deed, that he was a hero, a model, a wondrous new American.

Irene was born when her father was still a scrap-iron merchant unaware of celluloid. L.B. had married Margaret Shenberg, the daughter of a kosher butcher who lived opposite Mayer's lodgings on Rochester Street in Boston's South End. The butcher, Hyman, was also cantor at a nearby synagogue. Louis and Margaret were married on June 14, 1904, and on August 13, 1905, their first child, Edith, was born. They moved briefly to Brooklyn and business setback, and it was there that Irene was born, on April 2, 1907 (not far from where David then lived). She was named Gertrude Regina at first, but there was a change to Irene Gladys because Margaret Mayer couldn't pronounce Regina—"My mother was the sweetest, purest, kindest person, but no one ever accused her of being bright."

L.B. doted on his daughters as only a father could who wanted at least one son, but who was constitutionally averse to admitting failure. Coming to America was a game for him where winning was everything: in adopting July 4 as his birthday, he let the studio make it into a holiday for him. In turn, L.B. called Metro "a family"—he confused work and real family the way Pop Selznick muddled business and personal accounts.

The scrap-iron venture he ran with his father was Jacob Mayer & Son, but as Irene said, "Son did most of the work." L.B. never lost the physique of someone raised on hard labor or the emotional repression of someone abused physically. "Jacob beat my father—he was always down on him for being so hardworking. It left my father suppressed," said Irene. L.B.'s mother regarded him as a gift from God, but the son was deeply affected by Jacob's competitive hostility. He grew up in a crusade for power—wherever he looked, L.B. confused affection with contest. He formed an unyielding rivalry with his younger brother, Rudolph.

Irene knew Rudy as a charming rogue of an uncle: "He was as good-looking a man as I ever saw . . . a thief, maybe a killer. He made whatever money he had in armaments. L.B. feared and distrusted him because he thought he could be the downfall of the family. There was a time when Rudy came to visit us, and he gave me a large French doll, and my father was so furious, he took it away, and I never saw it again."

By way of Haverhill and Brookline, in Massachusetts, the Mayer family rose in prominence, wealth, and prestige as Edith and Irene grew up. L.B. was in the picture business by then and in it for keeps. He was like a diver holding his breath in his barrel chest, kicking for the surface and the light where movies might be respectable and worthy of America. He believed there were scoundrels, shysters, and the halfhearted in the picture business, people who, like Selznicks, had so little character or responsibility they behaved like pirates . . . and Jews. For all those who betrayed the cause, L.B. felt murderous disdain. He behaved rigidly well himself, or so he thought. He spoke of decent, truthful, loyal, and high-minded ideals until he made a tyranny of them.

Some said this left Mayer a hypocrite who boasted of probity and waved it like the flag in a time of war, but who secretly took advantage of his power. The cruelty and the dishonesty were more intricate. Mayer was so total a businessman he had no need to be sly, and he was too afraid of losing control for much personal indulgence. But he was the voyeur of others' weaknesses: that made him an ambiguous father figure to actors and actresses, and it helped account for his passionate instinct for movies—for they are the voyeur's fantasy. Mayer's dishonesty with himself—for he never faced his need for power and the cruelty of enforcement—is what made him into an actor. But to be with L.B., much less to love him, was also to have to take on the devices of acting.

At four, Irene had the waiting gaze of an inquisitor, with eyes so penetrating one might not see she was beautiful, too. L.B. told the girls he was delighted they were girls, for girls stayed with their parents, they were obedient and a comfort, and they were lovely. It was surely easier for L.B. to show affection with girls than it would have been with boys. Nor could he be so punitive if the mood took him. But he called Irene "his little

Margaret," and he poured his most intelligent energy into her. He would tell her as she grew up that if she had been a boy she could have run the studio.

Irene adored her father and rose to the challenge of being him in most ways. One of the few times she felt she let him down was when he took her to the 1914 World Series in Boston and she couldn't follow what was happening. Most of the time, he loved her "instant grasp" of things, and so, of course, she became quicker and more dexterous, with an early inclination for pouncing.

> My father had extraordinary reflexes, mental and physical. Being volatile and impatient, more often than not it was "move" or "think"; and he meant fast. It became a game I enjoyed. It's probably why I had a secret desire to become his secretary, be where the action was, anticipate him at every turn. But then, didn't every other little girl want the same?
>
> My father was not only omnipotent, he was omniscient. In a curious way, I got him mixed up with God, because of the word Almighty. Fortunately, I was saved by the Ten Commandments; many of them I didn't understand, but the first Commandment said, "Thou shalt have no other god before me," and I clung to it. If it hadn't been for that, I would have been afraid of my father.

By 1919, the family moved to California because that's where the business was going and because Edie was a victim of the influenza epidemic. Then she developed tuberculosis. She was sent away for over a year to the Palm Springs desert, and in her absence L.B. took a house on North Kenmore Drive. Irene was thirteen, with her father all to herself. But when Edie returned, it was with the status of an invalid, someone the younger sister had to serve and look after.

Irene felt that Edie returned from Palm Springs with a new sense of superiority toward the Mayers. Irene spoke of her own "survivor guilt" and of the dismay at no longer being an "only" child. But the childish rivalry was maturing. L.B. was a naturally judgmental man who could not look on his own daughters without comparing them. Irene was his favorite, but not necessarily always. He was a sentimental man swayed by the idea of an invalid, if not by the reality of Edie. Then at times, Irene said, "He would call Edie 'a lump and a log.' And he would tell me, in front of my mother and Edie, how I was the one his mother would have wanted to see. It was a curse on both of us."

A part of Irene wanted to object—and be seen objecting—to the unfairness. But a larger part succumbed to it. When Edie died in 1988, she and Irene had not spoken for years, and Irene said, "Edie was the worst person I've known, and she came by it honestly." L.B. had laid down such

Edie and Irene Mayer
"at a neighbor's in Santa
Monica, 1927"

a scheme of rivalry the girls could not rise above it. Decades later, Irene displayed an inability to love or enjoy her two sons at the same time.

In the early and middle 1920s, the rivalry between the sisters concerned romantic appeal, sexual potential, and marriage. Edie and Irene were good-looking girls, even if Irene showed darker reserves of character and intelligence. Edie had several small cosmetic procedures to enhance her appearance. She also took great pains to ensure that only the best photographs of herself won circulation. There were family pictures, but the Mayer girls were sometimes part of professional photographs, too, so there was plenty to check up on. Edie had a file of photographs that did not meet her approval for one reason, angle, or another. But Irene got hold of them and kept them close guarded in an envelope marked "Revenge."

When Edie came back from the Palm Springs sanitarium she was awarded first use of the girls' shared bathroom for medicinal bathing. This grew into what Irene regarded as a conceited and prolonged toilette. "She would take three or four hours—her pores, the clothes, the primping and the preening. And at last we'd be on our way, wherever we were going, but a few feet out of the bedroom, she'd stop and breathe on me, and say, 'How's my breath?' " Edie was also striving to rise above any suspicion of Jewish looks. "She thought I was swarthy, unclean. She was white meat and I was dark. I couldn't use the tub before her."

Irene had advantages in the contest. She had been healthy all her life; she was the smarter of the two, and she did not need to take time over her looks. But she was not secure, and there is only her natural inheritance from L.B. to thank for that. Moreover, by New Year's Eve 1926, their contest was on the threshold of its major challenge: whom would the girls marry? Or *would* they marry?—could their father let them go?

By then, the Mayers had a house on the beach at Santa Monica, designed by Cedric Gibbons (on the MGM staff) and effectively built in six weeks under the direction of production manager J. J. Cohn. The Mayers were characters in L.B.'s ardent version of the American dream. Irene was his true child, devoted to yet afflicted by his intensity and the great clash of savagery and convention in him. The David she encountered at the Biltmore that New Year's Eve was a display of eager confusion. In contrast, Irene seemed much more composed or premeditated. Yet there were contradictions in her all the more powerful because she kept them out of sight. And all David saw at first was the stuck-up aloofness of someone busy trying to stay "Miss Mayer." He thought *he* was a veteran of her young problems, of being a prince or princess in Hollywood. He was too arrogant to see she had the precision and the dreams of a kingmaker.

Of course, this Irene was also a kid still, anxious to fall in love, as innocent in 1926 as she could be when the censorious Mayer was her father and Jean Harlow had been a friend at Hollywood School for Girls. She was protected, and so she acted cool to seem more knowing. But even her innocence was strong. And as the friendship developed, very often on the tennis court, David—a clumsy enthusiast at tennis—felt the velocity of Irene's forehand as well as her guile. But he charmed her; he relaxed her and gave her daring. He told her to speak her mind, and he was the first person who made her laugh:

> *Irene*
> *A Rodin bronze of Helen Wills . . .*
> *Valkyrie of the Kinema Mills . . .*
>
> *Praxiteles adds a touch of cosmetics . . .*
> *The princess drops politics for athletics . . .*
>
> *The ingenue in an ermine robe . . .*
> *The worst-giggling dame in all the globe.*

So much happened in 1927, it was easier for their romance to develop quietly. On August 17, Rabbi Edgar Magnin married Irving Thalberg and Norma Shearer in the garden at 9401 Sunset, the house where the couple would live. Irene and Edie were bridesmaids, but no one can remember David being there. People didn't notice him yet. On September 6, Marcus Loew died. Rabbi Magnin led the memorial service on an MGM stage, and L.B. declared that Loew had been Christ-like. No one argued. On October 6, *The Jazz Singer* opened at the Warner Theatre in New York. Thalberg announced that talking pictures were a fad and L.B. jeered, "Let them develop it if they can. Then we'll see about it." But in a year, the stock of Warner Brothers (the company that had pioneered sound and made *The Jazz Singer*) climbed from $9 to $132. Studios would be refitted, theaters reequipped, and new talent put under contract. It was the business's most intense period of investment, all in time for the Depression.

Pop Selznick and Flossie moved out to Los Angeles and took another apartment at the Villa Carlotta. They surveyed the city and then went back to fetch Howard, Mildred, and the girls—though these trips were apparently paid for on advances from the luckless Charles Apfel. Howard's family lived down in Long Beach—as far out of sight as possible—but Howard liked to come into town, to roam and see the others, and to play the piano in the lobby at the Villa Carlotta.

Myron and David still shared the same apartment. Myron liked to open and read his brother's mail—no one ever wrote personally to Myron. Their friend Lewis Milestone was beginning to make a career as a director. He had an interview coming up with Myron's old enemy Johnny Considine. It may have been the urge for revenge that set Myron on his path, for he said he would go with Milly and do the talking. They would ask for $750 a week, and Milly was to shut up if Myron judged it necessary to go lower. So the meeting started and Myron began to shoot a line and threaten Considine. He said Milestone wouldn't work for less than $2,000 a week. They walked out with a contract for $1,500. Myron's 10 percent—earned in an hour—was what David made in a six-day, fourteen-hour-a-day week.

Myron took another drinking companion, the director William K. Howard, and talked Pathé out of his contract so a new deal could be made at Fox for $2,500 a week. Myron was already making $400 a week—for the next year or so, guaranteed. And these were just directors. David was thick with writers at MGM, and few of them understood the potential of representation. They made their own deals at the studio. Myron did not invent agenting any more than D. W. Griffith was alone responsible for extended narrative in movies. Myron had partners, the first of whom was Harry Rapf's brother Arthur. But Myron saw what agenting could be, and he

perfected the trick. No other Selznick had 10 percent of his influence in the
business. Today, Griffith is a name in history, but agenting runs the town.

In March 1927, David bumped into Irene again. The director Eddie
Goulding gave a Sunday housewarming party at the beach. David and Irene
collided on a spiral staircase and he made "a lunging, uncoordinated grap-
ple" at her. "Trying to kiss me!" She was alive with horror and thrill.

"You don't even know who I am," she told him.

"Sure I do. You're the dame from New Year's Eve."

But he couldn't keep up the tough act. He was clumsy—he had maybe
reached for her as an alternative to falling over. And her very firm gaze was
all he could handle. So he asked her would she like to go to the actor Matt
Moore's house where he and some of the fellows had a tennis court? She
went.

There was a gang of the guys there, in long white pants, including
Myron, Milly, and Bennie Zeidman, a young producer at Paramount. There
were no other girls. So David watched the impact his new friend made on
the gang, and she studied the talk and behavior:

> They played serious tennis, accompanied by a considerable amount
> of badgering and bantering, and they spoke in a kind of idiom,
> full of half-finished sentences and inside jokes. The quality and the
> tempo of the talk was something I hadn't previously met up with.

In that half-smart beach set it was possible to hear talking pictures
itching to begin. Myron came over to inspect Irene. It was a key moment.
He knew the coup she was as well as the danger in such a conquest. Irene
felt he recognized her immediately as "a maiden" and therefore lost interest.
But Myron would have understood the prospect of dynasty better than
David, and Myron was always aroused by his kid brother's girls. Moreover,
Irene was attracted to Myron; he had her raking, challenging eyes, and he
was evidently desperately intelligent. Irene was a good tennis player (though
she preferred golf) and Myron took her on as his partner in mixed doubles.
She played the baseline, and he was a killer at the net. "Myron was compact," she would write, "a man of few words, subtle yet cynical. He was
balding at an early age and, what's more, wore glasses, an unlikely portrait
of a Lothario and an athlete, both of which he was."

Myron commanded her attention—they were never to be other than
friends and confidants. They understood one another at the outset. But that
meant Irene heard the contempt Myron felt for all things, including himself.
What she liked in David was the sometimes foolish but idealistic talk. He
had such hope and innocence. Whereas Irene saw that Myron was incapable
of letting himself be loved. He was "as suspicious and jealous as only a

faithless man can be." So she placed him in her own life as an entertaining, tamed Iago.

Tennis Sundays became a routine. Irene struggled with the fact that though David was tall, he wasn't much of a player or very attractive. It was his talk that intrigued her, the lofty schemes, the mixture of arrogance and naiveté. She was also happy to be with a gang of young people and quite prepared to mask how little of life she yet knew, all the while listening and learning.

Sunday evenings were another matter. David and the fellows improvised, and Irene noticed young women gathering at the court as the sun set, not all with unblemished reputations. But it was the lack of a plan that worried her. She wanted order. So David invited her out properly: would she dine with him at the Cocoanut Grove? Her mother fixed it up with L.B., and they met outside the studio. He was late. But as they headed for the Grove—David had a car by now and a secretary—they passed the old Thomas Ince studio, "a lovely colonial building with tall white columns I had long admired." He told her it was the kind of place he'd like to have. She thought this was his worst foolishness. But he told her Selznicks had to be their own bosses. Wait and see.

She liked him better when they were alone together. Their talk had no flip interruptions from the gang. She ordered food modestly to match his salary. David ordered everything and then left most of it. He told her about his family history, and she admitted some of the difficulties in being a Miss Mayer. It was a quarter to two in the morning before he delivered her home and L.B. was awake still, standing at the head of the stairs, ready for her with violent temper. The problem was not just the lateness or a beau named Selznick. It was the threat of loss for L.B.

Irene had to negotiate with her father. She was determined to go out—so a curfew was set. She wanted to see David—so be it, but she must see other men, too, so that rumors did not grow. Irene had a hard time making other dates, but David was seeing other girls—maybe more than Irene knew. They were getting along very well, and David was rising at the studio. But in October, L.B. said he was taking the whole family to New York for an extended trip.

In that summer of 1927, David had a real project. He revived his old scheme of making two pictures at the same time. David was frank about it: he didn't so much want to make good pictures as "do something startling to attract attention." He fixed on the Tim McCoy pictures and sent the director, Woody Van Dyke, up to Lander, Wyoming, with McCoy, two scripts, and two leading ladies, one of whom was Marjorie Daw. The result was *Wyoming* and *Spoilers of the West*, made as a pair for $80,643, as opposed to $120,000 if they had been made separately. David supervised it all from Culver City as they were shot in nine days.

By October, therefore, he was a rising young executive, assigned to assist Hunt Stromberg on a big picture, *White Shadows in the South Seas*, about the impact of white men in Polynesia.

Irene was in New York, at the Ambassador Hotel, doing the "endless round" of the city from noon till the early morning. But she found time to write to "my disappointing but darling David." Her disappointment came from "the tardy, belated arrival of your 'little note' ":

> I'm doing my best to be dignified, decorous, and diffident. I'm not getting "Miss Mayerish" after all your hard work (?).
> And mother wonders why I'm pallid and nervous!
> I also saw *Sunrise*—the best made movie of all time (that's entre nous!). See it, David.
> Please write me all the "low-down" and *soon*.

Sunrise was a Fox film, the American debut of the German director F. W. Murnau, whose *The Last Laugh* had had a great impact in Hollywood. *Sunrise* won a special Oscar for artistic achievement, as well as one for actress Janet Gaynor (a friend of Irene's), and it was hailed by highbrow critics. But it had a depth of feeling and expression that marked it down as a director's film. It was not a great popular success, and it was not a comfortable picture for the studios, for it pointed toward an intensity of emotion on screen that was rare in America.

L.B. left Margaret and the girls in New York for a brief return to California. When he came east again, he asked Irene, "Have you heard from your friend Selznick lately?"

She said she hadn't, and he nodded, splendid and grim-faced.

"That's right. He's left the studio. We kicked him out. I didn't think you'd be hearing from him."

L.B. was letting Irene believe he might have been instrumental in firing David from MGM. The instinct for power never lets such opportunities pass by. But it was Thalberg who took the decision—with a show of reluctance. No one else in Hollywood had more reason to be wary of the young David.

White Shadows in the South Seas excited David as no other MGM film had done. He was "madly in love" with the romance between an alcoholic doctor and a native girl. He foresaw natural beauty and lyrical salvation, whereas Hunt Stromberg wanted to show the native girls' breasts. Stromberg told David his treatment lacked "virility and the personal conflict which is necessary to the story." David had proposed Woody Van Dyke as director,

B. P. Schulberg

but Stromberg wanted Robert Flaherty, the documentarian who had made *Nanook of the North* and *Moana.* Stromberg said let them direct together. But David thought it folly to have two directors so contrary in attitude.

Stromberg responded by telling David he was only an assistant. At which point, David sought out Thalberg for a showdown. The meeting took place in public, in the commissary. That and David's opting for "the rather strong language of youth" left Thalberg no room for maneuver. He backed Stromberg, and David blurted out that neither of his bosses knew what he was talking about.

Thalberg told him, "If you don't apologize to him, you're going to have to leave. We must have authority here."

"I've already cleared out my desk," David replied. It may have been so. In a business where far greater compromises are daily occasions, standing on principle is seldom unpremeditated. Thalberg could not allow David so large a victory. He was much higher up the Hollywood ladder, and there were days at a time when he had the unalloyed love of L.B. But Mayer used such claims as moves in a game. Mayer respected Thalberg's ability, his cult, and his reputation. L.B. could let himself think of Irving as the son he never had and as a loyal prince. But every king knows a prince waits to succeed him. So Irving let David go and very likely had the father's thanks as well as the superior's respect. Just like L.B., Irving had to wonder how important this thing between David and Irene was.

In New York, without more news of David than her father had brought her, Irene had a hotel Christmas. A basket of red roses came for Margaret Mayer, as tall as she was. L.B. supposed it came from Nick Schenck, but he read the card (before his wife) and threw it angrily away. The flowers were from David O. Selznick. There was nothing for Irene—

except the chance to see L.B. trumped. It was her first David Christmas, the subtlest he would ever mount.

Before she was back in town, Irene read in *Variety* that David had a new job, at Paramount.

This fact says everything about Hollywood's faith in David's potential. It also helps undercut the notion of lasting revenge for Pop, for Adolph Zukor's Paramount had been L.J.'s most steadfast enemy. Early in January 1928, the recommendations of Paul Bern at MGM, of the director William Wellman, and of Paramount producers Bernie Fineman and Bennie Zeidman had brought David's name before B. P. Schulberg, general manager of Paramount in California. David was kept waiting for his interview with Schulberg, and when it came he was told he would have to take a salary cut. On the contrary, said David, he required an increase. This was when other people had to persuade Schulberg to see the young outlaw again. At a second meeting, David asked for a two-week trial to prove himself.

For two weeks, David papered his new studio with memos, original story ideas, better titles for existing pictures: "I devised a whole new control system of the work of the producers and writers." After two weeks, he got a raise, the rank of associate producer, and the real job of assistant to Schulberg. Over the full year of 1928, a year of several raises, his salary would average nearly $650 a week—in other words, David had already reached an income that would be manageable now. In March, he got a Chrysler, for $2,250, and he started having accidents.

He began, conscientiously, to live as a man of the world. Irene must have given him great confidence in this, yet it was a confidence that extended to other girlfriends. When Irene returned from New York early in 1928, there was a fitting bouquet outside her door. But David was too much in love with floristry and card writing to confine himself to a single beneficiary.

There was a blonde in California who was taking David's fancy. She had a voice as high and quaking as Irene's was deep and imperial. This other girl was a contract employee at his new studio, Jean Arthur, two years older than David and already five years in pictures. As early as May 1928, David sent a note to Ben Schulberg saying, "The terms you spoke of for Jean Arthur are agreeable to her," as if to indicate some special care and protection. There were flowers for Jean Arthur, too, and when she was on location in the East for one picture, on her way to New Hampshire, she sent him a new photograph of herself with a letter referring to his lively New York reputation and requesting:

Please write—I think you might have written any way. (I shall tell you personally why you are such a difficult person to write to.)

Jean Arthur

David was rarely reproached for not writing, except in those early years when he was making a name at the studio and then moving rapidly between hotel dinners, the florist, the barbershop, the tailor's, and all the parties in town. On September 7, 1928, Schulberg had to write to David:

> I have your touching note of the 6th. Might I suggest that if you had not gone to a party last night and met Estabrook very late after you got home, you could have met him during the time you spent at the party—in which event you would have had more and better sleep and would not have had to write a memorandum about having to meet him so early in the morning after all these events.

Irene knew of Jean Arthur, though she was never sure she knew the whole story. "I desperately didn't want to know," she said later. Sam Jaffe had the office next to David's, and he noted that some evenings Jean Arthur was there and other evenings Irene. And David always seemed happy. Jean Arthur was never easygoing or confident. Few actresses had such nervous crises or changes of mind. All of a sudden, in 1928, Arthur married a photographer named Julian Anker—and then broke off the union after one day. At the time there was press comment that Paramount had reminded her of a contract that forbade marriage. Years later, the actress said she had simply realized how great a mistake she had made. But what part did David play in that realization?

Irene knew that David believed in Jean as an actress—"She was not one of the cuties who came and went, but a girl with whom he'd been in love and broken off. He couldn't beat me with her, and when I refused to listen to her reactions about me, he stopped talking about it. I never knew when she left the scene and his thoughts. In my passion for privacy, I had given him, unwittingly, the gift of freedom."

Perhaps, in Hollywood, with him an executive and so many girls around, she was taking a chance. But she believed in secret desiring, in waiting and watching. She was putting him to a test, and if she was curious about the result, she was in suspense, too. For she loved him, and she needed him to see that and to realize what love was. She knew he was mixed up, at war with himself whenever decisions arose. And fixing on that, it was easier to overlook her own turmoil of control and passion.

"How can two opposites be so congenial?" she asked herself and her readers in *A Private View*, the book she published in 1983:

> The girl most disciplined and the man least contained. He was reck-
> less, I was cautious; he was unconventional, I was conservative. The
> thing was, right there in the middle where it counts, there was a chunk
> of overlap. We had curiosity and we had appetites and an undue
> amount of energy. We were mad to know, to do, to see . . . and to
> listen. I discovered that underneath David's caustic tone there lurked
> an abashed idealism. All this and an idealist too—that was beyond my
> fondest hopes. His ideas were high-minded but not highfalutin.

She did kiss him—that was so much more proper first, before letting him kiss her. On September 14, 1928, she went east again, with Edie and Mary Brian as companions on the train. Her first letter was sent back to him from Albuquerque. This was the start for both of them of letters and cables sent to and from that train. They may never have been happier than when in transit, writing or reading.

Irene sent the letters to David at Paramount, not to home. Mary Brian had warned her that Myron spied on David's letters. As Irene admitted, it

was her first love letter, for in parting from him she had agreed to herself
to admit the truth: at the depot in Los Angeles, she had made the gesture:

> How amazed you appeared when thou wert kissed—second only to
> the shock you'll receive when a piece of lace emerges from the upper
> coat pocket of your newly-christened Watson.
>
> And so, my lovable lunatic, endeth my first love-letter (?)
>
> I have put my "mind," my "spirit," and my "heart" in your keeping
> (sort of a chance to twist me around your little finger)—guard
> them—my sweetheart—I love you.
>
> Irene

From Cleveland, she wrote again saying she hadn't yet removed his
going-away present, a bracelet, but kissed it every night. Rattling away from
him, she tried to grasp the special magic of lovers in different time zones
(coast to coast was a four-hour difference then):

> When you're nearly finished with your long day's work, and your
> young man's fancy turns to . . . the telephone—and it's rather close to
> half-past six—what do you think? I'm going to stop a moment then
> (10:30 here, I guess) and see if I can tell.
>
> My darling—this moment—you have me in your arms—and we
> are kissing—

But time and distance soured the mood—and some anxious need in
Irene to know and control surfaced. She was not, and could never be, too
easy with the freedom of others.

She stayed in New York at the Warwick and the Savoy-Plaza for over
a month. While there, she met Pop and Flossie, who were also in New York
on a visit. She told David his mother was "a *very* lovely person," an opinion
in which she never varied. But she had trouble with L.J. (he intercepted a
note Irene had sent to Flossie, thereby causing a long delay), which she
decided not to complain about. For she had never seen a father less critical
about a child: she may have envied this a little, but she deplored it much
more.

Irene was writing more than he was, and letters of hers—he said—
were lost. On October 21, she was acerbic with both the mails and David:

> Also you have not as yet enlightened me as to the fate of the other
> missing letters. Letter #4 had my address on it but has not yet
> returned. I think I shall destroy it. If I open it, I'll never send it—if
> I send it unopened, the contents will surely confuse you. That it was
> lost seems ominous, or should I say, significant? First, that you hardly
> troubled to trace and get it until it was out of reach—even tho I told

you it was being sent—again I had to be insistent, and . . . Second, as a warning to me not to write indiscreet and sentimental letters. However, I may yet send it—unwisely perhaps—if so, burn!

The tortures of so fierce a twenty-one-year-old who felt she had exposed herself were aggravated in New York by the stories about David's girls. "I see your friend Joan Bennett . . . everywhere," she told him. "And how is WA-4779? I can't think of her name—y'know, the tall blonde. . . . How is Jean?—remember me to her (if you like—tho possibly she remembers me sufficiently without reminder—but seriously, tell her I asked for her)."

Irene went to a dance in Harlem with "every pervert in town" and she couldn't sleep for five hours after seeing O'Neill's *Strange Interlude.* Talk of that led her on to the play David had talked about writing. If not a play, why not a letter? But Irene did not want to dictate or be thought a dictator: "I am not asking you to write—I am asking of you nothing except that dictated by your heart—and that you be sincere."

She hoped she was not nagging, but insecurity and demands mounted with the pages until by the end there was a strange note of ultimatum or of a lover who always expected to be betrayed:

> My dear vacillating idealist—I have only your interests at heart—please understand—if you do, you will forgive—and believe me to be, always, the dearest friend you will ever have.
>
> Everything is now in your hands—and my heart still in the palm—do as you wish. "To your own self be true."—and to me, Irene.
>
> The decision is definite—this time—you make it—and at least let me know even if you don't care to write it. *All my love* to you, my sweet.

6 · ACTING IN MY PLACE

IN NOVEMBER 1928, B. P. Schulberg sent a memo to his dozen supervisors (or producers) at Paramount-Famous-Lasky—a group that included Fineman and Zeidman, B.P.'s brother-in-law Sam Jaffe, Al Kaufman, and Henry Herzbrun. These men had seniority over David at Paramount. Yet as he anticipated the problems and opportunities of "the transitional period we are now facing" (the going over to sound), Schulberg knew it would not be possible for him to keep track of every aspect of every supervisor's work. He would therefore appoint an executive assistant for liaison: "It will be imperative, because of the impossibility of as many daily and hourly contacts as I would like to maintain with you, to look upon Mr. Selznick as acting in my place."

David's salary was raised to $820 a week, and he moved from the Villa Carlotta Apartments to a small house at 910 Benedict Canyon Road, close to the Beverly Hills Hotel in that square mile or so where he would reside for the rest of his life. His total salary from Paramount in 1928 was $33,462.

Taking his own house meant that David and Myron were no longer living together. Myron's business was growing, and around this time he was persuaded to take his own shot at domesticity. He had kept Marjorie Daw on a string for years. The silent actress was sweet and obedient, and she sometimes lived at the Villa Carlotta. But there were always other "dames" in Myron's punishing orbit. He had fallen into a flirty, hard-boiled banter with Irene, a routine that entertained her enormously. "Are your nipples far apart?" he would wonder aloud, out of nowhere. "I like breasts that are far apart." Edie may have heard some of this, and Myron may have considered going for the older sister. There was a time, in '28, when Edie was besotted with him. Irene remembered her in the bathroom they shared, Edie with both hands on the faucets sighing, "Oh, I'd follow him to the ends of the earth."

But Myron could shrug off all pursuit. "He looked at a woman the way she wanted," said Irene. "His confidence was enormous. But he laid a woman and never thought about her. He never called for them or took them home. There were no gifts, no flowers, no letters. It was just thirty minutes or an hour."

At Paramount, for Zukor, David was an executive in production, the very line in which Myron had led the way. And if Myron studied David to understand success, he saw energy, charm, and a readiness to please other people. The history books say Myron took up agenting to avenge his father, yet the deeper drive was to abuse himself and to confirm his low opinion of everyone. Myron did have a remarkable insight into the nature of the agent. He was a pioneer in so many of its tricks and reactions—not least, misanthropy.

Marjorie Daw never complained about being "family" without benefit of law. But in 1928, she went east to tour in a show with the tennis champion Bill Tilden. Her career was nearly over, but in New York she had a fling with Ronald Colman. Myron heard about it and pursued her. "We're getting married," he told her out of some perverse fear. It was done with abrupt simplicity by a New York City clerk on January 23, 1929, with no one else in the family present. "Then he brought her back to California," said Irene, "and forgot her."

Agents have to be like that. They go to the brink to make a deal and then move on. Myron and Marjorie lived briefly with L.J. and Flossie, and then they stayed at hotels or in rented houses. Myron acquired other company. Eataro Ishii, the family servant, had made his way to California, too, and he took up employment in Myron's household. Indeed, he ran it, which left Marjorie with little to do except have a child. Myron's use of other women went on, undisturbed, but the drinking increased, without any adverse effect on his clients and deals.

David was learning as much as he could at Paramount. B. P. Schulberg was an easier mentor than Mayer or Thalberg, for there was no immediate threat of dynastic complications. Moreover, B.P.'s wife, Ad, was especially fond of Irene, who had been on teenage holidays with the Schulbergs. Irene enjoyed Ad's "modern" thinking, her interest in psychology, and her common sense.

Schulberg was renowned for his managerial efficiency, and Paramount was producing seventy films a year to satisfy its distribution organization but giving greater liberty to good directors than was the practice at MGM. Although David had little to do with these projects directly, his years at Paramount saw the making of Ernst Lubitsch's *The Love Parade*, Josef von Sternberg's *Morocco*, and Rouben Mamoulian's *Applause*. Such films highlighted a program of great wit, glamour, and sophisticated romance. Moreover, Paramount made the boldest use of sound in its early days. No studio was more intelligent about seeking out players, directors, and writers for the new version of movies.

It was among this generation at Paramount that David formed associations of lasting value. One was with Merian C. Cooper, nearly ten years older than David, an expert pilot who had served in the war and then against the Bolsheviks. He had teamed up with Ernest B. Schoedsack, a former Keystone cameraman who had become interested in documentarylike films in remote places. As a team, they had made *Grass* in 1926 and *Chang* in 1927.

When David came to Paramount, Cooper and Schoedsack were in Africa doing location shooting for *The Four Feathers*. Schulberg assigned David to the picture in the summer of 1928, and Selznick proposed many "safari" elements that would be enhanced by the African material. He worked with Howard Estabrook to strengthen the script, and he urged the casting of Richard Arlen and Fay Wray as the leads—for very little of the story had been shot in Africa.

Cooper was nervous of David's youth, but he soon recognized his brilliance. The unit went to Cathedral City, and David followed Cooper's work from the studio. But when the film was previewed, there were problems of coherence and dramatic excitement. David masterminded the reediting and hired director Lothar Mendes to do some reshooting. *The Four Feathers* had been shot silent, but music and sound effects were added in postproduction. The rescue work excited David, and he promoted the picture throughout the studio. "I feel confident," he cabled Schoedsack, "that you and Cooper will both agree that the reediting has really been a tremendous game and that you will congratulate us as I now congratulate you."

Still only twenty-six, David had used the ways of the system to "improve" upon the work of more experienced men. Schoedsack was laconic: "If you say it's all right, then I reckon it must be, especially as you say so emphatically." Cooper was far more critical:

> I think your idea of switching the battle to the last was a good one and the picture is certainly speeded up but it has lost a great deal in sense of reality and I heartily dislike both the little boy and girl wedding in the beginning and the parade in the conclusion. I also think that your cutter made a great error in eliminating so much of the real African stuff.

He added that he wanted to take his name off the credits, but that was not legally possible. Nevertheless, Cooper had liked David enough to conclude his letter, "My association with you is really one of my most pleasant memories of Hollywood."

When *The Four Feathers* opened in June 1929, it was a hit. That same summer, David was preparing a picture he would later describe as the first that meant something personally. *Street of Chance* was written by Estabrook again, from a story by Oliver H. P. Garrett, another new friend. The subject of the movie was gambling, a family entertainment that was to become a preoccupation with David. The story had a central character, played by William Powell, who owed something to David's memories of Arnold Rothstein. This man sacrifices himself for a younger brother named "Babe." The two female roles were taken by Kay Francis and Jean Arthur.

B. P. Schulberg's son Budd (who was fifteen in 1929 and seeking David's advice about what college to attend) recalled David and Jean as a couple:

> Young David Selznick, who struck me then as an eager, alert St. Bernard, often dropped in with a young actress who was very pretty and very shy . . . I remember a Sunday afternoon when she sat on the floor and listened with a lovely and I thought loyal intensity while David was busy talking enthusiastically, as was his style, about some new picture idea.

To direct *Street of Chance*, David chose John Cromwell, an actor and Broadway director who had just come to Hollywood to handle dialogue scenes. The ties with Cromwell would last as long as those with another Hollywood novice, George Cukor, who had had several years directing for the stage in Rochester and New York. Cukor and David could hardly avoid the possibility of friendship, or enmity, at this time, for they looked so much alike. The two men did not collaborate at Paramount, though David helped get George his first job as dialogue director on Milestone's *All Quiet on the Western Front*.

There was another service that Cukor could do. David's dates with Irene were rationed by L.B.'s approval—to say nothing of David's alterna-

The menu and the contract

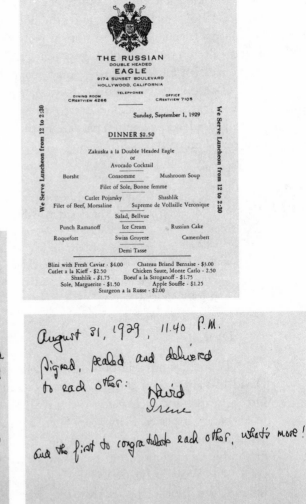

tives. L.B. believed that Edie, his elder daughter, had to be catered to first. But Edie had great difficulty getting and keeping dates.

> For my father [Irene said], I was to stay a virgin, keep quiet and keep David around until Edie got someone. And he said, "Can't David find someone for her—all the young men he knows at Paramount, guys coming off the train from the East." And at last David did come up with someone: respectable, overweight, in a black coat with a black fedora. And he took Edie out once—and never called again. It was George Cukor. And my mother said, "Is that the best he can do?" David couldn't even tell that George was homosexual!

David could not proceed too far with Irene. By her decision, there was no lovemaking, and by L.B.'s there could be no engagement until Edie was set up. All of which was magic to the born vacillator, and so Jean Arthur remained a friend. The actress was his big project and the recipient of many flowers. But on the night of August 31, 1929, David and Irene dined together at the Russian Eagle on Sunset. They made their own secret treaty on the back of a menu that offered the $2.50 dinner. By 11:40 p.m., they agreed to marry "signed, sealed and delivered to each other"; David took another menu and added a memo. That late in the evening, it still sounded stilted and out to impress:

> Darling:
>
> My felicitations, my good wishes, my highest hopes and my love to you. May I be worth the first; and may the second be ever unnecessary. May the hopes be justified, the love multiplied.
> —And may my sense of humor, which seems to have departed the while I write these words, return quickly!
> I'm just a little bit frightened, and yet ever-so-sure-of-everything. And I am, dearest,
>
> Ever your devoted slave,
> David

Tribute followed in bunches and pots from Felt's Palace of Flowers. David had an account there that often exceeded $100 a month. As late as October, roses and such went to Jean Arthur, too, but that could have been to encourage a player. Sixty years later, Miss Arthur did not want to talk about the matter. A better insight into the difficulties David had in making up his mind comes from Fay Wray, a friend and coworker from those years. Miss Wray had married John Monk Saunders, the writer of *Wings*, on June 15, 1928. Not long after that, they were in Los Angeles, at the Beverly Wilshire Hotel, where they saw David and Jean Arthur in a room talking together. There was a party in the hotel ballroom for David and Irene, and Miss Wray remembered Irene, tanned in a chalk-white dress, taking off her shoes to do a Charleston that "seemed very, very solo."

Some years later, at the Mocambo, Miss Wray was dancing with David when Jean Arthur passed by on the dance floor. Like a constant romantic chump, he watched her go, smiled to Fay, and murmured, "Oh, lost ecstasy."

There was need for subterfuge, still: the young couple had felt able to make their own secret agreement because Edie's engagement had just been announced. For a year, she had had an on-off relationship with Bill Goetz, an orphan, cared for by older brothers, and, at the age of twenty-six, out of a job after doing a bit of writing and a bit of acting. Some thought Bill was too much of a lightweight for the Mayers: he was always cracking bad jokes, and he went in fear and trembling of L.B. But Edie had had few beaux, and whatever scorn L.B. felt for Goetz privately, he masked it. He grinned humorlessly at the jokes and arranged a job for him as a novice supervisor at Fox. But when would Edie and Goetz get married?

David wanted to give Irene a ring, but could she wear it without questions? More to the point, could David afford a ring? His salary was $1,000 a week, but the family economy of the Selznicks was not yet secure. David and Myron earned, but Pop and Flossie and Howard and his family needed subsidy. David was beginning to use his salary as collateral for loans, and he was gambling more freely. He got an emerald-cut diamond ring from New York for $4,471, and in a few months Irene dared to wear it on a chain around her neck. But it was not until after their honeymoon that David actually paid for the ring.

What was L.B. thinking? And what did David or Irene imagine he was thinking? Extra allowance must always be made for the fear L.B. inspired and the threat of his tempestuous emotions. Irene was the daughter he looked to for quick answers. But she stammered. It was one of the things that accounted for her watchful air: "I was the sort of person, I let people know, 'Don't ask me what I'm thinking, and I won't tell you.'" Her stammering was most acute on the telephone. Sometimes she called David and was speechless. He would laugh and say, "If that's you, just whistle!"

L.B. must have noticed the ring; he knew how often David and Irene saw each other, for he would have grilled his wife to find out. He went so far as to announce that maybe Pop Selznick had mellowed—he was no longer a danger. (What's more, L.B. had an edge: Pop Selznick still owed him $5,000 on a debt from 1927.) And L.B. declared his opinion that Flossie was a fine and decent woman. Didn't that show he knew what to expect?

Irene established a fond relationship with David's mother, full of mutual respect. But she saw the wayward influence in L.J. still:

> Standing in their front hall [this was at 910 Whittier Drive], he said to me, "When you are married to David, you will give me a grandson. Never mind my other daughters-in-law, you're the one I count on. There's just one thing worries me: will he be a Mayer or a Selznick? Tell me," he said, pointing to the grand piano at the end of the living room, "will you let my grandson dance on the top of that piano if he wants to? I never said no to a child of mine. You shouldn't either. I want him to be a Selznick."

There is the confusion of affection and rivalry again, as well as the need for secret alliances. Howard had two children, but Howard was kept as much out of sight as possible. There is no record of L.B. being allowed to meet him or wonder where his problems came from, especially not with the increasing, involuntary nodding of Pop's head. Myron and Marjorie were already expecting a child. But there was L.J. telling Irene that hers would be the *real* one, the beloved.

On Sunday mornings L.B. would drive up past Malibu with Irene, talking picture business and asking her point of view. Once in the car he enquired if she was really serious about David, heard that she was, and made it clear she was to keep desire under control. She was not to go public, and she was not to sleep with David—the two imperatives were indistinguishable. Then he sang songs to her and rejoiced in the halcyon California life the Mayers had found. (Had anyone in history made a more extraordinary escape? Why should L.B. not feel blessed by gods?) Years later, Irene admitted their shared inability to tell all the truth: "We found those rides reassuring and felt we understood each other. This couldn't have been more misleading, as we were both to discover."

Sunday was the only day David had to be with Irene—L.B.'s drives were not casual or a gift to Irene. And Edie was left behind, whether she wanted it or not. Didn't she have her marriage to arrange?

In the fall of 1929, David had an extra opportunity at Paramount. A weary B. P. Schulberg took all his family off on a tour of Europe. David was left with the full responsibility of the West Coast studio. At this very time, he and Irene were discussing quite different careers—that David be the writer he was always promising or that he really go in for publishing. But with B.P. away, David played studio politics. The files show that he began to campaign with Jesse Lasky (vice president of production based in New York), the key figure at Paramount but someone David had had little to do with so long as Schulberg was at his desk.

David told Lasky about his vision for a little reorganizing while B.P. was away:

> With Ben gone a little over two weeks, I know that you will be glad to hear that things are running very smoothly indeed. I feel that my opportunity is both obligation and privilege, and when Ben gets back, I hope to have ready for his consideration a splendidly organized program. To this end, I am working on a schedule, in the execution of which there will be no "in suspense" period whatever for any writer or director; to accomplish this, I am assigning at least two, and in most cases three and four, jobs ahead to every writer and director on the lot so that the minute they complete one job, they can go right ahead with the next.

The letter to Lasky was five pages long, and it must have helped convince its writer that he was doing a conscientious job. There were many pictures discussed: *Manslaughter*, with Claudette Colbert and Freddie March; *The Man I Love*, an Eddie Sutherland picture with Richard Arlen and Mary Brian; *Sarah and Son*, a Ruth Chatterton vehicle, to be directed by Dorothy Arzner; *Street of Chance*, on which David was now insisting on the tragic ending; and many other projects that never came to pass.

But in the ending of the letter we can see how devious Irene's idealistic David could be. Not that he was behaving in any untoward way for Hollywood: production executives are no safer taking long vacations than ballplayers who get injured. But how does this disingenuousness fit with the "engaged" man who was talking of a literary life?

> Despite my feelings of complete assurance, thanks to Ben's patient teaching and coaching, I feel lonely without his guiding hand; and I should like to send you occasional reports such as this on the activities. Most of the things that I would like to take up with you go out daily, of course, in the night wire. I shall continue this method of communication, although I naturally feel somewhat more restricted than I would over my own signature. I have sworn to myself that under no circumstances will I disturb Ben's terribly-needed vacation by so much as a cablegram on business.

This was the moment when Paramount-Famous-Lasky became Paramount (notably, the name of the distribution arm taking over for production). Yet it was during Schulberg's trip that the stock market crashed—just when David was shooting his gambling picture, *Street of Chance*. There were immediate casualties in terms of people who had money in stocks. But it would be some time yet before depression struck the box office. For the moment, David was making his first serious investments. On September 21,

1929, he had purchased 200 shares of Paramount for $14,220—money he got on loan from the First National Bank. Then on December 23 he bought another 100 shares for only $4,482.50—the price had gone down from $71 to $45. The second purchase used the first as collateral! L.J. was acting as David's adviser in these transactions, marveling at any prudent objections the bank raised.

David and Lasky were communicating regularly, and whenever David felt intimidated by doubts Lasky urged the responsibility of decisions on him. In October 1929, he wanted to buy the newly published *A Farewell to Arms*. Lasky was wary of its "tragic unhappy ending" as well as the production difficulties, but he would not kill the project. There were delays, and it was not until 1932 that Paramount released a screen *Farewell* (directed by Frank Borzage, with Gary Cooper and Helen Hayes) that kept the tragic ending while trying to make it inspirational.

There was another problem building for David at Paramount, and it would not go away. For as David rose to a decision-making level in production, and as the Myron Selznick Agency took on more clients, so the brothers were obliged to make deals. The picture business has never liked to spend too much time examining conflicts of interest; it takes for granted that everyone is interested. For years, David boasted that he got no special breaks from Myron and that his older brother took every opportunity to screw him. That excuse does not stand up. David and Myron rose together. All through the thirties, David favored his brother's clients and Myron assisted David's career.

A feeling arose at Paramount during Schulberg's vacation that David was in collusion with Myron. Paramount was interested in the actress Jobyna Howland for a part, and before the deal could be concluded, she became a client of Myron's. Nothing could be proved, but David had employed several of Myron's clients as writers. M. C. Levee, in Contracts, proposed that any dealings between the studio and the Selznick Agency be conducted by anyone other than David. (This Levee had been on the committee to reorganize Pop after bankruptcy.) David could not stomach the implication:

> The proposed statement, that Mr. Levee "has given instructions" that Myron's office do business only with Mr. Levee and Mr. Herzbrun, is inaccurate because it will be absolutely necessary for me to do business with Myron's office so long as he represents as many important writers, directors and players. Apart from this, it makes it look as though a situation existed during Ben's presence in the studio which was corrected during his absence, which is, of course, absurd.

B. P. Schulberg was back at work in early December, and another problem arose. Oliver Garrett, the writer of *Street of Chance*, was a Selznick pal and one of Myron's clients. Before going to Europe, Schulberg had decided not to extend Garrett at $700 to $800 a week. But once Schulberg was away, seeing "how brilliantly he was doing on *Street of Chance*," David had urged Garrett and Myron to make no new deal elsewhere. On his return, B.P. concluded from the evidence of *Street of Chance* that while Garrett wrote good construction, his dialogue was bad—this distinction in screenwriting skills emerged with sound.

So Garrett went off to Warners to do *Three Faces East* for $10,000. Schulberg was taken aback: executives lust after writers or scripts as soon as someone else pays highly for them. He therefore told David to try to line Garrett up after the Warners picture and ended up paying him $950 a week. Schulberg felt confused, and his suspicions were only increased as he read David's fulsome explanation of his own clean hands. In all of David's memos, the most tortuous voice was that of self-defense:

> Up to this point I cannot understand how either Garrett or Myron can be suspected of the slightest bad faith. As to the late developments I believe Myron's statement that when Warners heard of his verbal agreement with us, they expressed their surprise and regret at losing him and Myron either suggested or considered the $1,250 offer with the express understanding that Garrett was obtainable only if you would release him from his verbal contract with me, which release I understand you gave but subsequently revoked for reasons that are naturally not clear to me. Entirely apart from my knowledge of these facts plus my belief that Myron's statements are honest on their face, Garrett is one of the most fastidiously honorable men that it has ever been my pleasure to contact. I should like also to remind you that Myron volunteered to waive his commission if Garrett would accept our $900 offer in order to help us obtain him. I am sorry if these statements are not in accord with your own recollection but I must ask you to accept them as a completely accurate record inasmuch as the retention of Garrett was so dear to my heart that I spent hours and endless energy on the matter and my memory is very clear on all these points.

Such talk of meticulous memory and unequaled hours was never politic, even if David believed it. Schulberg felt resentful and suspicious. He awarded David a $5,000 Christmas bonus, but criticized much of his work. And in one crucial respect he seems to have recognized the usurper. On December 19, David dictated and had typed a letter to B.P. thanking him for the bonus, regretting some of the mistakes, and looking forward to a vacation for himself. He added this:

> I have taken the liberty of sending a note to Mr. Lasky, the first and only note I have sent him since I have been with the company, in appreciation of the bonus.

Then some realization intervened. The letter to Schulberg was never sent, as if David had learned its lie was already known. He was tired: one flaw in the studio system was that it involved other people who might criticize and rebuke the stratagems of independence. That was discipline for which the spoiled child had no training or aptitude. Independence is a glorious slogan, but it is also a way in which connivers and egomaniacs may believe their integrity is unquestioned.

7 · SO HAPPY OR SO LONELY

DAVID'S FURTIVE MOVES against B. P. Schulberg were not only normal and expected. They likely had some support in other parts of the jittery kingdom. Jesse Lasky may have told B.P. how busy a correspondent David had been in Schulberg's absence, but not just to look after B.P. Informing was a sinister kindness, for Lasky and Schulberg were rivals in a Paramount that was having to change. The distribution business had been seriously intruded on by Sam Katz and Barney Balaban, powerful Midwest exhibitors. Not even Zukor was as commanding now, and Zukor was fifty-seven in 1930, already old for that business. Far worse, the Paramount stock was in a shaky condition.

In January 1930, David had to make a trip to New York. He went on Paramount business, yet another object was to fight the case against the Winik family over Flossie's jewelry. The trip was by rail: the Super Chief from Los Angeles to Chicago and the Twentieth Century on to New York. By 1930, it was a four-day journey and the closest to a vacation that David was likely to get. He might take secretaries, screenwriters, and scripts with him; there was always the show of work. But David loved the train because it allowed time for serious gambling as America changed from desert to pasture behind the windows. On this trip Joe Schenck was his traveling companion.

Schenck was more than twenty years older than David and a leader of United Artists. In theory, therefore, David could not keep up with Schenck's customary stakes, for Schenck was one of Hollywood's most persistent and successful gamblers. Not that David was susceptible to the friendliest cautions. To gamble in those circles was to put oneself up against people who prided themselves on instinct, nervelessness, the poker face, the skill to win, and the funds to stand losing. It was a way of acting tough and showing off; when gambling, the moguls were most free to behave like gangsters. Joe Schenck gambled with David from the beginning to very near the end.

There were stops across the country, and David used most of them to mail letters and send telegrams. From San Bernardino, in the early hours of the morning, while Irene was still driving back from the station to 625 Ocean Front in Santa Monica, he chased her with: "Train empty but heart full. Will you marry me?"

By Albuquerque, he mailed a letter, special delivery (an "oh! please rush" on the envelope), telling Irene how he'd had to open her bundle of going-away presents in front of Joe Schenck. There were English socks, a writing folder, a corkscrew, photographs of herself, and cookies to jeopardize his promised diet. So he kept a low light on to study the latest pictures of his Irene while Schenck slept.

From Newton, Kansas, he wailed, "It's cold and gray please wire your arms. Weakening Adventurer." But the wires were bright and singing. And by the time the train was at Chillicothe, Illinois, Irene was back to him (though only "Hopeful" in signature), "Darling as though you didn't know they are around that foolish wandering boy of mine. So why don't you weaken?"

In New York, David stayed at the Savoy-Plaza. A letter from Irene reached him there, reporting how they had made a spectacle on New Year's Eve at the Embassy, "standing still in the center of the floor embracing and gazing fondly at each other." At 625 Ocean Front, Irene had just begun to enjoy the benefits of a maid (even L.B. made concessions to his success, especially if they impressed his daughter). "I feel like a princess," she wrote to David. "I am gloriously indolent and fastidiously dainty." There was some guilt at having another human being whose chief interest and duty was her. "Nevertheless," she said, planning ahead, "ethics aside, don't you think we could economize on something else instead."

By January 22, David was exhausted: he made it to bed at 5:30 a.m. and 4:00 a.m. on successive nights. "All this morning I tossed restlessly (all chance of sleep spoiled by a thousand phone calls), and thought of you, and how glorious it would be to have you in my arms. And after a long while, I was not alone. You were with me, and we doing such bad, lovely things—such mad, happy things—Oh, darling, I love you."

He had just seen Noël Coward's *Bitter Sweet*, with Evelyn Laye, and he told Irene how magnificent the English actress was—"your respect for Myron would increase." There was a song from the show, "I'll See You Again," and it was made for separated lovers. Then he dined with Walter Wanger, the Dartmouth graduate who had been attached to Woodrow Wilson's mission to Versailles in 1919 and who was in charge of Paramount production on the East Coast. Wanger had more pedigree and smooth distinction than anyone in the film community. He had graduated from college! John Cromwell saw that as aristocracy and placed David as next of kin.

The socializing and the business meetings left him "a glorified wreck," and he conceded that he was no longer quite the Young Man of Manhattan. He loved her letters, he told her (they do not survive), more even than "Lasky-Schulberg wires re my work" or "those Mary-letters that I know I loved." He went up the Hudson to Nyack, where Ben Hecht had elected to live. Ben was still 90 percent the man David had known and "the only one of all my Eastern figures that has not been shattered." They walked in the snow beside the river and David revealed his publishing ideas.

Hecht had advanced. In addition to getting an Oscar for *Underworld*, he and Charlie MacArthur had had a great hit onstage with *The Front Page*. In the end, Hecht was impressed enough with David's dream to arrange meetings with the publishers Pascal Covici and Donald Friede. Another friend, Oliver Garrett, fixed David up to see Harold Guinzburg at Viking.

At the same time, David was sounding like someone who had seen through New York—"comes the astounding revelation that Hollywood is mature and civilized in comparison." He had been to a party in Greenwich Village where Robert Benchley and Harold Ross had bored him and his companion, Herman Mankiewicz. He found Ross "dull, heavy, self-important with affected fatigue."

He had a better time at the Mayfair in a high-class movie group: Zukor; Winfield Sheehan (head of production at Fox); "two silly girl-chasing Schencks; Goldwyn with a roving eye; Wanger, a smiling Casanova." Such men womanized all the time: they masked their lust in the necessary hunt for new talent for the business—thus the self-righteousness and the lack of human interest in their sex lives. David, evidently, was being tempted. Eddie Sutherland showed up with "an amazingly beautiful blonde—who bedeviled me persistently for a screen career and vamped me stupidly." But he decided she had promise and goaded his companions by leaving the party with her to cries of "Five thousand dollars not to tell Irene."

His thoughts were concentrating on the jewel suit, "which we hope and expect to settle out of court, thereby getting some money for the family quickly." Then David found a message at his hotel: a Mr. Meyer had called. David fancied it was an "ex-parasite," so he did nothing. Then he worried, and he did call back: it was L.B., come quietly to New York. "He gently chided me for not having called him, threatened to tell you of my bad treatment of him."

This led to an evening with Mayer and several Goetzes. L.B. said he and David would go together to the dinner, and then he ragged the tardy David with "Are you ready?" phone calls. David was put in a very poor mood, and he had not heard from Irene in eleven days. Had Irene withheld letters? Was she under orders from her father to let him see David without any epistolary interference?

Meanwhile, David was put to tougher tests. When the jewel case went against the Selznicks, L.B. had his scene ready. David was entranced: L.B. was "subtle, Machiavellian, likeable." He came to David's room at the Savoy-Plaza and laid out a collection of jewelry—this was no coincidence, the Winik case was in the papers. Then L.B. told David to choose something as "an engagement gift." David protested and delayed. He did not want to capitulate by accepting anything. Yet how could he have Irene without also bowing to the father? There might be debts to be collected later in the business, but this was an issue of raw power and one in which David had to wonder whether Irene could ever be free. So he asked Irene a key question, and as if a part of *him* needed escape:

> Irene darling, are you *sure*? I have been tortured these few days of your silence with some nagging instinct that tells me you are worried or uncertain; or perhaps merely not-so-much-in-love. Sweetheart, I adore you, I want you, as no man has ever loved or needed a girl before me. I love you so much, so jealously, if you will—so self-sacrificingly, if I may—that I had far, far rather lose you than suffer the suspicion that you are mine through some imagined obligation. —Now, to-morrow, ever, you are as free as all-outdoors.

Then a letter from Irene arrived, and he cheered up. The crisis of parting and of days without letters passed. He was soon on the train again, and then the cables became briefer and more urgent, from both sides of the country, rushing toward reunion like a D. W. Griffith montage:

February 1: New York to Santa Monica: "I'll see you again. Devotedly. Lucky Fool."

February 1: Santa Monica to Buffalo: "Morpheus has begun to evade me. Oh please hurry to save me. Love and mmmmm. Irene."

February 3: Albuquerque to Santa Monica: "My arms are frantic my mind single tracked and my heart in Pasadena."

February 3: Santa Monica to Needles, California: "I wish that engineer have mercy on the pit of my stomach. Must confess that I have flirted desperately but only with weather man in plea for a perfect day. Cannot decide if it is better to go to sleep and shorten the hours or to stay awake and think of how very soon my little one will be in the arms of Irene."

If train-swept lovers resembled one kind of movie—a romantic comedy in which the couple are never so in love as when apart but approaching—there was a greater drama coming: weddings that left scars. Weddings are famously the occasions of the young, but in these weddings there was no question about the central character. It was Louis B. Mayer. The weddings happened to him. His great need to be the actor playing himself dispatched the young to the wings, like nervous onlookers.

This Mayer was not an old man yet, and he had not lost any competitive vigor. There was talk at the MGM studio that he had been enchanted by a new star, Grace Moore, the opera singer, who had made her movie debut in *A Lady's Morals*, which had flopped. MGM was not succumbing to the effects of the October 1929 crash. John Gilbert films were failing, but Wallace Beery and Marie Dressler could do no wrong. Mayer was confident: he talked with President Hoover; the prolonged takeover attempt by William Fox was getting nowhere, and maybe Thalberg would live past thirty. Moreover, Thalberg had tax problems so that he needed not just a bonus from MGM, but Mayer's efforts in Washington to get the IRS off his back. Sometimes doing a good turn can be like a body blow. Thalberg had lost money in stocks, but L.B. had been less hurt: most of his money was in real estate.

As David anticipated marriage, he was more than ever worried over money. The Christmas bonus and the $1,000-a-week salary were all very well, but David had been educated in overspending. At the end of February, he sold the Paramount stock he had bought on credit, picking his moment well, for the stock had rallied to $67. He made a profit of about $1,500 on the whole thing, enough to keep him in flowers and new clothes for a few months. He was having some success in his diet, and taking care of himself in new ways. He had casts of his feet made so that shoes could be specially built to counter what he called arch problems. His chronic clumsiness began in those imperfect feet.

Irene was busy helping arrange Edie's wedding. This was set for March 19, and L.B. had yielded to her pleas: it would be a big affair. Never before had Mayer permitted personal or family ostentation; now, he felt challenged by the Crash. As Irene went shopping for part of her sister's trousseau (budgeted at $5,000), Margaret Mayer whispered to her to start looking for herself while she was about it. But David had not yet asked formally. So L.B. had not had to decide. Nevertheless, as he gave Edie a diamond bracelet, an ermine coat, and a Cadillac, so he made the same gifts to Irene.

Such tribute was beyond David: his flowers did die, and his sentimental verses were no more enduring. David told Irene: "L.B. can't control me. How do I know you can withstand him?" Irene knew there was something to the charge, yet she never understood her father's grip completely. She was too like him to share in Edie's growing antagonism toward L.B.

*David and Irene, engaged
to be married*

There was another family matter that took David away from Los Angeles for a few days. On March 11, he cabled Irene from Palm Springs: "Up the whole night pacing corridors with a black bearded papa. Congratulations in order. . . . Uncle David." Marjorie had had a girl, and she and Myron would call her Joan.

The marriage of Edie and Bill Goetz took place at the Biltmore with over 600 guests. It was "the event of the season," and it established a trend for white tie and tails for men. Irene was maid of honor and the bridesmaids were Corinne Griffith, Carmel Myers, Bessie Love, May McAvoy, Catherine Bennett, and Marion Davies. It seemed perfect; even Irene was urged to tears by Edie's radiance. The big wedding was the last apparent hurdle, and it was the better for being so grand that a smaller second wedding would be in order.

Giving L.B. time to breathe and pay the bills, David waited two days. He fixed an appointment at the MGM offices for March 21. They decided that Irene would go, too: she "couldn't resist watching them savor the best in each other."

David made the proper speech: he asked for Irene's hand. L.B. was benevolent, pleased, welcoming. David was "a splendid boy . . . the son he'd never had"—yet there was a team of such "sons" that included nearly every actor on the lot.

"What date did you have in mind?" he asked the couple.

"April 29th?"

Disbelief, horror, outrage—why so soon? "What was this, a fire sale of his daughters?" David said that the end of April was timed to fit in with the Paramount production schedule. L.B. acted aghast. Had the couple made plans behind his back? He turned on Irene: could he trust her? He became practical: how could people come up with more big presents so soon? David said they didn't want lavishness, whereupon L.B. seized the remark as a disparagement of Irene's merit. (Great movie men know all the lines of every scene.)

L.B. proposed June 14—six weeks later—because it was his own wedding anniversary.

"Wait?" cried David. "Do you realize how long I *have* waited? You cannot do this to me, Mr. Mayer. I cannot wait any longer. You're a man. What kind of hell do you think I go through? What do you suggest I do?"

This was a modern stratagem; it was talking pictures alluding to the urgent fact of sex. So L.B. elected to be shocked. "He spoke of character and self-control." And very likely this Mayer told himself, if *he* could gaze upon but resist all the actresses on the lot, then surely . . . ?

David pounded the desk with his fist. "I've had enough of this!" He flung open the door and turned to Irene: "Are you coming?" She should not have been there. She should have left with him. But she lacked the strength to make it out of the office, and she told David, "I'd better stay for a bit."

L.B. now turned to work on his daughter. Couldn't she see how impulsive this Selznick boy was? "If you can't balance him now, how are you going to handle him later? Use your head. He will listen to you and I can guide you. Then we have a decent family." He sighed. "For Paramount you'd do this to me?"

Irene said, "I cannot fly two flags. His flag must come first."

Irene went home, and her fearful mother told her, "I will stand behind you. I will defy him. For once in my life I will stand up to him."

Irene was in shock, incapable of anger or independence. She told David she couldn't marry him. So he was ruined and came pleading again. The crisis passed. April 29 was agreed to, but that had never been the point. Power had had to be demonstrated.

A few days later, David was haggling with Paramount so that six weeks of his honeymoon could be the paid vacation he had never taken since joining the studio. A "smaller" wedding was arranged, to be held at 625 Ocean Front. Irene selected her own trousseau, though she was too numb to spend more than $2,000. She would wear Edie's veil, a white satin Empire gown by Adrian, and carry white orchids. She said her mind was blank—"I seemed to myself like a somnambulist."

On April 29, the "small" wedding took place. Not even the death of L.B.'s father, Jacob—who lived with the family—ten days earlier postponed the event. Edie was matron of honor; Janet Gaynor, Mitzi Cummings, Margery Straus, and Marjorie Daw were bridesmaids, and Myron was best man. The throng included L.J. and Flossie, Howard, Mildred and their daughters, the Mayers and the Goetzes, B. P. Schulberg, Paul Bern, the Thalbergs, Herman Mankiewicz, Oliver Garrett.

The ceremony began, and Irene was still pleading with L.B. for forgiveness and understanding as they walked toward the "altar" wall of white roses. He had to tell her to be quiet so that Rabbi Magnin could begin the other script, the regulation one for weddings.

In the wedding pictures, David has a terrific grin, while Irene is reserved or like someone still in shock. The contrast has the effect of making her seem more certain or older than her husband. David had smiles for every camera, to signal confidence, but smiling faces fixed forever can look so vulnerable. In many marriages, the partners believe they are being rescued by their union. They feel they are soaring free. Yet here was a marriage that also kept the partners prisoners to a lasting pact and allegiance. It was the most serious deal David would ever make.

*P*RODUCER

1 · LEARN TO BE EXTRAVAGANT

THE FIRST FEW DAYS of marriage were baffling for young, inexpert lovers. There had been so much anticipation. Shortly before the big day, David had undergone a microscope examination of a smear to prove his wholesomeness. When he drove up to Santa Barbara for their wedding night at the Biltmore, the couple had a double police escort. Irene supposed this was her father's touch, but perhaps the police feared the testing drive for an excited David.

They did not reach the Biltmore until nearly midnight, and David had a production there ready to start: flowers with notes, a candlelit supper, champagne, and the ceremony of several waiters. To Irene, it was all overproduced at that time of night. What followed was no great wonder to either party: Irene was weary, and David was disappointed. They had waited too long for their humble bodies to survive expectation. "The poor man had a virgin on his hands," said Irene. "And he wasn't that sophisticated himself."

So as not to brood, they returned to Los Angeles to have dinner with Pop and Flossie in Pasadena before boarding the Super Chief on the start of their honeymoon trip. Myron sent his Duesenberg for them; after depositing the newlyweds, the chauffeur was to take the six bags to the station. But he went to Los Angeles in error and missed the train. When David and Irene boarded in Pasadena, the bags had still not arrived. Myron promised them he would see to it. Perhaps he had arranged the whole mishap: it sounds easier to design than have happen by accident, and it was not the worst practical joke to play on a lucky kid who had the best girl and more production values than gut instinct. Myron sent this cable to departing lovers forced to choose between one suit of clothes and nakedness:

After chasing from Pasadena to Los Angeles to Glendale from Tinker to Evers to Chance, over fifty-seven telephone calls, I finally convinced TAT officials that you were really quite a nice couple. All of this added together and divided by six means that your baggage will be put aboard the Chief at Albuquerque also that it is now 10:30 a.m. and I am due in court at 10 and besides who ever heard of a bride without lingerie. Please confirm receipt of baggage at Albuquerque.

It wasn't there. They were not reunited with it until Washington, D.C. But someone got the story into the Louella Parsons column; then the whole train knew and started taking bets. So as not to be a complete loser, David wagered the bags would never catch up with them. He won all round, for the couple started laughing at the predicament—it was as if they learned to goose their paralyzed romance with a shot of Lubitsch—and so at last they began to enjoy one another.

But then in D.C., at the White House dinner L.B. had laid on, David recounted the whole story in inordinate detail, and Irene had to mask her ruined privacy.

Then they went up to New York for liquor, parties, and the buying of clothes. David took Irene to Bergdorf's and commandeered the fourth floor. He had the models parade for her in every conceivable costume—was

Honeymoon, Paris

this life or Wardrobe? On the *Olympic*, she discovered he'd wangled a third room for their suite so that the maid he'd provided for her would have somewhere to sleep. The expense was not measured: on May 1, as his going-away gift, Paramount had raised David's salary to $1,500 a week.

"We were typical gauche, greenhorn, get-rich-quick Americans," groaned Irene decades later. Difficulties began on the boat, in the dining room, where David was intimidated by the French waiters and the menus.

Apart from that, Irene was cabin-bound, struggling to write thank-you letters. She discovered the many skills David had. "He said, 'What's the trouble?' I told him it was torture. So he showed me. He could write a brilliant note in a minute and a half—fresh, original, personal. Then another one while it dried. I took half an hour. He couldn't understand my problem."

They went to Paris—this was David's first time in a foreign country. He was hurt to discover the natives spoke French—never David's best subject. They went to famous restaurants and met many disasters. Irene liked one drink above all—brandy alexanders (she had a weakness for chocolate)—and she was slow to discover it didn't go with everything. Waiters tried to persuade David to broaden his young wife's tastes. But she was violently ill before wisdom dawned. "If you'd removed chocolate and thank-you letters," she said, "we'd have had a wonderful time!"

Irene had promised to write regularly to her mother. While David slept one afternoon, she went into another room to work on her letter. But he woke and walked in on her. Out of instinct, she covered up the pages. He was angry, and she became angrier still at being questioned. He hated the secrecy; she called it privacy. They had a full-blown quarrel, and she confessed how much she had had to guard herself against parental observation and control. "He said he had no curiosity, actually, and it had only been my gesture of concealment; that he trusted me." It seems like a trivial incident. But fifty years later, Irene had not yet settled in her mind a consequent unfairness, for he never saw or asked to see her letters, yet she often looked at his. Indeed, she sometimes believed he left them on his desk so that she *would* see.

They did the tour: Paris, Venice, Vienna, Budapest, Berlin, and finally London, the place David had most wanted to see. While there they met Sidney Bernstein, an owner of movie theaters and a friend-to-be. They also received a young actor and actress at their hotel, the Savoy. David was seeing them because they had prospects, and Paramount might be interested. She was Jill Esmond, and her fiancé was Laurence Olivier. They were only a couple of months away from their own marriage. Miss Esmond was the more established of the two, but Olivier was a comer: he had played

Stanhope in *Journey's End* and Beau in *Beau Geste* on the London stage (trying to look like Ronald Colman); in a few weeks' time, Noël Coward would ask him to appear in the first production of *Private Lives*.

The Selznicks sailed home on the *Île de France*. They were broke; Myron had to wire $3,000 to New York so they could get through customs. They were met in New York by Margaret Mayer, for the silent mother had been more devastated by Irene's going than L.B. This was the start of a melancholia that would make her even less suited as Mrs. Mayer. The three came west on the train, and Myron joined them at San Bernardino, pleased to see them and interested in Evelyn Laye news acquired in London.

David did not report back at Paramount until after July 4. They were out of money and without anywhere to live yet. So David elected to reside at the Ambassador Hotel. The bills drove Irene to despair, until Pop and Flossie urged them to come stay at their Whittier Drive house. Seeing David with his father, Irene understood how pampered her husband was—though we should allow for her wonder at the great, loose affection swimming between David and L.J. But Irene was learning from domestic agencies that the Selznicks always had a hard time keeping servants: the men in the family were so unreliable about time.

David's happiness had given Pop new daring, and at the wedding he had met Irene's Uncle Rudolph. The two men had things in common: L.B. despised the pair of them. So they dreamed up a plan for cartoons on topics of the day. By September, Pop could airily claim "a wonderful staff turning them out," in defiance of reality. Then as two plotters talked more, Pop discovered that Rudy was "an impossible man to get along with" and maybe insane. Still, if L.B. had got wind of the alliance, he had a fresh reason to be reminded of Selznickery.

Irene looked around for a place, and they rented 610 North Camden Drive (just south of Sunset), which belonged to Blanche Sweet. From the outset, David had three house servants and a chauffeur. The battle began between her prudence and his lavishness. She was buying secondhand furniture and darning his socks. He was horrified at such defeatism. He had the services of a business manager, Rex Cole, and Myron was his hardheaded adviser. But he couldn't stand for Irene to be preoccupied with the debts. He told her to "learn to be extravagant." That would prove her confidence in him.

Irene never mastered that trick; no torture could have made her put on its act. Among the immigrants to Hollywood who came out of Russia, some became conservatives and others preferred abandon. This was not a matter of political allegiance: most of the new movie moguls were Republicans. But as newcomers who had made fortunes (not always scrupulously), they were avid for ways that kept the rich secure. It was as if in Russia they had learned the unyielding aloofness of wealth and the rigor of the police. Louis B. Mayer had revolutionized his life, but he had the retentive grip of a banker bred from a mongoose.

There were others who believed money was ephemeral, mocking of human nature and desires and fit only to be spent. They taunted it with gambling—there are many ways to explain the urge to gamble, but one is the refusal to be money's slave. David had a habit of breaking the limits of budget: he did it to the companies he worked for, but just as much to the budgets he approved for himself. The Mayers thought his behavior was immature and unsound. But America—the new home for all these people— has lived like a reckless kid and shows no sign of reforming. It is worth repeating the request David made to Irene: if she could learn to be extravagant it would prove her confidence in him. David wanted all his life to be confident, and if he could not muster it himself then he sought it in those who loved him.

His final year at Paramount saw him less involved in particular productions than in corporate struggles. *Manslaughter* opened in July 1930, directed by George Abbott, starring Claudette Colbert and Fredric March, and November of the same year saw the premiere of the most enduring Paramount movie with which David was closely involved—Harry d'Abbadie d'Arrast's *Laughter*, with March and Nancy Carroll, written by Donald Ogden Stewart, with Herman Mankiewicz as cowriter and on-set producer. David was only one of the people at the party of its making, but few films are so good at getting the fast, sexy grace of early talkies.

In his increasing conflict with B. P. Schulberg, talent and material were frequently the issue. Two weeks after returning to work, he urged Schulberg to employ Dashiell Hammett as a screenwriter. If David hadn't himself read *The Maltese Falcon* or *Red Harvest*, he felt the stir those books had caused. He believed Hammett was "unspoiled as to money" and gettable for about $400 a week. Hammett wrote *City Streets*, the 1931 crime picture, directed by Mamoulian and starring Gary Cooper and Sylvia Sidney, the actress with whom B.P. was infatuated.

There was an unhappier end to Paramount's hiring of Sergei Eisenstein. Jesse Lasky had put the Russian under contract, and David was a supporter of the venture. However, by October 1930, Eisenstein and his associates had done a script for Dreiser's *An American Tragedy*. David thought it not only the most moving script he had ever read, but "positively torturing. When I had finished it, I was so depressed that I wanted to reach for the bourbon bottle. As entertainment, I don't think it has one chance in a hundred." He told Schulberg it would be brave to make the script "purely for the advancement of the art," but braver still and kinder to the stockholders not to.

This advice was taken, and Eisenstein—shabby, wild-haired, and so living it up in America that he seemed like Harpo Marx—invaded Mexico. When David heard the Russian was gone, he let it be known how wise and expert B.P. had been: "Isn't Mr. Schulberg wonderful? He waits and waits and chooses the right moment to strike, and always gets his own way."

In the fall of 1930, Paramount was approached by David Sarnoff, president of the Radio Corporation of America (and thus the head of RKO). He wanted David O. Selznick to run his movie company, and he was ready to offer Paramount $50,000 for trading him. Adolph Zukor declined the offer in October. But the outside interest forced Zukor and Lasky into a new vision of the future. They suggested to David that he would and should—very soon—replace B. P. Schulberg himself. That would have been a dramatic promotion, and it shows the impact of David's talent and energy. B.P. had not handled the transition to sound very well, and there was studio uneasiness over his romance with Sylvia Sidney. Moguls might screw actresses—but abandoning family for them was not professional or necessary.

For public consumption, David was a loyal defender of "Mr." Schulberg. B.P. had thrown a big party for David and Irene on the eve of their marriage. David said later that B. P. Schulberg was "a really great mill foreman . . . his strength was in the days when people had the movie-going habit, when pictures were sold en masse, and when a difference in quality made extremely little difference in the gross on the picture. But as the industry changed, and as the public became more selective, and as the method of selling pictures changed, the assembly-line method of making pictures obviously became outdated and destroyed its adherents."

David asked Lasky and Zukor what would become of Schulberg. They said he would be moved decently upstairs. David had politicked for this, yet he could not bear to have the deed done. So he went to Schulberg and asked the victim if *he* was agreeable. As a result, the move was put in abeyance and B.P. gave up talking to David—not just traitor, but informant, too. As a sign of the rift, and as evidence for David's maneuver, his files contain an undated, unsigned list of charges against B.P. At eight pages, the indictment is too thorough to quote in full, but these are some highlights:

- B.P. let Wallace Beery go to MGM
- he let Richard Dix, writer Howard Estabrook, and director Wesley Ruggles go so that they had the great hit of *Cimarron* at RKO
- he considered William Wellman "an incompetent, a has-been and a maniac," whereupon Wellman made *Public Enemy*

- he lost director Victor Fleming, "considering him old-fashioned and impossible for talking pictures" (*Note*: David was a believer in Fleming this early)
- he turned down Lewis Milestone
- he said *Street of Chance* would fail, *Honey* was "a hopeless mess," and *Sarah and Son* "bad management"—all were David's ventures and all were hits
- he refused to take on Constance Bennett
- he said Howard Hughes was crazy to let Milestone make *The Front Page*
- he turned down director Howard Hawks "as an absurd incompetent"
- he could never get along with Oliver Garrett
- he fired Jules Furthman, who had written *Morocco* for von Sternberg
- he turned down *Dracula* as "too wild and dangerous"
- he opposed the making of *City Streets*
- he never believed in Joseph L. Mankiewicz, the young dialogue writer hired by David
- he "regretted that George Cukor was under contract, termed his attitude 'much too sophisticated to allow his being a successful director' "
- insisted Janet Gaynor was finished

Not all these charges were fair or unanswerable. But there is ample reason for David and Schulberg giving up talk for memos. By the spring of 1931, David was pushing hard at a crumbling edifice. Paramount was in increasing trouble as theater attendance fell. But David was asking for more money, claiming his $1,500 salary was out of line with the rest of the business and reminding Schulberg of how they had "repeatedly bemoaned the fact that the largest percentage of the best brains in the industry are drawn to direction and writing, rather than to executive work."

Something else may be said of that list of B.P.'s failings: Estabrook, Wellman, Milestone, Connie Bennett, Oliver Garrett, and Cukor were all clients of Myron's.

No matter the studio's financial plight, David got action. On March 14, 1931, he won a raise to $1,750 a week, and on May 1, another brought him up to $2,000. In the same month, Paramount invited John Hertz of Lehman Brothers to guide their financial reorganization. He advised heavy cuts in the program and salary cuts across the board.

David refused: "I think I have the correct perspective on my abilities and the value of my services," he wrote to Schulberg on June 15, "and, judging even by present low salary standards, I do not think that I am being overpaid." He said he had another ten months on his contract at $2,000 a week, and he planned to take it. "Please advise me whether I may proceed accordingly."

B.P. did not reply to the ultimatum. And so, at the end of June, David was out of a job. He had come to the conclusion no studio could be run that way, with too many pictures being made and poorly qualified people in charge. He told B.P. he had not sought or received any other job offer, except for the RKO approach. That seems unlikely. But it was a tough moment to be so bold.

Only months later, anonymously, Schulberg wrote "a series of vicious pieces" against David in the trade press. David found the texts for the articles, in B.P.'s handwriting, and confronted the true author years later when Schulberg was a fallen figure in the town. Briefly, in 1944, David gave the older man a job. A few years later, he administered the final snub, a charity check for $500 in hard times.

2 · SHOOTING WITH BOTH BARRELS

BY MARRYING IRENE and then withdrawing from Paramount, David had made himself central to the politics and anxieties of Hollywood. He relished the attention; he believed it must improve the deal he was going to make. That July 1931, free of Paramount, he and Irene rented one of the smaller beach houses in Santa Monica—972 Ocean Front—and George Cukor threw a Fourth of July fireworks party for them and a few friends. When the accounting was done, in the spirit of the group, Cukor billed the guests on paper headed "Santa Monica Social and Fourth of July Club (No Jews Allowed)." Cukor was one of those at the party eager to hear David's news: Schulberg and Paramount were not happy with him as a director. But it was another guest, Lewis Milestone, who featured in David's plans. Milly and David were scheming for their own unit, probably to release through Paramount.

By July 17, W. R. Wilkerson was taking up this prospect on the front page of *The Hollywood Reporter*:

> This young production executive has ideas. Plenty of them. He knows a lot about pictures. He has the admiration and best wishes of every individual who ever worked for and with him. He is looked on as a highly intelligent producer. He can say yes and no and give you the reason for either answer.
>
> Selznick is going to launch two or three independent production

units. One is said to be headed by Milestone, and maybe others, around individuals who stand at the top of the production heap. Seemingly he is not worrying about releases, being satisfied that if the product is right the release is a cinch. . . .

David took the train east on July 23: in New York, he reckoned, he would put together the legal details of Selznick-Milestone Pictures. Since he was to be independent now, he surely needed an agent—so Myron went with him. For good reason: this plan was a serious attempt to break up studio monopoly and to give control and profits to filmmakers.

It was ferociously hot on the train, the hottest the Pullman conductor had ever known. On Irene's advice, neither brother was drinking or over-eating. They were restricted to melon, grapefruit juice, and learning contract bridge. "Enjoying Myron immensely," David wrote from Albuquerque, after a night of sleeping raw, reversing himself head to foot every hour. "And he me, I'm sure. He seems so young and quaint, somehow. I do love him so tremendously!"

This parting from Irene had a new sexual edge, and it was signed with an obelisk-sized phallus salute, his "Pie-Face Monument." When Irene wrote, her letters came from 625 Ocean Front, her parents' home. With David away, she had moved in with them. Whatever else this allowed, it brought her closer to trade gossip. She had been to a party on the Howard Hughes boat, and Irving Thalberg told her that Hughes had been wondering aloud, "Say, what is this about Selznick? I have Milestone's signature on a contract to me."

Irene was especially anxious now that David's brother might be feasting on their letters: "Darling, please hide & lock my letters from Myron. . . . If he's reading this now—Myron: I hope your tummy rebels against Scotch."

By Kansas on the train, David and Myron were being told they "could both easily be superb players" at bridge. "Keep kissable," David signed off. In Santa Monica, Irene reported that Ben Schulberg was now being complimentary about David, while Lasky was "saying that he thinks maybe you are right." Such word of mouth only inspired their needs. "I long to be once more in your arms," wrote Irene, "to sleep curled about you, and to have your precious mouth on mine. This is truly a very difficult life for a snuggler and a m-m-m-er—I cannot hold out much longer, how many am I entitled to?"

The same letter had one ominous note. Irene said she had heard "indirectly" that all the local moguls were furious. " 'Tis whispered at the Producers' Meetings that you're ruining everything." That indirectness may have been in her phrasing only. For L.B. was an interested follower of his son-in-law's tracks from 625. It is possible that Irene's worries about who was secretly reading the wires was misplaced. This came to her "at home" from David on July 31:

> To Swopes at Port Washington tonight for dinner. Very busy at Paramount today. To Otto Kahn's for yachting tomorrow and week-end at his home. Clarkson, Chairman Chase National Monday morning. Lunch with Payne Whitney Monday. Please tell Milly itinerary and that I am shooting with both barrels.

This was high-flying for someone who had been dead broke in Florida five years earlier. Otto Kahn was a hugely wealthy banker known for his interest in the arts and a force behind Paramount. The Whitney contacts were better still. When William Payne Whitney died in 1927, his estate was appraised at over $179 million, the largest in American history at that time. His heirs were John Hay Whitney and his sister, Joan. There was another Whitney on the scene, too, Cornelius Vanderbilt (or "Sonny"), the son and heir of Harry Payne Whitney and Gertrude Vanderbilt.

David was staying at the recently opened Pierre Hotel on East Sixty-first Street, looking out on Central Park, and liking it. He had a suite on the twenty-eighth floor, and he pronounced the entire operation far superior to the Savoy-Plaza or the Sherry Netherland. He was spending time with Myron and Walter Wanger in the smartest speakeasies in town. Wanger was a valuable friend, not just with his social connections but because he was a messenger back to Paramount. For David was weighing all options. Perhaps the most valuable contact he had was Merian C. Cooper, that irked but amiable producer from *The Four Feathers*. David had called Coop on arriving and had a very friendly welcome.

> Yesterday [July 30], [David wrote to Irene] spent hours with Cooper, here, and at an ultra-smart little club. How that Cooper does get the connections! Every member we met—and it was a tiny place—was a young Davison, Bruce, Whitney. We laid plans for our respective attacks on Chase National and on a Private Group ... How these moneyed bastards work! The week-end starts about Thursday. And if it's too hot, they don't come in Monday, or Tuesday, or Wednesday, or all three. Not that I don't agree with them!

He stayed one night at Walter Wanger's summer cottage at Great Neck—"formerly Ollie Thomas'—what memories!"—tried to play golf and got caught in the summer rain and the worse heat that followed it. But David was getting horny as well as hot:

> Have been ... thinking of those darling, spoon-bottomed little breasts. Stroke each of them for me—and go acrobatic if you possibly can: kiss other sweet delights for David.

A drop of sweat fell on the word "delights."

Then plans went awry. Myron—"Ooomskins" David called him in letters—had been asleep all the time, and he wasn't drinking. He was ill! Walter Wanger recommended a doctor, Sam Hirschfeld, who diagnosed appendicitis. There was an operation and a scare of peritonitis. On hearing the news, Irene and Marjorie decided to get to the Pierre as fast as they could. Irene wired David from Barstow:

> Warning have just heard your wife is speeding east. She has discovered all. She is on Chief Car 200 Drawing Room C. Hysterical but happy. Love—China Baby.

She arrived in New York late on August 4, and so they were reunited, she—as she put it—with her "Empire State." Their need for each other was very great, and Irene's political instincts should be included in that. L.B. must have regretted the loss of a letter writer in the house, but Margaret would be calling Irene regularly.

They had four rooms in their suite at the Pierre. The new hotel needed guests, but they were astonished by David's monopoly of the switchboard. As David told her repeatedly, in the promoting business grandness of manner was directly related to the offers that came one's way. So they lived beyond their means, trying to keep up with people of great wealth by showing how little they needed their money. Early in August, *Time* had announced the new company, praised the novelty, and played up the idea of that old Selznick enterprise being renewed. The family legend, it said, was "as lively as ever."

Then things began to go slower. Irene had to order fall clothes from California. The original notion entertained by David was that he and Milestone would form an independent unit. They would make seven films a year, two to be directed by Milestone personally. Paramount would guarantee them a release and put up the money for production. Jesse Lasky had been sympathetic to the proposal, and David had contemplated similar units with Lubitsch and King Vidor. But then Paramount became unhappy with the deal. Louis B. Mayer had spoken to them, and to the other studios, worrying that everything could get out of control if independent units became popular.

So David had explored other funding. After that meeting in the small club, Cooper had taken David to the Long Island home of David K. Bruce, who was then married to Ailsa Mellon, the daughter of Secretary of the Treasury Andrew Mellon. Bruce also had influence at RKO, a studio ever mindful of David's ability. Bruce had another angle to develop—for Cooper had told him the idea for a new kind of film about a gorilla, or rather a

Gorilla. Perhaps all interests could be merged? Cooper spoke to Myron and proposed buying the Tarzan books by Edgar Rice Burroughs as story material. Myron discovered that Burroughs had just sold movie rights to MGM for $25,000. He offered Thalberg double that to trade them, but Irving had dreams of Johnny Weissmuller, so he refused. Cooper was not put off. His partner, Ernest Schoedsack, and he had studied baboons in Africa and were sure of their appeal. Cooper had a notion to call the gorilla "Kong."

With Paramount losing interest, David was now torn between RKO and United Artists. But Joe Schenck, president of U.A., was party to the Mayer conspiracy. David's sometime poker pal on the train was offering him a studio job: head of production. It was tempting, and it was October by now, with David on no one's salary. He procrastinated, trying to improve the other offers, but the victim of indecision. Thus, he felt bound to tell Schenck there was another possibility "too important for me to ignore."

The Selznick-Milestone arrangement was now being pursued with RKO. The team would be paid $280,000 a year, and David was ready to split it $200,000 to Milly and $80,000 to himself—for he could no longer be sure of even his partner. They would each get 20 percent of the profits on their RKO pictures and be "in complete charge." In Hollywood, Milestone wavered. He felt the 25 percent overhead before profits that RKO had proposed was excessive, and he wondered if maybe their company shouldn't be called Milestone-Selznick Productions.

RKO was ready to defy Mayer's gang and go with the deal. David Sarnoff saw himself as not a picture man—he could do what he wanted. But Milestone was timid, and in a sudden twist he instead took up Schenck's opening for a head of production. That job didn't last beyond the making of *Rain* (in 1932), but the decision left David exposed.

So it was, late in October, that RKO came to David again. He had no unit or package now. But Sarnoff was convinced of his worth. Discussions went on into November, and a young Irish lawyer just out of Harvard, Daniel T. O'Shea, wearied David over the details. It was settled. David was to have charge of production for RKO on the West Coast; he would unite Sarnoff's two production outfits—RKO Radio and RKO Pathé—as one force. His salary was to be $2,000 a week.

David and Irene were much in love, with unexpected time to get to know the Pierre and the Whitneys. Still, the deal had taken three months, and the power of L.B. could not be disguised. We will never know how much information was passed from coast to coast or with what intent. L.B. had designs on David: he foresaw the chance that Selznick might take over at MGM from the increasingly difficult Thalberg. David there would be an asset and someone he could control. A David free in the business—truly independent—threatened not just stability, but L.B.'s leadership in his daughter's eyes.

Years later, Irene had this to say of the summer:

> Of course, David understood Dad's weaknesses, for which he made allowances, and my father returned the courtesy. He made no attempt to control David; he may have wanted to, but he didn't try. Wise old owl. On the other hand, it can't have been so uncomplicated as it appears now; perhaps I have unwittingly drawn a merciful veil.

David and Irene returned to California in early November, allowing the Pierre to subside. But the dates make it most likely that it was at that hotel they conceived their first son. There, or on the train.

3 · NO JEWS ALLOWED

IN A FAMILY that preferred to live in the future there was now much to concentrate on. Myron was well set up in the business he was pioneering; he was married, with a daughter. David was in charge of a studio, albeit a small one struggling to survive. He was brilliantly married, and now he and his wife were expecting a child. David and Irene were a wondrous couple to behold—she dark, svelte, knowing, and elusive; he ungainly and brash, but such a talker, such a charmer, such a smiler.

They had spent a part of that awkward summer being adopted by the best society that America offered. Part of the wonder and magic for them had been in being accepted—and liked—by people who were not ordinarily seen with Jews. "No Jews Allowed," George Cukor had joked about their little Fourth of July club on the beach, when probably most of the assembly were Jews.

Consider two salutes that came to David with the RKO job. From somewhere in the unfashionable density of Los Angeles there was this cable: "There is only one word. Congratulations. Your Brother—Howard." Whereas *Time* magazine used David's rapid elevation to make these observations about Hollywood:

> the crafty and extraordinary methods of one-time fur peddlers, garment dealers and second-hand jewelers . . . Jews . . . who padded their payrolls with relatives, settled their biggest deals over all-night poker games and . . . discussed the picture business in comic strip dialect.

Such talk was not furtive in 1931; mainstream America felt no need for apologies. And Jews had to decide whether or not to laugh along with the "jokes."

But the Selznicks were not quite sound. Howard was sometimes said to be in the agenting business himself. All that meant was that he would hang around Myron's offices in the Taft Building. Niven Busch had made his way to Hollywood in the early fall of 1931. He had been writing several columns for *The New Yorker* when he bumped into Myron one night at *George White's Scandals*, and Myron had said he'd take Busch on as a client. In Hollywood, Busch remembered Howard: "He would wait around outside the office, tap visitors in the lift and say, 'Myron wants you to lend me $2.' And then he'd take it to a cheap whorehouse."

Howard lived on Fountain with Mildred and the girls, and they were subsidized by Myron. But Howard was wandering all over the city, being brought home in taxis drunk. According to Mildred, "He was insulting and molesting girls on the street. I was getting telephone calls from neighbors complaining to me about his insulting their daughters." She had talked to the other Selznicks and told them Howard could be violent and that he was taking drugs. They had told her, stay with him and the money will keep coming.

But late in 1930, Howard had approached a friend, Sam Dubrow, and said he thought he was sick. Dubrow looked him over and took him to a Dr. Allan Gage. The diagnosis was a venereal disease. There was a family meeting (Pop, Flossie, Howard, Myron, and Mildred) in Myron's office. Pop conceded the merit of Mildred's earlier complaints—"I can't blame you. I would feel justified in knocking his block off." Howard said, "Oh, hell!" and stormed out of the office. Mildred agreed to stay with Howard on the promise of a weekly check for $75. Howard started a course of treatment, and Sam Dubrow took him three times a week to the doctor to be sure he went through with it.

The family hoped Mildred and family duties could keep Howard home at night. In the day, he was encouraged to be at Myron's office. But no one trusted him to do anything there, so the wandering set in. At least Pop Selznick stayed in the office. He had no occupation now, and his health was deteriorating, but Myron tolerated the old man reading his correspondence and offering suggestions and turned a blind eye when L.J. drifted after the secretaries and pinched their bottoms.

David and Myron were worried about their father's health. In New York, in August 1931, as Myron recovered from his appendectomy, they asked their newfound doctor, Sam Hirschfeld, to look into the case of L.J. So Hirschfeld had Pop Selznick go to a doctor in Los Angeles, Leo Kessel.

The report noted a twenty-five-year history of diabetes, regulated by no more than diet, a recent attack of glaucoma, head nodding for several years, and pains in the right hand and leg. Kessel found "deposture as a result of hypertrophic spondylitis"—some deformity as a consequence of spinal inflammation, for which L.J. walked with a cane. Unaware that L.J. no longer had steady employment, Kessel concluded, "As far as his return to work is concerned, I believe he will be much happier, as he is the type of man who has no avocation and retirement means for him boredom and a sense of futility with the usual worry about health."

Late in the year, Myron found a way of keeping his father busy. Merian Cooper arrived in Hollywood with a more developed scheme for his gorilla story: it was now Gorilla meets American Girl. Cooper and David Bruce dined with David and Irene; Pop and Myron were also in attendance. David heard the plan and "thought it was a showmanship idea but that RKO was in such a difficult financial situation that he felt it was wrong for him to have the studio put up the money for a dangerous year or two trip on the (feverside) West Coast of Africa." So Cooper thought of eliminating Africa and putting actors in gorilla suits.

Myron was nursing the project along and telling Cooper to resist David's invitation to go on the RKO payroll. But Myron had a favor to trade. Pop had come up with an idea for the oil business. Could Cooper fix a meeting? Cooper called David Bruce, who arranged an appointment with the president of Standard Oil of California. Cooper and L.J. took the train up to San Francisco, where they had two hours of the president's time. "He seemed interested in Mr. L.J. Selznick's presentation—which I thought unique and brilliant—and said he would let us know." The two promoters returned to Los Angeles, but three days later Cooper got a call from Pop saying he'd changed his mind, he had a better idea for another business. Would Cooper call Standard Oil and apologize?

There is no record of what these ideas were—only the trail of rapid brain waves and fresh tacks. But Myron was grateful, and in his subsequent representation of Cooper on what was to be King Kong, he waived his 10 percent.

David and Irene were back in Los Angeles in mid-November, and they moved into another rented house, 901 Rexford Drive. David started work at RKO, next door to Paramount, at Melrose and Gower, at the end of November 1931. He was a vice president in charge of production at a company where stock had lately fallen to an all-time low. David's predecessor, William LeBaron, was suddenly made answerable to him, and new people at RKO had been given a sixty-day warning against possible termination.

His first project there was one of his most personal films. The young producer Pandro Berman had developed a short story by Fannie Hurst called "Night Bell," concerning a Jewish doctor in New York. There was a screenplay when David arrived—by Bernard Schubert and J. Walter Ruben. But David took it apart. Berman observed that the new boss

> would come in in the morning with a hundred notes from which he would write memos. He had a roll of paper by his bed at night and would scribble things down when he'd get an idea. He was very meticulous, and didn't care too much about cost; he was more interested in quality.

In this first instance, David was restrained by budget. But he sought to give the project the scale of social epic. The script and the story were set in the doctor's adult present. David called for scenes of the man's boyhood. As he would never do again, he made an uninhibited picture about Jewish immigrants struggling to reconcile idealism and materialism in America. The story gained a new title, *Symphony of Six Million*, set against the rays of a sunrise and a line of city buildings:

> *A City—*
> *Six million human hearts*
> *Each with a dream—*
> *a hope—a goal—*
> *Each soul a vagrant*
> *melody in the eternal*
> *Symphony of life!*

Symphony is inspirational, sentimental, and melodramatic. It concerns the Klauber family: mother, father, two sons, and a daughter who live on the Lower East Side amid documentary shots of crowded streets. Anna Appel, who played the mother, was dark, sturdy, and providing, like Flossie Selznick: this is the closest family resemblance in the film. The father, Meyer, was played by Gregory Ratoff, a Russian-born actor from the Yiddish theater, making his feature film debut. The father is a tailor, an irascible but tenderhearted comic: he shouts and beats the table to show he is not getting excited, and he insists on playing chess with his studious son, Felix, though Felix always defeats him and reads a medical book while his father is pondering a next move. When Meyer gets indigestion from too much herring at dinner, the brilliant Felix advises bicarbonate of soda. In the scheme of such a movie, this announces the makings of a great surgeon.

The Jewishness is spread thick. Ratoff would never know another way, but neither the script, the director Gregory La Cava, nor the executive

Symphony of Six Million—
Gregory Ratoff third from right

producer, David O. Selznick, restrained him. David was not necessarily the author of these scenes. There is credit given to a James Seymour for additional dialogue. But at RKO he began to preside over the scripts of films he cared about. Their language may have come from others, but the concept was his.

The film jumps forward to find Felix (played by Ricardo Cortez) as an earnest young doctor at the Cherry Street Clinic, "in the ghetto," where waiting patients crowd the staircase leading to his office. He is filled with conviction about his work. He looks toward heaven when he says, "Just think, Mama, yesterday I brought life into the world!" Both parents are proud of him, and both have been secretly saving so that Felix may buy a microscope. His childhood sweetheart, the crippled Jessica (Irene Dunne), teaches blind children—nothing is left to chance. And Felix sees his vocation as a response to the poverty of the ghetto, not that there is any hint, even for 1932, that society or the state might bear responsibility.

But Felix's brother, Magnus, who has turned into a dapper, wisecracking "businessman," keeps saying Felix should treat medicine as a business, move uptown, and bill his patients. Magnus urges Mama to tell Felix to make a move so that the parents won't have to work so hard. The move comes on a fade-out and takes the film to ... West End Avenue and Eighty-ninth Street: Felix could have been practitioner to the Selznicks. The practice is smart and prosperous, and Felix is too busy with neurotic women to play chess with his father. But Felix is uneasy: he studies unexplained X rays of a spine and tells Magnus he intends going back to the ghetto. Magnus will have none of it. He urges Felix to go forward, not backward.

Another fade-out brings us to Park Avenue, where the patients are more decadent yet and Felix is smooth and ghostlike. *Vanity Fair* has a full-page photograph of "The million dollar hands of Dr. Felix Klauber." But "where's the inspiration that made them great?" asks Jessica when Felix misses an appointment to see little blind George and the boy dies.

There is a family religious ceremony, the Redemption of the First Born, for the sister has had a child and the family follows the Hebraic tradition of seeing the first child as belonging to the Lord until the family redeems it. At this gathering, the teary and unwell Meyer makes a speech: "When the children were all young, I said I wanted you to be educated . . . to give joy and happiness to others. We love to see all our children happy, and I am ready to go if the Lord wants to take my life now."

Before the Lord can stir, the script strikes—Meyer collapses with a brain tumor. An operation is called for. Felix is persuaded to be the surgeon, and Meyer dies on the table. Felix is at the crisis of his life. He gives up; he smashes the framed *Vanity Fair* picture. But he goes back to the clinic to see fine work carrying on. While there, he learns that Jessica is at last to have an operation on her spine. "Who's going to operate?" he asks her. "A very fine surgeon," she whispers. "Dr. Felix Klauber."

The picture was started on January 14, 1932, shot in five weeks, and opened on April 14 (five months after David arrived). It came in at $261,082, about $6,000 under budget, and it made a profit eventually of about $25,000. Such were the strict economics of filmmaking at RKO.

The Klaubers are not the Selznicks, despite outline resemblances. Meyer Klauber is a man of modest means and ambition. At one point, Mama tells him he might have been a success if he'd been more of a gambler. Nor are Magnus and Felix exactly Myron and David. But the issue of endangered idealism was always part of David's sense of himself. Above all, *Symphony* is a gesture toward family and religion. The father is seen warmly, as if *Symphony* had been made under the shadow of David's fears about his father's health.

Symphony alludes to an affinity between medicine and the movies. Dr. Felix Klauber has to take one path where the road forks: he gives up Park Avenue, wealth, fame, and *Vanity Fair* for "the Temple of Healing." But David had it both ways: he could be rich in Beverly Hills and famous in *Time* magazine, while bringing relief and consolation to "the millions" in those other temples, the movie houses. Thus, the ponderous moral of the film could be ignored by its maker. David felt better about himself because of *Symphony of Six Million*; it was an admission of Jewishness and a woozy, short-sighted hug for his father.

It is a terrible film, yet terribly effective, so well made that its half-truths slide by. When films are so powerful and so facile in their offering of fantasies, the distinctions of authorship are not important. *Symphony of Six Million* is an American movie, and Lewis J. Selznick was very happy with it. On June 10, 1932, he wrote to an old friend from Cleveland, where so much of his own past had been abandoned:

> My dear Jimmy:
>
> I certainly was happy to hear from you. David has turned your letter over to me and I had a great deal of time to think about it as I happened to be sick in the hospital. . . .
>
> I wish you would take a look at *Symphony in* [*sic*] *Six Million*, one of David's first pictures for RKO. This is a Jewish theme and it will do you good to see it.

4 · WHAT PRICE RKO?

FILM STUDIOS are as vulnerable to passing inspiration as film scripts. There is always the chance that some brilliant executive will come in—some new young genius—and stir them up. He may sound like Dr. Felix Klauber, or Dr. Klauber's dialogue writer; he may tell the gathered workers they have a sacred trust to bring truth, magic, and entertainment to the hard-pressed masses. He says they must all do good work, that he wants to hear every idea and every humble contribution. The hot shot means it as he says it: that is the thrill of moving oneself. But he also knows—in the way he knows his taxi to Tijuana is double-parked outside the studio—that these pictures have to *work* if he is to keep paid or if these workers are to stay employed. He knows box office. He calls the staff at the studio "all one family"—this is a telling encouragement, for many of them have broken family histories. Yet the new chief is also calculating how, if his reign doesn't work, he may move on and cut a better deal elsewhere. He smiles to the family: he has a great smile. But he has a private smile for himself, and with it the most viable intelligence in Hollywood turns to cynicism.

David O. Selznick was at times foolish and idealistic; at others, he was an arrogant manipulator. Usually he was both and struggling to stay upright or awake. It may be he was never more taken with the idea of the family at a studio than in 1932: it was a crucial year for all his attitudes to family. And it was a great year, even if RKO was going bust. But it is a time in which he moved with youthful ease from the sentimental uplift of *Symphony of Six Million* to the mordant analysis of *What Price Hollywood?* It is a time of which Irene Selznick wrote—with the utmost sincerity—

> Movies were like a great cause to us; to be pretentious, you could call it a sense of mission. I reinforced his aspirations. We had one romance with each other and another with the movies.

It was also a time in which, in *State's Attorney*, David could have the lawyer played by John Barrymore murmur to a judge in court, "Can you imagine people throwing money away, gambling, in times like these?" when the lawyer has just come from a gaming club. In 1932 also, in that grim year for banks and moviegoers, David was beginning to gamble as a habit, endangering his family economy and his marriage. In the same 1932, on April 29, their wedding anniversary, among all the gifts to Irene, one card said, "Second years, like second thoughts, are better/And better yet, my darling, are third. . . ." But at the studio he was also trying to screw any secretary who was willing. It was not serious, he told himself, no threat to Irene. He was only getting rid of his great energy.

There were long-term associations begun at RKO, where so many people saw David as the brightest producer in Hollywood and the most engaging personally. There were things to overlook: tantrums, excesses, lateness, seductions, lies . . . but look at his movies!

Marcella Bannett was a secretary at RKO when David arrived. She had worked briefly for Darryl Zanuck and for Myron before joining RKO. She was able, college-educated, and very good looking; she even made a screen test herself at MGM. Marcella would organize David's working life for the rest of the 1930s—as far as that was possible.

When David arrived at the studio, he started firing people, so Marcella took shelter in the mimeograph room: "Finally I came out with a message and I bumped right into this great big, tall, menacing creature. And he said to me, 'What are *you* doing? . . . Go see my secretary. I need somebody in my office.'" Marcella was promoted within days when the original secretary quit to work for Adela Rogers St. Johns. David made a pass at Marcella, as a routine matter, but she says she told him to be sensible and get on with business. He laughed; he was quite easily put off and bore no grudge.

If Marcella wouldn't oblige, then perhaps Connie Bennett would. The actress was queen of the RKO studio. Myron got her salary up to $30,000 a week. But actresses were also slaves to the bosses, and as Irene saw it,

"Connie was the smartest, shrewdest star there ever was, very wise about men—except when she came up against Gilbert Roland." Producers' wives needed another kind of wisdom, and so when Irene saw Connie she got anxious only because Bennett was such a great poker player and always looking for a game. If you screwed the boss now and then, you knew better when he was bluffing. "She was crazy about money and sex," said Irene, still wondering, fifty-five years later.

Some people said this David was such a romantic he always needed to be in love. Marcella saw it differently: "He was very sexually oriented. He had very strong needs. Which were not met at home, I'm sure. I think this was the promoting reason for his liaisons, most of which were trivial." David would sometimes tell other women that his marriage was more dynastic than personal.

For a negotiator, David grabbed the young lawyer who had worked out his RKO deal, Dan O'Shea. Marcella Bannett thought O'Shea had "a stern, agentlike personality." As time went by, O'Shea handled most of the contract dealings with Hollywood agents; not his least value was that David did not have to haggle directly with Myron.

In RKO's New York office there was a story editor, Katherine or Kay Brown. She had recommended Edna Ferber's *Cimarron* to the studio. She was small, feisty, and snub-nosed pretty; she had great contacts and good instincts, and she became the most trusted judge of literary material for a man who revered books but had little time to read them.

At a more direct level of filmmaking, David hired Merian Cooper before the end of 1931 to examine the cost controls at RKO and to proceed

Marcella Bannett

with *King Kong.* He had a gang of screenwriters that included Herman Mankiewicz, J. Walter Ruben, Gene Fowler, Rowland Brown, Jane Murfin, Wells Root, and Howard Estabrook.

David found a resident composer at RKO, the Viennese Max Steiner (a poker-playing friend to Pop and Flossie), and he encouraged Steiner toward large-scale scores that contributed an overall mood to a picture, as opposed to just overture and finale. Steiner worked on most of David's RKO pictures, and with *Symphony of Six Million, Bird of Paradise,* and *King Kong,* especially, he established a role for movie scores that has scarcely altered in sixty years. Another discovery at RKO was Slavko Vorkapich, a Serbian, who was in charge of the montage department, making those brief interludes for a film when time passes and the doings of the larger world have to be noticed. Vorkapich's work provided the greatest cinematic interest in films like *The Conquerors* and *No Other Woman.*

For his directors, David formed a team of old friends. No one went farther back than George Archainbaud, who had worked for L.J. at World and Select. He was director of *The Lost Squadron,* a picture about stunt pilots after the Great War, when David took over at RKO. It starred Richard Dix, Erich von Stroheim, and Joel McCrea, but the first cut did not work. David had more work done on the script, and he enlisted Paul Sloane to shoot new material. These were not just Selznick retakes, but fresh thoughts, rewriting in postproduction. By the time *The Lost Squadron* was released, on May 10, 1932, its budget of $475,000 had gone up to $620,000—it ended up in the red to just about the extent of the overage.

John Cromwell would make *Sweepings,* with Lionel Barrymore (a story about family business); Dorothy Arzner did *Christopher Strong;* Harry d'Abbadie d'Arrast made another fine film in *Topaze,* written by Ben Hecht from the Marcel Pagnol play and starring John Barrymore; William Wellman handled the epic *The Conquerors,* which starred RKO stalwarts Richard Dix and Ann Harding; Myrna Loy was borrowed to give enigmatic close-ups to the wacky thriller *Thirteen Women,* directed by Archainbaud, who was also entrusted with *State's Attorney,* a stiff film in which the director can only wait upon the languid, self-glorifying drunkenness of John Barrymore.

David was anxious to borrow the MGM director King Vidor to film the stage play *Bird of Paradise,* another romance of different cultures in which a San Francisco sailor (Joel McCrea) falls in love with a native girl (Dolores Del Rio). He gave Vidor the play and told him to read it overnight. But it was all Vidor could do to finish the first act. So the next day he asked David to recount the rest of the story.

"I haven't read it either," answered the boss. "I've been too busy since I took over this job to read anything."

So they talked it over, and suddenly David snapped his fingers. "Just give me three wonderful love scenes. . . . I don't care what you use so long as we call it *Bird of Paradise* and Del Rio jumps into a volcano at the finish."

Vidor was tickled. He was assigned Wells Root as a writer and, with piles of *National Geographic* magazines, they were ordered to sail to Hawaii—with the actors coming on a week later. So they had the voyage to discover a script.

The location was a paradise—they all stayed at the Royal Hawaiian Hotel on Waikiki Beach and Vidor fell in love with the script girl, Elizabeth Hill. But the problems of filming paradise with modern movie industrial methods were a model of what has befallen Hawaii. As soon as Hollywood brings its machinery to bear on the wilderness, it begins to destroy it. This was what David had always guessed about Cooper and Africa—not to mention the costs.

So the unit came home. They went to Catalina (the original thought), and they used the back lot at Pathé as well as the studio tank at First National. It was there that Vidor filmed the underwater scenes between McCrea and Del Rio that make the romance of *Paradise* arresting and dancelike. The photography was by Clyde DeVinna (who had done David's Wyoming Westerns at MGM), but it is Vidor's erotic vision and Miss Del Rio's apparent nakedness that really make the scenes. If only those two characters could have lived throughout the film as sexy fish, without having to speak.

Bird of Paradise went helplessly over budget: $450,000 ended up at least $725,000, though rumors suggested the studio was reporting the figure incorrectly low. *Paradise*, too, was a loser, but probably more people went to see it than went to any other of David's RKO films. This film is hokum; it lacks the eternal metaphor of savagery and culture that allows *King Kong* to surpass melodrama. But the love scenes are beguiling: Del Rio's laugh, her winged eyelashes, the peril with which flowers cling to her breasts, and the suggestiveness of the dialogue are still arousing. The erotic may have thrived in David's own mind, but he was usually shy of it on screen. Indeed, it would not return until *Duel in the Sun* (1946), also directed by King Vidor.

It is worth recalling David's disdain of Hunt Stromberg's lust for fantasy voluptuousness in *White Shadows in the South Seas*. *Bird of Paradise* is as blithely racist as *Time* magazine was anti-Semitic. Busby Berkeley choreographed the sacrificial dance, not an anthropologist. The "natives" are white extras in brown face and body paint. Nothing disputes the notion that civilization is "where people are accomplishing something." The princess may follow the orders of her script by consigning herself to fire and the custom of her own people. But Dolores Del Rio is palpably ready for

Vidor's rapturous close-ups, where she eats fruit and conveys juice to the aching McCrea by way of kisses.

Del Rio, Ann Harding, Irene Dunne, and Constance Bennett were actresses of note before David came to RKO.

The discovery at RKO was Katharine Hepburn, but that needs back-grounding first. When David came to the studio, he found that Laurence Olivier and Jill Esmond were contract players there. Esmond had supporting roles in *State's Attorney* and *Thirteen Women*, and Olivier shared the lead with Ann Harding in *Westward Passage*. Neither was impressive: Olivier was too thin, and not even a Ronald Colman mustache gave him a very forceful, romantic appeal. Miss Esmond was reckoned to have greater promise—she is briefly vivacious in *Thirteen Women*—and she was under consideration for the role of the daughter in *A Bill of Divorcement*, the Clemence Dane play. Director George Cukor had seen the test of a newcomer, Katharine Hepburn, who had done some stage work in the East. "She was quite unlike anybody I'd ever seen," said Cukor. "Though she'd never made a movie, she had this very definite knowledge and feeling right from the start."

David said later that he had wanted to cast Jill Esmond. But Olivier had had an appointment to see David: he was to be dropped. When David was late, the secretary—it had to be Marcella—let the actor wait in Selznick's office. At least, this was Olivier's contention in his autobiography, *Confessions of An Actor*:

> Well, there I was, alone in the boss's office, and it occurred to me that there might be some reading matter of possible interest, if I searched diligently enough for it. Well (again), I sort of found myself wandering casually round his desk, and from behind his chair my attention was caught and held, by God, by a document on his blotter. This turned out to be the agreement for a contract. My heart began to beat at what I read. It stated that Miss Katharine Hepburn was to be engaged on a three-year contract at a starting figure of $1,500 weekly for the first year, rising to $2,000 for the second year and $2,500 for the third year.

The actor performs his own slyness (and Marcella denies the occasion). He even lets us wonder whether he was not supposed to find the giveaway contract. (Not that the document Olivier reports ever existed. Hepburn was hired, in July, at $1,250 a week and a mere three-week guarantee.) But as Olivier describes it, his lucky discovery was a blessing to his wife; he was able to save her from humiliation and take her back to England. David's anger found expression seven years later, when Olivier had tried to impede the film career of another beloved. Referring to late 1938 and early

1939, when Vivien Leigh would be Scarlett O'Hara if a contract could be worked out, David wrote:

> the only reason Vivien became a great star ... was because I finally called him [Olivier] to one side and reminded him that he had cost his former wife, Jill Esmond, her one great chance at a career under similar circumstances. I had wanted to cast Jill Esmond in the starring role in *Bill of Divorcement* when she was under contract to R.K.O. Olivier was also under contract but was very callow and inexperienced at that time and we had decided not to keep him. He bitterly resisted his wife playing the part and insisted that she return to England with him. I believe she [*sic*] was motivated in that case as in the case of Vivien by jealousy and by the determination that his wife should not be a bigger star than he. Larry is the most selfish man I have ever met.

Not even the worst portrait of Olivier can prove Jill Esmond would have had the role. David was a great judge of talent and tests, however unusual the young Hepburn seemed. What seems most likely is that David had not made up his mind, that he was running at least two horses, and that Olivier's temperament assisted the matter. Cukor wanted Hepburn, and he helped her give a performance that inaugurated a magnificent career—and which had a lot to do with Cukor's own development. Yet neither Hepburn nor David could ever believe she was his discovery.

A Bill of Divorcement was the second of three films Cukor made for David in 1932. The others were *What Price Hollywood?* and *Rockabye*. And in 1933, there would be *Our Betters* and *Little Women*. In just over a year at RKO, Cukor moved from being a rather suspect figure to a leading director. Those last days at Paramount had been uncomfortable for him. He had directed some of Ernst Lubitsch's *One Hour With You*, yet Schulberg wanted him to have no credit on it. Cukor refused that compromise, and the matter turned into a lawsuit. Paramount settled, and thus Cukor followed David to RKO.

Not only was Cukor David's favorite director and his best. George was also a chum in high spirits, teasing, the bantering exchange of memos, and a shared attitude as to the desirability of grace and talent rising above the squalor of the picture business. It was as close a friendship as the bond between George and Irene. Moreover, the gay Cukor needed powerful protectors and patronage, just as David's own sensibility was best expressed by Cukor's asexual delight in women. Cukor had an odd way of giving cinematic life to the romantic in David, and the producer was more pleased by it, more at ease, than ever he was with the eroticism of a King Vidor.

Cukor encouraged exuberance in David, a delight in smart games, and David would build Cukor's career. Thus, at first, while they were useful to each other, it was easier to believe they were friends who enjoyed the pretense of rivalry and bitter jokes about their own unfortunate physical resemblance. That kind of embattled energy and superior gaiety would be vital to *What Price Hollywood?*

Selznick had wanted to make a movie about movies for several years. He bought a magazine story, "The Truth About Hollywood," by Adela Rogers St. Johns, early in 1932, and thought of putting Clara Bow in it. In the event, David cast his brother's expensive client, Constance Bennett, as the Brown Derby waitress who becomes a star. Jane Murfin did a script, and Ben Markson reworked it. But it was not until the last rewrite, with Rowland Brown and Gene Fowler, that the project came to life.

What Price Hollywood? is the antecedent of *A Star is Born*, the property David would make in 1937 and that George Cukor remade in 1954. All three films have a woman who goes from obscurity to stardom; they also feature an older man, her husband or lover, a falling star or declining director, who dies, and all are panoramas of Hollywood. But *What Price Hollywood?* is not just the earliest version, it is the toughest, the funniest, and the most interesting. In both versions of *A Star is Born*, the rise of one lover is locked into the fall of another, so there is no escaping the sentimentality of Norman Maine's self-sacrifice. Furthermore, in those two films, the woman (we cannot call Janet Gaynor or Judy Garland young) yearns to be in movies and a star.

The brilliance of *What Price Hollywood?* is in seeing the chanciness of elevation, the way any pretty face could be the one given the right circumstances. George Cukor said years later that *What Price* was "very dear" to David:

> Largely through David's influence, we didn't kid the basic idea of Hollywood. Most of the Hollywood pictures make it a kind of crazy, kooky place, but to David it was absolutely real, he believed in it.

Cukor sounds as if he had forgotten his own film or never understood it. *What Price Hollywood?* traces the power and wonder of Hollywood, but it appreciates the fine line between tragedy and exhilarating hype. The question of the title is real, sour, and still open at the end of the film. Yet *What Price* has a grasp of what movies were doing to America and its ways of thinking. It fixes on the effect of glamour, makeup, clothes, and appearance, but it understands the seepage of the movies' phantom romance into empty lives.

It is not a film about the Constance Bennett character making her way to heartbreak or happiness. The slightness of Miss Bennett's personality is better for the venture than the sincerity and emotionalism of Gaynor or Garland. Bennett is an empty beauty; she is skin and cosmetics turned into glossy armor. More important to *What Price Hollywood?* are the director Max Carey (Lowell Sherman) and the producer Julius Saxe (Gregory Ratoff again—the father from *Symphony of Six Million*).

Julius Saxe is Jewish, broad, crazy, funny, endearing, a rascal, and a visionary. He is more Goldwyn than Selznick and much more Gregory Ratoff than either.

Max Carey is based on Marshall Neilan, a director ruined by drink. Yet he cannot be separated from the dark presence of the actor Lowell Sherman, himself a director and a drunk and a man who died in 1934 at the age of forty-nine. Sherman does not act. His scenes with Ratoff present contrary philosophies whereby the show-off thrives and naturalness seems like a fatal illness. Carey is also a version of John Barrymore or Myron Selznick—men too intelligent and unyielding to ignore the insanity of Hollywood.

Carey has given up the ghost because he despises what he does so well. The picture never bothers being hopeful for him—and thus it never compromises his vision. He only pities the Bennett character when she makes it into pictures, yet he does not regret his own alcoholic decline. Nearly everything he says is barbed, and the wounds are his own. Saxe is his special,

What Price Hollywood?: Lowell Sherman (horizontal), Constance Bennett (couchant), Gregory Ratoff (rampant)—a story conference

merry torturer, his employer, and his devil. Whenever the two men meet they fall into inadvertent cross-talk. They are characters in a dazzling film, both played to perfection. But they speak to the ceaseless, unsatisfied rage of despair and idealism, which was so often at the root of David's difficulty in coming to decisions:

SAXE (finishing a cable): Send this cable to our London office, too. What's a big word for colossal?

MISS SPIEGEL: Tremendous.

SAXE: No. That belongs to the Burner Brothers Studio. Take it. Have just seen rushes of Chinese picture and it is positively stupendous.

MISS SPIEGEL: Stupendous.

SAXE: I like stupendous better than tremendous, don't you, Carey?

CAREY: One's as bad as the other. They use them both to describe flops.

SAXE: Make it "terrific." It sounds successful. Terrific box-office. Terrific crowds. Terrific talent. That's the word. Terrific.

5 · POP'S ETERNITY

ON MAY 10, 1932, David was thirty, "a doom he had dreaded for years," the end of his youth as he strove to impress a business that was a young person's domain. But, as in most businesses, the young held on as they grew older; even if the tension in keeping control made them age faster, the men said it helped them handle the next wave of young usurpers. Harry Warner, the Schencks, Louis B. Mayer, Zukor, Lasky, Goldwyn, and William Fox were all close to fifty. But David's youth was precious as an idea and all the more vulnerable in 1932. Not only was a new baby coming, a real baby, but Pop's health was so uncertain that David's role as treasured child was in jeopardy.

In that birthday month of 1932, in the joint account David and Irene held at the First National Bank, the cash balance hovered around $100. He gave a monthly allowance to Irene of $1,062, and one to Flossie of $400, for David and Myron were paying most of the expenses of their parents.

That same month, David lost $500 gambling. In June there was another $150 and in July $700. The scrupulous records of David's career at the tables date only from 1932, but he had been raised to play and wager since boyhood. During the courting of Irene, this habit had been restrained—or kept so secret she never knew. But in their first year of marriage, she found him out and discovered losses in one night close to what their servants earned in a year. Irene had taken him to task—it was the first time in his life he had been scolded by an expert.

In their early years together, David could lose his temper with Irene in public. His temper was always quick, and sometimes it seemed ugly to friends. She took it in, too discreet to make an open row. But his gambling allowed her in private to hold the high moral ground with David. He began to complain that she was spoiling his fun; she was making him feel guilty. They fell into a pattern of excess, recrimination, and woeful regret on his part. She disliked the lack of dignity or character she began to detect in her husband, but she harped on it.

In a way, Irene was fascinated. She was a keen games player: she and David played a lot together at home—Russian bank, bezique, backgammon, Chinese checkers—talking all the time. This was how, inadvertently almost, she gave him best counsel on business, as they concentrated on something else. But Irene played for the fun of winning. When she found out about the Clover Club, the place off Sunset where David went for real sport, she elected to go with him, hoping to restrain him. David was then a moderate gambler compared with what was to come. But that helps show how far what followed was—consciously or unconsciously—in defiance of Irene and her rectitude.

David was a wild present-giver, so Irene told him, gambling or gifts, but not both. He explained the release it gave him, and she said he was just

*David and Irene
at backgammon*

spoiled and undisciplined. Hadn't her father always warned her of Selznick failings?

There was one occasion that summer, at the Clover Club, when Irene, seven months pregnant, was begging David to take her home at three o'clock in the morning. He was overjoyed at the pregnancy, for a child would be continuity and a gift for Pop. He wanted a boy. But he did not want Irene to "show" or look less than perfectly desirable. So she had to dress slim that summer, and she must not remind him of the pregnancy by seeming tired or needy. David was already anxious: "Promise me, promise me everything will be the same. The baby won't make any difference."

David needed sometimes to play at night, and to lose gloriously, because in the day at RKO he was working so hard to be economical. That's what running production at a studio was all about. Before Labor Day of 1932, as well as running a program of forty films a year, with six Westerns and thirty two-reel comedies, David had made and opened *The Lost Squadron, Symphony of Six Million, State's Attorney, Westward Passage, What Price Hollywood?, Roar of the Dragon, The Age of Consent,* and *Bird of Paradise.* To this day, not one of those films is unwatchable. Several are silly, but there is a liveliness and flourish to them that any executive producer could be proud of.

He was doing this in the worst days the business had ever known. On June 4, Ben Kahane, president of RKO, sent David a statement of accounts:

> You will note that we show a loss to May 28th of $1,250,052 as against a loss of $142,840 for the corresponding period of 1931. My estimate for the full year 1932 is that the picture companies will show a loss of $2,271,528.

Kahane was not critical of David; he appreciated the effort and the quality in what was being done. But he could not be optimistic. He was certain there would be no more money beyond budget from the parent company, and he reported:

> the gloom is very thick and black at this end. There is no doubt that the conditions facing the industry are critical. The next six months will be crucial ones and it will be a case of the survival of the fittest. Theatre grosses keep declining and it is impossible to cut costs and expenses of operation quickly enough to keep pace with the drop in income.

Kahane's letter came down to one practical request: David must adhere to the average production cost of $238,000 per picture. Crack the whip, said Kahane. "I, of course, will have to be prodding you constantly, which I know you will not resent."

In practice, Kahane had others do the prodding for him. Frank O'Heron was a New York man reporting to Merlin Aylesworth, the president of R.K.O. Corporation. By the end of July, he thought Aylesworth should consider the following: Mr. Selznick had so far completed eleven pictures at an average cost of $353,942.50; delays had led to the loss of one picture each for Constance Bennett and Ann Harding; ten pictures then in production promised to average out at $336,000; there were also great fears in advance that *King Kong*—budgeted at just over $400,000—might go as high as $1 million.

O'Heron's function was to find fault, and David had exceeded first estimates on several pictures. But to make amends, he was striving to reduce the studio overhead. Still, he announced himself "greatly disturbed" at the doubts being raised. After all, he had to deal with a "chaotic studio condition . . . an unbalanced staff and foolish expensive commitments." He had merged Radio and Pathé; he had reduced long-term contracts, cut back on personnel and capital expenditure, and—as he read the figures—made a saving of about $5 million compared with the previous year.

O'Heron claimed David read the figures optimistically. In August, David had Merian Cooper work out a further $150,000 reduction in the overhead. But O'Heron's analysis was that box-office income was down by as much as 50 percent. The average cost expected of David was possible. But who wanted forty films a year of that mean quality? David was interested in projects whose ambition swept budget away. If he kept to budget, where was the excitement, the gamble? Thus, he began to argue himself out of the principle of his position at RKO. By August he was especially insecure.

A son was born at 1:45 a.m. on August 4, at Cedars of Lebanon Hospital. Irene insisted that David be there in the delivery room, an uncommon privilege of fatherhood in those days. So David was enjoined to observe the process of birth, though he could hardly bear to look if the shape of a whole creature—fish or fowl—was apparent in the serving of a meal. Irene was scarcely conscious during the delivery, but the boy was healthy. As she was wheeled back to her room, she saw family members "flattened against the wall" of a corridor. "Pop was resplendent—his dreams had come true. First David's success and now David's son."

In the small hours, David and Myron went out on the town to celebrate. They got wildly drunk, not just in celebration, but because Myron was bitter. He had had a daughter, when he wanted a son. If at first the fates came in for Myron's scorn, David was the more available target. The rivalry over this son never ended. Myron would say of him, "Give him to me, I'll make a man of him." The boy, Jeffrey, adored Myron for the eleven years they had together. And David resented Myron's tough, encouraging influence over his son.

The next day, when David returned to the hospital, he told the new mother a disaster had occurred. Their baby was gone. The infant in the nursery, the one with "Selznick" on its name necklace, that was not the baby David had seen born the night before. Pop had told David such mistakes could happen in hospitals—and the Lindbergh baby had been kidnapped that March. David was already upsetting the hospital with talk of an investigation. When Irene protested he was absurd, he turned on her: "Can't you tell the difference? How is it possible? How can you not care?" He warned her not to love *this* baby; wait until the real one was found again.

The drama held for a terrible day. "*He* was the baby," Irene said of David, more than fifty years later. "He was the youngest."

On the second day, David came to the hospital not quite reconciled, but abashed and prepared to concede that this Jeffrey Mayer Selznick, said to be his, was a handsome child. He had a poem he had written in the night, the only one of his that was ever published (in *Good Housekeeping*):

> So we are three:
>   My darling, and my darling's darling,
>   And, humbly, me. . . .
> And where, before,
> We thought there were no more
>
> To add to Happiness,
> 'Tis only now we know
> What Life . . . and Love . . . are for.

Some fuss remained over Irene's choice of a name. David's pals were telling him "Jeffrey" was an odd name. Rewrites were considered. "Nicholas" was proposed, but how could the world not regard that as a nod to Nick Schenck? "Daniel" was good, but David said keep it for the future. In a few days, "Jeffrey" had gained currency. George Cukor had presented the babe with a miniature ermine robe! "Jeffrey Mayer Selznick" was the name—at least for a few years. As Irene observed, "There were more flowers than at a gangster's funeral."

L.B. had been in Washington, for in 1932 he devoted much of his time to the Republican cause in the coming election. Mayer was a fervent Republican who loved to have Herbert Hoover as a friend. He neglected the studio, and he was not willingly absent from the great event. His telegram pinpointed his sense of the occasion:

> Dear little mother of my grandson miss you David and Jeff very much. . . . President delighted your happiness. Will hustle to return soon.

When mother and son were able to leave the hospital, there was a formal presentation at Pop's house. David "kissed his youth good-bye when he had a son, but it was made palatable for what it would mean to Pop." David propped the baby at the end of the bed in L.J.'s house, stepped back, and announced, "Pop's eternity."

6 · AN INTEGRATED AMUSEMENT ENTERPRISE

DAVID'S CONTRACT at RKO lapsed on October 27, 1932. In recognition of business uncertainty, though he had been taken on for a year at $2,500 a week, he had been paid only $2,000 a week. The accumulated overage—$26,000—would come to him if and when the contract was renewed for another year. When David said the executive regime at RKO was "utterly impossible . . . however sincere and pleasant and well-intentioned," this leverage should be borne in mind. With a substantial bonus hanging over his head, he was the more inclined to sign on for another year, even if his heart was not quite committed.

By the end of October, *A Bill of Divorcement* was in release, but Katharine Hepburn did not take quickly with the American audience. Long after the event, David would look back on the debut and claim credit. But his account speaks to the alarm in 1932 and the actual failure of *A Bill of Divorcement:*

> The world knows that startling Hepburn face now, but when she first appeared on the R.K.O. lot there was consternation. "Ye gods, that horse face!" they cried, and when the first rushes were shown, the gloom around the studio was so heavy you could cut it with a knife. Not until the preview was the staff convinced we had a great screen personality. During the first few feet you could feel the audience's bewilderment at this completely new type, and also feel that they weren't quite used to this kind of face. But very early in the picture there was a scene in which Hepburn just walked across the room, stretched her arms, and then lay out on the floor before the fireplace. It sounds very simple, but you could almost feel, and you could definitely hear, the excitement in the audience. It was one of the greatest experiences I've ever had.

That preview occurred only days after the birth of Jeffrey Selznick, but the realization set in a great deal later. Irene was to be far closer to Hepburn than David ever managed. "He was most unattractive around her," said Irene. "He heckled her. You were either her friend or you weren't. She was bossy. Men ate out of her hand. He wasn't her kind of man at all: not two-fisted, virile, tough, and colorful. David didn't fit into any of those categories."

Years later, Hepburn would say of David, "He was like a wonderful, brand-new, beautifully designed and very expensive shoe—he wasn't creative, but he was a piece of work." There was an odd rivalry between Hepburn and David. When the actress had come out to Hollywood, she had a companion—Laura Harding, very rich, from the Barney family, a would-be actress, but neither beautiful nor confident enough to command attention. There were rumors that the two women were lovers: Hepburn said such talk was absurd and came from the fact that they got their clothes from the same designers.

David and Laura fell in love, in a way that was not common with David. "I really loved him," she admitted, "and I felt he loved me. But he never made a pass at me. He was gentle with me and he told me I should not live Kate's life."

They spent time together—Marcella Bannett wondered if David wasn't thinking of trying to marry Laura. She was better connected for a producer in need of funds than she seemed to realize. But he never asked her for money. He liked the shy, retiring Laura, and she was never sure why. But she was touched because not many people did like her. David went to stay with her on her farm in New Jersey, and he enjoyed seeing the dogs and horses that were a big part of her life. They shopped together. Above all, he could be restful with her. Irene tried to dazzle and entertain David; she sought to fill his life, or the part of it she could reach. Kate thought that Irene was "cold and absolutely controlling." Laura was warmer, less demanding, and dull even. She hated Irene, and Irene would not have her in the house.

Before the end of 1932, RKO would release Wellman's *The Conquerors*, a saga of American achievement in which the most exciting passages were Vorkapich's montages on capitalistic collapse; *Rockabye*, Cukor's next picture, with Connie Bennett, Joel McCrea, and Paul Lukas; and *The Animal Kingdom*, directed by Edward Griffith from the Philip Barry play, with Ann Harding, Leslie Howard, and Myrna Loy given a chance at romantic comedy. *The Animal Kingdom* was one of David's personal favorites: it was an unusually sophisticated work and the movie that opened the theater at Radio City Music Hall.

There were others set to open in the new year: *Topaze* with John Barrymore; Bennett again in *Our Betters*, Cukor's adaptation of Somerset Maugham; and the *King Kong* we know now, a studio fabrication of superb special effects and the mythic subconscious. David never grabbed for credit on *King Kong*. He allowed he had done no more than preside over Cooper,

Schoedsack, and effects man Willis O'Brien. But he had defended the rising costs of the project, and over a period of years he had guided Cooper away from real jungles. This may have been a by-product of a need for executive control and economy, but David had assisted in *King Kong*'s realization as a dream.

A great production executive has the wit to let the right things happen. From the rawness of *Kong* to the sly, salon innuendos of *Our Betters*, from the Pittsburgh foundry scenes in *No Other Woman* to the sunny location of the Bill Boyd Western, *Men of America*, from Barrymore and Myrna Loy to the delightful partnership of Edna May Oliver and James Gleason in *The Penguin Pool Murder*, RKO was alive and adventurous under David. His year there was as good and as crowded as any executive ever had.

Nevertheless, as of October 22, 1932, RKO was running a net loss for the year so far of nearly $2.75 million. On the year as a whole, rental income was down by over $3 million. That was inescapable and indifferent to the quality or range of the pictures. A great deal of time was spent at RKO assessing different ways of assigning the overhead. Phil Siff, the man David had hired from Lehman Brothers, wrote a report on the clever ways in

*Passengers
for New York*

which, by playing with the overhead, big or small pictures could be made to seem relatively profitable.

Siff was trying to make the case that the bigger, bolder pictures worked better than RKO thought. A key to his report was the attempt to justify *Bird of Paradise.* But Siff admitted how, over the whole program, that required another $5 million in investment, no matter if RKO's theatrical returns were dropping. RKO was not quite a major studio. It had only about 300 of its own theaters, and it struggled everywhere for good terms.

David was again of the opinion that no one could make forty pictures a year, or be responsible for that many, while maintaining both quality and profitability. But a good producer might do ten or a dozen a year and have that work out well—more or less, David could argue, that was what had happened at RKO. He wanted the best of both worlds: a handful of special pictures without the overall budgetary worries of a studio. It was spoiled, special pleading.

But in October, as the deadline approached, he faced the acid test of being offered just the privileged opportunity he wanted. His father-in-law asked him, with very favorable terms of salary, to head a unit within the MGM operation.

At the end of October, David and Irene had a cash balance of under $6,000. They were living in rented property, at 972 Ocean Front, with a new baby. Earlier in 1932, the first payments had been made on a piece of land on Summit Drive, where the family home would be built. But L.B. had carried the payment ($42,000), for he was making the great home there possible as a gift to his daughter and son-in-law. It matched the property he had bought for Bill and Edie Goetz.

In October and November 1932, David and Irene went to New York; Jeffrey remained in Los Angeles with nurse and nanny. Irene would miss the baby, so David had studio cameramen come in to film him and then shipped the footage to New York for the mother's gaze. The journey took longer because David decided to go by boat, the *President Coolidge,* through the Panama Canal. He made a festivity of it: he would work on *Our Betters* and plan *Little Women* on the way, so he enlisted George Cukor, scenarist Jane Murfin, Marcella, and another secretary as traveling companions. David seldom let himself be alone with anyone—not even with Irene. Even if happy and relaxed, he wanted some audience to confirm the good time. David also paid for Pop and Flossie to go to New York by train.

Another purpose of the trip was to determine his future at RKO, and in this November David was paid the bonus of $26,000, recognition that he was staying for another year. But he was finding it difficult to settle terms for that year. Indeed, on November 12 he found himself able to write to L.B., turning down the MGM offer, adding:

> That you may know my reasons are sincere, I want you to know that at the time I am writing this note, I have not yet had a single word with the top RKO and RCA executives concerning my future. I do not know whether I shall be able to get together with them, and I have, as yet, not done a single thing to get myself an alternate position elsewhere. It is, accordingly, possible that I will be without a suitable proposition for myself. I do not fear this, but I say it is possible; and I point it out that you may know my decision is arrived at independently of any equal or better proposition elsewhere than the one I might possibly have with you.

David told Mayer he owed allegiance to RKO, which had let him spend their money "entirely as I have seen fit." But he conceded that it might be easier to make films at MGM. Still, he did not want to get in the way of Thalberg or be subordinate to him: "His record is too excellent for me not to regard him as the master of that particular situation; and I should think very little indeed of his organization if they did not regard him as their master." David knew that one of L.B.'s psychological motives was to weaken Thalberg's claims for more of the MGM profits. He understood how, as a son-in-law, he might be the instrument to dislodge a former, treasured "son."

Not that maneuver was alien to David, or to Myron, who was advising him closely. The letter of refusal was also a negotiating ploy:

> R.K.O. had an amazing faith in me at a time when my previous employer did everything to run me down, and when very few other companies in the business had even an appreciable respect for my ability. Notably, M-G-M did not change in its disrespect for those abilities from the time I left its employ about six years ago, up until a few months ago. Faith, I feel, should be returned with faith.

The letter was also to be read by Irene. For one passage raises the unfortunate aura of nepotism and the charge that might be leveled if David took a position at MGM. It makes a further point, one addressed to Irene's conscious eyes (reassuring her that he would never go to Metro) and to her deeper more secret feelings (asking her to see that he *should* not). It is a glimpse of a shifting triangular relationship of powers in which David was the least strong:

> Moreover, I believe there is a hazard to my life with Irene, which might lose a great deal of its balance were I an employee of her father.

> This is too personal a matter to do much writing about, but I may say,
> in passing, that Irene shares my opinion. I think, among other things,
> that she would lose her pride in me, which I may say I enjoy.

From the start of the second year at RKO, as well as the bonus, David received a monthly salary of $2,500. But he was asking for more in the new contract and pushing RKO for agreement. Aylesworth and Kahane promised a decision by December 15, but that day came and went without a word. David complained of having little chance to be in direct touch with David Sarnoff, and there were signals that the company was assessing its overall state in the light of David's demands. There were those in the New York office happy to have David gone.

On December 16, David wired Sarnoff saying he "would refuse further responsibility for the studio and its production effective immediately." There wasn't time left for anything except the maneuvering. He telephoned Kahane and Aylesworth and proposed a version of the old unit production system. David would find private backers to form a new company that would make a distribution deal with RKO that guaranteed the costs of production. The company would use the RKO facilities, and David thought he could take over several personnel contracts (which he had deliberately kept "flexible"), including those of Cukor, Connie Bennett, and Hepburn.

Also on the sixteenth, he asked David Bruce to act as a contact with possible backers. He thought that "total propositions would be swung for approximately $2.5 million," and he asked Bruce to go over it "with Sonny and perhaps with Jock also." The shape of such a scheme had long been in David's mind, but the detail was furnished in an hour, maybe even while he dictated the telegram.

Leaving no stone unturned, David wired Henry Luce, the owner of *Time*, to get the best promoting coverage. He specified that there would be four units, those of King Vidor, Milestone, Merian Cooper, and Walter Wanger. He hammered out an entire story for Luce and added a fascinating sidebar to keep RKO unsettled:

> If you want to get something up about rumored possible future
> associations you might mention Paramount, Fox, Howard Hughes,
> Metro-Goldwyn-Mayer although would appreciate omission from
> this article of any mention of any relationship. Wish you could also
> mention that Radio's last statement which I have just this minute
> received states that there is every likelihood that I will be with com-
> pany year from today which I am denying with statement that there
> is only very remote likelihood that I will be with company two
> months from today.

David Sarnoff urged restraint and patience on David, to say nothing of loyalty: "I ask you to reflect upon the difficulties which face the management at this particular moment in dealing with such questions as increased compensation to the highest paid officer in the entire organization."

In the last days of 1932, as Radio City Music Hall opened, RKO turned down the unit scheme but made David a "definite offer for [next] year at terms considerably better for me than I received last year." Nevertheless, he told Sonny Whitney, as he apologized for the cancellation of hopes for a new company, he was refusing RKO. He would finish those pictures in hand, but he was quitting. David knew he was going somewhere else. He even said of the new company idea, "afraid we will have to postpone it for time being at least and probably permanently." Even before the events of January 1933, David seems to have known he would be out of RKO by February 16.

Pop Selznick had been weakening for months. There are pictures of him with his new grandson, Jeffrey, where he looks like an old man holding himself in place. In the end, he died of a cerebral hemorrhage, but it is unclear what provoked it. Even in his decline, he ate unwisely for any diabetic. He liked to raid the icebox at all hours and then be idle and impatient at mealtimes. When Flossie tried to lay down diets and regimes for L.J., David said, "Pop would not want to live with restrictions." Irene felt David had an irrational confidence his father would live forever. That train ride east late in '32 had been meant as holiday, but it may have strained Pop.

By December 1932, the crisis in David's relations with RKO was matched by his father's collapse. With Myron in France on business, Ishii moved into the parents' apartment in the Sunset Towers. There were nurses around the clock, and Dr. Sam Hirschfeld was in attendance along with any specialist anyone could think of.

With the New Year, Myron hurried back to Los Angeles. As late as January 13, David was cabling him on the train to say that Hirschfeld was "tremendously optimistic." The doctor had said—or David believed he had said—that a recent incident had been only a spasm, not a hemorrhage. That explained L.J.'s loss of memory and his "difficulty in thinking."

Myron arrived. But on January 24, Pop had so bad a night no one left the Towers. On the morning of the twenty-fifth, Hirschfeld arrived and went in to see the patient. "Suddenly he flung the doors open and made a gesture indicating that all was over."

David lunged toward the bed on which his father lay. No one could restrain him. He was large and strong, albeit as clumsy as a child. He cried out, "Pop, it's David, speak to me! It's David asking you. Do it for me,

Pop." It was as if David could not credit the fact of desertion, as if he believed that will and need might still call Pop back. "For two years afterward," said Irene, "he cried out in his sleep for him. He was raw! And he *never* got over it."

Then the Selznicks left the Towers. "Take care of things," David said to Irene, in passing. "Ishii will help you." Everyone else took off for Myron's apartment at the Beverly Wilshire. Irene and Ishii were left to deal with the undertaker, the rabbi, the flowers, the cemetery, the casket, and the newspapers. When she got to the Wilshire, she found the family and a group of friends drowning their sorrows and chuckling together. David got up in surprise. "Where have you been all this time?" he wanted to know. Lubitsch and Milestone were members of the little party, professional friends, and they marveled gently that, left to herself, Irene had gone ahead with a full Orthodox funeral. L.J. had never been devout.

Florence Selznick decided then and there to move into the hotel. The Towers apartment was abandoned. In all that family, there had been little attachment to home; under pressure, the various members often resorted to hotels. To be closer, David and Irene moved into the Wilshire, too; they called up the staff at the beach and had the nearly six-month-old Jeffrey brought in. They would remain there until July.

The funeral services on January 26 were attended by the Mayers, the Schenck brothers, Jesse Lasky, B. P. Schulberg, Ben Kahane, Harry Rapf, and many others. Again, David collapsed at the ceremony. Marcella Bannett was there:

> I have never seen such a manifestation of grief as David's. It was hard for anyone to take. He was being held up, by Irene on one side and someone else on the other. . . . Myron was pretty good. He was walking along. Myron was not as sentimental, anyway. But David, his crying was so intense that the mucus from his nose just fell and drained right to the ground.

David tried to write a poem on Beverly Wilshire notepaper. It was not completed, and some of it is feebly scratched out:

> *Hours toward the dawn*
> *And music born*
> *Pop . . .*
> *Soul that gave me breath to draw*
> *And life to live and spend*
> *Pop*
> *Who knew what this is for*
> *And taught of life before the end . . .*

Gone the breath I borrowed
Gone my father
Gone, forever sorrowed
And he who gave me life has left
He for whom I fought . . . Bereft
I know no goal . . .
He who lived for me alone

Myron, the administrator of his father's estate, did not rush to probate. Pop had died without assets or property—he and Flossie had been isolated and stripped to avoid creditors. Still, there were claims against the estate for over $77,000. They would not be settled until 1946, after Myron's death.

On February 2 or 3, somewhere at the Wilshire, David sat down with parties from MGM to discuss goals and terms. Irene found it "incomprehensible" that David could think of rejoining her father's studio. She said the decision was entirely opposed to her advice and feelings. She believed the resignation from RKO and the move to Metro were decisions taken in distress and instability, prompted by what David said Pop had whispered to him near the end, "Blood is thicker than water" or, as he told Flossie, "Tell David to stick with his own people; they're the men you can trust."

There is no doubting the emotional volatility—for very soon after joining MGM David would be in agonies over the mistake. Yet David was not simply unhinged by the loss of Pop. He had made up his mind about leaving RKO. Nor was he so shocked he could not negotiate. The notes of his meeting with MGM are in his own hand, and they are lucid, terse, and hungry.

David would get $4,000 a week for two years to make only somewhere between six and ten films a year. Those films would bear the credit "Produced by David O. Selznick." The studio would put aside a building for Selznick and his staff (it proved to be the bungalow vacated by John Gilbert). He was to have his own unit and associates, including an art director, cutter, and a publicity man. On all production and authority matters on his pictures there was to be "no Thalberg." David was answerable only to L.B.

The contract was all to start straightaway, with the salary beginning the day David left RKO. On February 14 it took effect.

The press called the move "sudden." There were ill feelings at RKO as Merian Cooper filled the gap. Several pictures were left to the fates. *Little Women* is the best known, but there were two others, both initiated by David and directed by John Cromwell. *Ann Vickers* is from a Sinclair Lewis novel, with Irene Dunne and Walter Huston: it is unusually direct, subtle, and intelligent. *The Silver Cord* is none of those things, yet it is more intriguing. It comes from a play by Sidney Howard (who was to loom large in David's career), about a mother who so spoils and dominates her sons they are hardly free. Laura Hope Crews played the mother, Joel McCrea her prized boy (named David), and Irene Dunne the woman he marries. The picture is excruciating, yet fascinating. Everything is overdone—smothered, nearly—yet there is a feeling for parental power as a warping force in families. It might have been good for David if he had had to stay on and finish the project. But he escaped.

7 · THE TORTURE OF SELF-DISGUST

A CASE CAN BE MADE that David Selznick never had things as good as at MGM from 1933 to 1935. His temperament was blessed by the funding and facilities of a stable organization and the obliging authority of L.B. He could concentrate on making a few good pictures. There were prospects, too, even if filled with risk: his father-in-law was grooming him for bigger things. Irving Thalberg had had his first serious heart attack in 1932. He was on an extended leave that surprised no one. The wonder was that, with all the work and L.B. looking after him, Irving had lasted so long. David was easily seen as heir to the Culver City studio.

Even as David's agreement was thrashed out at the Beverly Wilshire, an attempt at reassurance was sent to Thalberg by Nick Schenck and L.B. It alluded to David's new contract and to his being answerable only to Mayer, and it said of Thalberg:

> That by consenting to the execution of such contract, you shall not be deemed to have approved the terms of the same nor the special conditions therein set forth. . . .
>
> . . . and particularly that you shall not be considered, by reason of such consent, as having acquiesced or approved the policy which has been discussed of establishing the unit system of production, and, finally, it is agreed that no concessions similar to that made to Mr. Selznick shall be made in connection with any other contract or employment without your express consent.

In the latter part of 1932, there had been fearsome battles between Thalberg and Nick Schenck in which Mayer stayed a clever onlooker. Rattled by the death of his close friend Paul Bern in September, Irving was

L.B. as yachtsman off the California coast. Marjorie Daw Selznick in the foreground

more determined to get financial protection for his wife and two children. The result had been a major concession whereby Irving was allowed to buy Loew's stock. When Thalberg's heart attack came in December 1932, it was pretext enough for the studio's effort to secure David. The face-saving letter was sent to Thalberg shortly before he, Norma Shearer, and their children departed for Bad Nauheim in Germany for rest and special treatment.

As he left the studio and the country, Thalberg responded in fatigue to Mayer—"There are, however, loyalties that are greater than the loyalties of friendship. There are loyalties to ideals, the loyalties to principles without which friendship loses character and real meaning." Irving had no hope of reforming L.B., but there was a Thalberg cult at the studio that would grow in his absence. Irving treated his coworkers well enough for them to believe they might be his equals. No one who knew Mayer could miss his need for control. Few were fully aware the extent to which Irving's fights with Loew's had been, quite simply, for more money. Thalberg's collapse was easily taken as a symbol of the struggle for quality and integrity. L.B. made things worse when he said he had only hired David "to spare Irving—who is so dear to me." Thus David was cast as the hit man and son-in-law.

Another crisis was less calculable. As Franklin Roosevelt took office in January 1933 (days before Pop died), it became clear that the nation's economy—and, eventually, the studio's—would be put on a fresh footing. In their own spirit of patriotism, early in March, the potentates of Hollywood called for a "voluntary" 50 percent pay cut across the board for eight weeks. L.B. led this movement, and he pointed to the closing of the banks as a justification. He made use of the Academy of Motion Picture Arts and Sciences to promulgate the policy so that it did not seem just the ploy of cunning studio bosses.

Of course, it did, and it was. David was now making $4,000 a week and L.B. close to $20,000. Chop that weekly income in half and it still surpassed what the majority of Americans made in a year. Plenty of Hollywood employees earned $50 a week or less. The drastic economy was instrumental in the formation or enlivening of the various guilds and unions in the business, and it initiated the panic of men like Mayer that socialism, and worse, was alive in the land. At the very least, as the bosses met, some argued against the manner of the cuts. Merian Cooper was one who resisted cutting the wages of the low-paid workers.

On the afternoon of Friday, March 10, the leaders of the industry were meeting at the Hollywood Roosevelt Hotel. At 5:45, they were still arguing the matter. Then Cooper saw the anger of the men take on terrified expressions: "suddenly the entire room started to shake like hell, it was bouncing around, and if you looked out the window the palm trees were all bent double."

An earthquake had struck Long Beach. Buildings wobbled, people fainted, and crowds filled the streets, looking up for falling masonry. There were fifty-four deaths and extensive damage, as well as the eerie sensation of natural disaster coming to join fiscal calamity. Irene was at the Beverly Wilshire, where she, David, and Jeffrey were living. She grabbed up the baby, put him in a blanket, and ran down ten flights of stairs to the street. A few moments later, a limousine came by, L.B. got out, and shouted to her, "Hurry up, get in. What's the matter with you?" A part of Irene had longed to get away from the Mayer household. Then her rescuing David had gone back into the dragon's studio. Now here was her father, turning up like magic—or fate's hero.

In the period of aftershocks, unable to sleep, Irene went away to Palm Springs and the desert. But this was more than just seeking a safer haven. It was also a separation. David was in agony at MGM already, intimidated by the support for Thalberg and humiliated by the trade press commentary about him, his salary, and the nepotism. *The Hollywood Spectator* ran an editorial that deplored the son-in-law who also rises.

In the dismay at being unpopular and losing his father, as well as the private wondering about having made a mistake, David was gambling with a new intensity. In the eight months of 1932 for which figures are available, David lost $2,500 and won $87.50. For 1933, the figures are as follows (note, they show when debts were paid; David paid these bills faithfully, but not always promptly): winnings, $298; losses, $23,024.

In March, for instance, as David conformed to the salary cut at MGM, he lost $2,955, nearly three eighths of his income. His unhappiness was spilling over into pathological behavior. David was an inept gambler. He bet on too many numbers at roulette. At poker, he always called an opponent's hand. He drank while he played. For Irene, it was too much to have to witness such self-destruction. She believed David was breaking down, so she left him.

He remained at the hotel, sitting up late with Myron, drinking. Irene had been all against the MGM contract in their talks, yet now she told him for God's sake, get on with it. (In all these troubles, David was making *Dinner at Eight*, directed by his good friend George Cukor, and with a cast that demonstrated the wealth of even a "hostile" studio: Marie Dressler and Wallace Beery, the Barrymore brothers, Jean Harlow, Lee Tracy, Edmund Lowe, and Billie Burke. No one could miss how like a Thalberg picture it was.) David wrote to Irene from the hotel telling her he'd been "pretty good" about the press attacks and saying he felt "about four times as valuable as most of the incompetents" at MGM. He said he would stop whining, but he couldn't manage it yet:

> I've only the hope left in the mess I've made of seven years of progress, and that's that I'll have character enough not to subject you to a repetition of suspicion ever that I blame you. I'm abject in humiliation over that. Believe me, darling.

Irene returned as the earthquake scare passed, but David still preferred a hotel life. Salaries were back to normal by May; in fact, the lowest salaries had been left alone. David's May salary was $19,500, sufficiently more than $4,000 a week to suggest some balancing out of his earlier sacrifice. There was antipathy to David at Culver City, but L.B. was working hard to make life more appealing for him. Nevertheless, in June, David sent a ten-page letter to L.B.:

> I write you instead of telling you verbally because I have learned that I write much better than I talk; because I want to be sure I tell you exactly how I feel, and by reading the letter myself before sending it to you, I know I am saying what I want to say; and because you might like to transmit the contents to Nick.

On the page, David's uncertainties started to mount. He wrote to find out what he thought—and the discovery frightened him. So much of the problem, and character, of the letters may lie in their being dictated.

"I want to get out of MGM," he told L.B., "and the quicker the better." He said he had made a mistake because of his "unique emotional strain." For the first time in his career he had followed the advice of his "immediate family." As he rehashed the past, David saw the mistakes he had made and the correctness of his first impressions. He now believed he should have taken the RKO offer of a share in profits rather than the high salary at MGM. He rued the day he had made himself vulnerable to the charge of nepotism:

> All past accomplishment is wiped out, because this is a business that forgets yesterday at dawn today; and any appreciation of future ac-complishment is impossible because I am not an executive here, as I believe, by right of six or seven years of struggle, but a relative here by right of marriage.

His self-pity eclipsed all reason. Only a month before, David had sent a seven-page report to Nick Schenck aglow with achievement and prospect. He was positive about his working relationship with Eddie Mannix (a Metro executive especially close to L.B.), and this tribute needs to be crosscut with the despair of the letter to Mayer:

> Eddie is doing an enormous amount of work, and I think he has a splendid grasp on everything. My own relationships with him have been simply splendid, and I think there is no one I have ever worked with so enjoyably—a condition which I am certain will continue. We are neither of us dignifying with attention any resentment which may remain on the part of others.

How can we reconcile the two? Was David subject to constant change? Did he become more cheerful as he tried to write positively? Or was he torn between being political and being sincere? There is an undertone in the report to Schenck of the newcomer anxious to show his abilities with a view to better things in the future. David saw and dreamed of *all* possibilities. As he made the report, he likely saw a day in which he might even take over from L.B. That wasn't so crazy, and it would end the nepotism slur.

But in the pleas to L.B., David had become the slave of misfortune. Even as he outlined a condition of manic depression, we can see how helplessly he was its victim. Just because David wrote pages of good sen-tences does not mean he was sane—at least, not on paper.

> My grief started from the first hour I came here, and has continued unabated up to this writing. I feel slightly better, at this moment, for

merely having written this letter, than I have for months. This is the first unhappy year of my entire life. No doubt the loss of my father had a large part in this, but I have a conviction that my moroseness has been aggravated enormously by my false commercial position. I have had other periods when things did not go so well, in fact a whole period of years from the time that the family went broke with the Selznick Company, and literally no one of us had a dollar to our names. . . . Never was there a hangdog moment, and certainly none of the mercurial moods of indifference and depression that have made me damned impossible to live with, and that have colored every side of my life.

Irene's health, David admitted, had been affected by her distress over his uncertainty and by the nights they had sat up discussing the problem. The bad publicity passed, and good pictures would banish it. For the moment, he hated his mistake and clung to the high-minded notion that money did not matter. But if he tried to demonstrate purity by gambling, then he aggravated Irene the more and put more pressure on her not to tell L.B. At such times, the Clover Club beckoned as relief and action. He dreamed of a killing there that would make him free. But the word was spreading that he was a sucker at the tables.

Dinner at Eight would open in August, the whole movie shot in thirty days and done inside six months. It would make a profit of nearly $1 million. In July, the Selznicks at last moved out of the Beverly Wilshire. They rented Colleen Moore's house at 345 St. Pierre, off Sunset and Beverly Glen. Jeffrey had his first birthday. Four thousand dollars a week came rolling in. There were plans for *Viva Villa!* and *David Copperfield*.

8 · HUMOROUS OR GROTESQUE

DAVID WAS SO BUSY at MGM that he took on more and more. There was not just the general hostility toward him at Culver City, to say nothing of learning how the studio worked with only Marcella, George Cukor, and Phil Siff to help him. There was the need to impress Nick Schenck about how quickly he could put the diverse affairs of the house in order, as well as the hope of persuading L.B. to let him out of his contract.

On the soundstages, there were the stormy temperaments in the cast of *Dinner at Eight* and George Cukor presiding over them like a magnificent, mobile, always flattering host who still had time to throw a raised eyebrow of horror and amusement to his intimates. Cukor was faster than David, wittier, lighter, and more accommodating. He was a director who would find a style in his need to get on with people, despite the possible stigma of homosexuality. And he was a man who could make David and Irene cheer up when the clouds seemed dense. The great fluent kindness of his best work grew out of self-effacing availability, the untiring ease with which he passed in a society ready to damn him.

Thus, in Cukor's files, for October 14, 1933, there is this hasty note. There are so many crises to which it might have referred—on the other hand, perhaps George had only found the right white peonies for a party:

> Darling George:
>
> What are words? Nothing! But you must know how very great my feelings toward you are.
>
> My appreciation is no end.
>
> Irene

At the age of seventy-seven, George Bernard Shaw visited Culver City. David and Marcella conducted him to the *Dinner at Eight* set, where John Barrymore took Cukor aside and said, "I'll be rather stupid and you can show me what you want, and they can see you directing." The stars worked together. The picture was made in a trice, and the prospect of life as a swell, catered affair was offered to 1933's America. The country loved it.

David had the Barrymores, Helen Hayes, and Clark Gable in *Night Flight*, Oliver Garrett's adaptation of Antoine de Saint-Exupéry's novel. He had fallen in love with the book's reputation and dreamed of a flying picture to rival Howard Hughes's 1930 epic, *Hell's Angels.* But when the novel proved earthbound in action, David tried additions unimagined by the French author, including the old-fashioned routine of a flying rescue over the mountains to save a child. Nothing helped *Night Flight*, yet somehow in years to come David would believe himself the only Hollywood filmmaker to be trusted with literature.

He had been assigned to *Dancing Lady*, a musical with Clark Gable and Joan Crawford. Here, he attacked with more relish and greater success. He got Johnny Considine to revise the script, and he cajoled new songs from Richard Rodgers and Lorenz Hart and Burton Lane and Harold Adamson. The Rodgers and Hart song "Rhythm of the Day" struck David as fine at first. But then he wondered aloud if the composers couldn't make it better. A song, they told him, is a song—you want another, we'll do another. It's a revealing anecdote, for David did not often trust the nature of things: he was as likely to think a song could be enhanced or a script polished as, say, that Jeffrey could have been better.

Joan Crawford was only doing *Dancing Lady* because L.B. had begged her. David won her over with a challenge. Screenwriter Allen Rivkin recalled a conference where the producer played on her professional pride:

> so David throws a curve at her, he says, "Joan, I don't know if you can play this part, it's kind of tarty. I think it's more Jean Harlow's style." Well, Joan kind of bristles at this and she says, "Look, Mr. Selznick, I was playing hookers before Harlow knew what they were, so let's not hear any talk about style because I know more about that than she ever will."

What did the producer and the actress say in private? David was in the habit of getting horny over the actresses in his films, and Crawford was rapacious and romantic. As Joe Mankiewicz put it, "Nobody had a long affair with Joan." If David didn't chase her round the desk, then it was only because he forgot. Such affairs were brief, chronic, and well known—which means that L.B. chose to turn a blind eye. He may have felt a secret advantage at finding his son-in-law unfaithful, for L.B. himself would never give up on Irene.

There was not much dancing in *Dancing Lady*, so David seized another passing opportunity. In his last weeks at RKO, the studio had been considering a movie career for Fred Astaire, already thirty-four and a famed dancer onstage with his sister, Adele. But in 1933, she had retired to marry the son of the Duke of Devonshire. Fred needed a change. David saw a rare charm in the way Fred talked and moved; he saw how the man might be both mysterious and appealing. On January 13, 1933, he wrote to Louis Brock, an associate producer at RKO:

> I am tremendously enthused about the suggestion New York has made of using Fred Astaire. If he photographs (I have ordered a test), he may prove to be a really sensational bet ... Astaire is one of the great artists of the day: a magnificent performer, a man conceded to be perhaps, next to Leslie Howard, the most charming in the American theater, and unquestionably the outstanding young leader of American musical comedy.

The test was not promising: Astaire had "enormous ears and bad chin line" (from a memo dictated the day after Pop's death); shortly thereafter David was gone. But RKO came to a deal with Astaire (for $1,500 a week) set to start on August 1, after the Broadway run of *The Gay Divorce* and after Fred's marriage. There was a window of opportunity for Astaire—the two weeks after July 15—and with David's offer, the new Mrs. Astaire spent her honeymoon watching Fred's movie debut. RKO, apparently, raised no murmur of protest at this, which suggests they had elected not to offend young Mr. Selznick.

Some projects were never made. Even in 1933, David was considering *The Garden of Allah*. He was thinking about a remake of *What Price Hollywood?*, and there was talk of *The Prisoner of Zenda* with Jeanette MacDonald. David looked seriously at what would become *The Paradine Case*. He was hoping to line John Barrymore up for *The Forsyte Saga*, and why not Lionel Barrymore playing the detective Pinkerton? But the apple of his eye was *Two Thieves*, a Biblical story, in which he hoped to cast Gable and Robert Montgomery.

Beyond all of this there were prospects and speculations. In 1933, David paid $5,000 of his own money for a story called "Dracula's Daughter." It was his notion that Universal (the studio that had made *Dracula*) would be obliged to buy it back from him to safeguard the character. Furtively, in correspondence, he referred to the project as "Tarantula," and privately he hoped for $50,000 for it. In the end he settled for a profit percentage deal from Universal that netted him about $15,000.

Somehow, money remained an anxiety for David. Since Pop's death, he was paying a monthly allowance to his mother, never less than $800. Irene's housekeeping allowance ranged from $2,800 to $3,500 a month. In 1933, the total income of David and Irene was split, for tax reasons, as it always was: $91,930 to him and $92,022 to her. Yet at the close of the year, their bank balance was $925.77. Of course, they were paying rent for 345 St. Pierre, just as they had paid lodging at the Beverly Wilshire. Their own house on Summit Drive would not be ready until the end of 1934.

But then, in the summer of 1933, L.B. was moved to greater generosity than the house. A new movie company was being formed, Twentieth Century, headed by Darryl Zanuck, who had made his reputation as a writer and producer at Warners, and Joe Schenck. While a leading executive at MGM, Louis B. Mayer became an investor in Twentieth Century. It was part of his arrangement with the new studio that Bill Goetz would be given a job. Zanuck had no illusions about Bill's ability, but "so long as he keeps his father-in-law's money in our company, he can work for me as long as he likes."

Looking to the future, L.B. chose to pass on part of his Twentieth stock to Edie, Bill, Irene, and David: he envisaged giving each one of them 12½ percent of what he held, a total value of $350,000.

David refused his share. In every way, he was at pains to deny their dependence on L.B. Very early in the marriage, L.B. had given Irene a diamond necklace. But David had sent it back, saying, "When I want my wife to have presents like that, I'll buy them." On their future home, David made no protest, but it would not be known for some time how it had been paid for. For David, it was enchanting to be provided for, yet it was hateful to both work for and live on his father-in-law. So his share of the Twentieth stock was divided between Edie and Bill Goetz. Which left the crucial question of whether Irene would accept hers.

She tried to decline, as if Cordelia could have explained to Lear that such gifts would not prove love. So L.B. said, very well, she could "buy" the stock, but he would loan her the money to buy it and the debt would be forgiven if he died. Again, she declined, and he told her she was being "a damn fool." No, said Irene, she hated ever to owe money:

> in the end I proposed a compromise to my father—a difficult one to be sure. If he was that determined on my having a share, he should give me the stock and pay the gift tax; nor would I mind if he reduced my share to compensate for paying the tax.
>
> It disappointed my father to find me such a stickler, but it was he who had instilled it in me. And although it was wounding to him, he took it with grace, his only comment being: "You have a very good character, but you are not flexible. I'm not sure I want to do business with you in the future." We didn't.

In that manner, Irene's conscience had been protected, though the gift had been delivered just as L.B. intended. By 1936, Irene was earning interest as the stock prospered. By 1942, when she sold the shares, she had accumulated $250,198 in interest. And in the sale, she realized $480,302. It might not be doing business, but it would enable Irene to have a substantially greater net worth than David at the time of their separation.

David was fretting by the late summer of 1933. In August, Thalberg returned from his convalescence. He would never again take on the full studio load he had had before his heart attack, but he had a unit, much like David's. The two men had adjoining bungalows, and they were friendly. Still, they could not ignore the appearance of rivalry, and David could not woo the many people at Culver City loyal to Irving. L.B. was not one to remove unease.

Thus, in the late summer, David put out feelers to RKO. *King Kong* had opened on March 2, 1933. Its first-run rentals would pass $2 million. The profits deal that RKO had offered David began to look very good in hindsight, and the labor of *Kong* and running the studio's production program had made Merian Cooper sick. David went to lunch with Frank O'Heron and apparently told him Cooper was in even worse health than reports stated. Not long thereafter, Myron approached the studio and intimated that with David restored to RKO, he might be able to deliver Gary Cooper, Fredric March, and Miriam Hopkins. Ben Kahane had heard of a "dog-fight" at Metro between David and Thalberg, and there was a rumor that David had also approached Harry Cohn at Columbia.

The possibility got into the newspapers, and by October 24 David was making vigorous denials. He wrote to Kahane saying that Cooper was "possibly my closest friend" and someone he would never wish to hurt or intrude on. He said that O'Heron had wanted David and told him that Selznick's departure had cost RKO "untold millions." Finally, David pitied "any poor devil" who tried to tackle RKO with its "utterly impossible" executive regime.

It may have been just talk and misunderstanding. But David's own nervy inclination would never stop trying new games. The letter to Kahane is bold and forthright, and nothing came of RKO. But another letter from the end of 1933 reveals the inner man. There had been more gambling backsliding, and David sent Irene a letter, handwritten in pencil, on RKO paper that he still possessed:

> Darling—
>
> It is after five-thirty in the morning, and one of the most miserable hours of my life. For perhaps the first time, sleep is unthinkable, and I shall not try to achieve it.
>
> I have lost a large amount of money—four thousand dollars. No loss of money could seriously upset me: this you know. But I have broken my most devout word to you, and I cannot tell you the torture of self-disgust that I feel. At last, and for the first time, I know the awful pangs of remorse, and I can not face myself or my work, or, most of all, *you* without the very mild but only slight relief open to me: Confession. . . .
>
> I went with the best of intentions, determined on bridge. But there wasn't a single bridger in the place. I was very late, and the house was already filled with games well along in progress. It was an awful party, an awful group. So I sat with Irving while he played poker a minute— and then, well, one small stack in an apparently piker-limit game— and then—well, then, collapse and increasing misery of conscience while I tried desperately to pull out and go home. This sounds as though the sin in my mind is the amount. Believe me, it isn't, and I know it isn't in your mind either. But the amount too is awful, when I think of what you do to save and conserve—and, oh how horrible!—the little luxuries of the house denied.
>
> I try to think of Pop, and how he'd have made me feel better about it. But all this does is sink me with memories of him, reawakening the depression over him I've been fighting, with your precious and un- mentioned help, to get over.
>
> I can't face you. I shall leave here when it's light. I'm going to sell

off as many of my stocks as possible when the market opens, for I've no right to jeopardize what capital we have. . . .

Please don't phone me. Just leave word with the office whether you'd rather I didn't see you tomorrow night, or whether you'd like to go way for a few days (or longer?) or whatever. I don't mean to be dramatic, but I feel so desperate and futile about it. "For each man kills the thing he loves." And I love you as I hate myself.

Your wretched David

9 · NOT ONLY WAS I INVITED

THERE WAS a restlessness in the Selznicks which bespoke their need for attention—as well as money, power, and yards of coverage in the press. There were afternoons and weekends when the Selznick brothers—by which people meant David and Myron—seemed to be taking over the town.

Myron chose to cultivate the myth that he was driven to redress the wrongs done to his father. But that was an outlet for a natural and even graceful hostility, and it survived the death of the father. At first, Myron was the more exultant because his success defied the nation's Depression and proved the absurdity in fate. He had time to screw around, get drunk and make trouble, and still run the most efficient operation in town. It made him seem like a prize hoodlum. Yet those who knew him well saw that he was also bereft. Despite all the deals and assistants, he had no plans or purpose. Once, the telephone company counted 550 calls going out of the agency offices in six hours—it was a frenzy of talk and capital accumulation. But the calls had never to stop. There was nothing else in his life.

Many people contrasted David and Myron, to David's advantage. Because Myron was the famous drunk, it was seldom remarked that David drank too much. The younger brother was not interested in money—that is what he professed, and David's single genius, amid so much talent, was for publicity. He wanted to impress people, and he began with himself. That sounds self-centered, yet David had true charm and endless boyishness. People of all sorts fell for him. But the best deals only left him anxious that some final embellishment had been left out. He was an actor playing David O. Selznick, always thinking of fresh touches and tricks of plausibility. He did not trust naturalness or simplicity. Thus, once, coming out of the barbershop, he couldn't resist the showmanship and the press release of cabling Irene (a few miles away only):

"I just got a haircut and you've no idea how handsome I look."

David was as much the victim of vivid emptiness as Myron. Myron was disappointed; he had far more money than public recognition; he was as much feared as liked, but he never had David's great triumphs, and he had no son. Myron was a willing antihero. He believed the play was a mockery, and he was ready to sneer at the audience. But David cherished the pretense so that he could not mock the stage or the audience, let alone his role.

David and Myron behaved badly. They were unfaithful to their wives; they fought and gambled and ruined dinner parties by turning up late. They had between them only as much social awareness or responsibility as would occupy a flat moment in a movie. And they not only got away with all of this, they thrived on it, for stories circulated about them in which their outrageousness seemed as fascinating as Cagney's way with a grapefruit.

One told how Myron had arrived very late at a fancy party being given by Edgar Selwyn. The guests were near the end of a two-hour dinner, in gowns and white ties. Myron was smashed, but he demanded to be served his dinner. David was there, and he felt compelled to ask his unruly brother, "Were you invited tonight?"

"Not only was I invited," Myron replied indignantly, "I declined!"

There is the brilliance of the drop-dead remark, insolent but irresistible. It could be the model for much of what the director, Max Carey, says in *What Price Hollywood?* That is how Myron played his role of agent. He could be just as dismissive of clients as he was hostile to the studios. Take him for granted, and he'd pound you in the nose. Be wary, and he'd turn charitable. His need was always to be unpredictable and remarkable. He could beat the desk on behalf of the wretched life to which Connie Bennett might be driven with less than $30,000 a week—beat it so that the heavy contract fluttered. Then he could turn on a client and tell him he was small potatoes.

Myron made money with monotonous speed and ease. The Connie Bennett deal had come in 1930, as the actress returned to the screen after retirement for one of her marriages and when Myron contrived to persuade the business that the world was agog to hear Connie's posh drawl. In January 1931, he pulled off the coup of getting William Powell, Kay Francis, and Ruth Chatterton away from Paramount and making better deals at Warners. (This evidently made David's position at Paramount more delicate.) By the mid-thirties, Myron's clients also included Carole Lombard, Fred Astaire, Fredric March, Merle Oberon, Myrna Loy, Ginger Rogers, and Loretta Young, as well as top writers like Gene Fowler, Dudley Nichols, and Casey Robinson.

By 1938, he moved from the Bank Building to a new, specially created office at 9700 Wilshire. This was an ingenious, one-story design, modernistic, laid out in a circle with an atrium. (In its day, it attracted as much attention as I. M. Pei's new building for Creative Artists Agency, erected over fifty years later, just a few blocks west.) When this building was opened, Myron threw a big party and another client, George Archainbaud, presented the agent with a six-foot-high "10%" done in flowers. As business expanded, the agency staff grew to fifty.

There were two companies at first, Myron's own and his partnership with Frank Joyce. It was also Myron's innovation to set up a range of services to assist his clients: he did their taxes and handled investments. For years, David took advantage of this service. Myron made big deals swiftly on the phone and moved on to others; he seldom dictated letters, but fired off confirming memos on the deals. In his correspondence, there is no trace of the soul-searching or second-guessing with which David destroyed forests. There was a practicality to Myron. He told his secretary, Maxine Graybill, not to waste time or brain space memorizing telephone numbers. Use the Rolodex. Thus at one o'clock in the morning, he would call her, drunk, having forgotten his own telephone number. She would tell him, so he could wake Marjorie and let her know what time he proposed being home.

Marjorie waited as Myron caused a stir elsewhere. "I think he adored her," said Maxine Graybill, "but he was a very bad husband. . . . He would invite people like Ben Hecht for dinner and then not show up himself until ten or eleven o'clock. It made her very nervous."

The sweet look of Marjorie seemed to others to mask blandness or vacancy. "Insignificant wasn't the word for her," said Irene. What's more, Marjorie lived in a household of three strong-willed people: Myron, Ishii, and Joan, who, by the age of four, struck her Uncle David as "the only person I have ever met more arrogant than Myron."

The running of the house was left to Ishii, and the domestic economy was controlled by Myron's office. From June 1935, Myron had a small house on the beach, 964 Ocean Front, and the actress Josephine Hutchinson remembered occasions there. She was married to Jimmy Townsend, one of Myron's associates at the agency. "Marjorie didn't seem to be the head of the household," she said. "Marjorie asked for a drink, but when it came it was something else entirely. And Marjorie was so meek, she didn't say anything to Ishii. But she whispered to me, 'He never brings me what I ask for.' "

Myron and the manservant enjoyed a splendid hostility, too. Time and again Myron would be half drunk at the dinner table. On one night, Ishii started to serve Myron carrots. Myron became furious. He slammed the table and roared, "Carrots! I told you—never carrots again!" Where-upon Ishii contemplated his irate master, gave him yet more carrots, and passed on without a word.

Myron made a comic performance of Ishii; it was like W. C. Fields with babies, one kind of tyrant bowing to another. Ishii was as efficient as his boss, and apparently above rebuke or discussion. Myron called Ishii "the Baron," as if to say the social order was upside down.

Myron's drinking was bad by 1934. Sometimes as dinner was served, he would simply go upstairs to bed. He began to eat less and less, and once, at Loretta Young's house, he started drinking straight from a bottle of cologne. The studios kept Johnnie Walker on hand for his visits. Sometimes he would call Townsend up at three in the morning just to talk. There seemed no relationship between him and Marjorie, and while he tried to like his daughter, he never knew what to do with her. Myron liked David, Irene, his racehorses, and drink, and more than all of them he needed the drink.

Another agency associate, Sig Marcus, said that Myron "makes great effort not to show his heart working; he hates emotion because emotion is the one chink in his armor." That was his way with women. He behaved as if needing to confirm his low opinion of the opposite sex; some said Marjorie was a wife taken in a mood of romantic despair. On the other hand, he loved to boast and conspire with Irene. And Loretta Young, one of the clients of whom Myron was most fond and protective, observed a helpless shyness:

> One night I was at his place for dinner with Carole Lombard and Merle Oberon—we were three pets of his as clients. And he was drinking. Not drunk, just drinking so that you couldn't quite get his attention. Myron's sitting there like a little cock-of-the-walk at the head of the table and here are the three actresses wolfing down the food. And he kept saying, "Oh, Merle, you're so gorgeous. Oh, Loretta, you're something. Oh, and Carole, you really—" Finally, he said, "Oh boy, would I love to have an affair with either of you, or all of you. . . ." And he's going on, and it's tough. And Merle put her fork down and said, "O.K., Myron, come on, right now!" Well, he looks, and he says, "Merle!" and he was just like a shocked old lady. She said it again: "Now! If you ever do this again, you've got to prove yourself right then." It stopped him cold.

David and Myron were very close in those years. They were often gamblers together, and Myron was the business adviser to whom David went most often. There is hardly a Selznick picture where David didn't use some of Myron's people, and there were some that amounted to package deals—before that term was known. In addition, they shared in providing for their mother, though Flossie was more open now in treating Myron as her favorite. Another of Myron's late-night activities was waking his mother up in her Beverly Wilshire apartment so that friends could see how wonderful she was. Then the two brothers had Howie in common.

Howard Selznick did not behave well either, but he got no reward for it. He, Mildred, and their two daughters moved many times, but nothing settled Howard or held his concentration. David paid money to Howard from November 1934 onward, but even before that it is likely that some of the money given to Flossie found its way to Howard's family. Flossie loathed Mildred and made life hard for her in any way she could. Flossie believed Mildred had always been out to make a killing off a rich family. But the marriage was fourteen years old by 1934, and Mildred had had no more than support and a hard life, with Flossie calling her "a whore and a bum" to her own children.

The Howie incidents mounted in seriousness. In the summer of 1932, he was sued for $36.50 by Henry Goode, a store owner whose bill had never been paid. Then in November 1933, David read in the papers that a doctor was suing Howie for $500. "I think that as soon as possible," David wrote

Howard Selznick in his days at Forget-me-Not

to Myron, "you and I ought to get together and talk to Howie about a little farm for Mildred and himself."

Howard would still spend time hanging out at Myron's office. But in 1934, he attacked a girl there and David ordered Mildred to "get him out of town until it blows over." As a result, they went to Catalina island for several weeks. On their return, they lived at 301 South Roxbury Drive, but now their monthly allowance was reduced. Howard was seriously involved with a woman named Christine McCoy and Flossie told Mildred they were afraid any money was going to McCoy.

So Mildred began talking divorce again, and David and Myron begged her to play along. They promised her a house. But there were renewed fears that Howie had picked up "a social disease," and there was a fierce row when David told his brother not to go near Jeffrey or kiss him.

Howard was said to be using dope, too. One day Mildred followed him to a club at Hollywood and Bronson, where he met the McCoy woman. She and Howard got into a fight and they ended up in jail overnight. Mildred waited for them outside. She recalled:

> I talked with her. I asked her what it was about. And she said that Howard and she—I don't know, they were having an affair, and that she said she was pretty tough. She said, "Don't hand me any of this stuff." She said, "We are both taking dope; we are shooting it up. I am going to get $50,000 from David and they are holding out that money on Howard." And Howard verified it and said, "Yes, I am fighting with the family about getting that money that belongs to me."

A flower shop was purchased for Howard, Forget-me-Not, on Sunset, near the Trocadero. Flossie and Mildred would work there to try to keep Howard in line. David pushed studio business their way. But nothing took with Howard or held him in place. There was one small crisis after another, with Flossie, Irene, and the secretaries of David and Myron called in to tidy up.

Marcella Bannett was sure Howard was brain-damaged but "never a menace to anyone except himself. He was a constant source of embarrassment." Flossie told everyone, including the daughters, that Mildred was beneath Howie. Then she would enlist Marcella in getting a truck loaded up with cheap gifts and turkeys and put Ruth and Florence (Howard's daughters) on board:

> Then we'd go down to the poor part of town and we'd give them away. Most of the people were suspicious of them and thought they were poisoned or something. It wasn't a successful venture, and it was humiliating for these girls, because they had to say, "This is a gift

from Mrs. Lewis J. Selznick." They felt terrible, they just hated that. But the grandmother loved it and she beamed.

Grand gestures ran through the family. But Howard was the shadow in the life of a man who was by now entertaining some of the richest and most discriminating people in America. Marcella was told to "look after" Howie and keep any trouble out of the papers. But no one saw a chance of reforming the brother himself. Perhaps it was damage at birth or a wildness that had to be independent.

10 · MOTION PICTURES AND SOCIETY

IN *WHAT PRICE HOLLYWOOD?*, producer Julius Saxe sees fresh continents for conquering when his new star, Mary Evans, the former Brown Derby waitress, plans to marry Lonny Borden, the prize of Santa Barbara and Oyster Bay, the best polo player in the country. "We got a merger of two big industries," says Saxe, "Motion Pictures and Society."

Across the crowded room of America, in the course of the 1920s, the stars of society noticed a new, melodramatic version of their old birthright—money and beauty—and they were intrigued. Equally, the sudden fame of Hollywood's newcomers left unschooled sensations greedy to be received in the great houses. The merger was filled with indelicacy, snobbery, slumming, and pretension, and it was a lot of fun, too. There were Hollywood actresses who took secret lessons on which fork went with which course, and there were real-life Lonny Bordens who hoped an actress might show them just what a woman could do when etiquette was put aside.

The rich are raised to marry the rich; it is genetic self-protection. But Hollywood people were rich, and none of them behaved as if wealth was as foolish as some of the well-born hoped it might be. If the producer wanted to forget those years in the sweatshop, or if the actress wanted the world to erase one winter of hooking, then the company of the rich and of aristocracy was happy cosmetics. The famous could marry the famous: that was another kind of genetics, with the extra benefit of bringing fresh blood to pale lines.

Hollywood and café society had something else in common—the wish to seem up-to-date and aware without ever being threatened by ideas or difficulty. This is the spearhead of America's leadership in its pioneering of the future—fashionable, yet old-fashioned, fond of charity and afraid of politics.

Adele Astaire had married into the English aristocracy, though the Astaires were Austerlitzes and acceptable company for the Prince of Wales and Jock Whitney. Fred Astaire could return the compliment in that same airy way the movie Fred hobnobs with society swells: "Jock was up to everything that was going on. He had a great willingness to appreciate life, and he enjoyed it very much. Doing anything with Jock was fun to do." Whitney rated high with Fred as a dancer: he did a superslow Charleston on a scale that had George Raft at the other end, so fast cameras could hardly catch him.

Raft was the buddy of gangsters, yet he might brush past Jock at a dance and trade partners with the Prince of Wales. There was a rage for crossover in which risk was most of the thrill. Gloria Swanson eloped with Wallace Beery when she was in her teens, next married Herbert Somborn, the president of Equity Pictures, before graduating to the Marquis de la Falaise de la Coudraye. When she had forsaken him for Joseph Kennedy, who was rich and self-righteous, the Marquis made another union with Connie Bennett.

David Selznick was enchanted by wealth, class, aristocracy, and all its devices of costume, pomp, and décor. At RKO, he made *Our Betters*, from the Somerset Maugham play, employing Elsa Maxwell as the film's adviser on how tables should be set, duchesses announced, and innuendos ignored. The jeweler's son honored the noble necks on which great stones rested. His respect for nobility would show itself in many period and costume films, and it reached a peak with *The Prisoner of Zenda*. The plight of a commoner who cannot marry his royal love was fueled by David's stir of emotions over Wallis Simpson and the Prince of Wales.

But David did not just romanticize the rich and the royal. More than anyone else in Hollywood, he saw the chance of getting society people to fund his small empire in return for introductions to show-biz parties and a dash of glamour. That is to put the transaction in an exclusively cold light. What is more remarkable is that David and Jock Whitney liked each other so much. Indeed, it amazed other people who knew David and terrified those careful men who gave Jock investment advice. But *Gone With the Wind* could not have been if David had not first swung so much class and old money behind him.

Or if David had not had Jock's steadying support. Whitney liked to gamble, he was mad about racehorses and susceptible to actresses. But he was no contribution to the notion of the idle rich. He wanted to be a solid citizen and a success in his own right. For some time, he had been determined to get into the movie business.

In late '32 and early '33, in that great crisis of David's, Jock and Sonny

Whitney had nearly put together a deal assuring the would-be independent of safety. As David went on to Metro in 1933 Jock looked elsewhere, to Dr. Herbert Kalmus, who had developed the Technicolor process and wanted money to promote it in a picture business that still regarded color as an unlikely development. David Selznick was not an early convert to color, or not until Jock took it up. Whitney liked color and saw it as the best available way into the business. He sold his own close adviser, John Wharton, on it and then, with Sonny, put up $450,000 to found Pioneer Pictures, dedicated to making color films.

For a year, Pioneer planned more than it accomplished. It did color tests of Katharine Hepburn as Joan of Arc and John Barrymore as Hamlet. But it was not until June 1934 that it made anything, and then only a two-reeler, directed by Lloyd Corrigan and photographed by Ray Rennahan. It was a piece of whimsy about a cockroach, *La Cucaracha*. David's own concurrent venture, *Viva Villa!*, released in April 1934, used the tune of the same name throughout as a jaunty salute to Jock's innovation.

From 1932 onward, the Selznicks and the Whitneys grew closer. Jock had been married, in September 1930, to Elizabeth Altemus. But Liz was her own woman. She had a mania for wild animals and sometimes kept dangerous creatures with her on a leash. She was tall and all the more striking for being bare-legged, with straight hair and no makeup. There were stories that she could not read, and it was no secret that she had her flings—one was with Bruce Cabot, Kong's rival for the affections of Fay Wray.

Jock adapted to this marriage easily enough. He had his own life to lead. He was often the guest of the couple he called "the Selzos" in California, and he enjoyed Myron and Irene as much as he did David. In July 1933, David held a luncheon for the Whitneys at MGM, using the kitchen in his bungalow on the lot. Dorothy Paley (wife to William Paley) could see some leverage to the friendship: "David was Jock's Jew and the Selznicks were very flattered. But Jock adored David. And neither Jock nor his sister, Joan, had any feeling against Jews at all."

There was a candor in Jock that never clashed with his consummate discretion. One day, he and Irene came searching for David in the house on St. Pierre. They found him, draped on a rattan chaise longue, out to the world. Even then, David's great energy could collapse in sudden sleeps, worthy of an infant. "Look at him," sighed Jock, "I could kiss him!"

Irene was taken aback by the remark: she had never been overwhelmed by David's physical attractions. Not that she had any doubts about Jock's sexuality. As the friendship developed, he formed the sort of private bond with her that she relished so much with Myron. Jock had romantic liaisons on both coasts and in England, too. He confided in Irene, and they joked about her keeping his diary straight. Something of this attitude made Jock and Myron allies, and Irene observed oblique, slangy, sexual talk between the two of them that left David wallowing in ignorance. Or maybe Irene preferred to believe in her husband's naiveté.

Dorothy Paley could see that, while he was physically quite unattractive,

> David was crazy about women. As a sex object he would not have seemed delectable. But how do you know when everyone wants careers? There's nothing sexier than royalty. David was crazy about attractive women. He adored Irene and would want to always stay married to her. But she was controlling. She had to know absolutely everything, and he did feel it was a little constricting. He was the

Dinner at Hill Haven,
clockwise from lower right:
Bruce Cabot, Vivien Leigh,
Laurence Olivier, D.O.S.,
George Cukor, Irene, Jock
Whitney, Merle Oberon

greatest romantic. He lived in this terrific world of fantasy about women, and sometimes rather ugly men go in for a lot of romance.

So there may have been several secret alliances in these friendships. And as the Selznicks became close to the Paleys, so Irene and Dorothy were one team, Bill and David another. Bill Paley was a leader in radio by the mid-1930s and more socially ambitious than David. He had set his sights on Jock. "Bill and David always laughed a lot. They were so compatible," said Dorothy. They played pool together, and Bill always lost. "They were two Jews," said Dorothy, "and two Jews can have a better time together than any two Christians. There is the bond of the excluded."

Dorothy Paley had been married previously to Jack Hearst, the son of William Randolph. She was sophisticated socially and very knowledgeable, and in her intense, rapid friendship with Irene Dorothy was a natural teacher who entranced the Hollywood princess. Irene saw Dorothy in this light:

> She was very bright, outspoken, clear, sharp, not warmhearted, but an extraordinary beauty with a small, dainty, oval face that turned into a moon. She was such a leader intellectually, striving, reaching, so fast on the uptake about flowers, psychology, medicine, design, pictures. Big blue eyes with black rims—she could stop traffic. But she had a terrible time with Bill! And she told *me* I was mishandling David. I told her, "Go scold Bill!"

Years later, Dorothy remembered an Irene who was herself brilliant but very difficult:

> David was the only person who could talk on Irene's level. I think she had a tremendous influence on his brain. She was so *interesting*, so beautiful, but terribly neurotic. She was sick all the time: hysterical physical manifestations. She was always under stress. She was a fabulous story-teller, if long-winded, and a great mimic. She was hot and cold about her father, but I think she loathed him. They were so alike; they had to run everything. She could make up out of nothing something in which she believed that had no basis in reality.

When David moved into their own home, 1050 Summit Drive, the house that Irene had designed and decorated, it became the Selzos' court, with famous Sunday parties. It was a great house, and for the next ten years David and Irene were the royal couple of Hollywood, with Jock and the Paleys as honored guests. Like most great courts, it had its intrigues and secrets, for there was a great deal of ordinary infidelity to put up with. In 1934, say, the ties between David and Jock were deepening, and David was the more encouraged in his dreams of independence as this lofty "outsider" was eager to assist him. But, as Irene saw it, there was always something too extreme and "pathetic" in David's love for Jock. He did not recognize the unbreakable differences. So much of friendship stays in the mind and the fantasies. Irene sometimes thought that it was David and Jock "so as not to be Jock and me."

11 • *VIVA VILLA!*

IF DAVID COULD NOT escape Metro, then he would rise above other producers there. For every avowal of not wishing to tread on Thalberg's toes, David was ready to beat him at his own game. Yet Irving was known for his prestigious productions. The smart company David was keeping could not hide all its squeamishness at Hollywood vulgarity. If he was truly acceptable and "decent," then he was obliged to make classy films. His thoughts turned to literature, in the way a politician takes up an exploitable issue.

In the first few months of 1934, he was all over the bookstores and libraries for material. He had an assistant, Jerry Sackheim, who scouted properties, especially those out of copyright but worth being registered— which kept the books out of others' hands. David said how deep the impression had been when L.J. read him the classic novels, and he would brandish the original editions he had had as a child. Some at Metro were skeptical. Joe Mankiewicz felt patronized by David in many matters. But Joe had graduated junior high school at eleven and entered Columbia at fifteen, where he was in the honors program in English. He graduated, and he was an honest reader and writer. He smelled humbug in David's literary background:

> He lied so dreadfully, and he had to live up to his lies. All this shit about "at the knee of Lewis J. Selznick" and having Dickens read to him, cover to cover, all 47 volumes. That's absolute nonsense. The old man was barely literate. If David registered the titles, the other studios couldn't. Well, he had all of Shakespeare, Thackeray, all of them, and he'd say, oh yes, I've read them all. You see, he had synopses. In those days, you had *David Copperfield* in any number of synopses you wanted. Thick to thin. He lied about all of that. This passion he had for literature! He had a passion for fucking!

David told Sackheim it was time to lift Joan Crawford to "adult material." What about Ibsen? The perplexed Sackheim thought *A Doll's*

House was the only possibility. Then David suggested Dreiser's *Sister Carrie.* He ordered up synopses for Gertrude Stein's *Three Lives, The Brothers Kara-mazov, Anna Karenina, The Hunchback of Notre Dame, Jane Eyre* ("one of my pets"), *Tess of the D'Urbervilles,* and *Wuthering Heights.* Sackheim was even required to read *Ulysses* twice, and David got briefly excited about Louis-Ferdinand Céline's *Journey to the End of the Night.* It was a great title; anyone could see Crawford and Franchot Tone in that.

Scott Fitzgerald's *Tender is the Night* was published in 1934, and David ordered the galleys early. Sackheim read it and passed on a synopsis with the comment: "a very involved bunch of tripe . . . I do not think abnormal psychology is very popular entertainment material." Some measure of Man-kiewicz's accuracy may be seen in David's response:

> *Tender is the Night.* I cannot get anything out of this synopsis, but I am such a Scott Fitzgerald fan that I hope to be able to read the book. If you hear of any company being about to close, I wish you would advise me.

Yet many of those dreams were realized as the decades rolled by. David may not have always had a reader's understanding, but he felt dis-comfort with original stories. He lacked the creative need that invents from nothing; he was not that independent. Even if he had not read a book himself, he could pose as its meticulous translator, keeping faith with the public that had read and loved it. This was an essentially conservative attitude.

Which may begin to account for the strangeness of *Viva Villa!,* David's pressing concern in the winter of 1933–34. This could only be a big picture: it had a large leading role, battles and banditry; there would have to be the sunny panorama of Mexico, whether found on location or near Los Angeles, and only spectacle and romance could disguise the innate socialism in a Mexican peasant's attempt to own his land.

Pancho Villa had been dead only ten years when the project was undertaken. But the real Mexico had made little advance from the condition that defeated Villa's naive mix of idealism and roughhousing. It was a country of poverty in the general, and privilege and corruption in the elite. David's own Mexico had never reached further than Agua Caliente, the resort just over the Tijuana border where whole families could have been bought for what David lost in one session at the casino.

The picture was inspired by a book, by Edgcumb Pinchon and O. B. Stade, from which it grew into a Ben Hecht script so long there was talk of making the film in two parts—rise and fall—until Nick Schenck asked how many people cared to see a whole film about Villa's failure. Thus the film omits the seven or eight years in which Villa "retired" and fell into apathy. Nor was it promising commerce if the revolutionary had an impeccable grievance against another country and its audience. Pancho Villa had always been a likely Hollywood radical in that he did not think his position through: he was happy-go-lucky, a boisterous rogue, and, in the personification of Wallace Beery, an ambling, dangerous buffoon who need hardly be blamed or taken seriously.

Metro sought official approval for Hecht's script: David hoped to start the film in Mexico to get the best out of authenticity and publicity. That ubiquitous go-between, Joe Schenck, was asked to win the support of the Mexican government and President Abelardo Rodriguez. The brother of actor Ramon Novarro suggested getting the advance okay from those forces that might soon oust Rodriguez. Later on, the widow of Pancho Villa was received in Hollywood by David so that she could accredit a movie that had the lazy lechery of Pancho ready to marry every woman he saw, tonight.

Ben Hecht had his approach, and he adhered to it whatever approvals came along. His friend Charlie MacArthur had been part of the U.S. military operation that had pursued Villa after his moderately murderous attack on Columbus, New Mexico, in 1915. That incident was not in the film; it might have reminded American audiences that Beery's Villa represented an enemy and a killer. But Hecht had seen a way to do the film that struck at the fabrication of modern mythmaking. It appealed to Howard Hawks, who had been assigned to direct, and reminded both of them of their 1932 collaboration, *Scarface*, in which the infant-beast Tony Camonte was turned loose on a hypocritical society.

Hecht had been hired for $10,000, with a $5,000 bonus if he could complete the opus in fifteen days: speed was part of Hecht's showy contempt for pictures, and it helped conceal from him his great need for the money. Hecht wanted to exploit Villa's confusion of character. His Villa was the sum of all rumors and a man so confused that he found salvation in a desperate, unprincipled American journalist sent to cover Mexico. This Johnny Sykes would be a kind of author within the action, a drunk who files one story erroneously saying that Villa has taken Santa Rosalia so that the good-natured Pancho has to attack that city to cover his friend's ass. Thus history would be turned into bunkum and Barnum, and in the contempt for integrity no special interest need feel picked on. Despite Hecht's flamboyant scorn, this approach had some instinct for what is now a respectable attitude: that the facts of history are compromised by reporting and perception, that "great men" are nothing without their wolf pack of journalists. The idea caught fire in the casting of Lee Tracy as Sykes, for Tracy was the perfect tough, embittered drunk.

Howard Hawks arrived in Mexico on October 10, 1933, and went deep into the countryside to find locations. The young Chinese cameraman, James Wong Howe, brought some epic dark landscapes to the film with clouds, as bright as Jean Harlow, piled up in the sky. It is gorgeous imagery, not without the romance of travelogue, but still we feel we are in remote parts of Mexico. But the extras—the peons—have the most soulful faces any assistant director could round up. We see no ugliness or cruelty in their poverty; we feel no anger on their behalf; these are the patient poor, abiding and picturesque.

The unit was living in hard and dangerous places. Hawks told droll stories later on about having to tough it out in meetings with real bandits. When Beery and Tracy arrived, they found that poverty of opportunity that horrified any movie star—nothing to do in the evenings. So Beery hired a private plane and flew into El Paso for revelry, while Tracy got drunk.

The unit was in Mexico City by November 19, in time for the anniversary of the Revolution, and in the festivities of the occasion, Lee Tracy was said to have urinated on Chapultepec cadets from a hotel balcony. A Metro publicist had much to do thereafter:

> The crowds in the street were in an uproar and the cadets were on the verge of coming after Tracy en masse. By the time I got to his room, he had just thrown out the first cop who went after him and then suddenly every cop in Mexico began to arrive. We were holding all these cops in the hall, they all wanted to beat Lee to a pulp. By this time Lee had passed out cold in his room, which was a blessing as we were able to convince them that he couldn't be moved.

Metro had no such problems. As part of the lavish apology that David wrote under L.B.'s name, Lee Tracy was fired. The unit was called home in disgrace and at high budgetary disadvantage. All of Tracy's scenes would have to be reshot with a replacement, Stuart Erwin. In addition, and for reasons never disclosed, Mona Maris was dropped as the aristocrat who is attracted to Villa. Fay Wray tested for the part in a rush: David assured her she would have to be very bad not to get the role. Thus those scenes were reshot, too. The budget of the movie would go over $1 million. And Howard Hawks quit, or he was let go.

Hawks was one of the most stubborn, devious, and truly independent men with whom David ever worked. He was a director inclined to go slowly until the mood took him and in the habit of rewriting scenes. He was also the ideal director to explore the unsentimental relationship between Pancho and Sykes that Hecht had laid down. Hawks might have made an audacious satire of Viva Villa!—reason enough for disposing of him.

A regular Metro director, Jack Conway, was assigned to the film, and losses were cut all round. Stuart Erwin could not help but be baby-faced and hapless; worse, he was encouraged to whine and pout. Beery's Villa was already a sentimental crowd-pleaser. Whereas the bandit leader needed the Paul Muni of *Scarface* or the wild-eyed mania of Edward G. Robinson. Why not a Rumanian Jew as Pancho Villa? There was even more interesting casting on the Metro lot: Gable? He was dark, and he had country boy attitudes. Yet Gable could have seemed adventurous and dangerous. Beery, as Hawks saw, ended up playing Villa as a lovable softie:

> It really could have been one hell of a picture. We had a great death scene. We made it up but they didn't use it. Villa was shot in a butcher shop where he'd gone to get some pork chops for a new girl he had. The reporter Johnny found him there. Villa said to him, "Johnny, I've been reading about what great men said when they died. What am I going to say, Johnny?" And Johnny says, "I'll think of something." Villa says, "No, I want to hear it now, Johnny." So Johnny went into a spiel about a great man shot and dying, faithful followers coming from far and near. The last thing he says is, "Forgive me, my Mexico! If I have harmed you it was because I loved you." Then Villa said, "That's okay, Johnny, but don't let my wife know I was buying pork chops for that girl." And then he died. I tried to make a strange man, humorous but vicious, out of Villa as he was in real life, but Conway's version had Wallace Beery playing Santa Claus.

Beery did not need much pushing; he simpers with the urge to be liked. There was a love scene shot in which he whipped Fay Wray, but it had to be cut—not because it was too sexual or violent, but because it was unbelievable. The ending is played for pathos and comedy, whereas it might have been the nihilism of two friends and a true extension of the tone of *What Price Hollywood?* David had tamed the project: he had served his obvious master—he had brought the picture in safely.

Viva Villa! is long still, and none too coherent. Episodes bump together with only Hecht's florid titles to join them. There is little sense of how much time has passed. Villa's politics are buried in his life-style—"He's a child, a bad child"—and the movie never explains what its Land Restoration Bill wants. No one was offended. The picture did well, or so Metro claimed. It won a nomination for Best Picture, though by August 1935, after sixty-eight weeks in release, it had only just covered its production costs. David's verdict was terse: "Cost high, due to the gods and Mexico. Result fine, I think. Can you point to a Beery success before or since, without a costar?"

He was talking business sense. Beery on his own had never been a reliable draw, and the Hawks approach might not have justified the costs, even if it had led to a film we could watch today with pleasure. David had escaped respectably—and among the first attributes in a producer is avoiding blame.

NINETEEN THIRTY-FOUR was not the worst year for a socialist epic if one considered the unemployed and disadvantaged in America. Yet *Viva Villa!* was doomed by practical good sense and self-interest. David had another encounter in 1934 that forced him to spell out the necessary credo for survival.

Two of Hollywood's princes had grown up as boyhood friends and then been dispatched together for Dartmouth, that model of Spartan conservatism. They were Harry Rapf's son Maurice, and B. P. Schulberg's son Budd. Maurice Rapf was as much an admirer of David as Budd Schulberg. Hanging around the studio, he had seen David watching the rushes of *Dinner at Eight*:

> He was *fantastic* in the projection room. . . . He'd sit there and he'd see things that I didn't see at all. Including minor things, but they were impressive to me—that he could notice that somebody's pocket was turned up or something. I said, Jesus! I was interested in movies in those days . . . but I could never be as perceptive as he. . . . He would be snap. It was quite extraordinary. . . . I think a lot of it was just, if you're going to be a boss, you'd better act like one.

In 1934, Maurice had visited the Soviet Union, where he believed he had found the answer to the world's problems. He had written euphoric letters to his father, which the half-proud, half-wary Harry Rapf had passed around the studio. The old guard read betrayal, especially the Russians among them. When Maurice returned, they called the errant student in for grillings. The Warners and L.B. were unyielding and horrible in their rebuke. But David was different, Rapf continued:

> He said, "You know, I read *The Nation* every week. So I understand what you're talking about. . . . Your father has asked me to talk to you, but I'm the wrong person because I really agree that the socialist system is a good system. On the other hand, I'm not convinced that it's going to work here or that there's any way of bringing it in here. If you're going to work in this business, I don't think you can devote your time and energy to this set of beliefs that you've got. . . . If you're going to concern yourself organizing the world for socialism, that's going to take your energy and you're not going to be a moviemaker."

12 · THE HERO OF MY OWN STORY

IT IS A TEST of any great producer or artist to suffer failure in the morning and then step into something like perfection after lunch. There must be no loss of confidence or momentum. Such skill shocks those humans who live with the producer. The ability to move on without wound or surprise can seem ominously insensitive. Family members require remembrance, consequence, and guilt.

Add this: even the lunch is a lie or a convenience of speech. There is no door between the rooms. The producer lives on the open plan, amid tumult, interruption, and a riot of simultaneity. There was a moment in the late spring of 1934 when a close friend warned David that he should do less. Merian Cooper was recovered from what had been his breakdown, and he saw reason to tell David:

> I've learned a little sense. I hope Irene will make you learn some; because you are the only other bird I have ever seen who worked and played at the same high pressure as myself. Anyhow if you do not learn any sense, I can tell you what to do if you break down.

No one ever made that advice stick. David's refusal to be educated was a reason for Irene's leaving him. But if a man is charging through synopses of great books, if he is caught up in the power plays of a studio, if he is finishing *Viva Villa!* and *Manhattan Melodrama*, if he has a two-year-old in yet another rented house (626 North Arden Drive for most of 1934), if he is going to lose over $20,000 again gambling in the year, if his family's new house is being built and the builder is requesting payment, and if there is no end of messenger girls and aspiring actresses, and if he still thinks of some setup whereby he would be independent, why he may need a picture of the most infinite delicacy, tone, and subtlety to divert him. Thank God for *David Copperfield*.

George Cukor's *Little Women* had been released by RKO in November 1933, for Cukor had gone back to shoot it, after *Dinner at Eight*. Both pictures were great successes, and so David proposed to Metro that he would make, and Cukor direct, a *David Copperfield*. There were doubters. With so much required of sets and costumes, and with such quantities of plot and caprices of character, classic novels looked unlikely movie material. People at Metro predicted the picture would only play in England or in those few places where reading flourished.

*In search of Dickens:
D.O.S., Hugh Walpole,
George Cukor, Irene,
and Howard Estabrook
in London*

Louis B. Mayer was a cautious supporter of the project; indeed, he did very little to oppose his son-in-law at Metro. But L.B.'s support only grew enthusiastic when he thought of Jackie Cooper playing the boy David. Cooper was a tough kid who had played with Wallace Beery in *The Champ*; he looked like a boxer's son and talked like his trainer. So David had to insist that somewhere there was a finer child, a boy who could pass for English, with a voice and eyes to match the narrative sensibility, a David fit to be David.

David, Cukor, and Howard Estabrook made the adaptation, though George was never much on construction himself. But the others could read scenes to him, and he had an ear for their tone straightaway. Apart from that, he was a leavening of amusement and teasing, the kind of friend who could laugh off every disorder with some whimsy.

In April, it was decided there would be a grand trip to England. There was still a chance that the picture might be shot there, for David and Cukor wanted as many English actors as possible. Cukor was anxious to see the sites of Dickens's life and those places that had been models for parts of *Copperfield*. In England, they would engage the novelist Hugh Walpole to polish the dialogue so that it was either pure Dickens or, better still, sounded like Dickens. Irene was excited to go on the trip, too, because she could raid English antique shops for their new house. They all sailed over on the *Majestic*, and Myron went along as David's guest, gambling partner, and all-round adviser. Jeffrey stayed home with nurse and nanny.

England was fun for everyone. Irene spent nearly $3,000 on furniture. David and George were lunched by J. B. Priestley and John Masefield. The

Dickens Society guided Cukor from site to site: "We photographed Betsey Trotwood's house and the White Cliffs of Dover. (But we shot the Dover scenes in California, near Malibu, and I have to say *our* cliffs were better—whiter and cliffier.)"

Meanwhile David was talking to David Lloyd George about the chance of a movie on the ex-prime minister's life, and he contrived a short escape to Paris. While there, he discovered a high-class brothel run by American Max Bercutt and was amazed and delighted by the oral techniques employed. He also met and signed up Fritz Lang, the director who was in exile from the Nazis. Lang was making a film in Paris, *Liliom*, and it was David who launched his twenty-year American career. (At Culver City, Lang was assigned with Oliver Garrett to develop a picture about the *Morro Castle* disaster. But it never happened, and Lang's Hollywood debut, *Fury*, was made after David was gone.)

It was in New York, later that summer, that David met the ten-year-old Freddie Bartholomew, an English boy on vacation. David Jack Holt had been in the running for the part, but Selznick was won over immediately by Bartholomew's "charming personality and distinctly English manner of speech." Freddie's aunt had put him up for the role, but his parents were against show business, and there were difficulties about bringing in an English child to work. David was on the point of sending Freddie home until a friend, Zoë Akins, reported that the London Home Office had said the matter was out of its jurisdiction. The boy was reclaimed from the ship in New York—or so David said—and thus Cukor had the angelic face that would be observer and conscience to the action.

As early as May, David had believed in the "vital importance" of Charles Laughton as Micawber. But even then he had thought of W. C. Fields as the next best bet. Laughton was under contract to Metro and the follower of Irving Thalberg. He was not keen, but Cukor persuaded him. The actor worked out a complicated makeup with a shaved head and "looked perfect." "We got on very well," said Cukor, "in spite of his strange habits, such as a terrific prejudice concerning Jews and needing strange off-stage noises to get himself in the mood for acting." But once Laughton began to shoot, his confidence faltered. This was not uncommon with him, for he often liked to draw a film into the beat of his own doubt. But David would not wait. He brought in Fields. (Both Laughton and Fields were clients of Myron's.)

Laughton was innately sinister and self-pitying—he would have stood a better chance as Uriah Heep—and there were those who saw the first dailies and got the feeling Laughton's Micawber might molest Freddie's David. Fields brought instant élan and slapstick verve. He was tough, brusque, and melodious in the great speeches. The stoicism of his attitude allowed the pathos of Micawber (and Pop Selznick), brave failures, to be felt. Fields was so proud, so impervious to downfall—he was a son's dream of how paternal virtue had not been impaired.

David Copperfield began production on September 27, 1934. Walpole had been shipped to Hollywood and he did his best to meet David's needs—drop Steerforth! make Agnes interesting! put Steerforth back! The film would be 132 minutes long. It has so many sets, costumes, and people; it is filled with scenes of doing, and yet it requires such mastery of what actor-author Simon Callow has called "the highly ingenious concoction of effects" in Dickens. The picture opened in New York on January 18, 1935. The bare dates testify to the efficiency of the Metro factory and the unstoppable drive of David O. Selznick. Such a schedule would not be possible today.

And no one alive now could come close to the beauty of the film. Drive in a producer may leave him capable of only energy on screen. That is not the case with *David Copperfield*. One may assess the film as simply a series of epic turns. But that suggests feeling has been omitted. The turns are flawless. Though derived from the original drawings by Phiz, the Metro *Copperfield* has given us versions of the characters that have not dimmed in nearly sixty years. There is an unerring casting instinct, but there is also Cukor's superb arousal of players that never disturbs the unity of tone or style. Basil Rathbone and Violet Kemble-Cooper as the Murdstones are charcoal dolls, possessed by the spirit of torture. Roland Young's understated Heep is clammy to the touch—Laughton would not have been so subtle. Lennox Pawle as Mr. Dick is so astonishing as to make one marvel at who Pawle was and what happened to him. He was English; he had worked on the stage; he would do *Sylvia Scarlett* with Cukor; he died in 1936. His Mr. Dick is one of the most blessed and noble fools the screen has ever had.

Then there is Edna May Oliver as Betsey Trotwood, whose magnificence is so constant, so mysterious, and so seductive one can only wish the real David O. Selznick had had that fictional aunt to look after him.

The filmic glory is Cukor's, but no one had trusted Cukor's talent more than David. Cukor said himself that he had only sought to render Dickens faithfully:

> It was a difficult thing, making these people funny and frightening at the same time. You achieve it partly by the casting but also by deciding on the style of playing. . . . I don't believe in "correcting" Dickens, "saving" him and all that. I just had to go with the vitality of the thing.

That is not the whole story. Cukor had strengths of kindness and optimism, and they are used in *Copperfield* to present the child's view of adult grotesquerie, danger, and impossible happiness. The boy David has a hard life, yet it is his treasury. *David Copperfield* is a pioneering work like Wordsworth's *Prelude*. For it is the first film that identifies the terrible beauty of a child's apprehensions and the way they burn unceasingly through duller adulthood. David never did anything better, and he would be a success if he had done nothing else.

David Copperfield had cost $1,069,225 to make. It would show a profit of $732,000. It was nominated for Best Picture and lost to Thalberg's production of *Mutiny on the Bounty*, which made an even bigger profit. *Mutiny* today looks like a film of its time—colonialist, overdone, but understandable and shallow. *David Copperfield* has lost none of its freshness. It stands midway between the Royal Shakespeare Company's production of *Nicholas Nickleby* and our dream of Charles Dickens reading his own work.

In Atlanta, Georgia, a Mrs. Margaret Marsh saw the film and rejoiced that the vastness of a great novel could be rendered with such drama and fidelity. She had her own novel, and it was getting on to be finished.

Micawber and his best boy (W. C. Fields and Freddie Bartholomew)

13 · THE EPOCH OF BELIEF

IT WAS A POINT of honor with David that he had never been settled
at Metro. This uneasiness was his way of countering the subtle opposition
to him among Thalberg loyalists and a stance that kept L.B. and Nick
Schenck leaning over backward to be helpful. Everyone at Metro in those
days was walking around at a slight angle, waiting to hear other timber crack
or to be there when Irving dropped. *Mutiny on the Bounty* and *A Tale of Two
Cities* were the proper works in progress for a palace expecting insurrection.

So there was reason for David to be jittery as contract renewal approached. In February 1935, his two years at Metro would be up. The old
agonizing would be joined again: to stay a company man or go independent?

Gambling was often the measure of his nervous state, but 1934 was a
moderate year with total losses of only $21,698 against winnings of $1,292.
But 1934 had not been without flurries and tendencies toward movement and
change. While the Selznicks had been staying at Claridge's in London in
June, Cooper had cabled David: "My judgment is that Sarnoff will act only
on advice of McDonough in whom he has always shown complete confidence."

Yet again, a return to RKO was being considered, for J. R. McDonough was now president of Radio Pictures. Cooper's cable arrived while
David was away in Paris. So Irene read it and added comments before she
took off. Her advice was calm, calculating, and excellent:

> I think he's right—I would neither mention nor attack Mr. McDon-
> ough but do as you will with the others. After all that can wait, and
> in the meantime he may cook his own "goose." You can still talk of
> complete control—demand it etc., but leave the McDonough situa-
> tion lay—because after all, you're being unfair—you don't even know
> him. You demand control and let him worry about McD. Because
> after all, if you ask me, you're being fresh enough. Now go do as you
> please—and God bless you!

There *is* a note of Betsey Trotwood.

Some dithery exchanges went on with David Sarnoff, all at arm's
length. By November, David had enquired as to whether, if he went into
independent setup, RCA would act as distributor. Sarnoff was circumspect.
He said RCA preferred to work through RKO. Still, he told David, "Some-

times I have the feeling that if you finally determine to go into that business for yourself, it ought to be possible to work out a contract or relationship between R.K.O. and yourself which should prove mutually beneficial, and I hope profitable."

As contract time came around, it was made clear to David that MGM was so desirous of keeping him that exceptional steps would be taken. Salary could be raised, of course, but those who thought of salary alone lacked vision. Metro and the Loew's organization were now prepared to cut David in on stock and profits. Why, said L.B., enlarging a little but not beyond reason, that could work out close to $1 million a year.

David was torn, and it served him in this negotiation to be two men, the Jekyll of obedience and the Hyde who needed to be bought off. Talks dragged on, with David being paid $4,000 a week. There were days when he did seem persuaded by Nick Schenck:

> During the past two years I have looked forward to the end of my contract and for the promised day. As the months went by, I was astonished to find myself slipping, slipping, slipping away from my long established dream; recently I had even become reconciled and had decided that the ideas of my future that I had cherished were childish ones that I should have gotten over in my teens, or certainly in my twenties, and that certainly I was almost stupid not to realize that what I had was something that probably not a dozen men of my age in America could boast.

But this unruly kid was touchy; some said slippery. The mood changed, and in the next sentence, he could be carried off again:

> But the hours came around again when I couldn't quite look myself in the eye without admitting that I was about to sell out for an easy life and a very high and steaming mess of pottage.

How did Irene and L.B. handle this fluctuating spirit? Irene always said that L.B. had the sense not to get at her privately, but was that just wishing and hoping? The screenwriter Frances Marion reckoned that, between D.O.S. and L.B., she "was being pulled like taffy." Nor was the Irene of penciled advice an unnatural or unskilled arbiter. But she knew her David well enough to realize there was no point in going beyond "now go do as you please." David had no other way, and only the wide-eyed actor in him could pretend to consider balanced arguments and reason's evidence. So L.B. pursued her, and she was caught in the middle.

One day, in the afternoon, when David was at the studio, L.B. came unannounced to their new Summit Drive house. He was exasperated, and he came in so fast, talking already, it was as if he was in his own home. Irene was caught on the stairs by his directness. "We talk to that boy every day," protested L.B. "He listens, he's interested. The next morning we have to begin again. Something happens overnight. Is this where my opposition is, right here in my own family?"

Then L.B. could turn away, wandering into the magnificent house, lost in perplexity, with Irene coming down the stairs behind him. And he could add quietly, over his shoulder to her, "I happen to know you people are broke."

This was the spring of 1935, and L.B.'s intelligence was correct. On May 1, 1935, David and Irene had a bank balance of $2,412. In the previous nine months, they had paid $82,821 for building the Summit Drive house. And in the first months of the year, David's gambling had been spectacularly disastrous:

Month	Lost	Won
January	$ 6,286	$ 655
February	18,805	916
March	3,304	2,401
April	4,222	———
May	4,457	2,975
June	6,712	750
	$43,786	$7,697

Flossie, David, and Jeffrey in the garden at Summit Drive, with the tools for perfectionist home movies

He had tried to take out loans to get by—but, on the other hand, he had never won as much at the tables, so he could believe something was coming up. Late in 1934, Myron had loaned him $25,000. By the end of June, they were overdrawn by nearly $3,500. He did try to economize: he scolded Irene for the time she spent on the phone.

Irene told her father she wanted to be happy, but this could not be unless David was happy, too. Surely she had learned how ingeniously he made himself anxious? The yearning has no end. That was when L.B. said it could be as much as a million, and then with Irving's health, and L.B.'s someday wish to retire. . . . Irene did not have to believe that; she may not have quite heard it as she struggled to defend the weakest man in her life. Of course, L.B.s do not retire.

David's life at the studio went on unabated in this period of indecision. He had felt trapped into making *Anna Karenina* with Garbo, and he could not hide his frustration. In January 1935, when it looked possible to escape Tolstoy and put Garbo in *Dark Victory* instead (a property owned by none other than Jock Whitney), David had written to the actress: "I, personally, feel that audiences are waiting to see you in a smart, modern picture and that to do a heavy Russian drama on the heels of so many ponderous, similar films, in which they have seen you and other stars recently, would prove to be a mistake. I still think that *Karenina* can be a magnificent film and I would be willing to make it with you later, but to do it now, following upon the disappointment of [*Queen*] *Christina* and *The Painted Veil* is something I dislike contemplating very greatly."

Garbo was not guaranteed box office. George Cukor did not want to direct the project, Gable was unavailable for Vronsky, and censorship would not permit warmth in the adultery. There was little time on screen for Kitty and Levin. Instead, using Freddie Bartholomew again, David focused on the role of Anna's son and its opportunity for pathos. *Anna Karenina* was made, with Fredric March and Basil Rathbone, and with Clarence Brown directing. It showed a small profit, and it is a film of minor interest, a novelette unaware that it comes from a great novel. There are lessons in this. For that which is truly literary—be it the voice of Dickens the narrator or the discourse of Tolstoy the psychologist—cannot translate to the screen, at least not to Metro's screen in 1935. The novels that "work" have a strong story line with evident crisis and appeal, vivid and immediate characters, and dramatic action. To judge by the movies of David Selznick, *Rebecca* must be a novel of more depth and intimacy than *Anna Karenina*.

The lessons were all the greater on David's last film at Metro, *A Tale of Two Cities*. The novel of the French Revolution seemed ideal casting for the producer of *David Copperfield*. But David found otherwise, and "found" is the word, for he sounded in June 1935 like a man who was reading the novel for the first time. He agreed with script adviser Kate Corbaley about her reservations:

> I know what you feel *A Tale of Two Cities* should be, but really, Kate, I am astonished myself at the fact that the more I work on it, the more I feel the difficulties of getting on to the screen what you and I both like to think is in the book. . . . There are twenty or perhaps forty living, breathing, fascinating people in *Copperfield* and practically none in *A Tale of Two Cities*, and herein lies the difficulty. The book is sheer melodrama and when the scenes are put on the screen, minus Dickens' brilliant narrative passages, the mechanics of melodramatic construction are inclined to be more than apparent, and, in fact, to creak.

There are problems of construction. The film is twenty-five minutes old before Ronald Colman's Sydney Carton appears; after that, there are long stretches when he is absent. But the love story of Charles Darnay and Lucie Manette is not very compelling: Dickens was rarely moved by normal love stories. There are large shifts in time and place: by comparison, the plot of Baroness Orczy's *The Scarlet Pimpernel* is tidier and more effective. Subsidiary characters seem like hangers-on, whereas in *Copperfield* they are all directly encountered by David.

Two Cities was assigned to Jack Conway; David wanted the melodrama to "pack a wallop" as he fancied *Viva Villa!* had done. But Conway does little with the people. Among the supporting characters only Blanche Yurka's Madame Defarge is memorable. Ronald Colman's excellent, quiet, and modern performance is almost overlooked. Without his mustache—for David's zest for research had established that Carton would have been clean-shaven—Colman seems stripped and deeply pained by life.

The crowd scenes in Paris were entrusted not to Conway, but to two youngsters: Val Lewton, the nephew of Alla Nazimova, who had been hired by David to do a script from Gogol's *Taras Bulba*; and Jacques Tourneur, the son of silent director Maurice Tourneur. Lewton became a story editor for David at MGM. He was an introspective man, whose reticence masked huge creativity. He admired David's energy and flair but flinched from his arrogance.

By the time the film was released (Christmas Day 1935), David was gone. The film cost over $1.2 million, and it returned only a small profit. In his absence, David believed, the old antagonism toward him at Metro was coming out again: the film was not being properly promoted or pushed. And so *Two Cities* became the object of anger between David and

Nick Schenck. On October 15, Schenck wrote to him, pointing out the absurdity of Metro spoiling its own pictures. He added a few remarks on Selznick arrogance:

> Estimate your position in the film business today. You are a very well-known producer, highly considered, and doubtlessly highly paid and sought after. When you came with M-G-M you were not so well known, and a doubtful quantity with sufficient promise to make us take the gamble. We consented to contract clauses with you which were designed solely to increase your prestige. We not only lived up to those contracts, but the spirit of the publicity department and your associate executives was such that you got far more than you bargained for.

Schenck listed the films that had flopped (*Night Flight, Reckless, Vanessa,* and *Meet the Baron*) and pointed out that they had been "inordinately costly . . . even the hits were not properly profitable because of your expensive methods. . . . You were spoiled by too easy accountability to money and people for production investment."

It was a tough letter, though it recalled "personal affection" and hoped "your little family is well." The budgetary charge does not seem fair: several of David's pictures had exceeded estimates; he never claimed to lack showmanship; he was never intimidated by what he had said a film would cost. Yet his greatest extravagance would come when he was independent. In truth, many Metro films went over budget and none more than Thalberg's.

Nick Schenck's attack is all the more dishonest granted that he had approached David the previous summer of 1934 to take over from L.B. That had been Schenck's grandest ploy to keep the young producer. As so often, it had been Nick's brother, the ever amiable Joe, who carried the treacherous message. David had told Irene and eventually she told L.B. When she and her father stayed with Nick Schenck one weekend on Long Island, and she beheld Nick's wealth, she had to speak. At night, she went into her father's bedroom and whispered the plot to him. It is a scene from Shakespeare, Verdi—or a Joan Crawford movie.

David was furious at Nick Schenck's letter. He drafted a long, retaliatory reply, but L.B. persuaded him not to send it. That fall, David was finishing *Two Cities,* but he was already his own man, dreaming of a great future. A man like L.B. always had the patience to look farther ahead. You might have to kill your friends and close ones, but there was no need to offend them. Even so, there were those at Metro who heard L.B. say, as David quit, "I'll get even with him!"

14 • THE BEAUTIFUL DANCING GHOSTS

"I HAVE MATURED considerably," David told Nick Schenck in the summer of 1935, as he looked back on his busy two years at Metro. "And with this maturing has come an acceptance that has almost made me into a different person—a person that I do not like very much." There was the rub that had become a wound: the failure in a pure narcissist, a great spoiled boy, to be pleased with himself. "I want very much now to retrace my steps and to get back to the ambitious and vital and, if you like, even erratic, but at least free, person that I was."

There is no freedom; there cannot be if the pursuit of liberty and happiness are to last a lifetime. This ultimate elusiveness affects every kind of life in the end. But it is inescapable in the picture business.

The making of movies is beyond the means of any individual. They cost too much. Thus the filmmaker, the director, the producer, the artist, the genius—whichever name is preferred—must find some source of money. He negotiates his dream with banks, and the dream begins to be compromised. But these are not regular banks. For the gamble of making pictures is crazy. Most movies fail; they lose money. Still, a few prosper so much that certain romantic or vagrant bankers are drawn to the business.

What seduces those people? It is profit, glory, and power; it is the limousines, the great houses, and meeting mythic beauties. But the gamble is too demented for such mundane satisfaction to be enough. No, the bankers are also moved by the idea of reaching so many strangers: there is a brief ecstasy of community in the diverse world when, say, the current of *Gone With the Wind* goes everywhere. That moment can only be called religious.

Even when it works better than it has ever done, or ever can again, the producer needs writers, directors, actors, technicians, editors, musicians, secretaries, publicists, wives, lovers, chauffeurs, chefs, and charlatans. He must command an enterprise to make prints of his film, send those prints all over the world, promote and advertise the screenings. There must be theaters, projectionists, and people to sell tickets. There must be reviewers, puffers, hypers, and columnists. Then there are audiences, as fickle as kittens. Yet he talks of freedom.

The scale of the operation is such that the producer's own proud bursting head succumbs to overhead. He may make five hits in a row and barely keep up. Then one failure destroys his business. Metro-Goldwyn-Mayer in 1935 was the most successful studio there had ever been and the most efficient. But it was doomed. In fifteen years, public taste would escape. Ironically, Metro's death was slowed because of the economic longevity of a film David had made—in a state of death-defying semi-independence—and which he then gave up.

David the daft gambler won. But he had to separate himself from the victory. He had to go back to being the boy he admired. Self-destruction was irresistible, even if it was the romantic fate of a man who had to play himself for all who knew him. As he confessed to Nick Schenck:

> I imagine you have received few business letters of this type; and to you it may seem that I have been reading too many plays and working on too many scripts, and that I am romanticizing and dramatizing to a nauseous degree. It may be that you will not even understand me, which I would regret very much because I want you to understand me. I want you to know of my appreciation and I want you to know I am not entirely insane in giving up what you offer me; and I want you to know that I recognize that I may be coming back in a year or two with my tail between my legs—but if that time should come, at least I will have had my fling, at least the ants will be forever banished, and at least the road I will travel for the rest of my life will be perfectly clear and the beautiful dancing ghosts that beckon now will have forever disappeared.

Of course, David had been available for independence for several years already, and time only complicated such matters as the courage he needed to summon up, the price to put on his own head, and the suitors he would consider. Nor was David adept at keeping such romances quiet. He had a habit of trying to play suitors off against each other. This should have persuaded his would-be bankers that if they did grant him his independence they might never get his anxieties out of their heads.

In November 1934, just as he was feeling out David Sarnoff and RCA once more, an item ran in the Louella Parsons column saying Jock Whitney had denied he was or might be financing David.

> Appreciate your willingness to give out statement [David wired Jock], but think this not necessary. If anyone asks you I would however like you merely say I have not approached you and you know nothing of my plans. Cordially yours.

Jock had been there for David from the beginning with money, understanding, and love in spite of that understanding and the gloomy warnings of his own advisers. But there must have been moments when Jock wondered just how much David believed he *had* approached the Whitneys. For there might be other plans that Jock had heard nothing about. By the end of the year, for instance, Phil Siff was in New York on David's behalf, introducing the prospect to Lehman Brothers, and in particular Arthur Lehman:

> He listened sympathetically, and expressed great personal liking for you, and confidence in your ability as a producer. He felt however that it would be extremely difficult to raise any such amount as you had in mind for the purpose of motion picture production, which is a field regarding which the monied men of New York have little knowledge, and even less confidence.

By the spring of 1935, David had so impressed Metro with his coming departure that Irving Thalberg asked him whether he had raised his money yet. "Not a dollar," Selznick admitted, whereupon Irving said he and Norma Shearer would be the first stockholders, to the tune of $200,000—all in Norma's name. Not to be outdone, Myron put up another $200,000, and then said that when David and Irene went to New York in May he would go, too. After all, the kid needed help, and Myron deserved a voice if he was a half owner of David's would-be venture. There were even occasions when the younger brother referred to the new company as "their" enterprise. Not that David had anything beyond his presence, his talk, and his talent to invest.

The three stayed at the Waldorf from May 9 to 19, and the talk got so loose that in June David was perturbed to hear how freely A. C. Blumenthal was making contacts on his behalf. "Blumey" was tiny, rich, and assiduous in putting people together. David was "extremely annoyed" to hear that he was being shopped by Blumey to Jay Paley, Connie Bennett, and "Lord knows who else." David wired Blumey telling him to shut up immediately.

David announced his resignation from Metro at the end of June, yet it was a holding measure for he was staying on to finish *Anna Karenina* and *A Tale of Two Cities*, and there was talk of setting up Fritz Lang's *Morro Castle* film. So David was still at the studio, having to implore his "groups" to wire him at Summit Drive, lest cables to Culver City fall into the hands of the front office—and David could not yet be certain that he might not be that front office one day. To resign was clearly a negotiating stance if the worst came to the worst. But there was a cocktail party at the Ambassador for 500, on July 9, to keep people eager for the new enterprise.

One of these groups was led by Harold Talbott, Jr., an industrialist and financier, a great polo player and racing enthusiast, and chairman of the

*Merian C. Cooper, John
H. Whitney, David O.
Selznick*

Republican Finance Committee since 1934. Talbott had met the Selznicks socially at Saratoga and Long Island. As late as the end of July, David was torn between deals offered by Talbott and by the Whitneys. But David was laying down sweeping laws for himself:

> I frankly want to feel protected on two points, first that under the management and corporate setup my management is assured of no interference, and second that I have opportunity of personally owning control of common [stock] for which control I would under optimal basis be paying and which degree of ownership is available to me without payment on some other deal. In connection with same major worries I should like to reiterate my feeling of importance of my having either management control with very wide powers or control of board of directors with common stock or preferably both.

The Talbott group fell through because David could not be assured of sufficient freedom. These were speculators, it seemed to him, ready to make a quick profit and unwilling to trust to the long term in which—he hoped—his success would enable him to retire their stock.

And so after an autumn of cables and furious haggling on both sides, there appeared the outline of Selznick International Pictures. David was back at the Waldorf from August 22 to September 25 (with a bill there for $3,194). The company was formed on October 15, 1935. The capitalization was to consist of 13,000 shares of preferred stock and 2,600 of common stock—the total capital working out at just over $3 million. Of the preferred stock, Pioneer took 8,031 shares, Jock Whitney 241, Sonny Whitney 221, Joan Payson (Jock's sister) 155; the Lehman Brothers took 2,188; Myron had 1,114 and Norma Shearer 1,000.

Jock was chairman, David was president, John Wharton (Jock's lawyer) was vice president, treasurer, and general counsel. The directors were Jock, Sonny, Bobby Lehman, David, Loyd Wright, Myron and Dr. Attilio Giannini, who represented United Artists (and Bank of America), the company through which Selznick International would release its pictures. David had made that deal (for three pictures) as early as July 17 as an asset for whatever arrangement of forces could win him.

David was to have a five-year contract as executive producer, and he would be paid at the rate of $40,000 a picture up to a level of $200,000 a year. He was also given 1,300 shares of the common stock. But he invested not one penny. He had pledged more than money—himself.

There would be offices in New York, and the base for production would be at the RKO-Pathé studio, just a little east of Metro on Washington Boulevard, the building that David had once promised to Irene. There was also an agreement to combine with Pioneer in the making of Technicolor films—in return for which SIP would receive Technicolor shares at favorable terms.

The first picture would be one David had already secured the rights to and for which he had L.B.'s promise of Freddie Bartholomew—*Little Lord Fauntleroy*, that perfect dream of the indulged and vindicated child. He was thirty-three.

GOING WITH THE WIND

1 · MY OWN LITTLE ROOM

IN THE SUMMER of 1935, Mrs. Margaret Marsh of Atlanta was hard at work on her large book. She had begun the writing ten years earlier, when arthritis had immobilized her and marriage to John Marsh kept her home. The writing had been done in the late twenties, but the author—who had published nothing else except journalism in the *Atlanta Constitution*—"never sent it to any publishers because, to be quite frank, I didn't think much of it. Written as it was at the height of the Jazz Age, I didn't think it would sell as a 'Victorian' type novel, almost as long as 'Anthony Adverse' and about war and hard times in Georgia. And, also there was precious little obscenity in it, no adultery and not a single degenerate and I couldn't imagine a publisher being silly enough to buy it."

But in April 1935, Harold Latham, a vice president at Macmillan, had come to Atlanta scouting. He was there because Margaret, or Peggy, as she liked to be called, had a friend, Lois Cole, who worked for Latham and who had heard there was a book, in envelopes and packets, here and there around the Marsh house. Latham spirited it away from the shy yet ardent writer, for the piles of paper were a hope that gripped her.

Macmillan accepted the book and asked the author to finish it—quickly. There were three chapters left to do and much historical verification to be pursued. So get on with it: Macmillan wanted to publish in the summer of 1936. Peggy Marsh could not be herself on the title page: she would be Margaret Mitchell there. Macmillan wanted some other changes, too: "Pansy O'Hara" hardly felt worthy of the written woman. So she became Scarlett.

Then there was the title. Peggy had all along had a title—*Tomorrow is Another Day*. Yet she thought it could be improved. She and her publisher exchanged ideas:

Another Day	?
Tote the Weary Load	??
Not In Our Stars	???
Bugles Sang True	????

until one day, when Peggy was dipping into nineteenth-century British poet Ernest Dowson, she found a phrase that seemed stricken with the very loss that had overtaken her South: "Gone With the Wind."

The pieces were in place, and the rapidly revised manuscript was delivered to the printer with the new title. Compared with Peggy's working title, this one looked back into the mists of nostalgia. There is genius in titling, a producer's genius, and sometimes it takes just one small click for elaborate locks to open.

By the summer of 1935, David, Irene, and Jeffrey were in residence at 1050 Summit Drive. Irene wanted a house that felt "in the country and yet in the city," and in 1935 the Summit Drive location matched those needs. It was only a few hundred yards north of Sunset and the Beverly Hills Hotel, yet it stood on a twisting lane where there were only a few other estates— the Chaplin house opposite and Pickfair higher up the road.

Irene wanted the perfect architect; she set out to find the best houses in the area. Everything she liked was by Roland Coate. So she persuaded him—this was in 1933, the bankers' worst year—not to close down his office, but to work for her. Roland Coate had been successful in the 1920s, especially in and around Pasadena, building new, larger houses for the wealthy.

The Summit Drive house won prizes and was featured in *Architectural Digest*. Coate began by reshaping the land and then designed a large, two-storied Georgian Colonial house. It had every possible modern convenience. There was a projection room and bedroom windows David could open and close electronically, without getting out of bed. Irene helped with the efficient layout of the kitchen and the bathrooms. But there were latticed porches, fireplaces with tiled surrounds, alcoves with display cabinets for porcelain. There was comfort, prettiness, grace, a certain ill-defined air of the past, and no gesture or flourish to disturb the conservatism of the occupants.

Those who lived there loved the house—and were devastated when the family finally disposed of it. Still, it testified to some urge toward historic origins in people who were settling or colonizing this Los Angeles, recent outcasts, suddenly rich, who wished to make their position manifest. To do that, they equipped themselves with a home and an atmosphere that looked gently backward in time. The other styles prevalent in Los Angeles then were Spanish and New England. It was happy serendipity that Irene and David chose a Georgian look.

The second floor of the house had the bedrooms, but there was a considerable distance between the quarters shared by Jeffrey and the nanny and those of his parents. Double doors guarded the bedrooms of the parents; they were open or closed by design, as a signal. The separate bedrooms had been designed with two different people in mind:

> My mother's was this absolutely wonderful shade of pale green. . . .
> There was a couch in pale green, there was an upholstered bed, with
> a back and headboard and footboard in embroidered pale green. With
> elements of white in it. Discreet little bookshelves that held about six
> shelves of books on either side of this presentational area of her bed
> . . . there was an area which was six inches off the floor which was the
> actual bed area, and this in turn was curtained, plus it had sliding
> doors. . . . I would call it a classic Freudian architecture. It's fascinat-
> ing, whether this was something of the architecture of the period or
> something that, on some level, my mother developed with her interior
> decorator and her architect, without really knowing what was involved
> in all that. . . . There were Marie Laurencins scenes on the wall, and
> two oval bed tables on either side of this huge, wide bed. Curving
> windows. . . . Very thirties. Classic, like a Travis Banton design in a
> film. . . .
>   My father's suite was paneled pine, brown carpet, forest green
> upholstery with its own massive, wonderful English-looking fireplace.
> Books in every direction, just massive, long bookshelves. A standing
> globe, for some reason . . . and this fabulous big desk.

The speaker there is Daniel Selznick; sometime in August 1935 he was conceived in one of those bedrooms. (David snored mightily, so the couple seldom passed entire nights together. Or woke together.) Conception could have occurred the night of the *Anna Karenina* preview, when Garbo had asked to have the lights turned on so she could play on the sunken tennis court, next to the space for the pool. There was no pool yet: David could not afford one. At the end of June 1935, David and Irene were overdrawn and David had lost over $35,000 on the year gambling.

In the second half of the heady year, as the SIP deal was being done and David was assuring his new investors of model economies, he lost over $94,000.

The pool would have to wait, and the furnishing and improving went on over the years. David's involvement was generally confined to his room, but it was the more chronic for that narrowness. As late as September 1938, when he had Munich and the nearness of *Wind* on his mind, he was driven to lengthy frustration by his reading lights. He fired off three pages to Tommy Douglas, the decorator, on lamps in the wrong place:

we agreed that the one light above the pillow was to operate on a switch that I could turn on or off from bed. This you apparently completely forgot about, because to use these lights I have to use all the lights in the room—and I would have to get out of bed and cross the room—which in this proletarian age is undoubtedly not too much of a burden for anyone, but it is scarcely my idea of a bedlight and for a dollar and a half I could probably get myself a light that would cater a little bit to my eyesight or my comfort.

There was much more—on wrong materials and undue expense— before David came to this conclusion:

Irene is hearing of my feelings concerning all this at the same time as you are. [So late home, so occupied, he might have to speak to her by way of cover copies of his memos.] Maybe she will let out a moan, because I am apparently a very peculiar guy about this one room, in all the world, in all my life, but she married me for better or worse, and she will simply have to help me get it the way I want it—or else leave it the way it was.

Wherever he looked, he began to wonder aloud, to query . . . on principle. Yet in making his own right home, he was as uncertain as a producer trying to find the best décor for a character. He wanted a portrait of Irene and Jeffrey for the new house. But, conservative and uneducated, he turned to Henry Luce and the art editor at *Time* for advice. He was fearful of falling into the hands of "a faker" and averse to anything "too stylized." He wanted a painter "who will give us actual resemblance rather than some eccentric, futuristic conception of what my wife and child look like." He was a society realist.

As David wound up *Anna Karenina* and *A Tale of Two Cities* for Metro, so Marcella Bannett was supervising the installation of the infant Selznick International at the old Ince studio, and David was working on the script of his first movie there, *Little Lord Fauntleroy*.

Marcella began with herself and five other people in Culver City: Franclien Macconnell, story editor; Silvia Schulman, David's second secretary from Metro; William Wright, as associate producer, an assistant at both Paramount and Metro; Barbara Keon, his script assistant at Metro; and as West Coast story editor, one more Metro colleague, Val Lewton. Yet another would make the short journey down Washington Boulevard: Hal Kern, the editor. It was a small staff, but a significant bite out of MGM's talent.

These people set up in the offices to the side of the impressive white, colonnaded administration building erected originally by Ince as a movie set and only converted to a serviceable structure by DeMille. This was the facade that would soon become the image of Selznick International Pictures—and it was another white house for the store of nostalgia, very close to the look of Washington's house at Mount Vernon that David had once employed in a 1920 color advertisement for his father's pictures in the *Ladies' Home Journal* with the caption "All America Loves the Beautiful."

David was delighted to rehire Kay Brown as New York story editor—so many of these first appointments were to search out good material and make contacts with writers. Kay had remained at RKO in the intervening years, but she had no doubts about the new operation: "Selznick had a marvelously impressive record of the kind of pictures I was interested in."

David had had to buy the rights to Frances Hodgson Burnett's *Little Lord Fauntleroy* from Mary Pickford, who had filmed it in 1921 (managing to play both the boy and his mother, "Dearest"). Little Mary charged David $11,500 for the 1886 novel, which only added to the surprise of a new outfit going for such old-fashioned material. Ben Hecht said David was helplessly affected by having done his real reading before the age of twelve. Never-

Freddie Bartholomew and Mickey Rooney in Little Lord Fauntleroy

theless, Hecht added polish to the screenplay David commissioned from Hugh Walpole. Other writing collaborators were Richard Schayer and David himself, for this story would not have gone far without David's heartfelt identification with a Brooklyn boy who passes into the English aristocracy.

John Cromwell was hired to direct. Freddie Bartholomew was to be the boy, Dolores Costello his mother, and C. Aubrey Smith the autocratic grandfather whose imprisoned kindness is liberated by his new American grandson. There were also several supporting players from Metro, notably Henry Stephenson, Jessie Ralph, and Mickey Rooney (whose discovery owed much to David). Shooting occupied the last two months of 1935 without mishap or budgetary fracture. David could point to it as an aus-piciously tidy start.

It was not hard for him to feel excited in December 1935, no matter the state of his personal finances. John Wharton was trying to restrain expenditures: he was especially keen to find a rational use of the telephone to control the gabby friendship of David and Jock. David was humoring Wharton and persuading himself about his own prudence. How would New York expenses be handled? "Checks could be signed by either you alone," he told Wharton, "or perhaps by you and Kay—this latter for the psycho-logical effect on her of seeing money go out each week."

Meanwhile, David and Jock were full of plans—to make a deal with Merle Oberon to play Florence Nightingale; what about Johnny Weiss-muller in *The Last of the Mohicans?*—for David believed he could borrow Tarzan from Metro, Robert Donat as Beau Brummell?, and maybe a ballet picture with Tilly Losch, the Viennese ballerina?

George Cukor had taken time off from his *Romeo and Juliet* rehearsals at MGM to supervise the Losch tests. He had signed a contract with SIP (on August 31, 1935) as its leading director. It was not to commence until after *Romeo and Juliet*, and then after *Camille*. Moreover, the Metro lawyers were of the opinion that Cukor's SIP deal contravened their own contract with him. But Cukor was actively involved in SIP plans and often at Summit Drive. David had offered him $3,250 a week for three years and "as many pictures as possible," with 5 percent of the producer's gross after recouping twice the negative costs. No director had had such an offer. But Cukor declined profit participation and took $4,000 a week for one year, with options and raises for following years. Ironically, though he served SIP through thick and thin, Cukor would never get a credit there.

As Christmas drew near, David and Irene went on a weekend visit to Lake Arrowhead. Myron was buying a property there, Hill Haven, a lux-urious lodge at 8,000 feet in the San Bernardino mountains that had belonged to silent director George Hill. The purchase was a measure of his own success and of his reluctance to be outdone by a kid brother.

On December 9, David wrote to Margaret Mayer, his mother-in-law, who had been sent east in an attempt to handle a nervous illness. David talked to her about Jeffrey, who was then three and a half.

> Jeff is developing amazingly and it is marvelous to see him emerge as a personality and also to see him grow mentally as well as physically. You would be astonished, for instance, to hear him point out on the map practically every State in the country as you call out the name.

That Christmas, Irene gave David their first painting, a landscape by George Bellows. She thought he would put it in his room, but David insisted it hang in the projection room for all to see. Irene was four months pregnant with their second child. *Fauntleroy* was largely shot, and its $500,000 budget had been adhered to. He was his own man, at last, and, for a moment, he had one film to make at a time.

2 · ALL THESE WONDERFUL CHANGES

NO ONE EVER HAS only one thing to do at a time. But few people are comfortable having to handle more than two or three things at once. In those years when Peggy Marsh was actually writing *Tomorrow is Another Day*, she had her husband to look after, as well as the socializings of Atlanta. But she was writing only one book or attempting to *find* the one book that hid among all the versions in her head.

A movie producer never knows that single-mindedness. It is so hard to get a picture made, and there are so many ways in which any hope can be forestalled or disappointed, he must have many projects on the go. If a schedule calls for six finished films a year, then there may need to be twenty schemes. And while no one of those twenty is to be taken lightly, or as less than one of the six, still none is ever regarded in the way Peggy Marsh thought of her book. The producer knows most of his progeny will be aborted. The author has the one venture as a part of her being. Indeed, she has written it for its own sake, without any guarantee of publication. She is so much more resolute than the producer.

In addition, this producer, struggling to survive and having to see so many possibilities abandoned, needs to find time to be with his wife, his son, his mother, his brother . . . to say nothing of friends. It may not be much time (there isn't that much time), but the relatives want to feel the time was precious and complete and that they had the best of their David. They grow to dread the harassment in his smiling, pleading eyes. The man who would be independent becomes the slave of meetings, appointments, obligations, and of anyone who has an idea to pitch to Hollywood's best producer.

In the spring of 1936, Peggy Marsh and Margaret Mitchell were joined, and the lady was disturbed; she wanted success and praise, yet she feared the threat to her settled life. The Macmillan "Spring Announcement" included *Come with the Wind* as one of five "great novels" it would be publishing. How vexing that mistake must have been and what a sign of the moment it is—a little later everyone in America knew the title. Publication was set for April 21, but a series of postponements occurred—to May 5, May 31, and finally all the way to June 30, so that *Gone with the Wind* could be the July main selection from the Book-of-the-Month Club.

There were other factors involved in the delay: the task of printing the book (1,037 pages) and the advantage in letting reviewers take their time with it. But by publication date, there were nearly 100,000 copies in print. This means there had been copies around, and galleys before them, since April, at least. In turn, that suggests the famed discovery of the book by Kay Brown in SIP's New York office may have been somewhat belated.

David had his own babies to look after: *Fauntleroy* and the one due in May. *Little Lord Fauntleroy* opened at Radio City Music Hall on April 2, a ninety-eight-minute movie, which, apart from the addition of sound, could have played beautifully in 1916. In its look and polish, it was made in the style of MGM: there is dimpled English countryside to behold, and the interiors of Dorincourt Castle are the first sign of David's taste for manorial décor. Just as his "small" room at Summit Drive sounds rather English, so David was always going back to some Manderley in his mind.

Despite the heartbreaking Freddie Bartholomew, *Fauntleroy* is not *Copperfield*. Rather, it is a shameless monster of sentimentality in which a Brooklyn boy, the only heir to the Earl of Dorincourt, goes back to live in the English castle with his grandfather. His American mother, Dearest, accompanies him but she has to stay in the gatehouse because the grandfather refuses to recognize her—a common American who seduced his son.

The boy, Ceddie, is a paragon. When given a penny-farthing bicycle, he exclaims, "Of all the events in my life, this is the most magnificent!" And Freddie is radiant with pleasure; his gratification is spiritually touching. David's own children must have marveled. If only they could have been like Freddie Bartholomew for their father!

The grandfather becomes human and is reconciled with Dearest. But the film remains uncritical of England, aristocracy, and the class system. In the Brooklyn scenes, there is much comment against the evils of privilege. When Ceddie sees the castle, Dearest murmurs the hope that "he mustn't be spoiled by all these wonderful changes." Whereas American ways of thought succumb like a maiden to the décor and retainers who knuckle their foreheads in reverence when the Dorincourts go to church. Mickey Rooney's Brooklyn shoeshiner makes it over to England for the climax—magnificent in a checkered suit—and he says of his old chum, Ceddie, "I bet you boys elect him king some time."

Why not? Even in Brooklyn this "American" Ceddie was dainty enough in elocution to outroyal real pretenders. Bartholomew is restored to his rightful place, and even Brooklyn bows to his natural regality. It might turn your stomach—if you weren't having such a good time. *Little Lord Fauntleroy* is an unblushing fantasy made with skill and cunning. That the film was such a hit shows David Selznick was not the only American who dreamed of being carried back to olde England and the nobility.

Bartholomew's trust saves the picture; it is hard to scoff at a child's conviction. David's attitude is stranger. He surely grinned when Ben Hecht teased him over the material; however soft his heart or head, he calculated the clichéd story. But this was the debut of his greatest venture and a property on which he was determined before SIP came into being. The producer might not have done it without Freddie Bartholomew's availabil-

David and Freddie, in mutual adoration, waiting for a telephone interview

ity: it was not just that David admired the young actor—he could identify with him.

Fauntleroy is a man-child, wise, grave, and tolerant beyond his years. He is the child a man might wish to have remained. The movie speaks of Ceddie as "a mixture of maturity and childishness," and that is something friends saw in David all his life. He had a softness, a readiness to laugh and be winsome that many people adored. Yet sadly, it did not make life easier for his own children.

David had no squeamishness about robust American methods in selling *Fauntleroy*. At the outset, he had hired Joseph Shea to run publicity. Shea had been with Fox and Twentieth Century, and he was an experienced man. But he made the mistake of believing what David said: "We're starting a new company. I don't want any personal publicity—we've got to sell the name Selznick International."

By November 1935, Shea had an assistant: Ring Lardner, Jr., a sophomore bored with Princeton. David met Lardner in the summer of 1935 at Herbert Swope's house in Sands Point, Long Island. Lardner was working for the New York *Mirror*, and he jumped at the job offer. In Hollywood, the kid could see that Shea was being too literal in his work: as long as it was not owned up to, David would stomach personal publicity—above all he just loved publicity. In December 1935 Shea was replaced by Russell Birdwell.

A year younger than David, Birdwell had been working for the Hearst organization. He would be David's employee for only three years, but his effect on SIP and David was enormous. There was a brash, cynical conjurer in Birdwell. He could hear out all of David's pomp and rhetoric while detecting the man inside. When Birdwell first came to David's office, he was stood before the portrait of L.J. and told the story of how Pop Selznick had pioneered electric signs on Broadway.

Birdwell went away and hired as many painters as it took to do a sign announcing *Little Lord Fauntleroy*. The "canvas" was two miles of Washington Boulevard, stretching from the Ince lot, way past Metro, toward the ocean. There had never been a bigger sign. All over the world, the press carried the story.

David was dazzled. Jock was tickled. SIP and *Fauntleroy* were household news. The two men knew the picture worked, and they felt the exuberance of coming success. On February 20, 1936, Jock cabled David: "Would we have as much fun together if we were married?"

Birdwell realized he was a wizard, and it gave him another idea: compared with the rest of Hollywood, SIP possessed genius, the new "it." So he hired an ex-G-man, Joseph Dunn, to guard this store of brainpower. Mr. Dunn was reported, fully armed, patrolling the premises against prowlers bent on stealing ace ideas. The press turned a little nasty. This was going too far; this was exploitation. David grew suddenly afraid that the stunt lacked "taste." Birdwell protested that a press agent with taste was a contradiction in terms. He made a show of resigning, looked up at the portrait of Pop, and said, "I've been working for the wrong Selznick." This was enough to win David over for as long as Birdwell wanted. Years later, David reckoned that "the most successful period in the entire history of Selznick International was those early months when Birdwell first arrived and worked with a secretary and his own inventiveness and drive."

Fauntleroy's final costs reached $590,000. But by the summer of 1939, it had returned a profit of $447,000—which is to say it was the most profitable picture SIP released before *Gone With the Wind*.

By April 15, SIP had started production on its second picture, and its first Technicolor film for Pioneer, *The Garden of Allah*. This, too, was a remake. The Robert Hichens novel (about a devout woman who discovers she has married an escaped Trappist monk—and the monk is the only person alive who knows the recipe for a monastery's famed liqueur) had been filmed twice already as a silent. David had even thought of doing it as a vehicle for Garbo at Metro, and he had to purchase the rights to the novel from them for $62,000.

Merle Oberon had been cast as the woman, Domini Enfilden (a name, not a crossword anagram), but as the budget for the picture rose, so David doubted her power at the box office. In early April, he discarded Oberon and filled the uncast male lead by scooping up Marlene Dietrich and Charles Boyer. This couple had just become available when the remake of *Hotel Imperial* at Paramount was postponed because of the replacement of Ernst Lubitsch as production chief by William LeBaron. Thus the stars, Russian director Richard Boleslavsky, full Technicolor equipment and crew, as well as camels, dancer Tilly Losch, exotic extras, and an "associate producer," Willis Goldbeck (Dietrich's lover at the time), were dispatched to the desert near Yuma. They took everything except a script.

David remained in Culver City, rewriting. The script would be credited to W. P. Lipscomb and Lynn Riggs, and that is no reason to rule out their contribution. But David and Goldbeck had their hands all over it, and when the young Joshua Logan arrived in Hollywood to serve as "dialogue director," he barely had time to hear some of the script in a story conference before he was sent to appease the mounting disquiet of Miss Dietrich.

"Logan," said David, "Dietrich's out there. Go talk to her. She'll tell you she doesn't like the script and blah, blah, blah. Listen to her ideas carefully, then tell her you think the script's great, and keep at it till she believes you."

The actress was waiting for the novice. She wore a silk blouse and jodhpurs, and her hair masked one eye.

"Look me in the eye and tell me the truth," she ordered her dialogue director. "It's twash, isn't it? You're a tasteful New Yorker. Admit it. It's twash."

"Well," sighed Logan, "maybe it's a *little* trash, but it's going to be improved."

This band of filmmakers went off, nevertheless, to a location called Buttercup Valley, "Journeying without aim, drawn by the mystic summer of blue distances," as one of the film's flowery titles puts it.

These titles smack of Ben Hecht, yet it is one of the few Selznick pictures that he managed to miss. So maybe David himself came up with the line, spoken by Joseph Schildkraut's Arab, "How curséd is the man with relatives. Do you have them in Europe, too?"

Family matters were much in David's mind. In April—as some demonstration of how successful he was—Myron set off for Europe for several months. To give the appearance of a splendid vacation, he took Marjorie and Joan with him. The tour included Holland, Ireland, London, Austria, and Czechoslovakia; they were not home until the fall. Of course, Myron had access to a telephone and to cables, but it was a remarkable absence, even if he was attending to his London office. Myron was often depicted as indifferent to his own family. But David never undertook such a vacation.

Myron would miss the birth of David's next child—and more. On May 13, with that delivery imminent, David wrote to Myron:

> By the time you receive this, you will have a new nephew or niece. Jeff has expressed a preference for a sister. We are still having name trouble and I wish you would have Marjorie cable any good ideas she has.
>
> Everything is about the same on the "florist front," with the exception that Howie has decided he has gone about as far as he can in the flower business and has just about reached a conclusion that it is time for his retirement from it and advancement into other fields.

The flower shop at 8788 Sunset, Forget-me-Not, had not done well; Howard had seldom been in attendance. In October 1934, there had been another incidence of syphilis. Howard was confined in the Hollywood Hospital, and Christine McCoy had a Wassermann test paid for by the Selznick family. From the hospital, Howard wrote to Christine: "Why do they keep you from me. They are killing me. If I saw you just for a little while. I'm going thru mental torture. Don't you believe me, Christine. I want to kill myself and I will if I knew they are doing anything drastic." That this letter is in David's files indicates the process of interception that had begun.

Mildred said there were mounting hostilities between Howard and his two brothers, with David especially concerned about the risks of Howie "kissing the baby." Then, late in May 1936, David and Irene (with Myron's support) arranged for Howard to be sent away to Johns Hopkins in Baltimore for examination—and simply to be somewhere else. Not that they acted directly. A Dr. Saul Fox escorted Howard cross-country to Baltimore. Then, on June 23, when David wrote to Dr. Henry Fox at the Phipps Clinic, Johns Hopkins Hospital, Howard was referred to as "James Roberts."

David was fussing over Howard's daily spending allowance, ascertaining that his mail would be "supervised" and also trying to get a singing teacher to visit Howard in the hospital. At the same time, David pushed for some kind of "brain operation." Uncle Charlie Sachs went to Baltimore to negotiate with Drs. Fox and Adolph Meyer. Charlie wrote to David about the very delicate talks: the Baltimore doctors doubted that Howard would do anything desperate; they wondered about the patient returning to California—the thing David most dreaded. Uncle Charlie was considering other hospitals, notably the Hartford Retreat, but he stressed that "there would be no chance of obtaining an order for his commitment." However, a Dr. Dandy did operate on Howard, and David sent a check for $500 to cover the costs.

Howard was dreaming that Mildred wanted him back—she refused outright. At the end of October, Dr. Henry Fox told David, "Further institutional care is not very practicable because he is really too well for it."

But Howard did not come back to reside in California during David's lifetime. Between May and the end of 1936, David alone paid $6,455 to cover travel, residence, treatment, and operation for Howard. But Howard was never certified, even if he had had no say in the operation. His problem was just distanced.

On May 18, a second son was born at seven in the evening at the Cedars of Lebanon Hospital. David got there just in time for the delivery. The baby, Irene recalled, was "fat, placid, and laughing." David's reaction was much improved over his performance when Jeffrey was born. But somehow this was different. Jeffrey had seemed, from the moment David saw him, like "a threat, competition"—these are Irene's words. Whereas, with the new baby, "There was acceptance on sight; an ally had arrived."

The new baby was named Daniel Mayer Selznick. Jeffrey Mayer Selznick (until May 1936) recalls the amendment this way:

> I remember my parents—I think it was both of them—confronting me one day to poll me on whether I would mind having my name changed. I found this alarming and I said how and why. They were very patient. They explained to me that they would still call me Jeffrey

but that my other grandfather had always been known as L.J. . . . . And they wanted my initials to be the same as his, in memory of him. And said they were going to take the Mayer and give it to Danny.

Jeffrey was renamed Lewis Jeffrey Selznick. But it surely was undermining. Irene said she saw nothing remarkable about it, and neither did her father. In the Selznick home movies there is footage of Jeff as a child playing with toy cars in a purpose-built garage. The edifice is large enough for the boy to enter, and it bears his name, as proprietor, "Jeffrey M. Selznick."

Myron was sore for another reason: now David had two sons. When he got back from Europe he said David didn't deserve boys, *he* did. According to Irene, he said, "You'd better turn Jeffrey over to me." And so, as the family increased, the subtlety and reach of its rivalries procreated, too.

3 · HOOP LA

IF YOU TAKE TRASH to the desert, sooner or later you raise a stink. So it was with *The Garden of Allah*. It is unfortunate that SIP filmed *Garden* and not the stealthy plotting among the gardeners. As the stunning close-ups of the film persist, the early Technicolor goes in and out like a virgin's blush, and the inane dialogue is passed through the hysterical enervation of Boyer and Dietrich, one longs for the camera to pan away to show some of the more interesting madness.

David did not trust Dietrich; worse still, he did not trust his own judgment. He had opted for her, rather than Merle Oberon, on alleged grounds of box office. Yet in the effort to beat down Dietrich's demands, he put it about that she was no prize. In August 1935, David had asked Gregory Ratoff to give Dietrich some "friendly" advice: tell her "she is no longer even a fairly important box-office star."

. As David saw it, Dietrich had been hurt by her films at Paramount for Josef von Sternberg: everything from *The Blue Angel* and *Morocco* to *The Scarlet Empress* and *The Devil is a Woman*. These films had done less and less well, and they had led to Sternberg's departure from Paramount, leaving Marlene to make *Desire* for Ernst Lubitsch and Frank Borzage, another failure. Dietrich was one of those strange cases whose fame and exotic uniqueness were not matched with popularity. She was a discomforting screen goddess, especially in the masterpieces she had made with Sternberg in which their own love affair made her a sublimely unattainable icon. There was reason to suspect

Dietrich's expressive range was very narrow. Make her sincere—have her play someone unalterably in love, without benefit of fatalism—and there was every prospect of empty beauty. Whether Dietrich understood this is one of the movies' great mysteries. It is only certain that Sternberg had told her how vulnerable she would be without him.

Dietrich and David were not close. Later on, she would offer the opinion that David O. Selznick must be the worst man to go to bed with in the world. I suspect that came from general disdain and David's obligatory, boyish attempt rather than prolonged horizontal enquiry. Dietrich was at war with her producer; in that cause, she could employ any rumor.

Russell Birdwell was irked when the publicity bungalow was turned over to Dietrich. He slipped David a caustic note of the kind that no one else at SIP could have mastered—easy, witty, and so aware of the pain in the neck of expensive talent:

> Rumor has it that, following our eviction, if this dire act comes to pass, Miss Dietrich will take over our little place, with all of its sentiment and the store of countless memories we will be leaving behind. Of course, we should suggest many things—for instance, sharing the place with Miss Dietrich in a spirit of true hospitality. This might not be advisable, however, because I would not care to hear Miss Dietrich say each morning at breakfast: "I do not see my storee on ze front page of ze Reporter. I only see my storee in beeg headlines in ze Examiner, ze Times, ze Daily News, ze Evening News, ze Herald Express, ze Hollywood Citizen News, and I onderstand eet only goes all ze way around ze whole world."

Dietrich was also suspicious of her director, Richard Boleslavsky, who had been an actor with Stanislavsky in Moscow. She called Joshua Logan to her hotel room in the desert one evening to suggest that "Boley" wasn't really up to it and maybe they could get von Sternberg. Inventive Logan evaded the request by falling asleep in her lap. But he was only seeing the lady because Boley was . . . well, in David's words:

> Now, Logan, remember this. Boley is the general and you are the lieutenant. Do everything he tells you and everything I tell you. Above all, I want our beautiful words spoken clearly. Remember, this is "desert poetry," and I want the poetry heard! Now, Boleslawski doesn't speak a goddamn word of English. . . . *Dietrich* doesn't speak English. *Boyer* speaks no English whatsoever. Schildkraut speaks bad English. That's why we brought you out here—to make them speak and pronounce every syllable.

The best chance for this desert bloom of a movie was if it could have been made in a foreign language—subtitles by Hecht. As it was, the dia-

logue was being worked out by the sweat of several brows in Culver City.
And it was always late. Arthur Fellows, the nephew of Marcella Bannett, was
an office boy at SIP who served as a gofer in the desert:

> We really didn't have a script on the picture—it was being written in
> Los Angeles and they put up a teletype machine in a railroad junction
> which was about six miles away from where we were shooting. Right
> over the sand dunes. And the company bought me a car with these big
> fat tires and I'd sit in this little hut where the teletype machine was
> and pages of script would come and I'd tear them off and get in my
> car, and drive back over the desert and hand it to the script clerk.

It was 120 degrees Fahrenheit in the desert. That part of Arizona was
bare of fun. The camels grew morose. The actors could not credit the
dialogue that did arrive. Technicolor was new and full of problems. Dietrich
was challenging Boleslavsky on camera angles and disputing her costumes
and hairstyles. So David fired off telegrams to the desert—so much more
striking than the script. He told Boley:

> I am getting to the end of the rope of patience with criticism based
> on assumptions that actors know more about scripts than I do, and
> am disturbed, worried, and upset by telephone calls that are now
> pouring in on the scene that precedes the confession, which definitely
> indicate that another situation is brewing of the same kind that
> happened before, where the actors are getting together and ganging up
> about scenes. Would appreciate your having a frank heart-to-heart
> talk with Marlene and with Boyer, either separately or jointly, telling
> them the problems that both you and I are up against . . . neither of
> them has ever had a single picture comparable with any one of fifteen
> that I have made in the last years. Tell them very brutally that this
> comes from me.

In person, people loved David: he was merry, warm, and understanding. Yet his memos could offend everyone on a picture.

The unit was recalled from the desert and put to work in the studios
with back projections to supply the heat and the space. But the lines were
still artificial, and Dietrich insisted on perfect coiffure no matter that palm
trees were aslant in the back projection. "Surely a *little* reality can't do a great
beauty any harm," David complained. But the actress was a serene saboteuse.
In another scene, she changed costumes for the pickup shots. Corynn Kiehl,
the script clerk, did what she could—

> At the time of shooting I spoke to Mr. Boley, to Eric [Stacey, the
> assistant director], and to members of the Wardrobe Department
> about the mismatch in Miss Dietrich's clothes. We held up produc-

tion for several minutes debating with Miss Dietrich in an effort to make her wear the burnoose—but nobody could force her to wear it because she had become convinced that the dull surfaced material was not becoming to her.

It was amid such folly that David made the most fruitful business decision of his life. On May 20, two days after the birth of Daniel, Kay Brown air-mailed both a synopsis and a copy of *Gone with the Wind* to the West Coast. She said it was a "magnificent possibility for Miriam Hopkins or Margaret Sullavan" and added the warning that another company had already bid $25,000 for it on a verbal recounting of the story (this proved to be Darryl Zanuck at Twentieth Century-Fox).

Val Lewton thought the book "ponderous trash." Silvia Schulman was David's top secretary by then (Marcella Bannett had just married Dr. Marcus Rabwin, and she had stopped working). Silvia went to some friends' home in Malibu and stayed up all night reading the book, with the waves beating on the house. "And I'm saying to myself, this is unmitigated tripe." But she couldn't stop reading the love story. David read the synopsis and heard the others' comments. He had doubts.

Kay Brown was on the Teletype again next day. "This is an absolutely magnificent story," she told him, "and it belongs to us." She thought of Bette Davis now for Scarlett and Gable or Colman (if he wasn't English) for Rhett. She had got another copy of the book for Jock Whitney, and she guessed that $50,000 would buy it.

David responded on May 25. He understood Kay's feelings, but who could play Scarlett? It had to have knockout casting or a huge sale for the book. He pointed to *So Red the Rose* (a Civil War picture, made in 1935, with Margaret Sullavan), which had been a great flop. A day later, David admitted, "the more I think about it, the more I feel there is an excellent picture in it." Still not convinced of color yet, he urged Jock and Merian Cooper to consider it in Technicolor with Gary Cooper. "Were I with MGM," he added, "I believe I would buy it now for some such combination as Gable and Joan Crawford."

Copies of the book were all over Hollywood; there had to be considerations going on at Metro—for nearly everyone who read the book thought of Gable as Captain Butler. Moreover, in New York there were rumors of collusion in Los Angeles. Had Zanuck arranged for no other bids so that his offer could be accepted? Or was there a bargain between unnamed parties as to which studio would secure it? Mervyn LeRoy was interested. He had made a film from the very long, best-selling *Anthony Adverse*, and he was married to Harry Warner's daughter, Doris.

On May 28, David asked Kay Brown what she thought of Ronald

Colman for Rhett. He and the actor had stayed up late the night before talking about it, and Colman "seemed very interested indeed." Had David yet read about Miss Mitchell's Rhett?—"He looked, and was, a man of lusty and unashamed appetites. He had an air of utter assurance, of displeasing insolence about him, and there was a twinkle of malice in his bold eyes. . . ." As late as August, Colman was talking to David:

> Gone With the Wind is tremendous, and I'd like to play Rhett. . . .
> If you think I could, and should, play Rhett, I'd do it like a shot, subject to the character not being too much emasculated for picture purposes, and conditional on a chat with you as to Scarlett, etc. etc. (K. Hepburn seems to me . . . to be No. 1!)

But in the same May 28 memo to Kay, David spoke of Colman "if Metro deal falls thru—and incidentally I understand there is no executive there who has any particular interest in it (but Thalberg is liable to take gamble without even reading it)." David was not so far removed from MGM that he had no contacts there. L.B. had permitted the loan of Freddie Bartholomew and of several other players; he had sold The Garden of Allah to David. For good reason: he wanted David back. Relations between L.B. and Thalberg had never been worse. Thalberg had laid plans to leave the studio, and he was seeing as little of Mayer as he could manage. Only Thalberg's death—on September 14, 1936—would prevent his departure. Yet legend has it that Kate Corbaley, the top reader at Metro, pitched Gone With the Wind to L.B., who then called in Thalberg for an opinion, and Thalberg said, "Forget it, Louis. No Civil War picture ever made a nickel." That sounds like the sort of legend that knows death comes next, for The Birth of a Nation had made plenty—it had made Louis.

It comes to this: at the end of May, David believed Metro was ready to deal on the novel. The sum of $65,000 was mentioned. Then there is that odd information that no one there was really interested. I think it likely that David had discussed the book and its prospects with L.B. and that Metro made way for David, not necessarily out of generosity or with a future deal spelled out, but with some elements of both attitudes and the glue of "wait and see."

A month passed. That is often overlooked in the story. For in a month in Hollywood all manner of arrangements can be made. All through June, David was fussing over Allah at the studio and Wind was showing every sign of a best-seller. Kay Brown remained a supporter of the cause, and she was able to work on Jock in New York.

Nor is there evidence that Myron was enlisted in the decision. Myron was in London by then, and David had dreamed of joining him there—but on agency business and to open an SIP office in London. On June 24, David cabled Myron saying that probably Jock would go to London instead. *Wind* was not mentioned:

> He flew New York today and will expect phone call from you tomorrow. He most anxious talk to you when you are sober so please please telephone before that first drink. He is fearful otherwise it will be another conversation in which nothing will be clear except that you have some terrific plans discussions about Pasha [a racehorse].

Two days later, it was decided Jock would go. David excused himself because "I am wreck and prospect of trains boats London and NY hotels passports customs frantic rush all for maximum of five days in London would return me more tired than when I left." He wanted to take Irene to Hawaii instead. So he would apprise Jock of any London deals that might be made. Jock was happy to travel: he had an affair going with the English actress Madeleine Carroll. Which hardly left him as the man pushing David into the key purchase.

That came only on July 7, and the parties involved were Kay and Silvia Schulman, who was carrying messages to David on the set of *Allah*. With the agent for the book, Annie Laurie Williams, in the New York office, Kay teletyped Silvia:

> She has not heard from Warners since this previous offer and with-drawal. Nor has she heard from Metro today. Where is Mr. Selznick and shall I keep her waiting here or shall I let her go over to Fox?

David was frantic on the set: it was the last day of *Allah*, and the final scene was being rewritten. Would Miss Williams wait? Could David come to a decision? "I don't know what to do about Williams," Kay teletyped Silvia.

> She just called her office and they told her Warner Brothers had called and left msg it was important. . . . It may be very foolish of me but I don't want her to get out of this office. How long do you think conference will be? If she only would go downstairs and have a drink with me but I don't think she drinks.

Silvia suggested tea—"I bet Annie doesn't get around much. Why not take her some place gurrand and I am sure you will have word from D.O.S. within the next half hour or at the very latest by five your time." Kay laughed back on the Teletype: there was a four-hour time difference then and it was after five in New York already. Silvia asked would Miss Williams wait until six? Six it was.

And so at some time close to 2:00 p.m. on July 7, 1936, from the set, David dictated a message to Silvia that she took to the machine:

> If you can close *Gone With the Wind* for 50,000 do so.

At 4:30 p.m. a woozy message came back from New York:

> Is Sylvia there.
> Here Ivoe Hold your seat I've closed for fifty thousand Marvelous Thrilled to death. Wait till DOS hears it.

The machines were crazed. It was late, and Kay was celebrating. But she got cold feet:

> You are sure there is no mistake in my authorization to close as I have worked my G-D- head off on this. There is no reason for you to baby me and say hoop la and no reason to telephone me if you are sure everything is all right. I'm in such a dither I was afraid I didn't read English. [Harriett] Flagg and I out to get drunk.

Silvia knocked out the last message of the wild evening:

> Absolutely certain your authorization. Close for 50,000. I still say Hoop La and have a drink for me.

At the last moment, Doris Warner had cabled in an offer of $50,000, too. Annie Laurie Williams had then asked for $60,000—but accepted David's offer. Why? She believed in David, and Kay had not let her leave the office. David had to save Warner's face by suggesting his price was a little over $50,000.

So David had his book. The agreement was drawn up on July 30. By then, David was away, on the *Lurline*, bound for Honolulu. On shipboard, for the first time, he began to read Margaret Mitchell's *Gone with the Wind* and was pleased to find many other passengers doing the same thing.

4 · AN AWFUL LOT OF STORY

THE DAY DAVID AND IRENE sailed to Honolulu, Daniel Selznick was two months old. But he and Jeffrey remained at Summit Drive in the care of nurses. Averell Harriman and his wife were the Selznicks' traveling companions, and they provided taxing bridge lessons during the trip. David tried surfing, too, on Waikiki Beach, and there is a 16mm movie of the attempt. But he fell off the board so regularly, he retreated to the Royal Hawaiian Hotel.

The reviews were coming in on *Gone with the Wind*. In the *New York Times Book Review*, Donald Adams called it "the best Civil War novel that has yet been written"; the Washington *Post* said it was "the best novel that has ever come out of the South"; in the *New York Herald-Tribune*, the historian Henry Steele Commager wrote, "It is dramatic, even melodramatic; it is romantic and occasionally sentimental; it brazenly employs all of the trappings of the old-fashioned Southern romance, but it rises triumphantly over this material and becomes, if not a work of art, a dramatic re-creation of life itself." In the New York *Post*, Herschel Brickell, a Southerner, caught the mood of many early readers: "I can recall a few books out of the thousands I have read since I began to write a daily column that left me feeling I'd much rather just go on thinking about them, savoring their truth and treasuring the emotional experience that reading them was, than to try to set down my impressions of them."

There were harsher comments. In the *Herald-Tribune*, Isabel Paterson was disgruntled: "The narrative pace is unflagging. And if depth and literary distinction are wanting—well, it is the lesson of Scarlett's career that one can't have everything. The style is commonplace." *The Nation* and *The New Republic* began to argue that the book was deeply conservative and none too sympathetic to blacks. Margaret Mitchell was jubilant at such attacks: "I would be upset and mortified if the left wingers liked the book. I'd have to do so much explaining to family and friends."

Ten days after publication, Macmillan reported sales of 140,000. By the end of July, it had sold a million copies. Margaret Mitchell was physically weakened by the success, the rush of public events, and the need for thank-you letters. David was beginning to realize he owned not just the best of properties, but the heaviest of responsibilities.

There were other things accomplished in Hawaii. Shortly before David's departure on vacation, he had been presented with a story written by director William Wellman and the writer Robert Carson. It was about a girl named Esther Blodgett who goes to Hollywood hoping for fame and meets a declining star, Norman Maine. She becomes a star; she wins an Oscar, but he causes a scene at the Awards ceremony. Because he thinks he is hurting Esther's career, Maine kills himself, swimming into eternity off Malibu. A broken Esther goes back to her home in rural Canada. Wellman and Carson called their outline *It Happened in Hollywood*.

Did they know how closely it derived from *What Price Hollywood?* Were they even writing at David's instigation? Or is movie storytelling based on so few set patterns that people can copy without having to be aware of it? Whatever, David felt the outline was too sardonic, too critical of picture

D.O.S., Cukor, Liz
Whitney, Irene,
William Wellman

people. So Wellman apparently told the story to Irene, just before the departure for Hawaii.

She loved it—so Wellman told Ron Haver, author of *David O. Selznick's Hollywood*—and worked on David on the boat. But Irene remembered that the story was largely David's—and David himself claimed it had been "a concept of my own, to tell the story of a rising star and a falling star." This remains a mystery, for when Wellman and Carson received the Oscar for "original story" on what would be *A Star is Born*, Wellman made a public statement that the Oscar really belonged to David—to this day, the Selznick family possesses that statuette. Irene said Wellman never spoke to her and did not conceive of the story:

> He never told me a story in his whole life. We had nothing in common: he was a terror, a shoot-up-the-town fellow, trying to be a great big masculine I-don't-know-what. David had a real weakness for him. I didn't share it. I never had an interesting conversation with him. He was so colorful—but he was on his way to being colorful, creating a personality. And I don't think he liked wives.
> *Star is Born* came about because I nagged and nagged and nagged David—since R.K.O. I said, "Hollywood—it's all around you—you can't avoid it." *What Price Hollywood?* came out of that, but it wasn't right. And David kept fellows around on it, and there was a whole pile of stuff. Out of the nagging came a lot of stories.

This account is important because on *A Star is Born* Irene admitted to her own influence as a project developed. Yet this way of working was not

uncommon. Kibitzing went on all the time. The part of David that wanted
to be a writer might believe he had given birth to the entire enterprise.
Whereas the people who came up with bits of business may have felt
exploited. Wellman's remark at the Oscars is unaccountable if he did not
feel David's role as an untidy provider of the story. And Irene was sure her
nagging was the cause of creation. It all fits, yet the untidiness allows for
misunderstanding and resentment. David never made a film in which the
writing was free from dispute or confusion.

Whatever its history, there was a Wellman-Carson outline. And in
Hawaii, on July 30, sneaking away from the rest, David put down some
notes on it: he was fighting the inherent sourness of a director and a writer
toward Hollywood. He needed to think well of his world and what he did:

> Suggest looking at what we did in *What Price Hollywood?* with the
> Bennett character and her husband. We must be awfully careful that
> the fall of the star won't seem to have started with his marriage. We
> should plant his faults very early and try getting over the idea that
> Esther feels she can help him if they are married. More importantly,
> after the death of her husband, we should keep the idea that she is
> through, she won't go on, the producer pleads with her to no avail,
> but then at the very end, we can have some sort of tremendous lift
> with the grandmother telling her that there are a few people in the
> world made for more important things—giving her a pep talk on her
> career and stardom, etc.

David asked everyone he could think of for ideas—didn't everyone
know Hollywood stories, and couldn't the film accommodate all of them?
If the fit wasn't exact, the whole thing could be rewritten. There was always
a plan, or a provision, for rewriting before the first writing was done. In
other words, everything was gathered, but nothing was ever quite chosen.

Irene had liked the notion of a Hollywood story just because it was
"there—it wouldn't cost you anything." But David began to add expensive
polish to the outline. Dorothy Parker and Alan Campbell were hired to do
dialogue for $1,750 a week. When George Cukor described a recent meeting
with John Barrymore in an alcoholics' sanitarium, that scene was borrowed
for Norman Maine—it is one of the best things in the movie, sinister yet
so lifelike it lets the viewer notice the rosy removal of so much else.

Parker and Campbell soldiered on, and when their ending didn't
convince David he found rescue in the bright idea of Ring Lardner, Jr., and
Budd Schulberg, whom David liked to think he was grooming. They came
up with the moment at which Vicki Lester describes herself as "Mrs.
Norman Maine"—great line, knockout gesture—give youth a chance.
Lardner was promoted from publicity assistant to writer, and so he found
himself in the office of Daniel O'Shea. For in July, David had managed to

hire the Irishman from RKO to supervise his contracts and negotiating.

Lardner and Schulberg were arguing their case with O'Shea: they deserved $100 a week, not $75. At that moment, the intercom interrupted them. It was David asking, "What about Sidney Howard?" O'Shea said, "He won't do it for $1,500—he wants $2,000 a week." "For Christ's sake, give it to him," said David, and O'Shea went back to haggling with the kids.

Sidney Howard was the writer for *Gone With the Wind*—or so it seemed. Time would prove he was only designated writer, the figure around whom other efforts congregated. His was the draft to be rewritten, the wall against which every other ball could be thrown.

David's first thought had been to get Margaret Mitchell herself: "that . . . is the only way to obviate any possible criticism of lovers of the book about any changes which must be made." Buy the novelist's presence and you get a protection that will excuse the changes you make. That was the order of August 31. David imagined the lady from Atlanta had been bursting to get to Hollywood all along, and he had heard the book's ending needed more work.

But Margaret Mitchell was no help. She had been ill, she replied, worn out by the furor and the interviews, scarcely able to see—"It will be impossible for me to go to Hollywood." David did not give up hope, and he never began to understand Margaret Mitchell. If he couldn't get an option on her services, "the next best thing would be to have her agree not to work for any other picture company . . . I assume that you will also get a first whack at any future books she may write, although I suppose that the next time she will write a *Gone with the Wind* it will have to be submitted to my son, Jeffrey."

The announcement was made in late September that George Cukor would direct *Wind*, and Miss Mitchell looked forward to meeting him or anyone else from SIP in Atlanta. She recommended the local architect and painter Wilbur Kurtz as an authority on the Civil War period. She could be coy, and there were surely moments when fame unhinged her—this *was* the creator of Scarlett, after all. But early on she found the right tone of amused, provincial complaint:

> Life has been awful since I sold the movie rights! I am deluged with letters demanding that I do not put Clark Gable in as Rhett. Strangers telephone me or grab me on the street, insisting that Katharine Hepburn will never do. It does me no good to point out sarcastically that it is Mr. Selznick and not I who is producing this picture.

Katharine Hepburn said that Margaret Mitchell had sent her the novel—in typescript: not just an invitation, but an early selection. The actress showed it to Pandro Berman, her boss at RKO, and he had told her it was a very unsympathetic part. But Kate was not persuaded, and she became more interested still when her good friend George Cukor was assigned as director.

Margaret Mitchell owned up to one suggestion: that Atlanta-born Lamar Trotti (head of the story department at Fox and writer on *Steamboat Round the Bend* and *Ramona*) might be engaged to do the scenario. David ignored this suggestion—much as he wanted Margaret Mitchell, he hardly meant to follow her advice. There was some early consideration of Jane Murfin as writer, but it could not compete with Sidney Howard. Howard was a playwright and a Pulitzer Prize winner in 1925 for *They Knew What They Wanted*. In addition, he had done screenplays of great merit and prestige, adapting *Arrowsmith* and *Dodsworth*. He was also the author of *The Silver Cord*. David felt that Howard and Ben Hecht were "probably the two best writers for pictures who are not tied up with studios, and they are both rare in that you don't have to cook up every situation for them and write half their dialogue for them."

Hecht was the friend, but Hecht was the rewrite man, at his best in dire emergency. Hecht would do the script—any script—immediately: but if it came that soon it would be an embarrassment, leaving David no option but to make the film. He had to believe that *Wind* was momentous, enormous, difficult, and not yet. He engaged a man he hardly knew, someone who preferred staying at home and working to strict professional schedules.

Negotiations went on in the first half of October, with Howard fitting the assignment into his playwriting plans. This alarmed David. He wanted to feel he could grab a writer whenever the urge seized him. A writer who had overly set ideas about how to work was not a natural kibitzer.

> I have never had much success [he wrote Kay and Merian Cooper] with leaving a writer alone to do a script without almost daily collaboration with myself and usually also the director. Actually, the only exception in my entire producing career in which I have had any success in leaving a writer more or less alone has been in the case of Hecht, and then structural changes in the script have been necessary as he went along, even after original discussions and agreement on treatment. I am hopeful and expectant that this will be equally and possibly even more true with Howard. . . . Nevertheless, I am fearful about no contact between Howard, Cukor, and myself between the time he has his conferences with us on the treatment and the time he completes the script.

But Howard evaded all entanglements. He would do a long outline first, send it to Culver City, and write the draft of a screenplay from David's notes. He would do all of this on his farm at Tyringham, Massachusetts. But he was ready to come to California to go over the treatment with David and

Cukor. Above all, he did not want to waste his or anyone else's time. On November 1 he wrote to "Dave":

> I have been re-reading GWTW and it is certainly quite a nut to crack. . . . It looks as though the best time for me to do the bulk of my work would be the month of December with a good prospect of delivering by the middle of January. Oh, brother, we've got an awful lot of story.

At David's suggestion, Howard had contacted Margaret Mitchell; evidently he had been led to believe the novelist would be approving the script. SIP could not persuade themselves that the lady was uninterested in their *Wind*. So Miss Mitchell delivered her most emphatic warning yet to Howard:

> When I sold the book to the Selznick Company, I made it very plain that I would have nothing whatsoever to do with the picture, nothing about additional dialogue, nothing about advising on backgrounds, costumes, continuity. They offered me money to go to Hollywood to write additional dialogue, etc. and I refused. I sold the book on that understanding. Not more than a week ago, I wrote Miss Katherine Brown of the Selznick Company and asked her if you were familiar with my attitude and she wired me that you were.

At that moment, if Margaret Mitchell had changed her mind and turned up in Culver City, she would have had nothing to do. For David was simultaneously putting *A Star is Born* into production and opening *The Garden of Allah*. *Star* began shooting on October 31, with Myron's client Fredric March and with Janet Gaynor as Esther/Vicki. That casting is further proof of Irene's effect on the project. David had considered Elisabeth Bergner and Margaret Sullavan for the role. Yet he settled on Gaynor, who was thirty in 1936 and whose stardom reached back to *Sunrise*, the movie that had impressed Irene. The actress had become one of Irene's best friends. Far from an ingenue, she was having something of a comeback in *A Star is Born*— indeed, that well-trod ground has never yet been tried with what the story calls for, a newcomer.

The Garden of Allah opened on November 19, 1936, and it did not do well. Its budget, including overhead and interest, had climbed to $1.586 million. This exceeded the top range then being predicted at SIP for *Gone With the Wind*. Three hundred twenty thousand dollars had gone to Boyer and Dietrich. Seventy-four thousand dollars had been spent on set construction, while travel and hotels at the Yuma location had consumed nearly $63,000.

The film was so costly in large part because it had run over. Technicolor was held to blame, along with desert difficulties and Dietrich's caprice. But the lack of script had helped push the original forty-eight-day schedule to seventy-one actual shooting days. Over 250,000 feet of Technicolor film had been exposed for a movie that ran eighty minutes, or 7,200 feet—a shooting ratio of 34 : 1. The film had gone over its original budget by more than $250,000, but David never heeded the budgets. How could they be exact if the script was an evolving organism? Independence permitted that indulgence, and when the only available watchdogs were Jock Whitney's men in New York, inexperienced with film, there was little chance of control.

Ray Klune, the increasingly important—and frustrated—production manager at SIP estimated the direct additional costs for making *Allah* in color were $154,695. But the picture had needed another fourteen days because of color, which added a further $103,600. Then there was the extra cost of prints. In all, he reported an increased expenditure of over $370,000. As it happened, the estimated loss on *Allah* by the summer of 1939 was almost exactly that figure.

The Garden of Allah was a wretched film, bedeviled by script problems and delays that owed most to David's consternation. And it was only the second picture from a company that had to turn out pictures to meet its mounting overhead. John Wharton was trying to explain such things to Jock Whitney, and Jock was cheerful still, the best ally David ever had, yet the helpless abetter of his shortcomings.

Jock had some other things on his mind. One old friend, Tallulah Bankhead, had prevailed on him to test for Scarlett. David had done all he could to cater to the sensibilities of the actress by telling her, "The tests are very promising indeed. Am still worried about the first part of the story, and frankly if I had to give you an answer now it would be no, but if we can leave it open I can say to you very honestly that I think there is a strong possibility." Jock was more warmly interested in Madeleine Carroll. Later in 1936, he took her up to Myron's Hill Haven for a weekend. "They bought groceries on the way," said Irene, "had it all to themselves and played up there in the snow." From that affair there came one fruit: Miss Carroll would play Princess Flavia in *The Prisoner of Zenda*. Fay Wray missed the part, though she believed it was because she tested poorly and resisted David when he made a pass at her.

By December 1936, *Zenda* was the latest enthusiasm. There were already several writers at work on it, and David grew passionate over the story of royal duty and the call of love when Edward VIII abdicated. Silvia Schulman was with him when the news from London arrived (on December 10), and David collapsed in tears—as if Christmas had been postponed. "It will wreck the Empire!" he cried out.

But Christmas did come, and Sidney Howard's present to David was the *Wind* treatment. Howard apologized that it was ten days late: he had had "a shot of grippe," his beloved dog had been poisoned, and he had a play that was forty pages too long. "This treatment," Howard wrote on December 14, "is not the perfect job I could wish. You cannot say that the picture is now in the bag and has only to be written. Its chief value—the treatment's—will be to make very clear the points in the story which most need worry and discussion."

Howard was ready to come west to discuss it, but David had a Christmas planned in Idaho, some winter sports while he assessed the treatment. So Howard said he would start on the real writing. He looked forward to Cukor coming east in January to see the pages off the typewriter. Meanwhile, David was wondering whether Errol Flynn was a possible as Rhett and he asked Myron to talk to Warners about it. In Austria, at Kitzbühel, a young actress named Vivien Leigh had also planned to ski for Christmas. But when she broke her ankle she read the book she had bought as she left London. *Gone with the Wind* was published there only just before Christmas. She was entranced by it.

5 · ALMOST WITH CERTAINTY

MOST OF DAVID'S working calendars survive, and sometimes it is instructive simply to repeat those terrifying lists of things done, attempted, or put off. Nothing else better conveys the simultaneity of running what was always a small studio. Here are most of the entries for December 16 and 17, 1936, as maintained by Silvia Schulman, with my explanatory comments in italic:

Wednesday, December 16

Birdwell would like to talk to you

Reminder Kohlmar [*Fred Kohlmar was a producer*]

Phil Berg is very anxious to see you [*an agent*]

Mr. Sheldon would like to see you [*from Paramount*]

Colman had an appointment at home at five and said you could reach him there if you wanted him [*the actor*]

Dailies are in [*the previous day's shooting on* A Star is Born]

Ginsberg re: Ross [*Henry Ginsberg was vice president and general manager, the appointee of Bank of America; Bob Ross was a unit manager, being let go*]

O'Shea and Williams: re insurance

O'Shea re: will

Behrman re: Zenda [*would screenwriter S. N. Behrman work on* The Prisoner of Zenda]

March re: arrangements for him to go to N.; also about cuts made in script [*fitting the actor's schedule into* Star is Born *rewrites*]

Call Mrs. Goetz re: "Let's Play King"

Reminder: write verses for Mrs. Selznick's book [*David had an ongoing project, the book of Irene, in which he asked famous people to write verses, etc., as a tribute to her*]

Call Loyd Wright [*studio lawyer*]

Richards re: Schildkraut, Mischa Auer [*Charles Richards was in the casting department*]

Call Mr. Whitney re: his Hit Parade message

Gaynor, March, Hal re: blackface scene and make decision concerning it [*a scene shot but not included in* A Star is Born—*Hal Kern was his chief editor*]

Scanlon—production bulletin and other notes [*Ernest Scanlon was studio treasurer*]

Dictate list of pictures Mr. Cooper has under consideration [*Merian Cooper was then in charge of production for Pioneer*]

O'Shea and Ginsberg re: Xmas and N. Year weekends

Townsend's piano [*the Selznicks were purchasing a piano from Jimmy Townsend, one of Myron's associates*]

Behrman will be in at four o'clock

Mrs. Thalberg said she could come in tomorrow. Do you want to see her here or will you go to her home [*Norma Shearer, a widow of three months, was a shareholder of SIP—there was also talk of her as a candidate for Scarlett*]

Mr. Markey is taking care of his Turf Club tickets [*screenwriter, friend*]

Were you interested in a Ford car? A Mr. Kline called and said he had seen you at the Automobile Club

The painted backing of the sky as a background for Mr. March walking down the beach is ready for you to see [*the glass painted by Jack Cosgrove for the suicide scene in* A Star is Born]

Al Kaufman called [*assistant to Jesse Lasky*]

Technicolor closed at 22-3/8 [*stock price*]

Auer is working with Hal Roach and when free there goes to Warners for a picture he is doing simultaneously with Roach picture. Richards will know after lunch about Schildkraut, who is working on a Paramount picture.

Reminder: O'Shea and Williams re: insurance

I see by the papers Lombard is going to Ketchum. Would you like to ask her if she wants to join your party? [*rounding up Carole Lombard for the New Year's party in Idaho*]

The insurance doctor would like a specimen from you for your new policy application. Will tomorrow be all right or shall I postpone until early next week? [*indication that David had to control sugar or even drugs before such a test*]

Reminder: write note to H.S. [*the need for a Christmas letter to Howard in Johns Hopkins Hospital*]

Wilkerson will come in tomorrow [*Billy Wilkerson, editor and publisher of The Hollywood Reporter*]

Schaeffer is with Mr. Ginsberg [*George Schaefer, an executive of United Artists, SIP's distributor*]

Thursday, December 17

O'Shea re: Sidney Howard (his treatment has arrived this morning and is in your mail)

Technicolor closed at 21-1/2

Reminder: Bill and Val re: Zenda writers [*talk to William Wright and Val Lewton about getting writers*]

Mr. Ginsberg advises Calvert not selling "Young Wife" but was holding for another title. He is now selling this story as Arnold-Menjou-Astor

In burning the letters on Jeff's bookcase, do you want fairly large letters or a very set motif? [*a Christmas present for Jeffrey*]

Jeff will be going to see Santa Claus after his nap—about 3:30. Shall Mrs. Selznick pick you up?

Mrs. Selznick would like to know if you can be home for dinner at 7:30 as she is not feeling well and would like to go to bed immediately after dinner—or do you think you will want to work at the Studio?

In view of pressure on you don't you think it would be best to postpone Richards' interview this week?

The dailies are in.

Reminder: wire New York about South American situation

Bill Woolfenden called to suggest Rathbone for the part of Black Michael in Zenda [*the part Raymond Massey played*]

Mrs. Selznick doesn't feel well enough to take Jeff down town today and said she would probably do it tomorrow

Do you think you will be able to drive over to Townsend's and see the piano?

Wells Root [*a writer on* The Prisoner of Zenda]

The insurance doctor will be at your home at nine tomorrow morning for a specimen. You will want to avoid sugar, etc.?

Harry Rapf has asked for "Allah" on Sunday to run at home.

There might also be secret associations or calls not committed to paper; so close to Christmas there would be gift suggestions to inspect and approve. But for the chief items from those days, SIP was nearing completion of principal photography on *A Star is Born*—which entailed the constant rewriting of scenes; the script for *The Prisoner of Zenda* was in development; the treatment for *Gone With the Wind* was delivered—in which case, it had to be responded to.

David came back from Idaho and sent a long letter to Sidney Howard—"very happy indeed over your approach to the story—rough as it is." He saw now that *Wind* might run two and a half hours, yet he still hoped for a $1.5 million picture ready by Christmas 1937. At this stage, he tolerated the exclusion of many things in the book so long as the atmosphere was retained—"it is much better to chop out whole sequences than it is to make small deletions in individual scenes or sequences." He argued over several of Howard's proposals, urged further cuts, and believed the Ku Klux Klan should be out completely. SIP had already received warning letters about filming a racially insensitive book:

> It would be difficult, if not impossible, to clarify for audiences the difference between the old Klan and the Klan of our times. (A year or so ago I refused to consider remaking *The Birth of a Nation*, largely for this reason. . . . I think we have to be awfully careful that the Negroes come out decidedly on the right side of the ledger, which I do not think should be difficult.)

Yet at the same time, David was wondering whether it would not be astute to have the otherwise unemployed D. W. Griffith as adviser to George Cukor.

Fundamentally, David wanted to impress upon Howard the size of their task. David's alarm was growing the more he studied the book—it is possible that Howard's treatment was the first time he had grasped the whole story:

> I feel, too, that we should not attempt to correct seeming faults of construction. I have learned to avoid trying to improve on success. One never knows what chemicals have gone to make up something

that has appealed to millions of people, and how seeming faults of construction have been part of the whole. . . .

I am embarrassed to say this to you who have been so outstandingly successful in your adaptations, but I find myself a producer charged with re-creating the best-beloved book of our time.

Howard was too busy actually writing for a lengthy reply, and he had George Cukor with him much of the time by then. But he wrote David, "The book is written in a series of islands: good enough novel technique, but you have to produce a picture, not an archipelago." It was a shrewd comment, and it bears on many of David's pictures.

The script occupied Howard from the middle of December to February 10. Though he gave some time to revising a play in the same period, he was devoted to *Wind*—except when he was complaining about Roosevelt stacking the Supreme Court. Cukor arrived at his side on January 6, but he had mislaid his copy of David's notes. He was encouraging and amiable, and he went off to have his teeth filled or to get belladonna for his eyes. More useful was the arrival in mid-January of William Cameron Menzies, an old friend and the designer-to-be on *Wind*.

By mid-February David had the script: 400 pages of it, enough for six and a half hours. Of course, that was too much, even making the book as two movies, but, still, the script contained the eventual film in its essentials. The large ball was now in David's court, even if it left no room for play.

Howard was again willing to come to Culver City to talk about the script. But David was in turmoil on *A Star is Born*. Because of Wellman's illness, he had enlisted Jack Conway to do some scenes, but then Wellman had wanted to reshoot the Conway material. By January and February, David was remaking his own film. He and editor Hal Kern were giving orders for the writing of new scenes or the retaking of close-ups that were not working. There was a preview in Pomona, where the murky color was not helped by the smoke that got into the theater from the neighboring orange groves—the "smudge" meant to avert freezing.

There were tonal problems in the story, too. The early comedy turned into tragedy. Was there a proper transition? And was the film too grim anyway? Did the audience understand Norman Maine had killed himself? If they did, was suicide acceptable to the Breen office? Was suicide box office? Lardner and Schulberg were trying rewrites, and David hired John Lee Mahin briefly (from Metro) for these reassurances: "After I looked at the picture I told him that he shouldn't think about making it into more of a comedy. The handwriting is on the wall when the girl first sees him drunk at the Hollywood Bowl. It has to be a tragedy." Mahin proposed a new setup for the ending and also reinvented the "This is Mrs. Norman Maine" line that Lardner and Schulberg had written. If it kept getting invented, it had to be used. So David passed it on to Wellman for shooting on January 25, but he ordered an alternative take, too—"This is Vicki Lester speaking"—just in case.

The editing and the music dominated February. But there were always other things slipping by. On February 2, Charles Morrison in casting asked Kay Brown who played the lady-in-waiting to Queen Elizabeth in Alexander Korda's film *Fire Over England*. Kay answered, "No one here has seen *Fire Over England*. Our guess is you mean Vivian [*sic*] Leigh with whom Mr. Selznick is familiar and about whom he is enthusiastic."

How did David know about her that early? A print of *Fire Over England* was rushed to Culver City by air—whereas the print Goldwyn had requested went by rail. United Artists told David, "You will have the advantage of two or three days at least." David did see the film, for he raved to Cukor about the photography: its cameraman, James Wong Howe, would be hired by SIP for *The Adventures of Tom Sawyer*. But on February 3, David had said, "I have no enthusiasm for Vivien Leigh. Maybe I will have, but as yet have never even seen photograph of her. Will be seeing *Fire Over England* shortly." Scarlett was not mentioned in any of this. Vivien Leigh was under general consideration. David had never seen her. But Myron had been in England in 1936, and that summer she had begun her romance with Laurence Olivier. They filmed *Fire Over England* in July and August of that year, while Myron was in London. And Myron was Olivier's American agent. In Myron's office files, the first item concerning Vivien Leigh is dated November 3, 1936.

In that same month of February 1937, Myron nearly died. He had pneumonia and so critically that on February 9 a plane flew serum from New York to Burbank. A car then rushed it to Santa Monica Hospital, where Myron was given only an even chance of survival under an oxygen tent. Myron pulled through, but the incident was indicative of his reduced constitution. In 1936, *The Bystander* had said of him that while thirty-seven, "he looks fifty-seven, and has packed more into his life than most men of seventy-seven." As office boy at SIP, Arthur Fellows sometimes made drinks when Myron visited David:

> The first time, he wanted a martini, and all I knew was vermouth and gin. And he spat it out when I gave it to him. He said, "Come here, I'll show you how to make a martini!" It was straight gin and then he took a toothpick and put it in the martini glass and used it to stir it!

Myron gave less time to the business and more to Hill Haven. He allowed no telephones at the mountain retreat, and he would go there for longer getaways. Loretta Young was at Hill Haven once, with William Powell:

> We had been up there for a week and Myron had gone home. Marjorie used to stay at their house at the beach with their little girl. I think I only saw her once at the mountains. And Myron was crazy about her. He really was and he treated her as if he was crazy about her, too. I mean, in every other way except he drank. . . . We knew Myron was going to have a meeting with Marjorie because he'd said something about it at breakfast. And I said, "I'm going to pray the whole time you're gone." Anyway, he came back. He looked fine. He didn't look like he'd been drinking. He came downstairs and said, "Oh, I'm glad to see you're up." And we said, "What's the news?" And he said, "Well, what?" I said, "Myron, you're dodging it—so it's bad news, isn't it?" He said, "Loretta, I *love* her. I would do anything on God's green earth for her, but *nobody* is going to tell me whether I can or cannot drink."

He was losing his wife and the company of his daughter—and there is no sadder sign of how Myron was receding as a person than the diverse opinions (from Irene to his secretaries) on how little or how much they meant to him. He could not quite stand up for himself, however tough he acted. David had two sons, a wife who ran Summit Drive and its parties, a wife Myron could talk to; David had some of Myron's money, and several of his clients, in the hot new production company in town; David was the Selznick in the papers, a kid in charge who still looked his age while Myron was deteriorating so fast people were afraid. And when David was broke, it was Myron who loaned him money. But David was now making a movie about a drunk who killed himself and casting one of Myron's top clients in the role. In the business, people felt Myron fed off them, exploiting, a parasite, a danger to the economy. But grant that Myron never had much interest in agenting, and it is likely *he* felt exploited. Time would come when David would employ the emergency serum incident in *Made for Each Other*!

The loneliness in Myron was pushing activity aside. He was not as regularly at his own office. Sometimes, in the daytime, he would drive up to David and Irene's house and just hang around. "He would explore," said Irene. "He loved the linen closets. He marveled at the order. And sometimes he'd sit at David's desk and drink his Scotch. I think he'd have liked to live there."

If the talent in Hollywood was a species of pampered livestock, then Myron amused himself by getting more interested in racehorses. That, and dames, were his meeting ground with the Whitneys. But Myron could hardly speak now, except with a sneer. A little later in 1937, he let a silly dispute over horses grow into a larger innuendo—and he jabbed at David with a copy of the letter:

> All over town about advantage the Selznicks are taking of the Whitneys. How much is it worth to him if I keep quiet about the advantage the Whitneys are taking of the Selznicks.

There was no question about how well the Selznicks were doing out of the Whitneys. If Jock was too proud or polite to mention it, John Wharton was speaking up. According to Irene, Wharton was an officious man and a snob. But he had aggravating messages for David, and he supplied them steadily, with copies to Jock. On March 8, 1937, he summed up the financial state of SIP after the release of its first two films. There was no emergency yet; the company had about $800,000 in hand. But it was already dependent on bank loans and a recent refinancing arrangement among SIP partners. Wharton foresaw a need for further loans, yet the rate of production was slower than had been promised—and the overhead was very large: by March 1937, SIP had 174 employees on the West Coast—and it was about to release its third film in the first two years of operation. At that rate, no *Allah* was affordable; every picture had to be a smash.

Where did David stand? For the year 1936, his income had been $93,335—and he had lost over $55,000 of it gambling. But Irene's income had been $154,862 (over $61,000 of that being her first dividends on the Twentieth Century-Fox shares). David was helping support his mother (usually $800 a month) and Howard ($700 a month). He had a mortgage on Summit Drive, and the loan from Myron, and he gave Irene a monthly allowance of $2,800. Her money, including half of his salary, went into her separate account. Month by month, David was on the borderline, despite the huge sums and the lavish life-style. He could not back off without losing the confidence and admiration of the business and the Whitneys.

The pressure came from within as well as without. And David's health was showing the strain. He had variously a sugar problem, a thyroid deficiency, or a lack of sleep. Nonmedical people said he was simply a terrible administrator who would not delegate. David responded by claiming a greater need for perfection than other people understood.

Doctors came and went like screenwriters. On the one hand, David wished to be assured he could live forever, in eternally suspended youth, like a great movie still; on the other, doctors were the seers for anxiety and the strange hypochondria produced by morbid narcissism. Such doctors need to hear confession.

Wharton was asking why take it for granted that *Wind* had to cost

$1.5 million. Why not assume $800,000 and let the inevitable inflation occur? David beat away at such reasoning: "I am aware that we can spend a lot of money unnecessarily on the picture. On the other hand, it is one picture which, if done perfectly, can almost with certainty return an enormous profit, in my opinion; and which, if cheated on, can cut down those potential profits substantially."

But he could not budget *Wind*, or do anything with it, until *A Star is Born* was complete. On April 16, five days before that film opened, he found himself acting out Wharton's worst fears. He was still in the office at midnight, not finished yet, and still without his dinner. He promised Wharton he would try to find new producers who could work on their own. He spoke of Gregory La Cava as a possibility—and then began to make a case against his own choice (all in one cable): "La Cava would drive me crazy as director with the rewriting he does on set, for as you know I don't like any projection-room surprises or shocks."

La Cava was not hired—neither was any new producer. George Cukor remained on salary for years, trying to put his heart into Southern research and valiantly auditioning would-be Scarletts. David's pressure found another escape. In the spring of 1937, Dr. Sam Hirschfeld recommended Benzedrine so David could work into the night with his old energy. The drug frightened David once he assigned his research department to investigate it. But he was always better at calling for research than acting on it. By December 1937, the American Medical Association had approved the pills, despite some evidence of increased blood pressure and cardiovascular disturbances. David talked to Dr. Myron Prinzmetal, one of the people who had worked on Benzedrine. The pills appeared on his desk.

6 · THE CRAZY QUILT

"I THINK THE BENZEDRINE was the worst thing," said Irene—fifty years later. She was not talking medically, even if she had once wanted to be a doctor. Others used Benzedrine and survived. David used it more or less all the time from 1937 onward, until about 1950—and in the fifties doctors said he had a very strong constitution. They were more concerned to have him reduce his cigarette consumption, which stood in the same period at between four and five packs a day.

The greatest effect of Benzedrine was on David's arrogance. Its use often exaggerates feelings of grandeur and self-importance, things in which

*Irene with Jeffrey
and Daniel, 1937*

David had an unfair start. The drug kept away doubt and the prospect of depression, as well as fatigue. He felt he could do anything and everything, and he never saw that the chemicals were putting armor plate on his difficulty in coming to decisions.

Everyone had to fight for David's time, while David fought for ways of putting them off. He gave such dramatic presents because he was guilty about not giving of himself. If a worker asked, reasonably, to have a project in hand pursued, David might invent another picture to divert him, to keep his nagging presence out of the office.

Once he had delivered his *Gone With the Wind* script, Sidney Howard was eager to do revisions and put the job behind him. He had another play to write; he hankered after a Mexican vacation, and Metro was asking him to do a polish on *Marie Walewska* for Garbo. Howard had read Margaret Mitchell's novel and struggled to understand it, even if he never seems to have admired it. His script is a model of care and intelligence—whatever happened to it, it worked on screen. But Howard had such a rational single-mindedness that he and David were bound to clash. David put off that meeting as long as possible: the writers he preferred around him were those who did not challenge him. An outsider might call them "yes-men," but David believed they were friends.

For six weeks in early 1937, David delayed Howard's coming west and tried to find something else for him to do. David was frequently discussing schemes with Merian Cooper, who worked out of the New York office on behalf of Pioneer. But the maker of *King Kong* was without a credit in three SIP years. He might have handled the Edward G. Robinson picture that was talked about so much or the Edward Arnold project—*The Man with a Young Wife*, a title David could not give up on; then there was *Blonde, Brunette and Redhead*—the Technicolor title of all time—on which Lardner and Budd Schulberg had been working. All of those ideas fell through.

But on February 23, 1937, David was writing to Cooper "to get definite clarification of the date John Ford will report here." Ford was an old friend of Cooper's, and David was figuring that Ford would do a Benedict Arnold story but that he would be on *Gone With the Wind* by May. George Cukor had no inkling of this, and Sidney Howard never dreamed that he was being regarded as the writer for the Benedict Arnold picture. David wrote Cooper:

> If, however, Ford does not report to us before July or August, this might work out satisfactorily. In this case, I would like Mr. Cooper to advise me whether he would like Sidney Howard right now for perhaps two or three weeks on Arnold, as I doubt there is enough time to start on *Gone With the Wind*. This might permit Howard to get a complete story line settled with Mr. Cooper before he returned to *Gone With the Wind*—and we in turn would have the enormous advantage of being able to cast properly, make production arrangements etc. It would have to be though that Howard would return to *Gone With the Wind* in order we could commence working on this, since a few weeks would at the moment appear to be an enormous advantage because of the pressure of *Prisoner of Zenda*.

Neither Ford nor *Benedict Arnold* ever happened. But when Sidney Howard reported for work on April 1, he was put on *Zenda*. Not that *Zenda* had been starved of writers. For several months, John Balderston and Wells Root had worked at it, often with David and John Cromwell, the director. Root, an old friend, thought it was a wonderful way of working in which he did the outline, Balderston supplied the dialogue, and David and Cromwell worked out how to film it, with David ordering in Brown Derby dinners for all of them.

But then the script was thought to lack comedy, and Donald Ogden Stewart was called in to supply that elixir. Stewart was not charmed: David was "a terribly overbearing person. He was *right*, and you weren't supposed to argue with him." He was only right for a few days. Howard was called on to do a new love scene: "Bad but better than Stewart's. Why can't they realize that Anthony Hope [the author of *The Prisoner of Zenda*] wrote that story better than they can." When he was idle, he started to revise *Wind*, but David and he had still not discussed the script. On April 14, Howard wrote to his wife about how the day before David had asked for a rewrite on the ballroom scene for *Zenda*—a large production scene. "Sure," said Howard, "how do you want it rewritten?"

"I don't know," said David. "I haven't read it yet."

He had more roles than ever at that moment. Irene had gone to New York to visit her ailing mother. As a rule, at Summit Drive, Irene suffered David's hours: he might get home at 4:00 a.m. and leave a note for Farr the butler asking to be roused at 7:30 a.m.—"Regardless of what I may say." Moreover, according to Irene, the gulf between David and Jeffrey (getting on for five) was growing. David didn't like having Jeffrey in the room while he was dressing or talking to Irene: "he would sign-language me to get him out. . . . David said, 'He's listening.' In other words, this fellow was an interloper . . . David needed Mama all to himself."

But with Irene in New York, David seemed to be having a good time:

> I am winning your sons [he cabled Irene]. You have no idea how they adore me now that you are away especially since it permits Jeff to wake me up at eight every morning.

A day later, he cabled her at the Waldorf in New York at 2:15 a.m.: "I am home from the studio. Oh Dolly where is your shoulder. I am so tired."

Sidney Howard never saw the domestic David—he hardly saw David at all. On April 19, he told his diary, "Bad day with thinking out how in God's world to get this job done." David could now not make up his mind whether to order Cukor west from New York or send Howard back east. But Cukor was busy entertaining Irene in New York; he had cabled her: "Dear Madame, Handsome slender Italianate young man in New York available. When does Madame arrive? Cukor service Hotel St. Regis." Nobody was more blithe or patient in waiting for the *Wind*.

On April 17, Howard told his wife he had had a 10:00 a.m. appointment with David "to discuss love interest"—on which film is not clear—but at 5:00 p.m. he was still waiting. He added, "Selznick hates color but has commitments. I am to see the best of all color films on Tuesday [the twentieth, the day before its opening at one of its locations, Grauman's Chinese]. It is called *A Star is Born*. I also hear that it is a terrible story."

HOWARD WAS PREJUDICED in advance, disposed to be vengeful. But arrogant bosses foster that malice in others. Writers told the funniest stories against D.O.S., even if their own humiliation was the point of the story. They felt the disregard of material or ideas in the manner of David's working. They sometimes despised a man who stole writing's pride without facing its loneliness. Writers must have seen that in *A Star is Born*'s Hollywood panorama there were actors, a producer, a director, technical craftsmen, and a publicist—but no writers. The film that had so many writing teams implied that the gang made the thing up as they went along.

Sidney Howard was wrong in one respect: the plot of *A Star is Born* is cute, clever, tidy, dramatic—it works. Hollywood has gone back to it already, twice in name and several other times in oblique homage. "This was really a concept of my own," said David, "to tell the story of a rising star and a falling star, and to try to prove something?" What was he after?

> the trouble with most Hollywood films was that they gave a fake picture—that they burlesqued it, or they over-sentimentalized it, but that they were not true reflections of what happened in Hollywood. My notion was to tell this in terms of a rising star, in order to have the Cinderella element, with her path crossing that of a falling star—to get the tragedy of the ex-star.

In *What Price Hollywood?* that contrast had been latent, but the actress and the director had not been in love—or not so that they knew it. In *A Star is Born*, the simplicity and the pathos of the arrangement hit the audience with force and novelty. The film was very warmly reviewed, and it did immediate business. It had cost $1.159 million, and it would gross about $2 million. By the summer of 1939, it was reckoned to have shown a profit of $181,000, not nearly enough to offset the total SIP loss, but that had to do with larger factors, including the United Artists distribution deal.

The SIP stockholders were apprehensive in the spring of 1937. *A Star is Born* could not remove the doubts, but it cheered everyone up; the wealthy Easterners could congratulate themselves on the public flocking to see a movie that made you laugh and made you cry and which carried the extra chic of seeming to "get" the glamorous world of Hollywood. For unaccustomed investors in the picture business, *A Star is Born* said this was a fine and honorable trade, entirely American, public-spirited and exciting. Jock Whitney wept whenever he saw the movie, and Jock had actually proposed the title, imposing on David's idea, *The Stars Below*. This was the first time the enterprise of SIP seemed to be working; it was also the first picture on which David used the studio frontage as a logo.

Then came the Oscar nominations, even if they were nearly nine months away: Campbell, Carson, and Parker for the adaptation, Wellman and Carson for original story (the only winner), Wellman for direction, Fredric March and Janet Gaynor, and for Best Picture. Six nominations, and the fourth year in a row in which David had been nominated for Best Picture (*Viva Villa!*, *David Copperfield*, *A Tale of Two Cities* earlier).

This also can be said of the film:

- the color is less vivid than in *The Garden of Allah*; this has a lot to do with the limits of Technicolor in 1936-1937, but rather more with the somber design of Lansing Holden and Lyle Wheeler.

This Hollywood is oddly cheerless and wintry. In the mind's eye, the film is made of blacks, whites, grays, and cold, grim blues. The melancholy imagery could be generated by the pale, tense face of Fredric March.

- but March's performance is the most compelling thing in the film: he makes Norman Maine quiet, edgy, very smart and alluring as he advances toward doom; the underplaying is gripping more than fifty years later, the drunkenness is very restrained (repressed nearly, as if to suggest that inhibition was one of Maine's chief problems).

- the alcoholism is the aspect of the story viewed most clearly. We can believe Maine is psychologically disturbed—though the origins of the illness are not explained. The self-loathing is frightening, and the scene in the alcoholics' clinic is among the greatest in a Selznick picture.

- Esther/Vicki is only a pretext for telling Maine's story. We do not believe she has extraordinary screen presence or that her stardom is earned. Janet Gaynor cannot give her youth or sexuality to arrest Maine's decline. Gaynor's personality is pretty, rather prim, and

A Star is Born: *Norman Maine in court—*
Fredric March and Janet Gaynor

too mature to be moved by fame or success. One can almost measure off the screen a content, subdued air, the decision on Gaynor's part to retire—as she did in 1938. And so we do not feel the love story or Maine's delight in her ability—whereas, in the remake, we believe James Mason's Maine is hearing a great singer so that he feels driven to promote her.

- the screenplay has several voices: there are many dark and funny lines, and they mostly belong to Maine or the publicist Matt Libby (played so well by Lionel Stander). It is tempting to attribute these to Alan Campbell and Dorothy Parker, for they are filled with scathing insistence on the squalid underside, and they urge the film closer to satire.

"What do they do with actors while you're away?" Maine asks Libby. The publicist sneers, "Oh, they cut 'em into slices and fry them with eggs."

But there is just as much raw sentiment and pleading pathos as another force tugs the film toward a benign view of Hollywood. The writing is never flat, and the film is very adroitly directed. But there are stretches of placid sweetness that leave us waiting for the pain and peril of Maine. Moreover, the movie is a series of set pieces joined together, but never linked. The honeymoon is a good example of this: a self-contained, uninteresting idyll that stops on an unanswered plot point. Not even music bridges the fade-outs. This is something that recurs in Selznick pictures; they feel like scenes worked over in isolation. This could be a direct consequence of David's writing methods, and it was often more than he, Hal Kern, or the music of Max Steiner could bring to flowing life.

- the whitest of white lies is the producer: Oliver Niles (played by Adolphe Menjou). This is the biggest name change David made from the Wellman/Carson outline. There the producer had been called Joseph Grantham. "Oliver" is not the only touch of David. We see Niles talking office business in his sleep, and it is David's handwriting that has signed "Oliver Niles" on Vicki's contract. But Niles is tranquil and unneurotic with his two actors. He goes along with their emotions, the self-effacing manager of the studio, not its god. Niles has no wife, and he lays no hand or greedy eye on the talent. He never interferes, and—in the urbane guise of Menjou—seems to have come fresh from the massage table. He has power in the world of the film, yet it is as hidden as possible— from him as much as from the audience. He does fire his friend Maine because his films are flops, but neither he nor the tough system gets any blame for it. "Letting Norman leave the studio was the hardest thing I've ever done," he says. "There was nothing else I could do." And so the pitiless practice of that kind of capitalism is passed over—Norman Maine simply went with the wind of changing taste.

- but now we begin to uncover fundamental implausibilities in the film—or let us call them necessary lies for 1937. David knew the ways stars were made and the cruelty with which they were dumped. But, just like L.B., he could stare through the squalor and miss his own brutality. To get into movies and stay there was desperately hard on the soul—that is one reason why a Joan Crawford looked so fierce. There have always been stories about how much of *A Star is Born* was drawn from life—the "courage" of Norma Shearer after Thalberg's death, the "tragic" fall of John Gilbert, and the suicide off Malibu in November 1936 of actor John Bowers. Those links are wishful thinking or humbug. There is an untruth at the core of the story as optimistic as the studio scenario that Paul Bern killed himself to "save" Jean Harlow: Maine kills himself *for* Vicki. That sort of altruistic gesture has no model in life. Picture people would never fall for the claptrap of making that sort of sacrifice for someone else. Maine's suicide is an adolescent fantasy; it is the kind of thing in films that cheapens life.

L.B. loved *A Star is Born*: "If there is anybody in this business who can take Irving Thalberg's place, David Selznick is the one. Did you see what he did with *A Star is Born*? He took that story—if it came to me, I'd say, 'Make it or don't make it, what do I care; it's been done forty times anyway'—he took that story and made a tremendous picture out of it." But if Mayer loved any movie about Hollywood, there was something wrong with that movie.

7 · MIXED LAUGHTER AND CHEERS

THE FIRST FEW MONTHS of 1937 were the most hectic of David's life so far. Benzedrine assisted the frenzy, but there were emotional chemicals surging through the brain, dragging the body in their wake—brilliance, need, recklessness, and foolishness. Whenever the stew was most active in David, he gambled. In the first three months of 1937—as *A Star is Born* neared release and *Zenda* began to shoot—David lost $13,313, $14,254, $18,265. These were the most depleting months in a row so far and a period in which he should not have had time to get away to the Clover Club. But neither should he have had half hours here and there to seduce typists and messenger girls.

As with nearly every woman he employed, David had made a pass at Silvia Schulman. But she and Ring Lardner, Jr., had fallen in love, and they talked of marriage. Whereupon David and Irene became highly disturbed. Silvia was Jewish, and Ring was not: he had come to David by way of social introductions through the Swope family. David and Irene advised against the marriage. They called Ring's mother in the East and suggested she come to California to help dissuade her son. No pressure worked. The couple were married, with David and Irene in attendance. But Silvia was offended, and she left SIP. Her replacement was Marcella—Marcella Rabwin now—ready to come back to work.

Silvia then wrote a novel with a friend named Jane Shore. *I Lost My Girlish Laughter* was published under the name "Jane Allen" by Random House in 1938. The girl of the title is secretary to a flamboyant, arrogant producer named Sidney Brand. The book went into three printings in 1938 and—despite David's strenuous efforts—Orson Welles adapted it as one of his plays on the CBS "Campbell Playhouse" series. It was broadcast on January 27, 1939—to honor the eventual start of production on *Gone With the Wind*.

The novel is no longer in print, but anyone entertained by D.O.S. should seek it out. Silvia Schulman tried to say the book was not based on David. But Marcella Rabwin regarded it, nearly fifty years later, as a disgrace and a betrayal. Here is a scene from when the new secretary ends her first day with Sidney Brand:

> Mr. Brand rises out of his chair and moves in my direction, all the time talking about the wonders of Hollywood and how he is sure I will make good because obviously I am very intelligent. I am about to open the door when I feel something moving over my back and I am stunned to discover it is Mr. Brand's arm and he pulls me around face to face with him.
>
> I am so taken by surprise that I do not think very fast, but one thing I do know and that is I will not be thrust into the undignified position of having to fight for my honor. So I look him straight in the eye and I thank him for thinking I am intelligent and the most intelligent thing I can think of at this moment for me to do is to find myself some food and get my girlish sleep so I can be bright and intelligent again in the morning. I am sure, I continue in a motherly tone, that he is very tired too, and tomorrow will be a big day for him.
>
> There is a puzzled look in his eyes when I finish, but his arms slack about me so I can breathe easily again.
>
> "You are a very naive girl," he says to me. "After all what's a kiss or two? Merely a friendly gesture."
>
> There is no answer to that one without being unmaidenly and one

thing I am determined not to be is unmaidenly. So I say that I think perhaps I will always be naive for I have discovered that it is more healthy.

When Sidney Howard at last got David to sit down, instead of *Wind* analysis, he had "an all-day discussion of love in Zenda." As that script procreated itself, David was becoming more enamored with the theme of sacrificed love and the impossible attraction princess and commoner might hold for one another.

The truth was dawning on Howard: "Selznick, a very nice and polite gent, has still to learn that there are several equally good ways to skin a cat." A week later, Howard was angry, for now any plans were doubly in jeopardy because David was both planning, and postponing, a trip to New York— for a vital SIP board meeting:

> This fellow Selznick [Howard wrote to his agent]—very nice, very polite, and very able—was born with no sense of how to organize his time. His troubles with *Zenda* which prevented my coming West again after Christmas are still continuing unabated. He has had no time to read my script of GWTW and has read the book only very hastily. In the five weeks that I have been here I have pretty much wasted my time completely.

Of course, Howard was being paid for that time. But David had a picture in hand, so why should Howard not serve up scenes and lines for *Zenda*? John Cromwell rebelled at all the new pages. There was a showdown, and thereafter Woody Van Dyke handled the fencing scenes while George Cukor took on love scenes. Under those circumstances of "teamwork," directors did not invest themselves in the work—and thus they helped support the Selznick theory of directors as replaceable technicians. Moreover, David was forever imposing scenes and ways to shoot them on whatever anyone else did. On April 12, he burst out with ideas on the taking of Michael's castle, and here we can feel fresh ideas ascending with the energy of dictation:

> In connection with the shot of the horses in *Zenda* that we discussed last night, I assume the horses will come charging, and not merely over the drawbridge but into the hall. I think we might try three or four different angles on this, including one in which they charge directly into the camera; a buried camera shot; and reverse angles as well. I think, too, that we should get the effect of them riding right over Michael's men, and that we should go in for saber thrusts. Perhaps one of our two "assistant heavies" is run down by a horseman, or perhaps one is killed by a saber, or perhaps both are killed by sabers.

Perhaps, too, we should cue Zapt's men into being so brutal by showing that the heavies start shooting first. Perhaps, too, one or more horsemen should go down, and I think it would be a grand effect if we could get one or two of the horses—horsemen and all—going headlong over the side of the bridge.

That sounds like an indulged child expanding his own game as he daydreams, flexing rules and budget to accommodate his excitement. But the spoiled boy has always been a model of leadership in Hollywood, even if condemning the other spoiled boys for immaturity is a frequent way of gaining power. "Independence" for David was a way of saying these are my toys and *this* is the game I am playing.

Rationally, practically, managerially, much of what David was urging was disastrous—worst of all for SIP, his say-so went unchallenged. No one on the West Coast could stand up to his energy, his desire, his great accumulated knowledge of moviemaking, or his good instincts. For many of his employees, David's fresh thoughts were as endearing and stimulating as they were frustrating.

SIP had its strict father, John Wharton, in New York, and he was preparing everyone for a crucial board meeting. On April 15, he sent an inescapably lucid analysis to Jock and to David. He foresaw that they were making too few pictures for the overhead:

> For example, *Prisoner of Zenda* is now estimated at a cost of about $1,120,000.00, including $107,000 for overhead and $40,000 for su-pervision. Allowing for retakes, the cost on this basis will probably be $1,150,000. If the picture were to do $2,250,000 we would have a distribution fee [i.e., to United Artists] of approximately $675,000, prints and advertising $175,000, Colman's percentage $100,000, which, added to a negative cost of $1,150,000 equals $2,100,000, or a profit of $150,000. If, however, the overhead charge has to be raised by $150,000, this profit disappears.

Wharton demonstrated that there was not enough money to meet staff undertakings, pay taxes, and repair the studio. These facts of life never quite permeated David's thinking—he could not credit failure when at least three out of four films were applauded. But four out of four would not have disproved Wharton's assessment: independence with just a few movies could not work. The Metro method was the answer, and L.B. had worked it out: a lot of pictures and your own distribution organization.

Wharton pushed his point further, with great care. He may have bored the Selznicks, but they could have learned diplomacy from him:

In my opinion we made a mistake in our plans last fall, and I feel that this mistake must not be repeated now. The mistake was the assumption that we could find producers who, with practically no assistance from D.O.S., could prepare scripts and productions which he would approve as suitable. A second mistake closely related to this was the belief in which all three of us, including D.O.S., joined, that D.O.S. could physically find the time to give detailed attention to production of pictures in process and have time enough left over to guide associate producers.

I am not criticizing D.O.S.; far from it, I think he has done superhuman work on *Star* and *Zenda*. I do criticize a policy which forces him to such effort.

Gaining confidence, Wharton now proposed another way of working: "I should like to make it a definite rule that the Company would never do a production, no matter how tempting the setup looked, if it meant that setup would take the vast majority of D.O.S.'s time." He surveyed the projects on hand: assigned *Great Riches* to Oscar Serlin, *Earl of Chicago* to William Wright, and *Gone With the Wind* to David and an assistant. David would supervise the others and scout for fresh material. But he would not take the other projects on his own shoulders.

The memo showed how quickly Wharton had learned the business and how well he appreciated David. SIP never made *Great Riches* or *Earl of Chicago*, and David never shaped up as an executive of the Wharton School. Wharton was not surprised: his memo was aimed at Jock, and it may have had the support of other SIP stockholders who had grown restive. Jock had his moment of anger and despair, but he was won over—by David and by Irene. For what a spoiled playmaking boy needs is another spoiled kid with bucks to back him. Jock's fling with Madeleine Carroll is no minor part of this. He wanted a discreet taste of adventure and slumming, just as David and Irene were angling for class. For a few years, David and Jock were a couple of guys on the town.

David did not relish the board meeting. He had good reason to stay on the coast and work with Howard. But he was not emotionally ready for *Wind*, and he flinched from sessions in which he could not mask his sketchy knowledge of the book. More important, he may already have seen an economic reason for delay: one of his growing concerns was that SIP was not getting the best distribution service from United Artists. For a year David had been nagging George Schaefer at U.A. over poor performance and talk of U.A. selling pictures in blocks, rather than individually. "After all," he said, "every picture I make is an attempt to be one of the outstanding pictures of the year."

A crisis was coming for United Artists, too. In May 1937, Sam Gold-wyn sought to buy out his colleagues there—Mary Pickford, Douglas Fairbanks, and Chaplin. He offered them $500,000 each; they asked for $2 million. With Alexander Korda, Goldwyn went in search of that money. The idea had been noted at SIP that perhaps Jock could be a contributor. If he bought into U.A. then SIP would have better control of its distribution. If there was ever a merger, then the overhead could be reappraised. But the resultant corporation would be another kind of major studio.

In this climate, David and Irene eventually set out for New York by rail early in May. Jock had been in Los Angeles, too, so they rode the train together. And because David had vowed to press on with new schemes, he took Wellman, Carson, and Hecht with him so the journey would not be wasted. These story-makers quickly grew restive, for as the train worked its way through the West, the Selznicks and Jock kept to their private drawing rooms, consuming Jock's stock of champagne. No work was done, and the studio workers felt excluded.

Their moment came in Chicago. For as everyone switched from the Chief to the Twentieth Century, Jock, Irene, and David took a private plane to Louisville to see the Kentucky Derby. Riding on their own, the writers liberated the Whitney champagne and reached New York feeling more cheerful.

The week in New York was no rest. If there were enough problems already, a few days nearly buried them in fresh prospects—all lofty, intriguing, and secret. Perhaps David managed to change the subject or the forum; perhaps he could not resist that part of him which, according to Irene, "would always sooner promote than make a picture."

Much as David had resisted the board meeting, he felt grateful for it afterward—a sign that he had charmed his way out of trouble. Not all the board really knew David. Jock had been trusted with most of the collaboration. Joan Payson and Sonny Whitney sometimes came to Hollywood and knew the Selznicks moderately. But John Wharton said he had wanted the others to see that David was no ogre—he may have had the notion that it was only in seeing David perform that anyone could grasp the liability he represented.

The talk about new arrangements had been giddy with possibilities. David had proposed, and Jock had resisted, going to other backers, like Averell Harriman or—again—Harold Talbott. There had been discussion of some merger with United Artists, even a takeover that would outflank the Goldwyn-Korda attempt. Using Sol Rosenblatt as a go-between, David and Jock learned that Douglas Fairbanks would be sympathetic to an SIP deal: "I believe I told you," David wrote Wharton from the train later, "that

Douglas Fairbanks, just before he left, told me that the Dillon-Read group was quite excited about the possibility of doing the banking on a deal for the purchase of United Artists that would involve control by us." So Rosenblatt was seeking an appointment for Jock with Maurice Wertheim on Wall Street: $20 million was in the air. But had David told Wharton? Or were there racing late-night talks between David and Jock which David counted on and Jock heard as if in a dream, while Wharton—the manager—never got it all straight?

At the same time, David had heard from Myron and Dan O'Shea that "the United Artists crowd is meeting right now with Paramount on a merger, and that the deal is ready to go through except for Chaplin's resistance." These household-name companies were as economically vulnerable as they were subject to rumor. All through that spring and summer of 1937, as if separately, SIP was also considering a merger with Paramount. In these dreams, SIP would have been the decisive and operative unit—the new young suitor in a field of rather desperate dolls all, in David's eye, begging to be taken. For a week, at least, David loved the thrill, especially when major Wall Street monies were involved.

Irene was in New York on this trip—but she never learned of the possibilities. David also renewed contact with Laura Harding, and she may have been a lead to other deals. Using the office and the hotel, and with his script girl Bobbie Keon as stenographer, David had a genius for keeping his lines of information untangled when intrigue was involved. Irene knew there were things not to notice, and, whether or not they talked about it, David and Irene understood there were lines back to L.B. so potent it was best for Irene not to know too much. And so the marriage was steadily compromised.

The brief romances with other movie companies seem sensational in David's letters. Yet they never materialized. He may have been kidding himself or misleading Wharton. There was always a better deal that beckoned. In David's New York calendar for May 17 there is the item "Nicholas Schenck—when do you wish to see?" But on May 23, summing up the trip in a letter to Wharton, David wrote:

> I read in the paper the morning that I left that Nicholas Schenck was in town. I regret that I did not hear this sooner (I learned he had been in town for a few days), because it is obviously important to us that the MGM deal be kept alive. I am wiring him my regrets that I missed him. Jock also said that he would invite him to lunch at the races, and I would appreciate your reminding Jock of this.
>
> I telephoned Al Lichtman [MGM executive] and asked Al to take up with Nick a one year deal. I pointed out to Al their confessed

anxiety to get *Gone With the Wind*, and the lack of risk to them as well as to us in making a one year deal that would include *Gone With the Wind* as compared with a five year deal. At the moment, and unless the United Artists situation clears to our satisfaction, I think we might very well want to make such a deal very soon if MGM were willing.

There was more fascinating detail in the New York trip. On the afternoon of May 18, David met Alicia Rhett—she was the single remaining possibility from the ballyhooed Southern search for Scarlett that Kay Brown and Cukor had undertaken. And she would actually make it all the way through, playing India Wilkes in the movie.

That evening for the first time, David met a man who had just turned twenty-two. The night before he had gone to see Orson Welles in *Dr. Faustus* at the Maxine Elliott Theatre. They got on very well: David had no doubt about Welles's talent, and they were two equally spoiled boys. On the spot, at "21," David asked Welles to run his story department (this sounds like Val Lewton's job). Orson was flattered, but confessed he was set on acting and directing. Instead, he recommended his associate in the Federal Theatre Project, John Houseman.

It is a meeting to conjure over. Welles was only two years away from his contract with RKO—one of Hollywood's rarest concessions to liberty. (In 1937, also, David had a paper plan for taking over that studio.) The portrait of Charles Foster Kane in Welles's first film at RKO applied to rogue geniuses like Welles and David just as much as it teased William Randolph Hearst, for it is a bittersweet tribute to the arrogance resolved to do everything its own way and believing in "love on my own terms . . . the only terms anyone knows."

On May 19, with Bill Paley, David talked about another novelty, television. Immediately, David saw the power and recognized its future. He flirted for half an hour with Herbert Bayard Swope about starting a newspaper and television company. He was so perilously open to anything; his eagerness or curiosity was death to concentration. For suppose, say, that Orson Welles had said, yes, I'd love to—when do I start? Then David's overhead would have grown, and he could have ended up making *Gone With the Wind* and *Citizen Kane* at the same time. Maybe David swooned with relief when Orson said no.

On the other hand, David could believe himself an unrivaled master of business. The suggestions for reform from Wharton had irritated him. He flat-out disliked Francis Altstock, an associate of Wharton's and an enemy from the RKO days, who had presumed in New York to offer advice and program charts that might help David. David had lost his temper, and he honestly believed that Jock had agreed Altstock must go. Later, Jock had second thoughts, or restated the first ones: David so often heard what he wanted to hear. Altstock was kept on, and he would prove a steady torment to David.

For the moment, as the train headed west, David took time to defend himself to Wharton. It was always his richest vein—that of a child lawyer defending a wayward brother:

> Contrary to any other opinions that may be held by anyone, I think I am a superb executive (sounds of mixed laughter and cheers), and as long as we continue to operate at a substantial profit I will continue to think so. I flatter myself that practically single-handed I have built a company that in its first year and a half of existence has a better record than any other company that has been started in the history of the picture business from the viewpoint of reputation and of prof- its—with the single exception of Twentieth Century. . . .
>
> It may be that I have done some wrong, but I have another principle that my father taught me, which is that anything above fifty per cent right is profit. . . . Put me in the automobile business and I would be as well an organized executive as you ever saw, but success in the picture business lies in deciding when to be a showman and when to be a per- fectly operating official. When these aims conflict I have long since learned that the only intelligent choice is to be a showman.

8 · TRUTH, CRUSHED TO EARTH . . .

BETWEEN INDIGNATION and champagne, Ben Hecht had achieved very little on the train coming east. There had been a notion that David, Hecht, and Wellman would concoct a comedy, for Jock Whitney com- plained that David's slant on material was too melancholy. (In haggling over Norman Maine's suicide in *A Star is Born*, David had admitted the number of woeful retreats from life in his pictures.)

Hecht had a story—about a socialite and a café singer—that lacked spark, even if it had *Nothing Sacred* as a title. David wrote it off, installed Hecht at the Waldorf for that wild week in May, and told him to try again. He threw in a short story, "Letter to the Editor," by James H. Street, that Val Lewton had found, for he wanted to make a newspaper comedy as fast and pungent as Hecht and Charles MacArthur's *The Front Page*. With David coming in and out when other appointments allowed, Hecht fashioned another story for the *Nothing Sacred* title.

It involved a reporter on the New York *Morning Star*, Wally Cook, who seeks to exploit Hazel Flagg, a young woman from Warsaw, Vermont, famed in pathos because she is dying of "radium poisoning." In fact, there is nothing wrong with Hazel, but she becomes a wonder for the modern world of media and wins the love of Wally. The story could be told in half a minute—Hecht knew his David. They would do it in Technicolor, to meet that obligation, and it would be another picture, to help defray the overhead. To impress John Wharton, David put a start date on shooting of June 12—only three weeks away. He was already committed to paying big money to Fredric March and Carole Lombard (Myron's clients), and the deadline on their services was approaching. Lombard was $18,500 a week. Hecht was offered $5,000 a week plus a bonus of $30,000 if he did the script in time.

Such desperate production needed the train again, and so Wellman, Hecht, and David traveled westward in a fury of invention and dialogue. They had distractions: George Cukor and Jock's wife, Liz, who was traveling with three dogs and a squirrel. There was a problem with the ending, but David decided to wait until the end to settle that. The script was an adventure in bravura bad taste and unquestionably funny. But he had misgivings over the character of the newspaper editor who doubts the entire Flagg scam.

Ronald Haver has suggested that David feared this character could offend his friends in publishing, like Henry Luce. But since the character was named "Oliver Stone," I suspect David's worry was more personal. Hecht could never stop needling those who employed him, and there is plenty in *Nothing Sacred* that alludes to America's mounting impatience with the movie of *Gone With the Wind*. At the start of the picture, the *Morning Star* is putting on a gala event for the "Sultan of Mazupan," a large black man ornately Technicolored in turban and jewels. But the Sultan is a fake from Brooklyn by way of Georgia, cooked up by Wally for publicity, and the gala event is interrupted by the Sultan's wife and many children telling him to come home. (The wife is the first appearance in David's work of Hattie McDaniel.) Because of the ridicule and criticism that follows exposure, Oliver Stone will later complain to Wally, "I've been through an inferno. I haven't been able to enter a café in the last three weeks without the band playing 'Dixie.' "

There was only one Oliver in the business crying "enough" on Southern publicity—when he wasn't asking for more. As early as November 1936 (when *Wind* was viewed as a movie for 1937), Kay Brown had invaded the South. There were several conceivable objects of this trip: to involve Margaret Mitchell in the production, to gain valuable research and atmosphere—if the elusive George Cukor could be lured along—and to gather a basket of young female talent, drawling peaches, who might furnish a Scarlett or a parade of extras for party scenes. There was also publicity, a way of delaying and building public interest.

Kay Brown was cheerful but skeptical about the scouring of colleges, drama groups, and junior leagues and was appalled when open calls in Atlanta produced 500 young lovelies. Such events cannot escape local press attention, and if David wanted professional dignity whenever possible, Russell Birdwell knew he also lusted after column inches and rising expectations. Kay took along with her the thirty-year-old Anthony Mann (a future director) to handle any film tests, but she doubted the chances of finding gold:

> My entire approach to this is that if I find a Scarlett it will be a miracle. What I hope to get are two Southern girls for secondary roles who have possibilities of development and I don't intend to pay them more than fifty bucks a week for the privilege of appearing in this picture. I plan to stop at Louisville on my way to New York because reputedly the most beautiful girls in the world live there and I am sure some of the Junior League girls will be worth looking at.

As she met the press along the way she felt "that this expedition is being conducted quietly and genuinely." But there were then mob scenes in Atlanta, and even Kay was conceding "the madhouse through which we have just gone." Margaret Mitchell had joined the search in Atlanta, sometimes trying to go incognito but sometimes yielding to a touch of celebrity. Cukor kept finding excuses for missing the South, and Kay signed off on one amused but exasperated letter, "How's you-all, honey chile? We're done in."

Kay reckoned the publicity and the fun were turning sour—yet no one had begun to foresee how long this publicity would be expected to stay fresh, and, as *Nothing Sacred* makes clear, yesterday's newsprint sensation wraps today's fish. Cukor did reach Atlanta in March 1937, still running his eye over girls, but more impressed with Margaret Mitchell:

> We arrived yesterday with a great fanfare. Margaret Mitchell was absolutely divine with us, helpful, cooperative, very intelligent about the whole thing. Yesterday, she took Hobe [Erwin, Cukor's friend and assistant] and me up and down the city, showing us where she imagined various houses to be; then we followed the road that Scarlett took to Jonesboro and "Tara." . . . I found it enormously helpful.

Cukor visited the Atlanta Historical Society, "where I was my usual gracious self and made a very good impression for Selznick International."

He also appreciated the possible value of historian Wilbur Kurtz and Susan Myrick, "a very intelligent friend of Miss Mitchell's who is very well born," who could help with women's costumes "and general behavior."

There were many scoops about Scarlett being cast. As well as Tallulah Bankhead, Louise Platt had been tested before the end of 1936. Liz Whitney herself got a screen test on April 5, 1937. From the photographs sent to him, David was intrigued by the Creole Adele Longmire. In Atlanta, at the Debutante Club, Miss Catherine Campbell was looked at closely—in time she would be the mother of Patricia Hearst. Scarlett was a kind of lottery for the top drawer and for deranged women from the hinterlands. In February 1938, SIP would receive a submission from Chester, Pennsylvania, which began:

> Honorable Gentlemen of Hollywood:
>
> One fine evening 12:01 I was reading the Chester Times. On our Society Page I glanced at the picture of our so-called modern Scarlett O'Hara??? Paulette Goddard! I wish to tell you all this:—She is much too pretty to play the role of K.S. O'Hara. Katie Hepburn is too cracked. Miriam Hopkins would probably do, but I Am Katie Scarlett O'Hara!

There followed a forty-two-page letter, including photographs and lurid drawings and page-upon-page which the writer had filled with the galloping scrawl of "I'm Scarlett O'Hara." Actresses were pretty and obedient at casting time—even the outspoken Tallulah Bankhead had reacted to David's "unlikely" letter by saying: "As to my being able to look the part in the early sequence of the picture, that is entirely out of my jurisdiction, but I have been assured by several ace cameramen in their vernacular that 'it's a cinch.' I claim no credit for *their* genius." Most aspirants were friendly, modest, pretty—just out for the fun of trying. But the letter from Chester roared with a madness worthy of *The Day of the Locust*—and it testified to how deeply some readers felt for Scarlett.

Hazel Flagg's "illness" in *Nothing Sacred* is like some unknown woman's "rightness" as Scarlett O'Hara. They are both myths begging for publicity. And just as Oliver Stone is a cheeky nod to a supposed friend, so Hecht's *Nothing Sacred* is a sardonic commentary on such careers as David's and Russell Birdwell's.

The picture did start to shoot on June 12: David cabled Jock, "You wanted comedy—boy you're going to get it, and be it on your own head." The film progressed in continuity, and some of it was apparently improvised. Hecht's preferred ending was considered too bitter an assault on Stone and journalistic dishonesty, so David sought a quick, romantic get-out from George Oppenheimer and Ring Lardner, Jr. It was a chaotic, headlong exercise, and David had come close to shutting down the production to get the script straight. But they charged through every problem, and the seventy-five-minute picture was finished, scored with just one lovely tune by Oscar Levant, and released on November 25.

The speed was part of the bravado. But the movie still works, pouring a satisfied scorn on all it beholds. It satirizes New York and Vermont and sees a world inhabited by only suckers or con artists—there is no ordinary existence. Hecht's opening titles talk of New York

> where the Slickers and Know-It-Alls peddle gold bricks to each other. . . .
>
> and where Truth, crushed to earth, rises again more phony than a glass eye.

But once Wally Cook reaches Vermont, he finds lean-faced and mean-minded people fearful of being spoken to, the superb arbitrariness of a blond-headed kid who launches himself at the New Yorker and bites him in the back of his thigh, and Carole Lombard's Hazel—eminently healthy but swooning for New York. Wally asks her, "You've lived up here all your life?" and she groans, "Twice that long."

Knowing duplicity—let us call it acting or show business—is the only proper state of mind once exposed to Hecht's merry contempt. He admires the film's lovers because they have so few illusions yet never give up their brightness. The actors are remarkably relaxed and natural: Lombard survives the insipid color and March ignores the secondary nature of his part. Both actors took it for granted that they deserved a small fortune for the work and remained too intelligent to act smart or grand. Such playing is uniquely American in the 1930s, and if it had a model then it may have been Myron rather than David Selznick.

Wellman's direction is more astute and witty than it was in *A Star is Born*; the self-observing tough guy warmed to the caustic attitude of Hecht's script. The wrestling sequence, for example, brings out the event's flashy brutality, as well as the innocent sentimentality of its patrons. The gonged ten seconds of reverence for the dying Hazel is poignant and hilarious at the same time, as is the immediate re-forming of the tottering tower of two wrestlers and a theatrically irate referee. So many people in *Nothing Sacred* are such daft, expert fakes that the audience enjoys hurrying along with them. It is a boisterous and invigorating film, rueful about sincerity yet full of life and enthusiasm. Just because it is a vein seldom tapped by David does not mean he missed it. For the producer of this film is the person so many men and women had a good time with. Life may be a set of frauds, but showmanship keeps it smart. It is true to David's big-shot foolishness that so much of the action takes place in "his" Waldorf Hotel and that the Oliver Stone character is described as something between a Ferris wheel and a werewolf. Only Hecht could get away with this—and only this once was Hecht allowed to be funny for David.

Zenda had its last retakes as *Nothing Sacred* was shooting—the contrast is so striking. For as Woody Van Dyke was brought in to do the swordplay in one film, actors fought with barbed lines in the other. The humor in *Zenda* is schoolboyish and archaic. At the same moment, David was making pictures a generation apart in state of mind. *Zenda* cried out for color, whereas *Nothing Sacred* would be better in the glossy satanic black-and-white of *My Man Godfrey*.

Sidney Howard was back in town that summer, still hoping for a moment on *Wind*. Yet again, he and Cukor were assigned to a new last scene on *Zenda*. David rarely made it to script talks, so Cukor "keeps screaming for more dialogue from the book and I keep screaming for more action in lieu of dialogue." If Howard became truculent, David had another diversion for him: he must write a verse for the book of Irene (an album of tributes, written by friends and celebrities). Still, by early August, Howard and Cukor had a revised draft, fifteen pages longer than the first.

To celebrate, David had Howard to dinner:

> Last night I dined at the Selznicks, big and formal. I got there at 8. The host got home at 9:15. The guests were still coming in a long time after that and we sat down to table at 10:20. I drank champagne— warm champagne.

At other celebrations David came more quickly. There was a wrap party at the studio for *Nothing Sacred*. Arthur Fellows brought a pretty girl as his date, but during the course of the evening he lost her. Fearing the worst, he headed for Birdwell's bungalow and found her there, being made love to by David. The publicity bungalow was David's hideaway at the studio. There were evenings when Birdwell hired a couple of call girls for him there.

Not that Birdwell fell down on the day job. In the spirit of *Nothing Sacred*, he had the highly paid Carole Lombard announce she was delighted to pay back most of what she earned as taxes "for the good of the country." And there was her picture in the papers with the story and the plug for *Nothing Sacred*. On another occasion, Birdwell "let" Lombard run his office for a day. Then he had all thirty inhabitants of Zenda in Kansas flown in for that premiere. The stunts were blithe with the assurance that the public were idiots, no matter that David insisted they be treated like adults. But the same clash of attitudes ruled David, too. It remains a small miracle that *Nothing Sacred* captures such riot so well.

The movie cost $1.262 million—hard to believe of something so short. *Nothing Sacred* lost nearly $400,000. *The Prisoner of Zenda* cost $1.25 million and showed a profit of $182,000. Together they won large audiences and good reviews. The ostensible reputation of SIP was rising, even as internal troubles became more severe.

Nothing Sacred had spent so much money on the talent—on March, Lombard, Wellman, and Hecht. Yet Hecht was a friend who could not resist salting David's wounds. After all, said Ben, he had hardly been paid properly for having to sit on the train drinking the Whitney champagne. In July 1937, he asked his agent, Leland Hayward, to inform David of an end to their association in a way that is comic and malicious at the same time. The sarcasm could come from *Nothing Sacred*:

> Dear Leland. David quotes me entirely correctly I made a suggestion about working a week in New York. However inasmuch as I worked three and a half days on train almost constantly while tired and inasmuch as I did a week's work in New York working constantly on no less a project than invention of an original cinema masterpiece why do I only get paid for my work in New York and not for my work on train. Have been feeling that David has notion I am overpaid and inasmuch as I have notion I am receiving fifty per cent of what I can get elsewhere our notions are getting too far apart to keep married. I am being so completely underpaid for work I have done that my staying with David was ninety per cent a matter of friendship. Getting chiselled out of three and one half days pay however puts the thing on a business basis. I think we will let my definitive resignation stand. Find me a job with someone else. I want no bonus but a straight six grand a week. Moment you receive wire me Gladstone Hotel and tell David I am only good as a hired man when I have feeling that my employer realizes all the time I am being trimmed and tries not to let me know it.
>
> Love Ben.

In 1937 or so, the picture business could be a lovely racket, and even a bundle of confusion like David might believe he was as happy and smart as someone living in a movie. Later that year, Myron came to David as agent for Russell Birdwell, asking for a raise. So David wrote Myron about the raises Birdwell had had already, for all his services, and he added a grinning postscript: "Don't be so generous with ~~my~~ your our money. And don't talk any more to him about it!" David had a great smile still, and he loved to give it. For he was a generous man who could savor a momentary babe and a sharp deal while he was waiting for some Great Writer to pen an ode to Irene. Why waste a moment?

9 · NOT THE SLIGHTEST INTERFERENCE

DAVID SELZNICK was not a movie director, an auteur, one of those people given responsibility for films by critics, enthusiasts, and would-be directors. He was a producer, and no one who worked for him ever doubted that he had all the power on a project. His daily agony in slogging forward testifies to how far he felt the weight of responsibility. But the power never helped him make up his mind. His pictures need to be assessed in terms of their creative personality. But there is a similar need to see them as the weary, frustrated product of indecision, confusion, luck, and accident. Here is the flux of choices that faced David in the summer of 1937, not so much as opportunity but nightmare that would not go away.

- There was trepidation over the chances of war in Europe. In January 1937, John Wharton had passed on the opinion that "there will be no war in Europe more serious than the late Ethiopian conflict, for the next five years." But every American film enterprise feared interruption to its European business. David's pictures did well in Europe and very well in Britain: the stress on literary classics, on historic values, on costume, grace, and English acting were David's strengths. He was a pioneer of what we now call "Masterpiece Theatre." More than that, Jock Whitney liked England: he adored the Grand National steeplechase at Aintree, and he had won the Cheltenham Gold Cup in 1929 with Easter Hero; he courted English ladies; and he was appreciated by English financiers, like Oscar Deutsch, who had promised to back him in any plan to buy out United Artists.
- SIP had its own arrangement, through Pioneer, with Technicolor. In hindsight, it is obvious that color won over the entire business. But this was as vexed a topic as the likelihood of war in the late thirties. Pioneer and SIP continued to secure portions of Technicolor stock for every color film they made. And they were obliged to make two every year, swallowing what David regarded as the excessive charges imposed by Dr. Kalmus at Technicolor. The stock would prove of value only if Technicolor flourished—until that time Pioneer and SIP were subsidizing the venture, and David had his choice of projects restricted. He had seen how much

color had boosted the costs in *The Garden of Allah*. *A Star is Born* was the first real hit in color, yet from David's point of view that film could have made more profit in black-and-white. He was always urging Kalmus to get more color commitments by lowering his prices. Metro, for one, had rejected color so far. So long as color remained at such a premium it was vulnerable: "A European war, or another depression such as many experts predict, or an epidemic of severe proportion, or any one of many things which we cannot presently foresee, would make the production of Technicolor pictures impossible from a business standpoint." Technicolor was most anxious to have *Gone With the Wind* committed to its process—but David was just as reluctant to surrender that advantage. Meanwhile, the technical quality of color was improving.

- *Gone With the Wind* in Howard's revised script seemed inescapably a three- or maybe a four-hour picture—or even two pictures. Its budget was revised upward to $2.5 million.

- In March 1937, the story was leaked to the press that MGM had refused the services of Clark Gable as Rhett Butler "unless the picture is released through MGM." This was their standpoint, but the news item may have been calculated to make an impression on United Artists in its consideration of a new deal with SIP.

- There was dispute and uncertainty over SIP's contract with United Artists. This had called for the delivery of eight pictures, and it had set a distribution fee of 30 percent—i.e., U.A. kept 30 percent of their proceeds from theaters and passed the remainder back to SIP. U.A. had never made a financial advance to SIP, yet the cost of *Wind* meant that SIP needed more funding. So David urged renegotiation of the U.A. deal, and he looked to nothing higher than a 25 percent fee for the distributor. U.A. was ready to talk, and very fearful of losing pictures, but. . . .

- This renegotiation was overshadowed by the chances of new ownership of U.A.—possibly a Whitney-led group that would effectively merge SIP and U.A. and put David in charge of a new studio.

- Then there was the chance that SIP might make some other merger—with Paramount or RKO—so as to secure a stronger basis.

- In summary: no Rhett, no Scarlett, no satisfactory script, no clinching deal, but no shortage of options.

David declared eternal ties of loyalty to Jock and SIP; he could, when it was prudent, voice the wish to play fair with United Artists. But he had used subterfuge at Paramount, RKO, and Metro. Loyalty was often only a bargaining chip. He had such enemies, or opponents, at SIP as to make clear the great personal rapport with Jock. But Selznick was also bound by other ties of respect to L.B. (no matter how much he disliked the man). There was not just Gable. There was also L.B.'s admiration of David, a tribute that had overcome rivalry. And there was David's certainty that Loew's sold pictures better than anyone else.

To the end of her life, Irene puzzled over the shifting triangle of forces that involved her, her husband, and her father. "My father had been so successful," she said, "he didn't like to acknowledge success in other men." And David was the greatest rival in L.B.'s emotional life, even if the father would have denied it. Yet just because David had won Irene, he had secured L.B.'s respect. Mayer would have liked to have David as son and heir.

It is clear from asides in the business correspondence that while SIP and Metro were discussing a deal, David was also talking to L.B. Why should a son ostracize his father-in-law, especially when he had no father of his own? How could a daughter not talk to her father? How could the son-in-law not wonder what she said or worry over how much she knew of his other prospects? He did not want her to know everything—but knowing was her vocation. Irene said, angrily, that L.B. had known better than to ask her about business matters. But the anger was evidence so many years later of the strain in that discretion. No doubt Irene was excluded from many discussions between David and L.B. And she was puzzled at the strength of her hurt, just as she would have been mortified to have been the betrayer. She was so much less flexible in deals than her husband or father. She was losing faith in her intimacy with David; that was a greater blow than his infidelities. Those affairs were manageable, if kept quiet—for she did not much respect David's emotional judgment. She was dependent on her own position and reputation—her integrity. But in that small vanity, she could lose sight of David's tireless deviousness. When she discovered it, nothing less than vengeance would suffice.

And so the prowling among the several companies went on. In early July, George Schaefer of U.A. stressed to David how closely Dr. Giannini (president of U.A.) was monitoring the situation and how eager he was to keep SIP. A couple of days later, David was airing out names with Wharton "if the big deal goes through . . . I should like to see the Selznick name part of a hyphenated new name, and I know that Myron feels this even more strongly than I do. We were motivated in forming SIP largely by a desire to see the name on top once more in the business." That sudden "we" may have made Wharton marvel, for together the "we" held a very small part of SIP stock.

In August, David asked Lowell Calvert of the New York office to ask

Schaefer the U.A. opinion on doing *Wind* as two pictures. But he let Calvert know the enquiry was something of a blind requiring careful legal wording:

> As you know our present plans do not contemplate our making *Gone With the Wind* in time to be delivered as one of the pictures under our present United Artists contract. We have been cautioned by our local attorneys against any literature, etc., that might involve us in an obligation to deliver other pictures beyond those that we are planning for this group of eight. I therefore urge that you immediately ask Mr. Wharton to prepare and send some kind of letter that will specify that our authorization to make the inquiry in no way involves us with an obligation to deliver *Gone With the Wind* unless it is our eighth picture to be completed—and please note the word completed.

This is the most concrete evidence that, more than a year before the eventual deal with MGM, David had decided United Artists would not handle *Wind*. This provides one very practical reason for the delay of that big film. Some legal advice said that SIP had to deliver eight films to be in the clear—and *Made for Each Other* would be the eighth.

Merian Cooper was also conveying the invitation to take over RKO. David's reply was among his most arrogant. He said he would need $1 million personally; the home office moved to Los Angeles; "protracted trips" to Europe, South America, and the Orient "to investigate business conditions. . . . I should like in addition, of course, vacation periods—as I have no intention, from this point on, of killing myself for any job or any deal." It did occur to him to wonder, "Are the others, notably Jock, to be under contract—and if not, what is their contribution to the company in the future?" He made further sweeping conditions and again could not refrain from referring to what was talked about at Metro:

> I do not want to undertake any kind of deal . . . unless it is clearly understood that there will be not the slightest interference of any kind. I want absolute power on both production and production commitments. . . . MGM was not merely agreeable but anxious to let me have complete control over their entire production operations with no interference of any kind whatsoever.

The decision on merging with Paramount was coming to a head when, in the first week of September, Universal leaped from out of the blue, offering itself into David's hands along with $5 million in capital. That studio was in a very bad state; still, it was doing at least $15 million a year in business, so David urged Wharton to investigate further. He had himself spoken to people at Universal, and when *Gone With the Wind* was mentioned it had sent them "into spasms of excitement and into speeches of what the one picture would do for any company."

The deals with Universal, RKO, and Paramount were rejected. For the moment, indeed, nothing changed beyond some refinancing at SIP. But in September 1937, MGM had also proposed a deal with four main ingredients:

- MGM would charge a distribution fee of only 20 percent
- it would want a portion of SIP profits, to be negotiated (in the 20 to 40 percent region)
- it would lend SIP working capital, maybe as much as $2 million
- Gable would do *Gone With the Wind*

In the early fall of 1937, SIP declined that deal, too, but it remained on the table. One other possibility arose in those talks: that David leave SIP, on a long- or short-term basis, and go over to Metro to produce *Gone With the Wind* there. The SIP stockholders were not disposed to block such a move. Some believed they were paying for the jittery whims of this David O. Selznick. Trade David away and they might have simpler lives. But David had refused the Metro proposition; if L.B. would end up controlling his destiny, still he did not deserve David's soul. There was no need to settle yet.

IN 1936, SIP released two films: *Fauntleroy* and *Allah*. In 1937, there were three: *A Star is Born*, *The Prisoner of Zenda*, and *Nothing Sacred*. But in 1938, there were only two—*The Adventures of Tom Sawyer* and *The Young in Heart*. The first lost $302,000, the other $517,000. It would be going too far to say they were made simply to bring U.A.'s allotment closer to eight. *Tom Sawyer* was one of David's childhood books. He searched long and hard for Tommy Kelly to play the part. Nevertheless, neither *Sawyer* nor *Young in Heart* nor *Made for Each Other* (released in February 1939 and a loser by $292,000) is of the same quality as *Nothing Sacred* or *A Star is Born*. David had at last begun to concentrate on *Gone With the Wind*.

On October 1, 1937, he went to New York for six weeks with George Cukor. They bullied their way into Sidney Howard's schedule, no matter that he was rehearsing a play. The three men worked hard, and even Howard was impressed. The script was not finished when David went back, but Howard wrote Margaret Mitchell that he was inclined to return to Hollywood in January to finish it off.

In 1937, David's earnings amounted to $103,127, and in the ten months for which figures survive he lost over $52,000. But Irene's income was $177,443, thanks to Twentieth Century dividends of over $74,000. The gap in their net worth was growing wider. At the end of the year, David's personal account was $1,855 overdrawn. All these dealings or thoughts of deals were the gestures of a man on the borderline of debt, who every year lost more than he had paid for the rights to *Gone With the Wind*.

While in New York in October and November 1937, Irene prevailed on David to see David Levy, the child psychiatrist. There was a problem emerging with Jeffrey, who "did not seem as gloriously happy as I wanted a child of mine to be." Of course, Jeffrey was in California those six weeks. Irene saw Levy herself, and he asked to meet her husband. At first, David was too busy, but at last the session was arranged.

> David came back to the Waldorf just before dinner, in the only total rage I had ever seen him in or ever would. He was beside himself, violent and profane. I couldn't make head or tail of it. Apparently my only crime was being taken in by a fraud like that. His fury mounted until he reached the climax of the terrible things David Levy had told him: "Can you believe it? It's incredible. Me, of all people. And when you think of Pop, it's not possible. He said to me that I have rejected Jeffrey. Imagine me rejecting our son! God damn him."

A little later, Levy told Irene that David seemed to him "completely opposite" to the man she had described. We must not forget that while Jeffrey and Danny saw very little of their father, he did not have too much time for Irene. Parts of his life were closed to her, and she was beginning to feel put off by his vulgarity. The book of Irene, for instance, was both a flattering of her and something that gave her horrors. Her feelings were violent and conflicted: fifty years later she had the bound volume still, yet she began tearing it to pieces in front of me.

For Christmas 1937, Ben Hecht submitted his offering for that book. It is a masterpiece of veiled hostility, so finely balanced one is not sure where satire meets dutiful hyperbole. The piece whispers to David that he does not quite like Irene:

> Dear David, Irene's eyes midnight roses. Hair is memory of Sheba. Body like exclamation point astride panther. Smile moonflash in Baghdad, teeth faraway angels marching in light of dreams. Am reminded Salome incident when Irene enters room also recall Egyptian barge when Irene enters taxi. Certain Irene's heart is Chinese bowl full of mignonette. Sincerely hope lovely archaic charm survives motion picture industry. Please believe memory of Irene is hill top temple in which many friends hang garlands. Can think of no better person to play Scarlett O'Hara. Forgot to mention Irene's wisdom. Solomon winks behind her words. My love and wonder she is still married to you.

10 · IT HAS BEEN OBVIOUS

THERE WERE FORCES at SIP gathering against David. Wharton, Francis Altstock, and Leonard Case were raised in law or finance, servants to the Whitney empire, suspicious of show business, much too careful ever to appear anti-Semitic, disturbed by David, and certain Jock was being beguiled. By January 1938, they could point to the mounting debt of the company, the diminishing product and increasing overhead, but they had not been able to rid their lives of the endless memoranda in which D.O.S. argued with himself.

None of them ever attacked David for this or for anything else. (Jock's affection ensured their dainty steps.) But the SIP memos and letters are notable for their clarity and practical sense and for their lack of emotion. Assemble the entire correspondence, and it is easy to feel the intrusion of David's emotional assertions. The more uneasy or threatened David felt, the more strenuously he argued in his own defense and the more blindly he wandered into cul-de-sacs of self-contradiction. No wonder David loved Jock, for Whitney took the memos without protest or demur.

On January 21, Leonard Case conspired with Altstock about priming Wharton for a decisive attack: "Inasmuch as you believe that the Company has now reached the point where hardheaded management is not only mandatory but is likely to receive the consideration that has long been due it, I

David and Jock: the pose says no, the eyes check the amount.

am setting forth a program which the management should follow in working out Company policy. There is nothing startling included in this outline, and in fact, there is nothing in it which is new to any well managed company."

David was not mentioned. Case proceeded as if the company made celluloid strip. But his most cogent point was to demonstrate that at a 30 percent distribution fee, there was no chance of profit if a black-and-white picture cost more than $845,000 or a color picture more than $870,000.

A month later, this preparation led to a memo from Wharton to Jock (without a copy to D.O.S.), offered as a suggestion but full of withering understatement: "The suggested policy is based upon the thesis that the Company cannot exist without production." At that moment, SIP had only one film in first-run release, *The Adventures of Tom Sawyer*, and nothing at all in production. Wharton's proposals were meant to stimulate production, but he allowed the need "to leave the Company free to really shut down its operations in case it is impossible to find satisfactory production material." A year before *Wind* started shooting, therefore, SIP was considering closure.

Wharton proposed economies, including disposing of Jenia Reissar (the London office) and a 20 percent pay reduction for Henry Ginsberg, Dan O'Shea, and Ernie Scanlon at Culver City. He wanted to fire William Wright and Val Lewton, and he was inclined not to renew the option on Jack Cosgrove in the special effects department. In general, he reckoned the California people—the coast idlers—had got off too easily for too long.

At this very moment, the coalition of disapproval had strange reinforcement. In the February issue of *Vogue* there was a drawing by Cecil Beaton used to illustrate an article on New York society by Frank Crowninshield. The drawing was a whirling montage of small details: the doorway to El Morocco, musicians, socialites and cocktails, newspapers, a camera, a telephone, a box of flowers, and so on. But Walter Winchell had looked very closely (he recommended a magnifying glass) at the newspaper and found:

> Cholly asks: Why?? is Mrs. Selznick such a social wow? Why is Mrs. Goldwyn such a wow? . . .
>
> . . . Mr. R. Andrew's Ball at the El Morocco brought out all the damned kikes in town.

Under heavy attack, Beaton had no passable explanation. He said it was done "unconsciously," yet if Winchell had needed a glass to see it then surely Beaton had had to do the writing with as much deliberation. He apologized and said he was not anti-Jewish, but Condé Nast required his resignation. In his diary, Beaton told himself, "if there is any possible explanation these quotes contained my subconscious momentary irritation at having seen so many bad Hollywood films."

He was not alone in that urge for vengeance. It is not the silliest notion of the twentieth century that Hollywood pictures have stilled thought and misled idealism. Hollywood fascinated and appalled, and nowhere was the battle more marked than in society, New York or elsewhere. All manner of people had been asking what Jock Whitney saw in the Selznicks.

Beaton had not doodled in the dark. He knew in England there were rumors that some homosexual affinity explained the unlikely closeness of David and Jock. As one who knew real homosexuals who had to be careful of exposure, Beaton felt bitterly toward two big boys horning in on the cult without paying the dues. And Beaton was a stylist, an aesthete who scorned most Hollywood movies and despised the attitude among their makers that they might be art instead of business.

Irene was one of Hollywood's most self-conscious hostesses, moving up in the social world, learning from Dorothy Paley and exulting in the company of the Whitneys. "Having" the Whitneys was a trump in her lifelong contest with Edie—this feud seemed to Katharine Hepburn "horrible, disgusting—they neither of them knew how spoiled they were or how they expected everything just so."

Irene was now a forbidding beauty of thirty, suspicious of others' intrigues yet devoutly given to her own. She took herself very seriously—and liked to laugh at others. She was deliberately mysterious and seductive, yet unavailable, both repressed and repressive, a flirt, an actress, sometimes a drunk, and a talker on the telephone by the hour. She was the center of

Irene—epitome, arbiter, and empress, for a moment

her own play, a character, idiosyncratic and so very smart it remained odd that she understood herself so little. Grant all those traits and it is no wonder she earned silent rebuke and hostility in some quarters, to say nothing of the judgment that, elegance, wit, and intelligence aside, she remained L.B.'s daughter.

Irene said there was never anything but friendship between David and Jock. She would fall asleep hearing them playing ping-pong downstairs, wagering kings' ransoms on every game, cronies caught up in the enthusiasm of making movies. David could never understand Jock's passion for "dames": he asked Irene, "How can you listen?" In his odd, hero-worshiping way, he did not wish to think Jock was like all the other guys—or like him.

As Joseph Mankiewicz saw it, "David just wanted to *be* Jock Whitney—his money, his style, his entrée." For Jock was American royalty, and David's films were steadfastly royalist. Of all the WASPs David could like, Jock was one of the most modest. He was a sportsman, but he was as shy as . . . Maxim de Winter in *Rebecca*. He personified David's idea of the well-born, gentle man.

Nevertheless, Jock could not ignore the reasoned objections of his trusted employees. He talked to David about economies and the need for more pictures. In conversation, David agreed. Then he withdrew, reflected, and delivered an eight-page memo that renewed his faith in a few pictures of unsurpassed excellence. He now said his time had been absorbed by building the organization, working out distribution, the *Wind* script, future material, learning color. David concluded that only a quarter of his time had gone on actual picture production. This was directly contrary to Wharton's complaint that the pictures monopolized David.

Jock had also argued that nothing was hurting SIP more than David's procrastination with scripts. David had the nerve now to use his faults as his best defense: "psychology and experience tell us it takes longer to complete a script in advance of production than it does to pound out sequences against a deadline." He launched into the virtues of "seeing the picture on the screen as it grew" and writing to keep up with it:

> There is, in fact, a great deal to be said for the method of developing a picture as it is shooting—creating it as you go along, getting the feel of the characters, seeing them come to life, etc. Thalberg invariably worked with this method, with such outstanding success that it isn't necessary to mention it. . . . I do not believe some of my pictures would have been comparably as good as they were but for this method. Even in such a picture as *The Prisoner of Zenda*, no matter how complete the script had been, it would have had to go into considerable rewrite after seeing Colman and Carroll perform, as was proven by the necessity of retakes on scenes which we had thought final.

One wonders whether Whitney checked any of this with the writers. In January, Sidney Howard was back in Hollywood: he had three good sessions with David (learning that "colour is now on the wane. . . . The talk, according to Selznick, is to lay off all further pictures in Technicolor and to wait for the perfection of the Eastman process"). Apart from that, he had many lunches with Cukor, "continued failure at Irene Selznick poem," and further postponement of *Wind*. He was in conference once at Summit Drive with David when the butler entered. " 'Oh, Farr,' says David, 'remind me to go back on thyroid in the morning.' "

There were these other pictures that kept slipping in ahead of *Wind*. Charles Bennett, an Englishman, was hired to write *The Young in Heart*. He had worked on several of Alfred Hitchcock's English pictures, and he was urged over the Atlantic by the Myron Selznick Agency. In the course of their work, Bennett found himself in sessions not just with David, but with William Wright and Lewis Milestone, who actually directed some of the movie that is credited to Richard Wallace. David asked Bennett how good Hitchcock was and what about another English director, Robert Stevenson, who had directed *Tudor Rose*? Which should he hire? "Both of them," said the ebullient Bennett. The work on *The Young in Heart* went well enough, with people being marooned at the studio because of floods. But Bennett knew David was not for him:

> I would come to the studio about ten o'clock in the morning. I'd work—things I had to do. Then, about half-past five, David would say to me, "Charles, I'd like to have a little chat about the script, the way it's coming. I'll get dinner sent in from the Brown Derby." I said, "Fine, fine." We'd sit there, and we'd have dinner—and I'd done a day's work already. Then we'd start to chat. About five o'clock in the morning, we'd *still* be chatting. I think David took things. Then the lovely thing was that, having spent the entire night talking about the picture, discussing it, discussing social life, too, David would say, "Well, Charles, I think this has been very rewarding. I won't be in till about noon. Do you think you could have on paper what we've talked about?" Bright as a whip. Always ahead of you, too. If you came up with a thought, he'd say, "Yes!" and develop it right then. Wonderful. But as regards working with him—it was murder!

David was earnestly intent on getting Hitchcock as a director. He screened his English thrillers; he sought the advice of Jenia Reissar and Kay Brown, but he felt that Myron was being so greedy, so neglectful, and so arrogant that the deal was in jeopardy. There were others interested in Hitchcock, and Myron was making a cockfight of it, allowing David to believe there had been a large offer from RKO. David got angry with Myron: "With any other agent we would raise unholy hell about such tactics

... they simply got our backs up and made us that much tougher in dealing for Hitchcock."

At the same time, another European was being drawn toward Selznick. From London, Jenia Reissar had recommended a Swedish film, *Intermezzo*, and its young actress, Ingrid Bergman. As it happened, a Swedish elevator man at 230 Park Avenue (the SIP/Whitney offices) had also been urging the movie on Kay Brown and her assistant, Elsa Neuberger. They got hold of a print; they liked it and sent it to Culver City. By August 1938, David had decided on a remake—with the Swedish director, Gustaf Molander, and with the actress (though her name would probably need changing).

That same year—in the spring of 1938—Val Lewton read the galleys of a forthcoming novel, *Rebecca*, and encouraged his boss to look at the book. David was immediately struck by its insecure and romantic heroine.

The horizons were always crowded for David. But that summer he was within reach of two of the most important people he would employ in the next few years. And in all the haste, the panic, and the mind-changing, he did recognize the talent of Hitchcock and Bergman.

However, there was another deal made in August 1938, more immediate and more lastingly important.

In March 1938, Warner Brothers released *Jezebel*, with Bette Davis. This was based on a play, by Owen Davis, that had a New York run in the winter of 1933–34. The story was set in New Orleans, but the heroine, Julie Marston, was lovely, headstrong, selfish, passionate. Bette Davis, until the end of her days, was one of those American women who knew she should have played Scarlett O'Hara. "It could have been written for me," she asserted in her 1962 autobiography, *The Lonely Life*. She had fretted when Warners gave up its option on the Margaret Mitchell book. "I was as perfect for Scarlett as Clark Gable was for Rhett. And many knew that. . . . It was insanity that I was not given Scarlett. But then, Hollywood has never been rational."

Who can doubt that the imperious Davis would have been remarkable as Scarlett—stronger, more willful and dangerous than Paulette Goddard or Joan Bennett, leading contenders late in 1938. We know as much from *Jezebel*, a black-and-white film only (despite its scarlet dress), directed by William Wyler. Miss Davis won her second Oscar as Julie Marston. If she had any handicap as Scarlett it was that she was famous already. (Another contender, Katharine Hepburn, also reckoned Davis would have made Scarlett too "unpleasant.")

Jezebel was made in David's time of delay, and Warners relished its own opportunism. It is also possible that Bette Davis welcomed the part because nothing could more forcefully demonstrate her case. The April *Redbook* ran a verse that drew attention to the comedy of *Jezebel*'s outflanking Selznick:

Hurry, Miss Mitchell, and mend your failing wall;
Weep, Mr. Selznick, weep from your wailing wall.
For rumors go forth by word of mouth
That a whirlwind blows from a different South—
Another vixen with velvet claws,
A forward woman as ever was,
A Jeze-belle gayer than all the others:
But the hussy belongs to the Warner Brothers.

David did not weep. But he tried to frighten Jack Warner into thinking *Jezebel* would be "damned as an imitation by the millions of readers, and lovers, of *Gone With the Wind*." There were several cheeky lifts of talk and business from the Mitchell novel. Yet it was the overall resemblance that was most striking. Warner was nonchalant in response; he sent David a copy of the Owen Davis play and thanked him for his "splendid interest."

No one was prepared to get too angry, for that spring there was a chance SIP might make its *Wind* with Warners. In June, David suggested to O'Shea that the company should let Warners have a project SIP owned, *The Drunkard*, "building up our list of favors to them toward the Errol Flynn loan." For Warners might fill both lead parts, with Flynn and Davis? In her book, Davis said the idea of Flynn as Rhett "appalled" her. So she refused the arrangement, just as it was George Cukor at SIP who was voting against her.

Actors were often passions and pretexts. In March 1938, David had felt that *Wind* must start shooting by June 1. He was then set on Gary Cooper for Rhett and, since Cooper was a property of Sam Goldwyn, he told Jock to "make clear to Mr. Goldwyn that there is no chance whatsoever of our distributing the picture through United Artists unless . . . we are to have Gary Cooper for the lead."

In May, Metro reentered the competition—if it had ever been away. David's calendar shows steady discussions throughout 1938. On January 10, there had been a meeting of David, Jock, Myron, L.B., Al Lichtman, and Eddie Mannix, a group of major powers with only *Wind* to consider. Myron's presence shows how vital a part of SIP he was. In February, Myron was asked by his brother to be in touch with Gable. By March 28, David was talking to L.B. about directors, and in April he was having Marcella draw up an "MGM calendar" for him to keep track of the availability of people there. The notes are all that exist, but contingencies were being explored as to other directors and actresses for Scarlett *if* Gable was ready to be Rhett. In early May, David went over to the Metro lot four times in seven days.

On May 27, L.B. made a personal call to David and wondered whether

SIP would consider selling *Wind* with its script and David's services as a package. SIP could expect a cut on the profits. David passed this news on to Whitney immediately, and it is impossible to tell how surprised he was by it, or how far it was a pressure play on Whitney and the other SIP stockholders. In fact, Jock was actively arranging for more money for SIP, and by then he was the only stockholder brave enough to offer it.

David had told L.B. that SIP could not shut down, to which Mayer had replied, with the two premises so close, couldn't David do *Wind* at Metro and then go down the street to handle SIP business? Selznick admired the system at MGM, and he told Jock that maybe he *could* make the picture better there.

David was agonizing. But, emotionally, he had decided to make the picture at, or with, MGM. Another huge memo went to Whitney early in June. The analysis showed that SIP by then had $394,000 invested in *Wind*, and Metro was offering $900,000 for the package. Cukor was part of the deal, on paper, but MGM preferred its own Woody Van Dyke as director. David would be paid $100,000 as producer. Metro would do the picture in Technicolor, thus ensuring more stock options for SIP.

"It breaks my heart to have the company sell the property," David told Jock. He believed other financing was possible, what with the bank loan Jock was trying for (at least $1 million) and a cash advance being talked about from United Artists. Above all, David still didn't know how the finished picture would fare.

> If the picture is a financial success, we might make $500,000 or $2,500,000—who knows? It is dependent upon the quality of the picture, conditions at the time of its release, whether the public interest in it is still hot or has cooled off, whether a war starts in Europe, and any other number of factors. . . . It is anybody's guess. . . . If we make the picture, my hair will turn white worrying about not merely its production but also its exhibition and exploitation and sales all over the world, for a period of two or even three years. If we sell the picture, my hair will merely turn gray producing it.

The discussions with Metro had been David and L.B. talking together, but David assumed Mayer could get Nick Schenck's approval in a minute. David did not want to take the SIP decision alone, and he feared, down the road, that some stockholder would complain. "Most of all, I want to avoid even the slightest suspicion that I have sold out to my father-in-law. Let them face the fact now that he is my father-in-law, and forever hold their peace."

The "deal" under consideration favored MGM, even in 1938. For a flat fee it would have the film *and* its natural producer. Had David made it under those circumstances (back and forth along Washington Boulevard), he would have been left high and dry by the film's success. No wonder Whitney argued for keeping the property and a part of the profits. That David had so easily let profits go suggests either that he was blind to all else except doing the film or that there was a further, private deal with L.B.

Whitney made SIP stand up as the originating party, not a supplicant. In the six weeks that followed, MGM and Warners were pitted against each other. A chart was drawn up of the terms the two studios offered. But now the deal was one in which SIP made the film. The vital parts of the chart are as follows:

Item	MGM	Warners
RHETT	Clark Gable at $150,000	Errol Flynn at $50,000
SCARLETT		Bette Davis "if we wish"
OTHER PARTS		Olivia de Havilland for Melanie
FINANCE	$1.25 million	Up to $2.1 million
DISTRIBUTION FEE	20 percent	17½ percent
PROFITS	50 percent	27.7 percent
BILLING	Joint presentation of MGM & SIP	SIP
SIP OVERHEAD	22½ percent	22½ percent
D.O.S. FEE	$100,000	$100,000
DIRECTOR	Probably Cukor agreeable, but not yet agreed to by MGM, who desire Fleming, Conway, or Van Dyke	Cukor or anyone else SIP selects
LENGTH	15,000 feet	At SIP discretion
ADVERTISING	Consultation, but final MGM approval	Complete approval
PRINT COSTS	SIP	SIP to certain limitation: then shared
OVERAGE COSTS	SIP—recouped only out of its share of profits	SIP up to $250,000—recouped out of 82½ percent of gross
RISK OF LOSS	50-50	50-50

Warners had three players and $850,000 more than Metro to put up. Its distribution fee was lower; other items were less tough. Only in the matter of profits—and with Gable—was it less appealing. However, David had a justified belief that Loew's would do a more effective job of marketing the film.

On July 20, David talked to Nick Schenck personally; he and O'Shea went over to Metro for lunch on the following day. The final deal memorandum—with Metro—was signed on August 9. But talks with Jack Warner and Errol Flynn went on till the end. Warners had even prepared jubilant announcements in which Miss Margaret Mitchell appeared to smile on the casting. Notably, David's office calendar includes no calls with Bette Davis. When the real announcement was made, it came from Jock:

> It has been obvious from the day Mr. Selznick bought *Gone With the Wind* that the public has felt an enormous concern in the bringing of this great book to the screen. As a company, we have been through a trying and difficult time involving unusual delay in order to satisfy this genuine interest. Mr. Selznick has felt all along that Clark Gable was the one and only "people's choice" to play the part of Rhett Butler, and only through an arrangement with Metro-Goldwyn-Mayer, to whom he is exclusively under contract, would he have been able to make *Gone With the Wind* as the world wants to see it.

The contract was drawn up. Metro would distribute. SIP would have Gable and $1.25 million. But if the budget went over $2.5 million, SIP was responsible for it, no matter that the profits on distribution were to be split fifty-fifty after Loew's had taken a 20 percent distribution fee. The contract was to run for seven years from the day of first release; thereafter, the film would belong 75 percent to SIP and 25 percent to Metro.

The contract was signed on August 25 by David and Al Lichtman, vice president of Loew's Inc. and an old employee of Lewis J. Selznick. But in the photograph, these two signatories stood, looking on, while Gable and L.B. admired the paper. By the terms of Gable's limited availability, the picture had to start no later than January 1939.

11 · THE BEST SCARLETT THAT SHOWS UP

THE NOVEL MADE CLEAR in its first words that "Scarlett O'Hara was not beautiful." But what did that matter if "men seldom realized it when caught by her charm"? Charm on the page became publicity in the late 1930s: the renown of the uncast screen Scarlett rivaled that of any actress. Astrologers offered their advice to David Selznick. Unknowns turned up at 1050

Summit Drive, and on the other side of America they sought the approval of Margaret Mitchell. Fans wrote in with suggestions, and SIP kept the score carefully. By the end of July 1938, there were 300 votes for Ann Sheridan, 228 for Miriam Hopkins, 58 for Joan Crawford, and 61 for Katharine Hepburn—not one of whom ever tested for the part.

There were plenty of tests done for Scarlett: thirty-five actresses, celebrities, or curiosities gave it a shot, and the tests on the whole film cost somewhere in the range of $80,000 to $100,000. But few established stars were willing to put themselves in public jeopardy of being turned down. David had often said he wanted a newcomer, and so most of those tested were little known and inexperienced. Only one unequivocal star tested— Jean Arthur—and then not until December 17, 1938.

Edythe Marrener tested in December 1937: she was a New York model, nineteen years old, and seen modeling hats by Irene. It was a lovely test, for a novice, and Miss Marrener would have a career, as Susan Hayward. Margaret Tallichet tested in March 1938 (with Kent Taylor as her Rhett), but her chief life in pictures would be as Mrs. William Wyler. George Cukor was involved in many of these auditions and tests, and he was generous in his enthusiasms. On February 11, 1938, he told David:

> It might interest you to know that Frances Dee reads absolutely thrillingly with great temperament and fire. She is a most accomplished and technically efficient actress. I have only one reservation about her for Scarlett, which we will see in the test—has she the shallow external minx quality that Mrs. Chaplin realizes so brilliantly in private life?

Mrs. Chaplin was, or was assumed to be, Paulette Goddard. She made three tests that February, two silent and one with sound, with James Craig as Rhett, all directed by Cukor. Paulette was the Selznicks' neighbor on Summit Drive, where she lived with Charlie Chaplin. Irene and David both liked "Sugar," though Irene scolded her for "borrowing" her favorite skin-colored bathing suit. Jock Whitney had sometimes taken Paulette out on the town. Her arrangement with Chaplin was vague. Paulette was one of Charlie's discoveries. He had put her in *Modern Times* (only the fourth film she had made, in 1936, and her first big part). Were she and Chaplin married? The question had different answers—silence, maybe, or yes; yes on a boat off the China coast or yes on Catalina island. But, in fact, by 1937–38, Chaplin had lost interest in Paulette except as a property. So she had a few romances, and she signed a contract with SIP for the lead in *The Young in Heart*.

"At first, we treated it as a joke," said Irene—the idea of Paulette the flirty, wicked-eyed neighbor, so full of mischief, as an actress, let alone as

Scarlett. But Paulette had Myron as her agent, and he was working hard for her. She was taking acting lessons from Constance Collier. Her tests were funny, full of energy; she was at least a possible. It was never certain for more than a few days at a time whether Chaplin would permit David to exploit her career. Paulette herself changed her mind, turned down roles, and schemed for others. She was not exactly a beginner, and Russell Birdwell reported that Paulette had been born with the name Levy, not in 1911 but in 1904. A Jewish Scarlett?

Cukor could not do all the tests himself, for at last David had pushed him into work. By January 25, 1938, David was horrified to learn that Cukor had received $155,000 in salary from SIP for some testing, some research, and the tours of the South. And his contract option renewal was up on February 10. There was already the beginning of ill feeling at such comfortable waiting. Cukor could say he had been preparing, and doing his best, while David delayed. But Cukor had also politely declined to do *A Star is Born* or *Tom Sawyer*. Then, early in 1938, David loaned him out for two quick films—to Columbia, for *Holiday*, and to Paramount, for *Zaza* (the one at $10,000 a week, and the other at $8,333—which meant that SIP picked up about $4,000 to $6,000 a week). In his enforced absence, an assistant did some of the *Wind* tests, but Cukor joked about the strain of making *Holiday* while thinking Rhett and Scarlett:

> Incidentally, this working in two studios is pretty tough going. In the mornings I roll around the floor saying "Rhett! Rhett! I am afraid of dying and going to hell." In the afternoons I am in my high comedy mood for Harry Cohn.

Katharine Hepburn was the star in *Holiday*, and she and her favorite director talked about Scarlett. Hepburn had called in at the studio on March 9, and she visited again on May 5. In that spring of 1938 there were serious overtures from both sides, no matter that David had decided to test her "only if we are stuck." The actress had said that if she could play Scarlett, she was prepared to commit herself to other films—it was David's intention always to get future pictures from the winning actress. In 1990, she said she had offered herself if David couldn't get anyone else. He reckoned in 1938 he could get her for $80,000—but "I am frankly not very excited by the prospect." Surely Cukor was encouraging the casting, for David said that he would look at *Holiday*: "I think this may have a large effect upon our decision as to whether or not we should do anything with Hepburn."

Talks went on into the fall, and a contract was actually drawn up, with Hepburn taking advice from Leland Hayward (her agent) and Howard Hughes. She was agreeing to SIP having an option on her for Scarlett for fifteen weeks' work at $1,500 a week. But whenever David talked to her, he got "a swift pain. . . . The more I see her, the colder I get on her." There was always talk of Hepburn doing a test, with David insisting on scenes "that require the most sex." By the end of November, the hesitant deal was broken off. Dan O'Shea told David that according to Hughes, Hepburn "now feels that any established actress who takes the part is sticking her neck out in that if she is less than sensational she will get nothing out of it but a lot of criticism. She further feels that we are not enthusiastic enough about her for the part."

Fifty-two years later, Hepburn said, "I could have done it, but I would have been acting. I was too strong for it. George said I was too noble." (The fact remains that Hepburn had delayed the stage debut of *The Philadelphia Story* in case Scarlett came her way.)

There were other tests in the course of the year: Anita Louise, Nancy Coleman, Shirley Logan, the eighteen-year-old Lana Turner, and four times, between October 17 and December 8, Doris Jordan. Before Vivien Leigh, this Doris Jordan gave the most intelligent, varied, and emotional reading. She was another model, discovered in New York. Cukor worked hard with her and David thought she was sexy—"I frankly would much rather see someone like Jordan play it if her performance is two-thirds as good as that of Hepburn." Miss Jordan did go on. She changed her name to Davenport and played the female lead opposite Gary Cooper in *The Westerner*.

There were other problems. In the middle of October, David had gone off to Bermuda to settle the script, angry that Sidney Howard would not break other arrangements to join him. By then neither man had much humor for the other. In place of Howard, David took Jo Swerling. But as soon as he returned, he called for Oliver Garrett. As start day drew nearer, the quantity of writers multiplied, and it was all the newcomer could do to digest the masses of material accumulated in the previous two years:

> It may be that Garrett will give us good enough scratch dialogue that, together with our efforts to use Mitchell dialogue wherever possible, even transposing it from scenes in the book that we are not using to our originally created scenes, will mean that the whole thing will not involve more than 100 lines of dialogue. However, it may turn out to be more extensive than I personally anticipate.

The panic was building and with it the desperate confidence that he could do more and more. David was tormented—by the untidiness of the script and the continued failure of Scarlett to appear. But he was exhilarated, too, for the picture was moving ahead without many distractions. SIP had not released a film since February. *Young in Heart* opened on November 3, and

Made for Each Other was in the editing stages. But David gave less than his usual attention to those pictures. William Cameron Menzies had made great progress with the production design of *Wind*. Walter Plunkett and his staff were doing costumes, and Ray Klune was beginning to build sets. There were many other parts to fill beyond that of Scarlett.

As the mania increased, so David's horniness became more urgent. Scrutinizing young women for Scarlett was not single-minded. For the producer always ready to make a pass and have a clumsy twenty-minute seduction in the office, it surely helped that so many of the women were outsiders and novices. How often did this occur? Evelyn Keyes, who got the part of Scarlett's younger sister, Suellen, was chased around the office once "in a rather obligatory fashion." It was not the frequency of screwing that inspired him, but the power that might command it. Finding Scarlett was a meat market for the imagination, a daydream for any emperor of the erotic. Bring on new girls! he ordered Marcella on November 12, fresh from Bermuda:

> While it is almost too late, I think that for the remaining time Mr. Cukor should set aside an hour daily during which he will interview applicants personally. Actually, if the thing were organized properly as many as fifty girls could be in and out of his office in an hour. . . . I feel that our failure to find a new girl for Scarlett is the greatest failure of my entire career.

What did Irene know? What did she allow herself to notice or be seen noticing? Ignorance was a shaky defense of dignity with a man as accident-prone as David or as determined to confess. Nineteen thirty-eight was a bad year for the marriage. There had been rumors and incidents, like the night at a party when David accosted Loretta Young—who, he said, was a Scarlett candidate, too:

> David loved the ladies, and he wanted his cake and eat it too. One night, he had had a bit to drink and he said, "Give me a kiss good night, Loretta." And I said, "No thanks, David, I know all about you." Anyway, David was strong and he pulled me by the shoulders and pushed me against the wall and said, "Give me a kiss, right now!" I said, "David, for God's sake, don't be an idiot." And Irene appears and says, "Oh, honey, give him a kiss. It's not going to hurt you. Give David a kiss." It took the silliness out of it.

But one night in June 1938 at dinner at the Chaplin house, David had met Joan Fontaine, the sister of Olivia de Havilland. She was nearly twenty-one, blond, lovely, the ingenue of a couple of pictures, English in her manner, very entertaining and very smart. She told him how much she loved the book *Rebecca*. What a coincidence, said David, I just bought it! Isn't that a coincidence? said she. (The wide-eyed look comes from never blinking for the camera.) Irene, if she was there that night, had no clever way of breaking it up. By June 21, David had ordered a screening of *Maid's Night Out*, Fontaine's latest B picture from RKO. As his biggest movie came closer, David would discover another complication—the face for his next one.

THERE WAS another possibility that faced David in the second half of 1938—it was aborted, and it is hardly known in film history; yet—if it had succeeded—it might have altered the affairs of the Selznick family.

Myron attempted to go into production. His plan was for production companies centered on leading directors or actors in which the talent would be producers, too, taking part of the profits of their films. This was the future of movies, and it was something against which L.B. had organized opposition in 1931.

In July 1938, Myron announced a plan to work with Ernst Lubitsch, who had just resigned from Paramount. In the next couple of months, similar schemes were proposed with Carole Lombard, William Powell, and Janet Gaynor as the featured attractions. *Variety* reported another scheme on

Myron and the ladies: Irene, Rosalind Russell, Loretta Young, Merle Oberon

Myron's part for George Raft, who was at that time under suspension by Paramount.

In all these cases, the stars would get "minimum compensation" against a part of the eventual profits. Today, this is called "participation," but in the late thirties hardly anyone enjoyed it. The trade press noted the plan was in line with reforms favored by Roosevelt himself. There were stirrings against monopoly in the movie business, but they were urged in Washington and New York. That same summer, in the Southern District of New York, the United States brought a proceeding in equity against eight motion picture companies (headed by Paramount) that alleged conspiracy against the Sherman Antitrust Act to control the production, distribution, and exhibition of movies.

This was the beginning of more than ten years of court process (much delayed by war) that would lead, in 1949, to the key decision whereby the majors had to sell off their theaters. But in 1938, for Myron, there was some promise of riding the bandwagon of official disapproval of the picture business. It was an idea ahead of its time—and the principle by which movie fortunes are now made by stars, directors, and agents.

By August 10 (the day after the *Wind* deal with Metro), David was telling Henry Ginsberg that SIP should do all it could to offer a studio "home" to Myron's venture. This was the spreading of overhead that SIP needed, though David was anxious that they be tough with Myron—"be careful that we do not make a deal with him that could be criticized by any of our stockholders."

Myron *was* one of those stockholders, and he and David were once more in a kind of collusion that David was shy of spelling out. However, David was a producer and just as vulnerable as all the other studios to a revolution in which stars and directors owned their films. He might wish to back his brother; he might want SIP's economy to be helped—yet he had no desire to lead the business into free agency.

That was Myron's dream—after all, if the talent benefited, so did he. *The New York Times* called the idea "one of the most startling developments in the picture industry in years." All the old antagonisms regathered, and they were still led by the L.B. who was now a partner to David Selznick.

Myron had a debut picture lined up: it was to be Lubitsch's *The Shop Around the Corner*, starring Dolly Haas. By the end of September, Lubitsch moved onto the SIP lot to begin preproduction. Then everything came apart. Myron failed in the attempt to secure guaranteed distribution. In other words, Paramount, Twentieth Century, Universal, Warners, Metro, and all the other outfits refused to carry his pictures. How the pressure was brought to bear is not clear, just as it is not certain what role David played.

On October 5, Myron wrote an "Open Letter to the Dictators" to Joe Schenck, Mayer, Zanuck, "et al." It was amused and resigned—"I really must congratulate you on your maneuvering abilities and on your foresight." But was Myron laughing it off or too proud to show the damage? Some press comment said the whole thing had been a ploy to get a better contract for William Powell at Metro. That sounds like Myron's sardonic self-defense. The scheme was simple, brilliant, and lethal—its defeat was a step in Myron's decline. So he made it another proof of the world's absurdity:

> In all fairness [he told the Dictators], I must admit that you warned me repeatedly that the day would come when I would learn that I was on the wrong side, and that a future on the producers' side of the fence would, in the long run, prove a good deal more dependable and profitable. Perhaps you were right.
>
> In the face of seeming defeat, I argue in justification of my error that you producers collectively are a lot smarter than my trembling and subservient colleagues in the agency business. It's pretty tough to have the Balkans for your only support.

The dismay showed only in the drinking. If David had been weak, it did not deter Myron. In two months, he would give the kid the best Christmas present he ever had.

In Europe, another actress was plotting her way toward David. Something will turn up, he had reassured Irene. When Ed Sullivan took him to task in the New York *Daily News* for messing up *Gone With the Wind* in delays and false starts, David told him the film had to start when Gable was done with *Idiot's Delight*. "And the best Scarlett that shows up by that time will play the role willy-nilly." It was a gambler's attitude (David lost close to another $60,000 in 1938) and not that great a gamble if he had Paulette Goddard, Jean Arthur, Joan Bennett, and Doris Jordan still to choose from.

He was not blessed or secretly protected. He did not know Vivien Leigh was coming. Why is that sure? Because he could never have kept quiet about it, before or afterward. If it had been his trick, he would have boasted, but it was—from his point of view—true luck, that thing gamblers take for granted, even if they seldom encounter it. That does not mean there was no intrigue: the lady had a plan, a vision, and an agent. She was also very like Scarlett: she was conniving and ruthless.

In the early spring of 1938, in London, Vivien Leigh had filmed *St. Martin's Lane*, with Charles Laughton. She had left her husband, Leigh Holman, and her four-year-old daughter, Suzanne, and moved in with Laurence Olivier. That summer, the couple were motoring in France when, at Vence, they encountered old friends—John Gielgud and Hugh Beaumont ("Binkie"), the theatrical manager. Binkie was homosexual, but he often declared that if anyone could have changed his nature it was Vivien. He adored her and understood her ambitions. He knew Vivien had had Angus McBean photograph her in the mood and look—as London dreamed it—of Scarlett's South. The four of them lunched in Vence, and Beaumont told her, "You want to play Scarlett, Vivien—then you need an American agent."

Vivien had an agent, John Gliddon in London, and so she went to him and suggested he be affiliated with the Myron Selznick Agency. This was in September 1938. Yet Myron Selznick's office in Los Angeles had been keeping track of Vivien for nearly two years and indicating that Olivier would work in America only if Vivien got a role. That coverage considered the likelihood of Vivien playing in *Wuthering Heights*—just as it wondered about Olivier for Ashley Wilkes.

William Wyler, the prospective director for *Wuthering Heights*, dined with Olivier and Leigh. Olivier wanted Vivien to be cast as Cathy in the Brontë picture Wyler was doing for Goldwyn—but the best Wyler could offer was the role of Isabella. He was annoyed that Vivien only wanted to talk about how the search for Scarlett was going.

On September 13, Vivien opened in the play *Serena Blandish* for an eight-week run. At the same time, Gliddon received an offer to her from Cecil B. DeMille to appear in *Union Pacific* at $2,000 a week for seven weeks. The Myron Selznick office had nothing to do with this proposition, and Vivien turned it down. She had a movie contract with Alexander Korda, but DeMille said that could be worked out. Vivien said no. When Gliddon argued, she said she was really a stage actress not much concerned about money. She waited; she was a gambler, too. But in Myron's files there was a copy of a letter from Vivien to Wyler (August 31, 1938): "Forgive me for being difficult but I find myself in such an awkward spot. Afraid I can't make things any easier."

On November 5, Vivien put Olivier on the *Normandie* at Southampton on his way to Goldwyn and *Wuthering Heights*. It was a lovers' parting, full of anguish and kisses, but it was also two actors going their separate ways. Years later, Olivier would write that when Vivien followed him to California it was for Scarlett, in part, but first and foremost, "pure, driving, uncontainable, passionate love, which to my joy she shared strongly enough to make the journey as speedily as possible." But Binkie Beaumont paid for her passage on the *Queen Mary*, set to arrive in New York on December 1. She traveled as a "Mrs. V. M. Hollman," according to Myron's files. One of the office people met her at the docks and took her straight to the airport for the 9:10 p.m. American Airlines flight to the coast. She had told John Gliddon she would be back by December 10, in time to play Titania in a Christmas revival of *A Midsummer Night's Dream*.

As Vivien left New York, more or less, Irene arrived. She was there for Christmas shopping and a hospital visit: something required a minor operation, something decades later she could not remember. But it was her drama; this being away from Hollywood seems as much a gesture as strict necessity. For Irene would miss the very start of *Gone With the Wind*: on December 9 or 10, weather permitting, David planned the first shoot. On the back lot (Forty Acres) there were many old standing sets (including some from *King Kong*). These would have 1864 fake fronts put on them and then a night fire would be staged for the burning of Atlanta sequence.

Irene stayed in New York at the Sherry Netherland, and in the first few days of December, she wrote to David:

> I have honestly thought of you the past week with an emotion which is very choking and which makes me feel not half the dream girl I'd like to be and perhaps occasionally used to fancy myself as. I've gone over your sweetness to me these past few weeks—and all your attractive and charming habits and traits and I can't understand how I could ever be upset with you over *anything!* Well, I guess that's putting my head in a noose! But I honestly don't mind—because I love you so very much and besides that old enchantment and those illusions I have been mourning this last year or so—have just come sneaking over me again.

David found time to dictate a letter, typed up by Betty Baldwin. He begged forgiveness in advance, knowing he might not be available to sign it. He had been up until 1:30 a.m. with John Cromwell and Hal Kern cutting *Made for Each Other*. He was also full of news of his sons, and his talk of Jeffrey does not quite match Irene's view of him as a father. David had sent Jeff's latest report card to Irene in New York:

> You may judge from my recent correspondence that since I have returned [from Bermuda and New York] Jeff is back in place number one with me. I am afraid this is true—although I won't guarantee that it will still be true by the time you return. Jeff is absolutely divine. His looks alternately fill me with pride and with sorrow: I am convinced that he is a completely handsome boy, but today I looked at him and he so resembled a picture of me at the age of about eight that I'll show you when you get back, that it just about spoiled my afternoon.
>
> He seems either to be growing less selfish, or to be covering it up more. Certainly his behavior with Danny is infinitely better, and he really has recaptured personality number one that we liked so much—and, if anything, his personality is much more attractive than it has ever been. He speaks more beautifully than ever, and seems to be developing the great gift for language that there has been promise of for so long. His use of four-syllable words continues to amaze me.

Also, he is really writing with great ease and fluency, and I spent the entire time I was dressing this morning calling out words for him to write. He asked questions about the spelling, wrote them out with ease and speed. I'll try to discourage this stunt before you get back, because while it was fun for once, I can't imagine either of us spending a half an hour each morning doing this with much joy for any length of time.

What rules could deter him from spending more of this fruitful time with Jeffrey? Especially if there was a difficulty between father and son. Jeffrey's answer may be the most helpful: as he saw his early life, it was his mother who ran the household. It would then seem horribly calculating if the mother complained of David's hostility to Jeffrey. Irene was never so cold-blooded, but she had trouble all her life keeping control and emotion untangled. The result was that to many people she seemed manipulative.

She entered the Private Pavilion at Mount Sinai Hospital in New York for tests, X rays looking for bone calcification, sugar tolerance, and so on. It's impossible to judge what it was or even whether it was: "As for the findings: they didn't really know what the 'lump' is—and they're not advising operations to find out except if ever an acute attack should overtake me with the possibility of a complete obstruction—but *I* assure you this emergency is *more* than remote. . . . I honestly think husbands ought to be able to send back an imperfect job like me—or at *least*, collect damages, poor Davido."

That was written on December 7. On the eighth, in Los Angeles, Vivien was out and about. Olivier had met her at Clover Field airport in Santa Monica on the second, "crouched in the back of a car" to escape gossip. They holed up at the Beverly Hills Hotel, and in a few days Olivier had taken her to meet Myron.

This is a moment of legend, and all tellers of the story like to be in control of it. Olivier said he had warned Myron that Vivien was coming—"there was someone coming over to visit me who might quite possibly be of extraordinary interest to him." Yet Myron's office had tracked her journey and may have known more about it than Olivier. Apparently, as late as December 10, Olivier turned up with Vivien at the agency offices. "I said innocently," Olivier would write, " '*I* think we ought to take her along to meet David, don't you, Myron?' He nodded slowly, realization beginning to dawn." As Maxine Graybill, Myron's secretary, recalled it, "It was around 6 p.m. and Myron got on the phone and he said, 'David, I'm looking at Scarlett. We're coming right out.' " Myron would deliver Vivien into the firelight of the burning of Atlanta.

But the office files show that on December 8, Jimmy Townsend of the agency took Vivien to meet people at United Artists and then to meet William Wellman (she was also being considered for his *The Light That Failed*). There is another story that a few days before the tenth Myron took Vivien to the races at Santa Anita, where they bumped into Dan O'Shea, who arranged for a screen test. Already, on December 8, according to the file, Vivien had made up her mind to get out of the London *Dream*.

There are always so many things going on at once, and not just the facts but the hopes and the possibilities. Only later is it all turned into a spiffy story with Myron arriving as the flames of Atlanta were subsiding and as the red glow was ideally pitched for suggestive minds, with Vivien in a hat and a fur coat and Myron saying—(take your pick):

"David, I'd like you to meet Scarlett O'Hara."

"I want you to meet Scarlett O'Hara."

"Hey, genius, here she is!"

Sooner or later, the facts hardly matter. But it was untidy, chancy, and devious at the time, with David cutting another film, worrying whether color shooting at night would work and whether the double for Scarlett would keep her face out of the shot, wondering whether he could protect George Cukor from the increasing opposition of L.B., wondering whether Irene would need an operation or whether it was all her drama, and waiting for notes from her such as did arrive in the next few days:

> You used to start without a script, now it's without a cast but heartfelt wishes anyhow.

and

> Please tell Miss Fontaine for me to take pity on you and would she please give you an evening. Besides I think she's a dream.

12 · DON'T SCARLETTIZE UNTIL I GET THERE

DECEMBER 10, 1938, was a grand night, with enough Technicolor flames on view to melt facts into romance. The night before, a weather forecast had predicted no wind but heavy ground fog from sundown on. If there was fog, the fire burned it away. Wind might have been a greater hazard, for the studio was in a built-up area. Three captains and thirty firemen were present in case the Shermanizing got out of hand. But there was no public warning, and Culver City locals were so alarmed they jammed emergency telephone lines. People thought MGM was burning down!

On the morning of the tenth, a Saturday, two trucks went to Technicolor to pick up its seven cameras. By one o'clock in the afternoon, the two drivers and the four doubles for Rhett and Scarlett (Yakima Canutt and Jay Wilsey, Eileen Goodwin and Dorothy Fargo) reported to rehearse the panic-stricken escape. They rehearsed in their own clothes, but the real costumes were ready, waiting for the shoot.

The general call was for 5:00 p.m. Production manager Ray Klune and assistant director Eric Stacey marshaled the forces. Howard Greene (of *Allah*, *A Star is Born*, and *Nothing Sacred*) was the lighting cameraman in charge of the evening, and he had seven operators, many of whom had large careers ahead of them (Winton Hoch, Charles Boyle, Giff Chamberlin, Joseph La Shelle, Henry Jackson, John Polito, and Clarence Slifer). There were assistants, a black-and-white crew, two still photographers, and a sound team.

They broke for "lunch" from 6:15 to 6:45: 235 hot dinners had been ordered, with 190 sandwiches and hot chocolate and coffee. (There were guests expected; David was making an impromptu party of the night.)

The old sets had been equipped with a network of gasoline pipes by Lee Zavitz so he could bring the fire up or down to order. Cameras turned over at 8:15 p.m. Myron, Olivier, and Vivien Leigh were a few miles away

Cukor and David, the evening of December 10, 1938, the burning of Atlanta, the start of Gone With the Wind, *and the beginning of Cukor's retreat?*

still, having dinner, and Myron was maybe saying, "Would you like to see a fire?"

George Cukor wore a thick coat and a white silk scarf, in case it was cold. He didn't have much to do except be enthusiastic. For the director of the burning sequence was William Cameron Menzies. This was not too remarkable: Menzies had directed several films, including *Things to Come*, for Korda; he was the production designer of the movie, and the fire was a graphic set piece worked out on paper in advance. Cukor had been actively engaged with Menzies in the planning so that the fire footage would be integrated with the "story." Cukor had approved a detailed drawing continuity and had suggested a few extra shots that might be useful. But he was not given charge of what was a great spectacle and an important public event. He may have said that such big action scenes were not quite his forte—or it was decided for him. It does suggest uncertainty, for in the fall of 1938 William Wellman had offered his services on action scenes, for free, and Cukor had said, no, he thought the film should have a single vision.

A few days after the fire, L.B. and David were talking on the phone: Ernst Lubitsch was about to sign on with Metro, and David's advice was sought—how often did L.B. and David talk? "During the same conversation," David wrote to Irene (in New York), "your Father made another stab at getting George off of *Gone With the Wind*. Incidentally, so far I am very happy with George on this job."

A reported 10,178 feet of Technicolor film were shot in seventy-five minutes—113 minutes of screen time. The evening cost $25,853.84, and it established the color scheme of the picture. When the fires died, Ray Klune began to build Tara and other sets on Forty Acres. That was clever enough. The greater and inadvertent genius was to have the fire signal the sensibility of the movie to all its makers. Two other points should be made: Technicolor was better, warmer, more natural and more emotional—the film stock was getting faster, but director of photography Howard Greene had done his last major work on the film.

And Vivien Leigh? David would say, a few years later, "I took one look and knew that she was right—at least right as far as her appearance went—at least right as far as my conception of how Scarlett O'Hara looked." He was not looking at a stranger: he had seen her early in 1938 in *A Yank at Oxford*, but still given the *Young in Heart* lead to Paulette Goddard. Her film *Storm in a Teacup* had been considered in March 1938—though largely to see whether Cecil Parker would be right for *Young in Heart*. There *is* something about seeing in the flesh, especially with firelight in the air.

George Cukor took Vivien to his office that same night and gave her some scenes to read. He was impressed, too, but struck by her very English accent—only two days before, David had told Cukor that Clark Gable "refuses under any circumstances to have any kind of a Southern accent." There is even a silent, color screen test of Vivien Leigh, slated December 10, but that is an exquisite error, one of all the slates from that night that was not corrected. Or maybe when she did test, in costume and makeup, the superstitious Leigh said, put the tenth on it, remembering her magical entrance.

David sent two cables that night to New York, but neither mentioned Vivien. To Irene, he said, "Sound the trumpets. The Big Wind started shooting at eight twenty tonight." As for Jock: "You have missed a great thrill. *Gone With the Wind* has been started. Shot key fire scenes at eight twenty tonight, and judging by how they looked to the eye they are going to be sensational." Two days later, he still felt exhausted, but now he mentioned Leigh to Irene: "Shhhhh: she's the Scarlett dark horse and looks damned good. (Not for anybody's ears but your own: it's narrowed down to Paulette, Jean Arthur, Joan Bennett and Vivien Leigh.)"

Irene was still in the hospital. On the tenth, the doctor told her she couldn't leave until the middle of the following week. She was "first-class depressed," afraid they hadn't the foggiest notion what was wrong with her—"That it was going to be the same old story all over again—or if a variation, that I was neurotic!" But then the doctor said he thought he had it: there was no need for an operation, three or four weeks' treatment ought to solve it.

David responded as best he could: "Your long tale of woe arrived this morning. Don't let anyone tell you that you're not a natural-born dramatist, because a more perfectly and naturally constructed piece I have never read. It had me practically dissolved in tears from the first few reels, and the climax and happy ending were wonderful. Please forgive me if I should appear wrongly to be facetious for even a single second about what you've been through. It must have been hell."

By December 16, she was back in the Sherry Netherland wondering about rumors she heard: would it be Ronnie Colman in *Rebecca*? Paulette had telephoned to leave "all kinds of cheery and affectionate messages. H-m-m," and Jock told her they had "at last found the girl." Whatever need there had been to go east, Irene now felt "out" of everything and isolated. "How is your romance coming?" she asked David, as if the bold joke could trivialize anything that was happening. "When I'm around, and you catch a slight yen, you stay within normal limits—but just let me out of sight, and you revert to type with a bang."

Irene liked to be the cool mistress of all gossip, a voice on the phone so deep with understanding it could sound too ancient for such modern inventions. John Huston would put it very well—and he had a romance with her much later:

> Irene was something of an oracle in Hollywood. There was an air of wisdom about her that led people to go to her for advice. She had a manner of speaking which contributed to that image: she spoke in so low a voice that you had to give her your undivided attention. You found yourself answering in the same hushed tones. It was like conducting secret negotiations.

But suppose some real talk was going on about her behind her back. Suppose there was something she did not know. Then she could become a worrier, an inquisitor, a nag; she could make herself ill or the center of a compelling drama that overshadowed all others. As she prepared to leave New York, she wrote to David with orders that were understandable yet absurdly demanding in view of all he had on:

> And please for heaven's (where does that apostrophe go?) sakes don't Scarlettize until I get there—please oh please don't decide even to yourself. And don't have a next-to-final preview on *Made* without me—in fact please do nothing, but absolutely nothing at all until I get there except *pant* for
>
> *Me*

She arrived back in Los Angeles by train on the evening of December 21. Much had happened by then. On Monday the twelfth, Cukor canceled his other appointments to rehearse with Vivien. For the remainder of the week, she worked with either Cukor or Will Price, a dialogue director. And on December 13, the Myron Selznick office traded back her return ticket to England on the *Normandie* (passage had been booked for December 10). No other actress at this time received such coaching.

The last round of tests began on Saturday the seventeenth, with Jean Arthur. Every evening beforehand David was busy with *Made for Each Other*, but Cukor worked with the temperamental Arthur, who was determined to wear a dress of her own choosing. She did three scenes (with Douglass Montgomery as her Ashley and Charles Quigley as Rhett). She was "no end of trouble," according to David: "I look at her as though I had never known her before!" On the twentieth, Joan Bennett tested, a candidate who had not even read before, or been named, but someone urged on David by her new husband, Walter Wanger. Paulette returned for the twentieth and twenty-first, and Vivien Leigh worked on the twenty-first and the twenty-second, in black-and-white, playing with Hattie McDaniel, Hattie Noel, Leslie Howard, and Douglass Montgomery. And on December 20, Vivien signed a contract with Myron's agency.

There is a part of the legend that has George Cukor telling Vivien she had the part on Christmas Day. But who can believe David did not seize that moment himself? On December 23, Sig Marcus in Myron's office cabled London for the immediate dispatch of Vivien's contract with Korda: the decision had been settled with those tests on the twenty-second, and Irene saw them that evening at home, with David.

The weeks that followed were not simple ecstasy for Vivien. She had to break it to her old agent, John Gliddon, that he was no part of this coup. The entanglement with Korda had to be worked out—and, as David saw it, Korda could have blocked the casting. Moreover, her being with Olivier now was not quite an uncomplicated pleasure. David knew the choice of a little-known English actress would be controversial, and he did not want to add public exposure of her life-style. Just before Christmas, a young woman in Myron's office, Sunny Alexander, was approached by Harry Ham, the agent who looked after Olivier and Vivien: would she move in with Vivien as her secretary and companion? Miss Alexander agreed, and they were set up at 520 North Camden Drive, while Olivier retained his residence at the hotel. A twenty-four-hour guard was put on the house.

Then there were negotiations. Years later, Olivier claimed he pro-tested David's meanness in offering Vivien only $20,000 to play Scarlett and for insisting on a seven-year contract. He quoted David as saying: "I'd be the laughingstock of all my friends if I paid her any more, an unknown, a discovery, for such an opportunity." The contract with Vivien attempted an intricate—and ultimately impossible—shared arrangement between David and Korda. She was to play Scarlett for $1,250 a week, with a guarantee for sixteen weeks ($20,000). There were also clauses to cover two films a year for seven years, building to a salary of $6,250 a week.

The facts in Olivier's account are correct. But was he just acting on Vivien's behalf? In 1944, David claimed the contract had been "all manner of trouble," not just thanks to Myron, Harry Ham, and the shadow of Korda, but because of Olivier: "Larry tried in every way possible to kill the casting of Vivien as Scarlett O'Hara. He advanced every argument conceiv-able against it, and . . . said that I wouldn't dream of going through with the idea of an English girl as a famous southern heroine; that Vivien . . . would be ridiculed in the role." David fought back by recalling the fate of Jill Esmond on *A Bill of Divorcement*, and he believed that Olivier was possessed by pure jealousy.

The stories are not inconsistent. Vivien was paid modestly for what proved such a powerful and onerous performance. She received more than $25,000 finally because of overages—but Gable, who worked seventy-one days to her 125, was paid $121,454. Yet Olivier's jealousy had a history and a future: Vivien Leigh's instability in the years ahead owed something to keeping company with the world's greatest insecure actor. And at the time of this contract, Olivier was still shooting *Wuthering Heights* (where he had not impressed Wyler or Goldwyn much) and remained uncertain whether he would ever make it as a movie star.

There is little indication of Myron's people being difficult in the negotiations. The notes kept by Dan O'Shea (who did the deal for SIP) reflect his use of the Paulette Goddard contract as a basis. Leigh's salary was talked up from $1,000 a week to $1,250, but the more serious concerns were over finessing her Korda contract.

In the first two weeks of January, Vivien worked hard on her accent with Will Price and Susan Myrick, who had just arrived from Atlanta. Myrick and Wilbur Kurtz, the other leading Southern authority on the picture, were impressed. "She's a honey!" said Kurtz, while Myrick noticed the very open sensuality of the actress: "Vivien is a bawdy little thing and hot as a firecracker and lovely to look at. Can't understand *why* Larrie Olivier when she could have anybody."

There are still stories to be found that Vivien Leigh was reluctant to do the part, that she shared some of Olivier's disdain of movies and Hollywood. These theories are belied by the brave and unscrupulous ways she had gone after the part—and the force of need and egotism that could resist her lover's objections. It was her drive that showed in the tests. For these are so much deeper and darker than her previous English films. Cukor and the dialect coaches had done great work with her, but the role of Scarlett released something hidden in Vivien. George Cukor made no greater contribution to the film than in preparing Vivien Leigh, finding a voice, a look, and an attitude and letting her lay sure hands on them all. She would never again be so intense or natural on screen. But David saw this could be so. He had a genius then for casting, and Vivien was the magic for this huge, unlikely picture.

The press announcement was made on January 13, and David was very apprehensive. The release stressed the actress's birth in India, an education on the Continent, French father and Irish mother, much of which was Birdwell slanting the facts. England was mentioned as little as possible, and Olivier not at all. Vivien was described as the wife of a London barrister. Nevertheless, in her January 16 column in the Los Angeles *Times*, Hedda Hopper regretted how after two years and "out of millions of American women" David "couldn't fine *one* to suit him."

Margaret Mitchell had a more open mind. She hadn't seen Leigh's movies, but she liked her looks: "She certainly is pretty. Naturally I am the only person in the world who really knows what Scarlett looks like but this

Wind *meets*
Wuthering Heights*:*
David, Vivien, Merle,
Larry

girl looks charming. She has the most Irish look I have ever seen with the
word 'Devil' in her eye." As to the voice, Miss Mitchell offered this theory:
the Georgians of the 1860s were pro-English. They took their vacations not
in the North, but in England.

On the same evening, as the news reached Atlanta, Miss Mitchell had
been more forthcoming on the other parts of the package—David had
protected himself with the simultaneous announcement of Leslie Howard as
Ashley and Olivia de Havilland as Melanie. Margaret Mitchell confessed
that in all the letters *she* had had, "an astonishing percentage" wanted Leslie
Howard. As for de Havilland, she was "made for the part." Even a novelist
could overlook Howard's being more than twenty years older than her
Ashley. David was already fussing over hairpieces and makeup for Howard.

He had sought him first when he was two years younger. But in 1937,
Howard had hoped to play Lawrence of Arabia for Korda. He also wanted
$100,000 for ten weeks. As the years passed, a way was found to Howard's
heart. He was ambitious to do more with his movie career and agreed to take
Wind if he could serve as associate producer on *Intermezzo*, as well as act in
it. That courtesy credit amounted to very little, but by the time Howard
came to shoot *Intermezzo* (*after* most of *Wind*), he would find he had another
chore.

As to Melanie, David had been interested in de Havilland since the possible deal with Warners. But there were problems in the way. On October 17, 1938, David had drawn up a list of Melanie possibilities: it included Julie Haydon, Dorothy Jordan (Mrs. Merian Cooper), Janet Gaynor, Andrea Leeds, Anne Shirley, Linda Gray (the girlfriend Arthur Fellows had brought to the *Nothing Sacred* wrap party), and two sisters, Olivia de Havilland and Joan Fontaine. De Havilland then seemed tied to Warners, but Fontaine was "to have a reading with Mr. Cukor."

According to Fontaine, she went to that meeting in a gray faille coatdress and silver-fox furs, having come from a Junior League lunch. "Too chic, too chic!" said Cukor. "Melanie must be a plain simple southern girl."

"What about my sister?" Fontaine says she responded.

And she has Cukor answer, "Who's she?"

Cukor's ignorance of the sisterhood is preposterous. He said himself that Fontaine did read for *Gone With the Wind*. On December 14, Wilbur Kurtz was in the office of SIP assistant director Eric Stacey when Fontaine walked in. Stacey looked up quickly and thought it was Vivien Leigh; Kurtz was left with the impression that Fontaine was definitely in contention for something. On January 19, 1939, Fontaine did a screen test of a scene from *A Bill of Divorcement*, with Alan Marshal opposite her. Whatever was happening, Joan Fontaine was much in evidence at the studio.

Her sister, Olivia, got a call from Cukor early in December. It led to a Sunday afternoon at Summit Drive, with David and Irene watching as George played Scarlett so that she could read as Melanie. They then adjourned to the projection room, where David ran some Melanie tests: they included Andrea Leeds, Elizabeth Allen, and Anne Shirley.

But David wanted Olivia. As he began to argue with Jack Warner, the actress took Mrs. Warner to tea at the Brown Derby to get inside support. The deed was done: Olivia would be paid $1,000 a week, but Warners also got a one-picture option that David owned on James Stewart.

After more than two and a half years, everything was being done at the last moment. The sets were going up on Forty Acres. Wilbur Kurtz fought for Georgia authenticity, but David, Cukor, Menzies, and art director Lyle Wheeler knew they were making a movie. Neither in life nor on the screen was David a realist. He was of his age: there had never been a notion of making the picture in Georgia. David had still not seen the South. But he put his people to insane lengths to get the right red look for the Georgia earth: they bought brick dust from a kiln.

Wilbur Kurtz was enormously impressed by David—by his desire and energy, by attention to detail without ever losing sight of the big picture, by the steady, cheery resolve to surmount all problems with skill, dedication, nerve, cheek, or blind lies, depending on the circumstances. He also admired David's reliance on what the novel did and said: the two of them had bets over recall of certain details, and David won some of them. But they had had one meeting, as far back as February 1938, at which Kurtz learned the nature of showmanship:

> As for Tara, they listened closely to my explanation of rural archi-
> tecture in north Georgia and Clayton County, in particular. They
> admitted that what I said was true and Mr. Cukor, who had seen
> Clayton County, knew that plantation homes down there, at best,
> were nothing wonderful, but since Tara was also on the fictional side,
> they indicated that the house should be "warmed up" a bit. . . . I think
> they are minded to ease off some of the north Georgia pioneer spirit
> and soften up the places a bit with a quiet elegance that would do no
> real violence to the spirit of the story. "After all," said Mr. Selznick,
> addressing me, "the Atlanta and Clayton County audiences are a very
> small percentage."

What was happening to the script was more questionable. David was working on it; he would have claimed it was always on his mind. But Kurtz and Susan Myrick, who knew the book as well as they knew Southern life, were perplexed. So many new writers were around the studio. Scott Fitzgerald was hired for some rewrites, and, when she heard that, Margaret Mitchell was amazed: "If anyone had told me ten or more years ago that he would be working on a book of mine I would have been stricken speechless with pellagra or hardening of the arteries or something."

David was moved to hire Fitzgerald out of nostalgia and a curiosity to see how far the author had fallen. Fitzgerald was on the film for three weeks in January (at $1,250 a week), expected to rewrite here and shorten there. He redid the bonnet scene and thought it better. "However, it is a page longer and if it is cut to the bone it will be as ineffective as any of her scenes when they are cut to the bone. Mitchell has absolutely no wit—which is another way of saying she has no brevity. She gets all her effects by repetition."

Cukor was present at story conferences with Fitzgerald. At the close of one of them, David told the writer, "Scott, I want to thank you for all you've done on the picture. Now, we've talked about these pages. Go away and write them—and we'll meet tomorrow." But as soon as Fitzgerald had left, Selznick picked up the phone and dictated a cable firing him, telling him not to report next day. As Cukor observed it, David had needed to act out his superiority to the once great writer. Yet he had not managed to do it face-to-face.

Somehow David had come to the eve of principal photography. Weariness, doubts, and ironic jokes had to be put aside. Nothing would suffice except enthusiasm in the face of reality. David knew how precarious the situation was and how vital it was to stay unrealistic. So he sent Jock the "script" as it stood on January 25 and told him, "Don't get panicky . . . the creative work that remains to be done is not of the type that leads to trouble."

He had his ideal Rhett and a Scarlett better than his highest hopes. He had a director he had defended against much argument. He had hired as director of photography Lee Garmes, an artist, the man who had shot *Morocco* and *Scarface*, but who had not yet worked in color. He had as good a corps of technicians as Hollywood offered. He had the money—just about—for a revised budget of $2.8 million. If he didn't have a whole script, he had the novel.

He veered between feeling confident and sick with trepidation. But, he told Jock, "the next couple of months . . . will be the toughest I have ever known—possibly the toughest any producer has ever known."

On January 26, they began.

13 · FROM DAY TO DAY

AND ON FEBRUARY 13, they stopped.

George Cukor withdrew from the project. He and David issued a joint statement: "As a result of a series of disagreements between us over many of the individual scenes of *Gone With the Wind*, we have mutually decided that the only solution is for a new director to be selected at as early a date as is practicable." It was not that Cukor had been fired; David was at pains to declare that George was "one of the very finest directors it has ever been the good fortune of the business to claim." Despite the public calamity for David and the disappointment for George, their friendship did not end or sour swiftly. Yet David's white elephant was now in danger of being a laughingstock, and Cukor had to feel an old friendship had been betrayed.

But directors then were not the figureheads they are now. Nobody in Hollywood believed they created their films. Directors did not believe it. Cukor had shot some of *The Prisoner of Zenda*—because he was available and under contract and because David had a need. The credits on the film did not recognize his contribution, and he never thought to protest. John Cromwell and David had their rows—and producers never lost those contests. Such things happened: a vehicle needed a driver, and neither cars nor highways, nor the community of traffic, can tell one driver from another.

Cukor's withdrawal was a measure of desperation and vast internal problems on the film. But it was not an outrage as it might be today if some studio fired Francis Coppola or David Lynch three weeks into production.

It is still said that Cukor was sacrificed because Gable was unhappy with him. Patrick McGilligan's 1991 biography of Cukor claimed to reveal this "ignominious tale." There is a danger of that explanation being colored by today's circumstances. In 1939, stars had more power, and less, than they have today. The public went to see them with religious faith. David had decided the film was not viable without Gable. Today, we take pride in being fickle with stars and in seeing through them. They are not sublime—yet they are bosses. If Gone With the Wind were made today, its Gable and Leigh would command profit participation in the film. They might be its producers.

Gable had been ordered to play Rhett, and he disliked his bosses while believing he had to obey them. A few stars had stood out against the system by 1939, but they were usually women and they usually failed. Gable was simultaneously the king and a slave.

There is a widespread feeling—half rumor, half legend, and without reliable provenance—that Gable was uneasy with Cukor because Cukor knew Gable had once been a prostitute who serviced homosexuals. Cukor was one example among many that discreet gays could flourish in Hollywood. There is no evidence that Gable had been a paid lover to anyone—though many people who became world famous as movie stars had "darker" pasts that they were anxious to keep secret and which became the material of blackmail.

In a preface to Cukor's last published interview, the interviewer, Boze Hadleigh, wrote:

> In reality, Gable insisted that "that fag" be fired, and producer David O. Selznick finally gave in. Gable, whose first two wives were much older than he—and wealthy—had reportedly been a heterosexual who wasn't above being serviced by orally-minded gay actors. One such client was leading man William Haines, a close friend of Cukor.

But in the interview itself, Cukor gave no support to this. He declined to talk about Gable and Haines; he maintained the accuracy of what he had always said about Gone With the Wind, but he did say of Gable, "As stars went, he was powerful, but that was little better than impotence, in those days."

In his book about the making of Gone With the Wind, Roland Flamini claims there were some days when Gable failed to turn up for work and that the actor told Russell Birdwell, "I feel very uncomfortable with George." Flamini talked to Birdwell, but there is no hint of Gable's absence from the set in the production records. As late as 1961, David told a Gable biographer that "Clark never opened his mouth. . . . Neither before nor after I made the change did I ever have one word of discussion about the director with Clark." The biographer, Charles Samuels, then reported that a friend of Gable's had said the actor told him, "I don't want Cukor. I'm going to have him changed." To which David replied, "This was reported to me as his feeling but he never mentioned it to me nor criticized Cukor. He worked with each of the directors just as professionally."

Ronald Haver adds in *David O. Selznick's Hollywood* that Gable had an "ace in the hole" in his loan-out contract, whereby Metro said, "We shall be in no way responsible to you [SIP] if, without our fault, the artist shall fail, refuse or neglect to perform for you the services above described." But such clauses were customary in loan-out deals: the contract for Olivia de Havilland had the same wording—and she was unhappy when Cukor left, but made no more protest than ask David to change his mind.

Gable was unhappy, and MGM evidently shared some of his feelings. He had never wanted to play Rhett, just because so many people said he was "perfect" for the most widely read book of the moment. The actor reckoned he must fail to live up to those expectations. David had similar worries over the picture as a whole. Just as David always wanted Margaret Mitchell's approval, Gable had nearly written to the author asking her to let it be known he would be "the worst possible selection" for Rhett. Gable thought the part was made for Ronald Colman.

It is possible that Gable also feared Cukor because of some complicated sexual history. But that fear would have begun in August 1938, when the Metro deal was done; Cukor had always been announced as the director. MGM did make noises against Cukor at that time, and L.B. asked David to use someone else. Gable may have had a voice in that, but would he have told L.B. the deepest reasons for his concern? And could an actor—the impotent king—have interfered with Loew's financial interest in the picture?

The issue that Gable and Mayer *could* talk about was the feeling that Cukor was a "woman's director." This was shorthand for saying he was gay, but it noted Cukor's special attentiveness to actresses and his inclination to have pictures gather around the sensibility of women. This is a travesty of Cukor's talent as a director and of his sense of life. He had directed Barrymore in *A Bill of Divorcement*, Fields in *Copperfield*, Robert Taylor in *Camille*, and Cary Grant in *Holiday*. He was, quite simply, a fine director of players, especially intelligent actors able to talk or follow his range of reference. But he was felt to be uninterested in great action scenes, and in story conferences he was likely to build up detail rather than move a film forward. He had never made an action film, much less an epic.

So what happened between January 26 and February 13? Gable came to the production late. He did not work until the sixth day of shooting: Rhett is in so much less of the film than Scarlett. But Gable had been aloof. Despite requests, he had not come in to test with any of the actresses. His absence had promoted the thing about which he was insecure: a special relationship between Vivien Leigh and Cukor. Thus, he found a director who was already talking a private language of understanding with her, excited by the feeling that he was about to reveal a new star in a great performance.

Gable felt Rhett's clothes were not flattering, but again he had been unavailable for proper fittings. In his first scenes, he had to dance, and Gable was a poor dancer. A platform on wheels was made to excuse his inept feet. He had to feel he was being cut down to size. In addition, he was disconcerted by Leigh: on a few occasions, she came to the set late, angering him; nor was the famous man's man happy with the blue language Vivien Leigh enjoyed—much less when it was uttered by a voice that could have ruled the best households of Belgravia. She knew her lines better than he did his—and she was a fearsomely rapid learner when the lines were changed.

Here we come closer to the heart of the problem. The script was a living thing, and Cukor was expected to adapt to it every day. Susan Myrick confided in Margaret Mitchell that it was not just a matter of Oliver Garrett "cutting" Sidney Howard's script:

> You are wrong, my duck. David, himself, thinks HE is writing the script and he tells poor Bobby Keon and Stinko Garrett what to write. And they do the best they can with it, in their limited way. Garrett is just a professional scenario writer while Howard knows dramatic values.

The unit would frequently get a two- or three-page scene as work ended one day which was to be shot first thing the next morning. Sometimes, then, a revised version appeared in the morning. In the opinion of Cukor and cameraman Lee Garmes, these scenes were poorer than the Howard script or the novel, so they had struggled with them and tried to restore some of the original quality.

The work was going slowly; the picture was falling behind schedule. But there were many reasons for that, including problems with décor and costume and the antipathy between Lee Garmes and the Technicolor consultants. In addition, as David saw the dailies, he began a list of essential retakes. Reggie Callow, an assistant director, said it was slow going with Cukor, but just as slow with Victor Fleming, his successor. Eric Stacey thought Cukor "had been damned patient not to have resigned before."

Cukor's tactful rewrites were getting him in trouble. David was so annoyed when he saw the changes on the screen, he felt compelled to take closer charge:

> I therefore would like to go back to what we discussed, and try to work out a system whereby I see each block scene rehearsed in full before you start shooting it. I am worried as to the practicability of this and as to whether it would lose too much time, but I should appreciate it if you would give some thought to it, as it might even save time in the long run. Also, it would avoid the necessity of my coming down on the set at any other time; any feeling on my part that I ought to go down to make sure a point we had intended has been made clear to you; would avoid projection-room surprise for me; and, conceivably, would be of considerable service to you. Therefore, unless you see something in the way of the plan, I'd like, commencing immediately, to be notified when you are rehearsing each block scene. If this means I have to get in at the same time as the rest of you, so much the better—I'll get home earlier and Irene will appreciate it!

Irene was seeing the footage at home every evening, and she argued on George's behalf with David: "I saved him his job only a week at a time. There was no magic. And fussy detail. As he went along, David said, 'I deplore George's lack of participation and contribution. He's growing further away and I'm spoiling him.' George was so busy with the talent and the parties and he didn't understand construction. The burden was twice what it should have been on David because of him."

The crucial dispute is whether David or George understood the film better. Irene was by then a closer friend to George than David. David did feel that Cukor had ridden along on *Wind* to his great financial advantage— but George was always ready to start. Cukor was interfering with David's script, and David was despoiling Howard's. In the end, in 1939, the script belonged to the producer. David insisted on being on the set, and Butterfly McQueen reported that he ordered changes in the line readings Cukor had called for.

The option on Cukor's contract had to be renewed by February 11; for a payment of $25, SIP had that date postponed until March 13—obviously Cukor knew about that. But there was a crisis, and as Susan Myrick saw it, it was Cukor finally who precipitated it:

> So George just told David he would not work any longer if the script was not better and he wanted the Howard script back. David told George he was a director—not an author and he (David) was the producer and the judge of what is a good script (or words to that

effect) and George said he was a director and a damn good one and he would not let his name go out over a lousy picture [and] if they did not go back to the Howard script (he was willing to have them cut it down shorter) he, George, was through.

And bull-headed David said, "O.K. get out!"*

The postponed option was never renewed. Cukor's contract was terminated. There was a going-away present, and David said he had waited to secure it before being rid of George. Cukor was immediately assigned—by MGM—to direct the movie of the Clare Boothe Luce play *The Women*. Its cast included several people who might be considered Scarlett rejects: Norma Shearer, Joan Crawford, Paulette Goddard, and Joan Fontaine. That picture would be released before *Gone With the Wind*.

What followed the withdrawal of Cukor also helps explain it. Vivien Leigh and Olivia de Havilland remonstrated. Vivien would say that with Cukor's departure she lost all hope of enjoying the picture. She also said it had been foolish to abandon the Howard script and then ridiculous for her to do costume tests after a full day's work. She wanted to fly to New York, and she complained about ever having agreed to do Scarlett.

David tried to get King Vidor to take over. Vidor went home with piles of scripts. He was overwhelmed and ready to decline. But by the time he saw David, Victor Fleming had been hired. Evidently, in the past, Metro had offered Fleming, a buddy of Gable's. At that moment, however, Fleming was busy directing *The Wizard of Oz* for MGM, a major project in its own right. L.B. was decisive. He shifted Fleming over from one project to another and had Vidor complete *Oz*. Fleming had directed Gable in *Test Pilot* and *Red Dust*; he had done *Reckless* for David at Metro. He excelled at action and the vigorous projection of old-fashioned male values. He was tough, handsome, and commanding, and he came to *Wind* with bad grace. Instead of a vacation, he got a huge problem. But he did as he was told and when he looked at the footage so far, he criticized not Cukor. "David," he said, "you haven't got a fucking script."

Later on, Fleming conceded, "George would have done just as good a job as I. He'd probably have done a lot better on the intimate scenes. I think I did pretty well on some of the bigger stuff. George came from the stage and taught us what directing a dialogue scene was about. . . . It's bullshit that he's just a woman's director. He's not. He can direct anybody."

---

* There was a very recent example to encourage Selznick. MGM had called a halt on *The Wizard of Oz* in October 1938, after two weeks' shooting. The footage was scrapped. Buddy Ebsen was replaced by Jack Haley; and director Richard Thorpe was fired. The new director was . . . Victor Fleming (after George Cukor had refused).

Those words were remembered by John Lee Mahin, the favored screenwriter of Victor Fleming, who was also assigned to *Wind* in its emergency by Louis B. Mayer. With David, Fleming and Mahin retreated to Palm Springs. Their task was to bring Fleming up to date on the story and—above all—to find order and line in the screenplay. While they were away, Mahin's wife spoke to a reporter, and her words seem as reliable as they were spontaneous:

> As far as I can make out myself, the whole trouble lay in not the cast or in the direction or anything—but the whole trouble was in the script. . . . When they came to shoot it, it wasn't as shootable as they had hoped it would be. So Mr. Selznick and Mr. Cukor apparently had some differences of opinion as to how it was to be changed. I've never known anyone so earnest about anything as David Selznick— he's really giving his heart's blood to it. Not only his money, which is considerable—but everything.

Mahin suggested they go back to the Sidney Howard script. This may not have been what David wanted to hear. In addition, there was press comment that MGM was taking over *his* picture. So he dropped Mahin and returned to Los Angeles with the exasperated Fleming.

At breakfast next morning, Ben Hecht found David and Fleming at his door with a car. On the way to the studio, Hecht talked himself into $10,000 a week, despite never having read the book. At Culver City, there was another writer waiting, John Van Druten (who was engaged on *Intermezzo*).

Hecht asked Van Druten if *he'd* read the book and what it was like.

"Fine book for bell-hops," said Van Druten, so David kicked *him* out.

Because there wasn't time for Hecht to read the book, David and Fleming acted it out for him, with David as Scarlett and Ashley and Fleming as Rhett. Hecht lay on the sofa while this was going on, until his two actors wore themselves out. Hecht asked for the script or a treatment, and at last he found the Howard treatment. He thought it superb, and he proceeded from there.

They did eighteen hours a day, on peanuts and bananas. A blood vessel exploded in Fleming's eye. David collapsed. Hecht kept to his sofa. After a week, he escaped, having tidied it up, he said, as far as the halfway point.

Hecht's account exists on tape, a rollicking comedy told by a man who often improved on facts. What can be said for sure is that Mahin and Hecht provided some help, and both recommended Howard's structure. But amid such panic, there was no time for thorough repairs. The hiatus lasted two weeks and added $150,000 to the picture's overhead. They would begin again. Fleming now knew the plot, and he was angry enough to cut through all petty human objections. Let Hecht have the last word:

> David had done a hundred brilliant things preparing for this movie. Menzies had drawn two thousand paintings, with set-ups for every scene. The costumes had been prepared. The casting had been perfect. The financing had been wonderful. There was not a bum in the crowd. The only thing he'd overlooked, in his great perfection mania, was a script. It's hard to remember that a script is also necessary, when you have all those other producer jobs to do.

14 • WHAT DO YOU WANT, DAVID?

VICTOR FLEMING came on the picture like Cagney sneering at rookie cops. When he walked on the set the first morning, he cornered Callow and Stacey and told them, "They tell me that you're supposed to be the best team in the picture business. But I'm going to put both of you in the hospital before this picture is over."

He didn't favor Gable; he didn't have to. All he did was bear down harder on Vivien Leigh, as if to say she was damn lucky to be there, when she thought it was her ill fortune to have lost Cukor. So Leigh's Scarlett became embittered, tougher, bitchier, and more dangerous—all to the benefit of the performance and never killing the tender wanton George had cultivated. It was something a cold-blooded genius might have organized, yet it was a happy accident for a flustered producer. And Fleming was a chump, too: when David offered him stock on the picture as extra inducement to take it over, big Vic said who wants stock in a folly like this?

Since his mind was made up—that the script was poor, but the picture had to be shot—Fleming took the daily pages and executed them. He had no love of the material, and it was only love, meeting Miss Mitchell, and the years on those test scenes that had entrapped George Cukor. No director ever rehearsed a Hollywood picture longer—and Hollywood mistrusts too much rehearsal. Go that deep and you may lose the line and its force. Hollywood's job was to make something anyone could understand immediately.

Fleming gave David no projection room surprises. He catered to the producer's whim, for he knew that, sooner or later, that's what directors had to do. Cukor had liked David—Fleming despised him: this was a more effective system, for only with a director who believed he was doing a job could David be delivered of his masterpiece. As Howard Hughes told Olivia de Havilland at dinner the night the Fleming news broke: "With George and Victor, it's the same talent, only Victor's is strained through a coarser sieve."

The movie resumed production on March 2. Ernest Haller was cameraman now, with a new Technicolor expert, Ray Rennahan. This was Haller's first color film, though not his Southern debut: he had shot *Jezebel*. The days averaged around ten hours at first, and there were six shooting days a week. Ideally in that system, the making of a movie is a manufacturing process whereby script is converted to celluloid. In 1939 more so than today, budget, schedule, and the minutes of screen time achieved in a day were the measures of progress. As to the magic, people were hired to deliver it, and they were expected to deliver on cue, without fuss, and for as many takes as it took. And look beautiful and be there on time tomorrow.

When shooting began, the budget had been estimated at $2.843 million. Two months later, on March 27, it had climbed to $3.328 million. The largest areas of that increase were for script work and for the director, the stars, cast, cameramen, and in raw stock and developing charges. The shutdown had kept people idle but on pay, and it had led to fresh hirings with some people being paid off. Hecht and Mahin, and anyone else involved, had added $32,832 to the writing budget. But they had also supplied new scenes that required more sets to the tune of $34,361.

By April 5, the daily schedule still averaged ten hours, but Ray Klune had to report another $44,836 on the budget largely because of retakes and new scenes added to the script. The new total figure was $3.374 million, yet Klune was cautious: these figures did not "contemplate any allowance for Scarlett's second arrival at the Atlanta Railroad Station and her trip through the reconstructed Atlanta to Aunt Pitty's House, which is in the new script which came through a few days ago."

On soundstages at Culver City, under Technicolor lights, the temperature was like that of Death Valley—and the actors had nineteenth-century costume to combat the heat. Which adds force to the story of Ann Rutherford wondering aloud to David about all the Val lace petticoats that did not show and David's response: that they helped the actress believe she was the character.

Between April 19 and May 24, on eight days the shoot lasted over twelve hours. It was in April that David was able to claim two more weeks from Sidney Howard. On April 5, he was shown the assembled film so far, for there was an attempt to shoot in continuity. His comments reflect his hostility to Selznick, and they were prompted by the roughest of cuts. But there is no reason to suppose his view was his alone:

I thought the stuff beautiful in color, dull and cold in action. Leigh quite extraordinarily fine as Scarlett though not really an actress of much accomplishment. Gable simply terrible as Rhett, awkward, hick, unconvincing. Melanie virtually cut out of the picture along with any scenes of heart interest.

Howard was charged with rewriting the end of the movie. He found a David who refused to cut the story even though the assembly already made a full-length picture. "How really astonishing," Howard told his wife, "that a man can spend the time and money he has spent and find himself so unready at the end. And he is as completely unready as though he had barely started."

On April 8, in the morning, David gave Howard a scene that was to be shot in two hours. "Rewrite it for me." Howard explained it could not be used because its incident and dialogue had already been shot in an earlier scene. David insisted that it be done and made different. Howard did his best. They shot the first page before David decided the writer had been correct. So everyone waited while Howard wrote another scene—never used. "The whole thing because Selznick had written the scene himself some weeks ago and just found it and because Gable said he couldn't learn the lines."

Sidney Howard was a visitor from another planet. One has to live with a film production to tolerate the rising neurotic behavior. A newcomer sees rare strangeness—madmen even—that the veterans now take for granted. Still, Howard saw the readiness for collapse, and the degrees of exhaustion and confusion:

> My own private weariness, apart from nausea whenever I look at a page of the script, is less my trouble than the miasma of fatigue which surrounds me. Fleming takes four shots of something a day to keep him going and another shot or so to fix him so he can sleep after the day's stimulation. Selznick is bent double with permanent, and, I should think, chronic indigestion. Half the staff look, talk and behave as though they were on the verge of breakdowns. When I have anything to say I have to phrase it with exaggerated tact and clarity. Then I wait and wait for the reaction which may or may not come. It is impossible to get a decision on anything. That in itself is really backbreaking. I say: "What do you want, David?" and David has not the faintest idea.

On the morning of April 17, there was panic when Vivien Leigh declared she was pregnant. Plans were made to give her five days off for an abortion before she reported a false alarm. David was terrified in case the rumor reached the press. Olivier had left for New York in early March to do the play *No Time for Comedy*, but even in the period while he was in Los Angeles after *Wuthering Heights* had finished David banned him from the set. That may have made Vivien more ardent or it could have been to stifle Olivier's opposition to her doing the film.

Sunny Alexander, still Vivien's chaperon, saw the actress's reaction to the pressure of the work and to her separation from Olivier. As shooting progressed, everyone recognized how the narrative and the movie depended on Scarlett. If few people knew it yet, Vivien Leigh was one of those actresses who, once into a role, were trapped by it. The talent and the startling outspokenness were equally influenced by her instability and her unusual sexual need. In her few relaxed moments, in Los Angeles, Vivien liked to play a game, Ways to Kill a Baby, in which party guests were expected to conjure up bizarre methods of murdering an infant. Once David flew Olivier back from New York for a weekend, and another time the lovers met in Kansas City for Vivien's sexual relief. As she said herself, in Kansas City, "Larry met me in the hotel lobby and we went upstairs and we fucked and we fucked and we fucked the whole weekend."

Whenever a film is finished, the publicity varnish of "team spirit" takes over. When a film is as monumental as *Gone With the Wind* those who made it begin to say that it was glorious, filled with endeavor and excitement. So it is important to hold on to clearer-eyed memories. Marcella Rabwin knew it was a great event of show business history, yet she was not sentimental or deceived:

> It was a case of utter chaos. They burned themselves, and out of the ashes rose this phoenix of a picture. I have never known so much hatred. The whole atmosphere was so acrid. Leigh hated Fleming. With a passion. Fleming hated her. He called her the vilest names. Clark Gable hated David. He was a very anti-Semitic man. He used to talk about "that Jew producer. . . ." Everybody hated David. He interfered in everything. He would call up in the middle of the night to poor Lyle Wheeler and say, "I can't shoot that scene now, get in there and put up Aunt Pitty's living room." Everything had to be done and redone. He was despised.

Howard made his escape, Vivien had her brief raptures, and then on April 29 Victor Fleming collapsed. There remains uncertainty whether this was a medical crisis or a gesture of frustration against David. That Fleming was exhausted was not in doubt: David had been worried about him for several days. So the doggedly healthy Callow and Stacey simply observed their tough director's retreat to Malibu and rest. Fleming was away for sixteen days; in his absence, Sam Wood was hired in, from MGM yet again, to carry on regardless.

By May 15, the day before Fleming's return, Ray Klune had grim budgeting news: $3.488 million, with a June 16 finish date.

To save time, Wood was retained for eight more days after Fleming's return. With Menzies also heading a unit, there could be three different shoots on the same day.

There was no longer money to pay for it all. The overall fiscal problems of SIP were mounting. *Made for Each Other*, released on February 16, 1939, lost money. As well as *Wind*, *Intermezzo* and *Rebecca* were coming up. By May, both Alfred Hitchcock and Ingrid Bergman had arrived at the studio, eager to begin their American careers. Wharton and Altstock were aghast onlookers at the toll of *Gone With the Wind*.

An attempt was made to get more funding from MGM. After all, its $1.25 million had been a notional half of the final budget. But L.B. had foreseen the likelihood of overages, even if he could never have imagined their extent. For Metro to pay more would deserve complete ownership of the picture. L.B. refused. So David turned to Jock, and Jock met the glum faces of the other stockholders. They had given enough. So he went to the Bank of America and secured a loan of $2.050 million earmarked as follows: $600,000 for *Rebecca*, $450,000 for *Intermezzo*, and $1 million for *Gone With the Wind*. The collateral on the loan was David's personal stake in those three films.

The wrap party for
Wind: D.O.S., Vivien,
Victor Fleming, Carole
Lombard, Clark Gable

David may not have noticed, but he faced personal disaster if this venture failed. As of that May, he had a little over $20,000 in his bank accounts—there had been no time for gambling, so 1939 was a reformed year. There was nothing else anyone could do by May 1939, and it was valiant of Jock to secure the loan. But the Wharton lessons had sunk in. In New York, at least, emotional decisions were taken to bring SIP to a merciful close.

Principal photography did end. The great spectacle of the wounded in Atlanta was accomplished, with its crane shot; after many early-morning trips to the Lasky Mesa location they got Scarlett and "As God is my witness" in the best dawn light; they shot an ending; there was a day on the lot when Olivia de Havilland passed Vivien Leigh without recognizing her, so great had been the physical and mental impact of the work.

On June 27, the four lead actors, Fleming, and David called a wrap party on Stage 5. David cabled Jock, "Sound the siren. Scarlett O'Hara completed her performance at noon today. Gable finishes tonight or in the morning." He had hired a yacht for a few days and he told the world, "You can all go to the devil."

Of course, it was not exactly over. There would be retakes, the editing, the process shots, and the music. But at the end of June, all units had exposed 437,949 feet of Technicolor film. That is nearly eighty-one hours. The cost of the picture stood at $3.576 million. The world was a little over two months from its real war. Everyone had survived *Gone With the Wind*. But everyone had been fired, let go, been taken sick, or had time off, except for David O. Selznick. Just as the horror of making a picture is very great, so is the sentimentality of having come through. Irene surveyed the wreckage that the film had caused and recognized the mercy "of great good luck." But David had the eternally boyish attitude that believed he had managed it.

15 · DREAMS OF LONG STANDING

IN *A PRIVATE VIEW*, Irene Selznick wrote of *Gone With the Wind*:

> After shooting began, it was like being under siege. We were in a war and we were in it together. I had the house organized "for the duration." Breakfast was earlier, dinner was later, and the children were neglected. So were the amenities. His burden was formidable. He had to lay it off on someone; it would have been intolerable to carry it alone. I didn't know what a beating I was taking until David told me what guilt he felt when he looked at me.

For years, mealtimes had been haphazard at Summit Drive, but there were plenty of occasions in 1939 when David never got home. He had a couch in his office, and a bathroom, and the work did not let up at night. There were also those who felt his lavishly provided for children were neglected as a matter of course. But how far were David and Irene "in it together"? They did not see a great deal of each other. David's feeling for Joan Fontaine lingered—for *Rebecca* was its consummation—and amid all the upheaval, David had had twenty minutes to spare in Vivien Leigh's bungalow if Sunny Alexander had been willing.

There were such brief encounters Irene did not want to know about, and the terrible effort of filmmaking in which she had no part. However much she felt "under siege," there she was sitting on the lawn at Summit Drive, on the afternoon of Saturday, May 6 (a fifteen-and-a-half-hour day on *Wind*), listening to the Kentucky Derby. Two women approached her: they had just been driven from Pasadena, having come by train across the country; they were Kay Brown and Ingrid Bergman.

"How do you do," said Bergman, trying hard to display correct English.

Irene hushed her and waited until the radio commentary was over. Then she was the perfect hostess, offering something to eat, taken aback that the Swedish actress had not come with several trunks, but inviting Ingrid to dinner at the Beachcomber with Miriam Hopkins, Grace Moore, and Richard Barthelmess.

"Is Mr. Selznick coming home soon?" asked Bergman; she was disappointed he was not there to meet her at Pasadena. For she was very idealistic about this American adventure.

"Mr. Selznick often works late at the studio," said Irene. "He'll be along later."

Whereas Kay Brown had thought Bergman more promising than *Intermezzo*, David had preferred the story. He wasn't sure about Ingrid. But in the late summer of 1938, Kay and Jock, with Jenia Reissar's help, opened talks for the rights. Then Kay sat Jock down in London and showed him the Swedish *Intermezzo*, and he'd said they had to have the girl, too. They found a phone and, with Jock plying it with coins, Kay got through to the home of Ingrid and Petter Lindstrom in Stockholm. But the husband had been dubious and difficult on the phone.

Jenia Reissar went to Stockholm in September; she arrived the day the Lindstroms' daughter, Pia, was born—September 20. "I waited for about five days, before I could see Ingrid," said Reissar. "I said to her that we were thinking of bringing Leslie Howard, one great trump card I had. And would she do it? . . . She said, yes, she would do anything to work with Leslie

Howard, she was terribly interested. But she said, 'Not for a year. I've just had this baby.' "

Miss Reissar made the deal for the rights to *Intermezzo*, and she established that the original director, Gustaf Molander, had too little English for the Hollywood job. Petter Lindstrom played the heavy in these talks, but he claimed Ingrid wanted it that way. There was bartering as well as a baby. Bergman was also considering going to Germany to play Charlotte Corday at UFA. Indeed, the question of her pro-German feelings was to loom as large as her height. David became the more eager as he realized he needed to get another "easy" picture in for SIP—a remake did seem straightforward. Kay Brown was brought back to America and then sent to England again in midwinter on the *Mauretania*. She then flew to Stockholm to "get" Bergman.

Petter would not accept the standard seven-year contract, so Bergman signed for *Intermezzo* only at $2,500 a week for eight weeks (twice Vivien Leigh's salary), with options on other pictures. The quality of unclouded idealism that made Ingrid so attractive was no indication of her careerism. From the outset, it was hard for Kay, Jenia Reissar, or David to gauge the balance of power between Ingrid and Petter, for the husband was made to seem awkward and demanding, while Ingrid was helpless. She was a great actress, and in April Bergman left her husband and baby in Sweden, went to England, and with Kay boarded the *Queen Mary*.

That night in Los Angeles, Ingrid joined Irene at her dinner date; Kay Brown was not invited. SIP workers like Kay and Marcella felt Mrs. Selznick never wanted them at social events. Stars were glamorous—if they behaved— but SIP people saw the snobbery in Hollywood royalty.

After dinner, Irene and Ingrid went on to Miriam Hopkins's home for a party. A movie was shown, and Ingrid was caught up in it when someone told her David had arrived. It was one o'clock in the morning, "and there was this man," in the kitchen, "lying *on* the table . . . well it looked to me as if he was lying half across it, and he was shoveling food into his mouth. As I came in the door he glanced across at me, and said, 'God! Take your shoes off.' "

He said she was too tall; he worried that her name was Germanic, and he began to appreciate she needed a comprehensive Hollywood makeup job. After all, David had seen at MGM how wondrously Greta Gustafson had been transformed into something called "Garbo." But Bergman drew herself up to her full height and told him no. "I thought you saw me in the movie *Intermezzo*, and liked me. . . . Now you've seen me, you want to change everything. So I'd rather not do the movie. We'll say no more about it. . . . I'll take the next train and go back home."

It had been a long day for both of them, and gradually David saw the light of inspiration. He would keep Ingrid "natural"; there would be no alterations. This was the new woman from Europe. He went straight for high concept; it was the speed with which he changed his mind that amounted to genius.

For her first week in Los Angeles, however great the siege at Summit Drive, Ingrid was the Selznicks' houseguest. The novelty of the invitation startled observers—the Selznicks had had no guests at Summit Drive except for Whitneys. Perhaps Ingrid's presence drew David home a little earlier.

The relationship between David and Ingrid was warm, troubled, yet curiously unproductive—she made her best films in the early forties not for him but on loan-out. No doubt, David went after her, and it is clear now that Bergman's career was marked by many affairs. Joan Fontaine has said that the first time she met Bergman it was in David's office, "where I saw her wince under his embrace." But Bergman was too good an actress ever to be seen wincing. Ingrid and Irene remained close friends for two decades. Whatever skirmishes there were, Bergman and David enjoyed one another. She was always taken by his foolish enthusiasm—she may have given it spur with her laughter:

> He was especially enchanting when he'd had a few drinks, and you were at his home and he was entertaining friends. He'd never stop talking and it was such interesting talk. He was so full of ideas. And he'd never let you leave. If you said, "I'm tired, I think it's about time I went," he'd rush to the door, hold his arms out wide to prevent you getting out, and say, "You're not going home. I won't let you. I've just had this marvelous new idea for you." So you'd stay and listen and it usually was a marvelous idea which left you pretty excited.
>
> Next morning you'd say, "That was a pretty good idea you had last night, David. Now what are we going to do about it?" And he'd look at you through his big glasses and say, "What idea? I don't remember any idea."

David had never meant to interfere on *Intermezzo*. The point of that film had been to slip through easily without his attention. The picture began shooting on May 24—a week after the sulky Victor Fleming returned to *Wind*—with William Wyler directing and Harry Stradling in charge of the camera. But after a week, Wyler was fired; a little later, Stradling was gone. David replaced the director with Gregory Ratoff and the cameraman with Gregg Toland. Ratoff—Julius Saxe in *What Price Hollywood?*—had directed a few undistinguished films. But he was a friend and a fellow gambler. Arthur Fellows, who worked on *Intermezzo*, was told that Ratoff was one of those few people who lost heavily to David and that his director's fee went to pay off the debt. In fact, said Fellows, the direction of the movie was left to Toland as far as camera work was concerned (Toland had done *Wuthering Heights* and immediately ahead lay *The Grapes of Wrath* and *Citizen Kane*) and to Leslie Howard for interpretation.

The picture was made quickly, but David was always concerned about the best way of capturing Bergman's natural look, and he retook her first appearance many times. Only sixty-nine minutes long, *Intermezzo* was done in less than five months—it opened on October 5, before the last retakes on *Wind*. But it cost $850,000 (about the same as *Citizen Kane*, for instance), and it lost $300,000.

ALFRED HITCHCOCK reported for work at SIP only a few weeks before Ingrid Bergman arrived—it is hard to credit how crowded 1939 was for David. Hitchcock would represent a kind of warfare very different from the tumult of *Wind*. It would be steady, quiet, and tactical; its subject was exactly how one made films and whose the responsibility was. The lesson of working with Hitchcock was that no matter how much the producer involved himself, there were secrets of craft, nuance, and meaning that only a director controlled. It was a war from which David emerged not just beaten, but demoralized.

In addition, Hitchcock meant *Rebecca*, and it is a matter of irony and real wonder that, in 1939, David Selznick produced his most intricate and effective film and the one over which he was most emotionally involved. That film was not *Gone With the Wind*.

David felt himself much in love with Joan Fontaine from the summer of 1938 into the early months of 1939. She always said that while David chased her, he never caught her. Indeed, she found him physically unattractive. Still, his chase was steady: between the end of June 1938 and the middle of July, David saw her in his office nearly every day. He wrote poetry for her; he made a fool of himself over her, and she moved on, before *Rebecca* was cast, toward marriage with the actor Brian Aherne. But even if she had ever flirted with David, she got her role in *Rebecca* for one reason—David believed in her.

David was heartsick. April 2, 1939, was Irene's thirty-second birthday. It was also a Sunday, a day off from the *Gone With the Wind* shooting. As a rule, David made a huge fuss of birthdays, but in 1939 he sent Irene this handwritten note:

Darling—

I feel a heel to have left you on Birthday Night. I hate to be in the light of making alibis, but I really *was* depressed, and I think I must have been as drunk as I've been in a long time.

I'd give anything to have comforted myself in your arms instead of idiotically drinking and gambling.

I guess I'm still not really "right", that I'm still without the courage and character to face a major disappointment with the equanimity I should by now have acquired—because so long as I have you, nothing else is worth bemoaning, even dreams of long standing.

I'm still sick at heart, and it isn't helping any to realize I could and should have stayed with you last night.

I'm confused. I need you as much even as I love you, and that's a very great deal.

The future seems so bleak commercially and creatively: I wish I could just be with you somewhere, away from need of money, habit of work, drive of years' silly hopes. Maybe—oh, I hope so—we can map a program: months, eight or ten, of hard work and drive for financial freedom, try very hard, I beg you, to forgive me and put up with me. I could weep, both for that vanished optimist that was me, and for you, who sat (perforce) through his disappearing act.

I'm really without deep emotions but for one: my overwhelming love of you.

Cry-baby.

The letter shows how bleak the future seemed to David as he made *Gone With the Wind*. But is the "major disappointment" a candid reference to Fontaine, or is it early realization of the funding problem at SIP? Is it simply a failed husband asking his wife to watch and help in his recovery from an infatuation? But how should the wife contain her mixture of grief and anger?

Hitchcock was working toward a treatment and a script for *Rebecca*, with Joan Harrison and Philip MacDonald as his writers. But Hitchcock did not yet comprehend David's devout approach to any book he was adapting. Hitchcock was a composer of films, a master of what worked on screen, especially in the way of suspense. He liked extreme physical action that uncovered the inner workings of a mind—and, to this day, that is not a bad working definition of movies. David had never met so pure and ruthless a technician or so subtle and cool a psychologist. Hitchcock was being free with the book, for he was of the absolute opinion that books are not movies.

David did not let him stay single-minded, however. Hitchcock was an available mind, and so David drew him in on *Gone With the Wind*. Hitchcock was asked to comment on the scene in which Union soldiers come upon Rhett, Ashley, and Melanie, the scene where *David Copperfield* is being read (in the book, it is *Les Misérables*). The analysis that Hitchcock submitted was cinematic and precise:

As I outlined on the evening of the 3rd of May, 1939, I feel that the lack of suspense in this reel arises out of the fact that it is deficient in three main essentials.

(1) That the audience should be in possession of all the facts appertaining to Butler's, Ashley's, etc., efforts to get into the home which is surrounded by Union soldiers.

(2) That the audience should be shown surreptitious exchange of glances by the pseudo drunken Butler and the character Melanie.

(3) That the end of the tension should be sufficiently marked as the Union soldiers depart with their apologies.

I suggest that these things can be remedied by the following method:

(a) To play the reel up to the commencement of the reading of *David Copperfield* and, instead of the LAP DISSOLVE to the pendulum, CUT AWAY to some location that has the house in sight and there show the desperate group of Butler, the wounded Ashley, etc. Establish that in the distance they can see that the house is surrounded; their bewilderment as to what manner they can pass the cordon; then, suddenly Butler has an idea. On this, we CUT BACK into the house and proceed with the reel until the family hear the arrival of the drunken group. Then, CUT outside to the drunks coming toward the house. Show Butler lift a sober eye in the midst of his mock inebriation, and from his eye-line show the military preparing to arrest their advance.

(b) Once inside the house it should be essential to see an exchange of meaning glances between Butler and Melanie in order that we know that she is in possession of the fact that they are only pretending to be drunk.

After the military have gone, there should be a slight movement, but Butler should hist them to silence for a moment while he crosses to the window; and then, turning, give the all clear. From this tableau of arrested motion, the whole room-full break into feverish movement around Ashley, etc.

Whereupon Hitchcock supplied, in script form, a list of "necessary shots" to turn the sequence into "one of the most magnificent" in the picture. There was always a teacher in Hitchcock. His movies demonstrate the informational dynamics of the medium, and he liked to have completely foreseen and comprehended shooting scripts before he undertook photography. Hal Kern, a veteran editor, looked at the notes and told David, "He surely has a great mind and better picture ideas than anyone I have met in months."

A month later, however, David was "disappointed beyond words" by Hitchcock's treatment of *Rebecca*. "Beyond words" was the gist of it, for Hitchcock was intent on making a self-sufficient film experience. On June 12, David sent a lengthy memo insisting on fidelity to the book.

In many respects, the Hitchcock treatment was crass and vulgar—Hitchcock was not a good reader, and he did not always grasp the depths of Daphne du Maurier's writing. David's specific objections were sensible and improving—and Hitchcock would incorporate most of them. But Hitchcock knew something David never quite worked out in his life: that films are impressions left on the viewer's mind by image, sound, hesitation, angle, lens, and light. For better or worse, David was shaped by stories that could be recounted verbally.

Hitchcock had wanted Ronald Colman to play Maxim de Winter, but had been unable to persuade him. Thereafter, the choice came down to Laurence Olivier or William Powell, and producer and director agreed on Olivier, who was signed on July 1.

As for the second Mrs. de Winter, there were five candidates: Vivien Leigh, who tested first after a day's work as Scarlett and then in New York with Olivier, Loretta Young, Margaret Sullavan, Anne Baxter, and Joan Fontaine. Olivier was anxious to have Vivien. On the evidence of the screen tests, any of the five would have been very good. David was also trying to get Olivia de Havilland as a possible. Vivien Leigh was ruled out, David said,

*Joan Payson, Irene, David, and Jock at
the Ocean Park Pier in Santa Monica*

said, because he, Hitchcock, *and* George Cukor looked at her test and thought "she doesn't seem at all right as to sincerity or age or innocence," and also perhaps because he feared the alliance of Leigh and Olivier. Margaret Sullavan impressed everyone, but would she be credible being pushed around by Mrs. Danvers? In real life, Margaret Sullavan was so commanding a woman.

On August 18, David wrote to Jock about the options; he was arguing himself back toward Joan Fontaine. She had been his first choice because she was "the only one who seemed to know completely what the part was all about." David had discussed the part with her more than with any other actress. But many people had scoffed at the proposal, and David must have feared being seen to cast someone he had been in love with. Then Hitchcock had had second thoughts. John Cromwell, who had directed Fontaine's first test, said they were crazy to look elsewhere. When the still invaluable George Cukor ran the tests he had said Anne Baxter was most touching. But she was very inexperienced and only sixteen. Cukor said he would pick Fontaine. There was a problem—though it was also a relief for David's need to save face: Fontaine and Brian Aherne were marrying on August 19— "Almost on impulse," according to Aherne himself.

Jock replied on August 21. He seemed to read David's mind, to give him that old unconditional support while making clear the approaching end to such generosity. He believed Vivien should have the part, but he knew that was a lost cause. His memo was full of fondness still, but the tide of belief was going out. It clinched the part for Joan Fontaine.

> The last test of Joan Fontaine was so bad that I cannot see her playing the role otherwise than as a dithering idiot, or as her other version—a talking magazine cover. I urge most strongly that if you are ever to consider her seriously any further, she should make the same test as the recent one of Ann Baxter. I should imagine that marriage with Brian Aherne couldn't interfere much with her time, so this should be comparatively easy to work out. If it can't be, then I think we all have a very serious problem. I cannot assure the Pioneer stockholders or the Bank of America that all is well with *Rebecca* until this most important part is cast. You must realize that although the money will probably be found to complete this picture—having gone so far, I am put in a very difficult position if I have to report with less than two weeks to go, the picture is not yet cast. Such procedure has not been and is not good business. You must realize, of course, that we understand that our opinion of various casting possibilities is invited only to assist you in making decisions which, in the last analysis must be your own, because the blame or the credit must be entirely yours. So that if you have a hunch about Fontaine and want to try her without further tests, for Heaven's sake go ahead and do it. You seem to have a pretty good

reputation in this respect. All I ask is not to delay it any longer. I fear these delays like at the moment the Poles must Chamberlain!

The offer reached Fontaine in the wilds of Oregon, where she was honeymooning with Aherne. He protested the interruption, but she took the opportunity and headed south. The couple had only met in June 1939. The marriage did not fare well. A few years later, she asked him one day, "How long have we been married?"

"Nearly four years," he told her.

"My God! I never meant to stay married to you that long!"

16 · MY FUTURE IS DRAWING TO A CLOSE

LONG BEFORE David had finished *Gone With the Wind*, he began his campaign of goading, advising, recommending, and second-guessing MGM on what to do with it. In May 1939, as Fleming fell ill, David was writing to Howard Dietz, director of publicity at Metro, thanking him for excellent advance ads for *Wind*, but wondering whether conventional ads weren't a little beside the point: "the picture is turning out so brilliantly that its handling will have to be on a scale and of a type never before tried in the picture business." He invoked *The Birth of a Nation*, foresaw a running time of between three and four hours, and did wonder if the gross might not go to "ten million dollars, perhaps twelve or thirteen million, perhaps fifteen million."

David was already showing bits of the film to Al Lichtman at Metro, building enthusiasm over the rough assembly. Lichtman had no doubts, and David refrained from passing his reactions on to Jock in case they seemed crazy. But "in his opinion it is generations beyond any picture that has ever been made, and that even *The Birth of a Nation* is not in the same class with it. So there!"

"So there!" is a clue to how David survived in 1939, that year as full as a lifetime. He believed he was going to be proved right, and the first proof came in late April and May, that worst of the bad times. Whatever the doubts of Sidney Howard, John Wharton, or even Jock, David looked at his film coming to life on Hal Kern's moviola and knew it played. After so many early photographic problems the colors shone. Gable and Vivien Leigh were natural yet larger than life. A Kern, or a critic even, could have seen those points of quality. But they were not enough for more than ordinary success. David felt phenomenon, and in this he trusted himself.

From New York, Jock was alarmed to see how far ahead David was thinking. For he was bombarding Lowell Calvert with plans on how to maneuver the best-selling operation out of Metro. And this was three weeks before the end of principal photography! Jock begged:

> I suppose it is inevitable that reams of correspondence will pass back and forth regarding this, but may I urge that you devote (I nearly said "waste") as little time to this as is humanly possible for the present. I had imagined that since M.G.M. is by contract solely responsible for the handling of the picture that we would give them as little chance to alibi and pass the buck as possible by placing the issue and responsibility squarely up to them.

Jock's innocence took David's breath away. A Whitney expected the execution of duties in a decent, professional way. Didn't he know this was the picture business! That some of these men were Russian! Fellow Jews! And relatives!! There was not one drop of the natural plotter in Jock—it made him a wondrous creature to behold, so different as to be energizing for David. So he told Jock (this was only two weeks after the crippling refinancing through the Bank of America), "I am afraid you are in for a disappointment if you think I am going to take a hands-off policy on something to which I have devoted three of the best years of my life."

It is easy to say the editing was a monstrous task: a grinning Hal Kern posed for horror pictures, hopelessly entangled in celluloid. Yet sections of the film were shown to Metro in June, and they evidently played. Two months after shooting ended there was a complete assembly that ran about 260 minutes.

Within days of the conclusion of principal photography, there was a screening for Lichtman and L.B. The length was more than Mayer's bladder could endure; the picture had to be stopped a few times. At the conclusion, Lichtman said it was a $30 million gross. There was no record of what Mayer said—fathers-in-law know how to stifle their pride, pleasure, or envy, even if the bladder has no master.

A few days later, the film was run (at 24,300 feet) for Nick Schenck and his wife and for Harry Rapf ("whom I invited because of a particularly warm feeling I have for Mr. Rapf, due to his being my first employer in Hollywood"). Schenck refused any intermission; he said it was "the greatest picture ever made" and he topped Lichtman: there was no conceivable limit to the picture's gross.

That was July 16. On August 3, A. C. Blumenthal wondered whether SIP would be prepared to sell all the picture to Metro. David said they didn't get rid of him that easily. He was already obsessing about the proper ticket price ($1.50 or $1.00) and where to open, whether to road-show, about how many theaters how soon.

By mid-August, therefore, David was as much caught up in that struggle as in watching the cut get finer, calling for retakes, setting Max Steiner up to do the music, and talking to Jack Cosgrove about the special effects. To say nothing, that mid-August, of cutting *Intermezzo*, finding time for gambling (losses bounced up to $10,925 for August), wondering about a war, and going off to a preview of *The Wizard of Oz*. Previews were on his mind, and he wanted to keep schmoozing with the people at Metro to see how they got ready to market a picture.

Irene didn't go to the *Oz* preview (it was August 8), and she had not yet seen *Gone With the Wind* in its assembly, so David left her a note to read. Compare the exhilaration here with the gloom of April 2:

> Angel—
>
> I took Hitch to the preview; saw Edie for a brief moment at the outside of the Troc, where I went just long enough to congratulate Vic [Fleming] and Mervyn [LeRoy] . . . and then went on with Hitch, for a drink and some dinner, to Lamaze, which I thought safe, with no need for explanation. We talked—stories!! Rebecca and Titanic and Benedict Arnold were my gaiety. He's not a bad guy, shorn of affectation, although not exactly a man to go camping with.
>
> *The Wizard* is a little heavy-handed, definitely not your dish, but damned good—and I think will be a big success. The Chinese audience and M-G-M lobbyists were as warm as ever. . . .
>
> I've been thinking of you, and have decided to marry you if you'll have me. I'm a little middle-aged, to be sure; I have a hammer toe and I run into things; I'm ex-arrogant, and once I wanted to be a big shot; I snore loudly, drink exuberantly, cuddle (i.e. snuggle) expansively, work excessively, play enthusiastically; and my future is drawing to a close but I'm tall and Jewish and I do love you, and I Jew mean you.
>
> David-in-Quest-of-his-Mate

One man in America had seen parts of the assembly of *Gone With the Wind* and disliked it. That was Sidney Howard. In the summer of 1939, he was at his farm in Tyringham, Massachusetts. He was writing a screenplay for Goldwyn, but there was much to do on the farm. On August 23, he was starting a tractor with a handle. But it was still in gear, and it leaped forward and struck him. Howard was killed—his is the saddest story of all of *Gone With the Wind*.

On Sunday, September 3, 1939, five days before the start of *Rebecca* and six before the first preview of *Gone With the Wind*, Neville Chamberlain announced on the radio that, unless . . . then a state of war would exist between Britain and Germany. It was the best of times and the worst—except that the best would get better yet and the worst would kill the age that loved and made *Gone With the Wind*.

So David, Irene, and Jock and all the cans of *Gone With the Wind* were driven out to Riverside on that hot Saturday evening, September 9. They are on the sidewalk still, outside the Fox, with its excited manager, waiting for *Hawaiian Nights* to end.

Hal Kern had made a further demand on the Fox. There would be an announcement of the preview—but the film must not be named. People could leave, but there would be no readmission once the preview had begun. What's more, no one was to phone out revealing the event. Once the show started, the theater would be sealed.

The manager said, "This is against the law. I can't do it."

"That's all right," Kern answered. "I'll do it for you. I'll close the theater."

So the manager considered the matter and asked if he could make just one call to get his wife over.

"I'll stand by the phone," Kern agreed. "Don't tell her anything except to come over."

There was an announcement made to the audience, and their eagerness mounted. William Erickson was a boy in the crowd. He and his mother had gone to the theater to escape the heat of the day. He wanted to see *Beau Geste*, but his mother told him to be patient.

As the film was set up in the projection booth, Irene panicked in the lobby. It was one of her nervous attacks: "There were a lot of strangers in there—what had they done to deserve to see this picture? I burst into tears and refused to go in." So David and Jock took an arm each and bundled this child of show business into the dark. They sat in a row and held hands. Kern was behind them, with a box that controlled the sound level.

There was very little of Max Steiner's score ready yet, so this assembly had some music from *The Prisoner of Zenda*. But it had the great opening title—the huge white letters sliding past like a dream train—for it had been done at Pacific Title the previous weekend.

The Selznick sign appeared, and a buzz went through the audience. This was close to Los Angeles. People knew the film business. The public had been waiting three years. War had been declared six days earlier. It wasn't world war yet, but no one in Riverside was stupid. David O. Selznick was about to have his moment when he put the show before the people. This was passion, and it is still why people do such insane things to make movies.

Hal Kern saw it and felt it:

When Margaret Mitchell's name came on the screen, you never heard
such a sound in your life. They just yelled, they stood up on the seats.
I was sitting here, Mrs. Selznick was here, and David was there. I had
the box, you know, the sound box. And I had that music wide open
and you couldn't hear a thing. Mrs. Selznick was crying like a baby,
and so was David, and so was I. Oh, what a thrill! And when *Gone With
the Wind* came on the screen, it was thunderous.

The movie, its story, had not begun. There has never been an audience
so ready. David's delays had made the picture. It was the greatest moment
of his life, the greatest victory and redemption of all his failings. The film
ran on past midnight. There was enormous applause when it was over. The
preview cards were astonishing—they were two-thirds excellent; people
begged that the movie not be cut; some said everyone everywhere should see
it; there were those who fell in love with Vivien Leigh that night; no one
found it untrue to the book. One person thanked all concerned for the
opportunity of seeing it. William Erickson asked if he could now see *Beau
Geste*.

The movies began to be altered. And David's future was over.

As Irene felt the mood in the crowd, "It was as though something
wonderful or terrible had happened."

17 · EVERY INCH OF THE FILM

RETAKES, CLOSE-UP INSERTS, and process photography on *Gone
With the Wind* did not end until November 11, and there was much cunning
sharing as elements of the antebellum interiors of the South served as
Manderley in *Rebecca*. Small corners of bright make-believe littered the same
soundstages, and sometimes a quick redressing shifted them from one story
to another. There had been a period when Leslie Howard was doing both
Ashley and *Intermezzo*, and there were anxieties over the continuity of his
different hairstyles. There were days, in the fall, when, desperately, across
the chaos of one stage, Scarlett O'Hara and Maxim de Winter gazed upon
one another, vast yearnings that pass under the same lights but never share
one frame.

It was at this time that Jack Cosgrove came into his element. Cosgrove
was a nineteenth-century artist who defied the modern eye to notice his

archaic enhancements amid all the lifelike photography. He did his finest work, painting on glass so that the backgrounds could be matted in with movie, a work so delicate and precise he had to be drunk to make it dangerous and interesting. Cosgrove's work was so good it remains hard to estimate how many shots in *Wind* have his touch. But what he offered was another way of rescuing a film in postproduction: one saving glass might let an otherwise useless scene play. The camera crews and Hal Kern looked on Cosgrove as a wild genius, up in the air doing the backdrops and always in danger of falling from the drink. No area of the film went over budget by a higher percentage than "Process Backgrounds." The work meant to cost $29,772 eventually came out at $89,832.

Cosgrove was also employed on the linking montages, the backgrounds for Ben Hecht's grandiose titles. As with so many things, these were left till late in the day. Hecht was home sick in Nyack, New York, when he got David's "frantic" cable on October 11:

> I realize it is an imposition to ask you to do these feeling as you do but if you cannot tackle them immediately I will have to do them myself which would break my heart as I have been counting, as you know, on your doing these titles ever since we started the picture. Can't you swallow a bottle of thyroid and a couple of benzedrines. My own metabolism was about minus thirty before *Wind* started. God knows what it is now.

The film's premiere had been promised to Mayor William B. Hartsfield of Atlanta, originally for November 15, 1939, the seventy-fifth anniversary of the burning of Atlanta. That date was too tough, so David resolved to get in and out of Atlanta before Christmas and open the film in New York and Los Angeles immediately thereafter. He had a hunch taking the picture to the South would be worth the trouble. And the publicist in David was now very confident. He held the flavor and the imagery of the film back: there were no early stills for magazines. So often consumed with schemes to get public attention, he now felt no need to seek anything. Let it go on the wind of three years.

He had another reason for being out before the end of the year. He wanted Academy Award nominations—in retrospect, he believed the January opening of *David Copperfield* might have deprived it of Best Picture. The Oscars, he guessed, would be awarded earlier than usual in 1940—with a war around, why wait?

Thought of awards led to considerations over the credits. How could such a film acknowledge everyone who had served? There is no Kay Brown, no Irene, no Jock, and no L.B. in the credits. Naively or not, David had approached Vic Fleming and had asked "whether he would like to see us include a card crediting people who had contributed greatly to the picture, but who had no place in the program credits." David was thinking of George Cukor, "who . . . has practically all of his scenes still in the picture," and Sam Wood (who had worked twenty-four days).

Fleming cut him off. He would tolerate no such thing. He had reached his limit with David—waiting for rewrites, enduring the changes, and, as Fleming saw it, saving the picture. In the retakes, there had been a bitter row between Fleming and Ray Klune. They were doing the scene where Scarlett, Melanie, and Prissy shelter under the bridge. Soldiers were the threat, but as the work went on a real rain began to fall. Fleming said it was not possible to get the scene. Klune argued, and Fleming exploded: he told Klune, "You do whatever those Jews want you to do, don't you?" Here was one more evidence of the animosity between director and producer. In Fleming's opinion, David had impeded the film, but now he was trying to steal credit for it. From David's point of view, Fleming had complained, sulked, and acted like a manager who believed the enterprise was a folly. David had believed.

He did believe it was his film, and that claim survives all scrutiny, for good and ill. But there was another side to the credits ledger that shows the very vanity in David that a Fleming found odious. In October, David told Dan O'Shea he had decided to let the writing credit stand to Sidney Howard alone—after all, no other writer was worth serious mention; the credits were cluttered enough already, and David didn't want to deprive Howard, or his widow, of the glory. But Oliver Garrett had objected, and so David felt compelled to make clear who had done what:

> When I mentioned to Oliver Garrett that I had some intention of giving him a contributory credit, he seemed rather upset and felt to my amazement that the credit ought to read Adaptation by Sidney Howard and Screen Play by himself, which would of course be ridiculous. But rather than get into any argument at that time I told him that when the script was finished I would take it up further. Since that time I myself did the last half or two-thirds of the script without anybody's help. . . .
>
> I don't think there is a chance of anybody else advancing any claim in connection with it even though, if you should discuss it with Garrett, you can say frankly that of the comparatively small amount of material in the picture which is not from the book, that most of it is my own personally, and the only original lines of dialogue which are not my own are a few from Sidney Howard and a few from Ben Hecht and a couple more from John Van Druten. Offhand I doubt

that there are ten original words of Garrett's in the whole script. As to the construction, this is about 80% my own, and the rest divided between Jo Swerling and Sidney Howard, with Hecht having contributed materially to the construction of one sequence.

The key credits of direction and writing went to one person each, and thus the legend of single-minded intent and execution in moviemaking was renewed. Success makes for the most rivalry among contributors; everyone is ready to desert a failure. But "construction" as David meant it covered only the blocking out of scenes and their order—it was a literary concept, based in complete trust about the accuracy of adaptation. A Hitchcock might have looked at *Gone With the Wind* and said it was truly constructed out of the emotional color, the uninhibited performance of Vivien Leigh, the design of William Cameron Menzies, the momentum that Hal Kern gave it, the glue in Cosgrove's transitions, and the ragbag of new themes and old Southern airs that Max Steiner threw on the sound track. The dispute over credits, and its bearing on David's identity, arrogance, and aspirations, was in a small way a discussion about the nature of film. *Gone With the Wind* was a success, so David assumed he was in the right.

Of course, he was in charge. If need be, he could insist. But there have been many executives who had as much power, yet could not exercise it. They surrendered to actors, directors, and technicians; they could not pretend to compete with writers, or they lacked the will to persevere against everyone. They did not care enough. They had not got the energy or the time to care every hour, to let no detail escape. They were not worthy of the storm that is filmmaking. David cared, and—much of the time—he tried to persuade others, to show them, rather than just bully them into line. For David, no matter how overbearing, the other makers of his films were the first members of his audience. He wanted their approval. This led him into a new tactic, crazier than just dictating long memos: it was dictating memos, having them typed, but not sending them. He filed them—so that history would understand him!

This happened with one of his genuine achievements in the film. The ending had always been a worry. The last few pages of the book have the events of Rhett's departure, interspersed with Margaret Mitchell's account of what Scarlett is thinking. Scarlett's last words allow us—and her—to believe she may get Rhett back (and the dream of sequels has always clung to that hope). But it is not a decisive enough ending for so large an experience.

Over the years, David had pondered, and he, Howard, and others had reworked the ending. Howard had made a deceptively slight change in Rhett's last line. In the book, he had said, "My dear, I don't give a damn."

Howard had put "Frankly" at the head of the line, and the addition may be our best remembered flash of Clark Gable. If David had traded so much away for Gable, "Frankly" was a magnificent gift to the actor and the film. But it was David who ordered the way the ending played: Rhett's going, Scarlett's collapse on the stairs, the voice of her father that rallies her with the thought of "Tara." On September 20, after previews had proved his instinct, David wrote to Kay so that she could tell Mitchell. Then he didn't send the letter. But it cries out with his feeling for the power of the ending:

> The part of each speech is repeated in turn with increasing tempo and volume; then the last phrase of each speech is repeated with still more tempo and volume; and finally, the voice of each of the three men saying in turn, "Tara." During this Scarlett has been emerging from her despair, raising her head slowly and reacting to the realization that she still has Tara. She lifts her head and, as the camera moves in to a big close-up of her, says: "Home to Tara! After all, tomorrow is another day." We immediately dissolve to Scarlett standing at Tara in silhouette in the very spot where we saw her standing with Gerald earlier in the picture and he spoke to her about the land. The camera pulls back just as it did on Gerald and Scarlett to an extreme long shot as we come to our end.

That moment would not be as it is without Max Steiner's Tara theme, maybe the best-known piece of movie music, the one great tune amid a

October 13, 1939, Vivien's last day of retakes

patchwork score. The legend has it that David went valiantly into combat with Joseph Breen and the Production Code to protect the "damn" in Rhett's last line. But this was a show-biz battle, a $5,000 fine, and more publicity. What is most impressive is the way he shaped that ending and the manner in which he discovered—in character, actress, and audience—the equal desire for adventure and security in a woman. *Gone With the Wind* is a film about a woman whose yearning makes her bitchiness and her duplicity bearable. That the film works so well, and still works, is because of the way two women—author and actress—and one man understood that.

That it worked so well in 1939 and 1940 must have something to do with Scarlett's final realization of the power of home. That meant so much on the eve of war. The film was lucky, we can say. But it is a great thing in life to be exhausted, crazed, still interfering, and cling on to a scrap of luck.

The picture had cost, so far, $4,085,790. When the last bills were in, it was near enough $4.25 million. It had run over by only $1.242 million. And it would play 220 minutes. It still does.

He would not shut up. The struggle with MGM was fully engaged. On September 23, he wrote Nick Schenck an eight-page letter, single-spaced. There had been few letters as long before, but there would be many more in the future. Finally, there would be nothing but those letters. Its style is crucial, for it expresses the disintegration and the triumph of David: the letter reaches a kind of rational hysteria in which argument goes on forever.

The letter to Schenck asked for many things, and it began to tell the story of how the film had been made. This song would last all David's life. He believed they should go for higher ticket prices—even $2.50—because this was a film everyone *had* to see. He wanted the picture road-shown everywhere—he wanted to reach the world. And he made a magnificent, heartfelt claim on the indulgence of MGM in seeing how fortunate it was to have the film on such generous terms: half the profit plus a 20 percent distribution fee for less than a third of the budget. He asked to have the deal rewritten.

And in that matter he won: MGM agreed it was lucky; it reduced the distribution fee to 15 percent. That and a world war in the same year.

But here is the song (in small part only). To be entirely true to David is to quote such letters in full, but that would require a life from readers, whereas a book like this tries to *give* a life. This is September 23, 1939, to Nick Schenck. David is thirty-seven, and ready to die:

> This picture has done so much to me physically, and has robbed me of so much, including my entire personal life, for so long, that my feelings about it go beyond mere commercial conviction, and are on the highly emotional side. To understand this, and, hopefully, so that

you will be more kindly disposed toward what I say, I take the liberty of reminding you that I staked my whole personal career, the whole existence of our company, on this one effort; I gambled millions of dollars of other people's money on my own conviction, and took full responsibility for every inch of the film, for the writing and reading of every line, for every prop and every camera set-up. I have taken a terrible beating from the industry and the press and even the public for about three years. No matter how well the picture finally does, it will always be questionable as to whether it has been worth what I have put myself through and my associates and employees through.

18 · THE SEASON OF PARTIES

WHENEVER SELZNICK INTERNATIONAL had raided the South for local color, patient beauties, or crumbs from Margaret Mitchell, Kay Brown had been its soldier. So Kay was in charge of many arrangements for the Atlanta premiere. She grumbled, but she liked to be given some opportunity to complain. She was a small, busy woman—a busybody, according to Val Lewton—full of ideas and the wish to be noticed. But she was tireless, ingenious, and seldom defeated. She got the best hotel rooms she could, while warning David that Atlanta was not New York, and she negotiated between two very different, but equally raw and wild enthusiasms for the picture—that of Hollywood and the South.

There was some pious sighing over the ballyhoo that might be turned loose in Atlanta. But no one would have missed it, and few of the sophisticates were more than a half inch out of the muddy waters of ballyhoo. As late as the end of November, David was putting on an act about keeping the fuss down and behaving with a little dignity. He sat in on talks between Birdwell and Howard Strickling, West Coast head of publicity at MGM. Those two men guessed at the disaster Atlanta could present. Birdwell wondered if things might not be thrown at anything as vainglorious as a procession. So David urged against too much showiness to Kay Brown. In his forebodings he described the events of which he would be a happy part in less than three weeks:

> He [Strickling] and Birdwell both feel, and I must say I agree with them 100%, that the parade or anything else in connection with the opening festivities that smacks of the reception of a conquering hero, is going to be so ridiculous as to make Gable, the picture, the entire

trip, MGM and ourselves laughing stocks of the whole country. After all, we have only made a motion picture, and we are only motion picture people, and the idea of a town receiving us as though we had just licked the Germans is something that I for one will not go through with. You couldn't get me into one of those cars for a million bucks.

Gable's going along for the ride was in doubt until near the end. He knew he would be a public spectacle, and he was bad-tempered about letting that benefit others. Neither was Vivien Leigh a sweet and obliging player now. Scarlett had changed her; as shooting went on, her toughness and her demands had made her less than popular. She had wanted *Rebecca* and was denied. Now Birdwell and company were asking her to go to a provincial town, for hicks, and wear Scarlett's costumes. Leigh and Olivier liked to think they were handling the Selznicks; they scorned them secretly and flattered them in person. They felt superior to Hollywood and American bosses, and there may have been anti-Semitism. Vivien was learning from Olivier the necessary smiles of careerism. She had seen *Wind* as a whole late in October and not been bowled over or quick enough to mask her feeling from David. So she wrote a vanilla letter to Irene:

> I was awfully distressed to hear that David was hurt by my seeming lack of enthusiasm the other night after the picture. I assure you this was not at all the case, as I was immeasurably thrilled by it—but it seemed vastly conceited to me, for me to enthuse as much as everyone else, being in every single shot, & a large proportion of the picture falling on my shoulders. I congratulated both David & Vic as much as I thought I unassumingly could and amusingly enough, in my bewilderment at the torrent of mutual congratulations all around me, I was somewhat reassured that my behaviour was alright by the fact that David said not a word to me!

Leigh and Olivier went to Atlanta: he was there in the background, composed, stiff, a little haughty (in character for Maxim de Winter still). Olivia de Havilland went, no matter that Warners told her not to, and she was Jock's partner at most of the proceedings. After much prevarication, Gable came, with Carole Lombard. From the rest of the cast, there were Ann Rutherford, Evelyn Keyes (raised in Atlanta), and Laura Hope Crews. Among friends and relatives, as well as Jock, there were the Goetzes, with an enthusiastic Claudette Colbert in their party, Myron, Flossie, and Uncle Charlie Sachs. There was no Leslie Howard, no Victor Fleming, and no Louis B. Mayer.

Kay Brown had run the hotel bookings for the celebrities. Yet the woman who had once insisted David make the film was no longer sure of her position. On the threshold of glory, Selznick International was beset with deficit. On December 20, John Wharton summed up the crisis: without taking account of the returns on *Wind* or *Rebecca*, the losses were $1.850 million. If *Rebecca* broke even, Wharton calculated, then *Wind* needed a distributor's gross rental of $10 million for the loss to be covered.

Wharton allowed that was possible, probable even. But David had declared his wish for a long vacation, and he was saying he was not adequately remunerated. Wharton knew Jock was coming to the end of his fascination with pictures, as much because of the vagaries of David as because of war in Europe. For the moment, SIP was on hold, waiting for the vital returns but at the end of its line. There were layoffs in the month before *Wind* premiered, and in November, Jock had to recall Kay from Atlanta to tell her that, as of January 1, 1940, she might have to be laid off.

There were other ugly incidents in all the fanfare of opening. The civic authorities in Atlanta would not allow a picture of Hattie McDaniel in the souvenir program given away at the opening—though David had pursued that program enough to ensure it had no cellophane wrapper so that it would not cause any noise problem in the theater. McDaniel was also prevailed upon not to risk embarrassment by attending Atlanta for the festivities. David deplored such pressures and kept the actress's picture in the program given out in New York and Los Angeles.

At 2:00 p.m. on Tuesday, December 12, at the Four Star Theatre in Los Angeles, *Gone With the Wind* was shown to the press for the first time. There were no privileges allowed. Paulette Goddard, who was leaving town, asked to be let in so she could at least see it—but her luck stayed bad. David had a great excuse: it was touch and go whether the finished print would be delivered to the Four Star in time from Technicolor. Seven hundred fifty members of the press saw it that afternoon.

When a movie is a huge, smash hit, it never matters what the press says. Even fifty years later, there has been little searching critical commentary on the film—as if critics were unwilling to tread too close to their own irrelevance. But in the next two weeks, there was extraordinary praise. *The New York Times* called it "The greatest motion mural we have seen and the most ambitious film-making adventure in Hollywood's spectacular history." *The Hollywood Reporter* said it was the "Mightiest achievement in the history of the motion picture." It then called David "the world's greatest motion picture producer."

The leading participants flew to Atlanta. David had said in advance that he would go by train because the train was less publicity, more reliable, and an opportunity for rest. But how could he resist the marvel of appearing in the South from out of the sky? Even Gable was astonished. He was a country boy, and he knew he was seeing the faces of country people who had journeyed into Atlanta for the holiday. How many? Gable said millions, his dark eyes on fire with public adoration.

There were balls, receptions, motorcades, parades of veterans, endless congratulations. David had a separate telephone switchboard installed in his suite at the Biltmore. Cables were coming in that ran the gamut, from classic show-biz finger snapping to true grace under pressure.

From Abe Berman:

Dear David: Tremendously happy that a Selznick made new motion picture history with *Gone With the Wind*. From now until the end of time whenever the great works of art and cultural accomplishments are written of or discussed that name Selznick will take its proper place. Wish that the great man among men and pioneer in motion pictures who with mother inspired you was with you, Mother, Myron and your wife to participate in the glory of this epoch making day. Congratulations, bestest and sincerest hopes for an American gross of twelve million dollars and an English gross of six hundred thousand pounds.

And from George Cukor:

Dearest Irene and David I don't know whether to be wistful, noble, or comic but I really send you all my love tonight.

Margaret Mitchell met her storyteller. She told David she had always trusted him because of *David Copperfield*. She beheld the beauty of Vivien Leigh and admired the cool-tongued Englishwoman's knowledge of Southern history. Then she did what everyone in Georgia wanted to do, she took Gable off to a private room for a chat.

On the evening of December 15, the picture had its world premiere at Loew's Grand Theatre on Peachtree Street. A Twelve Oaks facade was put up over the front of the theater. As the guests arrived, Gable said it was Margaret Mitchell's night. David spoke briefly, with a tense, beautiful Irene beside him. He was urged to look up so that he would photograph properly. But he was too nervous.

In 1939, the Civil War was not much further away than the premiere is from today. Of course, the "people" were not well represented at the premiere; it was an expensive ticket, much in demand. But the South was there, and just as Hattie McDaniel could not be permitted that night, so great reservoirs of old feeling were brought to the film. The response was not what it had been in Riverside. Evelyn Keyes saw the film that night and noted how at the intermission, "There was a hush. Nobody breathed, nobody moved for a moment. And when they did it was in slow motion. I felt almost that I'd never seen a movie before—and I haven't seen one since."

Movies are made to be new and sensational. Great movies reward re-viewing. But nothing can ever match the impact of the first time: it is primitive, sexual, a revelation. And in her few words, Evelyn Keyes says better than anyone else how that 1939 film came to embody not just a year or an age, but the magic of a medium. Poised between the Depression and the war, *Gone With the Wind* epitomized the movies' beguiling invitation to impossible happiness.

When the screening was over, Margaret Mitchell was persuaded to speak. The words and her voice are preserved on an old radio recording. She sounds older than she was, and her accent is so thickly Southern it is not easy to understand now. The South has lost that accent since television:

> I think all of you can understand that this picture was a great emotional experience to me. I know that fan magazines speak of lots of pictures as being that, but to me it *is* a great experience. I think it was heartbreaking, and I know I'm not the only person who's got a drippin' wet handkerchief! And I'm not the only person I heard secretly blowing their nose, and mine wasn't so secret.
>
> I feel like it's been a very great thing for Georgia and the South to see our old Confederacy come back to us. I felt that way all this week and I was practically giving the Rebel Yell tonight. It is not for me to speak of grand things these actors have done, because they have spoken so much more eloquently than I could ever do.
>
> But I want to speak just a minute about Mr. David Selznick. He's the man that every one of you all crack that joke about, "Oh well, we'll wait until Shirley Temple grows up and she'll play Scarlett!"
>
> I want to commend Mr. Selznick's courage and his obstinacy and his determination in just keeping his mouth shut until he got the exact cast he wanted in spite of everything everybody said. I think you'll all agree with me, he had actually the perfect cast.

God knows how David felt. This was a man with huge hopes and desires, and now they had been met. He had moved the people, even if the true people were yet to see the film. He had felt the ground of phenomenon begin to move. The show, the show—and such a business.

THERE WERE OPENINGS in New York and Los Angeles, with wondrous, romantic parties thrown by Jock Whitney. Surely Jock knew his life was changing and felt relief and elation because of it, as well as trepidation. The public response to the movie was already staggering as it

The Los Angeles opening of
Gone With the Wind*:*
Jock, Irene, Olivia de
Havilland, David, Vivien,
Larry

opened, on December 19 in New York at the Capitol and the Astor, and on the twenty-eighth, in Los Angeles at the Carthay Circle. A Wharton and an Altstock must have begun to see they might get the Whitneys out of this dangerous business with a little bit of profit. David could not stand to have the party end or slow. He browbeat MGM about other openings—couldn't New Orleans be as big as Atlanta? Was the show really over? Must it settle down to business as usual? He was actor and audience; he could not bear to leave the theater.

In New York, Jock threw his party at 972 Fifth Avenue, the old home of his parents. It was the moment at which show biz and society had their marriage, and that would never have been possible without the innocent, brave hopes of Jock Whitney. There are places in America—the Upper East Side, parts of Long Island, and in the silky pages of a few magazines—where the offspring of that marriage still dream. And in Los Angeles, there began the quest for a necessary class in the picture business that is evident now in museums, restaurants, many homes, and the new C.A.A. building at Wilshire and Santa Monica.

At Christmas, among other things, David gave Irene a medal with the inscription: "To the real heroine of GWTW from her Four-Eyed Rhett."

On the evening of December 28, Jock took over the Trocadero for his Los Angeles party. He had Irene make the arrangements—she had an A list, a B, a C, and a D: it was the sort of discrimination that once, in old Russia, could have paid off centuries-long vendettas or started small wars.

Nothing could deter a new year and a new decade. The business of *Gone With the Wind* was not just steady, it was an economy unto itself. But economies need managers, not showmen, and even David turned away in fatigue and bewilderment when MGM learned to ignore his daily measure of reproaches, urgings, and recommendations. You cannot send the same person cables twice in one season that begin, "This is the most important message I have ever sent" and maintain credibility.

There was only one more thing between David and eternity.

"For years," said Irene, "he had told me, 'There will come a night, there will be an Academy Awards night.' Told me! But told himself! The years of anticipation. The overstimulation."

This was 1939, and if no one bothered to notice it then, it was a great year: *Wuthering Heights, Goodbye Mr. Chips, Stagecoach, Dark Victory, Love Affair, Ninotchka, Mr. Smith Goes to Washington, The Wizard of Oz, Of Mice and Men, Union Pacific, Gunga Din*. When the nominations were announced on February 12, *Gone With the Wind* had thirteen. The Oscars would be presented at the annual dinner on the evening of February 29 at the Cocoanut Grove in the Ambassador Hotel.

There was a cocktail party at Summit Drive for all *Wind* nominees and their guests and for all those caught up in the great occasion. But what followed was not just a pinnacle of show-biz success; it was a family tragedy.

Irene saw it this way (and this is how she still saw it in May 1990):

The meeting place was our home and everybody was keyed up. They all came in limousines. And David was spoiled in things he had taken care of for him—the et ceteras. He had only to raise a finger. No one was appointed to say who goes in what car. Didn't occur to him that he was the host. If it had been a beach picnic it would have been in my lap. He was thinking ahead, of several hours ahead, what he was going to say—he *wasn't* thinking. Nobody knew we were going to win. But one assumed it.

Whereas that afternoon the Los Angeles *Times* had sneaked a list of winners—this was before the ritual of sealed envelopes. David must have known. Irene . . . did not know?

According to her, David got in a limousine with Gable and Vivien Leigh and went off without a glance or a thought. "I'd been forgotten."

So she came along behind in the last car.

"I thought—would he be pacing outside the Ambassador, waiting for me? Nobody. No message. Nothing. I had to walk upstairs—no one there either. I went in but I wouldn't sit down next to him, because I wasn't sure I was going to stay. It would have been unspeakable! But he kept sending messengers over."

Jock came over and said, "You're missing David's evening. For God's sake, nod, smile, anything. He's in misery."

"So am I," said Irene.

Jock left and came back again. She told him, "Don't you come back. You're making it worse."

So they sat at separate tables, neither one willing to get up and go rescue the other or save the idea of the pair of them.

There was din and delight to conceal much of the agony. Master of ceremonies Bob Hope called it "a benefit for David Selznick." There were

Vivien, Oscar, and "that composite of energy, courage and very great kindness," with cigarette

Oscars for Ernest Haller and Ray Rennahan for color cinematography, for Hal Kern and James Newcom for editing, for William Cameron Menzies and Lyle Wheeler for art direction. Sinclair Lewis presented the posthumous Oscar for screenwriting to Sidney Howard.

Hattie McDaniel won for supporting actress, beating out among others Olivia de Havilland's Melanie.

Gable lost to Robert Donat in *Goodbye Mr. Chips.*

Spencer Tracy announced that Vivien Leigh was the best actress and, instead of offering thanks as long as the book, she fixed on "That composite of energy, courage and very great kindness," David O. Selznick.

And David won the Thalberg Award, and then he got the Oscar for Best Picture of 1939.

"And what was desperate," said Irene, "was the expression on his face. He was pleading. He never took his eyes off me as he spoke. And he could still be pleading and I'd never move. When in doubt do nothing.

"We went home. I went to bed with no talk. And he went to his room. And there wasn't one goddamn word out of me. I never got over it and he never got over it. It hung on."

19 · THE TWO MRS. DE WINTERS

WHAT CAN ONE MAKE of the unresolved story of Oscar night in February 1940 and of Irene's being left behind? I have told the story from Irene's point of view because hers is the only one available. David never spoke of it. She wrote about it in her book and talked about it on several occasions. She was consistent in every telling and still disturbed by the wrong done her.

As with many things Irene said, she had a fixed version that left out some detail and atmosphere, to say nothing of how others saw things. This was not as clear-cut as lying or deception. Memories come apart, and they are reassembled by emotion. After all, what happened on Oscar night is ostensibly a story about forgetting. Irene had forgotten things or suppressed them. (Her account of that night does not fit with newsreel footage in which she enters the Cocoanut Grove a few paces behind David.)

Something else had provoked or aggravated whatever happened that night in 1940 and Irene's stormy emotions more than fifty years later. Did David leave his wife behind, or did she contrive to be left? Was a mistake, amid such fuss, so terrible? For instance, it is possible that David had said, of course, he had to go in a car with Clark and Vivien. Stars attract the photographers, so David should have been with them. He might have thought he had said Irene should drive with Jock—that would have been an appropriate arrangement. And perhaps she never heard the instruction.

Or perhaps something blocked the hearing. Irene had so many elusive illnesses when a young woman, problems doctors could never quite identify or treat. They were a way of attracting attention in a woman of great intelligence, character, and talent who had too little to do. Her husband did not see very much of her, and periodically she dramatized her sadness and her anger at the neglect. She had had no greater rival than *Gone With the Wind*, and that night was the end of its success. Irene knew her David and anticipated the depression that was coming on him. She may have needed to stand up for herself—may even have had a deep-seated urge to mar his evening, out of vengeance or some hope of saving their future. Things could not go on the old way. She could not stay so hidden in her own life.

David had wronged his wife. His family life was something of a sham. The marriage was smothering Irene, and David's affairs were undoing the tight stitch of her dignity. If David did forget at the house, then he would have remembered in ten minutes and retrieved the situation. It is possible that she—almost without being conscious of it—engineered the offense. For as she tells it, there is a feeling of her being in control and of a meaning she alone saw being made clear. Grant some of that, and then this Irene—beautiful, wise, intimidating—could have been a preying threat and a silent rebuke that the indecisive David needed to escape.

There was another crisis, of exactly the sort that might upset reason. Irene was pregnant again. She could have discovered this very close to Oscar night 1940. She did not want to tell David: it was a time of ostensible joy, yet she felt this was not good news. When she summoned the nerve, he replied that she must be mistaken. That could have prompted Irene's fury or distress and her making herself the unwanted person on February 29.

REBECCA GAVE DAVID uncommon trouble. Just because there were things in Hitchcock's method that David could never absorb or comprehend does not mean he was not learning to feel Hitch's stealth. And whereas *Gone With the Wind* is a film that stays on its rightful screen—a vivid melodrama once, a suction that draws us up there—so *Rebecca* slips off the screen and into our head, like smoke or rumor. Years ahead of his time, Hitch had a command of atmosphere that outflanked censors: the audience *knows* the "unnatural" ties that linked Rebecca and Mrs. Danvers, but no censor could find the place to cut them.

The competition with Hitchcock at the script stage had been David's victory because he cared more about the book and the virtues of story. The long attack on Hitchcock's treatment picks on many "mistakes": giving the second Mrs. de Winter a name—Daphne, showing the characters on their way to the actual Riviera opening, giving Max friends in France—and thus losing his solitariness. Worst of all, David believed, Hitch did not appreciate how the awkward young woman felt:

> As for Manderley, every little thing that the girl does in the book, her reactions of running away from the guests, and the tiny things that indicate her nervousness and her self-consciousness and her gaucherie are all so brilliant in the book that every woman who has read it has adored the girl and has understood her psychology, has cringed with embarrassment for her, yet has understood exactly what was going through her mind. We have removed all the subtleties and substituted big broad strokes which in outline form betray just how ordinary the actual plot is and just how bad a picture it would make without the little feminine things which are so recognizable and which make every woman say, "I know just how she feels. . . . I know just what she's going through."

David never talked about Scarlett with that concern; he rarely seemed to have read *Gone With the Wind* with such excitement. He was right in every detail: his attack on that first treatment rescued the project. Moreover, although it was contrary to Hitchcock's guarded, cocky nature to admit the benefit of others, still he learned a good deal on *Rebecca*. No character in his English films is as deep or neurotic as the people in *Rebecca*. Through David's eyes, the director began to see intimacy and secrecy. Hitchcock was on his way to *Rear Window*, *Vertigo*, and *Psycho*, pictures no one else could have made. But he was helped in a special way: he was able to observe the response David had to "the little feminine things" and the way the producer's heart leaped with every startled movement in the life of "I," the second Mrs. de Winter.

Hitchcock was an insidious watcher: the evidence of that is in his films. He was also, in 1939, an English filmmaker determined to make an American career. So, even in their daily contest, he did not go out of his way to challenge Selznick. In the casting, especially, Hitchcock accepted the boss's incontestable taste. He observed how much the gestation of *Rebecca* in David's mind had had to do with his feelings for Joan Fontaine. For if David knew how a woman read the book, the young actress was his best model. Later on, to sound superior as well as discreet, Hitch let it be thought the casting had been just a trick of David's:

Well, in the preparatory stages of *Rebecca*, Selznick insisted on testing every woman in town, known or unknown, for the lead in the picture. I think he really was trying to repeat the same publicity stunt he pulled in the search for Scarlett O'Hara.

He talked all the big stars in town into doing tests for *Rebecca*. I found it a little embarrassing, myself, testing women who I knew in advance were unsuitable for the part. All the more so since the earlier tests of Joan Fontaine had convinced me that she was the nearest one to our heroine.

David was not that calculating. He had been in genuine turmoil over both Scarlett and *Rebecca*, but in the latter he had an allegiance, for it was in talks with Fontaine that he had perceived the book's force. But by the time of casting it was all the more delicate and ambivalent a tie in that it was old. Should he cast as his showman's instincts dictated, as a former admirer, or as a reformed husband? Hitchcock was a cold connoisseur of such mixed emotions. And if Joan Fontaine was more sophisticated than the second Mrs. de Winter, still Hitch knew ways of pressuring her insecurities and making her his. He told her she was an outcast on the set, the sore thumb among so many English actors. When Olivier learned that Fontaine had married Brian Aherne, he wondered to her face whether she couldn't have done any better—it is a remark worthy of Mrs. Danvers. (Fontaine said she could never quite look at her husband in the same way again.) Fontaine was being paid less than a quarter what Olivier was getting—Judith Anderson (Mrs. Danvers) was earning nearly double Fontaine's salary. On October 22, 1939, Fontaine's twenty-second birthday, Hitch organized a small party for her on the set, but most of the other actors stayed away.

Her performance did not go well at first. This is not easy to assess, for outtakes do not survive and the final film has a magnificent "I," nerve-racked yet never grating—it is a better performance than the one for which Fontaine won her Oscar, in Hitchcock's *Suspicion*. But observers say the performance depended on much coaxing and coaching from Hitch.

As if that was not worry enough for the producer, he was perplexed by his director. Hitchcock did not bend himself to any SIP system, and he mistrusted anyone close to David. Two weeks into production, David was distressed at how hard it was to get a point across to Hitch, at the slowness of progress, and at the regular lateness of the director. Hitchcock refused to rehearse while the crew set the lights; he complained of the distracting noise. Thus everything was taking longer—"It is just infantile not to realize that these two processes must go through simultaneously, and if the noise disturbs you, then rehearse them on the side lines or somewhere," David fumed to himself.

He said that Hitch's shooting was very fragmented *and* very limited: "Cutting your film with the camera and reducing the number of angles required is highly desirable, and no one appreciated its value more than I do; but certainly it is of no value if you are simply going to give us less cut film per day than a man who shoots twice as many angles. . . . As somebody said the other day, 'Hitchcock shoots like [Woody] Van Dyke—except that he gets one-third as much film.' " David foresaw that he might have to rescue this film in the cutting room, but with very little film to choose from.

There came a crisis, and it took an unusual form. Irene had been a great champion of the book, and—she said—of Joan Fontaine in the lead. It is hard to say how much David had talked to her about the novel and its meaning: by 1939, Irene was a social lioness, but she had always felt herself the quiet, shy, stammering onlooker. It says something about the appeal of the book that even a Scarlett—even a Rebecca—could identify with the nameless "I."

"When the picture had been shooting some weeks," David asked Irene to look at the footage. I would guess this was early October. He called her from the studio and asked her to come over immediately. That was uncommon: Irene was not in the habit of going to the studio or the office. But "there was a vital decision to be made; I was to decide whether the picture should be scrapped."

There is no hint in production records that the film came so close to cancellation. Irene said David didn't trust himself: "he was hysterical, exhausted, there was some footage he had opposite reactions to every time he looked." She was shown a couple of reels in rough assembly, and she told him it was "superb." So the picture went on.

Was David simply too tired to be sure? Was he thrown by the emerging editing style made necessary by Hitchcock's way of shooting? (For in David's films generally, shots follow shots sensibly—if not ponderously; they do not overlap in our heads; sound and pictures do not work together chemically. Leonard Leff, author of the excellent *Hitchcock & Selznick*, has called the Selznick editing "stately" and keyed to showing us speakers speaking. Whereas Hitch often preferred to show listening faces—the moved, changing faces—in conversations.) Was the calling in of Irene a gesture of respect, love, and allegiance to a mistress of gesture? Or was there even a thought in David's head of showing her a strange story unfolding, about a man caught between two wives?

Was it during that visit that David had Irene supply a sample of her handwriting for the movie? There is a scene where the tremulous "I" goes into the morning room and finds Rebecca's stationery on the desk. There is an address book, with the name "Rebecca de Winter," in Irene's hand. In

Joan Fontaine and Judith Anderson in Rebecca

the novel, "I" says to herself, "How alive was her writing though, how full of force."

The shooting concluded. Hal Kern missed the Atlanta opening of *Wind* so that he could finish a rough cut of *Rebecca*. On December 26, two days before the L.A. premiere of *Wind*, *Rebecca* had a sneak preview in Santa Barbara—to great acclaim. But David remained irritated by Hitchcock's mise-en-scène, and he supervised some retakes personally to ensure more control in the re-editing. They had a last argument over whether, in the fire at the end of the picture, the initial "R" should be the embroidery on the bed pillow (Hitch) or a shape in the smoke from the fire (David). Hitch won, but he felt battered by David's command of the postproduction. The real winner was the film, for both men derived great benefit from their contest.

Hitchcock wondered what the English would think of this Holly-wood Anglophilia. Hitch was no aristocrat. His films often mocked the upper classes or those secure in wealth. He knew the model Manderley Ray Klune had built was as big as Blenheim Palace. Nor did he share David's reverence for the distinction of being a de Winter. In all the memos David sent the director during the filming, one minor gripe captures David's aspirations:

I refer to the service of the meal. We have one servant piling supper plates on top of one another as though he were in a beanery. The other carries one plate under his arm and against his body as though he were a discus thrower. If this be a luncheon service in an aristocratic English home, all I can say is that the servants in a Brooklyn flat are better trained. It may be that very few people in America would notice this sort of thing, and it may be that even in England it would get by unnoticed except for the few. But we have gone to such elaborate detail about props, furniture, and all the appurtenances of Manderley that I hate like the devil to have anything that even a minority would jeer at, especially when that jeering minority is likely to include our old friend Jock.

As David worried over the behavior of the servants, their real employer, Maxim de Winter, ignored the household and brooded over his two wives. We should not forget Maxim—such a big gun of a name, yet so inward and repressed a man. He is not the first neurotic in a Selznick picture—there is Carton in *A Tale of Two Cities*, Norman Maine, and even Kong, hesitating between savagery and worship—but he is the most clinically clear-cut. And he is one of four neurotic characters—there is really no one quite sane or sure at the center of the film. Mrs. Danvers is sinister, living in the past, immaculate, perverse—she is, really, the ghost of Rebecca; Maxim is pent up; "I" is distraught in her search for identity; and Rebecca de Winter? Well, she is absent, and she was a suicide. Yet she *is* the title, the spirit that presides over Manderley, and she *is* interesting. There are hints in the film that she was a lonely woman rather stranded by the house, her grim Maxim, and all the rules of society.

The film could not be the same as the novel, and David was afraid Daphne du Maurier would speak out against the differences. In the book, Max killed Rebecca, shooting her when she goaded him with the lie that she was going to have another man's child. She had cancer really, but she was brave and evil enough to make Maxim her murderer. Censorship would not permit that in the film. David complained to Jock, "The whole story . . . is of a man who has murdered his wife, and it now becomes the story of a man who buried a wife who was killed accidentally!" So Rebecca's cancer prompts a kind of suicidal accident. She seems too strong for that way out, and her death is the root of other small implausibilities that pass by. On the other hand, the new ending makes Max less powerful and more indecisive—now he is not quite sure how guilty to be. He has not been allowed to destroy this wife—so she hangs over him, remorseless and watchful. "Don't you believe that the dead can see the living?" Mrs. Danvers asks "I" in *Rebecca's* most haunting séance.

How far is a producer responsible for the story, especially one from a book? David tended to evade responsibility by attempting to adhere to a book. In his ending to *Rebecca*, he was compelled to use the accident. Producers are managers, not authors. But David was a romantic who always wanted to be a writer. There is a myth, or a fantasy, within *Rebecca* that seems to me suggestive. It is about a man who is rescued from the past and a potent wife by a young, innocent woman. That is why Olivier's Max is so good while seeming chained, constrained, infuriated by his own inner confusion. I do not think David was conscious of this myth or capable of articulating it. Yet I suspect Hitchcock saw what relevance it might have. David Selznick had brought himself to a point in life where he needed rescuing, and sooner or later some young woman was going to have to play the part. But she might then have to accommodate herself to a force in the first wife that would not go away.

BIG SHOT

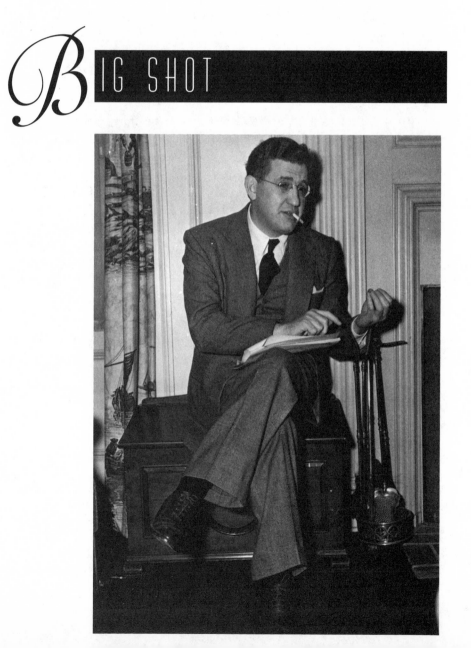

1 · STONY BATTER

ON MAY 10, 1940, David Selznick would be thirty-eight. He had two healthy sons—no matter if those boys had doctors and tutors the way Louis XIV had advisers. He was envied throughout Hollywood for the splendor of his home and the style of his wife—and she had been through hell for him, such as no doctor could ever treat. He had won the Oscar for Best Picture of 1939 a couple of months before. His next production, *Rebecca*, had opened to admiration and success. If poor in cash as yet, he would be richer than he could understand. He had played with the idea that he would relax, read, travel, be happy and content. This was the perfect occasion for some skillful arrangement of second honeymoon and first family holiday.

As late as October 3, 1939—in the exhilaration of completing *Wind* and shooting *Rebecca*—David had dreamed of futures. He was aware already that SIP was going to be put on hold:

> Jock is now as determined as I about the proposed hiatus. Make some definite plans [he wrote to Irene], and I'll work towards them. My mood is the Riviera—the Nile—houseboat—Greek Islands—yacht—Palestine—to Hell with expenses. I want to go gloriously in debt for a Great Cause. I want to loaf and play and write and love. I don't want to even try to make any money during the period. I'd like people if they're strictly fun-people, otherwise none. Maybe different people in different places. I think it'd be grand if we had Myron part of the time, Jock part. Maybe London for the "Wind" premiere (King and Queen there, I believe). I want to see you courtsey. I want to be gone three months. Four months. Six months—no plans for return—plans only for the first couple of months—stay as long as we like—

come home when we miss it. And I'll never forgive either of us if we
let *anything* interfere.

The refusal to tolerate *any* interference extended to the two boys: they
would have been an intrusion on the dream. Though handwritten on the tan
sheets of a desk memo pad, this rhapsody is David and Irene at the close of
their own *Made for Each Other*, soaring on the music, their embrace all aripple
as the curtains close over the screen while the image plays on. How poignant
to receive that note and then relate it to the endangered Europe, Nile, and
Mediterranean of 1940. Of course, David understood geography and what
war entailed. But no real havoc could slow a storyteller.

Fun and frolic never came; no companion to David ever knew such
peace or ease. Instead, David and Irene had an abortion. *Rebecca* opened in
Los Angeles on March 27, 1940. Three days later, the couple left for New
York, where the secret, medical deal must have been done.

Dorothy Paley was Irene's best friend at that time. They were the
closer for being wives who wondered how much they knew of what their
husbands were up to. Yet Dorothy knew nothing about either the incident
at the Oscars or the pregnancy and its abortion. There is no more frightening sign of Irene's isolation. She was a hostess, and she "knew" everyone,
yet she had hardly a soul to confide in. She sought out her own abortion—
"I procured the right doctor and the right hospital at a time when the
procedure was still so risky and sordid for most women."

Did David do that deal? Was he brave enough? Did Irene herself really
know how to call up the right people with the proper discretion? Or did she
need to turn to a man who certainly had such contacts and whose job it was
to ensure that young female talent stayed available for work? Did L.B.
arrange this for her? Or Myron, or Jock?

Irene had dreaded admitting the pregnancy to David, and after he had
told her she must be mistaken, the subject was dropped for another month,
when it had to be faced. "He made clear what he felt by what he didn't say.
The most positive response I ever got was, 'It's up to you.' I ventured that
perhaps we were being sent a message: we're supposed to have a baby, not
a trip. There was no answer. When I tentatively suggested an abortion, he
didn't demur."

At least one other person did know of the pregnancy. April 29 was
David and Irene's tenth anniversary. On that day, they received a cable from
Myron, even if by then they had canceled the prospect he foresaw: "Years
ago on April 29 you both made a mistake. If you can produce a girl you have
both won. Love and kisses."

How to answer Myron's greeting was just one of the questions that hung over David. What would he do next? What celebration of success could convince him? How should he address the state of a marriage when, by unspoken agreement, the two parents—young enough, rich enough—were not fit to have another child? Above all, how could he best capitalize on his success—how could he hold on to the most money from it? And how could he reward himself—with ease, splendor, or some higher task—especially when he had ongoing commitments to Hitchcock, Bergman, Fontaine, and Leigh and a studio of employees?

His answer was to wonder, waste time, and do all manner of little things. He was captivated by the reports of glory from local theaters all over America as *Wind* kept up its business. When the picture opened in Asheville, North Carolina, on February 5, he made sure the theater had twelve seats for Howard and his best friends from the nearby Highland Hospital. In New York, with Irene, he made it his challenge to see how many swell parties he could get into just because of his new fame. "You're David O. Selznick," strangers were telling him, and he had to agree. Mrs. Cornelius Vanderbilt asked them up for tea, and David charmed his hostess by saying he had only come along to see what it would be like. He was a hick, still, just as on the honeymoon. But now he expected celebrity and respect. And if it was slow in coming, he could turn surly. Both David and Irene were hiding unease in drinking. Dorothy Paley saw that they could be ugly drunks; she thought they were trying to muster some sexual interest in each other.

They returned to Los Angeles on June 4 for a family occasion. Howard's elder daughter, Ruth, was to be married. In 1936, aged sixteen, she had been on the beach one day at Santa Monica when she met Berman Swarttz, a senior at U.C.L.A. Despite the gap in ages, Swarttz was attracted to the very pretty and vivacious Ruth. They dated, and, by 1938, Swarttz was summoned to David's office.

To Berman Swarttz this felt like "a royal command"; David was not very cordial. He said he had heard a marriage was likely, so Berman should understand that David and Myron were not responsible for Ruth and that Howard was ill:

> he wanted me to know, if I was planning to marry Ruth, the nature
> of it. He read me a letter from a psychiatrist in New York . . . which
> indicated that it might have been birth damage, but that it was not the
> kind of thing that was necessarily inheritable. He thought I had a right
> to know that, she didn't have tainted blood, in essence.

That June, the wedding took place. Unwitting irony placed it in a hospital room at Cedars of Lebanon, where Flossie was undergoing treatment. David, Irene, Mildred, and Myron were in attendance, and David gave the couple a check for $1,000 as their wedding gift. It was a delicate occasion: Flossie was in the habit of decrying Mildred to Ruth, and Mildred was in constant need of financial support. The family was anxious to "place" Ruth happily, and Berman Swarttz was on the way to becoming a successful lawyer.

In late June, David attended the Republican National Convention in Philadelphia as a warm supporter of the dark horse, Wendell Willkie. No admirer of the New Deal, Willkie resisted the general Republican urge toward isolationism. He won, on the sixth ballot, surpassing Thomas Dewey and Robert Taft.

Later that year, in the campaign, David volunteered support and advice for Willkie. When a major speech was in the offing, he wrote to Willkie's close aide, journalist Russell Davenport, with a suggested insertion. "The entire election is at stake," said David. "And much greater things than even the election.... Maybe I'm slightly hysterical, but I cannot properly express my sincere conviction on the importance of the matter."

His suggestion was couched as a dramatic reading (with notes on direction). For the producer, sincerity had become the end result of timing and control:

> (After some loud-voiced dramatic climax, a pause, and then, in very quiet and serious tones:)
> Ladies and Gentlemen, Fellow Americans, I want to talk to you now, for a few minutes, about a very grave matter—a matter so important that I feel with all my heart and soul it deeply concerns the fate of America, the fate of Democracy itself, for generations to come (slight pause) I want to talk about—the Jews (slight pause)—about the Jews, and the part that they have been given in this campaign by one of the most vicious whispering campaigns that has ever disgraced the long history of free elections, by free people of all creeds, in this country. (Pause.)
> First, let me say that I do not believe there is any such thing as a Jewish vote, any more than there is a Catholic vote or a Protestant vote. (Pause.) And let me go further, and say that no matter how this election turns out, no matter what happens, nothing will ever make me believe it! The Jews in this country are voting—as Americans.

Even in defeat Willkie got more votes than any previous Republican candidate. But what did David mean by this Jewish vote in America? In finding it so vital, he was far out of the mainstream. Yet he did not quite stand up for Jewishness, his own or that under greater threat in Europe. Rather, he wanted a world that had forgotten Jewishness, which means he was either much ahead of his time or very insecure.

By early July, David was wondering how far to curtail the Culver City operation, but unable to stop thinking about new directions. He had agreed to go east again for a family holiday. But in the days beforehand, he messed around: he screened newsreel footage of the Atlanta opening; he wrote thank-you letters for small gifts; he got race tickets for his recovering mother; he wrote to Charles Lindbergh about the state of the world and took an ailing thumb to Marcella's husband, Dr. Marcus Rabwin. He repaid an earlier loan of $15,000 from Bill Goetz and tried to fill his days with small errands and missives. He was going through the motions of slowing down, while worrying about finding a greater challenge than *Wind*. He told everyone Dan O'Shea would be in charge while he was away—but no one believed a word of that.

On July 10, David, Jeffrey, and Danny took the TWA Stratocruiser and flew to New York. Irene had gone ahead. This was the first time the boys had flown, and it was—as Jeffrey recalls—the first commercial flight of a pressurized plane. Flying time was reduced from twenty-two to fourteen hours. Danny got airsick and secured family fame by saying somewhere over the bare Midwest, "I've had enough now, Daddy. I'd like to get off."

They stopped briefly in New York, at the Pierre. David took Jeffrey to see the sights. They climbed the Statue of Liberty and the Empire State Building. But if the boys thought David was theirs now, he quickly stepped back into his business life. Of course, there was a nanny on the trip, as well as a secretary.

The person David was most eager to exploit in 1940 was Vivien Leigh, but the actress had resented not getting *Rebecca* and been unhappy being loaned out to Metro for *Waterloo Bridge*. Against his better instincts, David had permitted Vivien to join Olivier in a stage production of *Romeo and Juliet*: this had been a failure in San Francisco and a disaster in New York, in May. Now Vivien was seeking permission to do another play, *Marie Adelaide*. From the Pierre, David sent out a refusal, no matter that he had no film for her. So he spoke grandly of a player's duty to the masses. War was turning the publicist into a propagandist. Miss Leigh should stop trying to cash in on her fame with "personal appearance":

> I am afraid that I still consider that from any standpoint it is more worthwhile to aim one's talents at an audience of between fifty and seventy-five million people the world over than it is to play to a tiny fraction of the audience. . . . It would be a very simple matter to prove that there are a hundred times as many people of adult intelligence and artistic appreciation in the audience of any film as there are in the audience of any play.

Then Whitey, the Selznicks' chauffeur, arrived in the limousine—he had left early to accommodate them—and he drove the family up into the northwest corner of Connecticut, to the holiday house—Stony Batter Farm, near Cornwall Bridge.

It was a charming house in unspoiled country. There was a swimming pool—albeit with a mud bottom. There was a quaint country store, walks to be taken, horses to ride, a lake for fishing. There was an opportunity for peace and family. But . . .

> Stony Batter was hardly pleasant [Irene recalled]. . . . I said, "Read!" It stretched out the summer. "What, *read?*" he said. I thought he could rebuild. It was a big, wonderful country place. It depressed him— there was nothing to do. Horse and buggy, ducks, geese, chickens, tennis court, a beautiful gentleman's room. Nothing stimulating! Nothing more than two kids and leisure! All he wanted to do was to have guests—exhausting people. He thought I was punishing him.

So the guests came. Jock Whitney arrived in a plane with pontoons attached so it could land on a lake. There were the Averell Harrimans and Clare Luce, as well as Bill and Dorothy Paley. David talked show business and society gossip with them. Irene took the boys riding. Myron came once, a Myron trying to give up drinking, by no means a natural country gentleman. But for Jeffrey, Myron was a much needed companion, someone to talk to:

> Myron would listen to me. He was interested in what I had to say. . . . I thought my father was a sissy . . . and that Myron was not a sissy and Grandpa was not a sissy, but my father was. I don't ever recall throwing a ball with Myron, but I knew that I could, and I couldn't with my father. This was always very difficult for me. I think Myron gave me a couple of lectures on not being a crybaby and not being afraid of things physical.

David could not rest or be alone with his family. He was not inclined to rustic sports and entertainments. So he brought in a movie camera and a studio cameraman to record the idyllic summer scenes. In the footage that survives there is one exquisite shot of the family in the horse and carriage that went with Stony Batter, riding away down a country lane, waving farewell to the camera. A professional shot it, and so it has the aura of fiction—but is it the first or the last scene of a movie? Are the family riding off to unknown happiness, or is the perfect moment waiting to be ruined?

As Irene saw it, David was getting worse at Stony Batter, paranoid about what was going on in Hollywood, bored, becalmed, resentful. He was stewing over thoughts of what to do with SIP, of how much money there was going to be, and of how to guard it best. He had even, in May 1940, sent off his first letter to Washington wondering if he couldn't be of use if war came for America. More and more that summer, he sneaked down to New York, went into the office, and got in a few hours of dictation the way some men abscond for golf or liquor.

On August 15, he delivered himself of a nine-page letter to Joan Fontaine. She was being "naughty," refusing to be loaned out to Universal for *Back Street.* David's letter is hypocritical, patronizing, shrewd, flirtatious, and filled with a fearful new need—the urge to write the history of the picture business in order to justify himself. It can only have determined Fontaine to be more mischievous.

It began, "Dear Joan: My very dear, very young Joan," and ends with a handwritten postscript and "Love D," which was rare in David's letters to his actresses. But whatever David's feelings had been for Joan, the tone of the letter sought to reappraise the actress as a willful, darling child. "It will always be difficult for me to get over my affection for you personally," wrote David, "but I like to think I know what will benefit your present childish pretension. But please, Joan, don't let me lose my enthusiasm for you as an actress."

What was more fascinating in light of the actual ordeal at Stony Batter was the portrait of his disturbed rest and meditation:

David, Joan Fontaine, and Alfred Hitchcock at the Oscars, 1941, when Rebecca *won Best Picture but Joan and Hitch lost to Ginger Rogers (*Kitty Foyle*) and John Ford (*The Grapes of Wrath*)*

I left California in the hope that I was going to have a vacation. But at a time when I thought that most people, or at least most adult people, were worrying about the shape of things to come, I find that there are still a few movie people whose minds are functioning as in the days of Jetta Goudal and Marceline Day (or don't you remember them? I think it would repay you to study the stories of their respective rises and falls). I have accordingly had to come into the office—but I do want to return quickly to the isolation and impassive calm of the Berkshires, where I can sit in contemplation of Dunkerque and Hollywood; and so I hope you will forgive me if I leave without waiting to sign this letter.

It would be a mistake to read that as simple dishonesty. David was the sort of chronic imaginer—always telling himself a story—who did cherish the idea of rural Connecticut, once he got into the bustle of New York. Being anywhere *and* liking it at the same time—that's what he found so hard.

2 · LIQUIDATION

DAVID DID NOT HANDLE victory well—there were many who felt it made him unbearable. As a young wanderer and failure—in New York, Florida, and Hollywood—and then as a junior mogul, on his way surely, but still with far to go, David was known for his charm and his grin. Not that everyone fell for them: Katharine Hepburn thought him "very ambitious and very cold"; Joe Mankiewicz and other writers saw the fraud in the man; Sidney Howard had been aghast at his chaos. Still, as David climbed, he was eager, funny, winning, naughty, ardent, and fiendishly energetic. Those traits forgave so many ugly memos and expedient incidents.

But as a success, he indulged in vindication and explanation. Benzedrine may have laid the groundwork for megalomania, but triumph was its edifice. David became immodest in his understanding: now he *knew* that he had always understood the business better than *anyone*—so why in hell didn't everyone listen to him? His memos grew more like proclamations; he did not bother with argument or consultation; he believed it would be hard for him to make mistakes.

Late in 1939, there had been several concerned parties who saw Selznick International as a disaster about to break—but then the rather ridiculous bounty of *Gone With the Wind* had loomed in view. As *Wind* opened to the public, the net worth of David O. Selznick stood at minus $112,795. He had some comfort: Irene's worth was plus $272,840. But the position of SIP was alarming. Nine pictures had been produced and released—*Wind* and *Rebecca* were yet to open. Of those nine, only three had been profitable: *Little Lord Fauntleroy, The Prisoner of Zenda,* and *A Star is Born.*

Whitney had seen enough of David's expanding disorder. David had not found or trusted producers to function independently of him; so many films had gone over budget; and in the crisis of making *Wind* there had been no time to describe, let alone deal with, the problem. David's independence had been won at the cost of Whitney's ever more generous supply of extra money. And this was in a concern where David drew salary and expenses, had a large stockholding, but in which he had made no investment. As late as December 1939, it was possible that Jock and the others had bank-rolled a catastrophe. All Jock saw at its center was a dear friend who was endangering his marriage, who was becoming ever more irrational in complaint, who insisted on being in charge, but who was in desperate need of a rest.

Altstock reported to Whitney, on January 29, 1940, that David's thoughts were lunging out in so many different directions: "Any plan for the future to be successful," said Altstock, trusting dryness, "must incorporate D.O.S.'s wholehearted and enthusiastic cooperation. Any solution offered for the future, therefore, as it may involve S.I.P., is first dependent upon D.O.S.'s wishes and ambitions."

David was all for cutting costs and making economies: so he would dispose of "such high-salaried people" as Henry Ginsberg, Kay Brown, and Marcella Rabwin. He might renew his contract with SIP or sell himself out somewhere else. Big-shot plans bounced around in his head. And if he stayed with SIP, "he was of the opinion that his 40% interest . . . was ridiculously low." Further, David was of a mind to clear out the lesser partners, including Myron, who "had no business investing in his production operations." He wanted to work with Jock alone. But it would be easier in this case if something could be done about the accumulated debenture interest and David's personal debt to Pioneer.

> As he termed it [said Altstock], these items provide "heavy clubs" held over his head. Without stating in so many words, D.O.S. indicated that some adjustment of the debenture interest that would increase his profits would be in order. He went so far as to suggest that he might designate a lawyer to act for him. D.O.S. stated that he "feels" he cannot talk with J.H.W. and vice versa, in the frank manner that is necessary to effect plans for the most desirable future. He suggested if agreeable with J.H.W., I act as a neutral middle man in the negotiations that would lead up to reorganization.

In later life, David said SIP had folded up its business as a clever way
of retaining the bulk of the money from *Gone With the Wind*: "The only way
I could see of getting myself some money that I needed and could keep was
to liquidate Selznick International. The other stockholders agreed; and we
thus created one of our lesser contributions to Hollywood, the introduction
of capital gains."

That gives the impression of acumen triumphant again. Whereas the
liquidation was an agony of mixed motives and shortsighted advice. The
exhausted part of David wanted just the biggest chunk of money possible,
what Irene called "a wad."

By May 15, at the instigation of David and Altstock, SIP engaged
Walter Orr of White & Case "to act as counsel for the corporation in
liquidation and/or reorganization." The most direct course of action was
liquidation of SIP over a set period of time with David forming a new
entity, David O. Selznick Productions (incorporated on August 7, 1940—
during that Stony Batter vacation) out of his share of the proceeds. To allow
the full playing off of *Gone With the Wind*, the plan set the finalization of
liquidation at the end of 1942. By then, its makers reckoned, there wouldn't
be enough left worth worrying about. But the plan depended upon agreement from the IRS—that proceeds from the hit could be claimed as capital
gain and not straight income. By the early forties, with war tightening the
screws, David faced an income tax top rate of 90 percent, whereas capital
gains were taxed at 25 percent.

The arguments on liquidation proliferated, and David carried them
home. Irene disliked legal jargon and she couldn't understand all the
refinements:

> I didn't approve in principle because there was a chance he might later
> have to sell his share of GWTW. . . . I couldn't bear for him not to
> keep some part of the film. That would be like giving up his child.
> The film was worth more than money. I called it unholy.

Altstock watched David dart around in momentary pursuit of many
other schemes. Lawyers were learning that to be involved with David
Selznick was first to have to teach him the law and then let him teach you
back. When David had so many points of view, the shrewd Altstock would
sometimes set him snapping at his own tail. Orr got the impression it was
the Whitney interests that wanted to be finished with SIP. But it was easy
for Altstock to explain "that it was Mr. Selznick who had instigated negotiations for a termination of the Selznick operation."

The cash in hand had enormous emotional appeal for David. He had
been broke; success hardly counted without manifest extravagance, and he

needed to splurge. In all his hounding of Loew's over its alleged mistakes in distributing *Wind*, David was becoming more obsessed with the details of distribution. He now saw how poorly United Artists was serving *Rebecca*. And he attacked the SIP New York office for letting the company be taken advantage of. In June 1940, Jock was drawn into the battle. He wrote David ("a very nice letter," David called it, "dealing with my vituperative attacks") a warning as to how David was becoming intolerable in laying down the law. David's letter is antagonistic, unwilling to be reconciled:

> I should like to observe that this is a business in which one has to fight every inch of the way; and that the people who haven't chosen to persist in violent tactics such as my own have fallen by the wayside. I don't consider the making of a picture in this business is enough. However good a picture is, the business credits or blames you according to its commercial success or failure; and I am more convinced than I have ever been in the past that whatever success or failure I shall achieve in the future is going to be dependent upon the extent of the competence with which my pictures are exploited and sold, and that this in turn is going to be dependent upon the extent to which I hammer at people.

The plan for liquidation was approved by the IRS. David O. Selznick Productions Inc. would take on David's 1,485 shares in SIP and then, shortly thereafter (at $1,000 per share), David himself received $1.485 million. DOSP Inc. took over the contracts with Ingrid Bergman, Vivien Leigh, Joan Fontaine, Alfred Hitchcock, Alan Marshal, Hattie McDaniel, and Robert Stevenson. *Rebecca* and *Wind* had another two years to play out, and the income from them would go to all the SIP shareholders.

By the start of December 1940, a month before this plan was to take effect, *Gone With the Wind* had grossed nearly $14 million domestically, and David foresaw $20 million worldwide. But as late as December 2, he was still stirring up the waters, wondering about eleventh-hour alternatives. He sought outside advice from Leo Spitz (a lawyer who advised movie companies). It was the bane of David's regular employees' work that he would second-guess them with opinions solicited from strangers he had met at dinner.

He wrote Spitz a nine-page letter, a mass of detail, referring the lawyer to many other findings and documents, testing the tax laws, speculating about selling instead to Fox or Universal, arguing out the turmoil of his hopes and worries so that the letter is barely coherent, let alone enough for Spitz to render a useful opinion in two or three weeks as the holidays approached.

I am sure that I need not call to your attention that this is December 2nd, and that you won't be reading these letters until December 4th at the earliest. It will take some time to study even the things I have in this letter, without the alternative and ramifications that will occur to you and Orr, and that will develop out of your conferences with him. The whole thing has got to be cleaned up before the end of the year, at least as far as the sale of my interest is concerned. Please check with Orr as to whether there is any danger to a purchase that goes through at the last minute. It will be just too awful if we reach the last week in December without having cleaned the thing up and I am faced with deciding on one plan which is the only one open, or even of deciding between two or more plans, none of which is desirable, with the absolute obligation of choosing and acting on one of them before December 31st—or an earlier date, if Orr thinks it must be earlier. Bear in mind that we have to draw the contracts, possibly put through a change in the charter of DOSP, Inc., possibly borrow the money at the bank—or, even worse, if we make the deal with Universal or MGM, they may have to go to their stockholders or directors.

This panic came after a year of rest from production, of vacation and fiscal confidence, of time to contemplate the best way ahead. But it was a letter impossible to understand, from a man beyond help or reassurance. David now had no patience to read or edit his own letters—he passed the burden on to others and demanded inspired salvation.

Three directors were appointed to preside over the liquidation: David, Jock, and Altstock. Jock was moving into fresh areas. David had his new company, and by 1941 he was already packaging some of his projects for other studios. Thus, Francis Altstock handled the routine business and inevitably incurred David's wrath and dismay. For Altstock was by now ignoring David's many contradictory requests and suggestions, proceeding at his own pace and feeling relief as Whitney's business eased away from pictures. Just as surely, David felt himself wronged and betrayed, and so, on June 30, 1941, he wrote a nineteen-page letter to Jock to deplore the liquidation management. Above all, this letter echoed David's distress at the loss of Jock:

> We have all along been aware that Fran has a steadfast policy of not expressing an opinion in writing. It is a basic tenet of his unfortunate political training that you can trace people's opinions, and show how wrong they were, by studying their files, and dragging out memos to prove how wrong they were,—and no one is ever going to be able to do this to him! From his standpoint, he is right. . . . As you so well know, I am not afraid of being in writing—and my records are open to those who desire to try me on them. . . .

I don't care whether you show this memo to Fran or not. As I have often demonstrated, I don't do things behind people's backs—and when I attack them I immediately apprise them of the fact, so that they may fight back in the open if they so choose. . . . I am perfectly content that only you, and not Fran, should receive this letter, if that be your wish. Possibly you can straighten this matter out in your own way, without adding fuel to the flame of the unfortunate situation. But if on the other hand you want to give it to Fran to read, or to answer, by all means do so. Whatever he may think of me, I am sure that to some extent he respects me for at least my frankness. I wish that my admiration for his qualities could extend to the same virtue. It is inevitable that he will go out to "get" me, through the years, as he has threatened to "get" other people. Revenge is always a characteristic of this type.

Jock was baffled by David's "violent personal animus." He resigned as a liquidating director and said he had "little patience for peace-making." David was threatening to withdraw, too; the last rites would be left to Altstock and Ernest Scanlon, acting for David. As to David's complaint, Jock would only note that Altstock "believes in doing business by tele-phonic communication and by actual meetings of the parties involved, whereas your habitual method is by correspondence." This is one of the first observations of the damage David did himself and his business in these huge missives. But as the letter to Jock makes clear, writing had become an emotional unburdening for David: the memos were his hope of clarity. David was saluted for his success and his ability. But he was like an athlete who had stopped to study anatomy—a kind of madness was growing in his self-analysis.

3 · AN IDIOT TAKING CARE OF HIMSELF

ON MAY 31, 1939—as the principal shooting on *Gone With the Wind* came to a close—David wrote to his sister-in-law Marjorie about recent talks he had had in which Myron "has come to the conclusion that he simply has got to cut out the drinking." David advised keeping fruit juices available, coaxing Myron to eat—prairie oysters, spinach, and borscht. "Another thing I have noticed is that he seems to be revolted by the sight of a great deal of food. A very small sized order without too many things on a plate and there is a one to five chance that he will eat it; but the minute a good big healthy plate of food is put in front of him, he turns from it as though it were medicine."

The letter does not ring with confidence in Myron's wife. By August 1939, the worn-out Marjorie had given up on her husband's resourceful neuroses. She left him and took their daughter, Joan, to Boston. Now David worried all the more. As he prepared to go to Connecticut for the summer of 1940—Irene's attempt to cure *him*—he wrote to Myron's secretary, Maxine Graybill:

> Myron is, as we all know, very careless with his health; and I am terrified as to what might happen, in view of his rundown state, if he were taken ill while I was away, and the right doctors were not called in immediately. For any illness, however slight, I am anxious that Dr. Verne Mason be called in immediately, before any complications develop. . . .
>
> It may seem that I am being very dramatic about nothing, but I know that Myron is simply an idiot about taking care of himself when he's sick.

It was coincidence that Myron's marriage came apart as David's triumph appeared on the horizon. But the coincidence could only make Myron's despair more savage. He had never been able to convince anyone—let alone Marjorie or himself—that he loved his wife. But suppose the drinker was especially vulnerable to solitude and aggravated by tedious company. Marjorie left Myron at Hill Haven, and she went to a lawyer for advice. Myron said he was bewildered, but ready to take her back. So Marjorie tried to explain:

> You must know that it is no longer possible for me to tolerate your fixed habit of excessive drinking which has accentuated an attitude naturally arbitrary and self-willed, and which also has caused you on

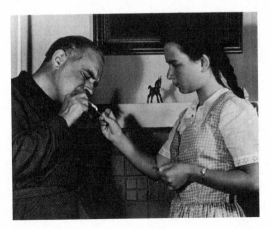

Myron, with his daughter, Joan

too many occasions to make me the butt of a constant stream of abuse, not only when we were alone, but in the presence of groups of people, many of them intimate friends.

In addition, Marjorie contended that Myron had had a very bad effect on Joan. The daughter was tense, inward, a worrier, yet assertive, arrogant, and gloomily precocious. A few years later, Joan wrote this poem about her parents:

> One day and I remember all too well
> For Father in a rage yelled across the room;
> He said that life with Mother was like hell
> And that she would drive him to his domb [sic].

The self-destructive agent acquired a new joke. He was forever giving up drink. Myron's lawyer, Barry Brannen, bought this "going on the wagon" routine. At the end of July 1940, as Myron prepared to visit David's family at Stony Batter Farm, Brannen wrote ahead, "In our discussion last night he seemed entirely prepared to recognize the facts. I have always said that the same judgment he familiarly exercises on behalf of his clients would impel him to stop drinking. He says that this is now the case. We reviewed fully Verne Mason's diagnosis, his analysis of the symptoms, and the extent and nature of his recommendations. You will know that Mason's conclusion was definite and authoritative that Myron stop, and that no halfway or divergent course was possible."

But Myron had another blow. In 1938, he had allowed his servant, Ishii, a six-month paid leave to go back to Japan to visit his family. When Ishii returned, in 1939, his natural authority had acquired a militaristic edge. "He didn't like the Jews and did like Hitler and was persistently vocal in both respects!" Ishii had no Marjorie to ignore or intimidate now. Myron was the only target, so the master fired the butler, who vanished into the Japanese quarter of Los Angeles.

Family lore had it that Ishii had gone back to Japan to be a part of the war on America. But from Los Angeles, he was taken by roundup and emergency order to the detention camp at Manzanar in the semidesert between Mount Whitney and Death Valley. Myron and David were not inclined to support his requests from there that he be helped to freedom. In their eyes, Ishii had become a dangerous "Jap." (He was released from Manzanar in 1944, and he returned to Los Angeles, but not to the Selznicks. Ishii died there in 1953, a hotel servant.)

Barry Brannen anticipated that a dry Myron would feel wretched for a while as his liver recoiled. But he urged relief from agency affairs. "If this means that the business will not run as well, I am confident that nevertheless it will run." Whereas Myron's longtime associates foresaw the breakup of the agency and began to steal the best clients. In response, Myron tried to set up a series of personal service agreements with clients.

David and Irene collected books on alcoholism; they surveyed the medical field. Amid their own growing troubles, here was something over which they felt a shared distress—for they were both losing a friend. But David could hardly talk to Myron without seeming a nag. David was such a part of Myron's problem.

And David felt guilty. In November 1940, he wrote a will in which he hoped his executors would seek the advice of L.B. and Myron in settling his business affairs. David went on: "Beyond this, I have no wish to express except that my brother, Myron, would take my death as a means of eliminating his drinking proclivities rather than as an excuse to accelerate them! And that he would take this as my final well-intentioned nagging of him."

Myron was not happy in self-pity—so if he felt sick, he was the more likely to take a drink. In the spring of 1941, he was sent a poem written by a fellow souse, W. C. Fields. Myron gave a copy to David:

> The horse and mule live 30 years
> And nothing know of wine and beers.
> The goat and sheep at 20 die
> And never taste of Scotch or Rye.
> The cow drinks water by the ton
> And at 18 is mostly done.
> The dog at 15 cashes in without
> The aid of Rum or Gin.
> The cat in milk and water soaks
> And then in 12 short years it croaks.
> The modest, sober, bone dry hen
> Lays eggs for nogs and then dies at 10.
> All animals are strictly dry.
> They sinless live and swiftly die.
> But sinful, ginful rum soaked men
> Survive for three score years and ten.
> And some of us, the mighty few,
> Keep drinkin' till we're 92.

Irene was always a spokesman for Myron. She was proud of the confidences he gave to her alone, the amused account of heartless flirtations, and, sometimes, the commiseration over David's excesses. For, boil it down: the sort of man Irene urged David to be—more economical, more businesslike, less gullible—that man had Myron as a model.

In April 1941, it was Irene who prevailed upon Myron to try a drastic cure at the Hartford Retreat. She flew with him across country, strength-ening his resolution, arguing away vacillation and alarm. It says a lot for Irene, and for what Myron felt about her, that he permitted this game. They went by way of New York, with panic rising in Myron.

"When the institution sent an attendant to the station along with the limousine," wrote Irene, "Myron asked did they think he was going to bolt? He almost did when we got there, because the reception hall was dim and there was a momentary illusion of figures moving in on us from both sides."

You can see the gloom of that April afternoon: this is another film, the sanitarium in *A Star is Born*, that grim place where Norman Maine dries out. In Hartford, a doctor welcomed Myron and offered him a drink. "Say when," the doctor asked, and Myron waited for a full half-pint measure. He drank it down because of the scare he'd had and announced that henceforth he was on the wagon.

Irene stayed in Hartford, explaining the family history to the doctors. Myron's nerves kept him walking about, except when he had to eat and when she pushed the cards in his trembling hands for gin rummy.

After a few days, Myron put her on the train. She went to New York first, and she was at the Waldorf when the hospital called. Where was Myron? No one knew. She waited a week, and then the wanderer strolled in, wondering where they might dine. Where had he been? Oh, in Boston, with clients of his, Florence Eldridge and Fredric March, who were trying out a play. Yes, of course, he was better. How could these people always know whether they were drunk or playing the part? The thing about going on the wagon as a career is that you have to keep getting off first.

But why the Hartford Retreat, so far away? The likely answer comes in this reverse angle view of Myron's trip there—a letter from Howard Selznick (another Hartford inmate) to his Uncle Charlie Sachs, on April 21:

> Last week Myron came up here. I believe to see me. I thought he looked either worn out or disgusted about something—anyway he looked bad and nervous. . . .
>
> P.S. Of course, Irene looked well—I guess that he is in the same boat as I am only I am better off *in many ways*.
>
> You know what I mean.

In such moments, we have to recognize how haunted this family was and how often the besieged David stayed cheerful. Howard was undergoing a variety of tests at Hartford. His "general efficiency" was "unusually poor"—"learning, motor ability, and repetition fall within the 'pathological' category." According to two tests, his mental age was in the eleven to thirteen range and his IQ was seventy-nine. X rays of his skull showed the possibility of hemiatrophy. In May 1942, Dr. A. A. Brill would go to Hartford to examine Howard for the Selective Service Board. Brill reported "a cerebral injury at birth, as a result of which he has never developed mentally and emotionally. . . . I concluded that the . . . patient is suffering from a paranoid condition on the basis of mental deficiency. . . . Whenever he has to face a problem, he immediately has ideas of reference and persecution. He is emotionally very unstable, and shows a definite deficiency in judgment, reasoning and insight."

Indeed: Howard had thought Myron was there to visit *him.* The staff at Hartford observed him writing to young women, and he regularly fell in love with nurses. "He likes to attract attention to himself, and he feels that he can be happier if he is the object of admiration and attention. . . . He has been advised to make his letters a little less frequent to everyone, but he says that he is 'a great letter writer' and that he has no intention of cutting down on his correspondence."

Howard wrote to an Eleanor in Jersey City. But the letter was intercepted by the staff and sent to David instead. "You are right, Eleanor," it said, "they are the lowest scum and my brothers are scum to see me suffer. . . . I sever all ties with them."

That was not so easy. David and Myron were paying for Howard's support and treatment, and on July 12, 1941, David himself went up to

The eyes that helped Phylis Walker become Jennifer Jones

Hartford to see Howard. This was only a few days before he would behold the astonishing eyes of Phylis Walker for the first time.

4 · FLESH-PEDDLING

IN THE EARLY SPRING of 1941, as David ruled the new world of David O. Selznick Productions Inc., he hired John Houseman, until lately the partner of Orson Welles in the Mercury Theatre and all its enterprises.

> He couldn't have been nicer to me [said Houseman]. I would be his associate, that was probably the right word, and I always assumed that that meant I would produce some pictures under his aegis and supervision. But I suddenly realized about two or three months into my tenure there that he hadn't the slightest intention of letting me produce anything—or producing anything himself for a while. He was aware of this. But I don't think he ever said, I'm going to let this poor boy believe I'm going to produce things—but ha-ha!—I'm not really going to. It never occurred to him. When you've got that kind of egomania!

Houseman had the posed manners of an English public school boy as managed by a deft actor, for he was crossbred from a French Jewish father and an English mother and born in Rumania; he could pass anywhere without seeming at home or at a loss; he was eloquent but cool and detached; he was genuinely creative, a man of ideas and a manager of more turbulent egos. He had guided Orson Welles through the richest years of the young man's genius, and if only in terms of their wearying effect on aides and assistants, Orson and David were alike. Indeed, it is possible that Orson Welles was still David's target.

"John and David didn't really get on," said Irene, who remained a friend of Houseman's until his death. "John was too intellectual for him—but David revered Orson." There had been the meeting of May 1937, the offer, and Welles's refusal. The genius had recommended his own associate, John Houseman, as if he might not be too sad to lose him. A year later, David had fallen in love with the idea of Orson playing the lead in a film about Beethoven, and Welles had come close to doing a test.

Only a few months after SIP had purchased the rights to *Rebecca*, Welles did the novel as a radio play (December 9, 1938—the night before the burning of Atlanta—David had so much to keep up with). It was a notable production, with Margaret Sullavan's breathy voice outstanding in the lead and Orson himself as Maxim. This was all part of the rising interest in *Rebecca*, as well as a casting note that made Sullavan a contender for the role.

But Orson and David had their teasing battles, too. After Welles did *I Lost My Girlish Laughter* on his "Campbell Playhouse" series, David asked Jock, "Have you tried Campbell's chicken soup and noodles? The rich, warm flavor makes one think of Orson Welles." In August 1939, Welles came to Hollywood, equipped with carte blanche to make a movie debut for RKO on his own terms. There was a party and David was so "pretty deeply immersed in wine . . . I remember only a portion of my offensiveness." There was real mutual admiration—albeit of the sort that resolves to keep its distance. David offered "on the level" help with what would be *Kane*, and Orson felt sure that *Rebecca* "is almost certainly going to be the best movie you have ever made."

Some of *Citizen Kane* was shot at the Selznick studio in the summer of 1940; David would have known the significance of it and the daring of Welles. He saw *Kane*, in March 1941, at an RKO preview. He was so much an admirer that when Welles's next film, *The Magnificent Ambersons*, was recut by the studio, David tried to have the original version deposited at the Museum of Modern Art. Yet he and Orson could do little more than exchange quips. Houseman was David's best bet, just the steady, tasteful intelligence he needed. As Irene saw it: "Put D.O.S. and John Houseman in a Waring mixer and you'd have something!"

Houseman's first task was to work with the English writer-director Robert Stevenson on *Jane Eyre*. Stevenson had come to Hollywood in 1940 under contract to Selznick; he had been loaned out to Universal for *Back Street* (with Margaret Sullavan instead of Fontaine). Houseman was still involved with Welles's stage production of *Native Son*, so Stevenson had done most of the work adapting *Jane Eyre*. "We finished it," wrote Houseman, "and presented it to our leader, only to discover that he had not the slightest intention of producing it." Instead, it was shelved until 1942, when Aldous Huxley came in to give the script some prestige and David packaged the script, Stevenson, his production designer William Pereira, and the troublesome Joan Fontaine and sold everything to Fox—who cast Orson Welles as Mr. Rochester.

That movie was eventually released in 1944, looking like a Selznick adaptation of a classic novel. It is a coherent, well-made picture making beautiful use of studio-built exteriors and the atmospheric photography of George Barnes. Why could it not have been made, under Houseman's control, for DOSP, with the same cast and team? The most powerful explanation is that David had become more interested in packaging projects: it would be hard to measure Selznick's investment in *Jane Eyre*, yet it was part of a sale (also including *Claudia* and *The Keys of the Kingdom*) to Fox on which he realized $2 million. Suppose a third of that sum is due to *Jane Eyre*—he could have argued to himself that this was as good a way of making money as actually producing the picture. He may have told himself—and the declining Myron—that he was doing better in the deal than any agent. It was the start of what Irene called "flesh-peddling." For if, in the late thirties, Myron had made moves to be a producer, so David now was teaching his sick brother a new kind of agenting.

There was also Hitchcock to handle. It was apparent to Houseman that David and Hitchcock welcomed a go-between, for they were both natural controllers, the one forthright, the other sly. With the young novelist Peter Viertel, Hitch was working out the future *Saboteur*. Houseman could see that Hitchcock "riled David all the time. Partly envy, partly that he couldn't make Hitch do what he wanted. He couldn't order Hitch around, and he knew that Hitch was saying terrible things about him behind his back. It was a prickly relationship. And David was no help on *Saboteur* at all. Early in the proceedings he said, 'I'm not going to make it anyway.' "

In retaliation, Hitchcock worked casually, at home instead of at the studio. The script was as slight as the film would prove to be. So David ordered Houseman and Hitch to go off on a tour of other studios to find a taker for it. This was humiliation to Hitchcock, and Houseman felt like a pimp as they pitched their story and were turned down. But eventually *Saboteur* was dealt: Frank Lloyd would do it as an independent production at Universal. There was one extra blow to Hitch: David made $100,000 profit, but the deal was so onerous to Lloyd that the producer insisted the film be done cheaply, so he commanded Hitch to use the lightweight Priscilla Lane as his lead actress.

Then there was the matter of United Artists. Selznick was always inclined to blame the failure of his SIP pictures on U.A. marketing. Its release of *Rebecca* added to his consternation. David was at the time talking to Frank Capra about some kind of collaboration, and he was pained to hear from him how well Warners was selling *Meet John Doe*:

> Only today I received word that even in those situations where *Meet John Doe* is not doing the box office gross that was achieved by *Rebecca*, the net film rental is greater because of the better terms, better playing time, and better selection of theaters.

United Artists was always fearful that David would take his pictures elsewhere. It had had to swallow the special circumstances of his defection to MGM on *Gone With the Wind.* But it was eager to retain his future works, and so it went after Selznick and Capra, volunteering stock in return for pictures. U.A. was also ready to help in financing the pictures and offered David $600,000 as a fund.

It was part of David's suspicion of U.A. that its effectiveness was hindered by the fluctuating commitment of Chaplin and Mary Pickford, who had too much say and too little concern for practical detail. Alexander Korda was striving to make David more a part of U.A. But David's neighbor Charlie Chaplin was too busy to take David's call. So David sent a telegram across the street to 1085 Summit Drive:

Dear Charlie:

I have been trying to get you on the phone for three days. If you do not want to talk to me please say so and kindly do not attempt to put me in the undignified position of pursuing you. I do not want anything from you personally and furthermore I know you too well to call you about anything that I did not think was for your benefit. My call is as a courtesy to a great many people including yourself and people very dear to you. If I do not hear from you I shall most certainly forget about it and you may be sure I have made my last call.

The volatile Capra gave up waiting. He went into the army, made major, and would soon be assigned to documentaries. As Capra put it, he got dizzy listening to the great deals being offered and could think only of Ed Murrow's broadcasts from the bombed London. David persevered, and on October 4, 1941, on sunny Pickfair's lawn, he, Charlie, Korda, and Mary Pickford signed the contracts. David was given stock in escrow (as much as 25 percent of U.A.) to be paid for in five years. He had board powers and dividends, and the company advanced him $300,000 to develop projects. There was a new board of directors announced for U.A., with Laudy Lawrence as David's representative. The board was to assume some of the executive power hitherto regulated by the owners.

David had three other assets, his discoveries: Vivien Leigh, Ingrid Bergman, and Joan Fontaine. Vivien was in America in 1940, waiting for Olivier's divorce to become final. They were married in Santa Barbara on August 28, 1940, looking eastward, toward England, as they took their vows. The Selznicks were not invited.

Olivier and Vivien stayed in Los Angeles to make *That Hamilton Woman* for Korda (a paean to being British and opposing tyranny, yet filmed at the General Services Studio on Las Palmas). By the end of 1940, the couple were on their way back to England, but they left behind hopes and assurances of when Vivien's commitment to David would be fulfilled.

A year later, on January 19, 1942, Jenia Reissar had to write to David:

> her refusal to return to California is based on personal reasons only;
> nothing else comes into consideration. She will not leave Olivier, and
> she seems willing to ruin her film career in order to remain with him.

Olivier had gone into the Fleet Air Arm. Vivien ran nearly a year on the London stage in *The Doctor's Dilemma*, and they engineered every weekend together. Theirs was a famous love, and wartime was its best context. For they were both of them aroused by danger; not to have been in England then, or to have been apart, would have reduced them as actors. The David whose own desire to serve was mounting could have been more sympathetic. But he felt he was losing a possession—and neither Olivier nor Vivien could bear to be owned. There has never been any suggestion that David pursued Vivien, if only because she was so intent on Olivier. But David fell in love with his own actresses, habitually, and none served him more magically than Vivien. The "romance" may have been only in his head—or in her cunning. But David never gave up on her.

When Jenia Reissar proposed *Jane Eyre* to Vivien, she said she didn't want to do that because Daphne du Maurier had stolen *Rebecca* from it and "since you did not consider me suitable for the part in *Rebecca* you couldn't possibly . . . want me for Jane!" Reissar then pointed out that Vivien had herself cabled David enquiring about *Jane Eyre*, hoping he might do it in England.

There was another factor at work, as Jenia Reissar recalled about forty-five years later, referring back to Jill Esmond and days at RKO:

> Olivier really hated Selznick. He never forgave him for throwing him
> out and wanting his wife, who wasn't very well known. . . . But Vivien
> had a mind of her own. She was iron, absolute iron. . . . Vivien refused
> to go back to Selznick because Olivier wouldn't let her do it. I've had
> lunch with the two of them, when I tried to persuade him to let her
> go and do one picture and come back then. He kept saying, "I think
> her place is here. It's the war," and so on. I knew he wouldn't let her
> go. But she didn't want to go either. She didn't want to let Larry
> go—in case she lost *him*.

David had to deal with another awkward husband in the case of Ingrid Bergman. Or was the problem, rather, a consummate actress whose urge to get on and be active was like water searching for a way through rock? Ingrid was always a personal favorite of David and Irene's. They had taken her and her family into their home. There was a young child, Pia, an infant on her mother's back, and a husband, a hardworking doctor, a fitness enthusiast,

Petter, who thought it natural that a husband advised in his wife's career. Moreover, the Lindstroms had no wish to go back to Europe—not yet, anyway. Ingrid was desperate to work. Ordinary life lay so heavy on her, she would overeat. So she begged David for pictures, and he found some for her, though he implored her not to do them, saying he would pay her anyway. But she worked, and not even wretched pictures could stop her becoming a star. So David loaned her out and made a fortune.

He always said that Ingrid was his natural woman. He ordered the makeup to be taken off her in tests and pictures. This is the legend. But any eye can see how much was left and how much effort went into projecting her beauty. David and Irene both thought her true and straight. But years later, long after the divorce from Ingrid, Petter Lindstrom would write to Irene:

> You are totally wrong when you characterize I.B. as non-materialistic. However, she never stopped acting and she evidently fooled not only me but you too. You stated that she was consistently generous. Yes, she continued to send flowers and gifts regularly to David and to those three famous Hollywood reporters, although she hated them all. . . .
>
> You may say that I.B. "knew nothing about money." That is totally wrong. Do you know that she did not spend one cent for Pia's living expenses, schooling, or traveling etc. from the time Pia was twelve years old and until Pia was about 23 years old.

Lindstrom was never a Hollywood person, and if he seemed strict or harsh it is in part because he was a middle-class Swedish doctor serving as his wife's agent and having to overlook her passionate affairs with those men who worked with her. In the early forties, alone, her conquests included Victor Fleming, Spencer Tracy, and Gary Cooper, as well as photographer Robert Capa and harmonica player Larry Adler. All this before the famous relationship with Roberto Rossellini.

The Selznicks believed that Petter was a tireless negotiator on Ingrid's behalf. He says she showed them smiles of ignorance and sent Petter in on the deal-making so that she could stay above it all and fresh for her work. This much can be said with certainty: Ingrid and Petter were no longer well suited once they left Sweden—Ingrid rose to every Hollywood expectation, while Petter remained a dogged outsider; when the divorce came, Petter got custody of Pia; Ingrid Bergman's later career was seldom free from storm and travail; she was the best actress—the most versatile and the one best able to win the love of the public—that David ever had.

David loaned her out: to Columbia for *Adam Had Four Sons*, to MGM for *Rage in Heaven* and *Dr. Jekyll and Mr. Hyde*, to Warners for *Casablanca* and *Saratoga Trunk*, to Paramount for *For Whom the Bell Tolls*, to Metro again for *Gaslight*, and to RKO and Leo McCarey for *The Bells of St. Mary's*. There are classic films and great roles there that are the basis, even today, of Ingrid Bergman's reputation. And in *Gaslight* she got her Oscar. But on *Gaslight*, dealing with his friend Arthur Hornblow, Jr., David received $253,750 for her services and paid Ingrid a little more than $75,000. On *Saratoga Trunk*, he again got $253,750 and paid her nearly $70,000. In the same deal, he got Olivia de Havilland for one film (at $30,000). Yet he traded that right away to RKO for a $100,000 profit.

All of which was legal and common practice in the picture business—it was something David had every opportunity to learn with Gable, Metro, and *Gone With the Wind.* Bergman was not unappreciative: she had yearned for the role of Maria in *For Whom the Bell Tolls*, and David fought a sustained campaign to get it for her. But he had only to look at Myron to see how depressing agentry could be—and David was making far more on these deals than Myron's 10 percent. Perhaps a part of him needed to beat Myron. The ugliest aspect of his dealing was the inability to understand the growing outrage in Bergman. At every protest, David's first defense was that the actress should be grateful, for *he* had made her. He wanted it both ways: to be a peddler and to be admired for it. Sometimes David could work himself up into an indignant blancmange at Ingrid's ingratitude—he would like Jennifer Jones all the more because she was paid so modestly without complaining, or even noticing.

The history with Joan Fontaine was more vituperative and comic. For in this contract, both parties seemed mortified by the recollection of David's earlier fondness for the actress. Fontaine's negotiating positions left David feeling bewildered and used. Joan refused films—she would not do *Back Street*; on others, she made herself so difficult that some actors and directors (David said) had blackballed her. She was on suspension; she encouraged the bad blood to get out into the press; she battled David from the word go.

Their correspondence is profuse and entertaining and best summed up in a ten-page letter of June 23, 1942, from D.O.S. to Joan's agent, Frank Vincent. It would make an interesting opera, with bespectacled tenor in the foreground while the mute actress tears out her hair behind him. Here are "fragments," as David takes the agent through his chronicles of Joan's career.

4. I announced Joan for the role [*Rebecca*] and was hooted at for an
   imbecile by everybody in town, many people predicting that I would

pull her out after two days. I determined that she would be a great success and proceeded with the picture, and with the casting, despite Hitchcock's warnings that the picture would take between a week and two weeks longer to make with Joan than with an experienced actress, at a cost of perhaps $50,000. . . .

5. Joan gave us great difficulties during the production, some because of her youth and lack of conscientiousness, some because of a temperament that was new-born with her selection for the role, and because of her extreme inexperience. Scenes were done over and over again until they satisfied Hitch and myself; whole sequences were re-shot because her performance was inadequate; literally hundreds of lines were re-dubbed when the picture was completed to get better and more professional readings by her. The result you know.

6. I do not think I am flattering myself to say that as soon as I select a personality, and especially when I announce that I have cast that personality in a lead in one of my pictures, he or she immediately assumes an importance in the eyes of the trade, and comes into demand. . . . Thus, the very producer who had accepted a cruel critic's designation of Joan as "the wooden woman" now wanted Joan on the strength of the fact that not alone had I cast her in *Rebecca*, but that apparently I actually was keeping her in the role! . . .

11. . . . I think it in order to point out to you that the "profits" that I have made on Joan have not yet commenced to reimburse me for the financial sacrifices involved in casting Joan in *Rebecca*; that the prices I have obtained for her have been secured over the threats of reprisals from other studios; that these prices could not have been received except for my management of her, and except for the skill and experience of Dan O'Shea; and that the "profits" on her have not commenced to pay the cost of managing an institution which has made possible, maintained and furthered her career.

IT WAS IN THE HUSH after such harangues that John Houseman felt "stirred . . . to revolt against the well-paid, tranquil, irrelevant life I was leading as a vice-president of David O. Selznick Productions." Instead, he accepted an invitation from Pare Lorentz to work on a documentary about the American industrial worker. By January 1942, he was at the State Department, meeting William Donovan, getting ready to organize Overseas Radio. "When I informed David O. Selznick of my new assignment he praised me for my patriotism, then notified me by registered letter that my contract still had eleven months to run, which he expected me to complete when the war ended."

All Houseman had wanted was to make pictures. The same was true for a lowlier Selznick employee, Val Lewton, story editor for David since

A Tale of Two Cities. Throughout 1941, Lewton did his best to attend story conferences with a cheerful face. He noted all manner of schemes: *The Pickwick Papers* with W. C. Fields? "Psychological stories. D.O.S. feels that there might be something of great value in Freud's life. Described Freud's life to him briefly. He also feels that an examination of certain case histories, particularly histories of dual personality, might furnish us with an unusual yarn for Bergman." Or what about Bergman, Katharine Hepburn, and Freddie March in Henry James's *The Wings of the Dove?* A China Relief conference was interrupted with talk of optioning P. G. Wodehouse's next Jeeves story. "He said [this is June 4] he would most dearly like to find the great American novel of the war—a story about the American people with not a single battle scene in it."

On November 14, 1941, Lewton got a clear hour with David:

> He began by announcing that he hoped I wouldn't be too upset at the news that he has parted with *Jane Eyre, Keys of the Kingdom* and *Claudia* to 20th in order to concentrate on pictures helpful to the war effort. . . .
>
> He then proceeded to outline his plans for a tie up between himself and the Reader's Digest, to make pictures to fill "a complete evening's entertainment" somewhat on the lines planned for the Anthology idea. He is to work very closely with me during the next few weeks selecting material from the files of Reader's Digest—all kinds; feature length subjects to run about 1-½ hours, cartoon subjects (Disney will do one for him); all kinds of subjects, both general and war, such as medical, educational comedy, etc. . . . we are to watch for things that normally would not lend themselves to pictures, such as the One Day Cure for Syphilis. . . .
>
> He says it may work into a very big thing and make a very big career for me.

Lewton did not leave easily; though full of dark, inner inventiveness, he needed external security. He was fearful Selznick would be angry if he left him. But the riot of good ideas hurled around, and the unlikelihood of any developing, was enough. Early in 1942, Val Lewton walked away to head a B picture unit for RKO, specializing in horror pictures. The first of these, *Cat People*, ran seventy-one minutes and cost $134,000—about the profit David made on one Joan Fontaine loan-out.

It was directed by Jacques Tourneur, an assistant director on *A Tale of Two Cities.* The story involved a girl with a fear complex—one of the ideas Selznick had entertained—and it grossed over $2 million.

In the next few years Lewton would prove one of the outstanding producers in the business. Myron remarked to David that Lewton "may have been a better man for your melodramatic subjects." A run of prosperous B pictures would have done so much to bolster the Selznick enterprise. But if David had made *Cat People* it would have had Bergman in the lead and cost $2 million. The cats would have been tigers.

5 · THE BIG-EYED GIRL

IT WAS ON MONDAY the fourteenth or Tuesday the fifteenth of July 1941, in the New York offices, that David saw her. He was taken with her before he knew what her name was. Anyway, he would change the name; he would create the star and call her Jennifer Jones. Names were incidental to those large hazel eyes watching him—for she could have been in no doubt about who he was. Perhaps her certainty made him think his turmoil could be calmed by this rapt unknown who had come into the office out of the hinterland. Love at first sight?—it is the only kind the movies trust. David may not even have spoken to her in New York—he was busy, he was rushing by, and she was Kay Brown's business (Kay had survived all the

Phylis Isley, age sixteen, Tulsa, Oklahoma

layoffs). But he noticed the eyes and the vulnerability and gathered that she had two children. She was upset about something; she broke down that very first time in the office. "Right in the middle of my reading," she would say, years later, on a radio show, "I had hysterics and was unable to continue . . . and the next thing I knew I was reading the same lines for Mr. Selznick himself."

Phylis Isley had been born in Tulsa, Oklahoma, on March 2, 1919. She was the only child of Flora Mae, or "Dolly," Suber and Phillip Isley. The mother, who was four years older than the father, had met her husband when she worked in an office that booked traveling shows in the Southwest. Phil Isley had wanted to be a Broadway actor, but he had given that up to have a roaming stock company and to own a movie theater in Tulsa. In later life, the high-strung actress in Phylis played with the notion that Phil was not her father, that there had been someone else who had gone off to the war in Europe.

By 1925, the family had settled in Oklahoma City. The Isley business did well, and Phylis entered the Monte Cassino Junior College in Tulsa, a Benedictine school. Phylis grew up tall (she was five feet eight), with dark hair, glowing eyes, long legs, and a full figure. She was devout and very shy. But she was desperate to be an actress, and very aware of how she looked. There was a family photo album in which she wrote wry comments about herself: "Isn't she *sweet?*," "My negroid period," and "Sweet 16, and truly never been 'kissed.' "

She had a year as a drama major at Northwestern, after which she entered the American Academy of Dramatic Arts in New York. It was there, on January 2, 1938, that she met the young actor Robert Walker. They were married a year to the day later, for they were wildly in love and sure they had the makings of great careers.

They went to Hollywood in 1939 and began to get parts. Phylis Walker had a six-month contract at Republic for $75 a week, and she appeared in a John Wayne Western, *New Frontier*, and in a serial, *Dick Tracy's G-Men*, without attracting much notice.

But she had two children: Robert, Jr., on April 15, 1940, and Michael, on March 13, 1941. By then, they were back in New York, looking for work and struggling to survive. She tried to get a job in the Chicago company for the Rose Franken play *Claudia*, in which Dorothy McGuire had had a great success. It was the story of a young bride coming of age. To that end, Phylis went to stay with Miss Franken in Connecticut for a few days to read and explore the role. That was how Kay Brown heard about her, for David had paid $187,000 for the movie rights to *Claudia*, and Kay was wondering who would best play the part on screen.

Kay Brown knew her David and how he noticed things. She was herself taken by the power of the girl's eyes beneath a wide straw hat. On July 16, as he traveled west, David's Culver City calendar bore this message from Kay—"the little girl (Philiss Walker) you liked so much for *Claudia*" had done a reading: "it needs a lot of work but was a very nice reading." David had confused her with Phyllis Thaxter, another *Claudia* prospect, who had been in the New York offices:

> Regarding Phyllis Thaxter: I think decision on whether or not you should test should depend entirely upon whether or not you think she is good bet for future apart from *Claudia*. . . . Is this the big-eyed girl we saw in the office . . . ? Incidentally, if it is the big-eyed girl I certainly think she is worth testing no matter when she would be available.

Kay Brown wired back, on July 23, and now a legend was growing: "Lovely big-eyed girl unfortunately isn't Phyllis Thaxter but Phyllis Walker." Two days later, on Friday the twenty-fifth, Kay did a screen test in New York after only fifteen minutes' rehearsal. On the twenty-ninth, David wired Kay, "You have really got me worked up with your series of wires about Phyllis Walker. I am terribly excited and looking forward to seeing the tests tomorrow."

Kay and David were focused on *Claudia*, for which Dorothy McGuire was the apparent casting. For most of the summer of 1941, David was arguing with McGuire's agent, Leland Hayward, over contract terms for the actress. But nothing was settled. Rose Franken had a great say in the movie of her play. Kay Brown went to see her and gathered that Miss Walker's best chance was if Franken believed *she* had discovered her. Never without nerve, Kay told Franken the reading had been no good, "but I didn't dare risk Franken's not seeing her because you [D.O.S.] liked her." Franken bit:

> She agreed to see her and has just [July 23] called me to tell me I am out of my mind and you are so right and that the kid gave one of the best readings she ever heard and she wants sign her for McGuire and Thaxter understudy.

Thus it was Rose Franken herself who came into the New York offices and helped direct Phylis's test on July 25.

Walker was Kay's favorite for *Claudia*, but the publicity machine was about to run stories on Dorothy McGuire, so Kay fired off a "please don't think me butinsky" note to Dan O'Shea to go slow. She envisaged Phylis playing the role for at least a week in Chicago when the play went on tour, and she ran a head-to-head battle of tests between Walker and McGuire. McGuire was not testing well—as David had said in June, "She has the 'cutes' to a great extent . . . and that prop smile of hers plus the showing of the teeth, etc. and all the other exaggerations and emphasis that she gives is in my opinion very overboard for screen purposes."

David saw the point about holding off and in one memo, to publicity director Whitney Bolton, he managed to reveal not just his excitement about Phylis Walker, but his own need to hedge a bet. This is August 2, and it is D.O.S. in a nutshell:

> I don't know whether you have heard yet about Phyllis Walker whom we have signed and who is in my opinion the best sure-fire female star to come along since Leigh and Bergman. For your very confidential information, there is a fifty-fifty chance we will cast her in the lead of *Claudia* instead of McGuire, even though we have signed McGuire, and this is the reason why we want to hold up on McGuire. Because of this possibility it may be wise to hold up on Walker also.

More searching tests were in order. On August 11, Phylis Walker flew to Los Angeles. Frances Inglis, David's secretary, met her at the airport: "I was so amazed, because this was a frightened little bird. She shook from head to toe. I couldn't believe that anybody at her age, with two children, a husband, could be so insecure."

David talked to her, and he told Kay Brown they would do another screen test, there at the studio, "and I should not in the least be surprised" if this Walker test settled the decision. He added to Kay that he felt for Phylis "a great enthusiasm, in case you didn't already know this."

In September, he was mounting a short but spectacular season of theater at the Lobero Theater in Santa Barbara. John Houseman was in charge of it, along with stage director Alfred de Liagre. There was a new play in the season, the one-act *Hello Out There* by William Saroyan, who had suggested Betsy Blair for the female role. David considered putting Phylis in it, along with either Alan Marshal or Henry Bratsburg (now known as Harry Morgan). On August 28, Phylis and Bratsburg read the play for David in his office.

Late hours in the office were routine, and so was the procedure. As Frances Inglis observed: "It was within a couple of weeks. He would ask her to come see him ten, eleven o'clock at night. I would hear the scuffling going on in his office, and Jennifer running around the desk and David chasing her, and Jennifer running out with her face as red as a beet, and getting into her car and rushing off . . . It was a sudden fusion of supply and demand. She needed his help, he desperately needed to give it to her."

Phylis Walker was cast, though David did tell Houseman and de Liagre that the play might require adjustment because of her: "We must face the fact that she is obviously a gorgeous looking girl and that there is much of the play that might be ridiculous in terms of Walker. I think that we must have some slight rewrite, and/or some cuts to meet this point—or get a less glamorous girl."

David had chased and caught many actresses, secretaries, and messengers in that office. He reckoned he had rights, and few in the business would have been other than amused if Phylis Walker had claimed exploitation. Some women would have got in their car, driven off, and never returned. Phylis came back and practiced her smile for the test. She wanted to be a great actress and famous. David may have had her there and then in the summer of 1941 and been smitten with her. Which does not mean he was in love with her. She was gorgeous, and he was the producer.

In Santa Barbara, John Houseman thought David was definitely interested in her personally, but he was not sure whether they were sleeping together. But Jennifer did very well in the Saroyan play: the Santa Barbara season was exactly the kind of thing Irene was always hoping David would undertake. David also said the Lobero season was mounted so that Irene might identify her own interest in theatrical production. He had the sort of confusion that believes you can be helpful to everyone.

Santa Barbara was presented with *Anna Christie*, starring Ingrid Bergman and J. Edward Bromberg, Geraldine Fitzgerald in *Lottie Dundas*, and *The Devil's Disciple*, with Cedric Hardwicke and Janet Gaynor. *Anna Christie* had been done in San Francisco first, and while there, Houseman had bumped into William Saroyan, who straightaway submitted *Hello Out There*. Houseman decided to do it as a curtain opener to the Shaw.

Phylis Walker was "damned good. She was very good," and she got rave reviews. On opening night, as she was in the wings about to go on, Houseman noticed she was still wearing her wedding ring. "Give me that," he ordered, and he took it off her. "She was very nervous. Her hands were always wet." When the play was over, she forgot the ring. There was a big party on the pier afterward, but Phylis never showed up. So Houseman was left with the ring. He found her on the telephone and she said she had to call New York and was too tired to come to the party. The ring was returned, and Houseman got the point:

> It was not until quite a bit later, from a press man, that I discovered what that was all about. David thought he discovered a sort of virgin goddess. The girl knew perfectly well that there would be a lot of press men at the party, and she had, in fact, made about four pictures for Republic—I think she really thought David didn't know.

Henry Bratsburg and Phylis
Walker in William Saroyan's
Hello Out There, *Santa*
Barbara, 1941

David regretted his discovery's absence at the party, but he was more concerned when the Hollywood screen test (done on September 5) proved a disaster. It was shot in the evening, so cameraman George Barnes came to it after a day's work. Selznick wanted Ray Klune to tell Barnes of his "bitter disappointment at this sloppy job." He was angrier still about the makeup since he had given notes on how Phylis's look should be kept natural. As for her hair! He had blowups made of the New York test for comparison. They proved that Phylis's hair looked good when she nervously ran her hands through it. In Hollywood, "she stiffened up terrifically and her self-consciousness completely destroyed her. She is aware of this."

Made-up, then made-down: the ordeal of perfectionism was beginning for Miss Walker. She would have years trying to be herself despite David's obsessive attention.

David had wanted her to do another test at the studio, and Stanley Cortez was mentioned as a replacement cameraman (he was about to photograph *The Magnificent Ambersons*). But Phylis left in a rush. She went back by train and wired from Albuquerque, "Sorry you were out when called to say goodby." Back in New York, she sent a handwritten letter on September 19:

> After opening night, which *was* something of a nightmare, I loved doing the play.

She was twenty-two, she was under contract, and she was getting $200 a week. As for the much maligned screen test, she looked no worse than enchanting in it.

When Phylis Walker went back east after the Santa Barbara theater festival, she found herself caught up in subterfuges and metamorphoses such as fall under the heading "publicity." She could seem like an innocent waif in all the plotting, but whatever happened between David and the woman who would be Jennifer, this was also the meeting of an actress who wanted to be a star and of a man who measured his potency by what he could get the public to buy and believe.

Kay Brown was trying to ensure that Phylis had the part in *Claudia*; that was a sign of David's inclination. Brown and Rose Franken lunched, and the playwright admitted that her two sons were not convinced by Phylis Walker. "To sum it all up," Kay reported, "Miss Franken didn't discover her."

> Of course, Franken is more than willing to direct the tests [further New York tests] and I suppose, perhaps because of her own ego, would do a decent job on them. But Phylis Walker will take such a shellacking during the preparation that I am not sure you want her to undergo this. But if you want her to go ahead, I'll watch her like a hawk.

Rose Franken was even hopeful that she might get to direct the film of *Claudia*, and she was, as Kay saw it, emotionally fixed on the idea of being the discoverer of three Claudias—one each for radio, stage, and screen. Selznick still encouraged collaboration between playwright and actress. The women met on September 24, 1941, and discussed some scenes from the play: Miss Franken was compelled in all honesty to write to David:

> She has undoubted talent, she is very pretty—overly pretty, and will possibly make a great success in a small part on the stage, or in carefully chosen picture roles. But no audience will be able to take her in the full dose of Claudia, as she has very little variety, a persistent breathiness, and a general naivete which makes a surprisingly knowing quality, poisonous to Claudia. You must also be aware that the child

moves badly, and that her body, for all her pretty face, has very little inherent beauty.

Dorothy McGuire was being led to believe the part was hers—if her tests improved and if she stopped giving signs "of being a daughter of the pixies." At the same time, David would answer Rose Franken with gratitude, regret, and a large dose of big shot. She was, he said, the only person so far *not* knocked out by Phylis Walker. But he stressed the value to any film of a new discovery, and he took a few hundred words to allude to his recent success with Leigh, Fontaine, and Bergman. Yet he seemed to appreciate Franken's criticism. He thought the problems were ones that good direction and Phylis's continued education could deal with. But "whether she does *Claudia* or not, I am grateful to you for uncovering and pointing out these failings."

There were also plans for Phylis to stand in for Dorothy McGuire in at least one stage performance of *Claudia.* McGuire to this day has no recollection of such a thing happening—"How could it? How could she know the part?" Yet Phylis Walker had been immersed in *Claudia* for some time, and D.O.S. did go to New York on October 7, 1941. More screen tests took place at that time, with Mel Ferrer (under contract by then) directing and John Monk reading the male role opposite Phylis. She was "jumping for joy" about Monk; there had been difficulties getting a good actor. "Phylis told me," Kay wrote to David on October 3, before the tests were done, "that she has no hesitancy whatsoever on having her performance in these tests be considered by you a complete indication of what she can do with the part."

Maybe there was one Phylis *Claudia* onstage; maybe the test was enough. For on October 14, David wrote to Dan O'Shea, "My present impression after seeing Walker test is that McGuire is somewhat better for *Claudia.*" He said that he still thought Walker "terrific . . . and probably better for *The Constant Nymph* than any girl in pictures."

Another worry had arisen. On October 24, David wrote again to O'Shea about a confession from Phylis. Evidently her awkward history at Republic had come out, and David's attitude was affected. "The girl is inclined to be a bit dopey about certain things," he wrote O'Shea, "and for all we know she is either on suspension at Republic or signed something that would prevent her from working for somebody else."

O'Shea found that Republic had let their option on her lapse. Still, the Walker situation was being reappraised. There had been interest in her from other studios, mostly from Steve Trilling, the casting director at Warners. Alfred de Liagre had wanted her in a New York play. Early in 1942, when he moved over to RKO as a producer, Val Lewton asked for her for the second female lead (the Jane Randolph role) in *Cat People.*

Instead, Phylis Walker was taken back to basics. Courses were set up for her in diction, dancing, and posture, and she took classes at Columbia for a while in English Literature and Fine Arts before she gave them up because "they were just too much." Her dramatic lessons were with Sanford Meisner, at $8 a week, and for $10 she studied diction at the American Academy. By December 1942, David estimated that $7,500 had been invested in Phylis (not salary).

Then her name was changed. Some have said this was a vital step in David's appropriation of Phylis from Robert Walker. The Republic affair, and Selznick's desire to keep Phylis a "newcomer," probably had more to do with it.

As often happened in such situations, suggestions were invited from many quarters. Alfred de Liagre facetiously proposed "Chloe O'Shea" just because he thought the change "utterly ridiculous." D.O.S. was irritated with de Liagre. He suspected that "Delly has spent most of his time with Phylis since last summer making cracks about me, and building up what he could do for her." He also called Phylis the girl of de Liagre's dreams—so jealousy may have been another reason for reappraisal.

"Jennifer" had come up as a new first name: Kay Brown liked it; she said she would use it if she had another daughter. "I still like Jennifer for a first name," David told Whitney Bolton on December 22, 1941, "and it somehow looks the way Phylis looks." "Jennifer Bard" had its hour of glory. But Phylis was wavering, and David despaired of "the numerologists and everybody else that they want to consult." "Jennifer Jones" emerged late in January 1942, and the name was announced for *The Keys of the Kingdom*—a part she would never play in another film that David would sell to Fox.

But "Jennifer" shied away: some friends said the new name sounded comical and plain. David was angry. In January, he had had to sign the payroll checks for once, and it irked him to discover that Phylis was getting $200 a week but had done nothing—at his orders. "Jennifer Jones," he said, had rhythm and romance. So the lady agreed, and on February 4 she sent a cable to Kay Brown:

JENNIFER JONES IS OKAY. LOVE. JENNIFER JONES.

With the name settled, promotion could move ahead. But Jennifer Jones would become notorious in the Selznick organization for her reluctance over publicity. This began with a radio spot in March 1942. Such "lifelike" occasions were usually scripted, and the Selznick people were horrified at the script submitted to them:

Stella Unger original script for Jennifer drips with goo and saccha-
rinity. She is introduced as glorious Cinderella latest DOS find who
will appear in that wonderful story *Keys.* Asked to tell how she was
signed, Jennifer says she will present facts for the other ambitious
boys and girls throughout country. . . . Marched into DOS NY office
for *Claudia* and broke down into Jennifer Jones crybaby act. Man
stormed into room asked about excitement. Unger asks whether DOS
was Prince Charming. Jennifer says Yes voice out of fog saying For
heavens sake if she can cry like that give her test.

The publicity people wondered whether they should demand changes
or withdraw the services of Jennifer Jones from the program. But the script
had grown out of talks with Jennifer herself. In 1942, David—as ever—had
too much on his mind: the whole liquidation issue; the question of whether
to go to war or stay in pictures; *Claudia, The Keys of the Kingdom,* and *Jane Eyre;*
what to do with Leigh, Fontaine, Bergman, and his latest discovery, Gregory
Peck, who was being groomed to play the priest in *The Keys of the Kingdom* and
whose contract David shared with Fox. There was not much room for an
affair, even if some in the organization were apprehensive of pointed press
comment about Jennifer.

Phylis Walker was the third great property Kay Brown had delivered
into David's hands. The first two were the novels *Gone With the Wind* and
Rebecca, and those were made and sold off before "Jennifer Jones" ever
appeared on a screen. Kay Brown would be gone, too.

The very acute Brown had only narrowly survived the aftermath of
Wind. Yet in the respite that followed, she had had little to do except remain
alert to something like the coming of a Phylis Walker and worry over
whether she had received proper thanks for finding *Rebecca.* The new projects
she tried to launch could only deliver galleys and synopses to David's desk.
Kay became certain that David was not reading them and that it was now
beneath his consideration to make anything like an ordinary picture.

By May 1942, David had a letter ready that fired Kay. He was too afraid,
or guilty, to send it. Yet he filed it away, as if to tell himself even a coward
could be right. His stated worry was the old one of overhead. The New York
office of DOSP had cost $75,000, $55,000 of which went on salaries—and
Kay was the biggest item. But David could not see a time when her talent
would be used. "Much of my uncertainty," David told Kay in June, in a memo
that was sent, "is of course due to my inability to get a clear picture of what
I should do, and what is expected of me, in the war effort." He regretted that,
by twenty minutes, they had missed out on *Mrs. Miniver.*

Kay was too able and too naturally busy for idleness. She had had
hints and warnings. But when the blow came, in early July, she felt extra

grievance because David had passed the writing of the letter over to Dan O'Shea—yet again, there was that wish to be liked making him more unpopular. Kay wrote back in hurt and anger, and then David called her feeling "only a very feminine approach."

David now argued that it was customary for Kay to deal with Dan—yet he had himself tried and abandoned a fateful letter. He had been trying to find a new job for Kay, and so he chose to be shocked that she was saying unpleasant things about him. For her part, Kay's uneasy self-importance had always felt ignored socially by the Selznicks, especially by Irene. There had been a time when she looked forward to a vice presidency at SIP and even a producer's job. Kay had her own fame and reputation: they would last her through a long career as an agent. But now in a mix of shame and pique, David condescended to her:

> Kay, my darling, you can do anything whatsoever you please to me. I daresay that I will survive, however feminine and bitchy you may be either in your attitude toward us, or in what you say to people working for us, or to people who have dealt with us. You once said to me that I was the only man in the picture business . . . who would treat with a woman as an executive on exactly the same terms as with a man. If this was true then, it is no longer true, and you may class me with the others. You have taught me that women are women, in business or otherwise.

In August 1942, David took another trip east, and on August 13, late at night, he wrote to Irene. This was once an eighteen-page letter, but only pages one, two, seventeen, and eighteen survive—or, at least, that is all Irene gave me:

Most Wonderful of Women:

It's almost four. I've had a shower to wash away the Washington mugginess and bad taste, and I'm alone. Remember: I came East partly to be alone; and here it's accomplished, however briefly and dreamily.

This letter will, I fear, have little form. I'm scribbling madly because I must talk to you—to you, and only you.

I've been depressed, as I've told you and wired you: a depression such as I haven't known in a long time, such as I didn't know in my most confused Hollywood hours. (Perhaps melancholia was the natural successor of . . . [the break]).

Whatever comes of this trip, it's good, I'm sure. The boil is coming to a head. I know I can't go on much longer without making any sense, or without going mad. So *please* don't be upset by this outburst: the thought of that possibility tempts me not to mail this—but I

shall, I know, because in my egotism I'm sure that *you* at least want all my moods—and for that, and for ten thousand other reasons, I am
Yours-at-the-pedestal's base,
David.

The next day he went up to New York, where he dined with Jennifer Jones. They had "a very good talk," and David painted a long-term future for her: more lessons and a seven-year contract before her first picture to justify the investment. "She didn't seem to react much one way or the other and I am not sure she knew what I was talking about." In which case, it is likely David only talked generally of parts and did not mention the prospect of the lead in *The Song of Bernadette*, a project which, with Darryl Zanuck's commitment to the army, now came under the charge of his stand-in and David's (and Irene's) brother-in-law, Bill Goetz.

6 · THE TIME OF REWARD

IN *A PRIVATE VIEW*, Irene Mayer Selznick described the sense of plenty that came from *Gone With the Wind*:

> The time had come for rewards. The most important, success, was already his. This time money could not be far behind. David had at last struck it big. And although the money had not yet come in, he was trying to share it with me; he offered me half, along with extravagant declarations.
>
> I thought he was crazy. I got very upset and backed away. In fact, David had almost as much trouble getting me to take money as my father had had. I was still so old-fashioned I thought it was wrong. I would agree only that what was his was ours and please leave things as they were. He said he couldn't do that because there was a deadline, something to do with a gift tax, which to me sounded pretty silly in a community-property state like California.

Irene's "old-fashioned" approach to money and David's generosity had meant that in all the years since their marriage, David's income had been divided: a half was paid directly to Irene. He told himself that was for the boys, later. They filed separate tax returns so that Irene's income showed the interest from those Twentieth Century-Fox shares given to her by her father. The house on Summit Drive was Irene's property, yet David gave her a monthly housekeeping allowance from his half of his income. In the SIP years, from 1935 onward, Irene had earned at least as much as, and usually a good deal more than, David. That was underlined by the way Irene kept most of her money, while David gambled and lost amounts ranging from about a third to close to all of his income.

No new system was put into practice as the returns from *Wind* mounted. The equality on which David had insisted continued to apply. For the year 1940, both David and Irene had salary incomes of $116,535 and dividend interest of $5,060. Their long-term gain (the first blast of *Wind*) was $370,876 each. The reason why Irene's total income was a shade greater than David's—

	IMS	DOS
1940	$499,772	$493,195

—was just that she continued to earn some money on the Twentieth Century stock.

Irene had never been a stockholder in SIP, so David was making a voluntary segregation of his gains, according to the principle on which he had always split salary and dividends from SIP. Under the community property laws of California, Irene would have had a claim upon that revenue anyway. However, there was a change in the structure of David O. Selznick Productions Inc., the company that took over David's SIP assets. Irene was now an equal co-owner: that is what finalized her ownership of half of David's gain from SIP, just as it gave her half the contracts with Ingrid Bergman, Joan Fontaine, and several others, including, eventually, Jennifer Jones. Irene would own half the career of her husband's mistress: the personal and the professional were, from the outset, damnably intertwined.

Nineteen forty-one was a quieter year financially: David's personal income was $129,094 and Irene's $139,922. For David that was more than he had earned in any year except 1940. Yet it may have aggravated him at the time to see a drop-off: in 1941, he was terribly inclined to panic and the more driven to loan out his stars at exorbitant rates.

Nineteen forty-two was a year of uncommon reward and decision. It was then that Jennifer Jones was loaned out to Twentieth Century-Fox for *The Song of Bernadette* in a deal made with Bill Goetz, the beneficiary of David's decision to take no Twentieth stock for himself. The tangle of interests is very dense here. From Irene's point of view, she was getting a portion of the Jennifer Jones loan-out profit; she would prosper as a Twentieth shareholder if *Bernadette* was a hit, yet she had to wonder how far Bill Goetz's picking Jennifer might have to do with what the brother-in-law felt he owed David. Add to that the possibility that, by 1942, the Irene who wanted to know everything may have had other suspicions about Jennifer.

Then refer to the much later account—very vague, but still troubled—that Irene provided in *A Private View*:

> 20th Century proved a success, and as the dividends came in, I grew
> very troubled. I thought what he [her father] had done for Bill Goetz
> was fine, and it was fine that Edie and Bill should keep their stock. But
> I asked my father to give up his stock and interest in the company. He
> had enough without it, and so had I; I would give up my stock with
> his. The whole thing made me very uncomfortable, particularly since
> MGM was lending its stars to 20th Century, thus helping the com-
> pany get on its feet more quickly than it could have otherwise.

It is hard in reading *A Private View* to be sure when these urgings
occurred—it seems to be the middle thirties. Whereas Irene did not dispose
of her Twentieth stock until 1942. And she did not give it away: she sold
her 6,910 preferred and 22,292 common shares (acquired in 1933) for a profit
of $436,552.

Something else required alteration in the summer of 1942. As the
liquidation of SIP neared completion, David, Jock, and the other participants realized they had to do something quickly with their last assets, *Gone
With the Wind* and *Rebecca*, to satisfy the IRS.

Jock was making many changes in his life. In May 1940, Liz Whitney
had gone to Reno and started divorce proceedings—the settlement was
quick, and it awarded her an estate in Virginia and $3 million. Not long
afterward, Jock met Betsey Cushing Roosevelt, who had been married to and
divorced from James, the eldest son of Franklin Delano Roosevelt. Betsey
Cushing had two sisters—Mary, or "Minnie," who married Vincent Astor
and then James Fosburgh, and Barbara, or "Babe," who married Stanley
Grafton Mortimer.

Jock and Betsey Cushing were married in New York on March 1, 1942.
David and Irene did not attend the wedding. According to Irene, the
nuptials were controlled by Betsey's mother, "and she didn't like show
people or Jews and she didn't like high living." Mrs. Cushing was also
resolved to have a wedding free from ladies who might have been involved
with Jock. David was invited, said Irene, but Jock called personally and said
"that Mrs. Cushing didn't want any wives. Would David be willing to come
under these circumstances? And David said, no, of course not. He was so
bitter about it. He felt like he was being systematically gotten rid of."

Irene felt a curious blend of mortification and pride, for there had been
rumors that Jock had looked fondly on her. Irene was flattered by the talk,
and Mrs. Cushing was not taking chances. There was another suggestion: that
David had led Jock astray and was hardly a fit companion for his own wife.

After years of favor, the Selznicks were getting their Whitney comeuppance, and the famously rich Jock had to go along with his ladies' design.

Disputes at SIP had already driven a wedge between David and Jock. Jock himself was now intent on the war and on having children. But, according to Irene, "David cursed Betsey for the loss of Jock. He blamed her. He had dinner with them in Washington and he wrote me a letter in a rage at their respectability!"

This could easily be the letter of August 13, the large central section of which is missing. For at about that time Jock shipped overseas to England as a captain in the army. He traveled with Bill Paley, and the two of them were at Claridge's, in the second half of August 1942, when Jock told Bill, "Something's happening." David had been calling in a great flap over *Gone With the Wind*. As Paley remembered: "Jock had to make a long-distance call to David when that sort of thing was very difficult. David sold Jock on a change in the stock. Jock said, 'If David wants to do it, I'll do it.' But he wasn't convinced."

As ever afterward lamented by David, the best advice he was receiving was that if he and Jock held on to *Wind* and *Rebecca* then SIP would be considered still in business, with its revenue subject to surtax, not capital gains. So, in David's words:

> they said that either the Whitneys or myself had to dispose of our respective interests in *Gone With the Wind* . . . or the government would challenge the liquidation. So in a quite simple meeting with my old friend Jock Whitney as to who would buy the other one out, I sold to Jock—for the simple reason that he didn't want to sell.

It sounds too simple, even if the talk begun at a tense Washington dinner was only completed on the transatlantic telephone. The deal done, dated August 31, 1942, was as follows: DOSP Inc. sold its 44.926304 percent interest in *Rebecca* to Jock for $67,500. The same percentage holding in *Gone With the Wind* was sold to Jock and his sister, Joan Payson, for $400,000 in cash plus the interest in SIP's accounts receivable then held by Jock, Joan, and C. V. Whitney. Two years later, those accounts receivable had amounted to $304,665. Thus, David sold out *Wind* to the Whitneys for $704,665.

This would prove the most disastrous decision of his career. Yet it was sensible at the time. David had made close to $3 million from the complete SIP liquidation. There were many who argued that, by mid-1942, *Gone With the Wind* had had its run. MGM had worked the picture hard. But in the third play-off in that summer of 1942, revenue was only a third of the second run the year before. Despite David's criticisms, Loew's had distributed the picture at high prices and won an uncommon rate of return from the theaters. When Metro had deducted every cost it could find, and some it could only imagine, there was still a profit of $8 million to be split with SIP. And then there were reissues at more popular prices to come. Moreover, although the picture did very well in England, many countries had not seen it yet—notably France, Germany, and Japan.

No one should now underestimate David's faith in the film or the frenzy with which he could dream. Yet it was beyond even his hunch to foresee that, by the summer of 1952, MGM would admit to proceeds of over $34 million. No one in the business then could have forecast *Wind*'s longevity, right up to its rerelease in 1989, not to mention the sale of the film to TV and to videocassette. It would have been fantasy to admit the possibility that, by 1987, in 1987 dollars, *Gone With the Wind* would have earned theatrical rentals of over $800 million.

But think of the terrible second-guessing as that future unfolded. The original contract between SIP and Loew's had granted distribution rights on the film for a period of only seven years from the date of delivery. Further, Loew's was not allowed to begin any reissue more than five and a half years after delivery. Thus, by December 1946, Loew's would lose control of *Gone With the Wind*. Loew's would retain its distribution, but the proceeds thereafter were to be split 75 percent to SIP (or its successors) and 25 percent to Loew's. It was spelled out that "after the expiration of said seven (7) year period the management and control of said property and material shall be vested in the Producer."

It is hindsight wisdom to measure the money that would have gone to David and his heirs from that setup. But David lived on hindsight wisdom, and he had intimations of mistake even in August 1942. He was short of cash; it was not just that he needed money at the moment, but he could not himself have paid Jock if the deal had been reversed. There is also that detail in David's version that Jock "didn't want to sell." A year later, in September 1943, Myron thanked David for making "a fortune for him, in advising him not to sell his interest in *Wind* at the time David was forced to sell his own in protection of all the stockholders."

By September 1943, Jock and Joan sold their ownership in *Wind*. Between them they then owned 86 percent of the old SIP half share. In exchange for that, they received not just over twice what Jock had paid David one year before, but $2.2 million. That is a considerable profit and shows a fuller appreciation of the film's long-term worth. The purchaser was MGM. There was, apparently, no attempt to find other bidders or to mount anything like an auction, as there had been in 1938 when the original contract with Loew's was negotiated. MGM was a natural buyer for the SIP interest, of course. It had a great deal to lose in December 1946 without some action. But in Hollywood, as is now taught in schools of business, a needy buyer is put to the test of bidding up.

As this September 1943 transaction went forward, David was frantically busy: *Since You Went Away* had just started shooting. But with the help of Scanlon and O'Shea, he did everything he could to round up the outstanding 14 percent of the other SIP holdings. He tried to get the Lehmans to sell to him, and he was ready to buy Myron's share. As always, the tax situation weighed heavily in the decision. Myron was in New York, at the Waldorf, with about six months left to live and 6.77 percent of SIP's half of *Wind* to contemplate. He told Scanlon that *if* he sold, David would have the chance to match any bid. Yet, all in all, he preferred to hold on. Was he ingenious enough to understand the thorn he was leaving in David's side?

The effect of the deals of 1942 and 1943 on the income of David and Irene was dramatic:

	IMS	DOS
1942	$1,055,476	$ 813,510
1943	494,169	474,114

But there had been one further change in the rules. On December 30, 1942, David and Irene had entered into a property agreement whereby:

> From and after the execution of this agreement all property, both real and personal (with the sole exception of insurance upon the life of either party) heretofore acquired by either or both of said parties, together with all property (excepting insurance upon the life of either party) hereafter acquired by them, or either of them, on or before December 31, 1942, and which is now, or would become when so acquired, community property under the laws of the State of California, is hereby declared to be and shall hereafter be the sole and separate property of each of the parties in equal shares.

They were protected against each other in the event of any breach, and Irene's financial advantage was secure against any claim. Years later, in May 1948, when the pinch of dispute and settlement claims were upon him, David would cry out to one of his lawyers about the generous steps he had taken to safeguard Irene: "After all, it was my foresight and desire to protect her that led me to my so setting up things, even when we weren't getting along, that she would receive half of even the new enterprise."

But in *A Private View*, Irene allows as how she let her arm be twisted in 1942:

> It was unfeeling of me to deny David the satisfaction that he had longed for, of making me independent. I would be safe, the children would be safe; he could spend, he could gamble without guilt, and if it suited him he could even "go gloriously broke." I hung my head.

I put it to Irene, in 1989, that "when we weren't getting along" presumed serious marital trouble by late 1942. She vigorously denied this:

> There wasn't a difficulty in the marriage. Just my concern for his fatigue, his overextension. The capital gains! The lawyers! I was victimizing him by not letting enough go—he wanted to be shed of everything. All I wanted him to do was to keep a minimum. I didn't want him to slam the door shut. He wasn't himself.

No one else can have much to say on the matter. But there is good reason to think that Irene knew about Jennifer Jones—and other affairs—early on. Her continued denial of such knowledge is the best indication of the pain it had given her. Irene also said that her father "never advised me—never one goddamn thing. He didn't know; he never enquired. He knew better."

On many matters that was true. Yet there is one other piece of testimony, that of Petter Lindstrom, the husband of Ingrid Bergman. He claims Irene told him, in later years, how, as the affair with Jennifer developed, so Irene and her father had taken steps to secure the revenue from *Gone With the Wind*. Perhaps Irene was boasting to Lindstrom and making the best of how things turned out to disguise her feeling of marital defeat. Perhaps Irene and Jock (always her friend—despite the wedding invitation) only took care to put *Wind* in reliable hands. Not everyone would trust so much to the whim of David Selznick at a time when he seemed nearly out of his mind. This much is clear: in 1938, MGM had to argue hard for a bit of *Wind*, but in 1942–43, the whole thing slid into its lap forever—or for as long as "ever" would last. As for David, he had created for himself a terrible model of self-destruction. But it seemed worth it: he was free from control and the power-mongering of the Mayers.

7 · A PATRIOTIC INSPIRATION

ON PEARL HARBOR SUNDAY, David and Irene were with the Paleys at their house in Manhasset on Long Island. Bill went straight to his office and into four years of activity in which he would become Deputy Chief of Psychological Warfare without ever letting CBS falter in the great need to bring news and encouragement to the public. Where should David go?

In the first flush of faraway excitement, he said he would be a soldier. Irene heard, and let him have it: "His spirit was fine, his idea impractical—he was nearsighted, slewfooted, overweight, overage. He didn't need an enemy, he'd kill himself."

David was clumsy and accident-prone. Irene had been reduced to hysterics once when, as he examined himself in a mirror at the Waldorf, he shut his privates in a drawer. Playing tennis at the Chaplin home, he had followed through on one shot so lavishly he broke his own spectacles and put glass in his eye. The great player Fred Perry got most of it out before the doctor arrived, and then Irene had had to watch over the performance of recovery. David was not resolute with physical pain; he could endure it in others even less well than when it was his own. "Oooh-oooh!" was a familiar cry at Summit Drive as David signaled the drama of pain or formed a sympathetic scrimmage at others' hurt.

Still, David protested, he had willingness and energy such as any country would need in war. But all on his own terms, said Irene. Suppose he went to training camp, how would they ever wake him? Her humor was merited. But it was also a scathing voice that encouraged ideas of escape. David had once taught Irene to speak up. But that had liberated her deep vein of disapproval. She was never a woman weak men enjoyed talking to.

David was an executive, an ideas man, a dictator, and it was on that basis that he started promoting himself in Washington in the spring of 1940. He was aiming high, seeking special attention, and fretting over official slowness. He was in two minds—his normal working method. As Bill Paley would say, "David talked about the war. But I don't think that he really wanted to do it." Which means David never recognized a need for patience with bureaucracy. He assumed the war would be lucky to get him. So the authorities should move swiftly and with decent respect. Otherwise . . . well, he had other options. To the authorities, it must have sounded as if David wanted a plum deal, his own theater of combat.

By the fall of 1940, he was in communication with Harry Hopkins, the Secretary of Commerce. But with every step forward, David backed off two. On November 23, he wrote to Sol Rosenblatt, an intermediary:

> The one thing that I don't think Mr. Hopkins quite understands is that as soon as I go back into business, I will take on commitments involving hundreds of thousands of dollars. In fact I am faced with the necessity of making a deal of one kind or another that will involve millions of dollars, and years of my future. It is difficult for me to say this to anybody that doesn't know the picture business as well as you do, but you can, I am sure, thoroughly realize the necessity of my knowing immediately whether or not I am to do this job for the Government.

Here was the David who worried himself, and his wife, close to ruin. When anxiety mounted, he could only reassure himself by requiring immediate action and talking like the big shot least likely to be welcome in a large, mass effort: "You might also find the occasion," he suggested to Rosenblatt, "to get over for me that I am at the very top point of what may very well be the most financially lucrative career in any industry in America—but that it means nothing to me if there is anything he [the President] would like me to do."

David had dashed off a proposal for Hollywood movies that would endorse the war policy. Rosenblatt showed this scheme to Lowell Mellett, administrative assistant to FDR, who was sympathetic but a little unnerved by such draconian control of a free business enterprise. Congress would not be impressed, and the government was inclined "not to burden the producers with suggestions or requests that would interfere with their normal operation." It was in Germany that entertainment movies had been most geared to war—and some saw that as totalitarianism. Rosenblatt regretted to David that top men "still haven't grasped the significance of your ideas." So he urged David to come to Washington himself and get to see "the Boss."

There were several trips to Washington in the early 1940s and a growing frustration on David's part. No one was more involved in fighting David's cause than Merian Cooper, a man nine years older than D.O.S., but who went from captain to major to lieutenant colonel between December 1941 and February 1942. Coop was in Washington; before long he would be sent to Chungking on secret missions.

He was busy and harassed, though he found time to write David asking for signed photos of movie stars and to draw the producer's attention to the novel *The African Queen*: "I would like to get first crack at this if there is any possibility of making it. I think with Wendy Hiller it is a natural." He teased David about his nineteen secretaries, while in the army Coop had use of one every sixteenth day.

David bore up as well as he could. Meeting with Robert Lovett, the Assistant Secretary of War, he got only polite responses. Still, he wrote to Lovett from personal experience about how low metabolism rates might make sentries fall asleep. He offered his own treatment. "A few thyroid tablets . . . change the metabolic rate, and guard against any such occurrence; so that no man needs to be placed in this position, and no one need be lost to the armed services because of it."

Cooper was a loyal friend. He passed on letters and ideas, and he wrote David, "I cannot tell you how sorry I am that you are not here with us . . . it seems almost criminal to me that your services are not being used now."

Bill Paley was just as upset at David's inactivity—so he said. Yet Paley was now much involved with Jock, for they were both active in the war effort, but rich and important enough to do things together. Alliances shifted very subtly, and David was left adrift, eager to keep the love of both his pals, but fearful that Bill had usurped him.

He never flagged as the "Idea Department" for Paley and CBS. In December 1940, for instance, he sent off a letter urging that Paley get Maurice Chevalier to record "The Last Time I Saw Paris," that a record be put out of "The White Cliffs of Dover," and that Paley launch a consumer's guide to radio receivers. "I will thank you for at least an acknowledgment of the above," asked David pluckily. But Paley did not always make time to answer, and he could be patronizing.

It was in the fall of 1942 that David came closest to getting in on the act. He had seriously interested James Forrestal, Under Secretary of the Navy, in establishing a Bureau of Photography for the navy. He submitted a twelve-page plan and gamely went along with Forrestal's public assessment that David was an "egomaniac." But a letter went to Forrestal with the plan, a letter that Irene sought to cut and moderate, in which eagerness and panic, modesty and big shot, are so much at odds that the result would have been predictable to everyone except D.O.S.:

> I had thought that you would probably want to commission me, and was prepared for whatever you would want to do, although I don't know port from starboard; but I recognized in advance the desirability of the civilian status which you stressed. I know full well that if I were commissioned I would be subject to the orders of every officer of superior rank in the Navy, and to whatever notion about motion pictures that each and every one of these countless superior officers might have. But the question is whether as a civilian I shall be able to act as an executive over Navy officers, some of whom obviously will have important rank. I don't know enough about the Navy to know how this works. . . . But I do feel I owe it to you to warn you that whether or not I will get the result that I presently visualize is going to be dependent to a very large extent on whether or not I will be free to function.

There was the nub of it: neither the navy nor any other branch of the war effort could quite satisfy David. His sadness and jealousy were real, even if naive. Coop, Jock Whitney, and Bill Paley were all by then away on assignment. In Hollywood, it hurt David's pride to see colonelcies *and* uniforms going to Darryl Zanuck and Jack Warner.

The disappointment never went away, and warlike notions kept coming back. In December 1942, he was suddenly taken with a scheme to make a movie about flying ace Eddie Rickenbacker's life. Again, he asked Coop to put in a word for him:

Telling him [Rickenbacker] that in the course of a conversation with an old friend, myself, you learned of my tremendous excitement about the possibility of making his life as my first film since *Gone With the Wind* and *Rebecca*. . . . I can sincerely promise you that you will be doing both him and the country a favor at the time you do this great favor for me, because I am determined to make this the finest film of my career.

But this idea shrank fast to the "Rickenbacker Belt," a device to be worn by all servicemen containing food, concentrate, vitamins, and sulfa drugs. This was after Rickenbacker had himself survived three weeks in a raft in the Pacific at the age of fifty-two. The official response was neutral at best, but David had such a belt made and sent to Forrestal.

His last great scheme occurred in March 1943. He had heard that swimmers of the English Channel kept out the cold with quantities of grease. Yet sailors and soldiers were dying from exposure in the northern waters. Axle grease was David's answer. Every ship should carry a substantial amount. More than that, it should

either be compulsory for each man in the Navy and in the Merchant Marine to grease his body once daily whenever the boats reach torpedo zones; or that it be made available to the men on a voluntary basis. Additional supplies might be on hand at convenient places whenever there is time (which I realize is rare) for the men to grease themselves between the time of the torpedoing and the time the ship goes down.

Forrestal replied in five lines, ending on "We are glad to have your ideas always." The fully greased navy was a subject only for Preston Sturges. By the spring of 1943, David Selznick was resigned to the inescapable resort of making movies . . . unless something else turned up.

The China Relief campaign in America was of questionable service to the interests of many Chinese. Its inspiration depended too much on political innocence and ignorance, and history has not been kind to its enthusiasm. But the world was at war, and to Americans in the early 1940s China was an infinity of noble poverty, inhabited by peasant legions such as Paul Muni and Luise Rainer depicted in *The Good Earth*, horribly threatened by evil Japanese. China was an ally, and Chiang Kai-shek was the head of its studio.

That's how David and millions felt about it. China Relief helped the war effort, and we can hope that some ordinary Chinese benefited from it. David Selznick *was* helped—he was able to feel busy and useful in the great cause. This was *his* bit, free from brass-hat interference.

The friendship of David and Irene with Henry and Clare Luce had China at its dinner table. It was Luce who persuaded David to be the Hollywood chairman of China Relief, and it was Luce who aroused the publicist in D.O.S. John Houseman was at hand at the outset, a good deal to the left of Chiang Kai-shek, but with not enough to do.

Houseman had mounted a radio show in the summer of 1941 in which Shirley Temple talked, through her tears, to the children of China. He had also had to dissuade David from a piece of living theater, a pageant across America: Central Casting would provide a crowd of Orientals, dressed as coolies; buses would ship them all over the country so that the troupe could march through American cities, rattling empty rice bowls, collecting money for the Nationalists. Houseman said no, really, no; it was in poor taste. You can see how David might come to regard Houseman as too prissy for showmanship.

There was also the poem. In *Life*, Henry Luce had caused a sentimental sensation by running a poem, *The White Cliffs* (on Dover and plucky England) by Alice Duer Miller: it became a book, a song, and eventually an MGM picture, with Irene Dunne. The challenge was out. David needed a China poem.

"Goddamn it," he said to Houseman, "haven't we got a poem like that we can exploit?"

"This is not exactly what I'm here for," replied the gracious Houseman. "But I'll help if I can."

He had turned to two Selznick employees known for their shameless invention: Val Lewton and Peter Viertel. First they attempted a collaboration, but that did not work. So the two men withdrew to quiet corners and produced an epic each. Viertel's had a New York taxi driver on the China Road, while Lewton did a pastiche of Kipling. When this was done, Houseman and his poets concluded that some judicious cross-cutting was in order. The assembly was offered—and published, in *Life* magazine.

This was small stuff compared with the visit to Los Angeles of Madame Chiang Kai-shek in April 1943. Madame was a better envoy than the Generalissimo: small, dark, attractive, intelligent, commanding—she was a lot like Irene. Moreover, David's evangelism on China's behalf would not have been as great or lyrical, if only Chiang had come. He felt history as the fate of heroines.

It was decided there would be two events in Los Angeles: a banquet at the Ambassador Hotel and a Sunday afternoon at the Hollywood Bowl, where Madame would speak to the public. On the one hand, David was bashful about being cochairman of all these activities, yet he started working night and day with floor plans, deciding where the photographers should

stand, what the music should be, the décor, the programs, the invitations . . .
if you want something done, do it yourself.

    The office staff was assigned: Ray Klune was general manager, Joseph
Steele was running publicity, and actress and old friend Aileen Pringle was
brought in to handle protocol, seating arrangements, and noses out of joint.
There were all the old problems of logistics, details, and changes of mind,
to say nothing of anomalies in a would-be free world. On March 19, in a
nine-page memo to Steele, full of thoughts, asides, objections, and new
ideas, David wrote:

> Miss Pringle should be told that there should be a negro table at the
> banquet, for negro actors who will be invited, and this should defi-
> nitely not be parked in the background or put against any corner or
> near any wall. Anybody that doesn't like it can lump it.

Another problem was that whereas unfamous people were eager to
attend the banquet, the necessary stars were not so willing. A few days
beforehand, Bobbie Keon was desperate that there were only 314 acceptances.
"Have asked Cagney to supply 20 more couples, telling him we have a large
waiting list, *which we haven't*, but that you thought, particularly since so many

The Hollywood Bowl and
the China Pageant

of his original group couldn't make up their minds or have refused, we should dress the place up with stars. He'll do his damnedest."

Madame stayed at Summit Drive while she was in Los Angeles and created such a good impression that Irene provided her own masseuse for the leader and was moved to become involved. "So Irene came to the Ambassador," said Aileen Pringle, "looked at the seating plan, and she changed it all. When I got there, everyone was waiting. They didn't know *where* to sit. When it was over, I told David, 'Your wife is a bloody fool.'"

The weather at the Bowl was kind on Sunday, April 4, and the house was full—30,000. The event started late and ran slow, but that was true of most Selznick productions. Spencer Tracy introduced Henry Fonda and Dr. Corydon M. Wassell, the hero of Java. There were honor guards and military bands, one led by Rudy Vallee. Flights of bombers flew overhead. When Madame arrived, she was presented with flowers by Mary Pickford on behalf of a reception committee of eighteen star actresses. There were the national anthems of the two countries and an invocation by the Methodist bishop of the California area. (D.O.S. had been worried about a musical intro for the bishop—"I don't see the harm in having music, particularly if it were discreetly chosen, before the troops marched in. But, as you may have suspected, I am no Methodist, and you'd better check.")

People needed value, so the next item was "China: A Symphonic Narrative," a flat-out pageant, with a narrative written by Harry Kronman and read by Walter Huston, with Edward G. Robinson as the voice of Chiang Kai-shek, and music written, arranged, and conducted by Herbert Stothart—the show directed by William Dieterle and produced by D.O.S. It was Scarlett in China:

> NARRATOR: China gives us, for this precious hour, a great and gallant guest. A woman. Slim and fragile as a woman is, with all of woman's immemorial strength. . . . These two small hands—a woman's hands—have swept the cobwebs from a nation's past. These hands have lit dark corners in its homes—have built its schools, cared for its young, and nursed its war-made wounds. These hands—a woman's hands—have helped to shape a nation's destiny. This heart—a woman's heart—whispers a simple woman's hope, and all the world must pause and heed.

When the last echo of what the script called "majestic finish" had died away, Madame spoke—for forty-five minutes. There was a translated tone to the speech that made three quarters of an hour feel like a dynasty:

> We shall not abrade the sharp, stony path we must travel before our common victory is won. But we, like you and the other United Nations, shall see to it that the four freedoms will not assume the

flaccid statutes of ethical postulates no matter how belated may be the final victory.

If the show had its comic aspects, many people there were moved. David didn't stop at that. He made a documentary film of the event, to be presented to the Chinese leader. But he sent another copy to John Grierson, head of the National Film Board of Canada. He admitted that the 8,000-foot film was rough in spots. Still, he hoped Grierson might see some use for an edited version, "particularly in showing the unity among members of the United Nations." Grierson examined it, admired the photography and the effort, but concluded:

> Hollywood Bowl setting does not create sufficient background strength to create importance for the Chinese story. Technically of course Madame's speech very long and attempt to relieve monotony by going away from speech and Bowl not successful.

David had to agree, and so China passed out of his immediate concern. It had been a wild time, getting the show on, and some other issues had had to be ignored. On March 15, 1943, *The Song of Bernadette* had started shooting, and David had been pursued by telephone calls from its lead actress, Jennifer Jones. Calls he had not returned. Jennifer's needs may be referred to in this note from Aileen Pringle that came as the China dust settled:

> Dear Davido,
>
> Enclosed, are two samples of my cerebral convolutions concerning little Miss J.J. As she isn't well known I thought the first article might arouse an interest in the young vampire but Harold Ross didn't share my enthusiasm or opinion. The second one Hedda used and I imagine breezed it up a bit.
>
> I called to bid you a lusty adieu after the Chiang debacle, but you were incommunicado.

A skeptic might think that as more immediate problems filled David's head, China was forgotten. Not so. For in December 1943, he sent to Madame in Chungking "as a small indication of my respectful esteem for yourself and the Generalissimo"—

> 182,500 multivitamin tablets. . . . You will be glad to know that these tablets contain the daily requirements of iron and all the vitamins required for good health and growth and are enough for one full year for either 500 children aged ten to twelve or 1,000 children aged one to three. We have all been thrilled by the news of the recent triumphs of the Chinese armies. Warmest personal regards from Mrs. Selznick and myself.

The China pageant had captured David's interest as an emergency. By thrusting it into his schedule, he could put off so many tougher decisions. Every day was like that, with appointments delayed and dodged while he talked to passing friends and pursued whatever was on their minds. There was no order or decency: sometimes he'd take a secretary into the bathroom and keep dictating while he sat on the john. So steadily the real work got postponed until the middle of the night. Here was a way of never going home while telling himself how exhausted he was.

Frances Inglis was his chief secretary in the years 1941–43. She dutifully executed letters that she considered "gibberish." Sometimes when David had been with Jennifer, he needed to dictate out of unreleased excitement, still pacing around the office in his socks. (So often, his feet hurt, and the size thirteen shoes dropped like debts and burdens.)

"You could just tell he was trying to get something out of his system," said Frances. "And next day he wouldn't use it." At other times, in disputes, there were tirades of self-justification: "He had to put it on paper, so he could say, I *told* you, it's not *my* fault, I made it quite *clear.*"

Eventually, Frances Inglis gave up. She thought she was wasting her time, and she wanted to join the Hollywood Victory Committee. David was shocked at her folly:

> Frances, you really are out of your mind! If you will stay, I'll send you
> to the Menninger Clinic for three months and they will straighten you
> out.

This wasn't quite persuasive enough. Frances thought the cure was better suited to her boss. She had typed too many letters like the November 1942 brainstorm in which David was ready to drop everything—war *and* movies—to promote a new odorless deodorant.

8 · *SINCE YOU WENT AWAY*

JENNIFER JONES had returned to California in the fall of 1942 to test for the lead role in *The Song of Bernadette*, adapted from Franz Werfel's novel. Her competition included Anne Baxter and Teresa Wright. But when director Henry King made the tests—of that scene in which the fourteen-year-old Bernadette Soubirous sees the Virgin Mary—he was left in no doubt: "All the others *looked*—Jennifer actually *saw* the vision."

David had waited a long time to launch Jennifer. He was still intent

on having her seem "new" and recent, a virgin to publicity. He even suggested she might test as that old "Phylis Walker" to escape attention. But
he had waited well, and it is arguable that he would never again cast Jennifer
Jones with such understanding. The veteran Henry King would remain one
of her favorite directors, and the role of Bernadette had a lasting influence
on the young woman who had been taught by nuns. More unexpectedly, the
story of Bernadette touched David, too, and made him interested in Ca-
tholicism.

In making the loan deal with Fox, David faced the Bill Goetz who
sometimes boasted about the plunder he'd made of him at the card table.
David scolded Bill: "I didn't know there was another Skouras brother named
William. I will be surprised if you haven't a Greek accent by the time I get
home." Goetz haggled. He thought Jennifer was "terrific," too. But why
should Fox invest in her without some long-term payback? "I just differ
with you on the amount of the girl's contract you think we should get if she
did play the part and if you would be willing to let us have half the contract
provided she played the role. I certainly would like to do everything you
suggest in your wire. When are you coming home? My best to yourself and
Irene."

David and Irene were in the East, halfway between a boating vacation
and Washington dreams. Yet he battled out the Jones deal by telephone and
cable, keeping the actress's service contract, but agreeing that Fox could have
her for a series of future films. This was family business as it often func-
tioned in Hollywood, but the association between Selznick and Jones was
also a business matter. He was loaning her out—and profiting—before he
ever put her in one of his own pictures.

Jennifer's salary from David rose to only $450 a week when she played
Bernadette—thus, she earned $6,075 on the picture. But on the loan-out
deal, David secured $12,300 from Fox. That was very little for what proved
an Oscar role. But Bill Goetz may have realized the favor he was doing
David.

By January 1943, David was sending names to William Perlberg, the
producer of *Bernadette*, ready to share his hard-earned experience in how to
photograph the actress. There were major press announcements with the
casting, and the press reckoned some pains were being taken to conceal
Jennifer's marriage to Robert Walker. David grew angry and began what
would prove a long line of warnings to publicity man Joseph Steele by
saying that "Jennifer was very uncomfortable during interviews."

The Song of Bernadette was in production from March 23 to June 24, 1943.
David then was in turmoil and in some sort of psychiatric treatment. How
did the relationship with Jennifer stand? It has been argued that he was
guarding her, not entertaining her in the grand style he had granted Ingrid

Nancy Kelly

Bergman. But David was properly proud that a discovery of his was being proven. In February 1943 he asked Steele to get him a portrait of Jennifer to hang in his outside office. "Joe tried," Frances Inglis reported, "but Fox said they wouldn't release any to us until the release of the picture, so I asked Jennifer to see if she could get us one—'for a friend.'"

David was surely drawn to Jennifer Jones whenever he thought of her or saw her—perhaps especially when he saw her in a picture or *live*, on screen. But it would be wrong to assume David was a steadfast lover. Sometime in 1942, David became infatuated with the young actress Nancy Kelly. Dorothy Paley served as reluctant counselor when she got a call from Irene—no less—who said she was ordering David to meet with Dorothy to be talked out of it. "This was Nancy Kelly," said Dorothy, "he was so adorable and honest about it—a fantasy infatuation, forty meets twenty. He was honest: it wasn't the dream of his life. But he couldn't resist the moment."

Nancy Kelly was twenty-one in 1942, and she had had leading roles in *Jesse James* and *Stanley and Livingstone*. In an effort to win her over, David would play Kelly the recording of Walter Huston singing "September Song," which he had made famous in the play *Knickerbocker Holiday* in 1938. This was the wistful, experienced woo an older man pitched to a younger woman. It was also a song that Jennifer Jones could not bear to hear.

Dorothy Paley was not a bad source of advice concerning Kelly, for she was married to a chronic womanizer. It is more important to David's life that Irene knew and was smart enough to seek the best advice. And David's infatuation with Kelly passed. There was also a wild pass made at Claudette Colbert that prompted a letter of great remorse to Colbert's husband, Dr. Joel Pressman. And, according to Shirley Temple, when David congratulated her on her seventeenth birthday (and her engagement to actor John Agar), he chased after her and threatened, "If you hold out, you could get loaned out!"

This would be monstrous and intolerable, if you were Irene. It may strike anyone as the spasm craving of someone in need of treatment or maturity. Yet it is worth recalling Dorothy Paley's opinion—"he couldn't resist the moment"—and putting it in the context of a kid brought up to assume a producer's droit du seigneur. David reckoned he was showing a kindness, a proper respect, in being aroused by the loveliness of all these ladies. He might have argued that actresses *needed* to be loved, that they could hardly shine without it. Of course, if we realize that David would chase all three members of his hallowed left-at-home family in *Since You Went Away*, there is something grotesque about it.

Since You Went Away had been recommended to David by the Paramount producer William Dozier, who had seen the galleys of a book of letters by Margaret Buell Wilder of Dayton, Ohio. The subtitle was *Letters to a Soldier from His Wife*, and most of the material appeared in the *Ladies' Home Journal* as a documentary account of those left behind living under the shadow of war. David bought the film rights and hired Mrs. Wilder to do a script.

In this process, Mrs. Wilder gave up the heartland for Bel Air and went on to suffer a losing arbitration at the Screen Writers Guild as she failed to obtain credit for the screenplay. Her competition in this struggle was David himself, for the credits to *Since You Went Away* announce "Screenplay by the Producer"—this after he had adopted the working pseudonym of "Jeffrey Daniel."

The credit is unquestionably deserved (the Wilder book was also named on screen as the basis). For *Since You Went Away* has no other auteur but David Selznick. At 172 minutes, slow, sentimental, and etched in melancholy, with far more detail than story, it does not play very often now. But for those interested in the life of David Selznick, no other film is more revealing.

The script was begun in August 1943—*after* Mrs. Wilder's departure—and it grew as shooting went on, seldom keeping far enough ahead of photography for anyone's comfort. This was Selznick practice, but on *Gone With the Wind* he had raided other people's scripts. Now he was author *and* raider. On one occasion he worked thirty-seven hours on the script when there were countless other business decisions awaiting him, to say nothing of family hopes at Summit Drive, children being paid tribute to in the author's pen name yet neglected, and an Irene left alone as David glorified a fictional wife and mother in the same predicament.

David had thought of doing more. He even wondered aloud whether he might direct the picture himself. Joe Steele argued against it: "Despite his amazing stamina, it was my opinion that he would kill himself." But when Steele heard D.O.S. pitch the story of the film, he changed his mind. David smiled and told Steele to tell Dan O'Shea.

"God damn it," O'Shea exploded, "why don't you stop talking like that? How do you think I feel? I think he should do it too, but what will happen to the rest of our business? Everything will come to a standstill until he finishes the picture."

This exchange comes from a publicity release never used. There may be a touch of hype. But David's grinning hope that O'Shea *might* permit him to direct rings true when put beside D.O.S.'s nearly simultaneous use of memo to lament to O'Shea and Scanlon the brink of chaos they all faced. On August 23, he listed the outstanding issues and problems, contracts and deals unfinished, the players howling at neglect:

> Also I'd like to urge once more, and perhaps for the 150th time, that it is increasingly apparent that we're going to get into trouble one way or the other unless Dan gets himself a first-rate man, and without any further delay. . . . I do hope that nobody is going to be hurt by this memo, but it's simply that I have had to revert to putting it on paper because Dan has obviously reached a point of impatience about my talking to him concerning it. I appreciate more than I can ever say verbally how hard he is working, and the extent of the burden that he is carrying, but worse than this wear on him is that he (and I am sure this is true from his standpoint also) faces the specter of it all being in vain, due to what I frankly regard as insufficient man power and an insufficient organization of his own time.

How did O'Shea stay so long with so frustrating a man? The only answer can be affection and admiration. In the event, John Cromwell was hired as director. He would handle most, though not all, of the film, but he was always servant to his producer and screenwriter. As shooting went on, David added characters and events and steadily built the role of Jane (played by Jennifer). And because he hired Cromwell late in the day, he argued that the director was unfamiliar with the script and should therefore rehearse scenes for David's approval before they were shot. It was on *Since You Went Away* that David became a presence, and a threat, on the set. Even when he was not there he was expected, and dreaded. It was not a happy production. There were many illnesses; a script girl nursed flu for a month, sharing it with many better-paid colleagues. It was also a 132-day shoot (from September 16, 1943, to February 15, 1944).

Since You Went Away is famous for marking the irreversible onset of David's love for Jennifer. Nevertheless, the producer's practicality should be stressed. Claudette Colbert was the star of the picture, and her role was central. Colbert was paid $265,000 for her work. Shirley Temple had been put under contract by David in May 1943. She was fifteen, and past her reign as child icon at Twentieth Century-Fox. But she was hired on at $2,200 a week. Whereas Jennifer Jones was loaned (on paper) by the Selznick Studio to Vanguard, David's new production enterprise, for $75,000—but paid only $9,866.66 for all of *Since You Went Away.*

"There was always a pleasant chaos," said photographer Stanley Cortez, "in working with David Selznick." And Cortez had taken over after twelve days in which George Barnes again failed to catch Jennifer Jones at her best. Further, Cortez, after shooting most of the picture, had to go off on military service and was replaced by Lee Garmes. But this was more than chaos: "It was embarrassing," said Cortez. There was real pain evident on the set. For, by November, when Jennifer and Robert Walker still had their most intimate scenes to shoot, they had separated. The news of it was in the papers.

One day, on a break, Claudette Colbert and Joseph Cotten speculated about the rumors and their implications. Cotten said he had heard nothing.

"If you haven't heard about it, then it's not true," said Colbert.

But within days, Alfred Hitchcock had come by, droll and malicious, wondering out loud how long before David and Jennifer got married. When Jennifer and Cotten were doing one scene, the actor noticed David watching them intently. So he turned to Jennifer and kidded, "Have you ever seen such an ugly man in your life?" Whereupon the actress ran off the set.

Why had Robert Walker been cast in the film, with love scenes to play opposite his estranged wife? Some reckoned this had been David's design—that he was needling the uneasy Walker, humiliating him, and that Jennifer by now was completely in his sway. But if David Selznick had been that assured a master of ceremonies he would not have ended up broke. People on the set were embarrassed, but that does not mean David had been so cruel as to arrange the melodrama.

He claimed that Walker was good casting. The actor had won a following with *Bataan* and *Madame Curie.* He was very likable on the screen; MGM was sure of his future. Robert Walker was a good actor, and he is excellent in *Since You Went Away* as the fearful soldier who has a brief love

Robert Walker and Jennifer Jones as Since You Went Away *began shooting*

with Jane before he goes off to his death at Salerno. Putting Jones and Walker together exploited the publicity value of the young couple. There is another case to be made, which is that the film was more important to David than his actress, that the affair with Jennifer might be beginning to weigh on him—even that he may have cast the couple to rekindle their union.

That ploy did not work, and that was in large part because, on the Metro lot, Walker had become romantically involved with Judy Garland. It is always tempting in David's relationship with Jennifer to see the dynamic producer controlling his hesitant actress. But Jennifer could influence the course of events: David was seldom resolute, and she did see visions.

Though better paid, Shirley Temple was bitter at the attention Jennifer was getting. There were many occasions when Jennifer retreated in distress, to David's office. At those times, the cast and crew were put on hold: Shirley began knitting an argyle sock. New scenes were created for Jennifer's character. Shirley sniffed—for she wanted a grown-up career for herself: "Personally, I detected little evidence that [Jennifer] was as exuberant as she deserved to be, with expanded opportunity raining down on her each new day. To the contrary, she always seemed to be suffering acutely. . . ." By the end of the shoot, Temple had completed a pair of socks.

Lois Hamby came to work as a secretary to D.O.S. just as *Since You Went Away* began. She remembered late evenings in the office: "Irene used to call. I'd say he was in the projection room. She'd say, 'Who are you kidding?' He was in there, in the office, on the couch with Jennifer." David's desk had a device that could lock the office door.

The affair became less cautious. There were raw, unwritten scenes on the soundstage. At one point in *Since You Went Away*, at a railway depot, Jane says good-bye to Bill as he goes off to war. The set was the depot from *Gone With the Wind*. As Stanley Cortez lit it, with just one lamp, the shot concluded with the most fateful image in a Selznick film: a high angle, diagonal view of the platform with Jane standing in a shaft of light as the train slides past her, paralleled by the long line of her shadow. At the close of the shot, Jennifer broke down in tears and ran off to her dressing room. Cortez gave the black-and-white a depth of psychological regret and pain that is uncommon in the history of American film. To look at *Since You Went Away*— not just the depot farewell—is to have rare access to the accumulated distress in David O. Selznick.

If anyone was asked to see the film, without any background information, and guess which actress the filmmaker loved, the choice would surely be Claudette Colbert. Her voice opens the film, and her face is its beacon. She is a wife and mother whose existence has crystallized as anxiety. There had been a plan of having the husband on screen, in flashbacks, to show the happiness sacrificed. Neil Hamilton was cast, and scenes were filmed. But that material was dropped, and Hamilton is now just a framed photograph on a dresser.

David Selznick was male enough that his libido controlled much of his life. Yet he was most comfortable with women. It is only when we think of the male stars he cast and encouraged—Charles Boyer, Ronald Colman, Fredric March, Leslie Howard, Joseph Cotten, Gregory Peck, Montgomery Clift, and Rock Hudson—that we may appreciate the threat presented by Gable on *Wind* and the great achievement of Gregory Peck in *Duel in the Sun*. David preferred charming, tender, passive men. There was a moment when he had to decide whether to put Mel Ferrer or Burt Lancaster under contract—he chose Ferrer.

In *Since You Went Away*, the men—Walker, Cotten, Monty Woolley— are like shadows to female brightness: we could be talking about work by George Cukor. David was never homosexual, and I doubt he ever entertained the thought. But in *Since You Went Away* his deference to women is clear, his devotion to their cause innate. The lesson helps us understand *Gone With the Wind*, too, for David had always perceived that film as the story of Scarlett's triumph by ordeal and endurance.

Joseph Cotten was very important as an addition to the Selznick entourage. The actor had had great days with Orson Welles—in *Citizen Kane* and *The Magnificent Ambersons*—before going under contract with David in 1943. Thereupon, simultaneously, he was loaned out to Metro with Ingrid Bergman for *Gaslight* (Robert Walker was part of that transaction) while

Joseph Cotten and
Claudette Colbert in
Since You Went Away

playing in *Since You Went Away.* Cotten quickly became a social friend and a regular at Selznick parties who carried over from the era of Irene to that of Jennifer. Cotten was a well-born Virginian, smart, funny, and the perfect backup to a charismatic leader: that was the very manner Welles had needed from Cotten in *Citizen Kane.*

Joe Cotten never lost faith in David's charm. He said of his parties that to be at one was "to be struck by the infectious joy which his enthusiasm for social communication generated. If anyone merely thought of leaving his party, he sensed it and a quartet of violins blocked the door. Driving home from David's parties required no headlights. The sun had always risen."

Yet Cotten was an uncommon Hollywood actor, not patently "strong" or commanding. His subtle performance in *Since You Went Away* is that of a hero in war who has not outgrown a boy's view of women as mother figures.

When James Agee reviewed *Since You Went Away,* he felt its immature gravitation toward softer, motherly company. Agee followed Selznick closely; he was intrigued by the "blend of serious talent with smart, safe showmanship," and he believed that this Selznick style would dominate Hollywood for a decade. For Agee, *Since You Went Away* could not be regarded as a good film, but he enjoyed it and was struck by the "innocence" of the approach (he did not know David had always seen the film as a version of *Little Women*—yet he intuited the link):

Mr. Selznick's attitude toward the Hiltons deprives him—like them—of any very clear psychological understanding, beyond fairly rudimentary and gracefully glossed-over stuff; yet now and then this innocence achieves remarkable things on its own. Mrs. Hilton's "Don't ever grow up," a request tenderly made of the bachelor who has spent his best years enslaved to her, is worthy of *Sentimental Education*; but I have no feeling that it was recognized as piercing and sinister, or that any irony or pity was intended when, with equal authenticity, Nazimova identified Miss Colbert with the America which she, an old, poor, working-class immigrant, had always dreamed of. I thought it just as brilliantly correct, and as clear of conscious malice, that both Hilton children were girls.

Anne Hilton in *Since You Went Away* is the madonna of ordinary American decency, the harder to take in a long film in that she is subject to much more idealization than scrutiny. But she has something of Irene in her, too, the neglected wife David knew best. So many details came oddly but emotionally from David's own life. The bronzed baby booties seen in the very opening belonged to Danny. When Anne goes to bed the first night after her husband's departure, she finds a note from him under the pillow. But it is in David's handwriting:

> *Wherever I am—always—*
> *I'll be kissing you good night.*

Now, it's possible David was sending such notes to Jennifer, too. But he was a romantic and a writer, and he knew fine sentiments could stand repetition.

The film ends at Christmas, David's favorite show and the one he produced best. There is a party, a parade of all the characters, as they play charades (a game he loved). In the fun and community, one can forget that the husband is missing in action. Late at night, alone, Anne Hilton (Colbert) goes to the tree and opens her present from her husband, a music box that plays "Together." Again, the card is in David's writing and the message is worthy of one of the world's best poets of the gift card:

Darling:

This powder box is not too gay, but the melody has told you already why I couldn't resist it.

   With it goes something I need no Christmas to send you—my eternal love.

The phone rings: it is a cable—the husband is safe, if not there. "Pop's safe. He's coming home!" Anne calls to the girls. The music swells. The camera backs off for an exquisite Cosgrove shot of the tiny house in the snow. There is a title: "Be of good courage, and He shall strengthen your heart, all ye that hope in the Lord."

No religion could beckon more to David than one not his. He neglected sons to make a film about daughters. *Since You Went Away* is sad and beautiful because its darkness gathers round great hope. But it is only hope, in a movie filled with foreboding. There is no Hollywood wartime movie made with less assurance. It is the most grown-up film Selznick ever produced, and all the more remarkable since he was breaking up his own family—for it has such a sense of loss, and such yearning for those things in danger of going.

W H E N A P R O D U C E R has had Best Picture twice in a row, how can the next film be other than a disappointment? Alexander Korda believed it was those two awards that eclipsed David's charm. *Since You Went Away* was not a failure. There were many good reviews. It was nominated for Best Picture; Claudette Colbert, Monty Woolley, and Jennifer were all nominated for individual Oscars. Rentals eventually exceeded $7 million—after final costs of $3.257 million ($1.25 million over budget). But for the first time in his life, David had yielded to expectations based on his past, and—as some saw it—on his inflated sense of himself. These are years of arrogance and paranoia: outsiders saw the tyrant and the big shot, while David felt envy ganging up on him, stealing his ideas and waiting for his downfall. David had made many jokes about the futility of trying to top *Wind*. But he had set himself a private hope of being acclaimed once more with *Since You Went Away*: that is how the quiet, small subject turned epic.

He was the more confused in that he had fallen in love with opinion polls and the services of George Gallup. The polls were hard to reconcile. On the one hand, in February 1944, 66 percent of moviegoers knew Selznick's name. The "combined marquee audit value" of the cast was 96.6 percent without Jennifer Jones, whose *Song of Bernadette* was only beginning to be seen. "Unfortunately," wrote David on February 19, "we have the curious contradiction of a picture which would interest 100% of the movie-going public, only 12% of which had heard of the picture."

Four weeks before the film's New York opening (July 20, 1944), Gallup found title penetration of only 24 percent—whereas *Jane Eyre* and *Claudia* both had 48 percent and DeMille's *Dr. Wassell* stood at 54. David felt he and his staff had erred in letting it be perceived as a Shirley Temple picture—the lack of strong male stars may have been more relevant. Nonetheless, as late as September 5, David was betting that *Since You Went Away* would outgross any picture made since *Gone With the Wind*.

There were grounds for thinking some parts of the business were laying for David. Don King, the director of publicity, had been trying to float a press piece on Selznick as "the master mass psychologist, whose understanding of what the public wants is irrefutably reflected in the box office success of your product." He reported it was a tough sell. One likely writer had been dubious about the article:

> He said that the attitude of his editors in New York with regard to you was very confusing; that they regard you unquestionably as a production genius, but their opinions are colored by reports they have heard of your personal relations, particularly with employees. He was asked, for instance, "What kind of man is Selznick, we hear reports about his kicking around people who work for him."

Irene had winced at David's "Hail the conquering hero!" act after *Gone With the Wind.* Among his great actresses, only Jennifer believed he was treating her fairly. Washington had shunned the budding commander in chief in David. Several employees did quit Selznick in the early forties, worn out by his delays and indecision, and alarmed at the sudden bursts of megalomania. United Artists had good reason to feel wronged and used by Selznick, and he accused the company of dereliction in the release and promotion of *Since You Went Away.* He even decided that some adverse reviews of the film were prompted by antagonism toward his Republican Party affiliation.

One person who recognized David's populist intent in the picture was Ben Hecht. He wrote to David on January 20, 1944, after an early preview, before retakes, and as Hecht and Selznick were getting *Spellbound* under way:

> My chief memory of *Since You Went Away* is that it made me cry like a fool and that the U.S.A. has made its debut on the screen. The film rings out like a song of America. It's a panorama with a heartbreak that will reach the theaters. You have wrangled on to the screen the amiable and indestructible face of democracy. I did not know till after I left the projection room that I had been looking at an all star cast. They all seemed too much like people ever to have acted before.

This coincided with something David told Don King. The publicist had looked at the picture and known it was unlike the regular Hollywood product—but where did this tone come from?

"Dickens," said David. "*Since You Went Away* follows the form of the classic novel. . . . I strive . . . to present a picture of the day-to-day life of a people. That involves not just the central figures portrayed by the stars, but scores of characters coming in and out of the action, just as they do in reality. I try to develop my story naturally, instead of seeking to dramatize it so as to lead to a single climax."

Is this David Selznick somewhere between novelist John Dos Passos and Russian documentarian Dziga Vertov? Hardly. The dialogue in the picture is predictable; the niceness and sweetness are as persistent as the velvety darkness that surrounds the resting faces. These *are* stars, yet they do not have the action or the melodrama that we expect in stars. But there is a feeling of so many people and stories to behold that individuals do not count as much as, say, Scarlett does against the story of the South. The clash in Selznick's own approach is borne out in the incongruity of the very mannered lighting and the well-researched treatment of shell shock, the attempt to contain all of Americana but the determination to do it on a studio soundstage, the urge to adore Jennifer while keeping her ordinary. It does not all work, yet the film helps explain David's later liking for Vittorio De Sica.

In the *Motion Picture Herald*, Terry Ramsaye called it "a strangely contrived examination of the United States at war. . . . It makes a velvety approach to realism, with suave direction and sleek telling of a story that is mostly moods which flow past like cloud shadows on a lake."

That *is* how the film feels—for the sadness is tranquil; particular loss is subsumed in the larger dismay and the resignation that sees all human incident as minor. All too busy to concentrate, far away from a civilian population put under real pressure or attack, buried in his own neuroses, David had been so moved by the idea of a war that he had had a vision of life and society quite alien to his own selfishness. He had been moved beyond his own creative limits perhaps. As Terry Ramsaye concluded:

> The picture seems to have at times dominated the producer. Mr. Selznick feels deeply.

Years later, *Since You Went Away* is David's most intriguing work, the one in which we grasp the sadness he worked so hard to hide.

9 · SO STRANGE A GUY

"MYRON SELZNICK LEFT US YESTERDAY," said *The Hollywood Reporter* obituary. "A great guy went. A lad brought up in show business. Who had his ups and downs a-plenty, and who at the finis of his career checked out a great loss."

The depot scene: Jennifer Jones in
Since You Went Away—
photographed by Stanley Cortez,
the still printed by Ansel Adams

He died early in the morning of Thursday, March 23, 1944, in the Santa Monica Hospital. Flossie, David, and Irene were at the bedside. But the disastrous abdominal hemorrhage he had suffered on Sunday—the immediate cause of his death—was so unexpected that Joan was not flown in from the East. Myron had eight blood transfusions as he lay in a coma. There were two doctors and consultants enlisted by David. But Myron was unconscious for the last thirty-six hours.

For over a decade, David had chided Myron about his drinking, and Myron made scapegrace jokes about it himself to play along with the notion that he was a hardened pirate. Myron was as laconic as David was long-winded. Everyone called him tough, and everyone assumes the tough will go on forever.

"He was very insecure," said Loretta Young, one of Myron's favorite clients. "For years, anytime anyone said, 'Myron Selznick' to me, I said, 'Ugh! Not my cup of tea. He's a bore. He's a drunk. He's insulting. He's absolutely insensitive.' Well, he proved me quite wrong. Because I think he was innately shy. A lot of shy men do this. They put on a tough act. The reason I know is, with women, Myron blew hard a lot." Katharine Hepburn believed that Myron was actually more sensitive, and less guarded, than David.

Yet Myron often entertained Irene with rough stories about how badly he treated women. Maybe both of them needed opportunities to exclude David: Irene was one of Myron's few intimates and one of the last ways he could top David. A part of her reveled in stories of someone riding roughshod over Hollywood's idiots. Her Myron screwed actresses, but never fell for them. So perhaps Myron made up some stories for her, excited to see her own humor exercised.

No medical solution worked with Myron. Years later, Irene thought Alcoholics Anonymous might have done it. But what was Myron going to do if he didn't drink? He was smart and cynical enough to be bored stupid earning $20,000 to $50,000 a week on work he found easy and demeaning. When he had offended every studio in town more times than he could remember, perhaps emptiness set in.

He had one routine in the tales he told Irene about how someday he was going to bed Joan Bennett, another of his clients. But Joan always put him off and told him she was a lousy lay. This went on for years, until one day Myron was with Irene and he admitted that at last Joan's defenses had yielded to weariness or kindness. And? asked Irene. He sighed: "She was right, all along," said Myron. He practiced a poker face, a mask of futility.

He gambled, he liked the horses, and he was good company to Jock Whitney and Bill Paley. But he couldn't get on with himself or give up on bleak self-portraiture. "He was very envious of David," said Joseph L. Mankiewicz. "Because it's a question of who loved the old man more or hated the old man more. The power of those tyrannical old Jewish men! Don't forget David still said, 'Yes, Daddy,' to his father. So did Myron. Here were two guys who between them were squeezing Hollywood by the balls, saying, 'We're avenging ourselves on what they did to our poor old dad.' Poor old dad was a schmuck! They were two very big egos!"

A part of Myron envied David's success with *Gone With the Wind* and said he didn't deserve it any more than he did Jeffrey. Yet his love for David barred him from direct rivalry. It was unfair and ridiculous that the chump had made it so big—but why try harder? And Myron knew how sweet the chump was. There is nothing in Myron's later life as poignant as the talk of returning to production or as forlorn as David's encouragement. Myron hadn't the energy or the concentration to be more than a killer in his dreams. And he was intelligent enough to see how thoroughly he lacked the "stupid" optimism that funded David's creativity. A Myron movie would have been a five-minute joke—savage, classic, the nutshell to contain all Hollywood nuts. But it could have no showmanship because Myron thought it childish to believe in audiences or love strangers.

If this made it harder to be Myron and stay sober, it is easy to see why Marjorie divorced him and removed Joan from his presence. There was a separation agreement on April 8, 1940, and the divorce became final on April 3, 1942. There is dispute over how much this hurt Myron. "Was Myron upset when Marjorie left?" I asked Irene. "Did he notice?" she asked back. But, she added, "Myron was so adoring and ineffectual with Joan. But she was a bore, cold, didn't like people." Still, Mary Rechner, Myron's secretary from 1940 onward, believed the loss of Joan was vital:

> There were days when he drank very little or none at all. The incidents or factors that accelerated his addiction could be laid, in my opinion, to having lost his young daughter's love. Joan lived with her mother and he could only see her part time. When she was permitted to visit for a couple of weeks he was happier. She did not show much emotion toward him, but he loved her dearly.

The Hartford "cure" wore off; other solutions met their defeat. By 1942, Myron was in a daze. His family gone, he moved into the Beverly Wilshire Hotel to be nearer his mother and found his only solace at Hill

Jeffrey—a picture sent to Myron

Haven. His mind darted around aimlessly: he would order books for Joan in the East, telling Mary Rechner that Joan was "old for her age"; he had horses racing—Can't Wait had had a good season in 1940; he, too, thought of a military job; then maybe the wise head of Uncle Charlie Sachs would save his consulting business—so could Charlie give up Pittsburgh and come west?

There was a weekend in 1941 or '42 when Jeffrey was with his Uncle Myron at the agent's beach house. "He was in a scruffy bathrobe and unshaven, and he walked over to the bar and took a shot glass and poured whiskey into it. He saw me looking at him, and he said, 'This is something you must never do. This is just terrible.' " It was ten o'clock in the morning.

By August 1942, David was trying to revive Myron's vague thoughts of production: "I think you would get some fun out of it as well as proving that you still know more about producing than anyone else in the business *except myself.*"

Myron wrote back: "I will give it considerable thought. . . . I hope that soon night will turn into day again."

Joe Mankiewicz's belief in the great rivalry between Myron and David is demonstrated by one of David's harshest memos—an eleven-page blast to Myron, dated November 11, 1942. It is a catalogue of complaints, a tirade prompted by Myron's neglect and arrogance and by David's long-held belief that Myron had always screwed *him* on every deal. But the memo starts with bitter rebuke as Myron's agency seemed ready to horn in on David's latest discovery:

> Just so there will be no question or dispute later on the matter of Jennifer Jones, let me *right now* give you the history of this:
>
> I know perfectly well that Twentieth Century is "hopped up" over Jennifer Jones. And just how do you think they became hopped up? I have been selling her on a systematic campaign to Bill Goetz for month after month, and finally I showed him her test. I then person-ally suggested her for *Bernadette*, a role it looks as though we are going to get for her. . . . So when your office reports to you that Twentieth is hopped up on Jennifer Jones they are simply reporting gossip that they picked up at the lot on *my* work, not theirs.

The memo called Myron "viciously unfair"; it lamented the "stagger-ing amount of commissions that you made on business that you did with us." It attacked Myron for his ingratitude toward Dan O'Shea: "That you should then turn on him and accuse him of being an enemy of yours is typical of an attitude that you have taken toward many people who were once your friends." David complained of Myron's poor memory for awkward truth and attributed it to "your attitude and/or ... Black Label."

But the climax of the assault was Ingrid Bergman's casting in *For Whom the Bell Tolls*. Yes, David had asked Harold Rose of Myron's office to help, and the help had been useless. For page after page, David detailed the persistence with which *he* got Ingrid the part and the deviousness with which Myron's office claimed credit: "I should say that I did fifty to one hundred times as much to get Bergman the part as did Harold Rose and your whole office. Beyond this I personally made the deal which your office heard about after the fact."

The memo reads better than most of David's: it is long, yet it is terse, full of fact, driven by emotion, and rising to a point of accusation: yes, David would be magnanimous in the end and grant that Myron did deserve—"purely to shut you up"—10 percent of the overage on Ingrid's salary. That meant $5,000. O'Shea had offered $2,500. David was prepared to go to $3,500. They agreed on $4,000. Eleven pages of hostility, backed up root and branch, with knowing, intimate jabs. Yet on *For Whom the Bell Tolls*, David received $90,666 for Ingrid's services, of which $31,771 was passed on to her.

A month later, Myron had gone east for a last "cure." It did not take, and his absence had a terrible effect on his office in Los Angeles. Ostensibly, Myron was seeking work in Washington—there was even a nominal $1-a-day position—but that was cover for time in Philadelphia, where he was under the care of Dr. Edward Strecker and Francis Chambers, a psychiatrist. The doctors believed Myron needed several months' treatment. They saw a mental breakdown:

> Myron has not yet gotten back to any degree his normal sleep pattern. His secretary just called me to change an appointment because he did not get to sleep until seven o'clock this morning. Emotionally, he is still off balance, though oriented. Anything like a normal emotional plane will be reached only after many months of abstinence. When we think of the hurt and hardships to his personality that was engendered by his alcoholic dependency over many years, a period of slow convalescence must be anticipated.

David told Dr. Strecker that the agency had been Myron's "Frankenstein, as it devoured him and obscured his real objectives." Production had always been Myron's aim; the agency had begun as a stopgap.

> Let me say in passing, however, that if he should be turned back to production, caution ought to be exercised by Mr. Chambers, perhaps in warning him that he can't expect to leap back into a field from which he has been absent for twenty years. Further, I believe I am correct in saying that the worst thing in the world would be for him

to turn to me, or to lean on me in any way, in such endeavors. This would be accomplishing nothing, other than perhaps increasing any inferiorities he may feel.

Well before 1943, Myron had become only a visitor at his own office. He was several times hospitalized in the prior years. His retreats to Hill Haven became more extended: in 1942, he was there from May 22 to July 30—in a house that had been designed without telephones. But the mountain home was stocked against a siege. Myron had installed a large gasoline tank in case of war rationing, and in 1943 the liquor inventory included 168 bottles of wine, 181 bottles of spirits, and over 60 bottles of champagne.

There were other blows. It was in 1943 that Mildred Selznick sued Myron, David, and their mother. With her two daughters married, Mildred claimed promises from the family that she would always be supported. Lawyers and detectives were hired. Nearly everyone in the family (except Howard) was deposed. The case dragged on as Lester Roth, the chief lawyer, had to argue with David as to how the case should be conducted. David wanted every detail spelled out, whereas Roth thought it imprudent to disclose the way the family had paid $10,000 a year for Howard and only $4,000 for Mildred and the girls. Myron was spared the final settlement: in March 1945 Mildred was awarded $30,000 and the house the family had bought for her.

Clients were deserting Myron, none with greater reluctance than George Cukor. On January 28, 1944, Cukor admitted that "in the last few years, I have felt that I have not had the full benefit of your handling," and so he was going over to the William Morris office. Myron said the letter came as "a terrific disappointment and shock."

Myron was forced back to California because the agency was coming apart in his absence. But once he had returned the disintegration continued. His most abiding role in the last year was still to aggravate David and provoke his irate memos. Myron may have relaxed now, collapsing but serene—he told Dan O'Shea that he had even wandered into St. Patrick's Cathedral in New York. What's more, Myron was alert enough to know—or hear—that both brothers were sick. It's likely Myron had heard rumors about Jennifer and could see David wavering at the brink. He was equally disturbed at the SIP liquidation, at the selling of *Gone With the Wind*, and at David's indecisiveness.

Myron had a spell of being businesslike. Then one night he was invited to dinner by Gregory Ratoff and persuaded to take a glass of wine. He was back on Johnnie Walker by the end of the night.

When Myron died, Francis Chambers wrote to David, saying that

Myron had long ago "so hurt himself that he was really not well enough to persevere or benefit by our treatment plan." David just wished they had all met Chambers years earlier. "But perhaps it wouldn't have worked: Myron was so strange a guy."

So the older brother was vanquished and David could feel guilty about having failed to save him. David had it both ways. But the needle was gone, the one voice that could tell David he was being foolish. So Myron's death left David free—and in jeopardy.

There was a dark joke in his death. Myron had died rich. By 1953, income from the trust set up by his estate had realized $1.85 million. Two years later, Joan would begin to acquire the capital and the property. Yet at the end, Myron's business was open to immediate plunder. Other agents were wooing clients during the funeral. David was devastated by the ceremony at Pierce Brothers. But he now had responsibilities to another business, for he and Uncle Charlie were the executors of Myron's will and the trustees for Flossie and Joan, the heirs. This duty would dog David for the rest of his life and serve as a steady reminder of what *he* had lost. For, henceforward, David had to watch and guard the income that came in on Myron's precious percentage of *Gone With the Wind*.

10   •   A CHARMED LIFE

ON MARCH 2, 1944, the Academy Awards for 1943 were presented at Grauman's Chinese Theatre. War modified regular practices: the banquet was abandoned, evening dress was no longer in order, the public was admitted, and the event was broadcast over the radio. David had requested Jennifer's presence as early as November 8, 1943, but he warned her not to be overconfident:

> As I have told you, I hope that Ingrid will win the Academy Award this year [for *For Whom the Bell Tolls*]. You are young and have plenty of time. But certainly you will be a strong candidate; and from what I hear from all who have seen the completed *Bernadette* you are practically sure of being nominated. Let's keep our fingers crossed, and not be too sure.

Jennifer could have had a hunch: that March 2 was also her twenty-fifth birthday. Moreover, *Bernadette* was released only on December 27; it was fresh in every voter's recollection. Irene Selznick was not at the Chinese Theatre to observe Jennifer's victory but in a clinic in La Jolla with a malady

Jennifer wins the Oscar for
The Song of Bernadette—
Ingrid Bergman lost in
For Whom the Bell Tolls

of imprecise nature. Asked about this absence forty-five years later, she said, "It rings a bell . . . but I don't remember. I never stayed away from the Academy if I was in town. But I recall very few Oscars. They were not memorable."

The day after the Oscars, Jennifer initiated divorce proceedings against Robert Walker.

A new star had been born, and stars are harder to handle than unknowns. It is harder to be quietly carrying on with a star than with a newcomer. But Jennifer Jones had now become a property that Selznick the producer was obliged to expose and trumpet. Not to have done so would have undermined the upcoming *Since You Went Away* and denied his own nature. Showmen keep no secrets. So Jennifer's success pushed David closer to the brink of decisions he may have hoped to avoid.

Less than two months after Myron's death, Jennifer was scheduled to do the Esther Blodgett role in *A Star is Born* on radio. She came to see David one evening "to seek my help and advice." The script had departed from the movie; the Norman Maine role (for Walter Pidgeon) had been built up so that "for the most part, Esther has nothing left but the silliest, most innocuous feeding lines. I am frantically busy," David wrote to Margaret McDonell, and I am frankly bitterly disappointed that I should have to take the time to even send this memo, when I had assumed that there were people on our staff that could relieve me of this. It is a pity that I even had to take the time to struggle with Miss Jones tonight and to send this memo.

But he launched into a detailed critique of the radio play, and warned that he would be listening on Sunday evening to make sure it was all "fixed up." He even suggested that someone from the Selznick organization be assigned to give Miss Jones the right direction. Finally, he made one of his best pleas for special care and the simultaneous denial of privilege for Jennifer:

> I also assume that Mr. King will take care to see to it that Miss Jones is not pushed around at the radio station by the publicity directors of the sponsor, and by the producers, who are apparently devoted to only one thing—Walter Pidgeon. Whatever is done for Miss Jones should of course be done in our name and not in her name. I want no impression given, even unconsciously or accidentally, that Miss Jones is being in the least bit difficult, because she was perfectly content and is still perfectly content to do her best with whatever is given to her. The indignation is entirely mine; the criticism is entirely mine. The desire to protect Miss Jones on Sunday is entirely mine. So please be careful that no impression is given that Miss Jones is making demands

Anita Colby, when she went to work for David

or that she is being high hat at the station, or that she is anything but the trusting young woman that she actually is. . . .

Perhaps Cam Ship could accompany her to the station, or perhaps Anita Colby.

David had just hired Anita Colby, a tall, blond model, known in America then as "The Face." It was a rare appointment that says so much about David. Colby had come to Hollywood to be adviser on, and to appear as herself in, *Cover Girl*, the Gene Kelly–Rita Hayworth musical. Colby knew makeup, publicity pictures, clothes; she knew society people and how to behave with them. And David hired her to school and encourage his contract actresses. A principal reason for Colby was to make Jennifer happier doing publicity, as well as to make her image more sophisticated. But Colby was also drawn into their relationship as confidante and go-between; there were even those who felt the decent and very beautiful Colby had been used as a front for the love affair.

Jennifer was the most high-strung of the Selznick actresses. She had an aversion to posing for still photographs; she was so insecure about her appearance she could need hours to settle on a costume, and in the buzz of press attention to her divorce from Robert Walker and her attachment to D.O.S., she had a horror of making herself available. Colby was to warm her to these tasks, and initially she was told to tell Hedda Hopper, Louella Parsons, and anyone else who asked that no, there was nothing to all the rumors. David did nothing to suggest the denials were less than the truth. By the time Colby appreciated the real state of affairs, she was trapped in friendship to both David and Jennifer.

In May 1944, Twentieth Century-Fox sued Jennifer for failure to do the second picture called for in the *Bernadette* contract. That project was *Laura*, which David decried on every ground he could think of. But *Laura* might have suited her—the lovely, yet slightly empty woman who dazzles but remains a touch ordinary and manipulative. The film would establish Gene Tierney, and it could have helped Jennifer.

Without her, Fox sued for $613,000, half a million of which was attributed to Jennifer's new "Oscar-winner" value. David countersued, and plenty of show-biz columnists guessed the inside story. In *The New York Times*, David was quoted as saying "the actress was busy on another matter." The paper added that this matter was a divorce from Robert Walker.

The summer of 1944 was the moment to capitalize on Jennifer Jones. She had an Oscar and an aura of dramatic arrival. Carrying her role for *Since You Went Away* into life, she was doing some work as a nurse's aide. Her next big picture was soon to open. But Don King, David's publicity director, was at a loss. There had been a *Look* interview with Jennifer, but photographer

Earl Thiesen had had great difficulty getting usable pictures. On July 3, King admitted the extent of the problem to D.O.S., and put the blame on Jennifer's "noncooperative and passive resistance":

> We in publicity try to understand, even if we cannot entirely sympathize with, an attitude which leads her to assume the character of the maid when answering the telephone at her home and inform us, as she did several times, that "Miss Jones is out of the city."

Colby saw something wonderful in Jennifer: "She looked like she'd just come out of the West. Country, apple cheeks, so pink, and no makeup. The most beautiful skin. And alive, her eyes sparkling, great big eyes and long lashes, and this dark, shiny hair. . . . The most untouched, unsophisticated person that I'd ever seen."

From very early on, David wanted the world to see what he had felt: whatever else Jennifer Jones represented, she is the peak of visual excitement in a moviemaker who was most impressed by structure and literacy in dramatic values. For years, David sought perfect stills. During *Since You Went Away*, he had the idea of blowing up frames from the movie itself, and he hired Ansel Adams to come down from Yosemite to make trial prints.

It was Colby's belief that even in stills Jennifer had to believe she was acting some other part and not being herself. "She'd hold on to my hand and I could feel her trembling—just the sight of people."

"Jennifer," Colby would say, "behave as if you're beautiful and you'll *be* beautiful."

"Oh, Colby, *you* can do that, but I can't."

"Yes, you can, I'll show you a walk, a model's walk. Be an actress. Perform. Come in and want people to notice you. Don't run with your shoulders down and folding your hips into the fetal position."

But should Jennifer act the bewildered child or the scarlet woman? Letters were coming into the studio that contrasted the character of Bernadette with the press portrait of her failed marriage. In January 1944, a letter reached Jennifer from the Ann Whalen Perfect Sodality: "As Catholic mother has movie industry taught you out of separation? After five years struggle, is this way you thank God for blessing? We need Catholic actresses maintaining Catholic ideals. We counted on you."

Sister Ursula, Jennifer's teacher at Monte Cassino in Tulsa, wrote to David, hoping and praying "that our Phylis will continue to give you the utmost in her beautiful and extraordinary talents. She is a wonderful girl. You will have to 'look out for her' just a bit until her little domestic troubles find some solution."

Out of some bizarre whim of publicity or marriage counseling David asked if Jennifer couldn't go with Robert Walker to the opening of *Since You Went Away*. Not even Colby could fix that. There were dark jokes inside the Selznick organization. John Harkins, a young assistant in publicity, wrote to David "a little concerned" about all the memos saying Colby was to go everywhere with Jennifer. "I am thinking particularly of the pictures, informal shots, and news shots that may be caught on the fly," said Harkins. "In art of this sort, I think Miss Jones may be at a considerable disadvantage, if Miss Colby also is in the picture."

Harkins was immediately fired, and David went so far as to urge he not be reemployed at Twentieth Century. He asked George Cukor to see if Ina Claire could coach Jennifer. And, in the middle of August 1944, as another part of her education, he gave Jennifer instructions to view ten of his old movies from the MGM and RKO days.

There was one other duty in the Selznick empire for which Anita Colby was ideally suited: the planning, selection, purchase, and packaging of Christmas presents. This work was the annual year-end production, and the record of status for those in Selznick-land. Christmas 1944 was Colby's debut; it was also the last unflawed festivity of the Selznick family.

Irene was still the object of a lot of gifts. On December 12, David cabled Harriett Flagg in the New York office: "Will you help on some Christmas gifts for Mrs. Selznick to supplement things I already have. To get these here on time you will have to either secure them and ship them personally or if this is dangerous President O'Shea can have the honor of having the gifts accompany him home." David wanted ideas for "anything cute." He ordered outfits by the page number in *Vogue* and wanted a couple of handsome black satin evening bags—"Nothing gadgety and no rhinestones or other such jewelry on it, in fact, no decoration at all if possible."

Jennifer received a string of pearls ($120) with this card—"I'm not a very deep thinker, but I lead a charmed life." And among the many others on Colby's list, against Joan Fontaine there was, "Nothing? What do you think?" But by Christmas day itself, judgment had relented and the lady got a $20 azalea. Vivien Leigh, not seen at the studio for years, remained a weightier gift: she received a suit and two dresses from Magnin's, total expenditure $343.33.

IT WAS IRENE'S TASK to overlook the rising tide of Jennifer, to absent herself from the Oscars and suffer the stonewall that Lois Hamby put up over the phone, and all the time stay smart, lovely, and cool. David did ask her opinion of Jennifer, professionally, as one co-owner to another, and Irene said: "I didn't like her looks or personality. I didn't see her developing. I didn't like the eagerness—she tried very hard." Nineteen forty-four was the last year Irene managed that objectivity. But there were other things that brought her to the breaking point. Another marriage ended.

L.B. got in first. For years, he and Margaret Mayer had been in despair with each other. Margaret was overwhelmed by the ambition in her husband and by the way he dramatized every situation. She could not keep up with him, either in his tirades or in his sweeping sentimentality. Irene had been the only woman L.B. could talk to, without hindrance, and she had "left" him—or she had tried. Margaret Mayer lost energy and will. She had a hysterectomy and was thereafter shunned sexually by her husband. He would delay getting home until the light in her room was off.

A David in that situation would have screwed around in the ways a movie studio allowed. L.B. knew this and watched his son-in-law from a distance in a mixture of envy and contempt. L.B. assumed he could have had the women guarded by the lion. But he denied himself, for he could not countenance his own weakness or compromise. He had several great loves in this period—Jean Howard, Jeanette MacDonald, and Ginny Simms—but they were goddesses seen, revered, idealized, and not touched.

Something pushed L.B. over the edge. In the spring of 1944, after nearly forty years of marriage, he left Margaret and moved out of their beach house. He was sixty (or more), whatever birthdate was in operation; he may have reckoned on a last chance. What was all his power for if he could not have a girl again? Perhaps war made change easier—so many dissolutions and social advances occurred in those years. But perhaps L.B. saw what was going to happen with David and asked himself why he should be different or come second. But what would his favorite daughter think?

There was a seismic tension in L.B.; it gave him physical strength and accounted for his several nervous illnesses. He believed in control and discipline, old verities and virtues (even if he had limited experience of them). Yet he made movies, the most subversive wind in American weather. Hollywood always pulled against that dangerous force; it tried not to admit futility, disorder, or madness. And David was part of that loyal striving, if never as fierce or hypocritical as L.B. All that got him was Mayer's scorn. The son-in-law, in truth, could never rise to the old man's level.

But David smiled, naturally and winningly. He was at his best when happy; he was youngest then, and people always hoped to see the smile. When L.B. smiled, as Leonora Hornblow attested, "it was terrible—it was better that he didn't smile." Nor was Irene an easy smiler. David lived with the disapproval she had learned from her father. There might be an indolence in life, a silliness or a looseness, a departure from order, that Irene could never share with David. It was a small thing, next to power and position. Single-minded empire builders would have put the idea aside. But David yearned for it. As Irene said: watch out for what you hope for—you might get it.

There was an Irene who intimidated L.B. as much as she did David. When her father told her he was leaving her mother, "My only answer was that permission was not mine either to grant or to deny." Irene handled her mother's divorce: Margaret Mayer could not be trusted to look after herself. In training for what was to come with David, Irene took L.B.'s breath away by getting the beach house and $3.75 million for her mother. Not that he was bitter. It was what he would have done if the positions had been reversed. He never faltered in his love for Irene. But when it was all over, L.B. and David were something like friends at last. They had both been through the wringer of Irene.

NINETEEN FORTY-FOUR was an election year, so David anticipated another convention. But now he felt the world-weariness of a promoting prophet hardly honored in his own party. There was even talk that he might be only an alternate delegate for California at the convention. This slight staggered David, for hadn't he been the one who had persuaded the party to regard Californian former attorney general and present governor, Earl Warren, as vice-presidential timber?

> Indeed, he was completely unknown to 99% of the American public outside California until I personally persuaded Gallup to include him on his polls on Republican possibilities, until I sold Henry Luce the idea of writing a big piece about him in *Time*, and until I discussed him with all the Republican leaders back East, including Willkie.

David did go to Chicago for the convention at the end of June, in a heat wave that rose to 105 degrees in the stadium. He even spoke to the assembly, late at night, protesting serious business as delegates called for adjournment. Thomas Dewey won the nomination easily: Willkie had been a bystander, and he would die before the election. Roosevelt's health alarmed anyone who could look at a photograph. But D day, the regaining of Europe, and success in the Pacific were backgrounds to the campaign. David labored to bring a touch of Hollywood into the Dewey attempt. He did not like FDR's politics, yet he loved heroes who played the audience:

> I cannot see myself in the role of a money raiser for the Republicans although I have indicated repeatedly my willingness to make personal contributions, have made them, and have offered to increase them. If this is what it is dependent on, then also and again I say that it is characteristic of the old-fashioned politics which have lost so many

elections for the Republicans, which have kept the Party in the Mc-
Kinley era and which make it so discouraging to be a Republican. . . .

I'm egotistical enough to think that I can shoot some showmanship
into the veins of the Party, showmanship which it sorely lacks to
compete with the greatest showman the country has ever produced,
Roosevelt.

11 • WERE I MORE SENSITIVE

DAVID BELIEVED he sought a noble aim, neglected in the rest of
Hollywood—perfection. That meant concentrating on one picture at a
time. But once he had hired the necessary staff, once the overhead set in,
there arose the need to be a regular or normal studio, making several pictures
and hoping one or two might be exceptional. By November 1943, David was
heeding the virtue of routine product—economical but revenue-raising pictures. This seemed to be what Dore Schary was doing at MGM.

Schary was only three years younger than David, yet he felt like the
next generation, worthy of David's teaching. For David often yearned for
junior producers, people to carry on the Selznick tradition—this urge would
eventually extend to his own sons, even if it could not embrace them. For
the protégés, the schooling was very hard: their personal relationship with
David might be exuberant and warm—loving even—but how should they
free him of the anxiety that they might take over?

Dore Schary had been a screenwriter first: he had done *Boys Town* and
Young Tom Edison and shared an Oscar for original story on *Boys Town*. From
1941 to 1943, he had headed the unit at Metro that produced low-budget
pictures, second features. Seldom more than eighty minutes long, these
programmers had won a great reputation and been the opportunity for new
directors like Fred Zinnemann (*Eyes of the Night, Kid Glove Killer*) and Jules
Dassin (*Nazi Agent, The Affairs of Martha*). No one saw those pictures competing for perfection. But they kept the MGM machinery oiled and were a
training ground. That was what David needed, especially with contract
players disconcerted at getting no work. Plenty enough times, he had to pay
people for doing nothing: that's what overhead entails. So he would use his
other company, Vanguard, to do "regular" movies. He only needed the right
person to run it.

Dore Schary was looking for a change. He had wanted Sinclair Lewis
to write an allegorical Western representing Europe in the 1930s and 1940s,

with characters standing in for Hitler, Mussolini, and Churchill. Louis B. Mayer had said it sounded like a great idea, but then he backed off. And so, within days, Schary and his agent, Lew Wasserman, were making the rounds. They came to see David and Dan O'Shea, and Schary recalled the first sight of D.O.S.: "A big, toothy grin was accompanied by an involuntary nod of his leonine head. His eyeglasses made his eyes look larger than they were."

"L.B. told me you're a maverick," said David to Schary. "Don't like to take orders. Tough to deal with. I told him you sounded like me."

On that competitive note, they were off: by the time Schary and Wasserman had reached Lucey's for dinner they got a call from O'Shea making the deal. Schary would be head of production at Vanguard: six or seven pictures a year, $700,000 top budget, and liberty: David "would approve of the basic idea, then I don't want to have anything to do with any of the pictures till you show them to me in rough cut."

Schary moved very fast (under cover of the *Since You Went Away* shooting). He heard a radio playlet, "Double Furlough," about a woman on parole from prison and a shell-shocked soldier on leave. David liked the idea, for the trauma of war moved him; he was dealing with it himself in *Since You Went Away*. He wasn't crazy about the "Double Furlough" title, but he gave the go-ahead. Schary hired Marion Parsonnet as writer, he was lining up Joseph Cotten and Dorothy McGuire for the leads, and he got a new title, *I'll Be Seeing You*, complete with a Sammy Fain song tie-in.

In a month, by mid-February 1944, Schary delivered a script to David. In twenty-four hours he had a memo back:

> It was long—it was murderous [wrote Schary]. He castigated the script—said he would not allow me to make it . . . that it was sloppy, hurried, and immature . . . for me to forget the project and look for something else. And forget Joe Cotten—and in any event, no star would ever play in the film because the film would never be made. In short—no compromise—junk it.

There was a standoff. Schary stayed at home sick. He tried to rise to the memo with a handwritten reply: "You applied the lash of sarcasm and the battle ax. The lash stung—the ax stunned." He reminded David of their original agreement. "You said . . . that if you became involved in my productions we would be in trouble. You had no time. You had been longing for someone to make good pictures for Vanguard. Someone you would rely on and leave alone to work out his own pictures." But now, "You outline a new plan for work with conferences, treatments. You pick new writers. You want to take over. David, you're beginning to produce this picture."

David gasped, groaned, argued—it was always provocative putting him in a posture of self-defense. A Hitchcock would have read the memo, called to agree and congratulate, and then quietly moved ahead in his own sweet way. But a challenged David would stop the presses to rewrite his own defense. He confided in Dan O'Shea, the most long-suffering of lieutenants. There were pages of it, the diatribe of self-justification. In this case, David had an immediate example to point to: the very shrewd observations he had made on the script and cast of *Gaslight*:

> Were I more sensitive, I would deeply resent a man who is working for us, and therefore for me, not accepting my opinions. The only thing I am sensitive about is Dore's yessing of me on the necessary changes, and then making them half-heartedly and superficially [*sic*]. . . . Arthur Hornblow [on *Gaslight*] is a producer of infinitely greater attainments than Dore, a producer of infinitely greater prestige. . . . Hornblow is not working for us, he has no obligation to me, yet sought me out for advice on his script . . . and sought my advice on the editing. . . . He followed ninety percent of my suggestions. . . . He has thanked me repeatedly. . . . I could get a huge fee from Metro just to read their scripts and give them the sort of analysis that I have given to *Double Furlough*. Yet we are faced with the ridiculous situation of a man working for us, with my money, rejecting these criticisms both as to operation (new writer, director, et cetera), and as to story and script changes. For me to put up with this is not alone being tolerant and patient, it is being Christ-like—and I am not Christ-like, in case you haven't found out.

Schary was still at home. On one rainy day, David came to call. He took a Scotch and told Schary what Irene had said: "Whether you like the script or not, Schary is right. You made a bargain—you ought to keep it."

The picture moved ahead, but without Cotten and fixed at $750,000. Then David had fresh thoughts: he liked Ginger Rogers for the woman— she agreed, and the budget jumped over a million. He wanted Alan Ladd, but Ladd was too expensive, so Cotten was restored. Finally, David wanted Shirley Temple in the picture. He was paying her $185,000 a year, so she had to work. Was there a role for her? There was one, an interloper who horns in on the central love story, and it was built up to justify Shirley's presence.

With William Dieterle directing, *I'll Be Seeing You* was shot, cut, and being previewed by the final week of September 1944. David was surprised how much he liked it, granted the need for a few "minor trims" which he felt he could entrust to Hal Kern and Bobbie Keon while Schary was on vacation in New York. But in the same cable of September 10, David moved on, changing his mind as he dictated: perhaps there were a few scenes that still needed retaking. He picked on three and said, "I am swamped with work; and I loathe the idea of stepping in on the picture at this stage of the game." He asked Schary: "Wouldn't it be possible for you to work on these three scenes wherever you are going to be, and then come back for a week to get the picture cleaned up, going away again if necessary? Anyway, I am terribly sore that you're on vacation when I'm back here, particularly in view of the fact that my vacation was anything but."

Two weeks later, there was a preview in Pasadena, with startling results. The film played "wonderfully," but the audience didn't like Shirley Temple. "Just as it is apparent that we have a very successful picture," wrote David, "it is also apparent that we have a very unsuccessful performance and presentation of Shirley; and under no circumstances can I permit Shirley to be destroyed." Seventy-five percent of the audience hadn't liked Shirley: Grad Sears of United Artists felt she was "just nothing."

David wondered how far this was the part, the heavy that she had to be in the story. Schary was too weary to remind David that her part had been contrived or to point out that Temple was not hurting the picture overall. The idea that followed was not employed, yet it shows the extent of obsession. For David was prepared to take this finished, ready, and "wonderful" picture, and

> create a whole new story for Shirley within the framework of the film. We have to get a characterization and a plot for her with a beginning, a middle and an end. We have to write good scenes for her and have them photographed and directed properly. We have to create a character that the audience won't dislike and will be interested in. Our problem is complicated greatly because if the other players, notably Ginger, should resent our attempts to improve Shirley . . . then our problem will be complicated by having to create scenes of Shirley alone or with the minor characters.

Very late in the day, David decided on new close-ups of Shirley to enhance her impact in *I'll Be Seeing You*. He asked George Cukor to be her director, for George was still some kind of Selznick loyalist. The emergency director had a hard time, and despaired of Shirley's ability. But Cukor did his best once more for David.

I'll Be Seeing You opened on Christmas Day 1944 in Los Angeles. It had cost $1.3 million, and it grossed over $6 million. Shirley Temple was by then sixteen: her grown-up life was beginning, but her sensation was over. There would be more films, many of them made on loan-out on her Selznick contract. But the one-take child of wonder and aplomb had become a cheerful, round-faced adolescent possessed of dull attitudes and flat timing. Hormones had made her the girl next door. At first, at least, as he looked at *I'll Be Seeing You*, David could not notice or admit that. It was an early

warning of his failure to keep up with changing times and to carry childhood to maturity.

Dore Schary liked David. He stayed on and would have more projects.
But they were all packaged away to RKO in a deal as lucrative to David as
it was offensive to United Artists. Schary did so well with them that RKO
offered him the job of production head. David said he wasn't surprised, and
Schary should take it. Indeed, he took credit for the appointment and never
really wondered how he had deprived himself of a right-hand man.

12 · MAY ROMM

THERE CAME A TIME in the woeful early 1940s when David would
not leave the bedroom of his suite at the Waldorf. Nothing could break the
depression. It scared him, and he told Irene "he was actually going insane."
From whom should she seek help but Dorothy Paley, "the analysis queen—
she had explored them all"? At first, David wouldn't see anyone, but Irene
went ahead of him, scouted out the man, Dr. Sandor Rado, and then

Dr. May Romm,
around 1960

dragged David with her. There's no reason to smile at the drama: David was desperate, and he never saw a doctor casually. This was honest self-dramatization, like Ingrid Bergman in *Spellbound* "saving" Gregory Peck from expressionist dreams and violin notes trembly with echo. The Los Angeles analyst that Rado recommended was May Romm.

May Romm was a doctor, pledged to treat disorder and confusion, with a practice in Beverly Hills where the Selznicks ensured influence and referrals. She was one of the first generation of analysts to discover business in the unhappiness of show people. She was also ironist enough to see they would be loyal clients, fans of hers, so long as she never put them to the acid test of saying they were well again.

May Romm was Russian and Jewish and a warm, clever, funny woman who might have been David's older sister—"she was humorous, lovable, magnetic, incredibly charming," says her daughter, Dorothy, "but my mother was lonely. She was looking for company."

She had been born in Vitebsk in 1891, and she came to America at the age of twelve. She took her medical degree in 1915 in Philadelphia at the Women's Medical College, and she practiced in Mount Vernon for twelve years. Only at the age of forty, inspired by the Freudian A. A. Brill, did she decide to take up psychiatry. Her studies were done at the New York State Psychiatric Institute. In 1934, she graduated from the New York Psycho-analytic Institute, and in 1938 she went to Los Angeles to set up a practice.

Dr. Romm had a daughter, but she had lost her husband. Why California, at the age of forty-seven? She had lived there briefly in the 1920s. She was by inclination a pioneer, and by 1938 it was already evident how many European exiles and refugees were looking for liberty and sunshine and a chance to settle their troubled thoughts. There are always fresh crazes and new kinds of gold in Los Angeles, and in the 1940s, psychiatry was one of them.

David delighted in her and did all he could to make her feel good about being his doctor. He took to her so swiftly it rather shocked Irene:

> Dr. Romm was a wise little motherly lady, and I envied David the privilege of having her to talk to and told her so. Arranging to see him every day on an emergency basis, she warned me not to let him discuss his sessions or permit him to tell me what he hadn't finished telling her. She would need my cooperation. I was delighted not to share honors with her.

As Irene saw it, David's treatment "went by leaps and bounds." Within weeks, the former recluse was seeing people and doing things. Dr. Romm warned him the treatment must be gradual to be thorough. He should go slowly, unraveling old knots. But David was impatient, and he wanted to please her. He picked up this new process quickly; it was so like the way one talked motivation to writers or actors. Yet this was more fun: it was talking about oneself.

Intellectually, David was enlarged by psychoanalysis—or inflated. But nothing in him was ready for responsibility. He felt cheerful again, so he must be better. Thus he subjected Dr. Romm to the old "healthy" D.O.S.—he was late for appointments, he kept her waiting into the evening, he sought her input on pictures, and she was added to Christmas lists. Dr. Romm waited, and advised, and accepted the white satin evening bags. She was star-struck, and no one ever found David less than exciting company. As her daughter says, "She was impressed by movie people and she loved their sense of crisis." In a while David was confiding to Irene that he fancied this doctor was falling in love with him. "He knew more than she did," he told Irene; "*he* could analyze *her.*"

Regular sessions stopped after about a year: Dr. Romm must have seen the impossibility of breaking through his enthusiasm. But by then, she was a family retainer, someone to be passed around like a good tennis coach. Irene would have her turn. Then there was the extended family: Jeffrey, Daniel, the Goetzes, and even Louis B. Mayer, who needed some justification for leaving a melancholy wife and becoming the womanizer of his fantasies. "She should not have done so many of them," says May's daughter. "And you couldn't change those people. So often they seek out the psychiatrist who is going to help them the least."

The Romm touch was everywhere. At one point, Dr. Romm turned to Anita Colby, recognizing another harassed retainer, and said, "Why don't *you* come?" Colby felt this was like the fortune-teller scavenging for good background: "She would have taken me, I'm sure, practically for nothing. But I said, 'No, I have my own means of coping with myself.' "

Still, Colby helped get Jennifer to see Dr. Romm. After *Since You Went Away,* Jennifer and Joseph Cotten had been loaned as a pair to Paramount for *Love Letters,* in which Jennifer had to play an amnesiac. But Jennifer couldn't understand the script or say some of the lines. "Take it up with May," David had ordered, and the doctor had counseled the actress. "She explained that when you lose your memory, you are going back, you have no recollection of good-bad, no-yes. Like a child."

One thing led to another, and Jennifer had plenty of her own problems to discuss. But she felt one great barrier with Dr. Romm, which she confessed to Colby: "David sends me to this woman, and she reminds me of Irene!"

Spellbound was David's reward for May Romm—a boost to her career, he hoped. In return for help with the script, she would receive screen credit as "Psychiatric Advisor." The film was a box-office success, but laughable from any medical point of view, as many in the profession felt bound to tell Dr. Romm. She had been used, in a kindly way—and she "sort of believed in the film" and in Ingrid Bergman as a beautiful analyst whose kiss could open inner doors. Irene's view was more caustic: "David was making the film *instead* of having an analysis. He was in a terrible state and the film is a terrible piece of junk."

This was not the first time Dr. Romm had been drawn into a movie's planning. She got no credit for it, but she consulted on *Since You Went Away* in which Albert Basserman played a doctor in a rehabilitation center for servicemen suffering from "nerve-shock." There was a similar theme in *I'll Be Seeing You* and the memory loss in *Love Letters*, and the trouble of the Gregory Peck character in *Spellbound* comes from war-induced nerve-shock. David's head was abuzz with the troubled mind as a subject.

Since 1943, David had wanted to put Alfred Hitchcock on some kind of psychological thriller, and Hitchcock had a novel in mind, *The House of Dr. Edwardes*, by Francis Beeding, set in a clinic in the Alps. Hitchcock had a treatment which seemed to David like a succession of director's tricks and traps. So David went earnestly in search of authenticity—the film they made is no evidence of this; it is one more proof of Hitchcock's confidence that film was a world unto itself, a screen where frenzies occurred. Nevertheless, David hired Ben Hecht as screenwriter, for Hecht prided himself on being an amateur analyst. Hecht was also someone David trusted to produce "a well constructed emotional story on which to hang all of Hitchcock's wonderful gags." Hitch might have groaned at "gags," but here was a crucial clash and an early sign of the old-fashioned in David: the producer believed in coherent dramas, whereas Hitch loved knockout scenes.

May Romm's chief duty was to ensure technical and professional accuracy in the dialogue. In the spring and early summer of 1944, working with Eileen Johnston, a recent student of psychology, Dr. Romm wrote copious notes on the screenplay drafts, along these lines:

> Page 28. Scene 77: Constance saying "That's a lie." This is not what Constance means. She means "That's a misconception or an erroneous idea or an illusion." No psychiatrist would use the word lie in this instance. . . .
>
> Page 77, 3rd speech: Instead of saying "The case is unusual" Constance should argue against J.B.'s being a lunatic—"This is not paranoia. It is not insanity. It is one of the complexes that any sane person can get under stress."

These were modest proposals, albeit deaf to the way people talked in movies. Dr. Romm held her peace on the larger implication of the story and the distortion of fact and reason in its mystery elements. David did not concur with many of her points. In the thick of work, he wanted her most as a seal of good intentions. He wrote to her on June 8, 1944, in humoring tones:

> I am paying Ben Hecht a hundred dollars on a bet I made with him that you would not approve the script technically. I told Ben the only explanation I can find for it is that you are in love with him—in which case I should like to recommend an analyst.
>
> I've told Ben that I am paying off the bet subject to recapture if you are unwilling to have your name go on the screen as technical advisor; as far as I am concerned, this would be the proof as to whether you are on the level or simply being agreeable.
>
> There will, of course, be a small charge for the advertising you will receive.

In fact, Dr. Romm was paid $1,500—she was one of the team. As such, she sometimes offered her own jokes at David's expense. At one point, she was asked to come up with some brief cutaways for a montage. She suggested a patient who

> writes furiously with incredible speed, and apparently indefatigably. NOTE: MANICS WRITE LETTERS BY THE HUNDREDS SOMETIMES WRITING THROUGH SEVERAL DAYS AND NIGHTS TIRELESSLY UNTIL THEY FALL INTO A COMA OR EXHAUSTION.

This may be the closest we will ever come to a clinical note from Dr. Romm on David O. Selznick.

By July 6, May Romm was looking over a revised draft and sending the word, through Miss Johnston: "Not only does Doctor Romm now approve the script, with the addition of these few minor changes, but she is genuinely enthusiastic about it. The Doctor is sincere and whole-hearted in her praise of the story and the technical accuracy of Mr. Hecht's writings, and the fine air of reality achieved throughout the psychological action."

The film was to have a foreword. There had been thoughts of having it spoken, and Dr. Romm struggled with many drafts, one over 700 words. David even consulted Dr. Karl Menninger on the foreword, stressing his recent dedication to psychiatric themes. He suggested that Menninger see *Since You Went Away*, "which includes a sequence that I personally conceived and wrote in the hope that it would have a value in making the American public aware of the work being done by psychiatrists to rebuild men who have been shaken by their war experiences." Menninger refused to be shaken by David's forgetfulness—for the doctor had already given some suggestions on *Since You Went Away.*

As to the foreword David had sent him, Menninger thought "many very unfortunate phrases and terms are used although the main idea is correct. . . . I think you do your gospel an injury by implying that one is either crazy enough to be locked up in a hospital or else perfectly well. The vast majority of patients with mental illnesses are not in mental hospitals— they are walking around in the streets of Hollywood, Topeka and other cities of our country."

The foreword as used is short, inspirational, and plainly Ben Hecht:

> The analyst seeks only to induce the patient to talk about his hidden problems, to open the locked doors of his mind.
>
> Once the complexes that have been disturbing the patient are uncovered and interpreted, the illness and confusion disappear . . . and the devils of unreason are driven from the human soul.

May Romm came in for professional criticism because of her work on *Spellbound.* She had been compromised by experts. In September 1944, she wrote to Karl Menninger, trying to extricate herself:

> I spent a considerable time with Ben Hecht trying to modify or eliminate some of the unscientific view points. It was no easy task, but a great deal was altered on the script for the better. However, it was impossible, according to Mr. Hecht, to eliminate the part, or to alter it, so as not to have the head of this private Sanitarium commit murder. . . .
>
> Naturally the question arises, why should I have had anything to do with a picture which many have interpreted as casting aspersions on psychiatry. Simply because had I not done so it would have been produced in a much more undesirable form than it is now.

By early 1947, *Spellbound* had worldwide grosses of $6.387 million. It was nominated for Best Picture, and Michael Chekhov was nominated as supporting actor. It did help draw analysis to the attention of the great public. Yet as a movie, it deserves Irene's censure. It is a collection of gimmicks, many of which are striking at the moment: the Salvador Dalí dream sequences (much modified in the making), Miklos Rozsa's main theme, the corridor of opening doors, the staircase and the razor, the red flash at the end, and the remarkable conviction of Ingrid Bergman as the face of sweet innocence. How that woman loved to work, and how her apprehensive beauty holds the implausibility together. The film has none of the anguish that would come to Hitchcock's psychological thrillers in the next decade.

Ingrid Bergman and
Gregory Peck in
Spellbound

From Selznick's point of view, *Spellbound* let him believe he was still up-to-date and in form, that he was equipped to draw novel material into popular entertainment. As far as analysis is concerned, the movie is a source of cliché and misunderstanding. It shows the conflict of feelings David had toward the new form of doctoring. He could not stop regarding it as the accomplice to narcissism. While *Spellbound* was in the works, David returned one day from a meeting with May Romm. Petter Lindstrom had been waiting for him in his office. The husband to *Spellbound*'s "doctor" had his own anxieties about Ingrid's extramarital imagination. David charged in, jubilant with new learning.

"You'll understand this," he said to Lindstrom. "I have a problem with Irene. I found this other girl, whom I love. It was terribly hard on me. How could I explain this to Irene and to myself? So I went to this woman psychiatrist. I paid her double her fee. She gave me a scientific explanation for why I had to leave my wife. I wanted you to know there is a *scientific* basis!"

The science in May Romm's analysis was like the statistics of Gallup polls—the two things only helped David believe in what he wanted. And with double the usual fee, then surely there was rationale for bigamy?

In July 1944, as *Since You Went Away* opened, David threw a party at the Scandia restaurant on Sunset. He became drunk, and he was talking too loudly. Both Irene and Jennifer were there that night, enduring the arrangement and their man's perilous exuberance. He had a sparring talk with his sister-in-law Edie and he told her, just wait and see, how he was surely going to have his cake and eat it.

A day or so later, David was sought out by Harry Rapf, the man who had got him in at Metro in 1926. Rapf was still at MGM, but he was unhappy or uneasy: he was wondering whether, at his time of life, he should break away from the big studio or stay put. He had sought David's advice, and David had managed to find time to listen to Rapf's worries. In the end, Harry stayed put—for the last five years of his life. But as he thanked David, he felt the need to offer a warning:

> You have made a lot of money and earned a lot of success—more than any other man in this business. You've carried the great name of Selznick to new heights, and I am sure your father, were he alive today, would feel very proud that his name is one of the most important and honored ones in the industry. You have also brought credit to the industry and you personally receive admiration from one and all—so don't burn yourself up to the extent I saw you on the two or three visits I had in your office. The business and the work will go on just the same—it's only the importance we attach to it that puts such a terrific strain on our shoulders. Begin to get some fun out of life . . . take good care of yourself.

THE JIG'S UP

1 · EACH HIS OWN AUDIENCE

AT CHRISTMAS 1944, Jeffrey Selznick was twelve and Daniel eight. As always, Christmas was a theatrical season at Summit Drive, with elaborate and unbreakable rules. For as long as either boy believed in Santa Claus, they would hang stockings above the massive "English-looking" fireplace in David's room. The two boys would then sing Christmas carols to these empty stockings before departing to their wing of the house and early bed. They were allowed back in that room at seven o'clock on Christmas morning, ushered in by servants. Then they opened their stocking presents, though the stockings were not large enough to hold all the gifts. Santa had piled them on the floor. But David, their Santa, a man who loved the idea of giving, slept through this. So spoiled in so many ways, he missed the most precious moments.

He was worn-out from the night before, when he and Irene had their gift-giving, after the boys had gone to bed. They did this in the living room, a place sealed off to the boys since mid-December, when the tree arrived. That, too, was said to be the gift of Santa. David and Irene usually had George Cukor over on Christmas Eve, even after *Gone With the Wind*. They dressed the tree, contriving its brief perfection. It was a long night, for David never had less than a score of gifts for Irene, professionally wrapped at the studio, but with gift cards he wrote himself. He watched her open every one in the order indicated. Here is a sample—it is Christmas 1941, with the gifts and David's descriptions:

1. Sonnets to a Dark Girl (book of poetry by Edna St. Vincent Millay)
2. The Nervous Wreck of a Whirl (pillbox)
3. Memory of Yesteryear (snuff box)
4. Tomorrow's Atmosphere (clothes sachet)

5. The Student Connoisseur (a book about silver)
6. Anniversary Allure (gardenia slip)
7. Rosemary—And Myrrh (perfume)
8. Sweater Girl's Purr (sweater)
9. Elegance O'er the Demi-Tasse (silver sugar tongs)
10. Casanova Receives the Coup de Grace (nightgown)
11. Miss Barrett's Snare (pink bedjacket)
12. Masseur's Nightmare (white bedjacket)
13. Odalisque at Mount Sinai (lamé velvet pajamas)
14. An Earful at Hollywood High (gold earrings)
15. Cents and Sensibility (Magnin black bag)
16. Presentability (emerald green evening gown)
17. Aladdin's Suitcase (large jewel case)
18. Oomph and Old Lace (Bonwit nightgown)
19. Roughing it at the Ritz (Chartreuse evening gown)
20. Mrs. Siddons Sits (gloves to match above)
21. The Souvenir Collector (small jewel case)
22. The Shulamite Dines the Rector (lace tablecloth)
23. Chit-chat After the Ball (white quilted robe)
24. A Tea Leaf Reading at Haddon Hall (silver teakettle)
25. Delicate Stuff (Worcester urns)
26. Rope Enough (evening bag and clip)
27. Colonel on a Small Scale (miniature lazy Susan)
28. Domestic Blackmail (rubellite and diamond ring)
29. Glamour on Cove Way (black lace evening gown)
30. Modernist's Holiday (Marie Laurencins painting)
31. And 31 ain't hay . . . (a check)

So David and Irene slept late, and the boys were clamoring for the opening of the living room. This generally occurred by 11:30 in the morning. Then came family presents at the tree, and Irene ran this show. "One gift at a time," Jeffrey recalls, "everybody must pay attention to the gift being opened. And she kept the lists for thank-you notes." Every year there would be checks, bonds, and sometimes cash for the boys from big stars in the business. The boys glimpsed these wonders, which then vanished, drawn away to a fund that David and Irene watered every year with some of their own money.

There followed a Christmas lunch, with relatives: Flossie Selznick, always; sometimes the Mayers, the Goetzes, and Myron. It was a literary Christmas meal, with turkey and plum pudding, and a great occasion, for on only two days in the year—Christmas and Thanksgiving—did everyone sit down to eat together in the dining room. The Christ in Christmas was not alluded to, but the Dickensian festivity was fully embraced and this in a household that never observed Jewish holidays. Even at Louis B.'s home—where synagogue was in order—there was a Christmas tree, too. Christmas was for David a willing commitment to Americana, a test of patriotism.

Christmas was only an exaggeration of year-round rules for the boys. Wake-up was at 5:45, whereupon Jeffrey and Danny took turns in the bathroom and doing their piano practice. They were in the breakfast room by 7:00 for a cooked meal and then off to school.

This routine was supervised by a line of governesses, but it was decided upon by Irene. "It started with schedules," says Jeffrey. "They were typed by a secretary and posted—really, every minute of the day was accounted for. Mother was the rule maker. My father never made a rule. If he did make one, he broke it immediately."

Danny recalls at least three governesses—"a Miss Dixon, who was English—"

"No, Dainton, Marion Dainton," said Jeffrey. "I absolutely adored her, a redhead. I remember seeing her nude once when I was quite young. My mother liked her enormously—but she was fired: it had something to do with men."

There were others: Ronnie Ramus, Carol Lang, and Dorothea Homer. These highly trained women ran the boys' comings and goings. "They had delegated authority from the parents," said Danny. "And they tried to keep the peace between Jeffrey and myself. Not easily kept. I developed intense personal relationships with each of these governesses. I think Jeffrey probably liked them all and had some affection—I can't imagine that he had a feeling for any of them to the degree that I had."

The governess kept the early morning on schedule and got the boys off to school. Then, in the afternoons, she would accompany them to the doctors, the oculists, the dentists, the allergists, to May Romm—and not always the same practitioners, for specialists, second opinions, and celebrated new figures all took their turn. The governess would report to Irene on medical progress and pass on any educational difficulties mentioned by the school.

School for Jeffrey was El Rodeo, at the corner of Whittier and Wilshire. He was driven to and from school, and it was his greatest horror if the family limousine was used, for that was a sign of privilege that earned teasing from his schoolmates. So did being collected to go home for lunch: Irene thought he was not eating the right things at school.

After school, there was a boys' club that went hiking or riding in the hills behind Beverly Hills. Then home to Summit Drive, a quick bath and six o'clock supper in pajamas and robe, supervised by the governess or Irene's maid. It was a three-course meal—soup, entrée, and dessert—and

Jeffrey recalls being made to clean his plate or the leftovers would be served up again the next night. After supper, the boys played games, and then Irene had her visiting time with them. She would come to their nursery, play with them, and talk about any problems, or they would go to her bathroom and chat to her while she got ready for dinner.

The boys had not seen David all day and would not until he got home sometime after 7:00. If he got home. Jeffrey, in particular, recalls nights when his father was late at the studio or never came home. But sometimes, before going off to school, it was possible to get a few minutes with him in the morning as he showered and shaved. There were days in succession when neither boy saw David—though each felt Irene took pains to spend some time with them every day. This was when the parents were in Los Angeles, living at home. There were many prolonged absences: the visit to Europe in 1934, trips to New York by one parent or the two of them together, Honolulu in 1936, and so on. There was no such thing as the four on a family vacation until Connecticut in the summer of 1940—and that had been no advertisement for the practice.

Of course, there was four years' difference in the boys' ages, as well as divergence in temperament. So their versions of their parents do not exactly coincide. Jeffrey cannot recall talking to his father as a child. Instead, he remembers being shut out of the room and going to talk to his mother:

> But I was afraid of my mother, and I didn't really want to see her that much. . . . Because of all the rules. She would find out. She could worm it out of me if I had broken a rule, and the inevitable punishments.

Jeffrey resented the rules and steadily opposed them. He wanted to ride his bike to school. He needed a man's company more and a man's admiration and encouragement. He loved cars, yet David was a lousy driver. He began to feel his father was not manly. If Jeffrey fell off his bike—"Dad frightened me more than the event. The thing I really hated him for—it's not too strong a term—is he taught me to be afraid of catching a ball."

There was a tension over money, too. Jeffrey recalls having no money, except for a quarter-a-week allowance. Flossie Selznick (Beauma, the boys called her) slipped him coins, but they were confiscated. He had a small coin bank, but when the contents approached $5 someone came in the night and emptied it. Jeffrey had a Victory vegetable garden and a few chickens, and he sold produce to the kitchen. But,

> I was never allowed to have any money, and so money assumed an importance which it didn't have, because it was forbidden. Another really stupid error my mother made. The result was I started stealing money from my father. Because he was very careless with change. I

knew he would never miss a nickel or a dime. The allowance thing kept getting adjusted, new rules and regulations. . . . But there was such a dichotomy about money, about my father's generosity and carelessness and my mother's *rigidity* about it.

Even as a child, Jeffrey felt that David favored Danny and regarded him as a more fragile, more interesting boy. Everything Jeffrey has said here makes a touching fit with Danny's account of another household situation—the frequency with which David's getting home late spoiled Irene's arrangements:

> I remember my mother saying to me, "That's not funny, Danny." But to me my father was such a colorful, funny character, sort of this jocular character who turned around at a party and broke dishes because he wasn't looking. There was a degree of clumsiness which I, being the child I was physically, obviously identified with. I thought, well, there's a man and he was probably like this when he was younger. It was all part of a larger picture of somebody who wasn't totally in control, who seemed to make life difficult for people who were in control. I felt sorry for Mother, in a kind of sweet way, that she had all these problems. Then I'd say to him, "Dad"—or "Daddy" as we used to call him when we were younger—"Mother's very upset about this." "I know," he'd say. "I can't help myself. What can I do, Danny? What can I do?" So I just had this bemused attitude toward it all.

Danny put on plays in the nursery. He wrote out programs and invitations to the staff, and he thinks David and Irene were there, too. But he doesn't recall Jeff. He made music for his plays, for he had a large record collection—opera especially. "I would put them on and sing along or dance along. . . . I remember my father coming in and listening to them with me and singing along himself." And Danny remembers David often tucking him in at night and leading him in prayers: "Now I lay me down to sleep" and a "God bless" litany that covered the family and the dogs.

Jeffrey feels he was left out. He recalls his father taking him a couple of times to the Ocean Park pier and "the great penalty of his existence was having to take me to the Rose Bowl. . . . But he enjoyed it when we got there. That's something he got genuine pleasure out of with me."

Jeff had his days out with L.B. when the old man would drive his grandson past Riverside to his horse ranch. Jeffrey sat up front in the Chrysler station wagon, beside the chauffeur, while L.B. played pinochle in the back with a friend. And they'd ride horses together. Jeffrey loved L.B.'s vigor: "He had a wonderful physical presence. He was kind of a rough-and-tumble physical man. He could be gruff, but you knew he didn't really mean it." Irene had laid down rules for these trips: she knew what to fear. L.B. was to cut out the bad language, and he was not to lose his temper. So Jeffrey got lectures instead:

> I liked Grandpa a lot. I always wanted to see him more than I was allowed to. He was very tactile. He loved to hug, kiss, hold me, rub my hair. The only thing that was disagreeable with him, I usually got a lecture, often centered on my father, about what a fool he was, that he could be the most important man in Hollywood but he wouldn't listen. . . .

It was in that stress on discipline that Jeffrey felt his mother and L.B. were alike, with David the rogue they could not control. Jeffrey was a handsome boy, yet he was insecure about his looks. There were rapid mood swings in the child, with sudden, rampant arrogance—big shot-itis, Irene called it—that David hated because he knew he had it, too. Danny was gentler, and in David's eyes he was a creative genius, so advanced at music, dance, writing. The playing of favorites had come with birth. The brothers fought, and Jeffrey was older and more attuned to combat. Yet he believed the fights started because Danny provoked them. But with Danny always in tears, Jeffrey took the blame.

David had never recovered himself with Jeffrey. Whatever threat the baby had represented in 1932 was sustained by the boy striking enough to play Tom Sawyer. Was it the irrepressible princeliness in Jeffrey, the kid who exulted in the Selznick name and Myron's office building on Wilshire, and who was nearly eight when *Gone With the Wind* swept the board, old enough to act like royalty? What was Jeffrey to do with all the domineering genes he had inherited?

Irene hired an exotic ex-cossack, a Captain Nasht, to do calisthenics on the lawn with Jeffrey: "She was mad about my body, very keen on my body, on my physical conditioning. Set great store by it. But like everything else, what could have been fun turned into a dreaded chore." And then, at eight, Jeffrey put on weight. It was the fall after Stony Batter when they all lived briefly in New York at the Waldorf Towers. Jeffrey was put in the Walt Whitman School, which he hated. Unhappy in the East, away from Summit Drive, he fell afoul of the Waldorf's creamed soups—

> and I put on a lot of weight. Up till then there'd been problems about making me eat, which was really my way of getting attention. (I mean, I learned later in analysis.) Then, of course, my mother tried to put me on different diets. I started the metabolism tests. Another string of doctors. They decided that I had low metabolism. These terrible diets, which for me was just another form of punishment.

Jeffrey was told his puppy fat came from indiscipline and moral failure—it could end up with him looking like David! But the boy had a half-savage, half-pristine look and the best smile in the Selznick family. When he needed glasses, Irene denied this for several years until Jeffrey's seat at school had been moved up right in front of the blackboard.

Danny was younger, more amenable and obedient than Jeffrey and inclined to tastes David and Irene hoped to see in a son. It is Danny's recollection that David had no time or patience for day-to-day care, but that he was a benign overlord to the immense scrutiny entrusted to Irene:

> School was just the beginning of my education. The number of things I was getting coaching in, both at the house and away from the house, was pretty extensive. She would supervise all that. At one point I was taking tap-dancing—was I with the right tap-dancing teacher? She had the wise and knowing involvement of almost a doctor. She took an almost unbelievable degree of interest in everything, I believe, and I'm sure the same with Jeffrey.

Of course, these two boys were among the most protected children on earth. And they had parents likely to be taken with fierce spasms of guilt just because of that. So money was denied, household privileges were withdrawn for a hundred small offenses. But a boy's pride and daily peace were ruined by being taken to school in a limo. Should he act ordinary and humble, or should he *be* the cock of the walk that schoolmates jeered at? Irene was already telling herself about the need to get the boys away from Hollywood and Los Angeles. She was full of principles about child rearing; she was so attentive to the notion of caring that one of her sons was intimidated. Yet she and David saw relatively little of the boys. These kids were simultaneously spoiled and neglected, and they were not spared that tendency, evident in both the Selznick and the Mayer families, that was competitive with affection. Much later in life, Jeffrey and Danny observed the weatherhouse effect in Irene—while one son was in, the other must be out. It was hard for them to be loved at the same time.

BUT JEFFREY AND DANNY did share many experiences and attitudes. They loved the Summit Drive house; they were deeply drawn to their governesses; they adored the spectacle of their parents. They both believed their mother had the nature of a brilliant detective. And they had no inkling of what was to come. They had met Jennifer Jones on the set of *Since You Went Away*, though for both of them in 1943 Shirley Temple had been the chief attraction. They had seen Shirley's pictures in the theater at the house—they never went out to the movies. The two boys believed their parents were made for each other, just like the couples in the movies—like Bill Powell and Myrna Loy.

"I would say that they were *very* warmly disposed toward one another," says Jeffrey. "And they laughed a lot." Indeed, Jeffrey thinks the closest Irene ever came to being at ease was when she was with David, while David, in Irene's company, was kinder to Jeffrey, better disposed.

Danny remembers David and Irene as being physically affectionate together and with the children, a lot of kissing and hugging, even in a playful spirit of competition: "I want as long a kiss as you gave your mother." But David did feel a kind of remove with the children, something that waited for the doors to the bedroom wing to be closed:

> They were markedly affectionate with each other, clearly, transparently. . . . At the same time, I had the distinct sense that they didn't want me to see past a certain point. I don't ever remember seeing my parents kiss one another on the mouth, for example. That's something that would have been done behind the closed doors.

Danny's recollections are rather subtler than Jeffrey's—was it this theatrical aptitude in his son that delighted David? So he and Irene may have played to Danny a little more. And Danny did feel he was part of an audience. For the parents seemed to need each other; they were a team, a great double act:

> I felt an unbelievable degree of rapport, similarity of humor, viewpoint, energy, rhythm, style, emotionality. Such a synchronicity, even though they were quite different physically. Many other people have said this, this is not just some romantic view of their child. . . . They were great audiences for each other. It's one of their great qualities as individuals, both. I can almost speak of them in the present tense. My father listened to you, what you had to say. He roared with laughter. He enjoyed, he wanted to know what happened next. "Did you do this, did you do that?" The involvement! He was a great audience, a great listener. For Mother as well as for us. Mother, an equally fabulous listener, involved, caring, interested, laughing, applauding. The two great listeners of the world. Each other's best audience!

Later on, Irene would say the performance had exhausted her. Yet she played it, with honor, until the end, but because she *was* playing she felt a loss of self. Danny was the fan they needed. Jeffrey had a skepticism that David could not seduce. Still, Jeffrey's greatest doubts about their perfection never guessed at the breakup coming—and he was four years older. Jeffrey and Danny were members of the audience at an intense, intimate show—their parents being together. And, just like the crowd at the movies, they knew the wistfulness that has to admit, sometimes, that the stars hardly know the individuals in the crowd exist.

2 · WANTING OUT

WHAT WAS IRENE THINKING? This was a woman who could not sit quietly and elegantly in a chair, in a good black dress, without building walled cities of worry. Moreover, the household was arranged so that she had not much more to do than sit and think, checking off in her head whether the schedule was being followed and wondering where David was. To Jeffrey, her son, Irene had too little to do:

> Well, she had a secretary, she wrote letters. She read books, she would play tennis with friends. She would go shopping. Conferences with the cook. Telephone—on the telephone a great deal. She didn't really get out of bed until noon. She'd have her breakfast around ten and then, from ten to twelve, she'd be busy with papers and telephoning. Then very often she'd go out to lunch. Be home, come home about three. Kills the day pretty well.

There have always been wives and consorts in Hollywood who have to kill time gracefully, without scandal or disturbance. They are given plenty and splendor, liberty and vacancy, a very cunning prison. And then they must take care that neither pain nor tedium spoils their looks. For the man does expect an eager, admiring, upturned close-up whenever he comes home, at least in the same league as those beauties from his business. The Hollywood wife has to watch and understand, but somehow stay serene. And Irene was not just a wife in the kingdom, but a daughter whose father had told her she might have run a studio if she'd been a boy. Irene shut herself up so much of the time, for she felt what she was thinking would alarm most people if they ever found out.

So she did something, in her unique way, something useful and assertive. In the early 1940s, she got herself a position with the Los Angeles Juvenile Probation Department. She started going about with a woman sheriff, rounding up troublemakers. As Irene recalled, "With her I encountered situations more vivid than a movie, vérité with a vengeance."

Her service in Juvenile Probation was another life to inhabit. She had a secret name, Irene Sells; she sought out costume—ordinary cotton frocks, standard shoes, and stockings—things she had never worn before and thus exciting. She purchased a drab, used car, what she called "a jalopy" so that she could arrive at work unnoticed, without the shriek of limousine. (It was a 1941 Oldsmobile convertible, Jeffrey noted.) She worked three days a week, nine to four. And so Irene went to the office—self-effacing, bureaucratic, laboring in welfare. Yet forty years later, she wondered about those files she had examined and said, "Marilyn Monroe's might well have been among them."

She thrived on it—"anonymity was a relief"—and yet she was tickled by the contrast of coming home to her luxurious bedroom to make the telephone calls there had not been time for at the office. Irene enjoyed the effect her work was having on other members of the family. Edie was horrified: "Darling, it is so sordid. It is a side of you I can't bear to think about. It disturbs me even to listen." David was often left in bed when she went off to her office, and he grumbled, "Are you trying to reproach me?"

Irene's work was not war-related—and she did not carry on with it after 1945, in Los Angeles or New York, as the serious industry of American juvenile delinquency got under way. This is not an attack. Irene never in her life worked casually at anything. She had reason to be proud of her "yeoman service"; yet in her stress on ordinariness, she was trying to redirect the conscience of other Selznicks and Mayers. She went into very poor homes and saw children who were "Mongoloid, imbecile, syphilitic blind, and severely spastic." She formed romantic plans for foster homes of her own, with residents to care for as many as twenty children. She was like a socialite played by Bette Davis seeing how the other half lived and plunging ecstatically into good works.

Even if she was the most clear-thinking of the Selznicks, the most intelligent, the most greedy for real knowledge, still she was cast in the culture of Hollywood romance. She could not pick up a knife and fork without being the actress. But actresses like to be moved, and Irene was stunned when she saw some details of how the audience lived:

> I couldn't absorb the shock of what I had seen. I lingered, trying to show them I was unaffected. It took all my control. Hours went by. It got dark. I tore home, trying to outrace the frightful screaming that was following me. I could hear nothing but "No!" over and over. It took me fully ten minutes to realize it was my own voice.

And in the troubled scenario of her life, this external shock was the harbinger of inner fracture. Irene was seeing the light. Whether she ever planned it exactly, her controlling urge had found a way of escape.

"I hadn't known the thought existed until I spoke it," she would say later. But Irene was the sort of person who could grasp hidden truths several times a week. Like a detective, she believed in discovery. She knew, that night in February 1945, she had a superb effect, a drop-dead line: she and David were in bed together, and she could not sleep.

"Why aren't you asleep?" said David. "What's the matter?"

"Nothing. I was just thinking."

"What are you thinking about?"

"Nothing."

There was a pause, and then she heard her own voice saying, "The jig's up."

"What do you mean?"

"I want out."

And then, before discussion or murmurs in the dark, she fell asleep. She was enough of a movie herself to fade out fast.

They were in bed together—this couple who kept separate bedrooms and who therefore had to admit how bound they were to think and plan ahead for the night. In going to bed there was always a decision; things could not happen naturally or by sleepy, half-dreamed accident. Yet there they were, with one person's insomnia keeping the other awake. And it does seem to be Irene's bed, for she reaches out to the drawer for a pill, knowing where it is in the dark. Irene told Petter Lindstrom she and David had had few sexual relations in the last years of their marriage.

There was another project afoot as 1944 turned into '45, a picture being made at Paramount. But in January 1945, David had the rough cut of the film, *Love Letters*, and he showed it to Irene.

What follows is part conjecture, part a reckoning of the dates, and part a reading of *Love Letters*, which was not David's picture, beyond his loaning of Jennifer and Joe Cotten to Hal Wallis for $200,000 against 10 percent of the gross. Thereafter, he had made many suggestions on the script (written by Ayn Rand, from a novel by Chris Massie). This was also the film for which he had advised Jennifer to ask May Romm about playing a victim of amnesia.

There is something of *Cyrano de Bergerac* in *Love Letters* and a true trail of David. Away on war service in Italy, the sensitive Alan (Cotten) writes love letters to a Victoria, in England, for a friend who is not really worthy of such gentle, lyrical writing. But Victoria falls in love with the written voice, and when she meets the alleged author, they are married.

But the friend proves odious. Victoria is an orphan—a foundling, the story says. The woman who became her guardian kills the wretched, undeserving husband. The killer has a stroke. Victoria goes into deep amnesiac shock. She serves a year in prison for the killing and comes back into life

"Singleton" and Alan in
Love Letters. *It is her
birthday, and Alan has
asked her to write some-
thing in the family Bible—
a ribbon leads from the
book to her gift (a car).
This was a ploy that
David enjoyed in life.*

as strange, innocent, and ghostly as David and Jennifer could make her. She calls herself just "Singleton." Alan comes back from the war.

The movie opens on the Italian front, with Alan writing a letter to Victoria for the friend. But it is David's handwriting, and David's hand in the shot—something he managed to fit in. Later in the film, in a flashback, Victoria is on trial for the murder, and in a ravishing close-up—shot by Lee Garmes, directed by William Dieterle—and in something close to rapture (for Jennifer was never more lovely or moving) she says:

> He wrote to me . . . I remember his letters. . . . You see, I think very few people are happy. They wait all their lives for something to happen to them. Something great and wonderful. They don't know

what it is; but they wait for it. Sometimes it never happens. What they want is the kind of spirit I found in those letters. The spirit that makes life beautiful. I loved that man. I loved him more than my own life. I still love him."*

David had not produced or written that scene, yet surely he had written love letters to Jennifer. And now, fate had given them both that scene. Then, I think, David sat Irene down and showed the picture to her. It was a kind of confession, a moment at which movie could deliver the message.

A character asks Alan why he writes these love letters for someone else, and the wistful Cotten answers, "Because I was able to write to her all the things I have never been able to say to any woman I know . . . things I always wanted to say to someone."

There is another point about the timing: by early March 1945, David planned to be in the area of Tucson, Arizona, as the location shooting for *Duel in the Sun* commenced. This was a project for which Irene had no appetite or hope. A Western was hardly David's kind of picture. Moreover, it was clear from the script that Jennifer Jones, in playing Pearl Chavez, was leading the producer, or being drawn by him, into a flagrantly erotic mood.

In the days after the bombshell announcement, David and Irene had monstrous talks. He argued, protested, defended, justified, set out the full, terrible extent of the pressures he was under, and she said not much more than "I must leave you while I love you" and "I'm unhappy as I've never been before. I don't have to be happy, just not unhappy and afraid to look ahead."

During these talks, he admitted he was having an affair, and then he told Irene it was with Jennifer. In her book and in conversations, Irene insisted she had not known about the affair with Jennifer until then—and anyway, the particular woman was not critical: "an affair is a symptom, not a cause." Irene said she was more concerned because she had *not* felt the affair, for that showed how much she had lost contact with David.

It is hard to credit such ignorance or such earlier restraint in David. Bill Paley believed "David lost Irene because he was foolish. He had a habit of falling in love and wanting to tell his best friend—and his best friend was Irene." Dorothy Paley, who was then closer to Irene than Bill was to David, thought it possible but unlikely that Irene didn't know about Jennifer. "If you're married to a womanizer, you know it's not fundamentally important.

---

* In 1983, in *A Private View*, Irene wrote of David in the 1930s: "He was then, and for many years thereafter, filled with the aspiration of which heroes are made. I thought that man was marvelous. I still do."

But you reach the end of the rope. There are too damn many. For Irene, leaving David was a salvation, and she'd been coming to it." Another friend, Leonora Hornblow, reckons if Irene didn't know, "She was the only person alive who didn't. David would go to public places with people—there was minimum effort to conceal Jennifer." Mrs. Hornblow had seen David and Jennifer hand in hand on the street in New York. Studio people saw them necking in a car on the lot.

Irene had wondered about Jennifer for years. The half knowledge had put her in the mortifying position of a queen not supposed to know what was going on behind her back. In public ways, she had played the part most likely to give her the shudders, that of a fool. And she was playing it in a community devoted to rumor and report: scandal was the telephone show for those ladies who came out of their bedrooms at noon. She had known about Jennifer, she had known others knew she knew, and so she had been driven into hysterical, lying self-dramatics, a way of pretending she did not know.

"Jennifer hadn't caused our situation," said Irene. "If it hadn't been her, it would have been someone else." That was wishful thinking, a hope worn out in the waiting. Irene had watched enough infatuations in David to learn patience would see them off; if not that, then down-to-earth advice from someone like Dorothy Paley—"Oh, come on, David, grow up." There were affairs ended by other affairs; promiscuity is one of the wife's last hopes. But Jennifer was more than the others. She was so meek, so young, so lovely, so entirely ready to be David's creation that she left all the responsibility with him. He could get out of this one only by being cruel to her, and Jennifer was wide-eyed, credulous, a victim in the making, an insecure, unhappy woman. Pearl Chavez was proof that in creating Jennifer David had swept himself off his own feet. He was out to make her the fit object of fatal passion. This was fucking her on the screen. Long before conservative America got agitated, Irene knew that *Duel in the Sun* was not decent. She feared something "pornographic."

Yet Irene guessed David would not leave her, not for Jennifer. He was not strong enough. The agony would go on a lot longer yet. So *she* took action; she resumed control. She began to play upon his indecisiveness. This was not merely cruel—and, if it was, she had been provoked. It was accurate.

Irene put a deal to David's head: he had six months in which to decide whether he would give up gambling or Jennifer. David's gambling had declined in the years since *Gone With the Wind*. He had a lot more money, and he lost rather less. There was none of that fearful going right up to the brink; the loss of excitement may have added to his depression. The figures are not complete for those years:

	Lost	Won
1940 (9 months only)	$56,378	$20,847
1941	33,055	9,131
1942	n.a.	n.a
1943	54,135	26,326
1944	n.a.	n.a.

He wavered and fluctuated. He complained that if he gave up Jennifer and Irene still left him, he'd be the chump because he wouldn't have anyone. Like a child, still, he was pushed back into the prospect of being alone, without anyone to listen to him—and he was appalled. "Then he did give her up," wrote Irene, "and he wanted sympathy for the hard time she was giving him. He thought me unfeeling not to listen."

It was in the course of these conversations that Irene's intelligence broke him. "Don't leave me," he said, "for if you do, I will have to marry her." With that, he had disqualified himself; he had become a jerk. Her power over him was secure. Whatever was left, Jennifer could have.

3 · FROM YOUR DEVOTED BOSS

BECAUSE THE SEPARATION between David and Irene can be portrayed as a fateful dance does not mean it was clear-cut or clean. There were dreadful scenes, fights behind closed doors, unending, wounding diatribes— the uncovering of all the hates that any long-term relationship has acquired.

There was drinking. In the forties, David and Irene had both drawn attention for getting out-of-control drunk, the two of them at the same party, yet not quite drinking together. "There was a good deal of talk about it in New York," said Dorothy Paley. "Nobody enjoyed it. David got exuberant, and Irene just got drunk."

Another schizoid approach to the cake had emerged, and it suggests that Jennifer was not always as demure as she seemed in the Selznicks' public spectacle. In the summer of 1944, D.O.S. had written to the local Salary Stabilization Unit, explaining his embarrassment over Miss Jennifer Jones. Because of wartime regulations, it was not easy to make radical changes in contracts. As Jennifer entered the third year of her original deal with David, her market value was about $10,000 a week, but David could pay her only $400. In notes to Dan O'Shea, David marveled how little Jennifer seemed to understand the money: he would have *known* she loved him, and, next to Irene, there was such comfort in an uncritical woman who ignored money.

Still, the actress's situation was very tough, as David protested to the Salary Stabilization Unit:

> In addition, Miss Jones, who has two small children, during the production of *Since You Went Away* was separated from her husband. . . . Indications are that no reconciliation is possible. I am informed that as a result of a settlement at the time of the separation Miss Jones is to receive no alimony or support for the children, of whom, I understand, she is to have custody. Her position in the industry has burdened her with a very much more expensive mode of living than heretofore was hers. I have been informed by her agents that after reservations for taxes, household expenses, rent, wardrobe, insurance, etc., she has nothing left out of approximately $307 a week, which is what her $400 a week amounts to over a 52-week period.

David hoped he might pay his star at least $1,000 a week. That would be serious underpayment, of course, for David found himself (just like a businessman) forced to loan her out at massive advantage to himself. He beseeched Mr. H. L. Ducker at the Stabilization Unit: "if such a situation is permitted to continue, there is a great danger that our relationship with Miss Jones will be impaired."

There was an accommodation; a $13,000 bonus could be paid without undermining the war effort. David heard the news in early November, but withheld it from Jennifer so that the check could be presented with the pearls that were her 1944 Christmas present. He sent a note, too, a sweet amalgam of the professional and the private:

> I would that the check were larger—and with the easing of salary stabilization regulations that will come with more normal times, and/or with the inevitable continuance of splendid and faithful performances by you, I hope for and expect the pleasure of sending you greater financial rewards. . . .
>
> You have won our hearts and admiration, and no wonder: Yours is a gift that accompanies talent with all too sad rarity—a silence and innate modesty that you will not lose.
>
> May the New Year be the best—I won't say of your life, because the years that stretch ahead will be, I am sure, ever better in an accelerating continuity of success and happiness; but may it be the best of years to date

> With deep affection from your devoted boss, DOS

Already, by the fall of 1944, David had a sultry vision in mind that would test Jennifer's "innate modesty." For now something in the boss wanted the world to imagine him eating the cake: he meant to display

Jennifer's sexual splendor on the screen. Of course, he could explain it to himself in another way: he was simply demonstrating her range as an actress and his Svengalian grasp of her talent.

There was a beach party where David and John Houseman met again. By then, Houseman was enjoying an affair with Joan Fontaine.

"You want to make a bet?" David asked Houseman.

"On what?"

"I bet you a thousand dollars that, a year from now, my girl will be bigger than yours."

An old friend of David's, Niven Busch, came back into his life. Busch had gone to Hollywood and done well: he had worked on several scripts (*The Crowd Roars, In Old Chicago, The Westerner*); he had married the actress Teresa Wright in 1942; and he had written a novel, *Duel in the Sun*, a Western in which a half-breed, Pearl Chavez, disrupts the life of the McCanleses, a wealthy ranching family. The book was not a big success when published. But Busch sold it to RKO, with himself as its producer. He hired Oliver Garrett to write a script, and John Wayne was lined up to play Lewt, the darker of the two McCanles brothers. As for Pearl, Busch was at a loss: he had thought of getting Veronica Lake to dye her hair black; Hedy Lamarr had found herself pregnant at the critical moment; Teresa Wright believed Pearl was out of her range. Then, Charles Koerner, production head at RKO, heard that David Selznick was looking to loan out Jennifer Jones.

As negotiations went on, Busch himself rewrote the Garrett script. But David was hard to please. He was dubious about Wayne in the picture: "he has represented to date the exact opposite of what this script requires; and if this doesn't come off as a powerful sex story, it is going to misfire." In a letter to Koerner (no copy to Busch, but a blind copy to Jennifer), David suggested more work on the script but claimed he had no wish to be the film's producer. "I have nothing against Niven Busch," he proposed, "and think he is an extremely talented young man." (Busch was one year younger than David.) "We have been friends since boyhood, and the fact that he came to Hollywood is entirely due to me. But this is his first picture as a producer, and one doesn't cast important stars with fledgling producers. . . ."

Busch's old wariness of David as a patronizing big shot was made more bitter when Selznick's story suggestions were so acute. In the novel, and in his scripts, Busch ended *Duel* with Pearl killing Lewt so that she could ride off into bliss with Jesse, the other brother. As early as September 1944, David wanted "to go whole hog on the finish." He didn't like the idea of Pearl becoming Jesse's bedmate when the audience knew how "desperately and unceasingly she had loved the man she killed." Thus, it was David who begged off Busch's overtly happy ending and wanted to pursue the fatal drive of passion:

> No, if it were my picture I would eliminate inference of a sexual or even romantic attraction of Jesse for Pearl; and would have her drawn from start to finish, irresistibly and right through to her death, to Lewt. I think there is a perfectly magnificent finish screaming to be written and played if, when she shoots Lewt, the retrospective dissolve of his hand coming toward her still has the same meaning and result that it did in the first instance. One of Lewt's bullets has gotten her just as one of hers has gotten Lewt; having shot him because she knows it is the only thing she can do, she is still drawn to him, and the two play their final love moments in each other's arms, both dying.

Busch was powerless: on November 17, 1944, RKO sold the rights to the novel, along with the Garrett and Busch scripts, to Vanguard. David set out on his own rewrite, and Gregory Peck and Joseph Cotten were cast as Lewt and Jesse. Busch was invited to the Summit Drive house, where he had to listen to David: "He tells me, 'You'd really be surprised what I'm doing with this book, how much better I'm making it.'"

His first thought for a director on *Duel* had been William Dieterle, a man Jennifer had appreciated on *Love Letters*. But David remembered *Gone With the Wind*, where a director sympathetic to the women had had to yield to an action man. *Duel* was to be in Technicolor; it had obvious epic scenes, and David wanted to exult in size. Till then, the Western had been an economical genre, but David was determined to make a huge picture such as matched his reputation. So he hired King Vidor to direct, the man who had made *The Big Parade*, *Billy the Kid*, *Bird of Paradise*, and *Stella Dallas*. But Vidor's instinct now was to concentrate on the intimate family story, and so he found himself in conflict with David, who wanted that *and* the range war. They started rewriting one another.

With Irene's ultimatum on his mind, David was in Arizona by the end of February with a large crew and cast, with cattle and horses, an estimated budget of $2.8 million, and a script that was work in progress. On the first day of shooting, March 1, there was snow on the supposedly burning ground at the mountain location outside Tucson—for most of that month the weather stayed wintry, with David and Vidor rehearsing scenes together when shooting could not proceed. They had begun with a script of 170 pages, and by April 7 they had shot only 52 pages, yet the script had grown to 199 pages. One day Jennifer was an hour and a half late on the set—she had to be driven in from Phoenix, for she didn't like the Tucson accommodations. But the hotel where she stayed in Phoenix, the Biltmore, did not then welcome Jews, which added to David's vexations.

Anita Colby had to make sure Jennifer would be sexy on screen—and some in the business doubted this could be done. David told Colby, "I want Jennifer to have more bosom at the top of the off-the-shoulder blouse. Go to Max Factor at eleven tonight, go in the back way so nobody will see you, and he will put her bosoms in some kind of form to make a piece of sculpture out of them and then make a rubberized thing . . . and so forth."

If this sounds like Howard Hughes at work, that may be because Hughes had lately made such a promotion of Jane Russell in *The Outlaw*, another Western. Jennifer was horrified. "I am *not* going to do it," she said, so Colby remembered Betty Grable had told her about a special uplifting undergarment she had once used. They found that, and it worked. Jennifer looked beautiful, hot, and voluptuous—in the great Technicolor prints of *Duel* she is a Rodeo Drive Gauguin. Jennifer was shy, yet she gave herself to the process.

"She did everything," said Colby. "She learned to walk off her hips, like a Mexican girl. She really concentrated on everything. . . . But, you see, she was doing it for *him*. He was having her do this to show the world—this is the sexpot I have."

The production had all manner of setbacks. After the late winter at Tucson, along with livestock difficulties, there was a strike in Hollywood and a day lost because of the death of Roosevelt. By June, they were seventy-five days behind. The budget had gone up to $3.45 million. The script was over 200 pages and rising. King Vidor was having dreams in which David urged him to visit a hospital, and the place became an insane asylum.

There were two pivotal scenes for capturing Jennifer's sexual glory: the night encounter where Lewt rapes her and then later, at the sump, where she dances for him. The dance was an agony. Not only modesty made Jennifer flinch. Colby thought the actress had an inborn problem in her hips. Tilly Losch, the dance coach, offered to perform herself instead, in long shot. But for David the scene was nothing if it was not Jennifer. He delayed for more coaching. He stirred up publicity and then closed the set. And they shot a great deal of Jennifer dancing, to Lewt's guitar, vamping a nearby tree. The material never worked, and there is none of it in the finished film, except the setting and the talk that followed.

The rape scene was another matter, and it remains arousing, a study in savage dark color, with Jennifer seen at first from the rear, on her knees, scrubbing the floor. Nor is it a scene in which one can imagine John Wayne half as dangerous as Gregory Peck. Anita Colby remembered that many people came to watch—never believing it would work. In this instance,

Jennifer and Gregory Peck in Duel in the Sun

apparently, David encouraged the crowd. And as so often on this film, he was there, behind Vidor's shoulder:

> I'll never forget it [said Colby] because when she was washing the floors and her bottom was wiggling around and she looked over her shoulder because she felt somebody looking at her, and she looked up, it was a very sexy look to begin with, then Peck pulled the hat off and went after her. She's fighting with him, and he is trying to kiss her and he just put his head down and got right on her mouth. . . . I can see it today.

The effectiveness of that and many other scenes aside, the pressure on the picture was mounting. Creatively, this had a virtue: Lewt and Pearl were destined for a grand death. But David had other appointments to make: August 15 was the deadline Irene had given him.

On August 10, King Vidor walked off the picture. Not only had Vidor endured David as kibitzer and second-guesser on the set. He had been expected to produce erotic abandon in an actress who had nightly consultations with her producer. And, in David's tradition, there were new script pages every day. Niven Busch was on the set occasionally:

Vidor says to me come on the set because I want to show you something. And he shows me how he's got the book marked, and he's putting the dialogue back. And Selznick is looking at the rushes and he's accepting it. And then he shows me what Selznick is sending down. He must have had fifteen writers on it, rewriting it.

There were two units at work on that August 10 at Lasky Mesa. With costs overrunning, David was complaining to Vidor about delay and extravagance. The two units were to set up that day, Vidor on first and Otto Brower on second. Vidor was to switch from one to the other to make the best use of his time. What follows is one of David's letters of self-defense, when Vidor was protesting any alteration to his credit as director. Vidor kept silent on the dispute and never gave up his friendship with David. But there was no need to speak when David's defenses were so windy:

> I went out to location and moved with King up to the Brower location. The camera was all set, ready to go. King rehearsed the action in my presence. Repeatedly I asked him whether the camera was all set and he assured me repeatedly and almost impatiently that I need have no worries on this score and that as soon as the actors were rehearsed, we would knock off the scene. When the rehearsal was finished, King moved over to shoot the scene and I went to a trailer to get caught up on some other work. Hours later, I went back to the

D.O.S. and King Vidor, on location

set to see how it was progressing and, to my horror, discovered that once again King had completely changed the setup and had ordered tracks built. . . .

When I took King to task, he quit; apparently basing his resignation upon the oldfashioned notion that he was indispensable. Fortunately, I am not a producer who ever had to crawl before unprofessional behavior of this type, and I was able to pick up on the setup, having in any case supervised in detail all the direction of the picture.

In a bizarre way, the picture began again. David hired William Dieterle to assist him. He wrote a whole new opening—the saloon dance by Tilly Losch and the Herbert Marshall scenes—to "explain" Pearl's mixed racial origins. The costs mounted further still. Vidor was one of the best American directors—but David could not see such practitioners as more than the producer's designated agents. It was confusion and megalomania up on Lasky Mesa. Yet it was also a sign of the naive artist in David, the wish to make all of a film himself, the assurance that he could have directed if he had not had better things to do. Whereas the look of the rape scene and the frenzy of the finale are in Vidor's composition, timing, and lustiness. Yet none of those things would have existed but for David. He had *seen* what *Duel in the Sun* could be. He had made it Pearl's story, and he had found its raw, bloody gold of *amour fou. Duel in the Sun* is still precariously pitched between the awesome and the ridiculous. But time has not tamed it. David was crazy and in love. *Duel* is truer than all his love letters. He was mad about Jennifer, and the feeling will show forever.

4 · THE DAY HAS COME

DAVID HAD MADE frantic efforts in the first six months of 1945 to believe life with Irene might go on as before, that somehow daily routines could wash away deadline. He met with Ben Hecht and Hitchcock on the plans for *Notorious*; he conferred with Dore Schary on other pictures; he saw the stills done of Jennifer at Paramount for *Love Letters* and wondered again why "those she makes for us are so invariably poor by comparison"—so he gave orders for the veteran director Josef von Sternberg, the Svengali of Dietrich, to come to their aid; he had evening sessions with Dr. Romm; he asked Anita Colby to take his niece Joan shopping so she could be outfitted for Dana Hall prep school; he told his secretary that no new secretary could be hired for Jennifer until he, D.O.S., had vetted her.

What should a man do with a wife and a mistress needing him and with a big film in turmoil? He might leave the country. From Paris, in March, Bill Paley wrote wondering if David was available for a European assignment. To most men, that offer would have been the final impossibility. But for David, it was a phantom of rescue. He cabled Bill:

> Terribly excited about the idea of coming over but do you not think it might put me in an embarrassing position just as the shooting ends. Could you tell me how long the job would take more about what it would be and whether in uniform etcetera. . . . Will eagerly await reply. Believe it would not take me more than two weeks notice to get things organized so I could leave even though I am in middle of production.

But like so many Paley notions, this one died away in the rush of other things.

On April 2, Irene had her birthday (her thirty-eighth), and on the twenty-ninth they faced their fifteenth wedding anniversary. David got her a $60,000 diamond bracelet and wrote a card:

> *One more tear;*
> *One more drink;*
> *One more year;*
> *One more link. . . .*

She said she couldn't wear it. He begged her. For show. For the sake of the big party he was throwing. She wore it. The party had another sensation to help distract from the unease at Summit Drive. This was the night when Errol Flynn spoke badly about one of the women to whom John Huston had been attached "and still regarded with deep affection." The two men went down to the bottom of the garden and for the best part of an hour endeavored to beat each other inert. They were seen, staggering about, in the headlights as guests started to leave. David was called—his home, his party—and he decided that, since Flynn must be in the wrong, as host he should assist Huston. There was more name-calling before Flynn was taken to the hospital with broken ribs and Huston was assisted back to the house. He slept the night in David's bed, with Irene putting compresses on his battered face.

In her book, Irene says David was reluctant to try more therapy. But on May 6 he went off to the East for a month, having made sure May Romm would be there, too. He had meetings with her (at the Waldorf, presumably), and then one night he took her for cocktails, dinner, and the theater. He was touching some old bases—looking for advice and reassurance. He saw Joan Fontaine in New York, and twice he took Laura Harding to the theater—to see *Oklahoma!* and *A Bell for Adano*. He slipped in and out of Washington, and had time for a weekend at the Paleys' Long Island estate, Kiluna Farm, in Manhasset. Only Dorothy was there; Bill was still in Europe: on May 9 he visited Dachau.

A young newspaperman was at Kiluna, Paul MacNamara. He observed a conversation between David and Herbert Bayard Swope, but Swope could never get a word in edgeways. MacNamara was fascinated:

> I instantly liked this slightly disheveled fellow with the pleasant voice and the eloquent way of talking. I was fascinated with the way he handled an endless chain of cigarettes, at the same time waving his well-shaped hands to emphasize his conversation. I found that his hands were necessary for him to make a point. With his hands in his pockets, David was a mumbler.

David invited "Mac" to lunch next day at the Colony and offered him a job. MacNamara had never worked in movies before, yet David appointed him on the spot his new director of publicity—be on the coast in ten days. "What do you say? . . . It will be a lot more exciting than what you're doing."

There was still time, on June 7, two days before he went back to L.A., for David to make an inspection tour of Deerfield Academy: it was his and Irene's plan to start Jeffrey as a boarder there one day. He went into the hospital for an overnight checkup on June 19, and he was seeing May Romm in July and August, while spending many days on the set with *Duel in the Sun*. Atom bombs were dropped on Japan, and David was getting three hours' sleep a night.

Irene reminded David that August 15 would be the day, for Jeffrey would be back from camp. The boys would have to be told; official announcements would need to be made. Irene let her father know what was coming. She launched into explanations, but L.B. cut her off, "Enough, enough. Don't make it too complicated. It went to his head." He offered and she accepted the services of MGM for her separation announcement.

She feared breaking down, so she planned a dinner party for when she would be on her own, and she sketched out the doorway farewell—Scarlett quitting Rhett now?—"I would kick over the traces along with the restraints of a lifetime and give him a good swift one in the behind. The thought kept me vertical."

August 15 brought unconditional surrender in Japan, the end of war.

After breakfast on that Wednesday, she told him, "The terrible day has come." He pretended he had made no plans—should he go live with his mother at the Beverly Wilshire? She went to the MGM office to handle the press statement, and when she got back David had done nothing to pack. What should he do? What had he expected? she asked. "Was he relying on his luck?"

"Frankly," said David, "yes. I had no other choice."

So she told him the news would be on the stands in hours. She had handled it, and gradually she got Farr, the butler, to start him packing.

Jeffrey had been home from camp only a day or two when he was asked to go to his father's room:

> It was four-thirty, five o'clock. He was seated in his favorite chair, which had a footrest which was always alongside the chair. . . . My mother was seated on that footrest. I was told that they were going to separate.

David said the words, but he added quickly it didn't mean divorce— "we're just trying a period of separation." Jeffrey recalls that in that same talk David said he would be renting the Miriam Hopkins house on Tower Grove Drive, a house Jeffrey knew,

> and he would see more of me, not less of me. I was in tears. I'm not sure, today, what upset me the most. . . . I think perturbation of the established order of things. A fear of what other changes might be in store, which may be hindsight talking. Or the real dread that they would get married to somebody else.

He was told he was being sent off to school and that he and Irene would be leaving for New York after Labor Day. Danny would stay in L.A. with the servants. David was crying by then, and Jeffrey was sent from the room to see Farr carrying suitcases out to the car.

Danny was next. He remembers seeing his mother first and then his father. David also told Danny that it might be only temporary:

> I think Dad was the one who tried to minimize it. . . . She was quite strong about it. I said, "Are you sure, so you really want to do this?" "Yes, yes." He sounded upset and reluctant, whereas she sounded like she had instigated it. Certainly, there was no inkling of another woman on the scene.

David told Danny, too, that now he could see more of him, not less. In their own separate ways, the boys discovered this was so. But at the time no one had calm enough to observe the irony whereby, away from the family home, a father might see more of his sons. Irene was once talking about an occasion when all four of them—parents and boys—were having a discussion together in the living room at Summit Drive. Asked when this had occurred, she worked it out that, if it was all four of them together in that rare room, then "it must have been after the separation."

Cars took luggage up the hill for the next few days: the Tower Grove house was only a mile to the north, but several hundred feet higher. (David had booked it in advance.) Jeffrey was sent off to see May Romm; he thinks he stayed with her one night. A few days later, he had a talk with David alone. "He said no, he didn't want it. Mother wanted it. He was hoping that she would change her mind and that the trial separation would prove that they should stay together."

Until the fifteenth, David and Irene acted as a unit. August 17 was Jock's birthday, and so they sent him a gift. His reply was distraught: "I cannot accept the concept that you can be irrevocably unjoined," he wrote to his "Dear, dear Selzos." He asked them to consider a temporary stay of execution:

> You haven't tried separation—a separation in which David can spread his newfound problem without benefit of illicit glamour. . . .
>
> I address this urgently to you both to postpone the drastic final statement because if I don't I may soon be simply discussing the post mortem with you separately. If that time must come I shall accuse David that this is the culmination of his only distressing—but none the less determining—quality of weakness; that of self-indulgence.

A story did run in the papers. Within hours Irene received baskets of flowers from the wives of Sam Goldwyn, Hal Wallis, and Darryl Zanuck. "Make what you will of it," she wrote forty years later.

A lot of stories ran: the press had been aware of the Jennifer Jones angle, yet restrained. On August 24, Louella Parsons wrote a sad commentary with quotes from the leading parties. Irene said, "We haven't been getting along and under those conditions the only thing to do was separate. Neither of us plans a divorce." David was in agreement: "I can't think our separation is final. We have been married so many years and I still consider Irene the most brilliant and beautiful woman I know. We haven't discussed divorce, but maybe a separation will clear the air. It was all my fault. I'm difficult. Irene has taken a lot of my temperament."

She had also taken the matter out of his hands. She had escorted him to the door, in tears, with no thought of a kick. She broke down at the instant of parting when he said, "I've had the best years of your life." Her arms around him, she took him—carried him nearly—to the car. The larger door was left open. There was time and space for David to reach his decision. Gambling or Jennifer.

David drove off and ordered bouquets to be sent to Irene. He had a long talk with L.B., and then he went to the Goldwyn house and lost $31,741 at gin rummy. That was sudden and dramatic, but it was the start of a new life. The frenzy of activity and evasion in 1945 can be measured in the losses. In the first half of 1945, David gambled "normally": he lost $41,898. But by the end of 1945, gambling losses totaled $309,692. In 1946, they were $581,621. And in 1947, $255,912. Well over a million in three years. From time to time, he sent Lois Hamby to the bank with a check for cash. Then she was driven around town in a limo to pay off Charlie Feldman, Eddie Mannix, Sam Goldwyn, Darryl Zanuck, Benny Thau, and the others. Some of them tipped her $100 for the delivery, and some made passes at her. It is a town where the boys love to act like gangsters.

5 · THE WAGES OF SIN

IN THAT SUMMER of 1945, Anita Colby, a convinced Catholic, was alarmed by what she saw in Jennifer, divorced from Robert Walker and at least one cause of the separation between David and Irene. "She's a Catholic convert," Colby told David. "She's disturbed and such a nervous wreck." This Jennifer was playing Pearl Chavez, a girl lured out of propriety in *Duel in the Sun*, brought before the "Sin-Killer" (Walter Huston) naked except for a Mexican blanket. "Why don't you pull yourself together," Colby ordered David, "and give me a chance with her." A friend of Colby's, a priest, was prepared to talk to Jennifer; Colby would take her away, somewhere quiet. There were trips to Palm Springs and Del Mar.

David said, "I think you're right, Anita. Then I could straighten out my life with Irene." Every half hour he could change direction; gambling or cutting *Duel* would have been mercy from such agony. He was exhausted— but he had always been exhausted. Jennifer was hysterical, but in those heights she was giving a great performance, and surely they both had to hope the performance, the film, would be some justification, something to stun the spreading gossip. David and Jennifer had become devout sinners, in love with the sin if only because it might lead to destruction and peace. They were so close to Lewt and Pearl at the end of *Duel*.

So *Duel* swelled with romantic need and megalomania. There was a screening of the assembly late one night for David, Dan O'Shea, and Dore Schary. When the picture was over, they went back to David's office; he kicked off his shoes, dropped his jacket, and "padded about the room asking us questions, 'How did you like it?' 'Was it too long?'" The others had liked it; it was "a rattling good Western," maybe a little lengthy.

But David was dissatisfied: "It needs a hell of a lot of work," he grumbled. "I want to do a new opening—giving the audience Jennifer's early story—her relationship with her father—it needs big scenes—a train wreck—confrontation—action."

Schary and O'Shea argued into the early morning until David "plopped down on the couch like a deflated life raft. 'I know my trouble,' he confessed. 'I know when I die, the obituaries will begin, "David O. Selznick, producer of *Gone With the Wind*, died today," and I'm trying like hell to rewrite them.'"

It was 3:30 a.m. when they went home. O'Shea sighed to Schary, "He's right about that obit—and it's going to cost him."

There were so many other things needing attention and getting away without it. *Notorious* was traded to RKO to avoid more labor, and who can deny that it is as good as it is because David had so little time to interfere? Schary's next projects were also sent to RKO, with David collecting part of the profits. Thus *The Spiral Staircase, The Bachelor and the Bobby-Soxer, The Farmer's Daughter, Till the End of Time, Mr. Blandings Builds His Dream House,* and *Walk Softly, Stranger* were sources of revenue, but not true Selznick pictures. They all did well, and they could only have helped the releasing company that David was about to form.

There were domestic issues. Though on the other side of the country, at the Cambridge School, Jeffrey was getting his father's attention. By the end of September, with Irene in New York at the Waldorf, David was lamenting a letter he had just received from Jeffrey:

> Dear Daddy, Although I am going to speak to you this Sunday, I am going to take this "free" moment to drop you a line. In the first place I want to thank you for the quiz stick it was nice of you to send it. Second, I am sorry I didn't phone you from New York, but I tried the studio and your house two different times but no answer, and when I reached Boston Mother said she would send a telegram and I would have this opportunity to phone you. The school is nice except the food is "lousy rotten," and the room was very dingy and extremely depressing but it is fixed (the room) now, and besides that I am terribly lonely here, so Daddy won't you please ask and persuade Mother to stay in Boston for a couple of weeks.

With Danny at Summit Drive, Irene lived for some time on East Seventy-fourth Street at the home of Dorothy Paley—she and Bill had parted on his return from Europe. Bill was seeking a divorce, rather encouraged by what he saw in David's leaving Irene. The ending to the Paley marriage was one more result of war and of a husband's need for new conquests. But Dorothy Paley and Irene came unstuck at the same time.

When Bill went to divorce lawyers he claimed the pretext that Dorothy was seeing film director Anatole Litvak.

But then Paley found a new love: Barbara Cushing Mortimer—"Babe"—the sister of Betsey Whitney. The Paleys would be divorced in July 1947 (a $1.5 million settlement going to Dorothy). Bill and Babe were married four days later, and allegiances shifted. "Jock was the most important thing for Irene," said Dorothy. "The property she guarded." So in the picking up of sides in the divorce, Irene stayed Bill's friend. "People are interested in where the power and money sit," said Dorothy.

David howled to Irene on Jeffrey's behalf that September 1945, and Irene agreed there had been some bad days but good work on a French test, and the appearance of some girls had raised Jeff's morale. Irene also referred to the anniversary bracelet: she had given it back to David at the parting. But then David prevailed on the jeweler Harry Winston to try to return it to Irene. In her book Irene says she felt helpless at this persistence, but on September 25 she did write David:

> At the risk of being slightly unrecognizable I must break down and confess that I'd adore to have it. I've even lost the most painful part of my reluctance which is probably a bit more understandable. However I do think he [Winston] ought to make a concession either in price or some token gesture about future replacement. Technicalities include I still think, if you will forgive the understatement that it's darned sweet of you. In lieu of other phrases may I say that I devoutly hope all is well with you.

A few weeks later, the bracelet arrived and in another wire, where she told him that Jeff "has to establish himself there first" at school, Irene admitted to David, "The bracelet . . . looks handsomer than ever. I am beginning to feel it is mine although only a small part as much as the gesture is characteristically and uniquely you."

While the gifts were nakedly an attempt to regain favor and wife, Irene understood that; the language of acceptance left open the possibility of reconciliation. Equally, she was already wanting something to do in New York and entertaining prospects of the theater. To assist that, David told his New York office to see she had whatever secretarial help she required, as well as a place to screen movies.

Jennifer was in a very bad state. Early in November, at the orders of Dr. Sam Hirschfeld, she was sent home from the unending set of *Duel in the Sun.* Hirschfeld "found her in an exhausted state after her long months of gruelling work on this production." Counting tests and those bizarre wardrobe trials, she had been Pearl now for a year. Another ordeal for her was the many efforts of newcomer Paul MacNamara to involve her in publicity on *Duel*—his first assignment. MacNamara had taken to the business, and David had a soft spot for him. Indeed, Mac could get away with more boldness and kidding than some of his predecessors.

"I am certainly having a hell of a time with Jennifer's 'free time!' " he would write David. "We set up a date for Monday at great expense and trouble. Everything was okay. Special photographers, hairdressers, the whole works!

"Then on Sunday afternoon—'How about making it on Wednesday?' Okay, Wednesday.

"Everything is set for Wednesday, then on Monday afternoon—'Please, what about Thursday? I can't make it Wednesday.' "

MacNamara was sympathetic. He recognized Jennifer's shyness and proposed making a virtue of it, turning her into another Garbo. But the press was increasingly hostile. The factory of fantasies, Hollywood was also firmly against divorce, the breakup of families, extramarital sex—all those consequences of encouraged fantasy. Rumors about *Duel*'s daring were now added to the liaison between Jennifer and David. Yet Jennifer resisted publicity whenever she could. This natural anxiety would have been all the greater with fears that *Duel* might be attacked and that David might yet go back to Irene.

David was deliberately delaying *Duel*, letting the stories build. But the delay hurt the budget and Jennifer's nervous condition. It was in November, for the first time, that David and Jennifer began to appear as a couple at social events: on the tenth, at the Zanucks at a dinner for Rex Harrison. They entertained at Tower Grove, although Jennifer was not living there. She maintained her own home at 635 Perugia Way, in Bel Air, just north of the Country Club.

At the same time, David had received a concerned letter from Jennifer's former spiritual adviser, Sister Ursula at Monte Cassino in Tulsa. He wrote back, referring to *Duel*:

> I must frankly tell you that Jennifer has occasionally experienced a fear as to how you would react to her appearing in this type of violent love story; I have tried to reassure her. . . . It has been a sore temptation to keep Jennifer only in very sweet parts, but in conflict with this has been my ambition that she should not forever be identified with one type of role, and that her great talent should have the free expression that is the privilege of an outstanding actress. In any event, when you see the picture please see it through before forming any conclusions on this point, because I think you will agree that the story preaches a very moral lesson, and that in effect this gets down to the simple precept that "the wages of sin are death."

A moment of humor:
Pearl Chavez poses as
Saint Bernadette

Without adequate rest, Jennifer was sent to Fox as part of that nagging contract, to start *Cluny Brown* for Ernst Lubitsch on December 3. As was customary now, David took it upon himself to consult with Lubitsch in advance. He urged that Jennifer have a week of rehearsal with costar Charles Boyer, for, he said, Jennifer's "self-consciousness and nervousness tend to result in only about half of what she is capable of during the first few days, or even the first week of a picture." Otherwise, David promised "a completely hands-off policy in relation" to *Cluny Brown*. If he wanted, Lubitsch could show the Fox publicity people David's letter because it would be wise to delay publicity sessions until after the shooting: "Jennifer has an absolutely one-track mind when she is working in a picture and any distraction from her enormously conscientious endeavors does startlingly bad things to her work."

Distraction was a small word for what appeared in Earl Wilson's column in the New York *Post* on December 15. The column reported that David had acquired a secret beach house in L.A.:

> So that Selznick wouldn't be revealed as the occupant, other persons purchased the house. Servants were discharged, and replaced with others, and finally when the secret was safe, came Selznick. Eventually,

after others visited him, his great star, Miss Jennifer Jones, came chaperoned to discuss a script. As they viewed the grounds they beheld large black-lettered legends all over the walls which shrieked, "Davie Loves Jennie!"

The sequence of events in December 1945 is not clear, but the climate of Jennifer's fatigue and David's uncertainty was brought to storm by the news that Irene and the boys would be coming back to Summit Drive for Christmas. The house had not been closed; servants had been retained; some kind of reunion was in the offing. But when Irene came back to California, David asked her to hire a guard "because he thought she would attack me."

Not long after *Cluny Brown* had started, late in the evening, Anita Colby was waiting to see David at the studio. He was in his office with lawyers. Colby had talked to Jennifer on the phone earlier that day, and the actress had "sounded rather down." On instinct, Colby called the Perugia Way house. The servant said Miss Jones was asleep after a massage. Something made Colby persevere; she asked the servant to wake Jennifer.

In a moment, the servant was back on the phone: Jennifer was in a very deep sleep, and a bottle of pills was gone. Colby broke in on David's meeting and told him the news. He said he would leave immediately, and he asked Colby to follow him, collecting May Romm on the way. A doctor was called to the house, and it was established that Jennifer would have to have her stomach pumped. In order to throw off attention, Colby drove down to the Bel Air gates at one o'clock in the morning to meet the car with the pump and oxygen cylinders. She loaded the equipment in her car and then drove back to the house.

It was touch and go. Colby put her rosary on the bed and asked David why this had happened. He said Jennifer acted things out and was threatening him: she wanted him to agree to marry her. But David had talked about it to May Romm and admitted to the doctor, "I don't know why I don't want to marry her." A few days later Jennifer was back on the *Cluny Brown* set.

David was furious at the New York *Post* and at its owner, Dolly Thackrey, a social acquaintance:

> in this case the victims include Miss Jones, a distinguished artiste and Academy Award winner who has worked hard through many long years to learn her craft and to achieve the acceptance of the American public; who, convent-bred, has lived quietly and in the most dignified manner, to achieve self-respect and the respect of her family, the nuns who taught and revere her, her two children (who, of course, are also your and Mr. Wilson's victims), and the community as a whole. She has scrubbed hospital floors and tended wounded, aged veterans at six

in the morning (when Mr. Wilson was gathering his choice and disgusting and unverified pieces of smokeroom gossip and lavatory scribbling for your commercial use), winning the salutes of Mrs. Lippman and the other Red Cross leaders for the unselfish labors which she refused to have publicized.

In a covering letter to his lawyer, Milton Kramer, along with the original Wilson column and the letter to Mrs. Thackrey, David noted "the main thing is the effect on my children." He claimed that schoolmates had drawn the article to Danny's attention.

Still, Irene brought the boys west for Christmas, and Summit Drive was much as it had been before. George Cukor was there, but David was houseguest and producer of the festivities, full of gifts and cheerfulness. He gave Danny books, records, artists' watercolors, a golf game, and cowboy clothes; Jeffrey got stamps, reference books, and a $125 chronograph watch; Irene got the matching diamond necklace from Winston to go with the bracelet. But there was some other crisis which no one can recall now, for on Christmas Eve an emergency call went out to May Romm. Her daughter drove May up to Summit Drive and sat in the empty living room amazed by all the presents under the tree, while the doctor was upstairs attempting to spread comfort to the family.

6 · A BLOOD-TINTED SCREEN

"NO ACTRESS IN THE HISTORY of the motion picture business has ever taken such a physical beating," said David. He was writing to MacNamara and Colby, in mid-September 1946 as *Duel in the Sun* drew near release. By then, David should have had no illusions about his own relationship with Jennifer bedeviling any scheme for handling her in the press. He was aware that Mac and Colby knew most of what there was to know. Yet even in interoffice memoranda to them, he could not be candid about the complication. He knew Jennifer had earned her media reputation for elusiveness.

To avoid facing real limits and difficulties with Jennifer, he began to elevate her to a glory where she could only be more uneasy. He could hardly describe her work and dedication without taking on the pulsing force he wanted in *Duel in the Sun*:

it is questionable whether she will ever get over the physical effects of the ordeal through which she went, including last but not least the sadism of the work in Arizona, during which she climbed up mountains of pinpoint stones and rocks for countless days, under a boiling and torturing sun covered with hideous make-up, with buckets of water thrown on her every fifteen minutes—all without a single murmur or complaint and with an insistence upon doing everything the hardest possible way if it would make for one tiny extra bit of quality.

It was as if he was seeing that finale to *Duel* in his head as he dictated, feeling a weird symbiosis of pain that linked action and character in film and viewer. For David with *Duel* was not just the producer, but the primal viewer, the ordering eye. Whose sadism was he talking about? There was never a movie over which David felt such passion for the imagery and sound themselves. As he searched for the right music for *Duel in the Sun*, David hired Dimitri Tiomkin. He was especially concerned to have "orgasm music" for the rape scene. He engaged the composer in talks about sex to put him in the right mood. Tiomkin arrived at a theme; he played it over several times for David. The producer nodded: he liked it, yet it was too refined. "It isn't orgasm music. It's not *shtup*. It's not the way I fuck." Whereupon Tiomkin responded, "Mr. Selznick, you fuck your way, I fuck my way. To *me* that is fucking music!"

It does not matter what the real fucking was like. The sex was in the most dangerous place—in David's head. There were rich creative possibil-

The finale to Duel
in the Sun

ities in that: *Duel in the Sun* is melodrama, cooked in the sun of Arizona and
the vivid chemicals of Technicolor. But it is breathtaking, and Jennifer Jones
was a perfect embodiment of wantonness for America in 1946–47: she was a
saint run wild. Such rages date fast. A movie is a sensation for a few months
at most. Ten years later, the fact of its impact shows how naive the world was
a decade before. But something of movie history had been captured: *Duel in
the Sun* made respectable people shudder—so they said. In its conclusion, it
dared to surpass many comfortable conventions, for a killer and his beloved
escape retribution. They wanted death all along, and they slide off into their
last great intercourse, without need of more than holding hands.

Jennifer Jones was a rare, nervy actress—but seldom relaxed and not
so beautiful that photographing her was easy. She could be very good in the
right role and in reassuring circumstances. But her private life had exacer-
bated her natural timidity, and the tireless championing of David would
prove exhausting and unsettling. There may have been an instant when—
without cunning, but with proper professionalism—she saw David and said,
"He could make me a star." She lived on to be the prisoner of his adoration
and of a career made impossible because of him. All of which was guessed
at in advance by onlookers and would not have been beyond Irene's pre-
diction. But David could not muster the necessary unkindness to drop
Jennifer. He had made her so frightened—and then her fear trapped him.

There was a lull in Jennifer's work after *Cluny Brown* and the *Duel*
retakes. With so many prospects, nothing came to fruition. Twentieth
Century-Fox had their claim on her for the *Bernadette* deal, and Darryl
Zanuck was pushing hard for more of Jennifer. But David was stalling him
with ventures of his own: he was going to remake *Little Women*—indeed, he
built sets for it and did tests; there was talk of *Joan of Arc*, though David
knew Ingrid Bergman yearned to play that part; he had a script for *Tess of
the D'Urbervilles*, written by Allan Scott, and he had a mind to put Jennifer
in that with James Mason, and William Dieterle directing; Metro was
asking him whether Jennifer could be loaned for *Cass Timberlane*. David also
was wondering whether Jennifer didn't need the experience of a Broadway
play. And, as early as 1946, he was thinking of putting her and Joseph Cotten
in a property he owned, Scott Fitzgerald's *Tender is the Night*.

Here are just a couple of those plans, as they worked out in 1946. *Tess
of the D'Urbervilles* was the kind of project that David did best. When Allan
Scott submitted a lengthy treatment in March 1946, Dieterle looked at it and
was excited:

> In the whole long and beautifully written novel I believe that there is
> one key which will unlock it. On page 434 Hardy says, not through
> a character but by himself, "She seemed like a fugitive in a dream, who
> tried to move away but could not."

According to Scott, Jennifer loved his script—"the best I ever wrote." Some second-unit photography was done in England. But then David changed his mind; he would trade the script away. His investment was $115,000, yet he put a prohibitive fee of $1 million on the script—and found no buyers.

Cass Timberlane was the story of a judge with a young wife. Arthur Hornblow was doing it at Metro, and he approached David for Jennifer's services. Shortly thereafter, David and Jennifer were dining with Leland Hayward and his wife, Margaret Sullavan. Jennifer mentioned the *Cass Timberlane* likelihood, and Sullavan, in a mood of malicious play, said, "Oh, yes, I was offered that."

Jennifer was upset at being less than first choice, and she was not the most adept in such delicate social situations. She attacked David for letting it happen. David complained to Hornblow, who insisted Jennifer had been the only choice:

> Far be it from me to call a lady a liar but unfortunately I have no alternative. Maggie was never considered by us for the part for a second nor would she be. She herself, being a bright girl, would know perfectly well she wasn't right for it.

Sullavan was persuaded to make apologies all round. But Jennifer had been thrown. "She never believed the explanation," said Leonora Hornblow. "Anyway, it began to snow in New York, and D.O.S. said, 'It's an omen— let's do *Portrait of Jennie* instead.'" *Cass Timberlane* ended up with Spencer Tracy and Lana Turner, and so a vagary of weather launched the misbegotten *Portrait* in early 1947.

Still, there was a full year in which Jennifer did not start a new picture—time to rest, perhaps, but time when she was no source of revenue, too, and already David was digging for money. There is also the chance that, on certain days, David was again thinking to detach himself from the actress. There were several press stories in 1946 that the romance had cooled. In September, in New York, David dined with a group that included a new young actress playing onstage in *Another Part of the Forest*. This was Patricia Neal. "He got very drunk, told me how much he loved Jennifer Jones, and then tried to get me into bed."

At last, a real picture opened: *Duel in the Sun* premiered at the Egyptian Theatre in Los Angeles on December 30, 1946. It was an anniversary of sorts, for the seven-year deal between MGM and Selznick International on *Gone With the Wind* would have lapsed that month. David might have owned three quarters of the epitaph he dreaded. Instead, he owned all of *Duel*. Not just the production, but the distribution, too. Weary of the chicanery and excuses from so-called distributors, he had set up his own company, the Selznick Releasing Organization, to distribute *Duel* and other films.

Paul MacNamara had the challenge of selling the film. One of his ideas had been to call up Walter Winchell and get him to run this item: "Paul MacNamara at Hollywood's Selznick Studios has been given a million dollars for promotion ideas for a new picture, *Duel in the Sun.* Anybody with an idea call MacNamara, don't call me."

MacNamara was in heaven: the phones rang off the wall. He paid $1 for ideas that would reach 1,000 people and $10 if it was 100,000. Ten thousand ideas were submitted, and 100 were purchased—maximum money, $1,000; minimum result, public furor. Pop Selznick would have been pinching bottoms till his fingers fell off.

One of these ideas was to release 5,000 weather balloons announcing the film, one of which had the number of the winning horse in the Kentucky Derby. The winning balloon was recovered from the top of a high-tension wire in Ohio with Mac and Lloyd's of London holding their breath.

The picture was talked about. There were disputes over the directing and the writing credits. There was the novel idea of opening the picture wide—in many theaters simultaneously—a way of cleaning up quickly and outflanking bad reviews: this was another of David's contributions to today's picture business. There was also, of course, the valuable notoriety of David and Jennifer themselves, which David did not have to admit or notice. The allure of the affair was being exploited, and so David courted a censorship struggle with the picture.

Even before shooting began, Joseph Breen, of the censorship office, had asked David to omit Pearl kissing Lewt as he dies, "to get away from

Rhonda Fleming in one of the many promotions for Duel in the Sun

any flavor of a glorification of their illicit relationship." Partly because the script was being rewritten every day and partly because the censors were eager to see, people from the Breen office had been on the set. Geoffrey Shurlock had watched the Sin-Killer scenes and confirmed that her serape did not adequately cover Jennifer's breasts. He drew this to the attention of David and King Vidor, who said they would take care of it.

But David had opened the picture without alteration. Hedda Hopper reared up in the Los Angeles *Times*: "*Duel in the Sun* is sex rampant. Jennifer Jones as Pearl Chavez is no *Bernadette*. Gregory Peck as Lewt McCanles is no 'Father Chisolm.' But these two are hotter than a gunman's pistol. . . . It's lusty, lush and lascivious and will make David O. Selznick millions."

The plan was simple and effective, and it was more brutal than David had ever been. Los Angeles saw a 138-minute film, and word spread. The picture would not open in the rest of the country until the spring of 1947. In that interval, Hopper and other gasps of outrage were syndicated. Archbishop Cantwell asked Catholics not to see it, and a battle went on as to whether it got a League of Decency B rating (Objectionable in Parts) or a C (Condemned).

David elected to be very difficult. Breen was grateful to magazine editor Martin Quigley for handling the unpredictable producer, who "might go off at a new tangent if you said something to him." The perennial futility of censorship, especially when confronted with a natural publicist like David, is borne out in this woeful memo from within the Breen office files:

> The duel in the sun climax is correct as a payoff on what has preceded it except for the very finish wherein Peck kisses Jones and dies, and she kisses him and dies. In this way they both get, not only what they deserve, but what they want and actually amounts to a scene of sublimation and exaltation. A great deal of the criticism could probably be ameliorated if, after Jennifer Jones' long climb up the rocks and crags, she was to fall back dead without reaching him. I know that it is more dramatic to have your leading protagonists die in a love embrace in a pool of gore, but the other ending would be more honest and, therefore, basically acceptable.

Which is why some people make movies and others go to see them. Paul MacNamara recalled a dinner at "21" with David and Jennifer during the censorship battles. Mac and O'Shea had spent the day with Quigley haggling over frames of exposure. At the dinner table, David demanded a complete recounting, and Mac became troubled discussing Jennifer's breasts so clinically in front of her. But David never noticed or responded to the droop of Jennifer's head.

Some small cuts were made; after L.A. *Duel* was 132 minutes. Editors were hired to remove the sump dance from over 300 prints—and every outtake was burned. The film eventually received a B rating, but David had been obliged to restrain his single case of personal expression. And so it became a little easier for him to begin to think of *Duel* as just "a pot-boiler."

By May, the picture opened in New York. Bosley Crowther led off his review in the *Times* with an attack on the plan to open in thirty-eight theaters in the New York area simultaneously. This was a new technique, said Crowther: "If the public's 'want to see' for a forthcoming picture samples higher than the reactions of test audiences, you sell your picture in a hurry before the curious have a chance to get wise." Still, Crowther had his say: *Duel* was "a spectacularly disappointing job," not least because of "its juvenile slobbering over sex."

As the money came in, so expressions of horror competed. On June 19, 1947, *Duel in the Sun* made the *Congressional Record*. John Rankin (Democrat, Mississippi—and a longtime enemy of Hollywood) had the floor, and he wanted to read a letter. The letter shocked him. He had read it to a colleague, and the colleague was shocked: "I took my daughter to see that picture last night," he said. "It was horrible, and even my little child was shocked."

The letter was from Lloyd T. Binford, head of motion picture censorship in Memphis, Tennessee. The letter was addressed to David, with a copy to the congressman:

> This production contains all the iniquities of the foulest human dross. It is sadism at its deepest level. It is the fleshpots of Pharaoh, modernized and filled to overflowing. It is a barbaric symphony of passion and hatred, spilling from a blood-tinted screen. It is mental and physical putrefaction.

At last, David had got Washington to pay attention.

As *Duel* opened, there had been the possibility of *Time* doing a cover story on David. Then he learned that because the magazine did not much like the film the story was being killed. He might have credited that to his friendship with *Time's* owner, Henry Luce. Instead, on January 9, 1947, he wrote Luce an ugly letter tacitly asking for the piece to be revived *and* made positive.

The letter boasted: *Duel* "will unquestionably be the greatest success in picture history barring only *Gone With the Wind*, and may possibly even exceed *Wind* in public favor and as to financial results." It threatened: David allowed that one day there might be a movie about a life like Luce's; if so, David would be "damned sure that if there was any bias, it was in your favor." Above all, it sought special treatment and mingled hopes, plans, and lies in a way that surely confused David himself:

> I have formed a new world-wide releasing company of my own. . . . I have opened the first ten of what will be a chain of at least fifty releasing offices through the world. . . . I have stepped up my producing plans and budgets by many millions of dollars. . . . I am starting a phonograph record company, a book publishing company, a theatre company. . . .
>
> All of this means that I am at a particularly crucial point in my career. I must deal with all manner of people, and with banks and other important groups. . . . Nothing could be more valuable to me than the right kind of piece in *Time* and/or *Life*; nothing could be more damaging than the wrong kind of piece. If I emerge as a figure of dignity and with my integrity unchallenged, it will be most helpful.

7 · SHADOW AND SUBSTANCE

AS 1946 TURNED INTO 1947, David seemed to have another hit. There was wicked talk about *Duel in the Sun* in the business. David had never been more aggravating than in his claims about his own literary respectability and unimpeachable dignity. The Selznick name, he averred to lowly rivals, promised "a tradition of quality." "Lust in the Dust," the lowly now responded. Moral guardians rebuked the film. Many critics were appalled. Paul MacNamara spoke of it being "slammed from hell to breakfast." But people went to see it, and David was left in the unaccustomed position of asking himself, if it works, who's worrying?

But was *Duel* a success? This is the point at which one must examine the business principle Selznick held most dear—being an independent. The close of 1946 presents an ideal opportunity for comparison between David and his friend and leading rival as Hollywood loner, Sam Goldwyn. For both men released films at the end of the year, both eager to qualify for the 1946 Academy Awards.

The Goldwyn picture was *The Best Years of Our Lives*, an astute reappraisal of *Since You Went Away*. Indeed, Jeffrey Selznick remembers being angry as a boy that Goldwyn's film had "beaten" *Since You Went Away* at the Oscars—whereas the pictures were two years apart. No, *Best Years* beat *Duel in the Sun*. David's Western got two nominations: for Jennifer and for Lillian

Gish as supporting actress. *Best Years* won seven Oscars: for editing, music, screenplay, direction, for Harold Russell as supporting actor and Fredric March as actor; then Goldwyn took the Oscar for Best Picture and the Thalberg Award. It was the cleanest sweep since *Gone With the Wind.*

In their first year of release, in the course of 1947, *Duel in the Sun* earned rentals of $10 million, while *Best Years* took in $10.8 million. The two films seem much on a par. But comparing them more closely, the contrast of efficient production and self-indulgence grows clearer.

Duel in the Sun had been initiated as a script purchased from RKO and then rewritten in 1944. Shooting began in March 1945. After 167 days of photography, the film went through more than another year of agonizing and was released in December 1946. Robert Sherwood signed to do the screenplay of *Best Years* on August 14, 1945 (*after* principal photography on *Duel* had concluded—in fact, four days after Vidor was fired). Sherwood delivered a final screenplay on April 9, 1946. Shooting began within the week, and director William Wyler was forbidden from changing a word. Production ran 100 days, and nothing more or less than Sherwood's script was filmed. The picture went into postproduction in August; it was sneak-previewed on October 17; it opened on November 22, *before Duel.* It ran 172 minutes (the length of *Since You Went Away*—yet it seemed shorter, for so much more happened in it). *Best Years* cost $2.1 million.

The Selznick picture never had a "final" script—as late as March 23, 1946, during the last retakes, David kept a unit waiting through the morning as he rewrote scenes; the rewrites imposed further delay in the afternoon by requiring a change in Jennifer's hairstyle. Similarly, the budget had to be flexible: the March 23, 1946, estimate of $2.82 million had reached $6.48 million by April 1947. The investment had to be tied up, draining away interest, for close to two years, while Goldwyn was able to start recovery less than eight months after he began production. *Best Years* cost $12,000 per minute of screen time; *Duel* cost $46,000 (*Gone With the Wind* had cost $18,000).

There must be a factorylike, productive aspect to the making of movies. It is the more vital when you are a factory owner embarked on the extra overhead of establishing your own sales force, rather than letting an agent distribute your film. Goldwyn released *Best Years* through RKO, granting it a distribution fee of 17½ percent. That deal was better than anyone else ever enjoyed—except for David Selznick. It meant that as RKO gathered its money from the theaters (*not* all that the public paid, but that amount less the "nut," the theater owner's costs, and his profit), so it deducted the costs of prints and advertising and then took 17½ percent as its fee. Very broadly—because this is the vexed area of "creative accounting," whereby a distributor can inflate his expenses and minimize the rentals—Goldwyn would have received about $7.5 million from *Best Years*. He didn't keep it all: William Wyler had 20 percent of the producer's participation. So Goldwyn's revenue was about $6 million, a profit of $3.9 million.

Whereas if David's rental income on *Duel* was $10 million, without any distribution deduction, still he had to pay not just for prints and Paul MacNamara's advertising genius, but for the structure of the Selznick Releasing Organization. In other words, although *Duel in the Sun* was hailed in its day for its box-office returns—and, in 1981, it was placed first among all Westerns in terms of rentals adjusted for inflation—still it is uncertain whether it broke even.

David liked to say SRO was the fulfillment of an old dream. Distribution, he would say, was inefficient, archaic, monopolistic, and dishonest. Independent film producers always had heartache getting their work out in the marketplace in good locations, on sweet terms, and with decent promotion. The majors had a lock on distribution and exhibition; they always favored their own pictures. The truth in such claims lay behind the very slow government advance in the old Paramount case. The monopoly was about to be formally broken—though that reform did not really give independents a better break.

People like Selznick and Goldwyn had to deal with a distributor to get their pictures into theaters. SIP had needed United Artists or Loew's, and it had been clever enough to pick and choose. After SIP, David had made his new deal with U.A., a deal so good for him that many at U.A. regretted it. Then David had taken arrogance (and greed) a step further by making up that package of films for RKO to distribute—the package that included *Notorious*, *The Spiral Staircase*, and *The Bachelor and the Bobby-Soxer*.

There was no question that D.O.S. had "contributed to" some of those films, and that broke his U.A. contract. So the board of that company, led by Chaplin and Mary Pickford, refused to handle *Duel in the Sun* and prepared to sue Selznick.

This was in November 1946, only a month before *Duel* was to open. In other words, the Selznick Releasing Organization sprang up not out of careful planning, but in crisis. Its performance never overcame that hurry, despite David's rhetoric about reeducating the stupid business. Not that SRO was simply a response to sudden pressures.

SRO would be a new company; it was in David's complete control; it did not have Irene as a half owner. If United Artists had released David's sexual fantasy, *Duel in the Sun*, proceeds from the distribution would have gone to the company that was shared by David and Irene. But why should she benefit from his dream—especially when the dream was his escape from her? Some mixture of tact and mercenariness kept David from embarrassing her. So he cut her out of the loop.

But SRO was a disaster. By March 1948, David had a note from Ernie Scanlon that said, to cover its operating costs, SRO required a weekly gross from pictures of $160,000—$8.3 million a year. For SRO was an enormous undertaking, as David vainly boasted in one of his pronouncements on the ills of the business and his own decisive pioneering:

> I was able to put into effect what I had long preached: that the whole method of distribution in the business was archaic, completely out-moded, and very wasteful. Within a matter of a few weeks, I arranged for physical distribution through existing nontheatrical channels on a per shipment basis. I was thus able, first, to cut costs of distribution by sixty percent (and this with extremely few pictures) and got far more efficient distribution.

This is one of the more grotesque instances of David writing for public consumption while trying to convince himself. He had a case in saying movie distribution was seldom efficient and never equitable. Jock Whitney had told him to shut up, stop interfering, take a vacation, and swallow the certainty that, in Albuquerque or Erie, Loew's selling of *Wind* could have been better—that its reporting of the revenue should have been more accurate. Let the proletariat of the business do it and if they cheated sometimes—*that* was the nature of the business.

United Artists was not a model operation. But David had joined U.A. in the hope of repairing some of its failings. And he had come with a deal fit to rival Goldwyn's at RKO. He had money loaned to him for produc-tions and a sliding distribution fee agreement: U.A. got 25 percent of the first $800,000 and 10 percent after that. (If Goldwyn had had that deal with RKO on *Best Years* he would have made an extra $690,000.)

The sliding scale deal was greatly to his benefit in the release of *Since You Went Away*—in one conversation with Chaplin, Charlie had told David "very candidly he thought we had too good a contract, and that he intended to use every means within his power to either break it or change it." Yet David had seen fit to prod and probe at every local mistake with *Since You Went Away*, grumbling that U.A. was running fewer ads for his success than Fox placed for the famously unpopular *Wilson*. At one point, in 1944, he was convinced of a conspiracy between the Los Angeles *Times* and those studios that put out a steady supply of pictures. He told an executive at U.A.: "I intend to go further in this business despite any attempts to gang up between monopolistic interest."

The personal rivalries at U.A. were considerable and comic. Summit Drive neighbors, Charlie and David had traits in common: they discovered young actresses. But David could not let Charlie off the hook. Not only did he provoke the U.A. board by selling off the Schary films to RKO for distribution, he was ready to attack Charlie personally when litigation broke out. When U.A. took suit against David in late 1946, he countersued for $13.5 million, highly indignant about ineptness and reneging on the old contract. Depositions were taken, prior to a hearing, and David fell with glee on Chaplin's testimony, alluding to the clown's sometime devotion to Joan Barry (who had since named him in a paternity suit):

> At the time Chaplin was trying to persuade me to make the new deal with UA . . . both he and Pickford talked about, and promised, as did Korda, future pictures in abundance, in reply to my argument that I was afraid to make the deal because I was fearful that either my pictures would have to carry the program or that they would take on a lot of junk. All three made elaborate promises. I believe Korda delivered a few pictures. Pickford delivered none and to this day has delivered none. Chaplin delivered either none (I am pretty sure of this) or possibly one (look up date of *The Great Dictator*. . .). Among Chaplin's other promises, which I think he might dislike having brought up, was one that he intended to make, in addition to pictures starring himself, many other pictures which he would not appear in, but which he would produce, INCLUDING A SERIES STARRING HIS NEW GREAT DISCOVERY, NAMED JOAN BARRY, the first of which would be "Shadow and Substance."

So Pickford and Chaplin were by no means despondent at settling in David's favor: he was awarded $2 million, but most of this was taken up in escrow holdings and outstanding loans. Only $164,000 changed hands. For that, they were rid of the sliding scale and David's browbeating. U.A. drifted badly, and lost a lot of money, until the early 1950s when it came under the control of Arthur Krim and Robert Benjamin. But the company survived.

Long before then, SRO had been shut down. There were never enough pictures to carry its operation. Those that David supplied himself were dramatic failures. Only a few of those he brought in did well. He declined others that turned out well—he refused Howard Hawks's *Red River* for SRO. And all the while, he was having to pay for offices and employees not just at home but in the world market. Even in Britain (the biggest element in the foreign market), and even when handling *Duel in the Sun*, the SRO office was costing more than twice its revenues.

By 1950, on the eve of shutdown, David was going spectacularly crazy with the waste of SRO. This actual dispatch should be put beside the airy overview quoted above:

> I repeat, and please paste it on your desk and in your hat: NOT ONE DOLLAR MORE WILL BE FORTHCOMING FROM VANGUARD FOR SRO BETWEEN NOW AND THE END OF THE YEAR. . . . SRO is going to be cut down, and at once, to whatever it can safely support. . . . There is just no further place to go, and it's the most disgraceful kind of fact today that we are spending $13,000 to *fail* to sell our product. . . . We are supporting men in the field for SRO that are too damned lazy and incompetent to go out and sell accounts because they are used to being swivel-chair admirals dealing with circuits, and because they either don't know how to sell accounts, or won't sell them. . . . Every time I saw Manny Reiner sitting on the beach at Puerto Rico through long afternoons, pretending to be working, I burned to a crisp, with the knowledge of the hard-working people at the studio who had been fired to make his existence possible.

SRO was an open wound that took away money Irene expected. She noticed the maneuver; she was as rueful as David at Vanguard money lost to SRO, and this helped her feel justified in her time of revenge. Her taste for David was not enhanced by his shouting around town for independence. David was as far from independence as any kid desperate to be liked. There has never been a viable independence in Hollywood—ask D. W. Griffith or Francis Coppola. The geniuses have to deal with the dirt, and sometimes, late in the day, they may realize how far their genius has been darkened.

Sam Goldwyn had the best working estimate of independence: make the pictures you want to make and produce them in the spirit of someone saving silver foil to build bombers; then make the best deal you can with someone who will take the risk and responsibility of selling your pictures—so that you may move on and make more. David had had the best shot at that of anyone in town—stockholders ready to bend over backward; a great deal. Nothing had been enough. He had impeded himself in every way he could find. He remained, in many ways, a brilliant producer, filled with courage, instinct, and drive. And he had not yet made a picture that the public did not want to see. What would happen if his pioneering ventured that far?

When Sam Goldwyn died in 1974, his estate was appraised at $16.165 million. The figure in David's case, from nine years earlier, was far sadder. Nor can one simply say, as an excuse, that David was a gambler. So was Goldwyn, and one of the people he played with was D.O.S.

8 · A FEW FIRST FLASH IDEAS

THERE HAD ALWAYS BEEN a matchmaker in David; it was an urge he followed in every scheme of casting or surrogate agenting. Suppose we put him with her? This is an innocent, airy divinity, hopeful, intuitive, yet sometimes cruel, and it is a kind of picture-making that goes on more easily if never trapped into real production. David had a genius for it—at picking people, newcomers often, and allowing them to flower. He loved such play, for it exercised his generosity. He might make money on it, but it was a true gift he was offering, a moment in the light so that the world discovered a stranger, even a girl from Oklahoma.

He wrote one delicious, ecstatic letter of casting notions—out of control, but so much in love. This was September 1946. Irene was by then edging toward theatrical production. She had been searching for the right play: "I wanted plays about just people in the here and now." She found a writer she liked, Arthur Laurents, and she bought his new play, *Heartsong*. It needed work, and so Irene sent the text . . . to David? Bear in mind, this was a woman who had quit her husband because he was impossible, permanently undecided, self-destructive, ruined in judgment, and generally overwhelming. The letter she got in response illustrated her every accusation, yet she invited it; some other heartsong was still at work, full of hope or habit.

David wrote back "awfully late" on September 17, "a few first flash ideas . . . before I finished reading the first act." It was a four-page letter from a kid trying to impress a girl:

> Are you sure you don't want to think about Joan Tetzel for Kate? What about Betty Field for this role? I think she is wonderful and well cast. Also I think she has a following in New York theatrical audiences. . . .
>
> Bob Sterling just got out of his contract and I think would be available. He is very good looking. You will remember him as the husband of Ann Sothern. I have a vague idea that he is a pretty good actor but I couldn't guarantee it but [Henry] Willson [David's talent director] knows all about him and is a personal friend of his in case you want to know anything further. . . .
>
> Don't jump on me, because I know how difficult she has become, but have you considered Jean Arthur for the lead? I think she is through with pictures of her own volition. . . .

I wonder if Connie Talmadge couldn't play Malloy, and if it wouldn't be a great publicity stunt. She may be ready to tackle something like this. . . .

A long shot idea: What about Gloria Swanson for Malloy? I understand she needs a job. . . .

. . . Mel Ferrer who is under contract to us, and whom we might be able to lend you. I have come to have enormous respect for his ability as an actor. He is the young man who played the lead in *Strange Fruit*. The thing in his favor, as with [John] Dall and one or two of the others above, is that they are not the usual good looking magazine cover type but that they have brains, and look it.

There were thirty-two suggestions in this letter (moreover, some of them took: Nancy Carroll was cast, for a while, and Mel Ferrer did join *Heartsong*, as director). In case this first response might seem halfhearted, a few weeks later David sent a fourteen-page letter analyzing the play, but recommending that Irene drop it and do "a distinguished revival" instead.

An idea had even been mounted within the Selznick organization that Jennifer Jones be proposed for *Heartsong*. On that, David restrained himself. But Jennifer made her own unexpected appearance in the play's life. Late in 1946, *Heartsong* was rehearsing in New York, when Irene was called to the telephone—it was said to be Dorothy Paley. Instead, it was Jennifer, and it was "life or death," she *had* to see Irene. Jennifer waited outside the theater for hours in a car until Irene was free. Then they drove through Central Park. "She was not crazy," said Irene, "she was crazed."

Jennifer was convinced she was bad for David: "he claimed his life was ruined and she blamed herself."

"He wants his children—not mine," Jennifer told Irene.

"I don't want to hear your woes," Irene answered.

And Jennifer said, "You must take him back."

At one point Jennifer made as if to throw herself from the traveling car. "David was always afraid of a suicide," said Irene. She did what she could to calm Jennifer: "I told her David was bad for himself, and nothing she did or didn't do could change that."

Some while later, after a performance of *Heartsong*, David came to Irene's hotel suite. He told her he'd seen the light: there was an abortion in the play; *that* is what had drawn her to it—it was their abortion that had made her leave him. They talked all through the night; he left only after he'd had breakfast. And Jennifer was in some other hotel in town, the Pierre, working on *Portrait of Jennie*, the picture David had decided to do—because the snow started to fall? Maybe that film was a pretext for being in the East as the play developed?

Casting is also a carousel to torture the uncertain. In *Portrait of Jennie*, until late in the day, David had retained thoughts of Vivien Leigh. He had never given up the dream of exercising her contract. He agreed to let Vivien appear in the film of *Caesar and Cleopatra*, yet he blocked her playing with Olivier in *Henry V*. The causes of England, of the war, and of their great love were always being invoked to explain Vivien's absence from Hollywood. But Jenia Reissar reckoned that Vivien felt guilty about it all, while Olivier was angling for more money and power. She wrote to David, on October 26, 1944:

> I can't believe that Vivien feels she has no obligation towards you, but she is influenced by Larry. I will put it more strongly and say she is bullied by Larry, and because she is still terribly in love with him, she can't or won't stand up to him. . . .
>
> The day Larry takes charge of Vivien's career, she will go right down the hill. . . . Unfortunately, it is impossible to point this out to Vivien, who refuses to listen to any criticism of Larry.

While filming *Caesar and Cleopatra*, Vivien suffered a miscarriage. The next year, 1945, David took court action to prevent her London stage appearance in *The Skin of Our Teeth*, without having honored her movie obligations to him. In the trial, Vivien's lawyers argued that if she did not do the play she might have to work in a munitions factory to make ends meet and to comply with National Service regulations. David's injunction was turned down: the judge decided he suffered no damage if Vivien appeared in the play, for she would not have gone to Hollywood anyway.

Yet David never repudiated Vivien. During the run of *The Skin of Our Teeth*, the actress fell ill with tuberculosis. He urged that she recuperate at his expense "and without obligation" in Palm Springs or Arizona: it was David's true generosity, even if his invitation would have brought the patient several thousand miles closer to Hollywood. Vivien chose to remain in England for a long convalescence from which she never completely recovered.

David had a short-lived dream of casting Vivien as Becky Sharp in *Vanity Fair*. But much more likely was *Portrait of Jennie*. On October 25, 1946, he asked her to make up her mind about it. She said she was "still fascinated" by the story but disappointed in the script's ending. Never mind, said David, what about *The Paradine Case*?

> If Larry delays departure for Hollywood until February and Vivien insists upon waiting for him this of course rules her out for

Paradine which would be most unfortunate since I still feel this is best use of her and I am of course still enormously worried about Valli's situation.

There had even been talk of Olivier and Vivien doing *Portrait of Jennie* together. But, late in 1946, David found himself forced into decision and covering action—of just the sort that Olivier might always have warned Vivien about: David's begging for you, but if you say yes he'll change his mind. David was a poor gambler: he wanted all the numbers at once, and in casting he was forever thinking he could have everyone. This cable to Jenia Reissar on December 9, 1946, gives further evidence of how upset Jennifer Jones might have been:

> With further reference to the *Portrait of Jennie* matter will be placed in a very unattractive and possibly damaging light with Joe Cotten and Jennifer Jones if either of them even gets the idea that we offered this property to either Leigh or Olivier and if they are ever told about it possibly by Vivien or Larry we may never even know of their offense and disappointment.

NINETEEN FORTY-SIX saw the end of the Ingrid Bergman contract. David had got himself into another awkward predicament with her, for he had been seen to promote Jennifer in *Joan of Arc*, when that venture had been among the first he ever discussed with Ingrid. No one had been as alarmed as Jennifer when she realized what was afoot, and she had stepped down.

Ingrid was still fond of David, still inclined to speak of him as her father. She would agree later that she and David had done well out of the association. She had won the Oscar and become a great star. He had profited enormously. In terms of reckless, romantic self-delusion and self-promotion, there was little to choose between them. In person, their farewell could have been warm, noisy, and prolonged. What everyone loved in David was the fun he organized, the easy, quick intimacy, the talk and the sympathy. He could have said good-bye to Ingrid with a dinner, a kiss and a hug, and maybe a clumsy enactment. Instead, he wrote her a letter.

It is among his most inventive and inspired—for it is a letter as if written from Ingrid to David. The purpose is to rub Ingrid's nose in her own good fortune and ingratitude. Interminably, and in her voice, it points out the lengths of wisdom and forgiveness to which David went on her behalf: the parts he won for her against great odds, the films he knew were worthless but which he let her make because she was so much in love with them, the sacrifices he made, her final heartlessness. It is a great idea for a letter, but one that a grown man should have abandoned in the morning:

> During the entire period of my many years with you, I was never directed to do a picture I did not want to do.
>
> During the entire period of my many years with you, there was not a single picture in the entire industry that I wanted to make that you did not secure for me. . . .
>
> When everyone else in Hollywood disbelieved in me and wondered why you had brought me over, and through the long period when you couldn't lend me to anyone, and through the secondary period when you were lending me at cost and at less than cost, you insisted that I was the great actress of this generation. . . .

Then there was a might-have-been. There was always Dorothy McGuire to cast, and all over Europe David had monies he could not get back to America because of limits on postwar currency exchange. There were kronor in Sweden, the profits for *Wind* and *Rebecca*, accounts receivable not yet received. And so he had the idea of making a version of Ibsen's *A Doll's House* based in Sweden, with McGuire as Nora. Once again, the indefatigable Jenia Reissar was involved in setting up the picture.

The film was to be shot in Norway with an American cast and a Swedish crew; the budget was only $214,000; Sweden's foremost director, Alf Sjöberg, was hired; and for the script, Reissar reported:

> People here also agreed that Bergman is one of the very best script-writers in Sweden. He is a queer looking individual: very young, terribly thin and tall, with hair almost down to his shoulders, and huge eyes deep in his head. He speaks little English, but said he understood me very well.

Thus, for $17,000, half in dollars and half in kronor, the twenty-nine-year-old Ingmar Bergman was the employee of David Selznick. He even gave the Ibsen play a more "positive" ending. But David didn't like the script, and the more he thought about the idea (with Robert Mitchum or Walter Pidgeon as the husband), the less he liked it. He thought of hiring Lillian Hellman for a rewrite. In the end, the project came to nothing but ill feeling and wasted investment. And David felt wronged:

> In addition, there was all the time that all of us, including yourself, spent on the deal, and all the great expense on both sides of the ocean; all the disappointments and embarrassment and damage in not going ahead. And why did we not go ahead? It was not through any fault of our own, but because they turned in a wretched script.

The fault in those years was always someone else's. The Bergman script remains in the Selznick files, and it is as odd as you might expect from this bold venture. Had it been made, the picture might have been awful—or the indication of a way ahead in world cinema. But in all the correspondence about *A Doll's House* there is not one hint that David ever noticed a play about a wife who has to get out of her husband's house.

9 · THE VERGE OF COLLAPSE

THE CLAMOR OVER *Duel in the Sun* corresponded with the intensity of his effort and belief. David could feel in touch, still, close to the audience, a showman at his peak. Now came a new experience. Crowded out with desirable projects and impressive scripts, still the master of many contracts, David embarked on *The Paradine Case*, his first complete failure since going independent. He wondered quite why he was doing it from the start of shooting. *Paradine* owed itself to the dying fall of helpless momentum: we make pictures—we have a distribution company that needs product—let us therefore make something.

The several actors for whom the film was a great opportunity—Alida Valli, Ann Todd, Louis Jourdan—had to swallow disappointment. For its star, Gregory Peck, it was a picture to forget or to burn. As for its director, Alfred Hitchcock, he fell into the view that *Paradine* was not just his last picture for Selznick, but a proof of why there should be no more.

The Paradine Case was a novel by Robert Hichens, published in 1933, in which Mrs. Ingrid Paradine (Danish father and Swedish mother) is accused of poisoning her husband, a military hero, Colonel Paradine. A lawyer defends her and, despite his successful career and marriage, falls disastrously in love with his client. Mrs. Paradine is acquitted, but she kills herself.

In June 1933, not long after he joined MGM, David had received an encouraging report on the novel from Franclien Macconnell:

A glove-fitting role for Garbo but an unwieldy story that will need considerable adjustment for the screen since, as it now stands, it is emphatically the man's story.

At David's urging, MGM purchased the rights to the book and had a script done, but the project never developed or provoked Garbo's interest.

In 1933, it was seen as the story of an unhappy, romantic woman, another chapter in Garbo's star-crossed love life on screen. David never lost that first understanding, and thirteen years later he had experience to reinforce it.

He bought the rights from Metro for $60,000, and by the spring of 1946 he had satisfied himself that Garbo was still averse to it—though David was then seriously campaigning for Garbo's return (as his seven-year contract player) and talking to her about *The Scarlet Lily* or a life of Sarah Bernhardt. But David let Hitchcock and his wife, Alma Reville, do a new adaptation of the book, and he then yielded to Hitchcock's advice, that James Bridie do a script.

What emerged was too poor to be shown to actors. So again, David became his own scriptwriter. Insuperable problems followed: the dialogue is often stilted when it needs to be hard and intimate—for by 1946–47, *The Paradine Case* should have been a film noir. Worse than that, David undertook the writing when he was desperately overextended. His delays became ruinous holdups on the picture. Yet he wrote *The Paradine Case* because he felt himself the harrowed possessor of its own story. Hitchcock regarded David's writing as a measure of vanity and inefficiency. But Hitchcock put less trust in the heart's conviction than David, and *Paradine* has been curiously overlooked as the confession of its producer.

Casting became a battleground. After Garbo, David had hoped Ingrid Bergman might take the role, but that relationship was at its creative end. Of course, he had flirted with the idea of Vivien Leigh, especially if it would help secure Olivier to play the lawyer—or the barrister. For with the participation of Hitchcock and Bridie, no one ever questioned the original English setting. Hitchcock planned a meticulous re-creation of London's Old Bailey, and a second unit passed five weeks in Cumberland's uncertain weather getting exteriors for the country home of the Paradines. Eventually, these exteriors would be supplied with five studio interiors that went to prodigious expense to imitate an English country house.

There was another way to go, one a less exhausted producer might have seen. *The Paradine Case* could have been set in Phoenix, Dallas, or Pasadena. The same characters could have been slipped into a contemporary American setting—war hero, older than his unhappy, foreign wife, ambitious lawyer on the make, the lawyer's wife afraid of losing him. It could have been Ingrid Bergman, an Americanized Peck (or Robert Mitchum, another Selznick property) as the lawyer, and, say, Kim Hunter as the wife (another Selznick contract player, never used). It should have been eighty-eight minutes, as dark and tough as an RKO picture of 1947, and it could have been called *Fascination*, one of the several titles David was considering until days before the release of *The Paradine Case*. Val Lewton might have

Gregory Peck and Alida Valli in The Paradine Case

produced it, with Jacques Tourneur directing. At RKO, in 1947, Tourneur did make such a film, the classic *Out of the Past*. And if Ingrid was adamant about not doing it, why Jennifer Jones could have played Mrs. Paradine.

Instead, David believed he would make one more new star with Mrs. Paradine. He was convinced the Italian actress Alida Valli could be his replacement Bergman. Valli was overweight to American eyes, her English needed work, and her teeth had to be overhauled. There were also allegations that she had been sympathetic to the Fascists. Those were false, but David had to invest over $30,000 in the right places to clear the matter up and receive a visa for Valli. He had not himself seen the actress—much less watched her work in English—until she came to Hollywood. Once upon a time, he would not have permitted such casualness.

For the role of the barrister's wife, David made a deal with the J. Arthur Rank Organization in England for Ann Todd, who had just had a success in *The Seventh Veil*, a film more likely to impress David because it dealt with psychoanalysis. There were problems with this actress, too, and with the husband, Nigel Tangye, who managed her career. Todd was determined to have a worthwhile part, and in London Jenia Reissar had been reluctant to show her the Bridie script just because the role seemed "a silly society woman."

Ann Todd stayed the course, but she was never happy with her part, and her American career did not take. Another actor signed but unseen in person was the French actor Louis Jourdan, and here a special friendship was born. "I met David in New York in 1946," said Jourdan. "Immediately, I could see that he liked me. He was happy that I had come. We got along beautifully, immediately. He was saying, 'I did not make a mistake. That was the *right* decision.' "

David took Louis on as a son or a kid brother. Learn, he told him. Don't go straight to Hollywood. Stay in New York first, as my guest. Then go to Washington, "so that you have a sense of this great democracy." Jourdan reveled in the kindness:

> I did go to Washington. Then I came back to New York. I was absolutely—he was right! A lot was coming in. I was like he was, when he was nineteen and decided to read about America. Then he said, "Okay, now you go to Hollywood. But now I can tell you what you must do. I'm not going to ask you to do it. I'm going to *tell* you to do it. You are not going to fly. You are going to take the train, because I want you to have a sense of this vast country."

Jourdan was twenty-seven, dazzlingly handsome; he spoke fine English. He was David's kind of man—gentle, attentive, an eager listener, ready to laugh, intelligent, philosophical. For Louis, David "had this wonderful faculty ... to put himself in the place of the other person." David lodged Jourdan in the Beverly Hills Hotel, but when his wife, Quique, arrived in America, he decided they had to live in a house. So the studio loaned the Jourdans the money for their first house. In addition, David changed the key supporting role of Colonel Paradine's valet (and the wife's lover) from Marsh to Latour. In one way, David was anticipating the times: he had an international cast, with Gregory Peck the only American lead.

Jourdan had dined in New York with Hitchcock and Anita Colby and gathered how hopeful Hitch was that it *not* be Peck. The director had wanted Olivier or Ronald Colman. At the time of the dinner, Hitchcock was talking about Emlyn Williams in the role. It was years before Jourdan discovered that Hitch felt the valet should have been Marsh still and that Robert Newton should have played him, "with horny hands, like the devil!"

Late in 1946, David had Ben Hecht with him helping on the *Paradine* rewrite. But Hecht left on December 7, "with an enormous amount of work remaining to be done," David wrote in agony to his perennial, if helpless, listener at such times, Dan O'Shea. Hecht did return, but by then he had forgotten the *Paradine* story.

"I am on the verge of collapse," said David: he was still marketing *Duel*, and *Portrait of Jennie* was about to start. The finances of the entire organization were dreadful, and talks had begun on a divorce settlement with Irene. At last David was admitting the consequences of disorganization: "Even though I continue to work eighteen and twenty hours daily, *Paradine Case* will not be what it should be, and may even be dangerous at its cost, which I predict right now will be between $3.2 and $3.3 million, with only one star of importance, Peck."

The Paradine Case fell two days behind schedule in its first four days. The hazards were everywhere, but nowhere with more significance than in the absence of production manager Ray Klune, who had left after *Since You Went Away*. For a decade, Klune had managed the daily shooting process and scheduled around David's changes of mind. Klune had been vital to *Gone With the Wind*. He had learned how to do it, but he had suffered terribly. Without Klune, Hitchcock was advancing slowly and a rivalry had grown among the several designers on the picture until sets became larger, fancier, and more expensive.

At the end of December, David wrote to O'Shea and Scanlon, predicting a $3.5 million budget:

> The old alibi that I hold things up that caused delays and additional costs does not apply in this case to the slightest degree. The script on these sequences was ready well ahead, there was rehearsal of the scenes, the picture was delayed at considerable cost as the Production Department was not ready.

David defended himself: he had not been on the set more than a few minutes at a time. "No," he said, "we must face the fact that Hitch is out of hand and that our whole general management is out of hand, and that we seem to be desperately in need of a firm hand on our production operation. This has been true for a long time, as I have repeatedly pointed out, despite the alibi of my interference, etc. I am sure that *Duel* cost at least a million or million and a half more than the identical picture would have cost anywhere else."

By the end of January 1947, the cost of the sets had gone to $275,000 ($100,000 more than on *Wind*). David was horrified to see ceilings being put on them: expensive, slow to build and slower to shoot with, and a denial of the old Cosgrove magic. Cameraman Lee Garmes and Hitchcock were feuding. Hitchcock was falling in love with long, elaborate takes—he was working toward the "ten-minute takes" of *Rope* and *Under Capricorn*. And, yes, the script was a delaying factor. "I will take full blame for the script situation," said David. "But there is no picture I will have made in fifteen years in which I have operated any differently." That was a fearsome boast, and it suggests how far David's daily behavior continued to defy his midnight perceptions of what was wrong.

A month later, a secretary sent pages 135 through 144 of the script to Geoffrey Shurlock at the Breen office for approval, without time to mimeograph them, "since the camera was waiting." Lavishness was dragging the film down: Ann Todd thought herself absurdly overdressed in one scene; she complained politely to David, and he said the audience in Arizona had to realize her character was wealthy. Hitchcock may have written the picture off in his own mind; perhaps he was allowing disaster to mount. But in many of his own staff, David saw ignorance, arrogance, and disorder. What he could never grasp was how his own life in the last few years had disappointed others. Morale at the studio had suffered terribly. *The Paradine Case* would be the last film Hal Kern edited for David.

Hitchcock's cut was nearly three hours long. With Kern, David got it down to 131 minutes for its Los Angeles opening on December 31, 1947. It remained unduly slow and static, too full of talk and seldom penetrating. Years later, when the picture had to be shortened for television, Arthur Fellows found a quick way of getting twenty minutes out of it—he excised all the country house interiors, and the picture played better. In the end, when the costs of prints and advertising were added on, the expense to David of *The Paradine Case* was $4.258 million (nearly exactly the cost of *Wind*). By June 1950, the income from the picture all over the world was $2.119 million.

STILL, IT IS A REVEALING PICTURE. There is not one word from David on record of his awareness that the triangle of Mrs. Paradine, Anthony, and Gay Keane could be a model for Jennifer, David, and Irene Selznick. That does not mean his troubled heart was not pumping through the chaos, sending out its courageous refusal to yield or ask for rescue.

The Breen office would not permit Mrs. Paradine's suicide: that way, a murderer escaped her guilt. So in the film, Mrs. Paradine will go to the gallows, leaving this curse on her barrister: "My only comfort is in the hatred and contempt I feel for you." Of course, Jennifer was never so fierce; she could not have matched the basilisk fatalism of Alida Valli. The blond, genteel Ann Todd is just as far from Irene. But this is a film about a decent man and good lawyer, happily married, who is led astray by his helpless love for another woman. With the best of professional intentions and personal generosity, Anthony Keane ruins himself.

At one point he tells his wife:

Mrs. Paradine is too fine a woman. . . . I've talked to her for hours, and I've done more than hear her words. There's a lovely woman behind them. And I intend that the rest of the world shall see her as I do.

And later in the film, Gay Keane addresses the two possibilities of her husband giving up the case or living on after Mrs. Paradine was dead:

I hope she goes free. . . . Not for any noble reason, but because I want an end to your being all mixed up. If she dies, you're lost to me forever. You'll go on imagining her as your great lost love.

10 • A MATISSE IN TRANSIT

YOU CAN TELL FRIENDS and relatives you are working eighteen to twenty hours a day, and that *this* is the hardest work of your life, only so many times. You can warn others you will not survive. But after they have heard this dire forecast a dozen times, the friends take heart: for there you are, soldiering on, beyond collapse or ordinary, merciful illness; they conclude that the tales of woe are only a comic, neurotic routine—something David was famous for. People assumed David Selznick was as strong as a bull.

After Myron's death, he had become the only stalwart the Selznick family could look to. Late in 1942, Howard had been moved from the Hartford Retreat to Appalachian Hall in Asheville. This was not only a medical facility, but a residence, too: Howard was likely to be there for the rest of his life, living quietly, listening to music, sending postcards to David. But David suspected he would die before Howard, and he was anxious to ensure that Myron's trust fund could support Howard without the uncle becoming a burden on the next generation.

By 1945, Howard had found himself a nurse, Rose Mary Phillips, who would be his companion for many years. Rose Mary was a kindly and reliable custodian, and, in 1947–48, David paid $3,286 so that the two of them could take a trip to Quebec and go on a couple of cruises.

And David had his mother to think of in these times of violent family change. Flossie Selznick had been devastated by Myron's death: she took to sighing "on a prolonged, descending scale." One night at dinner with David and Irene, unaware of the problems in 1945, she had groaned, "Myron is gone. I have nothing to live for." Later, Irene had asked her never to say such things in front of David. "Has he no feelings?" she demanded.

When the separation with David took effect, Irene invited her mother-in-law to lunch at Margaret Mayer's beach house.

"This is going to hurt you," said Irene. "There's no one who'll be more hurt than you. But I want to tell you everything, so that maybe I can forget some of the things. But I'm through. I'm going to dump him back in your lap. And take care of him, because he's going to need you."

Irene started to list her complaints. But before she was halfway through, Flossie stopped her: "The bastard! That's enough!"

"It's not," Irene told her. "You're going to hear it all." And she told her mother-in-law the whole story—there *was* a freight train of wrongs. At the end Irene said, "I'm sorry there's no Myron, now, because there's no me. It's you and him."

Irene and Flossie had always been admirers of each other's upstanding nature. But Flossie could never like or admire Jennifer—we can only imagine how many sighing laments there were over the years that David had done such a thing.

As he had predicted, David did see more of the boys, though sometimes they felt the meetings were further penalties for their father, eating up his time. Jeffrey was promised some kind of excursion every spring break.

David with his sons, late 1940s

In April 1946, David took him to Washington, Jeffrey's first sight of that city. They stayed in the Presidential Suite at the newly built Hilton. Jeffrey wanted to visit the White House, but David said no, wait for a Republican to get elected. Instead, they lunched with James Forrestal, Secretary of the Navy, and went to meet Senator Arthur Vandenberg. Jeffrey had been given a 16mm movie camera, and he shot his first footage in Washington.

Jeffrey was thirteen and in obvious ways not as sophisticated as his father. Once at the hotel, David asked Jeffrey to go down to the lobby newsstand and get "the tabloid." A sheepish son came back after a while to report there was no paper of that name. In other respects, Jeffrey was a better traveler than David: the son took care of the tips and the luggage. But the visit wasn't a great help to the relationship between father and son. "He was tremendously competitive with me," said Jeffrey. "His form of humor with me was needling me. It was always jokes at my expense, and I really hated it."

They had four days in Washington. From there, Jeffrey returned to school while David went down to Key West for a cruise of his own, to Cuba, on a chartered yacht, with Bill Paley as companion. It was a two-week vacation, with Jennifer waiting for him in Havana. With Paley, Leland Hayward, and Margaret Sullavan, David and Jennifer decided to invite themselves to Ernest Hemingway's house. The unexpected visit found an odd situation: Hemingway had a new wife, his fourth, Mary Welsh, and a lovely houseguest, Nancy "Slim" Hawks, married to, yet somewhat adrift from Howard Hawks.

Slim was one of the most beautiful and witty women in Hollywood, famous for her taste: she had been codiscoverer of Lauren Bacall and model for her in her first picture, *To Have and Have Not* (where Bogart calls Bacall "Slim"). "Slimbo," as Irene called her, had arrived in Hollywood in the early forties, young, blond, and very smart. "Hawks brought her to a party," Irene recalled. "Tall, slender, wide-shouldered. No one had seen her before: young, poised, dangerous. I said, 'She's like a dagger!' "

The afternoon in Cuba was delicate and dangerous. Hemingway was after Slim, Slim was beginning to notice Leland Hayward, and Bill Paley quickly made a play for Slim. Hemingway felt his ménage had been intruded on, while David believed he was being snubbed.

Louella Parsons used this news of David and Jennifer in Cuba to quash her own earlier reports that the relationship was "on ice." She added that while David and Jennifer were entertained by Ernest Hemingway, Irene was often with her own admirer, the pianist Eddie Duchin. Indeed, when David and Jennifer got back from Cuba, they bumped into Irene and Duchin at a New York nightclub.

Once returned to Los Angeles, David organized the search for a new home for Jennifer. Perugia Way had too many unpleasant memories, and Jennifer had definitely not moved in with David at Tower Grove. Irene had laid down strict rules about the boys' visits to see their father then: there were to be no overnight stays. They saw Jennifer at Tower Grove and realized she was a guest above the others, yet she was not even David's hostess at the house. And Jennifer had her own boys, Michael and Robert, Jr. She needed a suitable home.

The answer was 650 Firth Avenue, in the north of Brentwood, on the edge of wild canyon country. David asked Scanlon to seek advice from Florence Yoch on a landscape gardener; it was Miss Yoch who had done the gardens at Summit Drive. As to the interiors at Firth Avenue, David wanted Joseph Platt (who worked on several of his pictures, from *Gone With the Wind* to *The Paradine Case*). David set a top budget limit of $20,000 and said Platt would work after "discussing first with Jennifer and then securing her approval."

However, before long, David needed to take over the house. He sent a four-page memo to Scanlon to be forwarded to the people "in charge." There is something of a Mrs. Danvers in the meticulous attention to what a lady of quality expects:

> I would suggest that the closets for lingerie, blouses, etc., have deep but adjustable glass shelves, mirrors inside, and lighting, without drawers that open but rather only with the shelves, so that all one has to do is open the door and see everything conveniently on the glass shelves. . . .
>
> Overall lighting should be subject to two or perhaps even three degrees of lighting on the switch, so that Jennifer can try out her appearance for day or for night or for photography or anything else that she wishes, depending upon what she is dressing for.

Because of the remoteness of the house, and for the sake of the Walker boys, David ordered special security. He hoped the house could have the same system as Summit Drive, an emergency button that summoned police radio cars. While he was at it, he called for the same equipment at Tower Grove. Much of this work was done by Vanguard employees, and when it was completed Vanguard presented Oliver & Company (the account David and Irene kept for personal expenditures) with a bill for $44,448.95.

Christmas 1946 was another quality production, with Irene and the boys again at Summit Drive. Irene got her diamond necklace from Winston, and Jennifer had a mink coat. Jeffrey noticed the increase in what had always been a bad moment for David—when Christmas was over: "He had the worst Christmas afternoon depression of anybody I ever saw. Because he worked himself up to such a frazzle about Christmas—and then it was over."

Christmas was one of those glorious crises in which problems could be put aside. Similarly, what to do about Jennifer and Irene, Jennifer *or* Irene, could be blurred in every hesitation over black or red, fold or raise. Nineteen forty-six was the worst gambling year of David's life: losses of $581,621. The plunge carried on into 1947. In February, Jeffrey had another trip with his father—to Atlantic City. It was "a bit of a disaster" because David found an illegal casino and lost $130,000. In addition, he met a salesman from Winston's and undertook to buy more jewelry: he now faced a busy season of gift-giving—Jennifer's birthday on March 2, Irene's on April 2, and the wedding anniversary on April 29.

Jeffrey had a conversation with his father about the favoritism always shown Danny. In fact, an observer would think the two boys equally spoiled. Jeffrey was now at Deerfield, where he quickly took charge of film shows. Oliver & Company supplied the school with movie equipment, and Jeffrey tied up its telephone for hours, ordering in the print for a special screening of *The Paradine Case*. As for Danny, David seized upon a short play the eleven-year-old had written for school, had it copyrighted, and then circulated it in the profession. Didn't his boy have genius?

But at Tower Grove, Jeffrey—still conscious of being sent away to school, while Danny now lived with Irene in New York—rebuked his father. David explained his point of view to Jeffrey: "The thing that's so remarkable about you is that you're like an India rubber ball. The harder I throw you against the wall, the faster you'll come back. Whereas your brother Danny, I think of as a piece of Dresden china that's so fragile that even touching it could break."

More than forty years later, when Irene heard of that remark, she said no, David regarded Danny less as fragile chinaware than as a toy bunny. She was reminded of the occasion, in '46 or '47, when the four of them were in the Summit Drive house and David was cuddling ten-year-old Danny on his knee. The spoiling, the unwitting effort to retard maturity, the memory of Pop Selznick with David—all horrified her. "You disgust me!" she cried at David.

Danny, she claimed, was the helpless figure in "the last straw" incident. This was August 1947, with Danny scheduled for surgery at the Santa Monica Hospital. Irene arrived there with the boy at 7:30 a.m. Four hours later, there was still no sign of David, and no word from him. Irene telephoned and learned he was asleep, not to be disturbed, trying to make good for so many eighteen- to twenty-hour days.

"Goddamn you," she said. "God help you. You're doomed!"

There was a blind gossip piece in the L.A. papers to the effect that some woman was holding out on a divorce so that the wretched husband could not marry again.

"There's *this* in the papers," Irene accused David, "and I think it's you and your true love and I'm not going to stand in your way. I'm getting a lawyer and getting a divorce. You marry the bitch and the slut and see how you like it!"

Danny's operation became a pretext. Irene and David were in their own spiteful rhythm now: the indecisive one and the decision maker. The divorce went ahead from that moment; the settlement began, even if it would take four years. But the divorce was necessary to define the peculiar new form of marriage David and Irene would acquire. The terrible drift had to end. And Irene deserved her vengeful scene. Danny supports this reading of their interplay. He saw his father as forever needing to be guilty about something:

> He just carried an intense and extended guilt with him wherever he went. A guilt which I'm quite sure my mother was extremely aware of and, I felt, continued to exploit. Sometimes shrewdly and sometimes cruelly. And sometimes both. She did know how to turn the screws, so I felt she was responsible for a great deal of his distress. But he also inflicted it upon himself deliberately using her as the whip. Once he got used to it, I don't think he could do without it.

Sometimes the victims in such a relationship have a way of turning the screws, too. Which brings us to the Matisse painting. This is a striking picture, the full figure of a seated woman in a purple robe and a green skirt. The woman has black hair and sharp, watchful features: she looks so like Irene that Irene had to make herself blind to the resemblance. David bought the picture from the dealer Paul Rosenberg in 1946 for $18,000 and kept it at Tower Grove framed within a bookcase. Jeffrey felt sure David had bought it because it looked like Irene—and he reasoned that that made Tower Grove a tougher place for Jennifer.

But late in 1947, after divorce proceedings had begun, David called on Irene for "an enormous favor." Would she lend him $18,000 within the hour? David gambled throughout 1947, and sometimes such debts had to be paid immediately. As Irene told the story, she wrote out the check, and then David said she should have some collateral. Irene said there was no need of that. But David insisted and said the only thing he had of that value was the Matisse. So he sent the picture to her—daring her to be its witness. He also told her that if he couldn't repay the loan within a year, then the Matisse was hers.

Henri Matisse, La Robe Persane

The painting was never reclaimed. Whenever David visited her at the Pierre in the years ahead, there it was in her living room, a measure of fidelity or persistence. She told him she had left it to him in her will, but he was confident of dying first. With affection, tribute, and great skill, he had implicated her in the gesture. She was a part of him, still, and could not live without knowing he recognized her. The picture, *La Robe Persane,* had quietly become a portrait.

II · ANOTHER KIND OF DISTANCE

DAVID KNEW he should never have begun *Portrait of Jennie.* Once started, he wrestled with the possibility of closing it down—but those contests ended in "no decision." The movie seeks to invoke the dreamy, creepy context of "another kind of distance" to conceal its gulfs in narrative credibility. Perhaps it should have been a silent film or a film in a foreign language? If nothing else, we can lay to rest any romantic hope that, because of the title, this film was a love letter to Jennifer. Yet if *Portrait* had not been attempted, then its onlooker, Alfred Hitchcock, might never have begun to think of *Vertigo*. For *Vertigo* is the eventual realization of *Portrait of Jennie*—and it is a kind of horror film in which the depths of imagination are drawn up into life and love is turned to madness.

Portrait of Jennie was a novel first, by Robert Nathan, published in 1940. There had been some movie interest in it, but MGM never took up its option and David was able to purchase the rights in 1944 for $15,000. Among his staff, some thought it ideal for Shirley Temple as she grew older: in the story, Jennie has to advance from about eleven to her early twenties. But David saw no trace in Temple of exquisite spirit or acting technique. Jennie had always been earmarked for Jennifer, though it was seldom in the first group of properties discussed for her.

It would be incorrect to assume that, in early 1947, the bond between David and Jennifer was secure. On January 15, as Oscar interest grew, David told Colby and MacNamara that Hedda Hopper wanted to do a piece, "The Next Academy Award Winner," about Jennifer and *Duel*. This put David in a quandary:

> It is more difficult for me than I can say to ask Jennifer to do these things, perhaps particularly because I realize her extraordinary abhorrence of publicity, and particularly sincere allergy to anything connected with this role, her opinion of her performance in which she is at such variance with everyone else.

So he urged MacNamara and Colby to plead for him: "I think you should say frankly that I am embarrassed to talk to her about it." He recommended that Mac accompany her to the interviews, just to allay gossip that Jennifer "needed" Colby's presence. "I know that she will do anything in the world to be helpful to me," said David, in defiance of the very problem they faced, and he gave MacNamara this tactical advice:

> Perhaps also you could limit it to three interviews, and get them over with in one day, with one in the morning, lunch with a Martini forced down Jennifer's lips, then one in the afternoon, then another Martini.

David began to give parties at Tower Grove on Sundays to match the old Summit Drive act, and just because he adored parties. "He was more fun than any man I've ever known," said Jeffery. The Sundays began around 1 p.m. and ended after midnight. Guests who came early, for games, tennis, and the pool, brought a change of clothes for the evening. There were hamburgers served by waiters on silver trays. The cast had regulars—the Cottens, the MacNamaras, Dorothy McGuire and John Swope, and soon the Louis Jourdans. But David had the knack of getting the best visitors to L.A. and the hot kids in town. In his last decade, for instance, he had the instinct to invite

Natalie Wood, Tuesday Weld, Warren Beatty, and Peter Bogdanovich. These parties are now as important to the Selznick legend as the best films. Indeed, they are like the films: grand, extravagant, exuberant, sentimental, and all illuminated by the DOS grin. "They were the best times I ever had with him," said Jeffery. As Dad, David was at his best in a merry throng.

Jennifer left for New York and the *Jennie* location shooting on February 7, 1947. David sent instructions that she was to get off the train not at Grand Central, but at 125th Street, to avoid the press. She was to be checked in at the Pierre as Mrs. Phylis Walker, "so that she is not bothered by fans and other nuisances." The same day, he sent a cable to catch up with her on the train: "Dearest Darling. At last we can be away from each other without it being a separation. I'm so close to you, my sweet. David."

At the Pierre, Jennifer wrote a note to herself that is a touching portrait of her dilemmas: She listed tasks and assignments, and classic authors to read. She would work more diligently on the script and try to telephone David less often. Above all, she wanted to be "not so dependent on other people's response to me."

As David labored personally on *The Paradine Case* screenplay, he was having trouble finding writers for *Jennie*. S. N. Behrman was pursued, but he claimed no aptitude for fantasy—in fact, he did read and criticize some of the subsequent versions: a script by Peter Berneis, a new adaptation by Leonardo Bercovici, and a rewritten script by Paul Osborn. Needless to say, David was himself a supplier of new pages and dramatic reappraisals. At one point, he even called in the great stage producer of the 1930s, Jed Harris, so much on the slide by 1947 that he could be expected to provide advice in return for a loan. Harris's account of the meeting gives a portrait of David's state:

> It is now clear to me that, wallowing around in your bathrobe, as you were, answering offstage telephones, and intent, as you obviously were, on making me feel that I would have to start from the bottom and that I must expect you to pay me as little as possible, you never heard a word I said nor even learned what I had in mind in approaching you.

There had been every indication, early on, that David regarded *Portrait* as a modest venture, one he might trust to someone else. In April 1946, he had hired David Hempstead as a producer or associate producer at $1,000 a week. Hempstead had worked on *Kitty Foyle*, *Tender Comrade*, and *None But the Lonely Heart*, and as he settled in at the studio he tried to interest David in *Peer Gynt*, *A Passage to India*, and *The Odyssey*—evidently a dangerous influence. By the fall of 1946, Hempstead was managing producer on *Portrait*, trying to get a good script and making a schedule. David was surprised when he saw it: "I don't understand 56 shooting days . . . why so long on a story consisting of such simple little scenes for the most part?"

The story of *Portrait* is that of a failed painter, Eben Adams (Joseph Cotten), who one twilight meets a little girl in Central Park. She is dressed as if from an earlier age, and her name is Jennie Appleton. David was never quite sure how to present her, for Jennie is a ghost seen only by Eben, an unresolved spirit needing to find love so that she can die in peace. The couple fall in love. Eben paints Jennie, and she becomes, magically, a young, grown woman before meeting her death.

This is not easy material for film, for in movies all characters partake of both the real and the phantom and so actual ghostliness is an awkward status, except in comedy. David always saw the dangers, and as he tried to discover the meaning of the film he was also struggling to find a way of making the action plausible.

In a January 20 story conference, he said, "The minute that Jennie comes into contact with outside world, I think that your whole story collapses. For then she is no longer a creature of fantasy which we knew existed for him [Eben] but actually could not have existed from the world. For her to appear to the rest of the world, her ethereal quality evaporates."

David never lost that literal resistance to the story: he was not its ideal maker, for his movies seldom risked deliberate fantasy. But as time went by, and script arguments continued (no matter that shooting had begun), he did

Portrait of Jennie, *by Eben Adams, by Robert Brackman*

the only thing possible: he began to see the story as a version of himself and Jennifer.

By May 3, David was telling himself, "If this child is *merely* real, then Eben's interest in her is very dangerous and almost psychiatric, and her odd qualities, which serve as his inspiration become confusing." He was even feeling his way toward a climax that echoed *Duel in the Sun*:

> Another thing—the double tragedy at the end. I had a feeling that's more instinct than anything else that they both should die. In our final scene when she tries desperately to hold on—"Don't be afraid, Eben. Now we'll be together. Our love will last forever. We've finished our work"—my feeling is that if he lives beyond this in view of this legend, this mysterious thing that we can't explain—if the man's alive, it's hard to swallow the legend—and it brings up many questions: If he's done this one great portrait, what is he living on for? If she came to him to inspire this one great portrait, why doesn't she continue to inspire him? Is she coming back again?

David's nerve failed or muddle prevailed: this ending was not explored—yet it is the true line of the story, the fatal closure of *Duel*. *Portrait of Jennie* would end up a confused movie, pretentious and foolish all too often, but sometimes uncannily piercing. It was another picture in which David sought direct personal expression; it may have helped him recognize the real and the imagined Jennifer in his life—and it could be an astonishing and disturbing experience for any daughter he might have.

The shooting of *Portrait of Jennie* killed a part of David's love of picture-making and shattered the last vestiges of the SIP team. David Hempstead was a drunk. As shooting concentrated on the lower end of Central Park, in winter cold, Hempstead would drop into the bar at the Plaza for lunch and was never effective thereafter. Hempstead and director William Dieterle were running up a personal expenses bill at the Plaza of $2,000 a week. Scanlon warned Hempstead he would have to cover part of this personally, but nothing was done to remove him, despite the fact that he was often heard to announce that *Portrait* was turning into another *None But the Lonely Heart*, an atmosphere picture hated by the general public. Hempstead was not closed out until September 20, when principal photography had been completed.

There were hideous problems in the first days as they shot the meeting in the park of Eben Adams and the child Jennie, wearing the costume of 1910. The cameraman was Joseph August, a distinguished veteran who had not worked much recently. David saw a pattern in the rushes he viewed in Culver City: the long shots were beautiful—those in which Jennie appeared and disappeared are still among the most stirring in all of Selznick's work, though they have a sinister quality that needs more suspense or fear of the supernatural in the story. But the closer photography of the stars was

> wretched beyond words. We simply could not release film of the two stars with photography of this kind. . . . Perhaps one of faults is make up, but whatever it is, and both angles Cotten looks 80 years old and Miss Jones looks perfectly ghastly. Far from looking like a fourteen year old girl, she looks a very dissipated and tired forty.

David told Hempstead it should be easy to photograph Jennifer, who "looks about seventeen in life most of the time." Yet another cameraman had had difficulties, and now the nearly twenty-eight-year-old Jennifer was facing a severe challenge: her face was not childlike—her cheeks were filling out—and her body was mature enough to need concealment in the costume. But David didn't like her clothes, either, or the hairstyles. Jennifer was being asked to play half her age in a script that changed all the time; it was midwinter in the park; her lines were often odd or hard to say; she was undergoing mental torture—this is the period of her car ride in the park with Irene. And, though no one on the film knew it, Joseph August was sick: he would die of a heart attack in August, still shooting *Portrait*, in Hollywood. To the end, those opening sequences remained a violent contrast of moods and quality, full of ill-matching cuts, disastrous to the film's intended tone—that of fey mystery and high-class ouija board. (This *is* a movie that quotes Euripides and Keats, with music by Debussy, before the story begins.)

Only on March 1 could David get away from *Paradine* to go to New York. He found confusion, overruns, and ineptness. By March 12, he was asking Dan O'Shea to estimate the costs of postponing *Jennie* for two months: so much of what had been shot was already on the list for retakes, and now they had to puzzle over waiting for real snow or putting down fake stuff. Not only Hempstead and August were at fault; assistant director Argyle Nelson had given rash promises, the costumes were unsatisfactory, and S. N. Behrman was still happier saying what was wrong with the script than he was trying another.

> Everything about it in wretched shape [David cabled O'Shea], including the script, the casting, and the physical production planning and management which are a tragic farce; and it may be a lot cheaper to face the facts of a delay until we can get it properly organized instead of forcing it through in this cockeyed fashion as the most grossly incompetent of all our operations to date with all the costs that will

be involved in trying to repair a mess, and in being able to repair it only partially unless we retake the whole picture.

Arthur Fellows was ordered from Los Angeles to New York to cover for Hempstead. Not the least of his problems was getting the unhappy Jennifer on the set on time. Fellows was put in a hotel on Sixth Avenue. One day he got a call from David:

"He said, 'She's going to commit suicide. She's going to jump out of the window. Get over there right away.' "

Where was David? In all likelihood, he was out of town with *Heartsong* and its producer, having just put down the phone after an anguished talk with Jennifer at the Pierre.

So Fellows got a cab and rushed to Jennifer's hotel. "I'd go up to her room, open the door, and she's standing on something next to the window, waiting. I'm telling you—she wasn't going to jump! They had a fight or something on the phone. Nothing happened."

In that risky month of April, Dieterle and Hempstead took Jennifer, Cotten, and the crew to Boston for the boating sequence. They needed bad weather for the story, but whenever they got it the Coast Guard stopped them from going out. "Accordingly," said David, "what they are waiting for at our expense is a combination of exactly the right sky, weather and ocean, which might take a couple of years." David started to rant at O'Shea: wouldn't it all have to be done again as process work in Hollywood? Why not send just a second unit to Boston?

What is the difference between a lighthouse and an ocean on the West Coast and one on the East Coast, photographically, is not clear to me.

A man wise in the ways of his own productions, David worried aloud to O'Shea that the original budget of $1.15 million was already over $2 million. It's a strange tone, and it's there in so many of the memos: the complaining, bitter understanding of a good, but slighted, number two (a man like O'Shea!) forever writing to the boss and asking, why are you doing this to *me*?

David *was* the boss. He had chosen *Portrait of Jennie*; he had elected to film in the East; he was the force generating script confusion. He was responsible. Yet he could hardly write about the predicament without adopting the reproachful woe of its unlucky victim. Most people who worked for David loved him: they lasted an incredibly long time. But he broke this loyalty or endurance in the end. Even Dan O'Shea was thinking of fresh fields.

By April 21, David admitted that if the cost had been less he would have abandoned the picture. The investment was so crippling there could be no retreat. In May, there were script conferences deep into the night: "Can't commence to tell you what agony I am going through," said David, ". . . and how much it is like pulling teeth, with Hempstead present, he is trying hard, but I just wish I could be working with Osborn and Dieterle alone."

There were supporting actors hired, shot, and paid—yet their scenes are not in the film. David Wayne *is* in, for no plot reason, yet the saloon scenes that support him and the whole business of the mural Eben paints there consumed weeks of work. There were picnic scenes shot and unusable because August had let Jennifer's dark hair merge with the trunk of a tree. For four days they went out to Oldwick, New Jersey, with Jennifer and Cotten. They had an idyllic stream, with stepping-stones over which Jennie was to dance. Jerome Robbins was hired to do the choreography. Over 100 feet of tracks were laid, and in four days of rain they got one take—which was never used.

With nothing working, David planned rescue. He would change the ending and build up the hurricane and a tidal wave. "I hope to get a real D. W. Griffith effect out of this that will have tremendous dramatic power and enormous spectacular value." He gave orders to Mac Johnson (head of the art department) to storyboard the entire sequence—he had seen *Ivy* and been not just impressed by, but nostalgic over, William Cameron Menzies's planning of so much of it. Increasingly, David was forced to reflect on what had been lost: no one had done more to establish the Menzies method once than David, "and it is a little heartbreaking to see as undistinguished a studio as Universal now use these methods so effectively while we are going back to the methods of many, many years ago, with the consequent enormous loss in both quality and cost."

In July, just as the postproduction on *Jennie* loomed, Hal Kern gave up. Kern had gone to the racetrack on a Saturday when David came to the studio with Mary Pickford, eager to show her some of the *Jennie* footage. David was angry and so he fired Kern on the Monday. Two weeks later he knew it was one of his gravest mistakes. There was still much more to do on *Jennie*: the cutting, where David had to watch inexperienced men—and there are many poor cuts and continuity problems in the finished picture; the music, which ended up a mélange of Debussy and Dimitri Tiomkin; the script and the story—there is one breathless "explanation" speech from Joe Cotten near the end, where the actor comes close to cracking up.

Portrait of Jennie did not open until a year after photography had ended—again, money was tied up. It premiered in Los Angeles on Christmas Day 1948—it was eighty-six minutes long, black-and-white until the last reel. Then the screen itself grew larger, the music emerged from speakers all over the theater, and the storm was on green-tinted stock. Finally, there was a splash of Technicolor for the finished portrait. It had cost $4.041 million. By June 1950, its rentals were $1.51 million.

David would never produce another picture in Hollywood. He was very tired: the nights without sleep in 1947 and 1948 exceeded all other years. He was demented in his private life, waiting for someone to rescue him or for events to determine his fate. A cynicism had grown in him: when Jennifer went to stay with the painter Robert Brackman to have *the* portraits of Jennie done for the film, David had call girls in his New York hotel. Maybe worst of all, he had to know he had lost touch with his audience. *Portrait of Jennie* said nothing to its age—David never claimed any belief in its occult aura. The picture is a travesty, but in enduring it he learned his ruin: as he said to O'Shea, in July 1948, doing pickup shots, trying to edit, bemoaning the loss of the expert and cheery Hal Kern:

> The staff that made the best line up of pictures in history has been shot to the four winds. Step by step they have been eliminated and a lot of second raters substituted, so that we are left with the most expensive production operation in the history of Hollywood. . . . Thank God I am not starting another picture. . . .

12 • A THING CALLED ESTEEM

NINETEEN FORTY-SEVEN was also a year of legal proceedings in which Irene and David signed Custody and Property Settlement agreements and papers for divorce were filed. But as the language became momentous and inescapable, and as the first talks were held on the division of ownership in Vanguard and the Selznick Studio, so David found time to clamber aboard Irene's latest venture, a very challenging play and an unlikely hit, *A Streetcar Named Desire*. He was thrilled with his wife's success; it confirmed what he had always believed about her talent.

Irene had two angels ready to crowd her out of her seat with help: David and her father. When she had mentioned the theater to L.B., he urged that she join him at Metro instead. If she wanted a big job, she could have it. If she feared the idea of nepotism, start at the bottom. Irene persisted. She wanted to get herself and the boys away from the "sharpies" of Hollywood—which meant, in part, the air of power her father breathed so fiercely, his hawk's eyes always alert to competition. He turned on her with

Hollywood's practiced scorn for the theater, and just because he was brutal about it didn't mean he wasn't right a lot of the time. L.B. knew he had changed the tastes of America and the ambition of its most talented people. And he was unashamed:

> Why do you think people are in the theatre? I'm surprised anyone as intelligent as you can't figure it out. They're there in order to get what you already have, which is position and opportunity in Hollywood. You have friends, you're well known, you're respected. You've got everything right here. Name one person that didn't wind up broke in the theatre.

She had never had an easy time leaving, or believing she had left, her father. Irene was deeply susceptible to the unspoken plea in this bold defense of show business: personal desire, selfishness, his love for her. "He finally said what was really on his mind—that he needed me, that he was alone and I was alone and my companionship meant a great deal. He would move heaven and earth to keep me in Los Angeles, just to know I was there to turn to." If only David could have been so single-minded! L.B. invited her to live in his house with him. But she told him no, there had been too much sacrifice: "Everyone else's interests have always come first. I must try things my way."

Try as she might to be independent, she could never escape offers of services, talent, and "advice" from MGM and from David. David had taken it for granted that Irene's theatrical career would grow out of the company of which she was already co-owner, Vanguard. But Morgan Maree had counseled Irene (after talks with Scanlon) that "it would be unwise for your operation to be in any way connected with Vanguard, inasmuch as it might complicate matters should a decision be made to either sell, recapitalize or liquidate the situation." Nor did Maree recommend any use of Selznick Studio funds: "I am under the impression that you want this venture to be one that you thoroughly control and that you would only want to have David's advice when you were inclined to seek it."

Thus Irene formed her own company: the eventual profits from *Streetcar* would not be Vanguard business. Still, Irene did employ Vanguard for all manner of small services, and she could not stop David's letters. He saw *Heartsong* again, in March 1947, when it was clear the play was failing. The production was out of town, and Irene had to decide whether to take it to New York. Changes were going on all the time; the leads had been recast, with Phyllis Thaxter and Barry Nelson (both MGM contract players). But it didn't work, and in the end Irene took the decision that David's reasoning suggested, to close the play.

That was March. By April, Irene had taken on *Streetcar*, and she was talking to Elia Kazan as its director. At first, Kazan feared "the intruder from Hollywood," an amateur on the loose, but attended by the shadows of L.B. and David. There *was* a problem: Kazan found that Irene had learned a tradition from David—that the producer was more important than the director. But he was impressed by Irene; he saw "a beginner with a desperate will to learn and excel." He found a patient, gradual, meticulous listener, a surgeon ready to pare away her own inexperience until only will and excellence were left. *Streetcar* came to life: Brando was selected, the kind of actor David would never have tolerated, and in the part of Stella, Irene and Kazan chose a Selznick player David had never employed—Kim Hunter—despite David's argument that Joan Tetzel was superior.

Much work on *Streetcar* occurred in Los Angeles in the summer of 1947—that was how Danny's operation came to be done at Santa Monica Hospital. That same summer, David had another foot in the theater. Two of his players, Gregory Peck and Dorothy McGuire, were leading a summer theater company in La Jolla—it was like the Santa Barbara season. David was a financial supporter of the company, and there had been talk of Jennifer playing there in *The Voice of the Turtle*—enough talk to prompt rumors when she did not appear: that she was afraid to do a play, that she and David had quarreled over it. At any event, David went to La Jolla on July 24, the day after a sneak preview of *The Paradine Case* in nearby San Diego.

And it was in Los Angeles, in August, that the agreements on child custody and property between David and Irene were worked out. The custody agreement (August 30) called for the boys to remain with Irene during their minorities. On visits, education, medical care, and general access, "the Parties have confidence in each other's good faith, and it is the intention of the Parties to follow generally the customs which have prevailed since their separation." David was to pay Irene $5,000 a year for support of each boy; he was also bound to pay for their schooling and for medical expenses.

The property agreement (September 3) confirmed the agreement of December 1942. Further, it defined as belonging to Irene alone the art collection at Summit Drive, some office furniture and a couple of cars, an emerald-cut diamond ring, a pair of diamond earrings from Winston, and the Winston diamond bracelet. All of his insurance policies were to be David's property.

The parties to the agreement solemnly averred that it was not made "to facilitate any action for separate maintenance or divorce," but they agreed that it "may be offered and received in evidence in any action."

Meanwhile, on both sides, lawyers began to assess ways of handling the big thing—the fact that Irene remained 50 percent owner of Vanguard and the Selznick Studio. There was much for David to try to overlook or forget—to say nothing of how Jennifer could adapt to the notion that Irene owned half of her.

LATE IN SEPTEMBER 1947, the House Un-American Activities Committee had subpoenaed nineteen movie people to testify in Washington. The committee was headed by J. Parnell Thomas, but here was the start of what would be called McCarthyism. In October, the committee heard a series of "friendly" witnesses (including Gary Cooper and Robert Taylor, *Wind* codirector Sam Wood, Louis B. Mayer, and the mother of Ginger Rogers) who attempted to be afraid of the Red influence on American movies. Names had been named, and Sam Wood had attacked the Selznicks' old friend Lewis Milestone.

To smell Communist conspiracy in films like *Objective, Burma!*, *Pride of the Marines*, or *Woman of the Year* (works by some of the "unfriendly" witnesses) was more supernatural than hysterical. But there was no mocking the moment or its dangers. In Hollywood, a group led by John Huston, William Wyler, and Philip Dunne formed the Committee for the First Amendment. They said that HUAC was violating the Bill of Rights. There was no crime in being a Communist, and so Huston's committee advised refusing to testify on the ground that the proceedings were unconstitutional. Essentially, this stance was the one taken by Thomas Dewey in a famous radio debate with Harold Stassen in the Oregon primary on May 17, 1948. Dewey would then urge against outlawing the Communist Party so that its worm-like nature would stay above ground.

In October 1947, looking for a wider range of support for his committee, Huston asked David to sign on. No matter if it angered L.B., David did sign, once he had added the proviso that none of the signatories was a Communist. Then he tried to use his connections—with Stassen and Jock Whitney—to enlarge the protest. He insisted that this work go on secretly, and he did not want to be exposed in public—even if, with Huston, he was happy to take all the nobility going. So he wrote a fence-straddling letter to the director, one more piece of monstrous egotism and a warning to Huston that David was not quite his kind of man. "As it is," David despaired, "I still have not stopped my all night sessions; and I am falling further and further behind on my own work. Literally hundreds of people in my organization are waiting for my instructions on my own business—and I think some of them think I have gone out of my mind."

In the event, the first "unfriendly" witnesses chose to argue with the committee and to maneuver rather than trust the First Amendment. Huston believed the tactic was mistaken. Liberal support fell silent. And David turned to other diversions. As Huston put it, "A sickness permeated the country."

IRENE HAD BEEN TOUGH with David over *Streetcar*. She only showed him the text in October 1947, after rehearsals had begun, too late for his line readings. David's response when he did see it was quick and crazed, even if he still found a way of insinuating himself:

> I read it instantly. I am at an absolute loss for words to express my enthusiasm. Also I am much too moved to even try to make jokes about it. If he had written it ten years from now, I would be impressed. All I can say is that we have a great responsibility to protect and foster what I sincerely regard as his unquestioned genius and that I am grateful beyond words that he has the benefit of your understanding and wisdom.

David had his own opening for the end of the year, *The Paradine Case*. But he gave it rather less attention than *Streetcar*. He was always thinking of Irene. On November 22, he told her it looked as if he would be able to come east in time to see the preview in Philadelphia. He passed on an unusually economizing note: Paul MacNamara, in New York, had told David that "night after night" the lights were on until quite late in Irene's bedroom and elsewhere upstairs at 927 Fifth Avenue (the apartment Irene had leased)— "which I thought you might like to know, since the servants may be using the upstairs quarters." His fondness now could only be overbearing; complaining about his own late nights, he wanted to be part of hers. Jennifer did not go east with David: on November 10, after dinner together, he had put her on a plane for New York and thence by boat on an extended trip to England and France—she would not return until February 17, 1948.

So, with a conscience wiped clean, David went east for the play. There is no doubt he had read it, understood a great deal of it, and seen how vital Tennessee Williams was. Yet David would never have done *Streetcar* himself: it was too raw, too sexual, too dangerous—it was not his kind of thing. Irene chose it. Intelligence and cast of mind had played a great part in their parting. She understood things that were beyond him.

L.B. beat David to it: he got to see the play in New Haven. The reaction there was mixed: "There was too much respect floating around and not enough enthusiasm," said Irene. L.B. sat through the play, and he took Kazan aside afterward—Kazan had worked for him. This is what you do, you gotta do, he told the director: "make the author do one critically important bit of rewriting to make sure that once that 'awful woman' who'd come to break up that 'fine young couple's happy home' was packed off to an institution, the audience would believe that the young couple would live happily ever after." But for his daughter, he was a stalwart, the sort of friend you want in a fight. He dismissed the doubters: "They don't know anything. You don't have a hit, you've got a smash. You wait and see."

David saw the play in Philadelphia on November 28—and Irene never knew he was there. He was just as discreet about the New York opening: he asked her for a ticket, and she said they were all gone. He persevered. "Don't deprive me," he said. She found a spare seat, a single. It was a night of reunion. George Cukor was Irene's escort. He was to host the party afterward at "21." Jock Whitney was one of the play's backers, and he gave Irene a huge antique model streetcar with "Desire" painted on it. At the theater, David was so unobtrusive, he walked to his seat "as though he were folded up."

Streetcar was one of the sensations of modern theater, with standing ovations when such audience reaction was unknown. In one night, the potential of American acting had been changed. Irene had her triumph, but at "21" Cukor was ousted again as David greeted all the guests and spread his great smile around the room.

Irene said then, and later, that she disapproved of this. But she let David take charge: the fatigued George was sent home; Irene stayed until the last guest had gone. Then David asked if he might take her home. She was drained, and when they got back to 927 she "fell in a heap on the floor. . . . He was as tender with me as though I were a child. He undressed me and put me to bed." *That* was David's kind of scene, full of sentiment and heartbreak. Then he went away, like Norman Maine at the end of *A Star is Born*.

The dawn brought reality back. David stayed in New York until December 13. He saw Jock and the Paleys, and he found time to scold Morgan Maree for letting Irene "get into a straight income situation on her play"—think of the taxes she would have to pay. (In the years 1948–51, Irene's company made profits of $245,059—largely from *Streetcar*.)

He went back to Los Angeles early for Christmas, for on December 22 Mark Hellinger was to open an office on the Selznick lot, there to produce three films a year for two years, all to be released by SRO. Hellinger was a year younger than David, a great Broadway journalist of the 1930s who had become a producer at Warners and Universal. His credits showed a special taste for hard-boiled material: *Torrid Zone*, *They Drive by Night*, *High Sierra*, *The Killers*, *Brute Force*, *The Naked City*.

Hellinger was bringing an association with Humphrey Bogart and rights to many Hemingway short stories. David was putting up $200,000 as well as the studio facilities. Hellinger had been assured of independence. His first picture, *Knock On Any Door*, was to star Bogart and a Selznick discovery, John Derek.

On December 20, Hellinger had a heart attack. It was not his first, but cutting back on booze, from two bottles a day to one, had not helped. A few hours later, he was dead. Mark Hellinger was not David's kind of guy. That could have helped him remain independent, if he'd managed to stay alive. But desperate excess could not be denied. Like Myron at the end (and Myron had been his agent), Hellinger looked much older than his actual age.

On December 23, David got a telephone call from Irene. "She was obviously trembling with rage, and she said she had never been so angry in her entire life." Vanguard had just presented her with a bill for its services— the price of independence. The bill was very late, it covered eight months, and, as co-owner of Vanguard, Irene chose to be bitter about such tardiness, just as she was horrified at the charges. These covered the running of movies, as she looked for casting ideas, a sound track of thunder for the play, the services of a Vanguard employee to entertain the boys while Irene worked.

David was embarrassed as he tried to clear up the matter with Scanlon and O'Shea. Vanguard should bill more promptly, he said, and many of these charges should not be expected of Irene. He asked Scanlon to call her, "kid her about it, and tell her it will be a merrier Christmas for everybody if the thing goes over until the 26th." As ever, David wanted Christmas without any imperfection. That year his list of presents for Irene was topped off by a Vuillard. As Irene wrote later, with justice, it was

> of such irresistible appeal that I needed all my willpower to take David aside and protest. I couldn't possibly accept it, certainly not given the financial straits he was in. "Even the boys know; what do I tell them?"

But David insisted. He said Paul Rosenberg had given him a very favorable price, and it would pain him if she refused. The spiral of possessions from David to Irene took another turn. And years later, in *A Private View*, Irene wrote: "What I didn't understand—and still don't—is why he hadn't used the Vuillard money to redeem the Matisse!" Which only shows that neither of them could face everything.

It is one more gesture in their drama, but it underscored the emotional role of possessions and gifts for them. David's fortunes were crumbling, yet in gifts or gambling he allowed no concession to good sense. Shortly after Christmas, Billy Rose wrote a column that was a pointed sneer at David and shrewder fiscal warning than Rose could have known:

There's a one-set success on Broadway called *A Streetcar Named Desire*. There's a slick and shiny whodunit at Radio City entitled *The Paradine Case*. *The Paradine Case* cost millions to produce. I saw it the other night and it has as much guts as a papier mache Santa Claus. *Streetcar* cost one fortieth as much to put on. Its writing, acting and direction darn near took the top of my head off.

You say the movie will make more money? Well I'm not so sure. On one-fortieth the investment, *Streetcar* figures to make a million or better. But profits are only part of the payoff in show business. There's a thing called "esteem." And it's my hunch any producer who bathes regularly would rather have his name on one *Streetcar* than on a dozen *Paradine Cases*.

13 · WHEN WE ARE MARRIED

JENNIFER WAS IN EUROPE for the central part of the winter of 1947–48, allowing David to have fun with *Streetcar* and spared any publicity at the divorce hearing in January 1948. David talked to her on the phone regularly and then cabled her to say that "hearing your voice each day is all that there is to life at this time for your loving partner."

For Jennifer, the parting was more complicated. On the boat to Europe, she had found that Loretta Young was a traveling companion. Jennifer had her two boys with her, but she managed to see a lot of Loretta. "Then there was a message on the loudspeaker," said Young. " 'Miss Jennifer Jones. Telephone call. Please come to the captain's office.' So she'd excuse herself. Then three or four hours later, again, 'Miss Jennifer Jones—' "

Loretta said, "Jenny, what *is* going on?"

"Oh, David is driving me crazy!" said Jennifer. "I'm on this trip to try to find out what I want to do! And he won't leave me alone."

"Very simple," said Loretta. "Just don't answer him."

Jennifer sighed: "He would drive everybody on this ship crazy."

When Jennifer was in Italy, David fretted that she was going out alone, seemingly unaware that she would be recognized and followed—"she just has no sense about these matters." When she was in Switzerland, he wrote to her about Arabella LeMaître, a young woman Jennifer had met, and liked, and who might even be employable. Anita Colby had given up her problematic job with David in the spring of 1947, and David was anxious to find someone else who could be a friend to Jennifer, her adviser, as well as someone who watched her for him.

Jennifer's budget was a subject of real concern. When she was in Paris, David nagged her to go to Hermès to look at handsome alligator luggage. He wanted her to have three initials put on the leather—JJS—"since the next time I see Paris I don't expect my travelling companion to be a bachelor girl. These are orders." Later in 1948, however, Leonard Case and Scanlon were dismayed to find that, of the tens of millions of frozen francs David now found missing, 3.5 million had been spent by Jennifer on her trip. They wondered how much of this the Selznick Studio would absorb and "how much is to be billed to Mrs. Walker."

But where was Jennifer in David's head and in his plans—as opposed to his dreams? Where did she believe she stood? No one who observed them ever saw a tranquil relationship or one in which the two parties were able to discuss matters rationally. When Ann Todd was working on *The Paradine Case* she would cross paths with Jennifer in makeup or wardrobe, and sometimes Jennifer was very sad. Once she had a black eye. There were fights, sometimes "scenes," but sometimes out of control. Once in 1947, Anita Colby had been spending the night with David and Jennifer. In the early hours of the morning she was woken by sounds of chase and violence. Jennifer broke into Colby's room, with David in pursuit: "He slapped her hard in the face and she hid in the bathroom." Colby protested, but David told her, "Don't worry. She likes it."

Another friend to the Selznicks said Jennifer was "the unhappiest woman in love I have ever seen . . . they tore each other apart. He was enough of a playboy to make her out of her mind with jealousy. She set out to find out about his other episodes, and then she wanted to take her life. There were so many times when she went off at the beach. So many alarms. But there was such a love—I don't think there had ever been the same thing with Irene. David wanted a lovely, loving kitten mad for him. But he could be thoughtless and very selfish."

Jennifer became more and more anxious about her appearance. She would change clothes over and over again and then appear for his approval.

"How do I look?"

"What do you think?" he asked her.

"Well . . . I rather like it."

And he'd say, "I guess it's because you don't see your shoulders in the back." To be an actress is to surrender to a perfectionist's craze; it is to lose substance as a real woman. So Jennifer would retreat again to the dressing room, a little older, a little more desperate.

Jennifer was an actress, anxious to be seen by millions, yet terrified of the press. She had become a part of one of the great gossip-column melodramas of the time. Her ambition could be invoked to explain the breakup of two homes. Her lover had displayed her in *Duel in the Sun*—and had evidently alluded to their sexuality—in ways she found hard to look at. He had asked her to play a child. This lover was her boss, and the lover's wife or ex-wife owned half of everything she did, and already there were voices to warn her that David's interference might be damaging. She could see how fully David was still attached to Irene, how much he needed her. She had even gone to the wife herself, asking her to take the man back. There were surely days and nights when David and Jennifer thought of being rid of each other. But they were cast together. Jennifer might be the justification for what David had done. David was that powerful, decisive, wise judge in whose hands Jennifer could place her fate. That was the dream. But there was a nightmare, seldom suppressed for long, in which Jennifer was a neurotic, dependent child—a suicide even—and David was crushing the life out of her.

And they were going broke. This was not just the plight of SRO and the disastrous losses on *Paradine* and *Jennie*. The problem had been evident in terms of ultimate personal income. For here is what David declared for the years 1945–48, with what we know of the corresponding gambling losses:

Year	Income	Gambling Loss
1945	$197,766	$ 309,692
1946	433,655	581,622
1947	102,575	255,913
1948	39,293	23,000
	$773,289	$1,170,227

It was in this context, in December 1947, in New York, amid all of *Streetcar*'s excitement, that David had had meetings with Scanlon, his lawyer, Joseph Willard of White & Case, and that tax expert of yesteryear, Walter Orr, to discuss ways in which David might buy out Irene's share of Vanguard and then liquidate the company. Enquiries as to detail went ahead, overtures were made to Irene. She and David conferred together in New York on March 7. And on March 8, 1948, Scanlon wrote himself a memorandum as startling as it is concise:

> DOS says he had made an agreement, under the terms of which SRO is to purchase IMS's interest in Vanguard and The Selznick Studio for $3,000,000, payable at the rate of $50,000 per month for five years without interest, of course, on the unpaid balance.

Jennifer was in New York then, just back from Europe. She and David were at the Colony for her birthday dinner, and then again on March 20, dining with Leland Hayward and Slim Hawks, who was in the process of being divorced from Howard Hawks and getting attached to Hayward. Slim was a friend to David, Irene, and Jennifer. She saw a great deal of their lives, and in her opinion David and Jennifer "were the worst coupling. He took self and decision and individuality from her. He wanted to have all of it, so *he* could give it to her. So he could *be* David."

Not the least irony was that, at a time when David needed income, Jennifer was not working. In London, she had spoken to the Old Vic theater, but it had declined her offer to appear in a dramatization of *Tess of the D'Urbervilles* or in some other play. In Hollywood, Twentieth Century-Fox was close to writing off the chance of ever getting Jennifer in another film: whatever they proposed, David derided, and if ever anything was workable, then other commitments intruded. But Jennifer did nothing in over a year except retakes on *Jennie*.

There is no reason to endorse David's opinion of 1948 that Jennifer had no superior as an actress. She was beautiful, and she could be potent on screen; she could also seem lost or miscast. But the best years of her career were being squandered as these tortured negotiations went on. David's protective voice was likely to deter other filmmakers from using her.

Elsewhere, David was making the name of Jennifer Jones more infamous still. In the RKO film *The Miracle of the Bells*, a character referred to "Jennifer Jones" in the dialogue as the actress best suited to play a "noble, young girl" who died. David hounded RKO and its boss, Dore Schary, to redub the key lines. (Ironically, *Miracle* starred Valli and had been written by Ben Hecht.) "Genevieve James" was suggested and then "Janice James." Even when RKO had conceded, David sent orders that every print was to be checked for the removal of the outrage.

In that same crammed March 1948, on March 16, David told O'Shea of a talk he had had with Jennifer. It is a revelation of the fearsome interaction of two indecisive souls:

> I then had a long discussion with Jennifer about the various things she has been set up for and finally forced out of her some opinions which I have never been able to get out of her before, because of her insistence that I make the decision for her, uninfluenced by her, and I finally learned that her seeming vascillations [*sic*] have been due to her attempts to go along with my opinions as they have changed; and I actually got her preferences and opinions which I have long since found to be sound and based on excellent judgment and taste.

The things Jennifer preferred were scripts for "Come What May," "Mayerling," "Trilby," and a film to be directed by John Huston. This picture, *We Were Strangers*, set in Cuba, is the one Jennifer did, no matter that it ended up among Huston's poorest or that David came close to contempt and pity for Sam Spiegel, its producer. The script for the movie had not appeared by mid-August, two months after the appointed date. And so David tore into Spiegel with the sort of attack that might have been leveled at himself. Something in his panic needed to put on record the terrible ways in which *he* was being wronged. This particular letter to Spiegel was not sent: yet the six pages were dictated, typed, and filed. Somewhere in the advancing future, David saw his vindication resting in his archive—waiting for a biographer, perhaps the only person who would ever read all those memos:

> I know you are not a very experienced producer, Sam, but cannot I somehow make clear to you that you just do not do things this way? You talk about a great picture as though the greatness of the picture were going to lie in your hands only, without regard for the contributions of the director, of his staff, and—more apropos—of the cast. . . .
>
> Miss Jones does not even know how old the girl is to be in the picture, what her background is, whether she is supposed to play with a dark make-up or a light one, how she should do her hair, whether she is supposed to appear romantic or not, how she should appear in the romantic scenes as against the unromantic ones. . . . But what is the use, I could go on indefinitely, but apparently it is falling on deaf ears. Miss Jones is a very serious actress. She did not become one of the greatest stars on the screen in productions handled with this kind of preparation, or rather lack of it. . . .
>
> You are not dealing with a Zombie, Sam, nor with an extra girl. You are dealing with a creative actress, and you will treat her accordingly. Please note that this last statement is not a *request* that you treat her accordingly, it is an absolute *demand* that you treat her accordingly. Let me also give you this, straight between the eyes: Miss Jones will start the picture when you start making sense as its alleged producer.

As John Huston would write years later of the material of *We Were Strangers*: "It wasn't a very good choice, and it wasn't a very good picture." Jennifer turned up and did the movie. Huston was surprised to find how much she required direction: "She put herself completely in the hands of the director, more than any other actress I've ever worked with. And she was not an automaton. Jennifer took what you gave her and made it distinctly her own."

She needed a few days off in November for an emergency appendectomy. At the end of the year, as *Jennie* opened, *Life* ran a picture of her with what David, ingeniously, found a snide caption: "Jennifer Jones has been variously quoted The Enamel Girl (by dentists), 1947's Most Uncooperative

Actress (by a women's press club) and one of Hollywood's most beautiful women. In her biggest films she has been confined by her discoverer and admirer David O. Selznick to simple roles and simpler costumes."

In January 1949, the divorce would be final; David and Jennifer would be free to marry. Vanguard announced a roster of films for her. She had started *Madame Bovary* for Metro on December 1, 1948; she would probably do *Tender is the Night* there as well; and in England, she would play the lead in the film of Mary Webb's *Gone to Earth* for Michael Powell and Emeric Pressburger. Then she would do *Romeo and Juliet* onstage for the Theatre Guild and *Tess of the D'Urbervilles*, at last, in England.

14 · ZERO TO THE HUSBAND

IRENE HAD BEEN gravely and persistently wronged. Though she was always in her own mind a superior watcher of the parade, still she nursed a vast pride and stealthy righteousness. She was a woman in a world that did not rate women as serious opponents. She had seen a mother crushed and a sister satisfied with unkind small talk. But Irene truly admired her fearsome father and aspired to his power. When she was very old, she could still exult at the iron in her frail body and the fierce theater in her mind: once, in talk, she reared up and cried out, "Doom to all who lie to me!," without irony or shame—yet perfect on the first take.

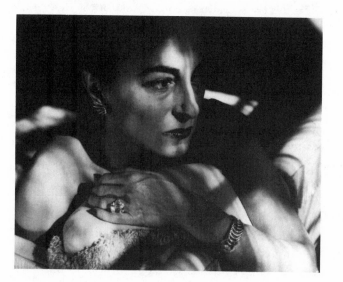

Irene solo

David *had* wronged her: there had been so many affairs and so many of them unworthy of him or her; there had been neglect and exploitation. She had had to keep her rapacious intelligence docile and well behaved, and for fifteen years her rules had been suborned, ignored, laughed at, and so finagled that she was left looking like a stern fool. It would have been out of character for her not to explore revenge. It would have been unfaithful to her father. If she had forgiven him, David, too, would have been disappointed. He was guilty, and he waited to be scourged. Only someone who loved him was fit for the task.

There was a battleground available where wrongs could be redeemed. It was very valuable territory, even if in their own emotional ways neither of them was single-minded about it. It was money.

On that August 15, 1945, Irene owned the house on Summit Drive; *she* had sent David away. With the Twentieth Century-Fox stock and the division of other income, with Irene storing and David indulging in gifts and gambling, their individual net worth progressed as follows:

	DOS	IMS
1944	$1,736,155	$2,542,509
1945	1,511,441	2,617,354
1946	1,430,843	2,977,396

Then came the meeting in the summer of 1947, in David's office, to settle child custody and the division of property. As far as the property was concerned, in her book, in 1983, Irene wrote as follows:

Then he offered to let me buy his half-share of our paintings at their purchase cost. When I questioned this as being unfair to him, David said the increase in value was surely equal to what I had lost by not taking a share of income-tax deductions and low brackets in the years of my 20th Century dividends. He had noticed that behavior and it was time he acknowledged it. I insisted on buying his half of my jewelry. I kept the house and half the new company and gave him all of our life insurance, among other things. No money changed hands, we simply "traded off." The two businessmen [Morgan Maree and Joseph Willard] were dumbfounded.

Irene had not recalled the agreement accurately or acknowledged how it favored her. She kept all the pictures and surrendered only her claim to his life insurance. By the time David died, much of that insurance had been lost, but the pictures were better than gold. In the agreement, the art collection was said to be just the "paintings at 1050 Summit Drive." These things were all to be the sole and separate property of Irene. Another point arises from this: the Matisse had been purchased after the separation, and it had gone to Tower Grove. It was from there that David had removed it and deposited it with Irene for that $18,000 loan. However, Anita Colby recollected that when the painting was taken from Tower Grove (leaving a hole in the shelving) it was because, as Jennifer told her, Irene had asked to have it. Perhaps that was just what David told Jennifer in the awkward moment of removal.

There was haggling over the company money, more messy and vindictive than Irene cared to remember. A note survives, from Irene to Morgan Maree, handwritten, undated but very close to this time. It suggests the intense alertness of negotiation and the suspicions abounding, and it makes clear—contrary to Irene's repeated assertions later—that L.B. was involved in the dealing:

> I suppose it would be petty to bring up the error about the art works. I didn't like to at the time I discovered it as (a) David had given me a $3,000 allowance on the $66,500—and (b) as DOS pointed out, the value had increased. Most importantly, I didn't want to re-open something that was presumably settled. However, do as you see fit. I'm satisfied at this point. O, no, let me amend that. Point it out (just for the record) and then *let it stand* as is.
>
> Will I ever be in any danger of having to pay the gift tax on the ring? On what else am I likely to incur a gift tax? How did I get myself into that? Just by being a good girl and offering to pay the tax on the bracelet alone? In any case, *please* don't register any complaints from me. Do keep it (this whole memo) confidential—but advise me on my questions.
>
> How is the big job coming? After all that commotion, I never heard such a silence. Has Dad spoken to DOS? Or vice-versa? And have you talked to either of them about it? Does the English thing still look so bad? What was the bank willing to lend?
>
> Anything that you want me to sign or initial re property settlement, just send on to me at the apt. (with envelope enclosed!) and I'll get it right back to you.

So many huge areas of confusion are alluded to in this memo written out on seven sheets of telephone-pad paper. Dad. The bank. The English thing. The big job. And the infernal interweaving of knowledge and secrecy.

To take the last first of all: at no time did Irene know more about David's business affairs than in this last visceral spasm by which she sought to extricate herself. For many years, she had felt able to preside over a successful operation, and she took success as her due, a family tradition. David's personal chaos was often evident, a mess tipped in her lap. But she did not have to examine the detail, and she was born to a sense of command that ignored the daily grind. Which does not mean she was incapable of detail. Irene was the sort of person who asked in advance for return envelopes and who could keep exact turns of phrase in her head over years. Like all natural detectives, she was possessed of a certain clerical fastidiousness, a torturer's respect for the rifling on screws. Irene could have run the IRS for King Midas.

Now, in 1948 and 1949, secure in New York, never a gay divorcée but a mordant connoisseur of new opportunities and a hit on Broadway, she was compelled to examine her husband's books. For they were her books, too. Over the years, she had remained aloof to the workings of Vanguard and the Selznick Studio: it was distasteful enough to be coproprietor of her husband's mistress—especially when it was a power she would not lose quickly. But Irene knew of the flesh-peddling, and she surely heard of the movies— she might have sneaked in to see *Duel in the Sun*, as solitary and wistful as the usherette in Edward Hopper's "New York Movie." Irene must have known about the crazed bank loans that kept it all going. She had to have seen the reports.

As a business, David had had a lot of revenue in the years since SIP: from the liquidation; from loaning out Bergman, Fontaine, Jennifer, and all his other contract artists; from the rentals on *Since You Went Away*, *Spellbound*, *I'll Be Seeing You*, and *Duel in the Sun*; and from his proceeds from the films that went with Dore Schary to RKO.

Against that, there had been the production costs on his pictures (often twice the original estimate), the money spent promoting and selling them, and the investment required to establish SRO all over the world. Then there was the gambling, the giving, and the extravagance with which David lived and worked. He had never taken exorbitant salaries out of the business, yet so much of his and Jennifer's living expenses were charged to it. Thus the business was struggling to break even as David made *The Paradine Case* and *Portrait of Jennie*. In just a few years, the plenty had vanished. And Irene had received, and preserved, only a portion of it in her annual dividends on her share of the business:

December 1945	$160,000
December 1946	$250,000
December 1947	$200,000

Irene was horrified at what she saw—and David was disturbed that she knew. More than ever before, she came to behold the detail of David's managerial incompetence and the deterioration in his taste. She charged that some of his new contracts were not worthy of "Selznick"; they were talent for the sake of making deals. Rhonda Fleming was not Ingrid Bergman.

Robert Mitchum was acquiring notoriety. As for Rory Calhoun . . . well, Irene could get the dirt on him from the Probation Department!

As early as 1945, David had known how to read the accounts. By being the big shot, in always changing his mind, he was suffering higher costs and overages than anyone else in the business. For years, he sang the same song of helplessness:

> certainly since we started on *Since You Went Away*, I have been scream-
> ing that our costs are untenable; miles above the cost of anybody else
> in town. . . . Such a situation is a terrible indictment of me and on our
> management, and must eventually defeat us.

The costs were one thing; overhead was another. David ran a very large operation still, on barely a picture a year. Every venture considered and abandoned added to the overhead, along with every trip, every hotel, every chartered boat, and every wonderful Christmas. But the books and the accounts belonged as much to Irene as to David, and so by 1949 he was in a perpetual alarm over the need for cover-up:

> In the event that before I leave I do not get the opportunity to go over
> the write-offs for the year, I should like to call to your attention that
> there is still a stockholder of Vanguard and of the Selznick Studio
> that owns 50%; that this stockholder and her representatives have
> accumulated facts and figures, as well as having looked down their
> noses at various accounts on our books; and that any write-offs are
> likely to be examined thoroughly and sometime in the not too distant
> future. Thus, write-offs which I might approve, in connection for
> instance with either Miss Jones' account or the accounts of some of
> the executives, might seriously be challenged.

Irene knew the people David employed: O'Shea, Scanlon, Beaman, and the others; she knew they were decent, professional men wearied by David's shifts of ground. For here was a man who in 1940 and 1941 had had the best reputation in the business, the income from the industry's greatest hits, plus contracts that were the envy of Hollywood. With what chilling ingenuity he had rid himself of those assets, using the reputation to raise crippling loans and proceeding toward divorce only after he had ensured that his wife could strip him bare. A genuine disgust arose in Irene for David. But disgust cannot kill love—it is an aid to memory.

David was terrified lest the details of his plight would leak out in the business. Driven to the point of destruction, and way beyond fiscal sanity, still he feared that bright new deals might be spoiled if the extent of his debt or the neglect of his own assets was appreciated.

He was forever begging Irene to be discreet and close-mouthed—more fuel for her dark mirth, for this woman had kept her mouth shut for fifteen years while suffering his young need to reveal every sin to her. (David had another dread: Jennifer, apparently, still had a party telephone line, and David suspected that some of their conversations had become public.) To diminish the circle of knowledge David and Irene shared one business adviser, the valiant Morgan Maree. One marvels that Maree allowed this conflict of interest (to say nothing of the invasion of his own time). But he may have been swayed by the fatuous justifications David and Irene made to themselves—and which Irene was still making forty years later, when she said of Maree:

> He was honest, square, a West of America man, good-looking, and dull. David and I could both use him because so much was agreed and no one was being greedy.

Irene infuriated David by bringing in her own lawyers at a later stage: their fees would be added to the sum total, and their ignorance of movie practice slowed everything down. More ominous still to David was his conviction that Louis B. Mayer was serving as his daughter's adviser. Irene denied that to everyone; she insisted most of all to herself that it was not so. But the documents make clear that L.B. was an active go-between, and L.B. was the man with whom David was trying to do business—over Jennifer and *Madame Bovary*, and on *Tender is the Night*, and it would be very surprising if, before Dore Schary was hired in 1951, L.B. did not say to David, come back to Metro, give up this fantasy of independence, rejoin the gang. L.B. was not just a vengeful instrument. He knew how merciless an opponent Irene could be, and he never lost sympathy for David, or admiration. L.B. had beaten David on *Gone With the Wind*; L.B. was still, just, cock of his walk, in 1948. But both now sensed their picture business was dying and felt the first cool of mortality descending on them.

The English thing was a deal with Sir Alexander Korda. Ostensibly, it was David at his most brilliant—seeing the need for cooperation with Europe, feeling the fresh approaches to film in England and Italy. The deal was an exchange: David got distribution rights for SRO in *The Winslow Boy* and *The Fallen Idol* (good pictures but not successes); Korda got *Paradine Case* and *Jennie* for Britain. The two producers would make two pictures in alliance, much more in Korda's control than David's, *The Third Man* and *Gone to Earth*.

As for the banks, David never believed in using his own money—he never really had enough money of his own for long. This heroic independent sought other people's money. At first it had been the money of the Whitneys and the Lehmans. But when David started again, after *Wind* and *Rebecca*, it was the banks' money—in particular, Bankers Trust and Security–First National. He borrowed for everything and went back for more whenever he was in danger of not meeting salary checks. The interest he had to pay in those years was only 4½ percent, on average, and for years the banks regarded him as the best prospect in sight. As pictures went 100 percent over budget, the banks carried the increase. It was not really until 1948—that most desperate of years—that the bank set restrictions on his business activity in return for more money to finish *Jennie*.

By August 1947, a total of $17.7 million had been loaned in less than five years. In May 1947, the debt reached a peak of $9.544 million. The monthly interest bill was $36,000, yet David was seeking more money within the year. He did reduce the debt: it was down to $6.950 million by the spring of 1948 and $4.226 million a year later. David was emotionally determined to pay off the debt, without seeking bankruptcy. Irene was in all of this the anxious co-owner, aghast at the disorder, eager to be rid of the responsibility, yet concerned lest her share of the business dwindle to nothing.

The "big thing" was always the sum at which David would buy out her interest in Vanguard and the Selznick Studio—and Irene was adamant that that transfer must be made. The solution did not emerge until a few years later. But the solution was never the vital element. For the settlement was a transitional stage in the marriage of David and Irene: authority changed hands, he was exposed as a disaster, and she could not disown her financial vengeance.

Dictation was the heartbeat of perseverance. There was a team of typists in the hotel suite, and the maid could never do the rooms because of the work, typewriters "going like the hammers of hell." Lois Hamby watched him once fall fast asleep as he was dictating, 120 words per minute trailing away. So she took off his glasses and crept out of the room. But a thirty-minute nap brought him back, ready for more.

"I was told D.O.S. would make a pass at me," said Lois. "He asked me if I could make a drink. He sidled up and sort of pushed me against the bar."

She told him: "Look, I was warned about you. If this is the way it is, forget it."

He laughed. "What are you doing? Saving it for college?"

"I can get it when I want it," she told him.

"Okay," he sighed, "take a memo."

And he'd laugh to show there were no ill feelings. Some women reckoned a refusal relieved him. He was so tired. But there were other typists, and some were happy to take a break. The memos, along with everything else, were a way of meeting women.

On May 4, 1948, he was at the Hampshire House in New York. He had been at work since 9:00 a.m. on May 3; it was now four in the morning of the following day. There was a deadline: at the end of the week, David and Jennifer were to go off to Bermuda with Korda. In the days beforehand, in personal talks, David had offered $2.5 million to buy out Irene. No, she had said; she wanted $3 million. Then, as a last straw, David had received the bill for Irene's divorce: $10,026.85. So he had an opportunity to write to Irene's lawyer, Maynard Toll. Every secretary had fallen by the wayside. "I am typing this letter personally," he proclaimed—but he did tell Toll, at the end of the second paragraph, "Incidentally, I am sending Irene a copy of this letter." Of course, it was primarily a letter to Irene: the bill for the divorce was a pretext for sentimental education:

> I must say at the outset that I was rather surprised by both your letter and your bill . . . (in view of the fact that there was very little to settle, even financially, by the time you were drawn into the situation, Irene already having received, by my prior action and—if I may say so— consideration on most of everything I had earned, and by passive but agreeable consent on the rest), but it certainly appears all out of proportion with the work necessary or required, or so at least it appears to me in my present financial condition. . . . Being rich through a business is a long way from being even well off personally. As you know, Irene received one hundred percent of everything left from what I had earned, with her very valuable wifely help to be sure, in fifteen years of fantastically hard and even fantastically successful work. She received in addition all the assets either of us owned—the house, the furnishings, the costly paintings (except one, fairly valuable, which Irene wanted back recently), the hugely costly jewelry, even all of our joint and very numerous wedding and other gifts. I of course do not mention what she had through her father, or what was earned on this, since I had always refused to touch a penny of this; but I hope it does not spoil what I had flattered myself was my generosity if I do mention that Irene received and still has literally millions which I made. . . .
>
> Mind you, I have no complaints about the division of one hundred percent to the wife, zero to the husband. I think this very equitable, I don't even complain about the fact that, on top of this, Irene has fifty percent of everything I have earned (and I've drawn practically no salary) through another very successful enterprise builded almost entirely since our separation, and still being built. Perhaps it's boorish of me to mention that Irene of course simultaneously received one hundred percent of what *she* has earned (admirably very large); both of you know I would have it no other way. . . . It's not her fault that I gave her half of everything that I made as I went along, that I paid all our expenses out of the other half, that I foolishly drooled away what was left of the half I kept.

This is a speech for John Barrymore in his last years—cunning, self-serving, self-abusive, manipulative—and *absolutely heartfelt*. Its tone goes beyond irony, alienation, or madness, and into the complete romantic glory of playacting. But it worked. David got no money back. But he kept Irene; he had remade her as his Rebecca. He had become her victim, and she his master (mistress was surpassed). The emotional groundwork for his special bigamy to come was in place.

15 · LIKE A LITTLE GIRL

IN 1948, DANNY SELZNICK was twelve. He lived in New York with his mother; thanks to David, he already had a precocious career as a playwright, and he had been wildly excited by the process of *Streetcar*. Yet he was kindly, generous, hopeful, and romantic: he loved his father, and he was ready to fall in with his love for Jennifer Jones. Whenever they were in Los Angeles, Danny and Jeffrey spent time with David and Jennifer, long days at Tower Grove, a feeling of ease and relaxation, of taking meals when people felt like it, not according to the printed schedules at Summit Drive. They were allowed to be up late and mingle with the starry guests at parties. Of course, they could not stay the night; that rule held firm.

Portrait of Jennie

Though David needled Jeffrey, still the son felt the father was happier and more relaxed not having to live up to Irene's code of what a father should be. Jeffrey was older, more worldly, and, as Danny saw it, more cynical. At Tower Grove, Jeffrey went secretly into his father's bedroom and found rubbers in a drawer. He guessed their parents would have no reconciliation—but that never stopped him hoping for it.

And Danny, to be more like his father, began to be moved by Jennifer. In the boy's eyes, *Portrait of Jennie* was the way into the mystery and the romance. So he cherished the film that had been his father's nightmare:

> I don't know how many times I went to see that picture. I felt the whole thing was his way of making love to her. My way of being close to the two of them in their romance, was going to see that movie. . . . There's a point at which the woman in front of you merges with the image on the screen. Perhaps it was an outrageous, childish conceit of mine, but in that film I really believed that I understood totally what my father saw in this woman. He was gazing at the image on the screen as much as he was gazing at the image in life and falling in love all over again every day at the rushes with the "fantasy" he had created. I imagined my father coming home and saying, "Darling, you'll never imagine this incredible creature that I saw today in my projection room. You looked so wonderful." "Oh did I?" . . . so that finally, I believe, she was in competition with her own image on the screen.

Again, in 1948, there was another competition and another yearning confusion of practicality and romance. In Italy, the director Roberto Rossellini craved a touch of Hollywood in his life. He was hailed for the vigor of his realism, yet secretly he wanted a real movie star. He had hinted broadly to the Selznick organization that he was available. He cabled Jennifer: "Congratulations for your wonderful performance in *Duel*. Hoping to be working with you soon."

Jenia Reissar had opened discussions with Rossellini, but at one of their meetings the director showed her a letter he had just received but could not understand. It was a letter from Ingrid Bergman—no, it was not the first letter, her truly notorious shot in the dark, the letter in which Ingrid had written to a stranger—"If you need a Swedish actress . . . who, in Italian knows only 'ti amo' I am ready to come and make a film with you." It was not that first letter, the one Irene had helped her good friend Ingrid write. No, it was a letter a little later in the correspondence, and the sly Rossellini gave it to Jenia Reissar to "translate" for him as a way of signaling to her that the director's heart was lost already to another actress. He had fallen in love—professionally, artistically, as well as personally: it was a package deal. So Jennifer never did her Joan of Arc in a neorealist style, and instead the world gained *Journey to Italy* . . . and Isabella Rossellini.

In the summer of 1948, David had another responsibility: Myron's daughter, Joan, came to California. She was eighteen, in search of the best plastic surgery, smoking "like a stove," and hitting the martinis. David had to advise the young woman about her future. Yet he discovered to his amazement that a year in Europe, at finishing school, had been enough for her to "become some kind of an American agent for two French firms—one of them a wine firm, and one the manufacturers of crates for citrus!" David showed Joan to Paul MacNamara, and the two men argued over whether she was "one of the most amazing and smartly aggressive young women" they'd met or "a child playing at being mature."

Joan was willful, an heiress, alternately worried about her looks and driven by the winds of romance. What horrified David most of all was that Joan had notions of giving up the Selznick name, and taking that of her mother's new husband, "Myers":

> I took the liberty of pointing out to her that I thought her father would be greatly upset by her giving up his name. Joan replied that she would not do it if her father were alive. . . . She wove a rather dramatic scenario of how difficult it was for Mrs. Myers to introduce her daughter, Miss Selznick; and that it led to all sorts of questions about divorce, etc. I told Joan that this was a problem which was now unfortunately faced by millions of children; and that in any event it did not particularly arise in her case, since all she had to do was explain that her father was not alive, and that her mother had remarried since her father's death. . . . However, Joan insisted that I had no idea as to how well-known the name of Selznick is in every corner of the world, and that it led to all sorts of repetitive questions about Hollywood.

Joan had no notion of how much wealthier than her uncle she was or how close the Selznick name had come to ruin. David was putting together a plan for retreat. Nothing had worked well for several years. Hollywood had begun a decline which many people saw as being prolonged and irreversible: movies had to yield to television, and the first, drastic drop-offs in attendance were only a prelude to changes to come. David needed to regroup; he had to meet his debts. He was thinking of spending time in Europe—traveling, enjoying himself—and maybe making a new base there. In that large shift of himself, it was taken for granted—and therefore not thoroughly examined—that he would marry Jennifer. By the spring of 1949, he wanted to be out of America.

So he completed *Jennie* and made his ideas known on *The Third Man*. He attended the funerals of D. W. Griffith and Harry Rapf. He took Jennifer to see *The Red Shoes* in Los Angeles in January 1949, the latest film by Powell and Pressburger, who would be making *Gone to Earth*. Jennifer was overwhelmed by *The Red Shoes*, the story of a dancer driven to her death by the passion of dance. David was still having his sessions with May Romm—wondering whether or why to marry—and he was also having to ask Morgan Maree to make sure Jennifer did not insist on selling some of her clothes to ease their financial woes. At the same time, he noted the chronic ease with which she mislaid the valuable pieces of jewelry he gave her.

And he met Hildegard Knef. She was a German actress, twenty-three in 1948, who had appeared in a few German films, most notably *The Murderers Among Us*. William Dieterle had recommended her to David—and he had put her under contract. Knef saw David in his office at ten o'clock at night on January 4, 1949. He kept her waiting while he made telephone calls, and then he asked her, "Tell me about yourself."

She began. She talked about her brief experience in a Russian prison camp. He made notes and said it might make an interesting story one day. He went into the bathroom—she heard water running, and when David came back his hair was wet and he had put on a fresh shirt.

"You're an interesting girl," he told her.

She stood up nervously.

"Don't you like me a little?" he asked.

"I don't know you very well."

"That could be changed," said David.

Hildegard Knef

He was still playing that scene, and even if he was broke and exhausted, he seemed menacing to the young German woman:

> Stiff spikes of hair waggled over his brow like chrysanthemum leaves;
> I stared at the wide neck, the tight smile, a smile that meant power,
> full power. . . . "I don't know any German girls," he said and tugged
> at my jacket. Two buttons sprang away like flat stones that one flips
> over water. The man, smelling of mouthwash and after-shave, was
> more menacing than the Russians.

She ran into the bathroom and vomited. When she came back to the office, David was on the phone again, loaning her out to MGM.

He was trading everyone away now, even Jennifer. Dan O'Shea had been given the batch of contracts and told to make the best deal he could. In the end, of course, David intervened, and by the time he left for Europe, he had divested himself of properties and stars, and he had about $5 million in hand, a magic step toward paying off the banks and Irene. Staff were laid off, never to be recalled. On April 25, after he had left for New York, there was an auction of production equipment and office furniture.

From David's point of view, this auction got out of control and reminded him of his own soft heart. Vanguard had employed Arthur Sachs, a son of Charlie Sachs. David was never happy about this. Only fools hired relatives . . . but David owed Uncle Charlie. Such compromise always turned into anger. One of Arthur's chores was the auction. MGM had let it be known they might scrape together $1,000 for Selznick's old props and costumes. Arthur had said they were worth much more. He proposed a proper auction as a way of raising serious money. David consented, and Arthur hired a relative of his wife as auctioneer. Just like a young Selznick, he promoted the occasion, with the result that David was horrified when, on April 5, *The Hollywood Reporter* ran a front-page headline: "Selznick Studio Goes on Block." Relatives! The auction cleared $100,000, but David felt humiliated. So he told his mother and asked her to rebuke the rogue nephew.

He was in New York a couple of months. On April 23, he, Morgan Maree, Irene and Irene's lawyer, George Cohen, met for eight and a half hours. He saw Bill and Babe Paley, and he went up to Deerfield to visit Jeffrey, saying nothing of what he planned in Europe. He had three appointments with a New York proctologist, and then on May 13 he left for Paris with Jennifer.

They went down to Antibes and were staying at the Hotel du Câp, where David chartered an English yacht, the *Manona*. He had arranged for traveling companions, too; he did not want solitude: Louis and Quique

Jourdan, Leland Hayward and his new wife, the lately Slim Hawks. The agent-producer Charlie Feldman nearly made the trip, too, but he got left on the shore. The *Manona* set sail, with an English crew and Slim doing the catering.

The boat was going east and south, after a stop at Monte Carlo, where Jennifer bought a bathing suit. They went by way of San Remo to Portofino. There was a game on the yacht, a guessing game: would David and Jennifer actually get married? Leland and Louis said they would not shave until the knot was tied. Quique Jourdan felt sure that

> David didn't want to get married. . . . He thought this was perfectly fine, his relationship with Jennifer. But he just was afraid to marry her. She was so unhappy that during the trip she wasn't sure and she was nervous. And we waited on the boat, and we didn't know what to do. Are they going to get married? We didn't want to spoil our vacation.

It was dark when they reached Portofino, but next morning there were paparazzi out in the harbor in small boats and they were spreading white oleander blooms on the water. The six of them went ashore and took a car to Rapallo. They had lunch there, and while Jennifer worried over what to wear, Louis went out in search of cuff links for David. Slim saw Jennifer standing on her head to make her cheeks pink. At 4:30 on the afternoon of July 12 they got in the car and drove to the town hall in Genoa for a six o'clock civil ceremony. Slim recalled "tiny men bubbling about, and the whole thing read out of a book, with translation for us, and when it got to 'in sickness, health and *debt*,' Jennifer laughed. But David laughed the loudest."

After the wedding, the other four wanted to leave them alone, but Jennifer said they must stay. They all went to Portofino for the wedding dinner, and Louis found a cake from somewhere. David was on the phone, sending cables. That's how the boys got the news and how Irene heard. Jeffrey recalled a conversation very shortly thereafter with Irene:

> And her kind of giving a sigh and being slightly apologetic. Saying, maybe not the same day, but certainly in that period of time, "Your father begged me not to divorce him because he would then be obliged to marry her." And that he had called her and accused her of having forced his hand. . . . I think if she had refused to divorce him, although I don't know why she would have, I believe he could have withstood the whole Jennifer thing. I think she probably would have wound up committing suicide.

The cable David sent Irene was one word: "DAVID." At first, she imagined there was something else omitted in transmission. So she checked,

Quique and Louis
Jourdan, Leland and Slim
Hayward—photo by
David

and it was confirmed. Years later, Irene said, "I assume he wrote and re-wrote the cable until he was at a loss for words. In any case, the message was clear."

David was a genius of the cable form. The uncommonly terse message is exact and infinite—not quite clear, yet unforgettable. It is like a bow of tribute to a victor, yet it is also the first sign of some new commitment the woman does not grasp. This is the boast of helpless fidelity, a dying word with sixteen years of life left still.

David had behaved like the showman again, consciously at the end of a major act, bringing down his own curtain with a flourish, but resolutely not grown up.

As if to detach himself from childishness, he wrote a poem about Jennifer. It survives on the back of an air cargo manifest, from that honeymoon summer of 1949:

> My wife is a little girl.
> Her hair has a curl
> Like a little girl
> She drinks, though, as if she were
>   adolescent,
> And when she's tight her eyes are
>   phosphorescent.
> You should see her when she smokes: there's a
>   laugh now!
> She's afraid people might see she doesn't
>   know how.
> The point is,
> My wife is a little girl,
> And pure like a little girl,

*And she knows good from bad, like a little
     girl
Uncomplicated by the subtleties that capture
     people
Till they don't know the True Cross from a
     church steeple
My wife's mind is translucent, like a pearl.*

End OF AN ERA

1 · QUICKSILVER WITH A FORK

IN 1949, for the first time in his life, David began to travel as a policy. He would spend enough time in London, Paris, and Italy to feel how drastically the war had changed ordinary lives. He was in cities affected by bomb damage, rationing, displaced persons, as well as the Berlin airlift and the threat of worse conflict. There is no sign this weighed on him: he never denied himself the best hotels, and he found his company still among celebrities and café society.

In postwar America, there was much to inspire confidence: the fact of victory, the reunion of families and a bounce in the birthrate, the prosperity that buoyed new families in suburban homes and which made it seem prudent to rid the country of un-American elements. For most Europeans recovery was slower and more painful. It was not as easy to believe in the gutsiness of a Scarlett ensuring survival. Though that fantasy still worked: as *Gone With the Wind* premiered in many countries after the war it did fabulous business. But there were new films more disposed to realism and less confident about fantasy. David would have his name on one in which a beautiful woman walked straight past the lovelorn hero at the end, as if he didn't exist.

This was *The Third Man*, and it was a big hit, but David didn't seem attuned to what was happening in it. There is a scene in *The Third Man* where Harry Lime teases his friend, Holly Martins, about believing in literary models applied to life: "Give myself up? This is a far better thing? The old limelight and the fall of the curtain? We aren't heroes, Holly, you and I. The world doesn't make heroes outside your books." Here was a pointed reappraisal of the chivalry of *A Tale of Two Cities*—yet David was considering remaking that hit of 1935.

The American audience began to give up on the movies a few years after 1945. At this distance in time, it is easy to suppose television made the change. But TV came after the trend had begun. There were larger, less certain reasons. People went back to school, they worked overtime to carry the mortgage, and they had new children. The Audience Research Institute reported a decline in weekly attendance at the movies from 81 million in 1946 to 69 million in 1948. Every studio suffered, and no executive knew what was happening or how to deal with it. Moreover, by 1948, there were only one million TV sets in America. Perhaps the movie trick no longer worked in the old way.

But as the audience dwindled—and the decline in numbers would accelerate in the 1950s—so there were other kinds of films. There was film noir, the last Hollywood genre, with not a happy ending in sight. *The Third Man* was Viennese noir, but as the decade ended there were many films made in America filled with disquiet and visual claustrophobia: *Letter from an Unknown Woman, The Lady from Shanghai, Force of Evil, Secret Beyond the Door, The Paradine Case, The Big Clock, Arch of Triumph, The Snake Pit, They Live by Night, Champion, Criss Cross, D.O.A.* Those were films such as, say, the Jennifer Jones character in *Since You Went Away* might have imagined if she'd had a breakdown. For in his uncommon turmoil of success and failure and his venture into psychiatry, David had approached the mood. He had some of the furious energy of a trapped soul.

He had a wife, he had two sons who became seventeen and thirteen in 1949, and in that same year he took on two stepsons, Robert Walker, Jr., who was nine, and Michael Walker, who was eight. He had an ex-wife, also, and every intention of making something of the failed marriage. He had massive debts and a collapsed business.

As if that were not enough, he got Alexander Korda, too.

KORDA WAS HUNGARIAN, nine years older than David and ready for anything. He had directed films himself for twenty years, as he moved from Hungary to Germany to Hollywood to France before settling in England in the early thirties. There he made a studio and an insecure empire at Denham, where he produced films to entice the American market. With *The Private Life of Henry VIII*, he discovered the American sentimentality over stories of English high life—it was a vein David might have excelled at, but Korda was quicker, more careless, and much less inclined to guilt.

He also had a grievance, for David had rather "stolen" Vivien Leigh from him. Korda felt superior in pioneering, even, for he had been the husband of two actresses—Maria Corda and, from 1939 to 1945, Merle Oberon. Before *Wind*, even, Korda had had a brief affair with Vivien Leigh.

Myron had warned David, years earlier. Trying to make a deal with Korda, he said, "is like trying to pick up quicksilver with a fork!" Korda was another family man, with brothers—Vincent and Zoltán—in the business and a larger clutch of Hungarians around him with whom to conspire. His nephew Michael Korda observed that "when charm failed, he was quite capable of rudeness, evasion and betrayal." David and Alex had been friends and rivals for over a decade. In the Selznick house there were often warning stories about those rascal Kordas, full of exaggerated shock and smothered envy. The two men were ideally cast as partners—so alike they could never trust each other.

David and Korda made their agreement through the agencies of SRO and London Films on May 14, 1948. It was a pretty package meant to produce four films in Britain or Europe which SRO would distribute in the "Western Hemisphere" (the United States, Canada, the Caribbean, Central America, South America, and the Philippines). The projects were *Tess of the D'Urbervilles*, from the Allan Scott script, with Carol Reed producing and directing and Jennifer as Tess; *The Third Man*, produced and directed by Reed from the original and unpublished story by Graham Greene; *A Tale of Two Cities*, to be made by Powell and Pressburger, starring Gregory Peck; and *The Doctor's Story*, to be written, produced, and directed by the English team of Sidney Gilliat and Frank Launder. Korda was to be responsible for the financing of these films in all respects other than David's provision of talent:

*David and Cary Grant,
with Grant's wife, Betsy Drake*

Jennifer, Peck, Joseph Cotten (for *The Doctor's Story*), Valli, and Cary Grant for *The Third Man*.

Not much transpired as intended. David and Jennifer had a brief yachting vacation with Korda in Bermuda, in May 1948. At that time, David read and liked Graham Greene's treatment for *The Third Man*, which took the form of a long story. In Greene's story, both Rollo Martins (not Holly yet) and Harry Lime had been Englishmen. In the contract, and in early talks, it was intended that Cary Grant play Martins, with Noël Coward as Lime, though David wondered if Grant would opt for Lime when he saw the final script. Grant's deal was separate and phenomenal: Korda was to make terms with him, but SRO would guarantee the first $200,000 of his fee. In addition, Grant was to receive half the net proceeds in Europe. This arrangement was undermined only by Grant's mistrust of everyone over money and the suspicion that Korda might fudge the calculation of "net proceeds."

We can only conjure with the prospect of Grant and Coward together. James Stewart was also considered as Martins, for the one effect David had upon the script talks with Reed and Greene was to make the hero an American. The two Englishmen had traveled to Culver City in August to hear David's thoughts. One meeting began only at 10:30 p.m. As it went deep into the early morning, Reed wondered if their secretary wasn't exhausted. "I'm terribly sorry," David said to the lady, "I should have offered you a Benzedrine."

David ended up giving them twenty-five pages of notes, and he spoke of their "grueling sessions" as if he had had much to teach them. Korda, Reed, and Greene reckoned they knew their story and their Vienna so well it was misery having David's advice. At all points, David was anxious to make the script acceptable to an American audience, and he was challenged by Greene's dark view of the world.

These script sessions—in La Jolla or in L.A., depending on whatever else David was up to—were fuel to the Englishmen's view of unbridled mogul vulgarity. David hadn't liked the title. Greene said he thought it was simple and memorable.

"You can do better than that, Graham," said David. "You are a writer. A good writer. I'm no writer, but you are. Now what we want—it's not right, mind you, of course it's not right, I'm not saying it's right, but then I'm no writer and you are, what we want is something like *Night in Vienna*, a title which will bring them in."

On another occasion, David had something in the script he didn't understand. He described the obscure piece of action. The startled Greene said no such incident occurred in *The Third Man*.

David groaned and sat down. "Christ, boys," he admitted, "I'm think-ing of a different script."

So he lay on the sofa, "crunched a Benzedrine," and waited for ten minutes until he was "as fresh as ever."

Greene produced a second draft by September 20; David liked it enough to take credit for the improvements. But he was perplexed because the rewrite had accommodated only some of his notes. Greene had practiced discretion and maintained authorship. It was a fresh experience for the very thorough David, and the things left undone spoiled his sense of the whole script:

> I spent countless hours going through with Reed and Greene, and getting agreement on, the treatment of the whole background of Vienna today, to give the picture size, and more importantly, to give it understandability from the standpoint of American audiences. . . . We frankly made the Russians the heavies, in pursuit of the girl. All of this has been eliminated, even what was in the original script. We must insist upon its return, for patriotic reasons, for purposes of the picture's importance and size. . . .

David came from a school in which everything on the screen had to be clear, whereas in film noir there is room for mystery and doubt. Also, David was at last becoming anti-English. Greene is not famous as a patriot,

David confers with
Graham Greene and Carol Reed.

and *The Third Man* was no defense of Britain. But David was in a ferment of anger and suspicion at the "faults" of the script and the cunning of the British film business:

> It would be little short of disgraceful on our part as Americans if we tolerated this nonsensical handling of the four power occupation of Vienna. We would be paying a huge sum of money, and supplying our stars, to foist a piece of British propaganda upon the entire world, including the United States and the rest of the Western hemisphere; we would be portraying an absurd falsehood from the standpoint of accuracy; and our American audiences and critics would be entitled to bitterly rebuke me.

At the same time, David was ingenious with casting suggestions. Vanguard owned half of Robert Mitchum's service contract; the other half belonged to Howard Hughes. Those pressures may have helped drive Mitchum to marijuana. On September 1, the actor was arrested, with two young women, for narcotics offenses. David's immediate defense was to call Mitchum "a very sick man in need of medical treatment." But within weeks, he noticed a remarkable upswing in audience demand for the actor's films. So he thought of Mitchum as Harry Lime:

> feel he would be precisely what is needed to further build gross of *Third Man* and that he would be superb casting. . . . There can be no question whatsoever about fabulous difference in gross here with Mitchum who is clearly star of first rank as against [Orson] Welles whom Gallup claims is detriment and who in my opinion would not add a dollar to gross.

But Mitchum ended in jail, and by October, Reed had gone to Vienna. Korda had sent brother and nephew to search Italy for his next best Lime, Orson Welles, who was seeking money to shoot a little more of his *Othello*—and so he took $100,000 instead of 20 percent of the profits. Meanwhile, David pursued Reed with more script notes, requests for an American writer, an SRO observer on the set, and for Korda or Reed to come to America to discuss everything. On October 7, Korda told David: "Jenia visited me today re script about which understand you worry greatly. If you keep on worrying about this script you will cause yourself and myself very distressing time without benefit to mutual interest and quality of picture. You cannot produce a picture seven thousand miles away."

Jenia Reissar was in an impossible situation. David sent his messages for Korda to her first—and she edited them to make them less offensive. Reissar had known Carol Reed for years, and she watched him throw the Selznick cables in the wastepaper basket without reading them.

"Carol," she'd say, "give me *something* to tell him."

Reed grinned and answered, "All right, tell him I'll do this . . . or I'll do that."

The strain told on Reissar, and when she had to go into the hospital for an operation some memos from David went straight to Korda without any tempering. The full force of Selznick's arrogance shocked Korda. At first, he blamed Reissar, for he thought it was her language. Then he realized the truth and came to a dislike of David.

The Third Man was shot in the winter of 1948–49, and any late script changes were due largely to Orson Welles, who felt some need to expand on the role and lines of his Harry Lime. Yet even as the shooting went ahead, David was "rather frantic" about what Welles might get up to: "For your confidential information" he wanted Reissar to tell Korda, "Cotten and Welles are both frustrated writers. . . . Cotten and Welles . . . are both experts at ridicule so will disparage any lines written by other than outstanding American and compete with each other in tearing dialogue apart with what could be resultant mess."

Dangerous actors—Joseph Cotten and Orson Welles on the set of The Third Man

To this day, *The Third Man* works as an entertainment and leaves one feeling morally vulnerable. The picture was a great success, and the size of the hit had to do with Welles and our difficulty in condemning Lime, who is ironically the only bold, cheerful, "attractive" character in the film. (In the 1950s, there was even a radio serialization based on the Lime character in which he became the hero.) And in that swaggering speech that Welles added, or adorned, the Ferris wheel comparison of Switzerland and the Borgias' Italy, of cuckoo clocks and great art, there is Hollywood's defiant insolence: take this deviltry as best you can, for it is essential to the power of the show—and showmen are not saints.

Thank God David was 7,000 miles away. Nearer at hand, he would have worried that ordinary American viewers didn't know who the Borgias were. To read the memos sent to London or Vienna is to tremble for the movie that has survived so well. David carped over all the old things, to which he added the proper weight of screen credit for "his" talent. By December 1948, Korda was valiantly beating off Selznick paper. He sent a polite letter to Jenia Reissar's secretary, a response to memos number forty-six and forty-seven from David. (Before the picture opened, the series had reached seventy-two!):

> Miss Reissar is mistaken. I did not wish Miss Reissar not to go to Vienna to Mr. Carol Reed because I was going to Vienna but because on general grounds I think it is perfectly useless for Miss Reissar to get in touch with Mr. Reed . . . about matters of production. . . .
>
> Mr. Reed is in the middle of a very hard and responsible job, working day and night. Therefore he cannot be expected, and I am sure Mr. Selznick does not expect him, to sit down and write copious answers on copious notes.

When David and Jennifer arrived in England on July 18, 1949, after their marriage, he was able to see *The Third Man*. He could not have made it himself; he would have spoiled it, given the chance. Yet he knew what it was. In later years, he conceded both that it was a triumph and that he had done "nothing that contributed greatly to its success." But it was "a substantial contribution to making me financially healthy again" so that he could get back into production. David did exploit *The Third Man*. There is no evidence that he ever carefully watched or understood the film, much less the lesson of its making. So there he was, in England, in July 1949, ready to give his new wife to Korda for another film. How could he recognize how thoroughly he had become a bore and a trial to the Hungarian? For if you are quicksilver, it is no fun being jabbed at by a blind man's fork.

2   ·   ME STILL TARZAN

DAVID AND JENNIFER had traveled in Europe after their marriage. But there was a film to prepare for. As many parts of the Korda deal fell through, *Gone to Earth* was left as survivor, to be made by Powell and Pressburger, with Jennifer as Hazel, the country girl, torn between squire and parson, but identifying most passionately with her pet fox. Most of the picture was to be shot on location, in the Shropshire countryside. The story was set in the nineteenth century and would be filmed in Technicolor, so there were costumes, makeup, and a long, chestnut wig to have tested.

The wig was the most pressing concern, but the Selznicks were in Switzerland. So Jenia Reissar arranged for the hairdresser to visit the actress over a weekend. The woman would arrive at five on the Saturday afternoon, do the measurements, and fly back the next day. The schedule was cleared in advance, but five came, the hairdresser was waiting, and Jennifer was not available. Jenia Reissar went up to Jennifer's room and explained the necessity of making a good impression: the hairdresser was on her own time, and in the British industry in 1949 starry temperament was not appreciated. David backed her, and so did Arabella LeMaître, who had quickly become a trusted friend to Jennifer and who worked for Jenia. The wig was tested.

The Selznicks came to London and stayed at the Savoy (Claridge's had been their choice, but that hotel resisted movie people). On the next day there were to be camera tests for makeup, with Michael Powell. Jenia Reissar

Honeymoon—David as photographer

*Jennifer in Shropshire,
with Michael Powell*

lived in Knightsbridge, and at four o'clock in the morning she got a tele-phone call from David:

> "Jennifer hasn't slept. She is in a very bad way. Ring up Mickey Powell and tell him that she can't make the test tomorrow." I said, "At four o'clock I'm not ringing up Mickey Powell. Anyhow, if it's a question of telling the director, you may ring him." That was one thing about David. If there was anything unpleasant to be said, some-body else had to do it. I said, "I will ring the production manager at 6:30 when I know he'll be up. Can you tell me how late Jennifer will be?" "No. She's got to get some sleep otherwise she's going to look dreadful." Six o'clock my phone rings: "Jennifer will do the test, she has had two hours sleep and she's feeling quite all right, and she will be on time."

From his office at the Savoy, David was soon bombarding Powell and Pressburger with his (and Jennifer's) worries. Did she have a work permit yet? Why were they called to England if the picture wasn't ready to start? Where was the promised Shropshire girl who would help Jennifer with the "intonations" of Hazel's speech? And did Powell realize that David, by contract right, was allowed to see the tests?

Michael Powell was known in England for his temper, his cutting remarks, and his calculated but intimidating aloofness. But now David was seeking to invade in every possible area, with the constant assumption of knowing better. "It was a shame," said Powell. "He might have been a good producer, but he had become a monster. And it was worst of all for Jennifer."

David was already plunged into the script, declaring how lucky it was he had got to it in time. He ranged farther afield when he met Cyril Cusack, the Irish actor whom Powell and Pressburger wanted to cast as Parson Marston. David looked at the deferential and dreamy Cusack and browbeat him about his unsuitability as a romantic lead opposite Jennifer. With a sigh—so David said—Cusack agreed that no, he wasn't exactly right. But he declined to make a test, and so David told Powell and Pressburger that the actor was too old, too short, and "about as far removed from being a possible proper mate for the girl as it is conceivable to imagine."

David was too humorless to see the delicacy of the ground he was stamping. Cusack was two years younger than David Farrar (who played the dashing squire)—and the junior of D.O.S. by eight years. He was also the same height as Jennifer. Moreover, it was the point of the Mary Webb novel, and of the film Powell intended, that he be gentle, pious, pale—the model of refinement as opposed to the sardonic and handsome squire. Not to see height accurately was one thing, but was David also blind to the very scheme of melodrama he had used in *Duel in the Sun*?

He went up to the Shropshire location with Jennifer, where he caught some case of the flu—or Powell put a spell on him. *Gone to Earth* was left in peace, as David dragged himself back to the Savoy to get ready for a trip to Europe with Jeffrey and Danny. He wired Jennifer in Church Stretton, assuring her that a doctor was looking after him at the hotel: "Be assured that I am not as broken down as I felt yesterday and that I will soon again be Tarzan."

Irene had brought their two sons to Europe for a vacation. She had to be in London by the end of the summer for the English production of *Streetcar*. They landed at Cherbourg on August 2—on the same day, David arrived in Rome. Irene took the boys to Paris for about a week before David collected them for *his* vacation.

He had his secretary, Lois Hamby, in tow, too, for there was never a break without some dictation. But David was making a great effort. This was the first time he had seen the boys since his marriage to Jennifer—and they were disappointed she was not part of the holiday. The trio went to Rome, and David took photographs with his new Polaroid camera as part of having a good time. He had organized some female company: not only Arabella, but the fifteen-year-old Marina Cicogna (granddaughter of Count Volpi, statesman and financier), who had a crush on Jeffrey *and* his father, and Afdera Franchetti, who won Jeff's heart, took him to parties, and appeared on the cover of *Oggi* with him.

They were in Venice by August 14, when Danny woke up with "a crick in his foot." Marina and Arabella worked the phones in search of the best doctors—David had a hunch it was polio! The doctors said it was not serious. So David had the wounded son carried by boat to a hospital. X rays were taken. "The doctors explained to me at some length the symptoms of polio and said it was absolute nonsense for me to have the slightest fear." To show good will, they put a plaster cast on Danny's leg. The crisis had been a Selznick production, and David lost no opportunity in writing to Irene about how solicitous a father he had been.

Then he shipped the boys off to Paris with a list of good doctors all over Western Europe, in case Irene needed them. He would stay on at the Excelsior on the Lido for a few days before meeting up with them again at Southampton on August 30 so that he could take the boys back to America on the *Ile de France*. And so, David was in Venice, on August 16, when he learned of a more serious accident: several days earlier, crossing a street in Atlanta with her husband, Margaret Mitchell had been struck by a car. She had been looking after her husband, who had had a heart attack in 1945. But on the sixteenth, Mitchell died, a world-famous novelist who had written only one book. She was forty-eight. Henceforward, her husband and then her brother Stephens would control the rights to her novel.

David had had fun as a self-promoter in Italy. He wanted to think well of his sea change in family circumstances. On the Continent, he was still a big movie man: as Jeffrey saw it, the economic facts had not yet caught up with the name, and David could live well in Italy thanks to the power of the dollar. The boys noted that when their mother handed them over to their father, their hotel or shipboard life-style moved from prudent excellence to heedless splendor.

He would have been hurt if he had not attracted attention with his informal court of Arabella, Marina, and Afdera, two great beauties and two aristocrats. This was a version of Zenda, yet David could tell himself it was for his boys' benefit. Some reporters misunderstood. They were struck by the absence of the new Mrs. Selznick, and they claimed David was seeing not just glamorous Italian women, but Irene, too.

David tried to set the record straight. He told Louella Parsons the stories had misreported his marriage to Jennifer (they claimed an uncertain mess) and that, false as they were,

> The whole tone and happiness of Jennifer's and my marriage are away to a wretched start as a consequence of these items, and notably of your own this morning. I ask you, in the name of that marriage, to do something to correct the matter immediately, and to restore to it the dignity which your item had robbed it of. . . .

There was at least one frantic telephone call from Jennifer, from Church Stretton to Rome, worrying over stories reported to her. The actress was deep in a complex role—a mixture of naiveté and sensuality—being deliberately played upon by an authoritarian Powell. He thought his method was working: Jennifer's Hazel is a daring performance, in many ways her freest and least self-conscious. Jenia Reissar believed firmness was the only way with Jennifer. "I think she was plucked out of darkness, so to speak. David took her into a life of luxury, of utter disregard for anybody's feelings or anything else, and she wasn't ready for it. She was scared stiff of that life. . . . It was this awful insecurity. Then she got more and more and more neurotic. Instead of slapping her down or being gentle about it and saying, 'Stop it, this is nonsense,' he was trying to be kind, to pacify her in the wrong way."

David had a few days in London at the end of August before he set sail. Powell and Pressburger gave Jennifer a holiday so the couple could be together. But David asked to see an assembly of the footage so far and then felt bound to itemize his dissatisfaction. *Gone to Earth* never had the originality or impact of *The Third Man*. But it is often beautiful, eerie, and emotionally powerful, and its vision of a remote rural world where magic and destiny are at work depends upon the barefoot, feral intuitiveness of Jennifer. David said the film was not working. Could he really judge, or was he bound by his own excluded heart to find fault?

The few days were not holiday or rest for a troubled actress. One night after dinner, David, Jennifer, and some friends were walking on the edge of Hyde Park. A row broke out between the Selznicks, and Jennifer ran off into the dark part of the park. David was very agitated. He found a policeman, and then they all came on Jennifer in the trees with a stranger. David said the man had accosted his wife, but the man denied it and said the woman had approached him. The policeman beat a tactful retreat. There would be many such flights and public arguments. David would never quite find a way of handling Jennifer or understand that his mixture of fatherly love and smothering control could unhinge her.

So he attacked Powell and Pressburger. On August 30 he wrote to them twice, once before leaving and once again from the *Ile de France*, with copies to Jennifer, Reissar, Dan O'Shea, and Korda. David had an old complaint: the script. He had accepted it only on certain conditions, and now those were being ignored. While ill, in Shropshire, against a doctor's advice, David had given of himself, explaining to Powell how it could be set right, but Powell had carried on regardless. Still,

> I shall find the time on the boat to go through the script once more, and to go through my points once more; and I shall advise you of the

degree of my insistence and the strength of my feelings, on each of the points which are not met. Believe me, I shall try to be no more insistent than is necessary; but in the interim, I am of course waiving none of them.

The language had one eye on lawyers yet to come. David had decided Powell was so stubborn, so stupid, or so English that he was not listening. This was the more baffling since, in Venice, David had seen the most recent Powell-Pressburger film, *The Elusive Pimpernel*. Here was a subject David could have made; it was such a cross between *Zenda* and *Two Cities*. But Powell had rather mocked the story and pushed it toward a witty, nearly surreal satire (the movie also had Cyril Cusack as its villain). David's comments won no allies:

> I hate to say this, but I am afraid that you and a lot of other people are in for a rough time on *Pimpernel* because of your obvious and very curious belief that there is some virtue in obscurity, and some artistry in confusion. . . . It really broke my heart to see such magnificent physical picture-making and such superb cinematic technique, all go for nothing, as demonstrated when the audience whistled at and loathed the picture, even those who understood English perfectly.

David was seldom all wrong. He could see Powell's brilliance. Yet *The Elusive Pimpernel* was a commercial failure. He might have been listened to more carefully but for one thing: the recent pictures *he* had made and which Korda had the task of distributing in Europe. *The Paradine Case* had been regarded in London as a major disappointment, and Korda was now making mournful noises as to whether *Portrait of Jennie* was worth opening. What did David know? Over forty years later, both *Pimpernel* and *Gone to Earth* seem alive, personal, and modern. Whereas *Jennie* is misguided and arty whimsy.

On *Gone to Earth*, David couldn't hear the dialogue for the dialect. He proposed recasting the Sybil Thorndike part. He thought the costumes were inelegant: "In the scenes in which Jennifer wears the shoes, the length of the costume, plus the shape of the shoes, makes her look bow-ankled and bow-legged. Apparently the shoes are turned out in such a fashion as to cause this startling result. I do hope it will be corrected." But the intent had been to make the wild Hazel seem awkward and constricted in proper clothes.

At their last session together, David had had a blazing row with Powell and Pressburger over a makeup effect they were attempting. As a parting shot, David promised he would be back and on the phone to Jennifer in the meantime. He may have believed he was defending film, actress, and wife, whereas he was putting her future employment in jeopardy:

Mickey, you simply must not deal with me as though my greatest star, and my wife as well, were not in the lead; or as though I did not have a huge investment in the picture; or even as though I did not know my business. . . .

Jennifer consulted with me about the "moonlight makeup". I think it is ridiculous and even amateurish. Anyone who has made as many technicolor pictures as I have . . . should know that you can get any degree of "moonlight" that is desired simply by printing to the extent desired on the "cold" side and on the "blue" side. I have no intention of having Jennifer made into a guinea pig for new experiments that could be most destructive. I have advised her not to wear this makeup and I assume that she is following this advice. . . . I trust that for your own sake you will not attempt to embarrass her, or to force the situation, or to punish her, because it must be obvious to you that I would not long tolerate any such attitude.

The boat left Southampton, and Powell got on with his movie. Jennifer had calls, and she and David would sometimes combine in the mutual hysteria of those who can only meet in uncertain transatlantic connections. So many people believed she did her best work when David was too far away to advise her.

He was back in Los Angeles by September 12, charged up with optimism yet oddly afflicted by tension. So he returned to one of his favored practitioners, Dr. Myron Prinzmetal, who diagnosed a spasmic condition, prescribed medication and relaxation. "Me still Tarzan," said David, as he signed off a letter to Jennifer.

3 · GOOD RIDDANCE

SIR ALEXANDER KORDA had been striving to keep at a chaste remove from the deals with Selznick. He was businessman and director enough to know that, eventually, films got made. The endless analysis of the process was not the point. He had done what he could to protect Carol Reed and Powell and Pressburger. But Selznick and Korda had to face each other: that life-style of bravura extravagance to mask penury demanded a meeting.

David was putting himself through the extra ordeal of travel. He had five days in Los Angeles in September 1949 before he went back to New York and took to the boat again. By October 5, he had returned to London and seen the assembly of *Gone to Earth*. That prompted twenty-two pages of single-spaced notes, many of which were to the benefit of the film, some of which were hectoring and offensive. But the notes forgot the picture was more than halfway done.

The sound in the whole film was a problem, and David foresaw days of postsynchronization and looping. He told Powell that Jennifer loathed such work, in part because she was not good at it. If only the sound work had been good enough on location and Jennifer had been encouraged to be natural.

Michael Powell could point to how well Jennifer did if she was treated firmly. He saw in David a complainer, who "never had the guts to direct a picture himself. He shunned the responsibility." Yet how he craved the power and its emotional taxation—he could hardly bear not to be vital! "But he was very likeable," said Powell, "I suppose because he aimed high. But how erratic was his aim! How naive were the judgments upon which he based his decisions!"

Yet David came so close to the real passion of film. As part of his October notes on *Gone to Earth*, he had a late-night brainstorm. He had heard

Gone to Earth: *David Farrar and Jennifer*

David and Dan O'Shea

that Powell was to shoot a key scene on the next day, October 6. He kept a secretary up all night as *he* saw how the scene should really be done. He went back to the Mary Webb book: his old security and policy. There he found wisdom and typed it out. Of course, Powell never acted on the advice and likely never read it. But here is the exhilaration of Eureka!, at the Savoy at maybe 3:00 a.m.:

> I gave myself this beating because of some convictions at which I arrived, which I believe in as firmly as I have ever believed anything in my long career concerning a script.
>   I take no bows for the contents of these things. Practically every line is called out of the book. I have attempted merely to keep them within your present continuity, with the exception of one additional scene. I will therefore say without fear of seeming to pat myself on the back, that I consider them two of the greatest and most heart-breaking scenes ever written for motion pictures—and I emphasize that they were written by Mary Webb, not by me; and I call to your attention the fact that the whole basis of our arrangement was your enthusiasm and my enthusiasm and Jennifer's enthusiasm for the book.

David could manage only five days in London. He had to be back in Los Angeles again for a lawsuit that should have been warning enough to keep out of the courts. William Bacher was a minor producer who had taken advantage of SRO's desperate need for product to get a commitment on a picture, *If This Be My Harvest.* How binding the commitment was was the cause of the suit. For the script had turned out lousy; David had held up the money and warned his own people away from it: Valli, Louis Jourdan, and

Robert Mitchum. But the case was filed and would not go away. Louis B. Mayer asked David how had he got involved with such a second-rate picture? L.B. was more openly critical of David than he had ever been. So David had tried to explain: he even wondered about having L.B. as an expert witness, ready to declare the project worthless. This meant telling Mayer how broke he was.

L.B. was sympathetic and surprised, but he found it hard to reconcile the mixture of brilliance and sentimentality in David. He offered him a large personal loan, which David declined, according to the rules that had prevailed through his first marriage. (He was divorced from Irene, yet L.B. was still father-in-law in David's mind.)

At the end of October and in early November, David was on the stand for four days: even as a witness he was exhaustive. Then it was back to New York and London (this time he flew across the Atlantic). It was during this absence that Jenia Reissar had gone into the hospital and one of David's vituperative letters went straight to Korda. Korda said the letter was so full of "fishwifely insinuations" he was compelled to speak out. Now he reassessed history and posed himself as Solomon, with David as a reprobate:

> After long discussions we decided to make a business deal together. I had a long talk with you and I begged you to forego your customary toughness and meanness in concluding a business deal with me and to try to make it on a friendly basis and to behave with that sense of moderate generosity and gentlemanliness which is the basis of civilized life.

Korda wrote a shorter letter than David, and he had more instinct of how to make the whip crack. He knew how vulnerable David was to any claim of old friendship and gentlemanly honor. "Now, because of Miss Reissar's letter, I feel something ugly has happened to something good and decent. I felt a deep friendship for you and now I feel it has been spoilt."

David could not hold back. He told Korda only wounded pride and business worries could explain these "ungallant, untrue and slanderously vitriolic remarks" which were "so unfaithful to the traditions of British Knighthood." He had been preparing a long list of the ways Korda had broken their contract—they were alarmingly trivial, but David refused to notice this. He listed some of them to Korda with grandiose assumptions of how the courts would rule. And he hurled Korda's dark reputation back at him:

> I have always maintained that everyone else was wrong about you. Apparently, I was a bit naive. Seemingly, no affection for you or relations with you can possibly survive any kind of business association. If your every unreasonable demand is not acceded to, the other man is unrea-

sonable and mean and ungrateful and petty; if your own breaches are called to your attention, then the person who properly performs his or her function in calling these to your attention is stupid and a liar and a fishwife; if credit is extended to you, it is ridiculous because it is not enough; if you trade out a deal and it turns out well for you, it was typically brilliant of you—but if it turns out badly for you, the other man has taken advantage of you; if the other man does work on your pictures that you should have done in the first instance, you are fearful that somehow he will get credit for it—and particularly, (and whether in one case through coincidence or in the other through some kind of contribution of effort and personalities, is besides the point) if there is a contrast with past pictures; when things are going well for you, you are Openhanded Joe—but if things are going badly for you, it doesn't matter whether you are obligated to make payments you can make; if you're in trouble and you ask for help and get it, it is immediately forgotten, and the next time you ask for help and don't get it, you are outraged. . . . I can only say, "Good riddance."

In one sentence of 240 words, David had captured the nature of the picture business. Korda would have laughed to see how well the description fitted both of them.

Gone to Earth finished retakes in a wet Shropshire on November 3, with Jennifer the victim of what Powell called "an old English cold." But he admired her and called her "the best loved trouper." David was in London by November 15, as the postsynchronization was carried out. Jennifer failed to report for several days in a row, and Korda told her he had to reserve his "rights against yourself and to complete the production of the film with or without your assistance."

David and Jennifer returned to New York eight days before Christmas and he visited the law offices of Donovan, Leisure, Newton, Lumbard and Irvine to put the case in their hands. An outstanding newcomer at the firm, Frank Davis, who had just graduated from Harvard Law School, was put in charge. He went to call on David at the Hampshire House, where he was given several files thicker than Tarzan's arm.

In the new year, Davis went to London to meet Sir Lancelot Joynson-Hicks, Selznick's English lawyer. Action was pursued in both countries, and David reported woefully on the legal costs. The case came down to Korda feeling *The Paradine Case* and *Portrait of Jennie* were poor return for *The Third Man* and *Gone to Earth*. His goal was to regain all rights to *The Third Man* (the only success of the four) by claiming that *Jennie* had been delivered late and was then so bad all the circuits in England had refused it. In retaliation, David said Korda had not yet delivered *The Third Man* and had departed from the script of *Gone to Earth* so that reshooting was required. In addition, Selznick put the English *Paradine* income in escrow.

Joynson-Hicks had sought an injunction against *Gone to Earth* in London. But on April 4, 1950, he had to report failure. The case involved so many technical terms, witnesses who testified only by affidavit, and a judge who never saw films. "The tragedy of the thing was," said Joynson-Hicks, "that the man who had the final say took the view that substantially the Defendants had produced a film which did comply with their contractual obligations in so far as it followed the story line of the book and the script in so far as D.O.S. had not dissented from it."

There remained an arbitration decision in New York, to be made by Judge Robert P. Patterson. He held nine days of hearings. He read the scripts and the correspondence, and he saw *Gone to Earth*. At the end of all the fuss, paper, and delay, and for an arbitration fee of $6,000, he let everything stand. *Portrait of Jennie* had been late, but not unreasonably so. *The Paradine Case* receipts should be released. *The Third Man* reached America late, but not so late as to worry. Selznick did not have to pay the £250,000 Korda was claiming for *Gone to Earth*. But, on the other hand, the arbitrator felt that film was close enough to its script. If David wanted to make changes for the Western Hemisphere, that was his right. But it should be at his own expense. As Jenia Reissar saw it, Judge Patterson had washed his hands of the foolish affair.

The waters were ready to settle again. But David would not relent or back down: he said *Gone to Earth* was unfit for America. There were yet further negotiations on how it should be improved. Korda cheerfully bet Joynson-Hicks sixpence there would never be an end to it. But by October 1950, Joynson-Hicks offered these terms: Selznick would undertake all personal and financial responsibility for the reshooting; Korda had only to supply scripts and costumes—plus the proper foxes, if required—and do all he could to persuade Powell, Pressburger, and the English actors to go to Hollywood.

On October 19, 1950, Korda accepted the deal and sent the lawyer a bankers draft for sixpence. Joynson-Hicks had the piece of paper mounted and framed in his office as a tribute to the folly of movie people who go to law.

4 · CONFIDENTIALITY

DAVID'S OFFICIAL POSITION was that he would not be in production until "the debt" was paid off. But that was a cover for searching. During those five days in early October 1949, while he was in England, the days in which he gave Powell and Pressburger so many notes on *Gone to Earth*, and even those small-hours scenes, "two of the greatest and most heartbreaking" ever done for pictures, he still found time to be in Manchester, which is an easy car journey from Church Stretton, the *Gone to Earth* location.

In Manchester, just prior to its London opening of October 11, Irene was battling with Laurence Olivier over the English production of *A Streetcar Named Desire*. Olivier was directing his wife, Vivien Leigh, as Blanche, but he was not happy: he did not like the play too much, he foresaw censorship problems in Britain, he felt overshadowed by Elia Kazan's New York success, and the marriage to Vivien was no longer idyllic. So he was making changes to the text and shutting Irene out of rehearsals. Reason enough for David's gallantry to believe Irene needed rescuing.

David had further thoughts—the movie. From New York, as he set out for England, he had cabled his ex-wife (and still business partner at Vanguard): this was someone he *had* to impress now, and if he could also find a pretext for working with her . . . ?

> Just before leaving for Los Angeles Charlie Feldman approached me on going in with him on a deal for *Streetcar*. I would possibly be able to do this because of deferments Feldman can arrange. Also possibly I could do either this or handle alone through deal I have pending for financing future production in New York confidentially with the Fabian group or alternately with new English company. However thought it rather ridiculous for me to deal with Feldman and therefore stalled him although he has very successfully courted both Audrey [Wood, Williams's agent] and [Tennessee] Williams in Hollywood threw big party for Williams. . . . Quite apart from any possible benefit to me and apart from chance Vanguard could handle it especially if money limited by means of Feldman partnership and deferments thought this information might be of value to you but please please keep source confidential since Feldman can be very useful to me in immediate future. I still do not know why you do not make it yourself and might be able work this if Fabian SRO arrangements pending work. But if you have resolved not to make it then I do not know whether work with Feldman or direct with you since fearful apparently new love match Audrey Williams Feldman may take enterprise elsewhere. Lost none of my faith in value of enterprise because of its showmanship and low production cost.

This moment had its layers. Feldman was talking to David to get an inside track with Irene. David was speculating over the venture just to talk to her *and* to get closer to having the funds to buy her out. Irene said she was reluctant to produce the movie herself: she wanted David to know she had now moved up in the entertainment class structure. In fact, Irene had played an active part in the movie sale and had been tempted. She treated

David's effort with amusement. But however belated or sly she thought his cable and telephone calls that tracked her down at her Manchester hotel—in the lobby—she did entertain David's visit. He had old dirt on Olivier.

"Breathing good will and advice," David took over the hotel in Manchester and talked to the Oliviers. He saw the show: back in Los Angeles, Charlie Feldman waited to hear how Vivien was doing as Blanche. If there was to be a movie of the play, then a star actress would be required. David chartered a plane to get back to London, and he took Irene and Binkie Beaumont with him. Irene explained to the impresario that the plane "wasn't his wealth, just his extravagance." To charter a plane in England in those days was so unexpected no one would have been asked to pay immediately. Beaumont felt excluded by David's constant confidential chats with Irene.

"I thought you people were divorced," he murmured.

And Irene said, "You should have seen us in the old days," leaving Beaumont to wonder whether they were gabbier then—or happier now.

It is not clear how much Jennifer knew of this side trip. But once *Gone to Earth* had wrapped, and the Selznicks were restored to Los Angeles, David did pursue Feldman, who by then had secured the rights, set the picture up at Warners, and wooed Kazan to be his director. As David reminded Feldman, on March 1, "Kazan volunteered to me, out of the blue one night in Hollywood, that in his opinion the girl to play it was Jennifer. Then you volunteered, out of the blue on another Hollywood night, the same thing to Jennifer."

To the extent that Irene had any say, she voted for Vivien Leigh. But as the spring dragged on, David neither gave up hope nor let himself seem eager. Kazan was stalling, said David, and then jockeying the Selznicks into a position that was "annoying and embarrassing." No one likes to be up for a part too openly and left hanging. Kazan wanted an actress who would revive his excitement in the old project. There were censorship problems with the script. In Europe, Jenia Reissar was talking up other projects on Jennifer's behalf, Dreiser's *Sister Carrie* was in prospect at Paramount, and "my own production plans and where I shall be this summer are naturally going to be affected by where Jennifer is going to be." At the same time, David said—and it was always David speaking for Jennifer—that to work with Kazan appealed to the actress even more than the role itself. He got Arthur Fellows to assemble a reel of extracts from Jennifer's work so Kazan and Tennessee Williams could "get the almost fantastically chameleon-like variety that she gives automatically to her appearance."

By early May, Vivien Leigh was cast to play her second Southern romantic. Kazan wrote to Jennifer with regrets and the hunch that if he had been able to shoot a test with her, then Tennessee Williams might have been persuaded. In the same note, he told her he'd seen Robert Walker the night before: "He looked better than I've ever seen him. Seemed calmer and completely in control of himself. Some kind of inner torture has evidently been lifted."

Walker had had very difficult times. In 1948 he married Barbara Ford, the daughter of director John Ford. It lasted six weeks. There were drinking bouts and enough of a breakdown so that by the end of the year the actor entered Menninger's Clinic in Topeka, Kansas. He remained there for several months, but by the spring of 1950 he was at work again. In a few months, Hitchcock would cast him as Bruno Anthony in *Strangers On a Train*. Jennifer and Walker had two young sons who were very close to their father—there was an intense physical resemblance. She kept up with the events of his life and remained affected by guilt. Her new friendship with Arabella LeMaître was assisted by Arabella being Catholic (like Anita Colby). Since *Bernadette*, Jennifer had been susceptible to the rules of that church, especially those she had broken.

Once the decision was made on *Streetcar*, Jennifer told David she was relieved not to have the part. But she had not been able to speak up before. David was by then at the end of the road with Dan O'Shea, yet he urged his contracts man into renewed efforts on Jennifer's behalf. For he could not survive with her out of work, and he had to admit that *Portrait of Jennie* and recent loan-outs had done her standing no good. However, he added—as he waited for Judge Patterson's arbitration—"I think *Gone to Earth* will do fine things for her prestige." He asked O'Shea to find out everything he could on the status of *Carrie*.

That was on May 4, 1950. In the previous month, David had finally lost the services of his most loyal retainer. O'Shea had done all the loan-out deals, and he patiently applied himself to selling off rights, stories, and talent contracts to repair the debt. He was a tough negotiator respected throughout the business. He knew the history; he had joined SIP in 1936 and never left his volatile boss. By April 1950, O'Shea was tired, disillusioned, and listening to outside offers. But he knew David was under great pressure: indeed, O'Shea had made him a personal loan. Then, on April 7, David picked up another loan: $50,000, interest-free for five years, from Bill Paley. This was not for business; it was for his and Jennifer's living expenses, and Paley asked no questions. (By 1950, Paley's own worth was close to $10 million.)

David was touched by the loan, but it was a moment to feel the full weight of disorder he dragged wherever he went. So he lashed out at the dogged O'Shea in as terrible a memo as he ever sent—a five-page, personal delivery, day-rate telegram, the least economical way of communicating:

You know what you set out to accomplish or rather to terminate on this last trip to Coast. You also know whether any more time there can bring any more successful result on Dracula-like overhead or on apparent impossibility overcoming destruction to players and our attitude concerning them which was wrought by small town grocers we ridiculously left behind as executives, managers and showmen despite every continuing proof of idiocy of such assignments. What worries me is fear I shall have to send hatchet man unfamiliar with operation to end this unbelievably fantastic incredible impossible waste. . . . I hope to heaven you have not found still more reason why those near morons have to be kept on still another week and another week as has happened for two years. I want studio closed I repeat closed. I repeat emphatically closed except for Ruth Madelon. This means auditing department complete except for Beaman and assuming all tax rebate papers on which Beaman needed help have been completed. I repeat auditing department completely closed except for Beaman to New York. I mean also offices given up. I repeat offices given up. I do not care how cheap they seem. It is apparent that so long as they are open you will not turn off the faucet from which is running out my health and nerves on top of everything else. Please Dan do not give me any more jokes in reply. Each joke now gives me spastic memories of what its predecessors have blinded us to.

In April 1950, this was the man pursuing Korda in any court that would hear him; considering how to buy out Irene for $2.5 or $3 million; offering Jennifer for *Streetcar*, *Carrie*, for a film in Italy to be directed by Rossellini; beginning a campaign (as trustee to Myron's estate) on how MGM had underpaid on its profits from *Gone With the Wind*; considering countless new projects to replace those he was urgently selling off; and alienating the last lieutenant.

Was this man entirely sane? Robert Walker had got drunk and violent in public, and he had turned himself in to Menninger's. Howard Selznick had chased women and squandered money, and he had been in hospitals in the East for as long as Dan O'Shea had worked for David. Howard's two daughters, Ruth and Florence, were already showing signs of mental illness. Myron had drunk himself to death. All the while David had lived in defiance of reality, unable to keep control or give up the display of pomp and mastery.

Dan O'Shea had had enough. He cabled back his resignation. David was immediately stricken and contrite, yet he knew this jig was up, too. He did not fight to hold O'Shea. He paid off the personal loan and did all he could to retain friendship:

Believe me, Dan, I greatly regret both our separation and its manner; and I'd like to believe that after all these years a little cooling off period will remove any trace of misunderstanding or bitterness. I have been quite ill and doped up for the past week or ten days, and it may well be that this, together with my nerves being at the ragged end as a consequence of our seeming inability to come to grips with our problems over not merely days and weeks but actually months and even years, led me to statements which I could not have made without so many drugs in me.

O'Shea was somewhat mollified. His going was drawn out, and he helped secure his own replacement: Frank Davis, the young lawyer who had handled the Korda case. Apart from that, Davis had had no other experience in the picture business. Yet David liked him, and Davis was tempted when offered three times his existing salary. Davis asked O'Shea's advice, and the veteran didn't know what to recommend. He tried to explain the tangle of David's affairs, but any description simplified. The problem lay in David's inability to see the net was made of strings, not holes. In the end, O'Shea admitted, David was rare company and fun. So Davis took the job.

In June 1950, David was serving virtually as Jennifer's agent; she had a real one, Ray Stark, but he was trusted with little more than 10 percent. David was pressing on *Carrie* and dealing with its director, William Wyler. At first, Jennifer had seemed cast in the role, but then Wyler and Paramount decided to make Carrie younger. Cloris Leachman was being considered. The bookman in David was horrified by this distortion. Yet as he protested he failed to see how Dreiser's story of Hurstwood and Carrie, of an older man who leaves wife and family for a younger woman (a would-be actress) and who is driven to steal as he falls in the world, had a bearing on himself and Jennifer.

On June 22, 1950, David poured scorn on Wyler and could not help but reveal himself:

> I just cannot imagine how you failed to see that casting an adolescent in the role distorts the entire story, and makes it unpleasant, and makes Hurstwood neurotic, if not actually degenerate. . . .
>
> Clearly the story has no point unless Carrie is a girl of obvious gentleness, despite her lack of outstanding talent and despite her lack of educational opportunities. The audience must understand why the man . . . falls hopelessly and irrevocably in love with *Carrie*, and goes headlong into doom and disaster.

In *Gone to Earth*, Jennifer had responded to the notion of a naive girl emotionally overpowered by older men. When she did *Carrie* it was to make a movie—one of her best—that seems enriched by her situation in life.

David lectured Wyler. He enlisted his past triumphs and turned a blind eye to some of Jennifer's limitations. He knew that Olivier was already set to play Hurstwood:

> As for the age differences ... I cast Olivier as the very much older man than Joan Fontaine. Joan at this time looked, and was, years older than Jennifer looks or is today. [In 1950, Jennifer was thirty-one; in 1939, Fontaine had been twenty-two.] And today Olivier looks and is *twelve years older.* So the notion that Olivier is right for Hurstwood and that Jennifer (who has just finished her very best performance as an 18 or 19-year old girl in *Gone to Earth,* and who preceded this with successful portrayals of girls respectively 12, 17 and 20 in *Portrait of Jennie*) would have been insufficiently young for Olivier and Sister Carrie, is so manifestly myopic as to require small argument.

Perhaps Wyler read with enough insight to gain some understanding of *Carrie* itself. He cast Jennifer. Shortly thereafter news broke that would have been more serious if the picture had not called for turn-of-the-century costumes. Jennifer was pregnant.

5 · WHAT IS COMING TO ME

FITFUL, SEARCHING, trying to escape, dreaming of a lucky strike, the prospector in David could still come close to gold. Evelyn Waugh's *Brideshead Revisited* had been published in 1945, and in July 1950 one of David's people in London urged it on Selznick and sent a synopsis. With slightly askew prescience, Waugh himself reckoned the story was perfect for Joan Fontaine and Laurence Olivier, Though, in 1950, he saw Olivier as Charles Ryder (the Jeremy Irons part).

Waugh was enthusiastic, if spared personal publicity. His spirits rose higher when his friend Graham Greene said he would like to do the screenplay. But it fell through because David could not muster the resources. He may never have got as far as looking at the book. If he did, then Brideshead was an interesting development of Manderley and Tara, the great home that has lost its treasured past.

That summer in Los Angeles, David was in an entertaining mood, even if distressed by the domestic economy at Tower Grove. Irene had presided over Summit Drive with complete vigilance. Her greatest problem had been explaining David's unpredictability to the servants. Now that was *his* job. Jennifer was neither housewife nor hostess; she was his David, subject to anxiety, retreat, agonies of makeup and dressing, so regularly delayed he had to start being prompt.

David now was checking the cost of their Fourth of July party, ordering boccie balls and croquet for the lawn and examining the liquor inventory. He believed he and Jennifer were being exploited by their servants. So used to signing checks without reading them (as if they were his letters), he was now forced to closer study. One couple got $128 for a day's work—"I can scarcely think that there has ever been . . . any colored servant . . . in all America that has been paid $64.00 a day." So he nagged Morgan Maree about ledgers, accounts, the way servants bought and ate luxury foods, and the estimate that he was paying $1,000 a month more than was necessary. Taxes were biting, and David was beginning to perceive a relationship between business money and personal expenditure:

> Also, and very important, it should be the problem of whoever has charge of this—and the obligation of such person—to make notes each day as to who was entertained the night before, for purposes of income tax deductions on proper business expenditures. I cannot justify the tightening up of expenditures around here [at the studio] while there is such a niagara of waste at home. With taxes now what they are, I could not possibly have enough to live on if I made half a million a year, at the present rate of expenditures *and this should be made clear to the staff* since I believe we have the reputations (handed around from servant to servant) of being chumps and easy marks.

Between them now, David and Jennifer's annual income was far from $500,000. In 1948, David's salary (from Vanguard) was $103,250, but after business losses and deductions, his net income came down to $11,278. Jennifer's income (from the Selznick Studio) was $129,250. For 1949, he earned $83,478 and she $130,000. And in 1950, filing taxes jointly, their net income after losses and deductions amounted to $43,080. (In that year, Jennifer's salary from the studio had been $154,333.) The figures seem worse than the facts: this *is* the presentation for the IRS, and David had advisers clever enough to move money around. Equally, it is clear that Jennifer's salary was vital to their life and that she hardly got to touch it. David was also behind on the monthly support payments to Irene for Jeffrey and Danny.

His predicament was underlined at one dinner party at Tower Grove that summer. On July 26, he and Jennifer entertained Myron's daughter, Joan. In February, truculent and intent on being her own woman, Joan had eloped to Las Vegas with "some gent in the paint business," a man named Grill, who had three children. He was thirty-five, and Joan was nearly twenty.

There were suspicions on David's part that Joan's marriage was a way of detaching herself from the "Selznick" name while staking a claim for legal independence. She seemed to him "a curiously and indeed unattractively suspicious person" who would only begin to acquire the capital of Myron's estate in 1955 and could not get it all until 1975. In the meantime, Myron's assets were in trust, and the income went 60 percent to Joan and 40 percent to Flossie. David was not just an executor of his brother's will, but—with Bank of America and Charlie Sachs—one of the estate's trustees.

In that position, he reviewed the continuing returns made by Loew's on *Gone With the Wind*—for Myron's estate held 6.774376 percent of the producer's share. Between Myron's death and mid-1949, the estate had received $226,357. By May 12, 1949, Loew's was admitting income to itself of $31.6 million—that is to say, the net income after all "adjustments" that they reported to the "producers." There was a major reissue of *Wind* in 1949, and the receipts on that surge alone were $4,646,000. Had David held on to his share (granted that in December 1946 the producer's share went up from 50 to 75 percent), he should have received about $1.45 million from the reissue.

This was the start of an obsessive campaign driven by naiveté, greed, and a belated fiscal education. As David examined the returns, he guessed that Loew's had all along been tricking the figures. He turned to his treasurer, Earl Beaman, and proposed a complete reexamination of Loew's ledgers:

> It is clear that up to the time I disposed of the picture, my own interest was very much greater than that of [Myron's] estate: I believe something like seven or eight times as great—so that for the years up to my disposition of the interest in the picture, which was subsequent to the time when it earned the largest part of its revenue, my interest would be very great indeed. And since I need money, I hope that you will lose as little time as possible in computing what is coming to me, and in getting it.

The effort would be unrewarding, but it was loaded with extra chagrin as David's lever—the estate—served an increasingly rich, and unsympathetic, niece. It would have been easier for David—and saved him a great deal of time—if, after 1942, *Gone With the Wind* had ceased to exist.

He was looking after Joan for Myron's sake: "I continue to have the feeling that one of these days he is going to bawl me out, as he used to love

Joan Selznick

to do, for judgments of mine with which he disagreed." As David planned for the baby Jennifer was expecting, he thought that if it was a boy, he would name him Myron.

David and Jennifer dined with the Oliviers on August 14. They were in Hollywood together, she for *Streetcar* and he for Hurstwood. D.O.S. had backed Olivier for the role on account of his "spurious elegance." Equally, Olivier was watchful enough to see how much his costar's life might help her with the part. When David tried to teach William Wyler the meaning of *Carrie*, he said it was rather like *A Star is Born*: "An ambitious girl rises to the top while the man who has supported her and adores her goes to the bottom. She never ceases to love him, despite the fact that the relationship becomes more and more impossible." The business reckoned that David was hurting Jennifer's career, yet he began to see himself as Norman Maine, the falling star who balanced her glory.

Meeting Vivien had been a great test for Jennifer. Here was the icon of David's art, the moment of his glory, as well as the actress who had won

Blanche on screen. When the evening was over, Jennifer sighed, for this had been a meeting of Tulsa, Oklahoma, and Vivien's most polished London act. "Oh, David," said Jennifer. "She's lovely! I wish I were like that."

There was another family landmark that summer. In August, Jeffrey Selznick was eighteen. In the fall, he would start at Yale. This was not by his choice. Jeffrey wanted to get into the movie business, at whatever level he could manage. When he heard his father talk, he noticed David's early start and the way the big producer had never finished college. David saw it another way entirely: "As I think you know," he told the reluctant Jeff, "I prepared for Yale, and I made a mistake that was akin . . . to that which you are making: I, too, thought that I was ready for business and for the motion picture industry. . . . As I have told you over and over again, I did not achieve whatever success I might immodestly claim because of my mistakes or shortcomings: it was in spite of them."

If he had to go, Jeffrey hoped for somewhere in California. But U.C.L.A. would seem too close to pictures for David and Irene. So he argued for Stanford. Then they dangled the carrot of a car, a convertible, if he got in at Yale. Jeffrey adored cars as much as he did movies. His grades at Deerfield were not good, but he did well on the college boards and he had a letter supporting his admission to Yale from a godfather who was also a benefactor of the institution—Jock Whitney. He begged to drive the car cross-country to Yale, but his parents feared his dramatic instincts at the wheel. The car was shipped to New Haven.

On August 28, David left Los Angeles, for a month. It was a time when Jennifer might have expected unusual attention. But David was engaged in a constant effort to sell off his pictures country by country, and though he was paying others to do that work—notably Victor Hoare in London—he liked to be doing it himself. In addition, he wanted to be at the Venice Film Festival for the first proper year of his creation, the Golden Laurel Awards. These were a response to the new creative strains in European film, an attempt to promote pictures with "universal themes." David even foresaw a "European film academy, modelled after the American Academy," and he could quickly bring himself to expect State Department support. For wasn't this a great cause in war-torn Europe? "I feel that we could in this fashion make a tremendous contribution to ideological unity during this, the most critical period of propaganda in the history of the world."

David had an Englishman, Anthony Downing, running the Awards, but he put more confidence in the charm and connections of the sixteen-year-old Marina Cicogna. He told Victor Hoare and Jenia Reissar what a treasure Marina was, in terms that might have made Jeffrey groan with frustration:

She is going on 17, and is one of the most brilliant people I have ever known, regardless of age. I am not one to rule people out either because they are too old or too young. When I was Marina's age after school hours I was running a publicity department of 100 people, and I think pretty well too, if I may say so.

He said Marina was "very near to being as close to me as though she were my own daughter." In Italy, in 1949, Jeffrey had seen the affection blossom. He was sure it was not romantic—"but it was more than a daughter, it was a super-daughter. He was much more interested in her than in Danny and me." David gave Marina his new Polaroid camera and then supplied her with film. The relationship was a portent of what a daughter might mean to David.

One of the films in the Venice festival was *Gone to Earth* (it had opened in London on August 21). Korda was there, too, and the warriors of the courts sat down to dinner grinning. A few hours later, David liked the film. At 5:38 in the morning, after celebrating, he cabled Jennifer to say "delighted beyond my greatest hopes with picture, and with your performance." He was always very tender in his comments about her work, for she so easily believed she was a failure.

As it happened, Jennifer was in great distress. David had gone away after some unsettled dispute. This was aggravated when no messages appeared. The Italian phone and cable system had ensured a complete sepa-

David with Marina Cicogna

ration. Jennifer was distraught: "I have sent several cables with no answer-sand I am ill and worried and can't work.

David got Arabella and Arthur Fellows to work out the problem. Contact was resumed quickly, and the panic passed. Olivier learned that Jennifer was pregnant and promised he and Vivien would take care of her while David was away. David talked of a trip to Egypt in the new year for both of them, but business kept him abroad. He moved on to Rome and Florence and sent Jennifer a postcard of the Michelangelo *David* (in an envelope) with Selznickian spectacles added in ink to the nude statue. "God, how hungry I am for you!" he wrote to her. "The mere thought of you does such things to me that I wouldn't be surprised if strange things were happening, in sympatico, anatomically to our friend whose photo is en-closed."

He did not make it home to Tower Grove until September 29. *Carrie* finished shooting in early November. Later that month, David took Jennifer to Palm Springs and then—to honor Myron—he decided to have a Thanks-giving party up at the Hill Haven house. Little had been done with the house since Myron's death. For the journey, David hired a bus and musi-cians to play for them. Whether the road was rough, or the party too rowdy, is not clear. But Jennifer felt ill and uncomfortable. They went back to Tower Grove and, by early December, she was in bed, "flat on her back . . . not daring even to move to one side, day or night, because she has been fighting desperately to stave off a threatened miscarriage."

David's mother was in the hospital for tests, also full of fears. And Jeffrey was flunking out at the end of his first term at Yale. He hadn't liked his living arrangement. He had had trouble getting up early for classes. One teacher, a survivor of the concentration camps, had picked on him for being a privileged Jew. The car had enabled him to get to New York when he wanted—and Irene had opened her play *Bell, Book and Candle* in November. As Jeffrey saw it, "I didn't know how to prepare my work in college. . . . I was thrilled to have movie houses available to me and I'd go see a double bill every night of the week."

The wariness that David had always felt toward Jeffrey came to a bitter head. It was a tragedy that the man who had learned so much from, and felt so much for, his father could not get on with his elder son. Most damaging of all, Jeffrey was lashed for emulating his father.

David had much to be guilty about, but on December 6, the pent-up worry and the mixed feelings exploded. Did he really want another child now? Would Jennifer miscarry? Could he save Jeff's place at Yale? With Jennifer in bed, David wrote Jeffrey a 10,000-word letter that invoked every point of shame: parents, Dr. Boyden, the headmaster at Deerfield, Pop

Selznick, Jock, not repeating the fateful mistake of D.O.S., and even the reputation of Hollywood Jews. Every insecurity was laid out in pages so relentless, so self-serving, it is unlikely a son could see to finish the letter. These passages are from a single-spaced twenty-page letter (with a blind cover to Irene) that concludes "With deepest devotion":

> My father wanted me to go to Yale, but his experience was not such as to be able to help me get there. Had he known what I know, surely I would have gone. . . . It has been my assumption that you would have the things that I have missed; and that you would be free of at least those faults of mine that, with the limitations that always exist as to one's objectivity about oneself, I could recognize. Certainly I do not attempt to defend those of my habits which you seem to be emulating, consciously or subconsciously: my regrettable lack of punctuality, my grotesque hours, my impositions upon people who work with and for me, my delusion that I "work better to a deadline." As the years have gone by, and with the help of psychiatry, I have conceded to myself, that these things are great weaknesses in my character, which I am now trying to correct. . . .
>
> It is surely no secret to you that, disgracefully, Jews are not the most welcome commodity at the leading American universities. Whether or not this will continue is entirely dependent . . . upon the performance of the Jews who do get in. . . . And how do you think your behavior is going to react upon other Jews seeking entrance to Yale? Don't think the entrance board doesn't consider how many Jewish boys they are taking in! Don't think that there is no danger that when the next son of prominent Jewish parents applies for admission, there isn't going to be the inevitable crack, "Probably another spoiled Jew like Selznick."

Ten days later, on December 16, Jennifer had a miscarriage.

6 · PAYMENT ON PRINCIPAL

IN THE EARLY WINTER OF 1950, as David sent Irene copies of his epistles to Jeffrey, he signed every message to her with "love," and he meant it. He would have been pained if his ex-wife had claimed there was anything else between them more problematic or less warm. He had never intended letting Irene go or seen her as less than his best audience.

As well as love, marriage, and family, they had shared partnership and the intricate forces that possess money yet cannot always keep a clear-eyed account of it. David was not mercenary or a miser. So many people in pictures sold their souls and disgraced the business for money. David had to believe of himself that he was not doing it for the money, so he ignored the figures and gambled his cash away. He was never more splendid or aglow in later life than when estimating how selling off *Gone With the Wind* had cost him maybe $15 million. That mistake was the entrance to infinite might-have-beens.

Irene had been raised to loathe the idea of debt or waste. Nothing guarded against it better than the hoarding of assets. Her family had always been secure, yet she anticipated disaster—it was as if she could not shrug off her father's upbringing. Yet she was fearful of money; she believed it distorted human relations, that it made people venal, dishonest, and un-sound. So she could not acknowledge how much she had or how steadily she accumulated. Money became a kind of ghostly character, an asset more potent in being neglected or locked away—it was something like sensuality in a frigid personality.

The pressure took its toll on the marriage early on. David was too knowing a member of the film community not to wonder whether he hadn't married Irene to move upward in the business. In giving up Jean Arthur for Irene, had he sacrificed True Love for pragmatism? Not even the fun and success at Metro had made up for the agonizing over nepotism. He had never quite decided whether he had gone there in 1933 out of weak greed or good sense. But he *never* made the tough decisions; he hoped action would chase them away. L.B. had become an overlord of David's imagination, the more compelling because he offered wisdom and opportunity for so simple a thing as fealty.

So theirs was only a "perfect" marriage. Irene was attractive, wise, brilliant, a fine hostess; she helped David make that social journey into the world of the Whitneys. Two family kingdoms merged, and surely, one day, David could have MGM? Yet David guessed that was only possible if one first vanquished or killed L.B. And he was not a killer. A man more determined on profit, power, and position would have kept *Gone With the Wind* and outplayed L.B.

Even the husbands of "perfect" wives have casual affairs. No matter the self-effacement of the wives, the men are led by the horn of opportunity and fantasy and by that immaturity which feels irked and smothered at the thought of a freedom given up. David's escapades had all those character-istics. But there was something more profound, in search of escape, gener-osity, and sensuality. He wanted someone as free from controls as he hoped he might be. He wanted silly, untidy, impractical love. Emotionally, he feared he might be nothing if he did not go for broke.

And if his private life with Irene had always had money and power as its drums, so in 1949, 1950, and 1951, there was a marching rhythm fit for the scaffold. That was when settlement was reached.

By the time he married Jennifer, David had reason for bleak pride in what he had accomplished fiscally. In May 1947, his debt to the bankers had stood at $9.5 million. Thereafter, he had had to teach himself to read financial reports. Once he read, he started to second-guess the men he paid to run the money. Thus, the repair work became the more tortuous and destructive to his ties with people like Dan O'Shea. Still, by the end of July 1949, David had paid off $10.679 million on principal (there had been fresh loans since 1947 amounting to $5.29 million) and $573,000 on interest. The outstanding bank loan was $4.155 million.

The means of reducing it were various. By June 1951, David had over $2 million in revenue on *The Third Man* and $685,954 in profit. In addition, he had close to $100,000 from royalties on the record of Anton Karas's zither music. There were the talent contracts steadily traded away in the late 1940s, and there were scripts and story properties. There had always been frozen funds in other parts of the world—one reason for David's venturing to Europe was to live on pounds and lire that he could not convert into dollars. By the end of October 1950, the bank debt was down to $1.715 million.

In these slow and painful acts of recovery, Irene was his auditor. From time to time, she did speak up, nagging at David for getting so little for, say, Louis Jourdan's contract when David had once promised how great a star the Frenchman would be. Irene was a demon for spotting waste and mistake—there was a payback there for having overlooked so many sexual flings and follies. She had it in her power, through lawyers or over the phone, to remind him of details of ineptitude or carelessness. He longed to buy her out, and she was anxious to be free from the risk. But she had some appetite still for squeezing him, and he was not without the masochist's desire to be pained by the woman he had betrayed.

David's distress was never closer to anger at Irene. On July 26, 1950, he asked Morgan Maree to send a letter to Irene's various advisers (and thus to Irene herself):

> Henceforth, I am ceasing my attempts to add new assets to Vanguard. So far as I am concerned, I shall continue feeling my obligation to the banks, who have repeatedly and consistently demonstrated a complete confidence in not only my ability but my integrity.... While I gather that Irene, and at least one of her advisors, feels perfectly willing to

let me pay the entire price of this moral obligation to the banks and their stockholders, I gather that it is the opinion of Irene and her representatives that she should receive fifty per cent of the residual beyond that payment of the debts. I think for the sake of the record we ought to summarize that Irene made no investment in money, no investment in time or effort, no contribution of any kind, in advice or otherwise; that she volunteered no contribution of any kind during the critical periods when we were in danger of going broke; that she drew large sums of money out of the enterprise during those years on a capital gains basis, and on top of the money made out of the previous enterprises; that she wishes, under no circumstances, to be involved, even remotely, in either any financial responsibility or any moral responsibility for the continuing operation of the enterprises; that she resists paying even her share of the taxes, even on the money that she has drawn from those enterprises, and even though other portions of it were earned on a capital gains basis; that she expects those enterprises not only to pay her the profits, but also to pay the taxes on those profits; that she expects me to continue to work without salary, and the sacrifice of my career, to the end that her fifty per cent of the profits may be increased; that during all this period, as during the years of our separation before the divorce, she made considerable money from enterprises of her own, from which she made no contribution whatsoever to these enterprises, and in which I never claimed the slightest share, even though to a large extent they

What do you do with contract players? Louis Jourdan, Ricki Soma, and Robert Mitchum on tour in Mexico. Soma would marry John Huston and be the mother of Anjelica.

were earned during the period when she insisted upon her half of the community property, limited to what I earned and without including anything she earned; that she wishes to continue to earn half of what is earned by these enterprises, under my direction (without salary), as a consequence of efforts necessary to repay the bank; that she would prefer to anticipate what these earnings might be and sell them now for a substantial price in order to make the risk entirely my own and the profits certain only to her. . . . This viewpoint seems to me to be so extraordinary and so incredible that I have decided it is worthwhile to put it down on paper once and for all, in all its ugly truth.

But during the course of August, crucial emotional holds were relinquished. On August 28, for $92,000 Irene sold David her half of the Selznick Studio. The bill of sale specified that this included "all her right, title and interest in and to all employment contracts to which The Selznick Studio is a party (including, but again not by way of limitation, the contract with Jennifer Jones)."

This was foreplay. Vanguard had always been the big thing, and David had been prepared to give up $2.5 million to be in the clear. But that was a cold-blooded sum to pocket, one that could take explaining to the boys. More than that, it would have ensured bitterness and separation afterward. And Irene could no more manage without David than he could stop talking to her. So, at the brink, she forgave him—then she could go on scolding him for the rest of time. This is what she said in August 1990:

> I didn't like the climate. I said, "Where did my David go? You're running down the thing that was most precious." I sat there and wept. He'd never heard this before. I had carried on about the gambling— but this was worse. This was corrupt! I let him off all kinds of things. He had already been so generous. I never saw anyone so generous. I had enough money. You can't be demanding with someone who is so generous.

Ten months later, on June 9, 1951, Vanguard was liquidated and David (and Jennifer) took on its remaining assets and liabilities. What followed was the start of yet another problem for David. For the year 1951, he reported liquidated assets of $1.006 million (this was comprised of accounts receivable for SRO, furniture and fixtures, remaining talent contracts, and petty cash). Vanguard receipts continued from June 9 to the end of the year to the amount of $801,019. Against that, they paid off $1.447 million of bank loans and deducted the original cost of the stock, leaving a capital gain of $249,853. David was advised to follow the "Carter Case" tax principle by which no valuation was put on the films and subsequent income was reported as long-term capital gains.

In the following years, that income was reported as, from June 9, 1951, to December 31, 1954, $3,121,791.

But by 1955, the IRS had caught up with the ploy. The Carter principle was rejected, and the examiner decided that the movies had had a value. He set it at $6.665 million. Thus for the year 1951, David had a tax deficiency of $1,510,208. The debt changed shape and color, but there was no escaping it.

At any time, David could have elected bankruptcy for Vanguard. When Frank Davis took over from Dan O'Shea in 1951, he marveled that that had not been done. It would have saved so much time and paper. Yet it would have smashed David's romantic sense of honor and fractured his relationship with Irene. Jennifer had been an infatuation and a passion. She had seemed to him the medium's great actress. And she had been a strike against the coldness and vigilance David felt in Irene.

But he did not break with Irene. He was too much in awe of her and too understanding of her. She was necessary as friend and scourge. And so, from the middle of 1951, they entered into their steadiest relationship, that of separated marriage. The condition that had long existed in truth was now legitimized.

For Irene, 1951 was a summer of grim, full harvest. Vanguard was liquidated, so she could tell herself she and David might start again. Now, he could woo her in safety, for she was resolutely unattainable and the romancing could burn for as long as life lasted. In time, it might even resemble friendship. That was order, peace, and victory. But there was more: her father was made ordinary.

After the divorce from Margaret Mayer, L.B. began to sell off parts of his racing stable. No one believed his financial difficulty could be that great. Losing his horses was a public atonement, a gesture. For years, Mayer had been famous as the highest-salaried man in America. He held no stock in Loew's Inc., but he got a bonus that was a percentage of the company profits. Between 1947 and 1949, Mayer sold his horses, in part because Nick Schenck was remarking on the distraction they presented. Mayer had other pursuits. In December 1948, he went to Yuma, Arizona, and married Lorena Danker, who was only one year older than Irene.

The vibrant triangle that David, Irene, and L.B. had made up went suddenly slack: two divorces and two remarriages in the space of two years. It gave the men another kind of affinity. L.B. might concede now that Irene was a tough partner. David could see, or guess, how close the older man had come to his end. In her way, Irene had overcome both of them. All three could feel a little weary, older certainly, and relieved after the fierce ordeal of intimacy. David and L.B. found in an odd way that they got on. And Irene could regard them both as older brothers—foolish, but hers.

L.B. and David had another thing in common: Dore Schary, who, in 1948, had been appointed head of production at MGM. It was the old Thalberg job and a position L.B. had offered many times to David. Schary was not in their league, but he had a few good years that helped Nick Schenck ignore the inevitable decline of a great studio. L.B. could not subdue his jealousy or keep pace with the changes in the picture business. He contrived a showdown and demanded that Schenck back him.

He had put his head on the block. Schenck could easily live with the younger success. L.B. announced his resignation and waited to see whether some force of nature would avert the evil day. But on August 31, 1951, after twenty-seven years of unrivaled power in the business, he left the building and walked to his car. Producer Arthur Hornblow watched from a window: there was no crowd, no party, no nothing. There was no one who had known L.B. who did not have something to treasure at having lived to see the moment. And that included family. Who else knew how much that old man deserved?

Irene had better rewards yet. Dore Schary had involved Bill and Edie Goetz in the cause of Adlai Stevenson, not just candidate for President but Menace to America in L.B.'s angry eyes. There were rows between Mayer and the Goetzes. L.B. refused to talk to Bill. Edie could come to call, but alone. She said that was an impossible demand. So she was rejected, too. L.B. dropped her from his will. The Goetzes still had their box at the racetrack, right behind L.B.'s. But the Goetz daughters, Judy and Barbara, were forbidden to speak to their grandfather, and he refused to notice them. Hatred and rivalry were institutionalized. As Irene put it, "When he said, 'my daughter,' he referred to me."

The feud between Edie and Irene is a vital yet elusive theme, hard to research yet important to remember. Edie's elder daughter, Judy, believed that Edie saw herself as L.B.'s favorite—the very role that Irene said was hers. There are those who think Irene always scorned Edie as a vulgar, lightweight Hollywood hostess and a mischief-maker; others claim that Irene was jealous of Edie's lasting marriage to the amiable Bill Goetz. In the end, the outsider has to regret the hostility and its ingenuity. For example, both sisters believed the other had neglected Margaret Mayer in her illness, just as both claimed credit for negotiating her divorce settlement. In the Mayer family, no one was allowed to feel secure—and that, surely, was the climate of L.B.'s making. Yet Irene believed that Edie had fomented Hollywood's and history's baleful view of Mayer. As if L.B. needed help. When L.B., Edie, and Irene had all passed on, the Goetz daughters and the Selznick sons were left in bewildered, pained relief.

Daniel Selznick was fourteen in 1950, an avid admirer of his father and closer to him emotionally than Jeffrey, just because Danny was more supporter than threat. Sometimes David would allude to the great loans he was carrying and Danny would say, "Dad, that's terrible, is that true?"

"Oh, don't worry," said David. "If you knew the plans I've got. I've got this, and we're going to do that. Then I'm going to do this. So-and-so wants to do that."

Danny lived with his mother in New York, and he went to school at Dalton. He felt he was her confidant and her helper, though there were matters she might lead up to but never discuss. "I felt that she turned to me a great deal and that she was extremely maternal, in the best sense of the word, in terms of problems I was having with girlfriends, with schoolwork, whatever it was."

And sometimes they would talk about David and his money problems.

"He's getting increasingly in debt," Irene told Danny. "It's getting worse."

The boy wondered, "Is there something I can do? Should I say something?"

"Don't say anything," Irene told him. "I just thought you should know."

Danny knew that David and Irene still talked and met whenever they were in the same city. There were presents and telephone calls. He did not feel the break was complete. Indeed, there was a suggestion that Irene was somehow watching out for David or watching over him:

> There was an unspoken implication from her—if he'd stayed with me, he wouldn't be in this trouble. Then they'd get together. And it sounded like she'd given him good advice, and I'd say, "O.K. he doesn't have her in his life on a day-to-day basis, but she's met with him and she's given him her advice, and now maybe things are going to turn around."

7 · KNOWLEDGE OF CHILD PSYCHOLOGY

DAVID WAS CONCERNED about Jennifer's depression after the miscarriage—even if he felt some relief. Irene believed he had not wanted the
child. Jeffrey reckoned the timing had been wrong: David was too worried
over money in 1950. But Danny saw another side to it, a Jennifer who feared
being ranked as "number two," what Irene wrote off as a symptom rather
than a cause of the divorce. To have a child by David could win him—"If
there was twenty percent of his attention going back to Irene, or to other
women, if she had a child then she'd have him 98.6 percent."

In the last days of 1950, with *Carrie* completed, David wondered
whether it wouldn't be best to get Jennifer back to work, if a film could be
fitted around the "protracted trip" he wanted to take with her. He asked
Charlie Feldman to enquire on their behalf and act as agent. He had heard
about *The Story of Ruth* in the offing. What were Joe Mankiewicz, Anatole
Litvak, and Henry King planning? A few months earlier, the teasing Michael
Powell had sent Jennifer a cable with a poke in the eye for David reading
over her shoulder:

> My dearest Jennifer: We are thinking of making a film of *The Tempest*
> next Spring. Would you be free to play Miranda? Would she, David?

That *Tempest* was never made. Nothing came of the approach to
Feldman. *Carrie* would not be released until July 1952, eighteen months after
the end of shooting, for once Paramount had looked at the film they
reckoned on commercial failure and even feared its jaundiced view of
America. Jennifer would do nothing in 1951 except the reshooting that David
decided on for the American version of *Gone to Earth*. In America, there was
a gap of nearly three years between the release of *Madame Bovary* and the
Selznicked *Gone to Earth*.

They went to Santa Barbara for a few days in the middle of January,
to the place where Phylis Walker first worked for D.O.S. But they stayed
at the Biltmore, where David and Irene had spent their wedding night. There
was always shadowy history looming over Jennifer. Early in February they
visited Mexico for a week, and then later in the spring Jennifer went to
Hawaii as David took off with Jeffrey on his spring break trip to the
Caribbean and Haiti.

Haiti was a vacation with a mission, for Jeff was failing again at Yale.

David hoped the French-speaking island would improve Jeff's linguistic skill. But while they were there, father and son had "one terrible row" in which "Jeff made it very clear to me . . . that he was not responsible if we made extra efforts on his behalf, and that he felt no obligation as a result of our having done more for him than was done for other boys by their parents." There was a radical in Jeffrey (he told David he believed the extra efforts were damaging), but he was a fearful mixture of hope and insecurity and more unsteady in nature than any advice or psychotherapy could deal with.

In the spring, Jennifer went to Korea to tour military hospitals, for she had allegiance still to her nursing efforts at the time of *Since You Went Away*.

David had a dinner party while she was away, and Jennifer herself asked the Swedish actress Viveca Lindfors to be his hostess. At the end of the evening, David insisted on riding home with her in his chauffeur-driven limousine. "The battle began the moment we hit the highway," said Lindfors, and she realized the chauffeur had enough experience not to notice the boss's backseat groping. Lindfors thought it "ridiculous and pathetic," and she wondered how much Jennifer knew.

David wanted to give Jennifer the most restful time possible that summer, so he rented the old Thalberg house at the beach. With the Walker boys and the Selznick sons, the Tower Grove house seemed too small. The house at the beach had a good pool, a fine projection room, and an ideal room for Flossie, as well as playrooms and guest quarters.

The dean of freshmen at Yale broke it to Jeffrey: he had failed Logic, and it was felt that "I was just simply emotionally too immature." His options were summer school and try for reentry or get a job. But both in the East. Then the son parlayed another arrangement: he could live at the Thalberg house with David and Jennifer and do summer courses at U.C.L.A. Jeffrey saw it as a tough deal: without a car, he had to use the bus, and he was expected to conform and behave. David had weakened, for he knew Jennifer flinched from Jeffrey's hostility. Somehow he strove to believe he could please everyone.

The "invitation" to Jeffrey was twelve pages of love and rebuke, of warning and lavish daydreaming. On the one hand, David supposed they could play golf together, "develop a comradeship," and generally look after each other. But then David recalled Jeff's sloth and selfishness: "It is some kind of commentary that my doctors are trying to get me to cut *down* my work to forty hours, by comparison with the sixty and eighty hours I have put in for twenty years or more, while I am trying to get you *up* to forty hours!"

David said Jennifer was exhausted after Korea, so he could not "have her summer spoiled by having in the house either a prisoner, or someone who is here ungratefully or miserably." He did invite his son nevertheless, but on terms that guaranteed wariness:

> Thus, if—as I genuinely and deeply hope—you really want to be with us, and you do come to stay with us, I hope you will make yourself the attractive member of the household which it is so very easy for you to become. You have enormous intelligence and enormous charm—but, boy, how this disappears when you live like a slob, with your room a disgraceful mess, stuffing yourself like a pig, nasching [*sic*] at all hours, sleeping at irregular times, stretched out on the bed or the couch half-dressed and with the lights on, yelling at the servants, complaining about little slip-ups in luxuries available to one-hundredth of one per cent of boys of your age, whining and complaining, dramatizing yourself, going through all sorts of pitifully transparent maneuvers and petty artifices to accomplish some minor objective, or even some major objective.

Jeffrey went there for the summer, took the bus, did his classes in the morning, and got an afternoon job at Technicolor. He did not warm to Jennifer. He saw a woman who sat on the floor on bright silk pillows, who practiced yoga, and who was late whenever there was a party. He saw fits of anxiety over clothes and makeup: she might change her outfit half a dozen times before an event. Jeffrey felt she and his father were just two people who lived in the same house. The only sympathy he had for Jennifer came on hearing that needling tone in David's voice, the attacks he had thought were for him alone.

Father and son talked. David said times were hard, and he counseled austerity. Then he'd throw an extravagant party. If Jeffrey remarked on the inconsistency, David would wave him off and say, "You don't understand. If anybody thinks I'm broke, I'm dead. So I have to keep up the appearance that nothing has changed."

This was the summer of L.B.'s departure from Metro. Jeffrey noted that David and his grandfather talked on the phone and often had breakfast or lunch together. David was outraged at L.B.'s fate, according to Jeffrey: "He thought it was criminal. He thought this was the end of an era and that it was suicide for Metro."

Near the end of August, Jeffrey went back to New York, his future uncertain. David and Jennifer left, too, on their way to the Venice Film Festival. But they got only as far as New York. On August 28, at his house on Sunset, just east of Pacific Palisades, Robert Walker died.

Walker had a day off from *My Son John* at Paramount. He spent it at home, without visitors. In the early evening, his housekeeper called Dr.

Frederick Hacker, his psychiatrist (as well as consultant in the cases of Howard and Ruth Selznick). A friend of Walker's, Jim Henaghan, was at the house when Hacker arrived, to be followed by another doctor, Dr. Sidney Silver. According to Henaghan, and on Hacker's order, the three men restrained Walker and he was given sodium amytal, a tranquilizer. The young actor never regained consciousness. Another doctor was called in— Dr. Myron Prinzmetal—he arrived at about 10:00 p.m. and said Walker was dead.

Henaghan had already phoned Dore Schary, for Walker was a Metro contract actor, and Schary managed to reach David and Jennifer in New York. They flew back, incognito, and David got Arthur Fellows to retrieve the Walker boys—they had been staying with friends. David did everything possible to suppress publicity, and he would attack Schary for the releases handed out from the MGM offices. On September 1, he told Schary that "in every decision that has been made during these agonizing days, the welfare of the two boys has . . . been the uppermost and dominating factor in the minds of everyone."

The same concern applied to Jennifer and might save her some bad publicity. In many quarters, her screen sweetness had been contrasted with two broken homes. Walker's breakdown was easily interpreted as the inability to cope with the loss of his wife. The circumstances of the death were odd. Hacker cosigned the death certificate, which reported "natural causes after receiving a dose of sodium amytal and had been a victim of schizophrenia of an undiagnosed nature." David admitted to Schary that "the doctors and the psychiatrists spent many hours (of course this is confidential) struggling with the death certificate, although they were naturally most scrupulous about being accurate, but the phrasing of it was a matter of great importance to the future welfare of the children."

There were arguments over how much Walker had been drinking, whether he was truly schizophrenic or just unhappy, and as to how suicidal he had been. It was another burden for Jennifer's guilt, and it brought David added responsibility for the Walker boys. He was part of the decision to switch Walker's funeral from Forest Lawn to his hometown of Ogden, Utah, in an attempt to escape reporters. When that was dealt with, David and Jennifer set out for Italy once more, this time with Michael and Robert Walker, Jr.

Getting away might escape the photographers and the gossip columnists who had "portrayed a startling and depressing and even frightening ignorance of the most elementary knowledge of child psychology." This was the David who once had scarcely been able to listen to what Dr. David Levy had to tell him. How should children equip themselves to handle the unstable energies of such parents and guardians? How may they relax when their elders are not just stars of the screen, but featured players in psychiatric serials? For the travels to Europe were also a means of letting Jennifer take discreet therapy in Zurich. No one who knew her then felt easy about her state of mind or the acting out that might seize her.

There was never quite a home: in all of 1951, for instance, David and Jennifer were only at Tower Grove for scattered weeks. Otherwise, they clung to change and lodging: the Thalberg house at the beach, hotels, New York, London, Paris, Rome, Switzerland. Nineteen fifty-two was just as fitful and nomadic, even if the residences were luxurious and even if the children had to be sheltered from difficulties over how to pay the hotel bills. Do not let the world see you are broke because in those audience eyes one must be smiling, successful, and lovely.

The kids were torn between shyness and grandeur, yet whenever doctors appeared, David went into a version of script conference with them. In Paris, in October 1951, "little Bobby Walker" was taken ill. One doctor, the one recommended by Anatole Litvak, said it was appendicitis. There should be an immediate operation. David second-guessed. He sought further recommendations, this time from David Bruce (the U.S. ambassador in France). Bruce was out of town, but the governess to his children suggested a doctor in whom they had enormous confidence. This lady examined the young Walker. Food infection, she declared. The first doctor said it would be a calamity not to operate. "Well," said David later, "to cut a long story short, Bobby recovered the next day; as soon as we got to America, we had him checked and double-checked, and of course the woman was completely right."

The lessons of this adventure were not consistent: do not trust doctors—but seek other doctors; favor women doctors—"forgive my seeming predilection toward women," but they do have less "egoism"; and seek further opinions until someone urges masterful inactivity. A cynic might say that is the favorite treatment for hypochondriacs and imaginative invalids. David only reported Bobby Walker's "close call" to Irene because, in 1952, Danny had "a thing" on his neck that was prompting talk of operations and removal of a gland. An ocean away, David had described this case to his Parisian doctor, Dr. Raymonde Grumbach, and she wondered if it didn't sound like the "fake meningitis" that was so prevalent.

David was doing business in Europe, too, in the fall of 1951, selling off assets, getting pictures into release, and looking for fresh ventures. He had been impressed by Ingrid Bergman going off to Europe and Roberto Rossellini. Perhaps great actresses needed European directors. Marina Cicogna's father had been a backer of Vittorio De Sica's *Bicycle Thieves*, a film that had been offered to SRO, only for David's Italian representative to urge against it.

So David had sought to make amends. Through Jenia, he had been pursuing De Sica. She warned him the Italian spoke no English, was not a writer, and—despite his artistic identification with impoverished people—wanted a three-year contract, at $2,000 a week the first year, rising to $4,000 in the third. Still, David believed this Italian neorealist might show the world the greatness of Jennifer as an actress. Talks went on.

From Rome, the family moved to England and the Savoy. Jenia Reissar was asked to get a tutor for the Walker boys for the week they were in town. She found a teacher who led the boys off to museums, galleries, and the Festival of Britain on the South Bank. He came back a few days later and said, "I'm through. I'm not dealing with those hooligans. I just won't have anything to do with them. They have no manners whatever. They have far too much money. I have no control over them. They spend their time chewing gum and sticking it under everywhere."

They were all back in New York in time for Christmas—"at one of the nice hotels," said Frank Davis, the new vice president, who was invited with his wife to the Christmas Eve present-giving. It was just David and Jennifer: the boys were sent off to their room. "And he had gone through the whole apartment with a long, beautiful white ribbon with 'To Jennifer—I love you' all numbered. There were sixty-two presents to Jennifer that she would unwrap in sequence."

In the New Year, on January 16, David went to Philadelphia, Pennsylvania, to preview his American version of *Gone to Earth*. It was called *Gypsy Blood* for the moment. Powell and Pressburger had declined to come over for the "salvage" job, so David hired Rouben Mamoulian. The costumes were sent over, and David Farrar and Cyril Cusack came, too, in a daze, to do new close-ups and new lines of dialogue. David was tidying it all up and pouring another $165,000 into the picture. He reduced Powell's version from 110 minutes to 82, and he elected finally to call it *The Wild Heart*. As such, it opened in Los Angeles on January 17, 1952, and in New York on May 28. It did no better commercially than in England, but David's shorter film had lost the power of Jennifer's performance for Powell.

At the end of February, David and Jennifer went to Jamaica to stay with Bill and Babe Paley. *The Wild Heart* had had bad reviews—*Carrie* was still not in release. But David had arranged for Jennifer to begin work soon on a new picture for King Vidor. It was called *Ruby Gentry*, and it had affinities with *Duel in the Sun*, not just in story line and the study of a destructive passion, but in the way David was already telling Vidor how to do the picture. "In Jamaica," said Bill Paley, "David and Jennifer had terrible fights. You could hear the arguments. They weren't meant for each other. But she was a very nice girl."

Others said David and Jennifer had neurotic personalities that might have been designed to fit together in bouts of serenity and hysteria. She was the spectacle, he was the showman. She was the helpless vessel of anguish and desire, he was the controlling genius. She always changed her mind—he never could make up his. She seemed beset by malady and tragedy, and yet she owned a secret, inner durability. He was energy personified—but he was weakening, and slowing, and he had less will than ever before to be David O. Selznick.

In the first half of 1952, again, David avoided Tower Grove by traveling; he was angry when Morgan Maree failed to secure the Thalberg beach house for another summer. David had promised that to himself as a "reward" after "this bitter and last year of recovery." Tower Grove was not big enough for all the fun David wanted. He began to think of building a separate cottage on the grounds for the Walker boys. Jess Morgan in Maree's office, David complained, had neglected the negotiation with Norma Shearer for the beach house. He had got married instead, and so his "honeymoon plus his indifference to the welfare of my family and myself and to our desires and to what we have looked forward to all year has taken all the joy out of returning to California."

Before going back "home" at last, David sent a memo to Margaret Nilsson, the housekeeper at Tower Grove, with twenty-five points. He gave orders about special light bulbs, notepads by the phones, ashtrays, "first class fruit," drinking glasses in the bathrooms, Kleenex holders, his special soap,

David with Morgan Maree

a teaspoon by the bed, one tomato juice rather than another, "Tastychips" potato chips . . . and:

> There is something wrong with the way the beds are made. The sheets are tucked so far under the end that they don't come up high enough; also, they are not turned over enough at the tops so that they are a nuisance in the middle of the night. Or maybe they are turned over too much. But anyway, I wish you would instruct the girls on how to make up the beds.

In the spring in which he was fifty, D.O.S. visited the same anxious obsession with detail, the same clerical attention to his proper spoiling, the same interference *and* indecision on *Ruby Gentry*. This was a Twentieth Century-Fox release, with a producer of its own, Joseph Bernhard. David had no credit and no role, except that of husband to the star.

There are some critical apologists for King Vidor who claim *Ruby* was his vengeance on what Selznick had done with Pearl Chavez in *Duel in the Sun*. In an early draft of the script "Ruby" was actually named "Pearl," and in its conclusion, in a mist-laden swamp, as the loving couple stalk one another, there is a clear allusion to the finale of *Duel*. But it is a pale, black-and-white parody of what was once unbridled insanity. Despite fleeting bouts of dynamism, *Ruby Gentry* is small and trashy, only eighty-two minutes long, close to exploitation. At the box office, it did well enough, but David was rather ashamed of the success.

There had been a new note of potboiling in his intrusions. He wanted something for Jennifer that was not another flop. Vidor had apparently indicated his intention of making an artistic film. David turned on this, like McCarthy spotting a Red: he was an uneasy showman in changing times, desperate to get back to old virtues. American movies were becoming bolder with material, if only because of the confusion as to what played commercially. David allied old-fashioned attitudes to the best modern market research. He was beginning to sound like anyone in Hollywood:

> Reliance upon the intelligence and knowledge of an audience, to the extent that King indicated it is his intention to do, makes no concessions whatsoever to the immaturity of that section of the audience which can be disregarded with impunity only on rare subjects which are certainly outside the field of *Ruby Gentry*. This picture, if it is to get its costs back, not to speak of making a profit, must play not only to adult audiences but *also* to literally millions of people of the actual ages of between five and fifteen, and to still millions more of this mental age.

The movie previewed in Pasadena on September 24, 1952, and it would open on Christmas Day. In the process, David boasted to his old pal Al

Lichtman, now a vice president at Fox, as if old times and the D.O.S. style had not changed. But the boast was ready to settle now, to take some money and run:

> I have just finished thirteen uninterrupted hours during which, jointly with Vidor, his cutters, and my cutters, I did a complete overhaul and recutting job from beginning to end of *Ruby Gentry*, about which perhaps best comment is that Vidor is wildly enthusiastic, not ninety-nine per cent, but one hundred per cent. It is a job on which normally I would have spent a month. I resisted any and every notion of any kind of retake whatsoever, even when Vidor suggested them, and excepting only for inserts. I am contributing out of my own library several vitally important stock shots without cost. Think I have combed almost all of the junk out of the picture and that it can now not only get money but even actually be a respectable picture.

David was emerging from the old debt, very slowly, but he was close to being broke personally. He was harassed, unstable, traveling, searching, and tiring. With his two sons and two stepsons he was well intentioned, generous in person, and extravagant in plan, yet seldom truly helpful or considerate. Having never known calm himself, he could give it to no one else.

There was something else. Of the four boys for whom David was now responsible, Danny was the most stable, the most star-struck, and the one most sympathetic to David. Jeffrey had seen so many movie actors growing up; he knew the false glory and the real shabbiness, and he felt superior. Yet Jeffrey was desperate to make movies himself, and he could not rid himself of the psychic urge to be like his father. Danny was younger. He gave David adoration and admiration, and he worked hard but naturally to think as David did. As a result, he fell in love with Jennifer. His view of her, and of her with David, is valuable as a mirroring of what David felt. It begins with a theatrical comparison—for to be a Selznick, without terror or faltering, one had to live as if in a story or a movie:

> I remember that when I acted in Ibsen's *The Master Builder* at college [Harvard], there was a character, Hilda Wangel, and the director said, "Can you understand what Ibsen means when he says that Hilda has this life force?" I understood it completely. Because to me, Jennifer had it, this tremendous capacity for life. That's something that she had in common with my father. . . . It was a driven energy. It illuminated the space that she was standing in. There was like a fire inside her that made you want to pay attention to her on screen and in life. I felt myself drawn towards it and I know my father felt it. Part of it was her desire to please, something that does seem built into an

actress. But there was also this tremendous life force, which I suspect made her exciting sexually. She wasn't a towering intellect, but I was never bored with her. . . . I think that my father loved me very much and I think that he told her that. He found it difficult, at times, to express that love: he didn't interface with a child very easily. So what Jennifer did for the two of us, in a strange way, was that she extended the relationship. She made me feel that my father loved me very much and that her feeling for me was partly inspired by his feeling for me. The way she talked, the way she hugged me, the way she wrote me. Passionate. . . . I think my mother was very puzzled by it. She had her own view of Jennifer, as a creature of limited intellect, limited charm, not really quite figuring out how she could appeal to my father except in the most base levels. She would ask me questions, and I would be careful. I was really smitten with Jennifer and I would talk about her warmly. And my mother would say, "When you're older, you'll know better" and "I certainly hope you never fall in love with an actress." But I have to say that I saw Dad extremely happy with Jennifer on many, many occasions. She fulfilled something for him. . . . You see, Irene was judgmental and critical. And Jennifer was not. She was totally supportive, giving, tolerant of the most outrageous excesses. If he wanted to smoke three packs of cigarettes a day, it was all right with her. If he forgot things, he'd say, "Forgive me, darling, forgive me." She had temper tantrums, and there were plenty of times Jennifer was angry with him. But she would always forgive him, instantly. He was like a little boy. If I'd said to him, "Dad, which woman is better for you?" he'd have said, "Irene's much better . . . but Jennifer makes me happier."

8 · SHOULD HAVE BEEN UNTHINKABLE

IN THE EARLY 1950S, D.O.S. was ahead of most American contemporaries in sniffing out fresh breezes in European cinema. From a seat in the dark, he could be moved by neorealism. Yet as soon as he saw *Bicycle Thieves*, he wondered about the story being remade in some American city . . . with Cary Grant as the father? Somehow, he was immune to the irony of De Sica's father figure needing a bicycle to keep his job of pasting up Rita Hayworth posters for *Gilda*.

Of course, his motives were mixed. He wanted to escape a home community greedy for his new failure. He wanted the admiration of Venice, an occasion for Jennifer to see her Swiss analysts, and splendid hotels. But he also saw the innovative opportunity for coproductions and breaking down barriers. When he acted, though, he often fulfilled Europe's worst idea of the overbearing Hollywood mogul.

That image now was encouraged by some American films. On September 18, 1952, before leaving for Rome and *Stazione Termini*, David sneaked into a theater in Pacific Palisades to see *The Bad and the Beautiful*. This was an MGM movie, directed by Vincente Minnelli and produced by John Houseman, in which Kirk Douglas played a charismatic and unscrupulous producer, Jonathan Shields. David had had Frank Davis check the film out in case of a need to sue Metro. Davis said leave it alone. Yet for anyone in the business the brotherhood of Shields and Selznick was apparent and entertaining. It ranged from the emotional influence of a father to Shields having David's habit of kicking off his shoes. Houseman had suffered a little under David, had felt used and patronized.

David huffed and puffed, not sure whether to be flattered or offended—for the film had a deeply ambivalent attitude to Shields: finally, the rascality of his snake charmed all the flute players. There was another message to read in the film and in *Sunset Boulevard* (1950). They both breathed with the relief that "Hollywood," the Golden Age, might be a thing of the past, fit to be mocked.

The Selznicks were in Rome by the end of October, ready to engage with the Italian director of *Shoeshine* and *Bicycle Thieves*. De Sica wanted to make a movie about the variety of life at a great railway station. The realist saw a panorama that had to be filmed in a real station (in Rome), with many stories, or incidents, spilling over so that the viewer could see how insignificant each story was in the sea of affairs. David was excited and challenged. But he could only grasp many fragmentary stories if there was one compelling story holding all together: it should be the last meeting of lovers—an American wife and an Italian man. David had memories of *Anna Karenina* and David Lean's recent *Brief Encounter*, and he pictured glorious images of Jennifer's lovelorn face.

Coproduction requires self-deception on all sides. David wanted art, prestige, Continental sophistication; the Italians wanted American money, big stars, and a chance of getting to Hollywood. So all parties agreed the contradiction could be reconciled, that Jennifer would look like a goddess and Montgomery Clift pass as an Italian.

There were two teams of scriptwriters, for there would be American and Italian versions. De Sica's group, led by Cesare Zavattini and Mario Soldati, were busy generating background action. Soldati had even suggested that the man should be a cad relieved to have his American mistress depart. That offended David's wish for unmitigated tragedy. But he conceded that "his" script, by Carson McCullers and Paul Gallico, was not working. He found rescue in another American writer wintering in Rome, the twenty-eight-year-old Truman Capote. Capote didn't much like the story, but he needed money, and he and David got on famously.

The shooting began and winter set in. But because De Sica wanted the real station, and David insisted on story, stars, and dialogue, they had to work through the night, for six days a week, without coffee, soup, or tea, in great cold. The electricians were paid extra so as not to ask for meal breaks. Clift arrived so late they could not shoot in continuity, and then the actor grew uneasy being directed by an interpreter. David was delivering memos to De Sica every evening before shooting, with mounting distress at the quality of the sound and the photography.

In Italy sound was redubbed after shooting. The station was not an easy place to record. The Italians were inexperienced with magnetic recordings or live dialogue. So David insisted on Dick Van Hessen being flown in to supervise sound. More serious, he felt, was the photographic problem. The Italians were not trained in glamour, and De Sica did not favor close-ups. Realism required long shots and unadorned faces. Jennifer, David complained, was looking terrible and unlike her real self. So he imposed himself once more. The Italian cameraman G. R. Aldo could do everything up to full-figure shots. Anything closer was the responsibility of Oswald Morris, the English cameraman recommended by John Huston, for whom he had just shot *Moulin Rouge*.

As Morris recalled, "It was made absolutely clear to me by D.O.S. that

David and Jennifer listening to Vittorio De Sica

he held me responsible for Jennifer's appearance in the movie, that I was to tell him exactly where Aldo was going wrong and all her scenes were to be retaken! We eventually did this very thing much against De Sica's will . . . Aldo and I were just about on speaking terms at the end. De Sica was quite wonderful with his handling of nonprofessional actors he pulled off the streets. He would show them himself how to play the part and then bully them into submission and they loved him for it. D.O.S. simply could not come to terms with this style of moviemaking, even though De Sica was merely doing what he had always done in his many previous successful movies. The sad end to all this was, of course, the two entirely different movies. The chemistry was doomed to failure from the outset."

The memos grew more dismissive; even in translation, the Italian was stung. The hysteria of the lovers never worked on screen, but in the freezing station at night, Jennifer and Clift discussed another kind of scenario. "Jennifer is madly in love with David," Clift told a friend, "but she talks openly about his emotional instability to me. She says it's almost as bad as her own." Clift called David "an interfering fuckface."

In the small hours of one morning, Jennifer ran from the set in unstoppable distress, and David had to call up a limousine to pursue her through the streets of Rome. David was not an unaided runner, but, like Hazel in *Gone to Earth*, Jennifer had an urge to desperate flight. And, as it seemed to onlookers, it was David's presence that made Jennifer berserk.

Yet again, David's convulsion of guilt and desire over Jennifer did reach the screen. Early on, the woman writes a farewell letter to the man: we see the page and the handwriting—David's. He was always afraid the character was being turned into a cold exploiter and that Jennifer might find herself compromised by having to play sex scenes for the Italian version. David wanted passion *and* chastity:

> The man has to have some kind of feelings; and if he does not feel shame and horror and remorse at having dragged the woman into this situation, cheapened her, brought her to the verge of ruination of her own life, of the life of her daughter and of the mother's relationship with the child—and if instead of this he is still thinking in terms of passion—he is just a sex machine and not worth writing about or showing on the screen.

David and Jennifer flew back to New York for a rushed Christmas at the Sherry Netherland. By January 1, 1953, they were at the Suvretta House Hotel in St. Moritz for ten days. On the eleventh, they returned to Rome, and on the following day David was able to screen an assembly of *Stazione Termini*. It was too long, and anyone could tell it was not working. De Sica was reduced to talk of miracles in the editing, while his lawyers sought concessions in the contract. Some retakes were done in the Piazza Navona to correct what David called "the distortion of Jennifer's face and figure into a monstrosity because of what I regarded, and still regard, as the almost irrational insistence upon giving superior consideration to the photography of buildings."

Lawyers were gathering, with interpreters for the lawyers. Frank Davis was even compelled to seize some of the film and take it out of the country. David's wrath became very great at Italian insinuation against his integrity. He was the more bad-tempered because of increasing pain in his rear. The dramatist in him had wondered about cancer. But the doctors had only piles to report, and they recommended an operation soon. He had laryngitis, too, for which David knew "the cure is more sleep, less smoking, less talking and less dictating. But that's a little bit like that old gag of getting the horse used to doing without food just before the horse died."

There were other pressures. Jennifer had been contracted in advance to go directly from *Stazione Termini* to John Huston's *Beat the Devil*. She had wanted to work with Huston again, and so David had taken the worst of deals and a mere sketch of a script. As it happened, *Beat the Devil* was no project for the solemn.

As he tried to outmaneuver De Sica in Rome, he was groaning over Huston's script for *Beat the Devil*. Having seen Jennifer in black-and-white, he tried to argue Huston out of that medium for the next film: "there just is no comparison in the way Jennifer looks in color as against the way she looks in black and white. She is far more beautiful in color, and also looks younger." With that provoking ingenuity of his, hovering between genius and cruelty, Huston had cast Jennifer as an Englishwoman in a blond wig. David asked could she maybe play the part Irish? Only one of David's many suggestions was accepted: Truman Capote was hired to help on the script. David was very impressed with Capote: "he is easy to work with, needing only to be stepped on good-naturedly, like the wonderful but bad little boy he is, when he starts to whine."

Huston was an old acquaintance; if not the warm friend David assumed, at least a wary Selznick-watcher. The current and fourth Mrs. Huston was Ricki Soma, a model-actress David had once had under contract. Huston welcomed Capote into the strange assembly that would make *Beat the Devil*, but he was anxious to keep that other bad boy, D.O.S., away.

From Rome, David took Jennifer to North Africa for a trip: by early February, they were in Marrakech. The cable system was not as sure from there, so David fell into an unusual telegraphese, such as most people use in telegrams. On February 12, he sent Huston and his coproducer, Humphrey

Bogart, a five-page condensed cable in Ravello, where *Devil* was to be shot. Among other things, it marveled at the inexplicable script: "difficult even determine whether intention drama melodrama comedy farce satire or even in third act slapstick akin Abbott and Costello in Africa."

Huston was not fazed. The more moods the merrier. There was drinking and gambling in Ravello, as well as moviemaking. *Beat the Devil* was a moment of elegant collapse in Hollywood earnestness, a serene making-it-up-as-you-go-along, indifferent to commerce or the staccato cables from Marrakech. At one point, Huston told David he was going to pull the movie out of his hat. David did get in and out of Ravello a couple of times to find an ongoing party that included Huston, Capote, Bogart, Gina Lollobrigida, Peter Lorre, Robert Morley, the future director Jack Clayton (as associate producer), the young Stephen Sondheim as an assistant, Ossie Morris as cameraman . . . and Jennifer. In the view of Morris:

> I do not believe that Jennifer ever thought she was playing for com-edy. She played it straight all the way through with that terrible, phoney English accent and Huston felt it best to leave her alone and let things slide. Off the set things were as mad and daft as they were on the set but Jennifer held herself in total isolatic n. She had her own Selznick-appointed entourage who took care of her twenty-four hours a day but she never joined any of her fellow actors after shooting hours or even at lunch.

Whatever her intention, she is comic; the movie that confused David as much as any he ever saw is now a classic of parody and irrational motivation. From Marrakech, David sent signals, but in *Beat the Devil* the communication is never straight or tidy. He was in pain, dreading his operation, and losing a lot of blood.

He went back to America for his operation in April, and he was reunited with Jennifer in London in May for a belated birthday celebration. They dined with a group that included John and James Woolf, backers on *Beat the Devil*. Around midnight, Jenia Reissar was woken by a ring at the door. It was David with a friend who was carrying Jennifer in his arms. David gave orders for his wife to be put in Jenia's bed. There had been trouble in the car. Jennifer had insisted on getting out and running away. She lost a shoe and a valuable earring, and they had had trouble restrain-ing her.

The chauffeur went to the Savoy to fetch Jennifer's maid. David used Jenia's phone to call Jennifer's psychiatrist, in Zurich, and have him come over immediately. With Jennifer asleep now and the maid arrived, David went back to the hotel to catch up on his sleep. Jenia was awake still when the doctor arrived from the airport. The doctor talked to Jennifer and gave her something, and then slipped back to Switzerland. The maid returned to the hotel to get some day clothes for Jennifer. Life picked up on normal again, without shame. But by the autumn of 1953, after fifteen years' work for him, David had to let Jenia Reissar go. There was no real future in coproduction or maintaining a London office.

The Selznicks returned to Los Angeles, and now they lived at Tower Grove. David was busy editing the American version of *Stazione Termini*. He previewed the picture in San Francisco and Berkeley over the Labor Day weekend and had depressing reactions. So he went back to it again, with a vengeance. By October 21, he had news and recriminations for De Sica, mixed in with wild optimism. *Terminal Station* would not do as a title, David believed. But he was getting a good response to *Indiscretion of an American Wife*. By advertising that forthcoming title in an alluring way, he prompted Columbia to put up $500,000 for American distribution rights.

He told De Sica that not even on *Gone With the Wind* had he "devoted so much time and care and energy and even money to the cutting and recutting of a picture." With all the footage to look at, David was dropping more and more scenes that did not work. The movie ran barely an hour! Why worry about that, he told De Sica: "There is no reason on earth for a picture running any particular length, and the 'experts' who talk to the contrary are the very same people who thought I was out of my mind in making a picture, *Gone With the Wind*, that was almost four hours in length."

When De Sica asked to have his name removed from the wreckage, David sighed with fatigue at the ingratitude. For D.O.S. had spent months attempting to rescue a film that, irrevocably, had to carry the name of De Sica. He complained about the difficulties De Sica had given him and the poor reviews in Europe. When the full dangers of fifty-eight minutes were pointed out, in February 1954, D.O.S. borrowed a duplex apartment in Tudor City, William Cameron Menzies to direct, James Wong Howe to do photography, and with Jeffrey and Arthur Fellows as assistants, he hired Patti Page to film and sing two songs that would afford record tie-ins and swell the running time to sixty-three minutes. *Indiscretion of an American Wife* opened at last in Los Angeles on May 27, 1954. It was a disaster.

Beat the Devil was out of David's reach. Huston edited it languidly: no one had great hopes of coherence or success. David did not see a cut until December 17, 1953, in New York, and he began a seven-page cry of distress to Huston by saying he intended to say nothing: "I have taken very much to heart your counsel that I stop giving so freely of my advice." But he was bewildered, and he could not contain that or any other emotion in silence. He would speak up, just because Huston was such a good friend and because "I can't tell what is going to happen with this mad picture. . . . It is so utterly insane, it is in such complete defiance of all the rules."

Still, he believed it might be saved—*if* his advice was taken. So he advised previews and close response to what audiences said, he worried that the sound was unintelligible, and he did grieve that the former salvation, Ossie Morris, had delivered some "terribly damaging photography of Jennifer." To his credit, David realized Huston had produced something novel and disconcerting—he suggested calling it *The Big Wink*. But he believed it was fatal amateurism indulging itself—instead of fatalistic professionalism striving to escape the rigidity of Hollywood in the 1950s. *Beat the Devil* did not open until March 1954, and it was another failure. Since *Duel in the Sun*, Jennifer had made eight films, of which only *Ruby Gentry* got into profit. She was magnificent in two of them—*Gone to Earth* and *Carrie*—though neither appealed much to David. No actress had been subject to more care, promotion, and cosseting—or provoked so many complaints about the interference of her husband. David was a movie producer, and the facts were undeniable. He had led Jennifer into trouble, no matter that he had winning reasons for blaming others over *their* interference.

Then in the spring of 1954, Jennifer was offered a great role, at Paramount, in *The Country Girl*. Grace Kelly would win her Oscar in it, for Jennifer had to let the chance go. She was pregnant again.

9. · REMNANTS OF THE OLD SOUTH

FEW THINGS became simplified in David's life as he grew older. But in 1954, he had Bobby and Michael Walker to worry over and some sort of father's role to serve for them. Danny was to start at Harvard in the fall, while Jeff had done classes at City College in New York and got a job as an assistant at CBS, unknown to David or Bill Paley. Then he became an assistant director on some B Westerns in Utah, the 1950s version of David's first films. In time, Jeff worked for David a little, under Arthur Fellows, but Fellows had to fire Jeff, as David confided in Irene, for "shirking all unexciting or undesirable assignments despite repeated warnings although worked extremely hard and brilliantly those things which appeal to him." David was the more outraged by Jeff's chutzpah in hoping to gain introductions to Audrey Hepburn—yet this was the father who had always told the boys how many famous people he had on call.

Howard Selznick was still at Appalachian Hall in Asheville. He was paid for by the family, and David kept in amicable contact with him and sent gifts faithfully for Christmas and birthdays. By the early 1950s, Howard's daughter Ruth, married to Berman Swarttz, was having emotional problems that led to sessions with Dr. Frederick Hacker, paid for by David. Ruth and Berman had a son, Steven, in 1945, but Ruth's deterioration kept on. In 1945, David had warned Berman that he could not continue to carry the medical bills. "I am very fond of Ruth," he wrote, "and think she is a splendid girl with superb potentialities once she gets a decent chance at life."

The younger sister, Florence, was a graver case. During the war, Florence had married a man named Phil Howard, while Phil's older brother, Al, a boarder in Mildred's house, had an affair with Florence's mother. Florence and Phil had a son, too, named Myron. A few years later, Florence broke down, and she was hospitalized at Chestnut Lodge—"pretty much like her father," said Berman Swarttz. But who would pay for Florence? Her husband had no means. Mildred professed poverty. Berman and Ruth could help a little so long as Ruth's own needs became no greater. Everyone looked to David and assumed he was wealthy.

And since 1951, David had another duty: he felt some responsibility for L.B. What could Mayer do after MGM? He was too large a figure to be taken in elsewhere, and he was too adrift from the times to function on his own.

In early 1952, L.B. had presented David with an unexpected question. Since David was spending so much time in Europe, could L.B. occupy the Selznick office space in Culver City? David had to think very quickly—"it distresses me to have to advise you that I really do not think it will work." Why? Well, "I have paid a fortune in rent to maintain these offices, for a period of years during which I have been there very little." They were crammed with files, "trick equipment, reversible projection equipment, etc.," and they were "terribly run-down." "I myself feel now, when I go there," said a David as wistful as Scarlett at the ravaged Tara, "as though I were living somewhat in the broken-down remnants of the Old South; but I was there in the Studio's better days, and it isn't the same thing as your moving in for the first time."

In the event, L.B. worked out of his new home in Bel Air. From there, he devoted himself to plotting against those he had left at Metro, supporting the right wing of the Republican Party, serving as chairman of Cinerama, and pursuing a few personal projects. He had the rights to *Paint Your Wagon*, *Blossom Time*, and a script for *Joseph and His Brethren* commissioned from John Lee Mahin, the one MGM veteran who had followed L.B. when he left the studio.

Joseph was a Biblical epic that brought L.B. and David closer together. The lure was to propose that Jennifer play Potiphar's wife. Again, David had to hedge: he felt much sympathy for L.B., but he had never wanted to work with him. Yet Jennifer might be interested, other projects permitting, though Potiphar's wife was "probably too consistently villainous to be believable." The problem was the script, which, David believed, needed much more work "if it is to be sufficiently better than the cinematic debauches which have been based upon careless and sloppy raids upon the Bible."

In the fall of 1953, there was correspondence and discussion between the two men which David carried to a higher plane. *Joseph and His Brethren*, he felt, only illustrated the danger of L.B. doing anything commonplace. On October 1, he sent ten pages of counsel to L.B. with a blind copy to Irene. "My reason for sending it to you," he told her, "is because I feel that I owe it to you and to the children, and to L.B. also, to try to enlist your efforts in getting your father to have a better perspective on his great potential and on his future activities."

David urged L.B. to retire from pictures and to devote himself to "such avocations as interest you": politics, charities, a Louis B. Mayer Foundation perhaps "to serve laudable objects." The letter was a masterpiece of flattery, artful direction, inspired sympathy for the wounded tyrant—and self-deception. For David understood L.B.'s innate need for vengeance; Mayer had wanted to be avenged even when he was successful and boss at Metro.

Mayer had money to spare. He had had such eminence that mere profit could look shabby or petty: "The enormous contribution you made to the industry was . . . in the building of a great machine, in which you could act in a transcendental capacity, surrounding yourself with the greatest talent available in all branches of the theatre arts, and utilizing your unparalleled perspicacity in the selection and management of personalities."

It shows how imperial a picture D.O.S. had of movies. Here was the sense of an estate in the nation, respected by all and influential of so many ways of life and thought. Such self-importance failed to recognize how, in the 1950s, America was beginning to regard Hollywood as an archaic and disintegrating country of warring domains, its rhetoric equal to its squalor. A Mayer, and to some extent a Selznick, too, had risen from anonymity to great wealth, fame, and power and never seen how fleeting or insecure the precious perch might be. Humility was only a style for these men—their vanity had outstripped their talents, and they believed America needed them. David was humble talking to L.B.; he could take up the pose and beseeching of "a lesser man." But he could never apply the lesson to himself:

Do, please, L.B., think first and foremost of your own happiness and peace of mind, and equanimity. I have hesitated long before saying this, but I am not alone in feeling that you are letting your bitterness about your mistreatment at M-G-M color your thinking to a dangerous extent. Since no one else will tell you, I feel obliged to tell you myself: the extent to which you unburden your heart and soul and mind, in relation to Nick Schenck and Dore Schary, has become a source of town gossip.

What was it David foresaw for L.B. instead of Machiavellianism in the business? It was to cultivate his friendships—with J. Edgar Hoover, Earl Warren, and President Eisenhower (no matter that L.B. had preferred Taft and thought Ike soft). "Isn't there a far better life waiting for you than that possible in the world between Washington Boulevard and Vine Street?"

L.B. must have smiled. He had cultivated those notables for their power, and they had acknowledged him for the same reason. Without power, what need was there of relationships? Only David believed in being liked for himself. L.B. knew there was just death after vengeance. If David believed what he preached then he might have changed his own life, especially with a new child on the way. L.B. reckoned men of power should beware of children, for they deflected concentration and made for betrayal. Hadn't Edie aligned herself with Dore Schary in supporting Adlai Stevenson?

David's magnanimity was swiftly put to the test. On the night of February 14, 1954, Ed Sullivan's television show, "Toast of the Town," celebrated the thirtieth anniversary of Metro-Goldwyn-Mayer. According to Dore Schary, he simply turned up at the studio and read a narration put in front of him, a script prepared by Sullivan's writers and checked by Howard Strickling, Metro's head of publicity. But as Schary admitted, "two dreadful oversights were recorded. One, Mayer's name was hardly mentioned, his efforts and record slighted. Two, and more serious, when *Gone With the Wind* was recalled, the name of David O. Selznick wasn't heard or seen."

What did the public care, or know, that Mayer and Selznick had been disowned? Such omissions and distortions were the privileges of power, made worse for David by Schary "and this pose he assumes—this kind of benign, kindly gentle man, and—"

He was "nearly" apoplectic in a conversation with Hedda Hopper two days later. Yet no one ever had real talk with Hedda. David was supplying anger and quotes for her column. "I think it's the most disgraceful thing I ever heard of," he shouted.

"So do I!" Hopper egged him on.

"I didn't know which burned me up more—my selfish resentment on the *Gone With the Wind*, trying to make that not only an MGM picture but Schary's picture, or more for Irving or L.B."

"Nothing can disturb your record," David had told Mayer a few months before, but these men were reluctant to die without some assurance of posterity. L.B. handled himself like an old vaudeville player. He brought the house down at a business banquet when he told the gathering demurely, "You know I *really* was at MGM." In print, he called Schary "a ham." Would he sue? "Can I say I'm the great Louis B. Mayer?" he asked. "This is impossible." He played it like a movie and let his sad, silver hair catch the light.

A couple of weeks later, David talked to Hedda, "off the record," and revealed his strategy. MGM planned a significant reissue of *Gone With the Wind* in May 1954, and it needed the music tracks that David had held on to. "We're being plenty tough with them. I must say I think this man needs a psychiatrist or something. I ran into Ed Sullivan and Ed said he was terribly embarrassed. Don't quote me saying I think he needs a psychiatrist because I don't want to give them anything they can pin anything on. I said to L.B. let's us stay as aggrieved parties until we get remedied."

In March, David and Jennifer came west again after three months in New York. They had thought of Jamaica, but the doctors would not let Jennifer leave the country until the baby was born. It was due in August. The parents-to-be went to Palm Springs for a holiday. David spent increasing amounts of time there, at a rented property, 796 Via Miraleste. But he came back to New York in May. After spending the day with the Paleys at Manhasset he drove into town on the evening of May 23 for his own turn on "Toast of the Town," having his say but helplessly promoting the reissue of *Gone With the Wind* for Loew's. He used the occasion to condemn showmen intent on "message" pictures—but how many knew that referred to Schary?

The 1954 reissue saw several modernizing alterations to *Gone With the Wind*. Technicolor was losing its monopoly, and its fierce dyes were changing as popular taste shifted. So the reissue was brighter, cooler, and more "up-to-date." In addition, the proportions of the frame were altered to give a "wide-screen" look. It was damage that could never be repaired. The public hardly noticed. Some reclaimed their old pleasure, while a new generation discovered the classic. The reissue was so successful it established the film's capacity for being revived regularly. In those days, most movies had their first run and then disappeared. There were few ways of seeing "old" movies, and the business scarcely thought to exploit them. But now a second life was at hand, on television, where the color, the frame, the sound, the rhythm, the integrity could all go to hell once it was proved that people would sit through "old" pictures.

David had been thinking television for several years already; he was always ahead of his time. And when he saw the 1954 bounty for *Gone With the Wind*, he had to appreciate just how far ahead of himself he had been. David knew what he was dealing with: the restrained returns reported on the film were one of those Metro traditions laid down in the great age of L.B. So David asked for audits and leverage and tried to overlook his conflicts of interest. While he protested about his mother and niece being cheated, he haggled over the *Wind* music tracks and sought to get back in on the picture with a deal negotiated with the Margaret Mitchell estate to give him the right to do a stage or television version of *Gone With the Wind*.

By December 1953, David was so compromised he retired as a trustee to Myron's estate. That did not diminish his agitating. Now he could believe he was acting altruistically. And so he wrote to Joan Grill, urging her to be busier on her own behalf. The audits were unsatisfactory; only an exhaustive study of the figures from all over the world would uncover the facts. As lawyers were commanded to be threatening, Loew's did release a little more money. The obsession for David was only aggravated by the events of 1954. By the summer of 1955—at which time, he was also engaged in negotiations to return to MGM as an independent producer—David wrote to Joan Grill and every other trustee, banker, lawyer, and accountant who contributed to the files:

> There is something *drastically* wrong about the situation in relation to GWTW payments. . . .
>
> . . . let me point out that, *by the statement of Loew's own executives,* THE DOMESTIC GROSS OF GWTW ON ITS LAST REISSUE WAS IN EXCESS OF SEVEN MILLION DOLLARS!! [In former times, D.O.S. might have hoped to pocket $2 million of that personally.] The figures rendered to the estate show a domestic gross from Nov. 26, 1954 to May 12, 1955—*the period which would seem to be the very heart of the period of the last reissue*—of $527,408.43.

And so the proper gratification over a film still beloved by the masses, and the expectant pleasures of a new child, were a little marred by calculation and resentment. David had encouraged his former father-in-law to retire. But he had to press on himself: he had responsibilities—old and new—and a name to repair.

> Lest I subject myself at a subsequent date to a charge of hypocrisy, as a consequence of doing myself what I recommend you do not do [he had written L.B.], I must point out the differences. To begin with, I am considerably younger than you are; secondly, my career at this point is not at its peak, by contrast with your own; thirdly, having

successfully devoted myself to my moral obligations to pay my debts,
I should now like to insure my own future and the future of those
close to me, through the accumulation of at least some material wealth
that I do not now have; fourthly, if and when I do achieve a position
of wealth, I assure you that I am entirely sincere in saying that I hope
I shall be able to put it to good use in other than entirely selfish ways.

In that spirit, in the spring and early summer of 1954, largely paid off
(or having shifted part of his debt from the banks to the IRS), he prepared
to have another child, to make an unprecedented television show about the
diamond jubilee of light, and to put his wife onstage in a version of Henry
James's *The Portrait of a Lady*. He was still young.

10 · HAVE A GAY EVENING

THE FUROR OF "Toast of the Town" in the first half of 1954 suggests
David Selznick had inadvertently blundered into television. But always a
willing kid for new inventions or gadgets, David had loved television from
its early days. Here was a toy that made a knockout gift; and he was full of
ideas for what it could do.

Most of the geniuses who ran Hollywood tried to ignore their upstart
rival. David was incapable of ignoring anything, let alone something as new,
silly, or potent as TV. One of his best friends was William Paley, the man
who had bought into CBS in 1929 and who was president of the company
or chairman of its board throughout David's lifetime. The opportunity for
association there was more obvious than it had ever been between David and
Jock.

Paley was generous and sociable, but he was also a rival. In 1952, when
he learned that Jeffrey Selznick had been working at a lowly level at CBS,
Paley said he would recommend the young Selznick to Columbia University
if he thought of finishing his education. (The parents who rule show
business are often kinder to the children of colleagues than to their own—it
is a bizarre one-upmanship.) The Paleys and the Selznicks socialized whenever they could. They liked the same kind of life and the same bright people.
It was David who had introduced Truman Capote into the Paley circle,
though the first time he had said, "Can Truman come, too?," Paley had
thought he meant the ex-president.

On January 15, 1954, just as he was about to spend a weekend with Bill
and Babe Paley at Kiluna, David was able to repay the $50,000 Paley had

loaned him in April 1950. The money came out of the $500,000 Columbia had advanced on *Indiscretion of an American Wife*. David was now prepared to admit the emotional value of Paley's gesture: "it was *the manner* of your loan that made it the only one I could accept, if I was to preserve my pride and self-respect." There had been other offers, including one from Jock. Paley was closer to David now than Jock. Bill was more intimate and understanding. (He *was* Jewish, of Russian descent, and he was in the audience business.) He read David very quickly, and so he had just written a check, unasked, and handed it over. It was how a friend should act in a movie, as well as in life, and David had been touched.

For over fifteen years, David had made it his business to send Bill kibitzing notions for CBS. He sometimes wrote in the person of "Wallingford" or the "Idea Department." In May 1939, David found time amid *Gone With the Wind* to propose long-playing records to Paley. No idea was dull, a few were brilliant. And David never let up. Paley did not always acknowledge them—which sometimes hurt David, for his letters were a quest for love as well as the flourish of egotism.

Between 1948 and 1954—the years of D.O.S.'s "rest" and his travels in Europe—a battle had been fought in America between big screen and small screen. In the twenty-five years after 1946, movie attendance fell by over 75 percent. A television set went from being a luxury item to a household appliance. Movie theaters began to close. The Supreme Court's 1948 decision in the Paramount case broke the monopoly of production and distribution. The major studios had to sell off their theaters. There was no longer a guaranteed outlet. In time, the studios were obliged to sell some of their Los Angeles property, and they let many people go—crews, writers, directors, and actors. TV absorbed them. By 1954, Jack Webb and Lucille Ball (an actress from movies, yet never quite a big star there) had become national houseguests, as familiar as Kellogg's.

Hollywood fought the small screen with bigger screens that proved a hindrance when old movies were sold to TV. Yet at first it disdained such deals and regarded them as collaborations with an enemy. Some major studios forbade the appearance of television sets in movies as if they were pubic hair. More fundamentally, the studios had never thought to consider the chance of buying into television early on, of even sharing in its ownership.

David offered Paley wizard ideas for TV programs, but he missed the great opportunity. When war came to America, David had felt at a loss. He yearned to be useful in the larger theater of public service; he wanted to be a showman, too. In 1943, the Supreme Court required that NBC sell off one of its two networks. The Blue was purchased by Edward J. Noble, of

LifeSavers, for $8 million, and he renamed it the American Broadcasting Corporation. It is not inconceivable that, in 1943, David could have mustered the funds to compete for that purchase. As potential head of a future network, he had stories, contracted talent, and ideas. But he couldn't see that future in 1943.

Even in 1954, when belatedly David came to the party of TV, it was as a self-conscious VIP, honoring the upstart and not as a creative visionary, a cross between, say, Bill Paley and Slavko Vorkapich, who saw that TV was already a seething montage of live events, news, commercials, and bargain-price Hollywood as well as Lucy, Jackie Gleason, Paddy Chayefsky's *Marty* and the whole range of live TV theater, the Army versus McCarthy, Nixon's "Checkers speech," *and* Ernie Kovacs. Instead of just changing the switch at random, David occupied all three networks at the same time with a grandiose celebration of the seventy-fifth anniversary of Edison's invention of the light bulb. David lacked the humor that knew light was commonplace, not a subject for statuary.

"Light's Diamond Jubilee" was a commission from the power companies of America for a two-hour variety program of David's own devising, so long as it contained proper tributes to electricity. There were to be no other commercials, and there was a promise that President Eisenhower would make an appearance. Frank Davis did the negotiating for Selznick, by way of Charles Miller of MCA and Dwight Van Meter at the Ayer advertising agency. The production budget was set at $350,000, and David's fee was $75,000.

As early as April 1954, David was restless about the show. Now there was talk of commercials, and doubts about Ike; it was even possible that ABC would back out of running it. "Entire project is becoming less and less attractive," he cabled Davis. He began to see that he was "creating two hours original story for films, without even basic story; and this is made many many times a tougher job as it would be for a motion picture in consequence of my being circumscribed as to type of material. Obviously there can be no profit in this thankless job, on which my entire career will be at stake. . . . I am undertaking backbreaking six month job that is actually far more difficult than making ten or twenty million dollar grossing film."

He talked of getting out of it, yet the foolhardy public spirit that had taken the job on would not be deterred. His protests went toward his old cause: getting and keeping a free hand. In fact, for some of the six months he took things easily, living at Palm Springs, visiting New York, and looking for a beach house at Malibu where Jennifer's pregnancy might be most comfortable.

By July, however, he was at work, often at the beach, with Ben Hecht, his writer for every crisis. Hecht had never been far away. He had put pen to paper for D.O.S. on *The Wild Heart* and only he could supply the opening title for *Indiscretion*: "Rome: Eternal City of Culture, of Legend . . . and of Love."

But Hecht had fallen on harder times. He had done many movie jobs for little pay. He had taken time off to write his autobiography, *A Child of the Century* (published in March 1954), and he was behind on his taxes. His wife, Rose, had written to David in January, sending a proof of the book and asking whether D.O.S. could loan Hecht some money. David was taken aback by the book a little. He was warmly treated, but "I don't recall having said what he quotes me as saying," and he did consider that it "could be harmful." The passage that worried David was not cut: it has him in a melancholy mood, uttering obituary sentences that were awkward if he planned living on:

> Walking at dawn in the deserted Hollywood streets in 1951 with David, I listened to my favorite movie boss topple the town he had helped to build. The movies, said David, were over and done with. Hollywood was already a ghost town making foolish efforts to seem alive.
>
> "Hollywood's like Egypt," said David. "Full of crumbled pyramids. It'll never come back. It'll just keep on crumbling until finally the wind blows the last studio prop across the sands."

Perhaps David didn't say this. Still, it was his kind of wistful foreboding, and Hecht had been his writer long enough to know what D.O.S. ought to say.

As for the loan, David wasn't quite that flush yet. He said he would do what he could to persuade some banks to help the Hechts. But he could go one better by giving Ben the "Light" script and about $10,000 for the job. The "script" required was a concept and a structure for the show, as well as whatever running narration was needed. There were inserts that were adaptations of stories by Irwin Shaw, John Steinbeck, Arthur Gordon, Max Shulman, and Burton Benjamin. As these were shaped and edited, David met a new kind of problem: Irwin Shaw, for one, had had links with Communist organizations and had been cited in *Red Channels*, the report on Communist influence in the media. David faced and rejected the pressure against Shaw, whose story "Girls in Their Summer Dresses" was a highlight of the show.

The show was an assemblage, and every piece needed contracts. By July 21, David was desperate. "I simply cannot any longer be negotiator, lawyer and businessman on this show at same time I am its creator," he told Frank Davis, and so he begged Davis to come help, even if that meant leaving the reissue of *Duel in the Sun* for a while. (That much assaulted movie was given a second run in America—to raise revenue and to help maintain the Selznick reputation. It did well, grossing $1.3 million, about $400,000 of which was straight profit.)

And so, with Hecht busy on the beach and a production once more getting out of hand, David became a father again. On August 12 (eight days after Jeffrey's twenty-second birthday), Jennifer gave birth to a dark-haired daughter. They named her Mary Jennifer. At fifty-two, David was euphoric. But he had little time to sit and watch the child. To give Jennifer peace in the house and to press on with the work, David and Hecht moved into a bungalow at the Beverly Hills Hotel. By September 18, Jennifer and the baby came to the hotel to join David and Hecht returned to Nyack. The matter of the presidential contribution to the show was still not settled, but on September 26 David flew to Denver to consult with Eisenhower. As a result, David himself wrote the speech that Ike would deliver, based on these notes:

"His admiration was 100% for the theme of faith—that's what he wants to talk about. . . . He didn't indicate that he wanted to get into any interfaith message. But he does want faith directly coupled with free government."

In David's two-page script, the President "turns thoughtfully from having looked at TV set" and duly raises the topic of "faith" that would be beamed out to the most prosperous, strong, and insecure audience the world had yet known. David had always been the man to write such stuff, and he knew as well how an Ike should talk as Ben Hecht could play ventriloquist with David:

> We carry the torch of freedom as a sacred trust for all mankind. We do not believe that God intended the light that He created to be put out by men.
> (PAUSE: The President changes his tone, smiles a little)
> Very soon now it will be Halloween. I hope to have a little fun with my grandchildren. For Halloween is one of those times when we Americans let the *little* individualists be free too. . . . I hope you and your children have a gay evening. Let's all give a little prayer that their pranks will be the only kind of mischief with which we Americans must cope. But it can be a confident kind of prayer, because God has made us strong—and faith has made us free.
> Good night.

Ike liked it, and on October 3 David returned to Denver with Arthur Fellows and William Wellman as his director to shoot the sequence. Then on October 24, with filmed and live segments, the show aired from 9:00 p.m.

to 11:00 p.m. That night, for a moment at least, some Americans may have turned off the light and thought of eternity. The show had gone $73,000 over budget, and David had to swallow much of that himself. It played on the three networks and on the DuMont network and was estimated as having been seen by 60 to 70 million people.

The show was popcorn, with some corn stale and some fresh, but David had never known as colossal an audience so quickly. Eisenhower was no more awkward or persuasive than the on-camera narrator, Joseph Cotten. Dorothy Dandridge sang wonderfully, Eddie Fisher was syrup. Guy Madison and Kim Novak made "A Kiss for the Lieutenant," directed by King Vidor, worth all of *Ruby Gentry*. David Niven and Lauren Bacall did "Girls in Their Summer Dresses" with wit and feeling in a sketch about a man's helpless attraction to women. Other sketches were ponderous. Most remarkable of all was a standup act by the young comedian George Gobel, so funny it established his career in American TV.

The show was only politely received, and even its best parts were slow and old-fashioned. A television critic in San Antonio cabled David: "While viewing the disappointing light era program it is difficult to believe the name Selznick is connected with same. Proves in a way what the country generally believes Hollywood lacks—the knowledge of what America really is and is about."

David came away battered personally and perplexed by the medium. How did a showman in business for himself reconcile an audience of 60 million with a debt of $73,000? Yet he was intrigued by TV technology, and he had fallen in love with seeing rehearsals on a monitor. He was asked whether he would stay in television or do more. He said the show had been exciting, but "just like everyone else, I hated to see the whole thing end and then disappear forever." He had had talks with Bill Paley over the years, and Paley had said David would be a fool to try—but was welcome if he insisted. He did have plans with NBC, which was interested in his library of stories, scripts, and treatments. He was intrigued, but it never developed. David remained a visionary of TV: he foresaw cable and pay-TV, and he was certain of the power old movies would come to have on the small screen.

TV was modern America; it came and went like the day's weather. If anything dissuaded David from going further, it was not the disappointment of "Light's Diamond Jubilee," but the insignificance of the people who made TV. In the end, the medium could hear only the cash register of the network, the jingle of the ads, the static-like din of the montage, and the deep, digestive sounds of the audience. TV was so modern it was as if it simply happened, without makers. There was no room for a personality like Selznick.

II · SELZNICK INSISTS

TOWARD THE END of the summer of 1954, as "Light's Diamond Jubilee" neared critical state, and with Mary Jennifer two weeks old, David looked for suitable New York accommodations for the baby, himself, and Jennifer in the coming fall and winter. That season, she would appear in a play adapted from James's *The Portrait of a Lady*. David took it for granted a lengthy campaign was in view.

Mary Jennifer's doctor and nurse advised proximity to the park. That eliminated the Waldorf. But Jennifer wanted to be close to the theater district, and that excluded the Carlyle. "We must rule out the Pierre for obvious reasons," he sighed. Irene had purchased an apartment there in 1949. "This would seem to leave the Sherry Netherland, the Savoy-Plaza, and that old wreck, the Plaza."

David had a new East Coast talent executive, Nancy Stern, who was recommended by none other than Kay Brown. Nancy was charged to search out the best base, but it had to meet several requirements: a hotel suite with a kitchen ("so that the baby's formula can be prepared"), five rooms, and four bathrooms—that is, a living room, two master bedrooms and a bedroom for the baby and nurse, and another room for the office.

As soon as the theater was chosen, David wanted Nancy Stern to inspect Jennifer's dressing room "so that I can perhaps spend a few dollars to get it fixed up a little . . . but of course not doing anything that would seem pretentious or 'Hollywood.' "

The play was of the highest importance; the prestige of a Broadway success might settle Jennifer's eminence as an actress. There was also her urge to work, for Jennifer Jones had not acted since *Beat the Devil*, which had finished shooting in the spring of 1953. Of course, her pregnancy had intervened and lost her *The Country Girl*. But for Jennifer's agent of that time, Sam Jaffe, pregnancy must have come as both a merciful relief and the culminating frustration in trying to handle any actress who had David as her adviser.

Jaffe had acquired Jennifer as a client when David gave up on Ray Stark. As soon as Jennifer had dealt with her prior commitments (*Stazione Termini* and *Beat the Devil*), she was Jaffe's to conjure with—except that David was discussing *Mary Magdalene* for European coproduction and might come up with other things himself.

Sam Jaffe labored a year and a half. He had Jennifer in contention for most of the significant female roles of the time. Long before his end, Jaffe could have seen that he would never place Jennifer in anything as long as David was there to imagine the alternatives. In all his efforts on her behalf, Jaffe hardly ever spoke to Jennifer herself.

In March 1953, the possibilities included a film from Zola's *The Human Beast* ("a terribly morbid and heavy subject," David feared) and *East of Eden*, on which Jennifer herself had "a particularly strong hunch." In time, other projects came along: not just *The Country Girl*, but Joseph Mankiewicz's *The Barefoot Contessa*; the movie of *Picnic*, in which, David had heard, playwright William Inge had had Jennifer as his own original choice; *Mary Magdalene*, still, a role that waited on Jennifer's horizon, ageless and patient, for years; and even Kazan's *On the Waterfront*.

Hindsight knows how foolish it was *not* to do *On the Waterfront*: after all, Eva Marie Saint won the supporting actress Oscar in the film. But David did not want Jennifer in roles that might end up as supports. In advance, *Waterfront* looked risky and rough-textured—it was not a film where the proper care would be taken of how Jennifer looked. Then again, pictures waited on timing: *The Country Girl* would go as and when Bing Crosby was bored with golf. A picture might be right with a good costar, but unthinkable without him. David was squeamish over *The Human Beast* and doubted it could be done as censorship then prevailed. But it looked better if Brando would do the lover, and David began to get very excited when he thought of Alec Guinness as the husband. (In the event, the story was made, as *Human Desire*, directed by Fritz Lang, with Gloria Grahame, Glenn Ford, and Broderick Crawford.)

David taxed Jaffe to be more active *and* more discreet, to get early looks at scripts without being seen to be considering those scripts, unless people got the wrong idea about Jennifer's taste or position. As likely projects came up, so David's elaborations of pros and cons, to say nothing of his behind-the-back contacts and discussions, put any decision in jeopardy. As early as February 1953, the unfortunate Jaffe was saying, "I have learned, through many years of experience in this business, to be a good loser; but I don't like to lose when I haven't been given a proper chance."

The Barefoot Contessa was something David really wanted for Jennifer. He was proud of her "barefoot" past in *Bernadette, Duel in the Sun*, and the gypsy girl in *Gone to Earth*. Mankiewicz's heroine was a Spaniard? No problem, for Jennifer had won the Spanish equivalent of the Oscar for *Portrait of Jennie*. David pressed. After all, he had known Mank as a kid and ordered him around then, and now Joe had made it. He couldn't believe Mankiewicz was actually thinking of Ava Gardner for the part, especially since David had heard from a very good inside source that, when writing the script, Joe had had Jennifer in mind!

So David volunteered a cable which Jaffe should send to Mankiewicz to squeeze a decision out of him. Jaffe refused to send it, but it was a composition for which Mankiewicz could easily have guessed the true author:

> Selznick insists your disinterest Jennifer obvious and my arguments that role still open placing me in difficult position particularly since Columbia pressing for *Mary Magdalene* answer with almost certainly conflicting dates. Have managed stall Columbia on basis awaiting rewritten script which however due momentarily and even if David Jennifer dislike this have two other pictures available for her prior *Country Girl* on which must also give replies. Therefore would appreciate as personal favor actual lowdown even if your reply is only that you are not interested. [Bert] Allenberg agrees with me that you making terrible mistake if you pass up this outstanding costarring opportunity for your first independent picture and that even if you find new girl you do not have comparable showmanship values also combination Bogart title ludicrous without important female co-star. . . . David inquiring whether you saw Jennifer as barefoot Welsh gypsy in *Gone to Earth* which could be run for you Italy although dubbed version available there would not reveal her extraordinary ability accents which caused highly favorable reaction England despite unpopularity film . . . she is actually the only actress I know who can successfully accomplish transition from savage peasant to sophisticated world figure capable of being accepted as countess infinitely better than Gardner even and certainly no comparison in acting talent. Therefore believe you actually fortunate Gardner unavailable from both commercial and quality standpoints. Why not discuss with De Sica for whom however remember that her integrity as actress led her to deliberately make herself older with mature mother appearance which proven by successful very young characterization she did for Huston immediately after De Sica. . . . Kindest regards.
> Sam

Jennifer went to see Mankiewicz personally, against David's wishes. Apparently the meeting decided the director-producer not to pick her. For Jennifer was nervous, constrained, ladylike—an actress for whom the "barefoot" attitude had been a courageous departure. No one, now, can doubt that Mankiewicz made the "right" choice. *The Barefoot Contessa* has not aged well, but its rather innocent view of a Spanish peasant girl who can command men with a glance is more directly served by Ava Gardner, who seldom looked insecure. Worry is a hard faith to keep out of a face, however much one pretends. Jennifer had torments that took her time and again to Swiss analysts, but in addition she had a career that David might be managing to death. Because she seemed vulnerable, he took power and responsibility away from her, and thus she became the more insecure. "It was like a surgeon operating on his own wife," said Sam Jaffe. "There's a law against that."

By the end of 1953, David believed Jaffe's agenting for Jennifer was "getting nowhere." He persevered, and her pregnancy (evidently a surprise) took a lot of the pressure off. But Jennifer was still concerned. Looking ahead, she called George Stevens personally about the female role in *Giant*. Then Jerry Wald, at Columbia, wondered about doing *Tender is the Night* (which David owned), with George Cukor directing. Here was another of those projects over which David pondered far too long. But in early 1954, he did court and pester Cukor, who was then shooting his version of *A Star is Born* at Warner Brothers, with Judy Garland and James Mason. (David had retained some foreign rights in that property, and he was daring Warners to go ahead without full clearance. The dispute would not be settled until late 1955, when Warners got the complete territories plus $25,000 from David in return for the remake rights on *A Farewell to Arms*.)

In 1954, Cukor was irritated by David's intrusiveness. He told his old friend off in the closest he ever came to taking revenge. Cukor was working steadily, in one of the richest periods of his career, while David was behaving more and more like an agent.

Sam Jaffe's last effort was *The Galileans*, another Biblical project in which Jennifer was being asked to play Mary Magdalene. It was to be directed by Douglas Sirk, but David admitted he was not familiar with Sirk's pictures. So much in Europe, he had missed many films. By spring 1954, Sirk had been in Hollywood a decade, and when *Magnificent Obsession* opened in August 1954, it was a great hit. Its male star, Rock Hudson, was being proposed for *The Galileans*, too, but David had to tell Jaffe, "that I have never seen him." He was shaken to discover that this Hudson was the truck driver who had been brought to him a few years before by Henry Willson, Selznick's homosexual talent director. David then had discounted Hudson, but here he was, a star.

By that spring of 1954, David was thinking of the stage for Jennifer. They were both aroused by the prospect of *The Lark*, Jean Anouilh's play about Joan of Arc, with Lillian Hellman doing the adaptation and Wyler directing. *The Lark* required auditions, and David was against that on principle. "He forgets that I had to audition for *him*," Jennifer told Nancy Stern, in a flash of independence. In the event, Julie Harris got that role, as she did Abra in *East of Eden* and Sally Bowles in *I Am a Camera* (another of the parts considered for Jennifer). *The Galileans* was never made, and Elizabeth Taylor played in *Giant*. Taylor was thirteen years younger than Jennifer, and about to become a dominant actress in Hollywood, along with Grace Kelly, Audrey Hepburn, Kim Novak—a new generation.

Sam Jaffe was terminated. He bore no grudge; there was no room for it in the relief. But he did tell David, "I can truthfully say I have put in hundreds of hours of work in the interest of Jennifer Jones, and in making this statement, I am not pleading for sympathy. Every time a note (which you knew was unusually lengthy) came in from you, it required days of my time to follow through in order to get the necessary information and reply to you."

A week after the night of "Light's Diamond Jubilee," David went to New York. Jennifer had gone earlier, with Mary Jennifer and a nurse, for rehearsals. *Portrait of a Lady* was a play written by William Archibald and directed by José Quintero. Cathleen Nesbitt, Robert Flemyng, and Douglas Watson were in the cast with her. David was in attendance in November for the tryout performances in Boston and Washington, and he was doing all he could to improve the production and the play.

Three times in that period—on November 22 and 24 and on December 9—he had dinner with Irene, sometimes with Danny or Jeffrey. He also took Bobby and Michael Walker down to Philadelphia on November 27 to see the Army-Navy football game. Jennifer came back to New York on December 19, and two days later, *Portrait of a Lady* opened at the ANTA Theatre. Christmas was a tough time for such a debut. The play ran four

Jennifer onstage with Marcia Morris in Portrait of a Lady

performances. Jennifer was devastated. She said she wanted to run away and hide; early in the new year, David would take her off to Jamaica. *Variety* ran a mocking headline, "Where Was David?" He was left feeling he should have interfered more!

The reviews had been poor but polite. In *The New York Times*, Brooks Atkinson called it "a decorous but colorless play." In *The New Yorker*, Wolcott Gibbs regarded Jennifer as "beautiful and grave but somewhat lacking in depth." Louis Jourdan was there on opening night, and, while he felt Jennifer was fine, the play was simply uninteresting. Nancy Stern believed she wasn't very good: "She had a strange tic sort of thing that she'd do with her mouth, it was like a string on a horse's upper lip, when she'd get upset. She was so scared."

Did David ever dare ask Irene what was wrong with *Portrait of a Lady*? Did he get her to see it and give him a few notes? Irene could have begged off, for at that time she was intensely engaged with Enid Bagnold in rewriting her own next production, *The Chalk Garden*.

Miss Bagnold, who was both fascinated and daunted by Irene and her "carved eyes," wrote about this experience in her autobiography. She described a titan of dedication, eccentricity, and silent-engined power. What a model for D.O.S.! This producer inhabited *The Chalk Garden*, at the Pierre or in Bagnold's chilly home in England:

> She never wrote one word of the play [wrote Bagnold], and this was her pride. And it was true. She pushed and poked me into rearrangements, into doing things I thought I couldn't do. Nobody has ever got so near writing without writing. Out of the heart of the play, and always from what I wrote, she kept her hand on what she called the theme (we never mentioned it because I got cross at the very word). She was like a stalking Indian who (through the forest) knew the only track.

The playwright saw how much a character Irene was, how deeply set in gesture: hours on the phone, in magnificent black dresses and diamonds, with gifts of champagne. Irene was a very good producer, but the more strenuously she declined to write, the more she unnerved her author. There *was* a touch of that melodramatic ex-husband in her: she hired George Cukor to direct *The Chalk Garden*—and then fired him.

But there was a darkness that never left Irene, a certainty of ultimate loss and a refusal to be optimistic. It was the best lesson she had from her David experience, even if it meant they could not live together. When *The Chalk Garden* opened, it was a hit. Enid rang Irene, but the producer was in tears.

"Irene!" said the author. "It's a *success*."

Irene answered "in the excessively deep voice, made deeper by tears: 'I know. I was all geared up for failure . . . and I just can't *take* success.' "

12 • AN ALL-TIME GIANT

HE HAD BEEN fleetingly exuberant in the spring of 1954. There had been the new baby on the way, and the lovely coincidence of his old debt settled at last. So David had talked of getting back into picture production. In his own mind, he had been at rest since *Portrait of Jennie*, the last film that had been his alone. Everything since had been some kind of coproduction, situations in which he felt constrained to let others make the films. Those others would have marveled at his belief in the limitations. But David could point to the fatal area of compromise as reasons for the failure of *Gone to Earth* and *Stazione Termini*. He had made great sacrifices; he had become policeman to his own operations; he had denied himself his true vocation. Didn't such a good boy now deserve reward?

He would make *War and Peace*. "It contains many of the things found in *Gone With the Wind*," he said in his formal announcement in June 1954. He had been dreaming of the project for twenty years (since the Garbo *Anna Karenina*, in fact). Something had altered in David that left him incapable of making small pictures. But Natasha Rostov is fifteen when *War and Peace* opens and in her early twenties when the book ends. Jennifer's elder son, Bobby, was fourteen in the spring of 1954, but David's Tolstoy venture was founded on the idea that she would be Natasha.

Selznick registered the title, and once upon a time that would have been enough to warn others off. But now Mike Todd and Dino de Laurentiis jumped up as rivals: *they* would make *War and Peace*, too. Despite his unhappiness with MGM after the Ed Sullivan broadcast, and no matter his indignation at its accountancy on *Gone With the Wind*, David had been ready to make a deal with Nick Schenck for *War and Peace*. MGM would finance and distribute the picture. He would function at the studio as an independent producer, suffering some controls but taking so much smaller a risk. The banks he had paid off were no longer happy to fund him in fresh ventures.

But Paramount said it would back the De Laurentiis version, and it was ready to hire a team of scriptwriters who could deliver the pages to shoot in a month. This was a grotesque way to treat Tolstoy. David considered options: Niven Busch nearly sold him on a way to do the book that omitted Pierre. In the end, Schenck had challenged D.O.S.: could he guarantee his picture would be ready first? Speed had never been David's specialty. So De Laurentiis had the field. He hired King Vidor to direct and the twenty-five-year-old Audrey Hepburn to play Natasha. This *War and Peace*, 208 minutes long, with Henry Fonda as Pierre, and with moments of real glory, opened in November 1956.

Nick Schenck was not prepared to let David stay disappointed. If David had been willing to go to MGM for one thing, then why not for another? When he came east for *Portrait of a Lady*, he began serious discussions with the studio. Yet again, Morgan Maree and Frank Davis were acting for him; at David's request, Eddie Mannix represented the studio.

The outlines of a deal had appeared by early 1955. David would go to MGM for two pictures, the subjects to be agreed jointly. The studio would supply all the money at a 3 percent interest rate. Profits would be split fifty-fifty, and, as an advance against profits, David would be paid $100,000 per picture. He was to have "autonomy," but Metro would supply a general manager. There were penalties if the pictures went more than 15 percent over budget. The distribution fee would be 25 percent domestic and 30 percent overseas. An overhead charge would be levied on each picture, in return for which Selznick had the run of the studio. If the pictures went 50 percent over budget, then Metro had the right to step in and take charge.

This was to become a predominant way of making pictures as studios shrank their own contract staff and as producers, directors, or stars wanted a place to call home. The system let pictures be made, and it allowed reasonable freedom to efficient operators. At the same time, such deals could leave David, say, with a picture and just a moderate salary. He knew the ingenuity with which Metro could fall short of reportable profits or profits to match a producer's dreams. But this was the first independent production deal MGM had been ready to make.

Early in February, David, Frank Davis, and Charlie Feldman (who acted as David's agent) flew to Miami for a celebration meeting with Nick and Pansy Schenck. "We stayed at the Fontainebleau," said Davis, "which had just opened. We had dinner and we shook hands and expressed our love and good wishes for success and so forth and then flew back. Then it started."

Particular projects were in discussion—the Françoise Sagan novel *Bonjour Tristesse* and *Fanny*, a Broadway musical derived from the plays of Marcel Pagnol. But when the draft contract appeared from Metro, it didn't reflect the handshake agreement. Frank Davis now was dealing with J. Robert Rubin and Ben Melniker from MGM, yet having to submit every report to David and getting extensive memos back on every worry. The dispute hinged on the definition of overhead and profits, and grew out of Metro's sense that they could now push a needy David.

For Frank Davis, in the trenches of negotiation, the frustration became disillusioning. Here was a D.O.S. claiming to be in earnest about a deal, yet filling every delay with new problems and forever warning him about the rascality of MGM. Look at *Wind!* said David, and Frank Davis told him forget that, for David's time and nervous energy were serving no business end. His only excuse was that he was looking after his mother's interests. On the same day, David might utter eternal damnation on the deviousness of MGM while attempting to complete a production deal with them.

Now David was the first of the new breed of would-be filmmakers who devoted all their time to working on deals. To Frank Davis, it sometimes seemed that he was there only so David could measure his own capacity as a lawyer. By May 1955, David was writing to Eddie Mannix, ostensibly on the overhead (which seemed to work out at $150,000 per picture), but really as a pilgrim in search of vindication. Even the hypocrisy now was gilded and varnished—the old enthusiasm and spontaneity were deserting him:

> I want freely to concede to you that we have no intention of kicking over the traces—i.e., the deal—on this overhead point. We want to make the deal, very much. . . . It is now a full seven months since the deal was first discussed. It was late January, I believe, when we agreed on the basic premise of the deal in Miami [February 4 in fact], and it is now the first of May. We could have made a picture in the length of time it has taken to make the contract. So from your standpoint, as well as our own, we want to get it pinned down and over with. But, as in so many other things, and as through the years, I have relied upon the finest man I have ever known in this business, one E. J. Mannix.

This was no casual compliment. Eddie Mannix had been a fellow gambler in David's worst years, and he still held substantial IOUs. It was not until 1960 that David was settled with Eddie, at which time Mannix congratulated David for his sense of honor. Most people would have written it all off.

David's absorption in the metaphysics of the deal left one beneficiary: Jennifer. For in that spring of 1955, for Fox, she made *Love is a Many-Splendored Thing*. David tried to be involved. He wrote to its producer, Buddy Adler, about Jennifer's appearance as the Eurasian woman and the "unnecessarily mature appearance" of the hairstyle. "If this makes her look much older, I think you will harm your love story . . . and that the reaction will simply be, 'My, how old Jennifer Jones has gotten!' " But he was too busy, and much of the picture was shot in Hong Kong. It proved Jennifer's biggest hit since *Duel in the Sun*.

By the middle of the year, David discovered his new financial crisis when the tax returns for 1951 were reopened. As a result, he was found to be in arrears by $1,510,208. There would be appeals and discussions, and it was not until 1957 that the teeth bit.

The threat accelerated his decision to sell some of his old movies to television. The airwaves were desperate for material, and most old movies had not been seen since their first release. The marriage was inevitable. But in its early days, it occurred at incredibly low terms. Studios sold off hundreds of titles at as little as $10,000 to $20,000 a picture. It would be a decade before the long-term value of this old product was recognized, most of it entirely free from residual payments to the talent.

RKO made a breakthrough deal in 1955: for $25 million it sold out the studio and the back lot to General Tire and Rubber. In a subsidiary deal, 740 RKO films were made available for TV showing. As part of the changes at RKO, Dan O'Shea left CBS and became president of a studio whose most important tenant was Desilu, a television company founded on the success of "I Love Lucy." That appointment gave David more ruinous ideas. He had always foreseen the place of old movies on television, and he was in no position to block the invading medium. David was a better showman, always, than a proprietor: he could never resist the public and the chance that it would like him. There was a new generation looking for entertainment that had little inkling of what a Selznick picture was. For ten years, he had had few pleasures as intense as showing *Gone With the Wind* to Jeff, Danny, Bobby, and Michael, and their young friends, and then asking them when it was over, "Did you like it?" He showed *Wind* so often some kids fell asleep—and then David lost his temper.

How perfect if Bill Paley could have bought the Selznick films for CBS. Friendship might then have concealed the loss in scale, beauty, and integrity. CBS did make an offer, but it was not generous: Paley never confused business with sentiment. So David looked elsewhere.

National Telefilm Associates was interested in a package of fifteen films to exploit on television. On August 18, 1955, David, Victor Hoare, and Frank Davis met with Ely Landau and Oliver Unger of N.T.A. at the St. Regis Hotel in New York. Thus another set of negotiations commenced, this time with people David neither liked nor trusted. He realized something else, the drab absence of audience contact in TV and the harsh ways films would be edited, interrupted, and reduced. But N.T.A. was offering $2.25

million for a ten-year license, with an option to David to buy the pictures back after five years.

As David flew back to Los Angeles from New York on April 26, he felt compelled to write out his agony for Davis, Hoare, and Earl Beaman, lamenting the very deal he had instigated.

> These are the thoughts of the sleepless night imposed upon me by those monkeys concerning the delivery of my name, trademark, and all that I own of my brain children of my entire career, for a mess of pottage and tax-money.

He was afraid of delivering precious negatives to "this gang." It was like experimental surgery to think of having the films cut to fit TV time slots. He kept going back over the figures and repurchase, wondering if there wasn't a better deal. But the snob and purist in him was horrified. Flying over Kansas, writing on TWA paper, the script larger with every page, David did get a comeuppance, a vision of what had become of movies by 1955. The fun was slipping away, and he was trading off his great assets to pay debts he never fully understood.

> Nor is it only the pride, for the pride was our inspiration, and our inspiration was our financial success. Can't we afford, having paid our debts, to shun the company we wouldn't keep when we were on the verge, week after week, of bankruptcy? What has happened to us and to our thinking that I could be led to association with the Dead End Kids? Morgan [Maree], who knows what we were and can be again, told you how I passed up Harry Cohn though we were desperate.
> Yet I am tired—horribly, unprecedentedly tired.

Nearly every prolonged memo slogs toward that realization. Doctors agreed with him and said the fatigue was exceptional; but they seldom found more warning signs. His favorite doctor was Connie Guion in New York, a recommendation from the Paleys. In May 1950, a previous doctor had given Guion a report on David: "His habits are not conducive to good health." No vacation and no exercise, twelve to fourteen hours work a day, along with eighty to one hundred cigarettes. Benzedrine "daily" for a decade and a basal metabolism rate of minus 30 percent. Dr. Guion had urged "the great importance of your reducing the strenuous life which you live to one of more reasonable activity. You are no longer a young man, and after all what's life worth if you can't get a little pleasure out of it?"

David had sometimes justified his travels to Europe as part of the relaxation. But then he had found himself in hotels at three in the morning, dictating, waiting for the phone, hovering on the edge of frantic worries.

In February 1952, Connie Guion found normal cholesterol and a basal metabolism of minus 9 percent. The electrocardiogram was normal. But David was still taking thyroid extracts (when he remembered), and the doctor was concerned about doing that on so low a basal metabolism. She begged him to cut down the smoking to a pack a day, but he admitted he hadn't the character for it. With dictation, the cigarettes left him permanently hoarse, but without cigarettes, his weight went up.

By the summer of 1953, Dr. Guion recommended at least seven hours of sleep a night as well as regular exercise. But when he tried that, he was short of breath. "You spoke of having pains in your chest when you were tired," wrote Guion. "I believe that these are due to your having an insufficient supply of oxygen for your heart muscle due to a spasm in your small coronary arteries. Such spasms are due very often to the absorption of the coal tar products in cigarette smoke." By April 1954, his weight was up to 222 pounds.

He had the best doctors, yet consistently defied their advice. At the same time, he plied them with tiny, alarming signs he had detected. They told him he was overimaginative or worse. He felt he was somehow not recognized, if his condition went unspecified. During the making of "Light's Diamond Jubilee," he had been hit on the head by a studio door "weighing perhaps a couple of tons." He claimed a brief concussion that sometimes brought on "unceasing pains" just above his left ear and running down his neck. "Also, perhaps it may be my imagination but I seem to feel some sort of dent in my skull at this point and below it. . . . Perhaps not unnaturally, I have a worry as to whether there is some kind of tumor, caused by the blow or otherwise—maybe by business problems!"

By August 1955, MGM had come around on most of his anxieties on the deal. A new contract was ready to be signed, whereupon David concocted a superior offer from RKO and Dan O'Shea. He had a telephone talk with his old friend, the man who had left him too pained and frustrated to bother with self-defense, and conjured up another independent production arrangement: three films with funding of $7.5 million.

For Frank Davis, this was the climactic sidestep. He had spent months in the Metro negotiation, and it was at last ready to go. He believed it was a good deal for David. MGM was more stable than RKO; its facilities and human resources were superior. But O'Shea was the man Davis had replaced, and Frank knew what mixed feelings the Irishman had about David. Davis did wonder whether D.O.S. wasn't in a kind of unwitting panic that would deal forever, so long as nothing was settled.

> I had the feeling early on [said Davis] that Dan O'Shea, notwithstanding his love and respect for David, wanted no part of his old boss coming in to work for him. He would not be the boss. David would be. But Dan couldn't say that and I don't think he ever said it

to me, but I sure had that impression from my discussions that they would temporize by screening *Alice Adams*, which David thought maybe we would want to remake with Jennifer.

An announcement was made very swiftly, and O'Shea and RKO were rattled by the implication that maybe David was going to take over the entire company—hadn't he always believed RKO needed rescuing? O'Shea was groaning at the lofty press releases David wanted, to say nothing of the major advance advertising to the effect that *A Farewell to Arms* and/or *Tender is the Night* at RKO would be bigger than *Gone With the Wind*. Dan, said David, don't you remember how I used to do it? Within days, David had picked up their old relationship and began lecturing the man who now ran a studio:

> You simply must realize, Dan, that the news angle of this story, from the standpoint of the press of *its value to RKO*, is myself and The Selznick Company.

From David's point of view, O'Shea was trying to be cautious and prudent, as if the business was in a bad way. Whereas they had to be bold and remember what showmanship was! Make big announcements. Let the public know that huge things were coming. *Tender is the Night* with Cary Grant or Gregory Peck or Bill Holden, and Jennifer, and why not Elizabeth Taylor, too? With Lillian Hellman or Arthur Miller doing the script. *A Farewell to Arms*—"I am trying so desperately to build a picture that will be as eagerly awaited as anything since *Gone With the Wind*." Dan had to see that the only hope of the business was in big pictures . . . "an all-time giant."

The harangues went on, and O'Shea fell silent. David had a long two-column memo to himself on reasons to favor the RKO deal or the MGM one. It was like 1938 again, wondering whether to go with Metro or Warners. But in 1938, those studios had wanted him and his project, and he had been resolved to make his movie. In 1955, he was so tired he looked for problems. The deal with RKO broke down. By the end of the year, Frank Davis quit and went to work for Charlie Feldman.

Only one deal was done, the one that least appealed to David. By November, he had had to settle with N.T.A. But he had compromised even there: instead of fifteen pictures for $2.25 million, he sold ten for $1.11 million. He let them have TV rights to *Intermezzo*, *A Bill of Divorcement*, *The Farmer's Daughter*, *The Garden of Allah*, *I'll Be Seeing You*, *Notorious*, *The Paradine Case*, *Portrait of Jennie*, *Since You Went Away*, and *The Spiral Staircase*.

He had kept back five especially valuable properties: *Duel in the Sun*, *Rebecca*, *The Adventures of Tom Sawyer* (which he was reissuing theatrically), *Spellbound*, and *The Third Man*. By January 1956, he was telling Bill Paley about these plums and bragging about his N.T.A. deal:

It looks to me as though your people are going to find out that they enormously undershot the mark at evaluating these pictures. From what I gather of N.T.A.'s plans, which are quite extraordinary, they seem certain to gross between $300,000 and $350,000 on each of the films. . . . It seems clear to me, from my talks with not only your people but also N.B.C. and A.B.C., that the independent distributors are many miles ahead of the syndicating departments of the big chains in their ingenuity, sales and terms.

And so, by 1956, "independence" had become a synonym or a disguise for loneliness. It was a way of always telling himself he was right, the only survivor, the all-time giant.

13 · YOU MUST FORGIVE ME

THERE WAS ONLY one person with whom David could ever discuss his end. In March 1953, he had written to Irene about getting back into production one day, "although if I had any character at all, I would find myself an ivory tower somewhere, gather together all those books I have never read, prove once and for all that I don't know how to write, and be very happy."

Imagine what might have been. After his death, television ran "Hollywood: The Selznick Years," with great success, but without David. He might have been the host to a parade of Hollywood's history in the way Alistair Cooke led a tour of America. David might have founded film studies programs. Could he have written a great autobiography? Or would it have piled up the unedited prose of self-justification? He never tried. But he paid storage bills on his papers at Bekins depository when he had no money to spare.

Two years after the wistful admission to Irene, in June 1955, he was telling her:

I am arriving at my decisions slowly and carefully; for my next moves, during the coming week or two, will determine the shape and course of what is left of my career. With some reluctance and some sadness, I have come to the conclusion that I might as well accept, without further resistance, my preference for continuing hard work and do whatever seems to offer the most exciting opportunities, rather than attempt leisure and semiretirement, for the enjoyment of which, other than briefly, my gifts are much more limited than I wish were the case.

Some could have argued that David needed the ambition and stimulus of a son. By 1956, Jeffrey had paid his dues; he had worked as an assistant at Republic and for the producer Benedict Bogeaus; he was an assistant director on *Giant* in Texas. David did talk about passing his business on to his sons, and he was moved by memories of the collaboration he had known with L.J. and Myron. But he could not see Jeff as a partner: he did not trust anyone so like himself.

Jeffrey had found a more understanding mentor in John Huston. The nomadic director had a desire to go to Tahiti to make a film of Herman Melville's *Typee*. He offered Jeff a job, but then became preoccupied with his new pal Billy Pearson's success on "The $64,000 Question" on TV. *Typee* lingered, and Jeff went to California in the spring of 1956. It was the moment at which David had chosen to reissue *The Adventures of Tom Sawyer*, and he enlisted his son in the work. There was to be an important preview screening on the night of April 27, and David loaded the detail on Jeff: clean the print, check the splices, nag the projectionist, rehearse the curtain arrangements—

> Would like after first picture for lights to go up and curtain closed just for about thirty seconds (but being prepared to delay this on signal from you in event people are milling in and out of theatre, until they are settled). Would like curtain to be about half way open again when the trademark goes on at start of picture.

The instructions ran three pages, so filled with the possibilities of mishap Jeff was bound to make mistakes. The son resented this and became more surly and difficult. When the father saw that, he felt confirmed that Jeff had a "Crown Prince complex."

Around the house, and in front of David's friends, Jeffrey was inclined to call his father "an impossible reactionary." Jeff's stay at Tower Grove was a constant battle. As David saw it, his son abused and exploited the servants, took breakfast in bed in the middle of the afternoon, and generally acted the role of a spoiled liberal:

> The notion that 50% of Americans, who like myself are Republicans, are rich reactionaries, is fantastic enough—for among the tens of millions of people who think highly of Richard Nixon, not to speak of the President, are huge armies of day laborers and other hard-working people doing jobs that you consider beneath you. But what I find so offensive is your criticism of any followers of Eisenhower and Nixon as reactionary, while you behave in a fashion that went out with the Romanoffs.

Jeffrey stormed off to Europe, feeling victimized and unsupported. Danny was beginning to falter, too: he was on probation at Harvard. But his shortcomings were easily explained: "He is such a remarkable human being," David told Irene, "that I think we must both be on guard against judging him severely for deviation from his own high standards."

As David raised and then squashed deal prospects, Jennifer worked steadily. After *Love is a Many-Splendored Thing*, she took the role of the school-teacher in *Good Morning, Miss Dove*, going all the way from youth to old age. Then she played the wife in *The Man in the Gray Flannel Suit*. Gregory Peck had the lead role, and now he and Jennifer were playing a middle-aged couple, tired of each other and grounded by everyday compromise. It was a movie in which Fredric March played a media tycoon—Paley or David—who had neglected his family. David fired off many memos. But Nunnally Johnson, whose film it was, found an exquisite way of putting David in his place:

> In case your wife is too modest to tell you, I want you to know that she did a scene today that was absolutely marvelous. P.S. Don't answer this.

In the spring of 1956, Jennifer was cast as Elizabeth Barrett Browning (the Norma Shearer part) in a remake of *The Barretts of Wimpole Street*. The filming was to be done in London, and John Gielgud was cast as the father. So David and Jennifer set off for England and a two-month stay. Had David wearied, or had Jennifer told him off? While Jennifer worked, he went to Paris for a few days, he watched the tennis at Wimbledon, and twice he dined with Lord Beaverbrook, the newspaper magnate.

Twenty years after the abdication, Beaverbrook remained the friend and supporter of the Duke of Windsor. He found he was talking to the right royalist among movie producers. The memoirs of the Duchess of Windsor were being published, and Beaverbrook wondered about the possibility of a movie. David's trip to Paris was to meet the Duke and the Duchess and to discover they were both pleased "over the idea of Mrs. Selznick's essaying the role of the Duchess." There were many problems, notably the question of whether the Windsors really wanted this movie, with its inescapable vulgarization. But for the rest of 1956, talks went on, and as late as December 10, in Paris, David and Jennifer dined with the Windsors to consider ways of proceeding.

Nineteen fifty-six and 1957 were difficult years for moviemaking. The audience was fickle, yet it was ready for new challenges, too, and not all the best films were big ones. There were epics that had their rewards—Vidor's *War and Peace*, *Giant*, *The Bridge on the River Kwai*, *The Ten Commandments*. But if only because of David's search for size, we should remember the smaller pictures. Not all of them were immediate hits, but they inaugurated careers and showed a way ahead: Don Siegel's *Invasion of the Body Snatchers*, Stanley

Kubrick's *The Killing* and *Paths of Glory*, Vincente Minnelli's *Lust for Life*, Kazan's *Baby Doll* and *A Face in the Crowd*, *Picnic* with Kim Novak as the woman, *The Sweet Smell of Success*, *Fear Strikes Out*, *Twelve Angry Men*, and Billy Wilder's *Love in the Afternoon*.

It was in this climate that David remade *A Farewell to Arms*, never knowing it would be his last production, yet somehow advancing like a man enacting his own tragedy.

Of course, it had to be a big picture, not just because of David's expectations for himself, but because of the war background and the wish to shoot in Italy. So David was obliged to hire himself out to a studio as an independent producer, the thing he had found impossible with Metro and RKO. He made his deal at Twentieth Century-Fox, the studio that had made *Love is a Many-Splendored Thing* and Jennifer's next two pictures. It said it was eager to have her play Catherine Barkley from Hemingway's novel. Spyros Skouras, president of Fox, agreed to let David make the picture for $3.2 million. There was as yet no director decided upon, and no actor cast for Frederic Henry.

David turned to Ben Hecht for his writer. Over sixty now, Hecht was still a careerist. He had not had a credit on a hit since *Monkey Business* in 1952, but he knew how to write music for David's ears. And while he was a fast, facile writer, he was a trimmer who would not fight his boss. What was worse, he envied Hemingway, another Chicagoan, but a few years younger, and the recipient of high critical praise and large sales.

David with Ben Hecht in the Dolomites

Once Hecht and David got to work on the script, the writer "discovered" that Hemingway was not ideal material for film. So much of his best writing and fatalistic character are in the tone of the narrative. The war aside, not a great deal happens. If censorship cannot permit something close to real lovemaking, then even less happens. Add to that the gulf between Hemingway's English heroine in her twenties and Jennifer Jones, who was thirty-eight when the picture was made. Some movies are wrong before a foot of film has been exposed.

Writer and producer labored. By late October 1956, they had done five drafts. In the process they learned that just transcribing Hemingway produced unplayable scenes. Yet David the defender of literature still did not grasp how much of writing is in the arrangement of words and in the rhythm of narrative.

It had always been his desire to have John Huston as director; Huston was so close to being a character out of Hemingway and such a master of action scenes. Contact with Huston was made in August 1956 by Arthur Fellows, an old friend of the director's and David's right-hand man now. The onetime office boy was to be associate producer on *Farewell*. Huston had gone to the island of Tobago in the fall to shoot *Heaven Knows, Mr. Allison*, and he wanted to do *Typee* in the summer of 1957. But he was excited about *Farewell* if it could fit in the middle, and he suggested Gregory Peck for Frederic Henry.

Huston and Fellows had something else in common: they had learned to see David through the experience of Jeffrey. Just as the director had been ready to hire Jeff, so Fellows had been a kind of uncle figure to him, watching over his ups and downs. Huston said he was happy to have Jennifer in *Farewell*, yet *Beat the Devil* had taught him how oppressive the husband's interest could be. Huston and David were "old friends," yet there was little warmth. A director like Huston never trusted producers, and Huston would one day write that "David never did anything worth a damn after he married Jennifer."

There were other directors considered: Wellman, William Wyler, and even some Italians. Huston did not commit himself until the end of the year, and he went along with David's proposal that $250,000 was a handsome fee for simply directing. Huston had little part in the preproduction; he agreed to leave the editing to David. Huston always had a lot on his mind: he had a family safely lodged in Ireland but requiring some visits, he had sports and romances to pursue, and Humphrey Bogart was dying. That said, he was wary of the project, unconvinced of the setup but needing the money. Huston was a gambler, too. He liked to make "Huston pictures," but he never lost the habit of doing throwaways for the loot.

By October, David had Rock Hudson lined up for Frederic, for Hudson had become a major star in the space of three years and David was not the man to feel that Hudson's romantic nature was more gentle than manly. In cabling Huston, David was very candid about the need to stay on budget and schedule, and he gave Huston an opening to say "no":

> and also because extent to which I personally produce in every sense of word I am perhaps not unnaturally worried lest unquestioned eminence of your present position would cause you to resist and resent functioning as director rather than producer director.

Huston promised to deliver himself in time, and he gave notes on the script. The first draft had made Huston ready to refuse the job—but it was that draft which had been the most faithful. As the drafts progressed, he grew happier or more resigned. As late as December 19, David was urging more revisions on Hecht, mindful of Huston's wish to have a heroic film, but also increasingly shrewd about the book:

> I wish you would think about what we are going to do with the opening sequences of the love story. . . . I know, I know: we did much more than Hemingway—but this is another instance of Hemingway "writing on water" as you put it, or successfully telling his story "in the white spaces between the lines" as Huxley put it. Unfortunately or no, we haven't the white space and have to really get this love story going. This is quite apart from, and in addition to, the unanimity of criticism of the girl being the aggressor as to the affair, which I think we now both realize is wrong. And apart from the actual relationship between the two principals, everybody asks the same questions we asked each other, and that we apparently kidded ourselves we had answered: What is Frederic Henry all about? . . . What is there about him that makes him the long-awaited answer to this maiden's prayer? (and it's not fair to the actor to make it solely dependent upon his good looks, for as I am sure you would be the first to agree, an actor should never be made to be a substitute for a script); What is the girl all about? (Huston particularly objected to her being so seemingly nutty in the first scene—a probably bad carry-over from Hemingway).

Much of the novel disappears once one removes Frederic's narrative: the final film does begin with a few sentences of voiceover, but they are stilted, and Hudson's delivery so uneasy, no wonder the scheme was dropped. After that, it is a story of a wounded man in a hospital bed and a nurse who comes to him as easily as fantasy. The dialogue may play, silently, in a reader's head, but actors have rarely found a way to utter

Hemingway's lines. The lovers needed recklessness and passion: let us say the twenty-year-old Vanessa Redgrave and the twenty-nine-year-old Christopher Plummer (an actor David had admired onstage the previous summer in *Measure for Measure*). But Plummer and Redgrave then had no box office. And for David not to have used Jennifer would have been sacrilege. Some people believed Jennifer knew she was wrong for the part. But neither of them could escape; that is a pitiless consequence of romantic rescue.

Arthur Fellows had gone to Italy months in advance to prepare. He had been production manager on Vidor's *War and Peace*, and he was charged with finding locations, extras, and army support from the Italians or the Yugoslavs. At first he had no script to work from; then it was a script that changed as every wavelike memo broke on his shore. Fellows was quick-tempered, and he feared David could never trust the ex–office boy. David always said he wanted to promote his own people. Now that this had occurred, with Artie Fellows, it left him suspicious and condescending.

In his autobiography, Huston said he was signed on before he found out how far the story "had simply become a vehicle for the female lead." This is not true: the deal came after he saw and helped refine the script. But he was disturbed. Bogart died on January 14, 1957, and Huston read the eulogy at his funeral. Around the same time, he met Hemingway and learned the writer was getting no more money from the picture. His rights had been disposed of in the early 1930s when Paramount first filmed the book. There was ample atmospheric reason for Huston to believe the intrusive David was going to spoil the book's masculine ethos. A more detached opinion could have said that Huston had never proved himself with love stories: the closest he had come to one was *The African Queen*. Love was not the womanizer's theme.

The script was never fixed, and the producer's plans changed at every turn. That is what alarmed Huston and urged him to get himself off the project.

Nothing is as instructive as the letters David sent to Arthur Fellows during preproduction. They are cruel, mocking, and absolutely counterproductive. They ring changes in script and schedule, yet constantly assume superiority in foresight, local knowledge, and movie experience. At first, David believed his production designer, Alfred Junge, was a genius greater than William Cameron Menzies—later, he acknowledged he had been a terrible disappointment. Fellows bore the burden of those changes without apology or realization from David of how badly the picture had been set up. The problems ranged from uncertainty over Hudson's start date (he wanted to stay in Hollywood until the Oscars, for he believed he might win with *Giant*), to the question of when and whether snow would be in the mountains.

The tone of David to Fellows began to undermine the film in advance of shooting. Here is David, on January 9, 1957, writing from Los Angeles. It is maybe 0.05 percent of what Fellows had before the start of photography:

> You simply must get over the feeling, Arthur, that because I get help from others it is any reflection on you. . . .
>
> You are far too sensitive. When you have had more experience in an important job you will realize that the bigger the man, the more he not only seeks help from others, but the more he needs it and the more he is willing to give credit to others, even if it is excessive credit.
>
> I do hope that you won't impose upon me to spend more time worrying about your feelings. You are worse than a jealous bride.

The following day, David was at Fellows again, not at all mindful of sensitivities. Here was a picture where Fellows was waiting on so many things—whether the right hairdresser could be found for Jennifer, when Huston would arrive, whether Jack Cardiff could be obtained as photographer. Yet David mocked him and sought to trap him in error and inconsistency.

> It's difficult at this distance to figure out your gyrations as to a starting date of March 15, or March 17 (which incidentally is Sunday), or March 30 (which incidentally is Saturday). You must forgive me if I suspect that these gyrations are not due to the Hudson situation, as you state in your memo, but rather to your belated discovery that my repeatedly expressed fears concerning the snow were justified, and that your assumption that we had no problems about the snow if we started on March 30 "because we could go higher" were based upon either amateur information . . . or improper realization of the cost of going higher. . . .

David arrived in Rome on February 12. Huston came later. The director asked for Hudson's hair to be cut very short, as was the practice during World War I. David said that diminished his appeal. The producer called for rehearsals. Huston was reluctant and tardy. They were in the Dolomites, based at Cortina d'Ampezzo, in dismal weather, planning the complex long shots of troop movements. Rock Hudson arrived only days before shooting was to start. He needed special help, yet Huston was so unimpressed with the actor he neglected him. On March 19, David dictated a sixteen-page letter to Huston that began, "I should be less than candid with you if I didn't tell you that I am most desperately unhappy about the way things are going."

The letter looked back eighteen years to the moment when D.O.S. had let Cukor go on *Gone With the Wind*. It went into details of script and shooting and expressed horror at Huston's readiness to rewrite the script on the set. Sixteen pages, of over 600 words to a page, nearly 10,000 words at a time when, David said, there was not time enough for the vital work. (At the very same moment, he learned from America that his mother had had a heart attack.)

The letter ended:

> Because every hour counts, in order to minimize the losses of a possible change in direction, I shall appreciate your immediate choice as to the course of action you wish to follow. The only single favor that I ask of you is that you *not* decide to do the picture without any enthusiasm, or with anger, or with resentment, or with a feeling that it is going to be bad that will eventually communicate itself to what I know could be a wildly enthusiastic unit if it only had the kind of guidance directorially to which it is accustomed. . . . As you are an individualist in your way, so too am I in my own. In this case, there cannot be two individualists: there can only be one—and, under my obligations and by my training, and consistent with our discussions and agreements, both before and after you agreed to do the picture, this can only be myself.

Huston never read that far. He put the letter aside after a few pages and called his secretary to pack. Then he turned to Fellows, who had delivered the memo, and said, "I can't tell you, Art, I'm really so relieved." He went home, rescued and carefree, without shooting a foot of film.

14 · SUDDENLY REMOVED

HUSTON NEVER REPLIED to the memo, but on his way out of Italy he gave a press conference and suggested the problem was David and Jennifer again, as well as David thinking himself superior to Hemingway and his directors. The story got about that the producer was enlarging his wife's role and that he had other writers at work. It was alleged that Ben Hecht was as angry as Huston. But Hecht remained on the picture, and only two weeks before the crisis with Huston, he had asked David that "you and I alone decide what you want me to write and that I see you and receive information from you alone. A three-cornered taffy pull will be dangerous." Hecht had dropped out briefly, but from disgust with Huston. He was back in time to remind the press, "The last time Mr. Selznick had a directorial change was on *Gone With the Wind.*"

King Vidor could have corrected that kindness. Others in Hollywood were mindful of David's history. Slim and Leland Hayward sent a cheeky one-word cable: "Copycat."

As for the other writers, David had engaged a young poet and screenwriter to bring vigor and authenticity to the trio of Italian soldiers. This was Pier Paolo Pasolini. David had no idea of the man's Marxist approach, nor had he really considered that Hemingway had a special, colorful way of rising above the realities of his supporting native characters. Pasolini wrote dry comments on the script that define the huge gulf between showmanship and politically correct neorealism:

> I am confronted with a problem which, perhaps, is unconceivable to an American. I mean to say: do those three soldiers belong to the low or middle class? (To the "people" or to the "bourgeoisie"?) . . .
>
> In the latest interpretation that was explained to me, the three Italian soldiers have opinions of their own, an ideology of their own, they protest in a conscious way, and finally they make a choice which engages them morally and totally. All this would lead one to think that they are young men belonging to the middle class, to a rather elevated cultural level.

Pasolini was an intellectual diversion for David—the "myth" of literature—someone to court and be baffled by. Yet in Huston's wake, Pasolini was alleged to have done an entire and different script with more Jennifer and less Rock. Without saying very much, Huston had helped damn the movie in American eyes; he had acted out the clash of creative liberty and producer's megalomania. There had always been enough of this in David for the caption to stick. But Huston had behaved badly, David had been David, and the project was doomed.

Second unit director Andrew Marton handled the spectacular troop scenes that began at the snow line on March 24. Early in April, David and Jennifer made a fast trip to L.A. and back, as Flossie had an operation. Then Charles Vidor was hired as the new director. Vidor was neither Huston nor a hack. He was versatile but impersonal: he had had such diverse hits as *Cover Girl, Gilda, Hans Christian Andersen,* and *Love Me or Leave Me.* Brought in at such short notice, Vidor's only aim was to do what David told him. He began to be distressed as that telling changed course day by day. Vidor persevered. But his misery—and the film's inert blandness—give the real clue to why Huston left. For all his languid air, Huston was a decisive creature—and David made him nervous. When Vidor

Lunch on location for A Farewell
to Arms: *Rock Hudson, Jennifer,
David, Charles Vidor*

arrived, he was telling the story how he had been given a going-away
party in Hollywood, with the promise of another in two or three weeks,
when *he* was fired.

Within a month, Vidor was in tatters, lamenting his inability to please
David and inadvertently alluding to *Gone With the Wind* when he wondered if
there shouldn't have been "a two week hiatus in production" when Huston
departed. The locations were difficult, the weather was worse, the Italians
and the Americans had little common ground, and David was increasingly
of the opinion that Vidor could not do the job—so that David was obliged
to supervise every shot, including those he had rewritten the night before. In
his departure, Huston had been heard to say that David had hired a conductor when he wanted no more than a first violinist. Vidor picked up on
that idea:

> You are harping over and over on the fact that I have damaged the
> quality of the picture, and you feel the solution would be for you,

Ossie and I to get together before each scene to discuss set-ups that would satisfy you. Dear David, I have been directing for twenty years, I have never done that before and I am too old to start with that now. It seems to me you don't even want a first violinist, you want a piccolo player. If you have no faith in me, if you don't think I am the man to make this picture, please come out and say so, and I assure you, with sorrow but without hard feelings, that I will retire as gracefully as possible.

Also, I want you to know that I am not sending a mimeographed copy to our fellow workers to embarrass you, as you embarrassed me.

"Ossie" was Oswald Morris, Huston's favorite cameraman, who had stayed on. He tried to hold the picture together and remained for twelve weeks, being "the 8th or 9th person to quit." Vidor was too afraid to look at the rushes himself, so Morris screened them and reported over breakfast.

Jennifer seemed to have her own rule, that David should keep away from her on the set. So David lurked in the shadows and whispered messages to crew members for them to pass on to Vidor so that he could speak to the actress. Most of the crew elected to playact the whispered instructions.

Ossie Morris was told in person by David that the rushes were fine. But then, outside his hotel door, Morris found files of devastating criticism, worrying over the look of Jennifer's hands, hair, and chin. Morris could not endure the contradictory approach or the impossibility of trusting David again. He quit the picture.

Whenever anyone protested to David, or argued, he told them this was the most important film he had ever made. Because he had so much at stake, he had to be attended to. He began every memo by urging the recipient actually to read it. The self-dramatist could hardly think now without feeling a turning point: "Because I feel that in the subjects dealt with may lie the entire difference in the status of the film, I must earnestly request you to read this memorandum carefully."

No one clashed with D.O.S. as regularly as Arthur Fellows, whose task it was to get the talent, material, weather, extras, and scenery in place each day. Fellows had so many handicaps: he had known David twenty years; he had seen decline and he thought he knew how to handle him; he was also keen to prove himself to the boss he adored and certain that someone needed to assert control over their chaotic project. If he had a model, it was the young David—so David told him he had a "Hun-like attitude" that offended everyone. On May 14, they had a quarrel so severe that Arthur challenged David: "Do you want me to quit?" All Fellows got in answer was a memo that drove anger deeper:

I don't know whether your resignation today was just your customary weekly hot-headed demonstration, or whether you meant it. But I do want to say that I think the time has been reached when you ought long since to have grown up; and that if you don't govern your temper, you are going to constantly get into trouble wherever you go and whatever you do. . . .

I am perfectly willing to give you this spanking, and then forget it, if that be your desire, conditioned solely upon assurances that I won't be subjected to this kind of insulting behavior again.

Jeffrey was in Paris working as an assistant director on another Fox film, *The Young Lions*. His special job was making sure Marlon Brando and Montgomery Clift showed up fit to work. But over the July 14 weekend, he went to Italy to visit his father. He was cornered by Vidor and Fellows before he ever saw David. Then David admitted there were fearful problems and wanted to know how *Young Lions* was functioning effectively. "He said, 'You're obviously doing something right, and we're doing something wrong.' " When Jeffrey went back to Paris, D.O.S. pursued him with calls and cables, asking for help and advice. But Jeff was already bone-weary from his real job.

In all the physical confusion, and often adding to it, David remained the sleepless writer ready to be struck by visions. On July 30, he finished the day "vaguely disturbed that we were missing something" in the final scenes. So he pondered, until he *saw* it. New scenes came to him, "pure Hemingway." He wrote them out in the white heat of inspiration and sent them to Vidor––wanting to be liked and appreciated.

It would be tough as hell to play. You would have to work like mad with Rock on it. I would, in any event, strongly urge you to work with Rock if you have to keep him up all night, on whatever version of the scene we use. I think he is taking this section a little bit too much in stride, possibly as a result of too many compliments even if justified on what he has done to date. I think he needs to be goosed into the realization that in the scenes he is about to do, starting with this scene, may lie his Academy Award, and his enormously increased stature as an actor. I think if he works all night tonight and is tired, it can only help the mood of the scene—and anyway we know he is a big strong hulk and if he can go without sleep for play purposes, he can go without sleep for the most important scenes in the biggest picture of his career to date.

The more I think about this, the more I dictate about it, the more I feel that we may be on the verge of something wonderful here.

Early in August, the unit was at Lago Maggiore, preparing to shoot the escape of Frederic and Catherine to Switzerland. There was a big shot

*Wedding anniversary
during* A Farewell
to Arms

required, of the rowboat and a German gunboat with a searchlight, and it had to be done at magic hour, the brief twilight. Arthur Fellows had set it up, with lights and a field telephone. Jennifer was in her hotel, waiting for the call, a hotel that looked out over the lake. People went to get her, but she never came. Twilight passed, and the cameraman—Piero Portalupi, who had taken over from Morris—said there was no longer enough light. Then Jennifer appeared.

Fellows gave the order to wrap. They would have to come back the next night; it was more money wasted.

David approached Fellows. The producer and husband had been around all evening, but he had not gone to fetch Jennifer. "If you knew your business," he told Arthur, "you would have had the army get enough searchlights so we could shoot it."

Fellows replied, "David, why don't you call the army if you think that's what we should do."

Selznick said, "Arthur, you're impertinent," and he slapped his associate in the face.

So Fellows punched David. The blow broke his glasses, and David was crying that glass had gone in his eye.

"I don't know whether he said I'm fired," Fellows remembered, "or I said good-bye first. But, anyway, the whole relationship went up with that."

David was taken to a hospital in Milan, but the damage to his face was minor. Fellows went back to America—he would get no credit at all on the film after a year's work. From the hospital, David called Jeffrey in Paris and said he had to come down to take over. Jeffrey was touched but reluctant: he had a job, yet he was bursting to do well for his father. So David went straight to Darryl Zanuck, who reassigned Jeffrey from one film to another. Thus, as David and Jennifer returned to America, on August 27, Jeffrey was left to handle the outstanding second unit work, using a double for Rock Hudson. He planted poppies on a bare hillside to get the right look and trucked loads of snow from higher up a mountain to match the footage from April. But David was soon displeased. Even at a distance, he reproached Jeffrey for being arbitrary and domineering with the Italians.

On August 28, David dined in New York with Irene and Danny. As he hurried through postproduction on *A Farewell to Arms*, he saw her for dinner again once in October. His film was not the only worry. In that summer of 1957, L.B. fell ill. He was afraid of cancer, and he had had many X rays to search it out. Suspicious of L.A. doctors, he went to Boston to Dr. Sidney Farber. The doctor told Irene her father had leukemia.

She was very close to him at the end, and Edie was still excluded. Irene was in charge of whether or not L.B. should be told. L.B. was sick but he did not ask, and Irene said Farber was to wait on her father's question. Irene was advised she should leave L.B. in bed at home and go back to New York—surely then he would believe he was all right? David visited him, and L.B. told Irene he was a fine fellow. But L.B. was still distraught; he asked her, was he dying? His will, he said, was not the way he wanted it, his affairs were in an untidy state, so he had to know. Irene reassured him: she said there was no question of death, and she went back to New York. Irene waited in the East, but the strain was too much, so she flew back to L.A. secretly and waited in a hotel.

At 12:35 a.m. on October 29, Louis B. Mayer died. He had asked for Irene, but he was unconscious before she arrived. When the death was confirmed, she told Edie and then she called David, who took on the funeral arrangements. He also telephoned Italy and asked Jeffrey to fly over.

David helped write a eulogy, and Spencer Tracy delivered it. There were notable absences at the funeral, including Nick Schenck and Bill Goetz. The feud between Irene and Edie was not healed. It was terribly increased when the will was read, and Edie was omitted. The estate worked out at $7.5

million. Five million dollars went to the Louis B. Mayer Foundation. Their home and $750,000 went to his second wife, Lorena. Irene and Lorena's daughter, Suzanne, got $500,000 each. There was $250,000 each left in trust for Jeffrey and Danny, but nothing for Edie's two daughters. Power went as far as it could, and it never bothered with forgiving or forgetting. There were those not quite confident that even death would hold L.B.

Jeffrey had lunch with David and Irene. He told his father how the last shooting had gone in Italy, and David talked about the editing and the music. Then they got down to business. Jeffrey had some inheritance now. That summer, he had turned twenty-five, at which time he began to receive trust money from Margaret Mayer's estate. With that, and inheritance from L.B., Irene needed to make a matching gesture. She therefore determined to turn over all the Christmas-present money from the past, as well as the sums David and Irene had put aside. The total was $109,000. "You can buy a brothel in Barcelona," David grumbled, "or do the right thing." In time, Danny would collect a similar amount. Irene also told Jeffrey that it was probably her fault he had inherited "so little" from L.B. If she had told her father the truth, then he would have called in the lawyers and been more generous.

When David drove Jeff back to the airport, he was gloomy. He told his son there was no future in pictures. *A Farewell to Arms* was at least $800,000 over budget, and David had no illusions. Without illusions, a producer cannot function.

The picture would open. You cannot burn a finished picture when it is not good enough. It previewed on December 16, eighteen years and a day after the Atlanta opening of *Gone With the Wind*. Jennifer was not present— she had gone off on a trip to India. But she was home in time for the December 19 premiere at Grauman's Chinese. At first, in L.A., business was promising.

Danny came from Harvard to be at the New York screening on January 24, at the Roxy. Danny had not been involved in the film. He had not known how to reconcile his feelings for father and brother when Jeff told him, "Dad behaved so terribly, so monstrously." Danny went in to see the picture hoping for the best:

> Dad had built it up in his letters to me. What a great picture it was going to be. "We're all going to be up for Academy Awards." I just remember feeling sick with disappointment. . . . I saw shots and I thought, John Huston would never have allowed that. And I had seen the very first script, which I thought was pretty good . . . but he showed me the final script, and it was 7,000 colors, bloated, it lost its central thrust. . . . There was some applause at the end. But it seemed

something less than the sum of its parts. I tried to reassure Dad, and I said, "It's very good." And he said, "But, it's not wonderful."

No one now thought it wonderful. The East Coast reviews were crushing, and they were fair. Elaine Stritch and Mercedes McCambridge were good in two small roles. The last scenes were somber and affecting, and Jennifer was moving in delivery and death. But the film did not work, and for 152 minutes, in CinemaScope, it was a stately bore.

The coincidence of L.B.'s death held the meaning of 1957. Overwhelming as that man had been, rival as he always was, his death left David that much more lonely and more reconciled with Irene. L.B. was the end of the great glory and unsettling success of immigrants. David was only fifty-five, but in the eyes of the business, he had been of the same generation. Indeed, if he had been as rough and willful as L.B. then *Farewell* might have been wonderful—or never made. But David had wanted to be of the next, improved generation. For a decade he had managed it. Now, he was stranded. He wrote to Irene, trying to make sense of it all, but conscious that he had lost his second father:

Afterwards

Dear Irene:

How strange, this vacuum he has left. It is not love that has been lost, nor tenderness, nor even paternal protection. Rather it is as though we had all lived fearfully in the shadow of a magnificent, forbidding Vesuvius, which is now suddenly removed: no more the little arbors huddled up on its slope, no more the threatening lava. . . . You, above all others, know that I never ate of the grapes nor feared the eruptions. Yet I could stand in awe. And I can feel that the world this day is different than all the days of our lives before. . . .

Even this vein of writing is so foreign to me that I am amazed: what power the man had, even over those free of the best and the worst of him alike.

The best of him, obviously, was yourself. Yours too is the brain; yours too, is the Power, whether you wish to exercise it or not—and yours too is the over-rated, under-rated thing called Glory, whenever if ever you want it. But you have what he, poor man, did not have: the understanding that is Greatness, the comparison that is Genius.

Let me say it, Irene, for I know that it is remotely possible for you to believe it only if it comes from me: the world needs you. And it is high time you did something proper about it!

You know the little religion that I have clung to—that what matters most is the continuity of life, and its improvement from one generation to another. Never has there been a greater example of its potential than in you. What are you going to do about it?

You remember too that I've always felt that every set-back or calamity has its purpose, if we but have the patience and the perspicacity to find it. Because I have been so unexpectedly shaken by your father's death, I have sought its meaning. I think I have found it. The strange finish of your father's bizarre life can have meaning if, and only if, your own life is the fulfillment of what his might and could have been, if only he had had your character.

And that, L.B., is that! I agree with you. And I know—indeed, there is ample evidence: you knew it all the time!

David

SECOND CHILDHOOD

1 · 1958

NO ONE IS MORE of an embarrassment than a producer without pictures or prospects. Directors are allowed to lose the talent or their touch. Producers are never forgiven for fumbling power. And until they die, they have no other real calling except trying to look prosperous and keeping the grin fixed on their faces. David Selznick managed this rather well. While waiting for the obituary that he could predict in detail, David kept his nerve true and tempered. He was an entertainer, always.

In September 1957, once back in Los Angeles, he went to Dr. George Griffith for a checkup. David was short of breath whenever he climbed stairs, he was sometimes dizzy when he woke, and he felt exhausted. There were also "short, sharp stabs" of pain in the chest, never more than a second in length. Dr. Griffith put those down to a shortening of the left leg by as much as an inch that curved the spine and produced intercostal neuralgia in the left chest. This discrepancy in David's legs is observable in some photographs. He was given a complete electrocardiogram test, but the results were normal. His weight was down to 198½ pounds. Griffith recommended a lift in the heel of his left shoe, a careful diet, reduced smoking, rest, and exercise. David had given up tennis in 1955 because of shortness of breath, but he claimed that in the course of dictation, he "probably travels as much as 10 miles" a day.

Doctors didn't have to believe in that exercise program—it was sufficient that *he* fell for it. And this is a key to the last years: anyone examining the evidence must share the feeling of many contemporaries that David was slowing down in a race that had passed him by. But he never quite saw he was no longer in the lead. Whatever he was doing had to be "big"—because *he* was doing it.

If anyone was *not* David's fan after 1957 it was his son Jeffrey. Yet Jeff saw the charm working, in what was surely a major cause of death:

It's very difficult to understand what occurred when he stepped into a room. It was magic. He didn't have to open his mouth—suddenly there was electricity and everybody picked up a beat. He would start to laugh, and the laugh was infectious. It could pick up the mood of a party or a gathering. . . .

He would put a cigarette in his mouth, and it would stick to his upper lip, and he'd never move it. He would talk, but never take it or use his hands to smoke. Ash would fall on shirtfront, suit, the floor. . . . There has never been anybody who could get an ash that long on a cigarette. It would mesmerize people while they were talking to him. They couldn't concentrate on what he was saying, waiting for the ash to drop. . . . Finally, it would fall, of course, in a shower. It was part of the personality.

In January 1958, when he traveled east for the New York opening of *A Farewell to Arms*, David saw Dr. Connie Guion. She found him "very tense, grey and fatigued" and scarcely able to keep awake: completing the film had been a desperate drive to get the sound and the music done in time. His cholesterol was at 260 (very high, though less alarming then than now), and his blood pressure was low. But Dr. Guion could find nothing more specific: "On the whole you are in astonishingly good physical condition. Don't impose on this elephantine constitution of yours! Get your smoking down to under twenty a day; get long hours of sleep, some exercise and fun."

The full release of *Farewell* did nothing to encourage fun. During the heyday of preproduction, Fox had predicted domestic rentals of $10 million. If the budget had held at $3 million, that would have left profits for David. But by the end of 1958, worldwide rentals were $6.889 million. Against that there was the Fox distribution fee of $2.202 million and sundry deductions (including prints and advertising) amounting to another $2.238 million. Thus, only $2.475 million had been "earned" to offset a final negative cost that climbed to $4.353 million ($803,506 of which David was required to pay).

Farewell had earned about $6.9 million for Fox (which means it took in about $20 million at the box office, all over the world). Fox would have made a little money on it, for it earned a fee on top of its expenses. But Selznick was left stranded. Even if the film had been a hit (of any ordinary nature), he would have done far less well than the studio. This was the thinking that had driven him into SRO and his own distribution setup. The chances of independent production flourishing were so very unlikely.

Not even Twentieth Century-Fox was safe. In the next ten years, despite some hits—*South Pacific, The Longest Day, The Sound of Music*—the studio would suffer the calamity of *Cleopatra* and such flops or abortions as *Something's Got to Give, Doctor Doolittle,* and *Star!* In 1969 and 1970, Fox would lose

over $110 million and have to sell off half its lot to survive. Century City had a better chance in the twenty-first century than the movie company.

But the summation on *A Farewell to Arms* came at a paining moment. For it was in June 1958 that David had to face settlement with the IRS after all appeals had been exhausted. Earl Beaman drew up a statement of assets and liabilities for David and Jennifer and the Selznick Company to prove to the IRS that payment of the tax debt could only be gradual.

	DOS & JJ	*Selznick Company*	*Total*
Cash on hand or in banks	$ 3,917	$257,966	$ 261,883
Accounts receivable	44,094	25,276	69,370
Insurance policies (less loans)	150,398	23,375	173,773
TOTAL (current assets)	198,409	306,617	505,026
Motion picture assets (less amortization)	950,266		950,266
A Farewell to Arms		803,567	803,567
Others	64,767	65,167	129,934
Studio/office equipment	6,740	11,985	18,725
TOTAL (motion picture assets)	$ 1,021,773	$880,719	$1,902,492
Real estate (Tower Grove & guest house)	288,485		288,482
Accounts receivable by D.O.S. for Selznick Co.	$2,732,941		

Of course, there was no way David could ever recover that debt from the Selznick Company. Still, the total assets came to $2,737,905, including his house, his insurance policies, and even such things as his Hillcrest Country Club membership (worth $10,000) and a mausoleum at Forest Lawn (worth $22,180). Against that, he faced these expenditures in the thirty months beginning July 1, 1958:

Operating expenses	$ 675,000
To purchase film properties	204,750
Accounts payable	233,149
Federal tax debt	1,662,942
California tax debt	188,000
TOTAL	$ 2,963,841

According to these estimates, he and Jennifer would be in the red by $225,000 unless they could generate other income. The estimate also allotted them personal expense money for those thirty months of $187,500, or $1,442 a week. David and Jennifer could have just about survived on that figure—if it was per diem. In the meantime, David agreed to pay the IRS $80,000 a month while "continuing to exploit every phase of possible transactions which will constantly increase the possibility of raising funds to continually aid in the liquidation of the tax liability."

On January 16, Jennifer and David, with Mary Jennifer and her nurse, flew to Montego Bay in Jamaica, avoiding the New York opening of *Farewell*. They stayed at the Paley house, and Bill Paley heard quarreling. By early February, Jennifer went off on another trip to India. She had become fascinated with the study of yoga and mysticism, and she had formed a friendship with the ambassador to India from a South American country. For his part, David had been having an intermittent affair with one of his secretaries, Shirley Harden.

The night David put Jennifer on the plane to India, Irene was having dinner with Arthur and Leonora Hornblow—"And at 9:30 the doorbell rang. It was David, merry as a bird. . . . He was there to take Irene home. They had grown very close with L.B. dying."

For Christmas 1957, among other things, David had given Irene the original of a Charles Saxon cartoon from *The New Yorker*. It showed a settled, middle-aged couple, the woman reading on a couch, the man at his desk. He says to her: "Well, Irene, I just figured it out. If I walked in front of a truck tomorrow, you'd be worth one hundred and four thousand dollars."

In the first half of 1958, when David flew to New York on January 3, with Shirley Harden, he went straight to see Irene at the Pierre at 11:00 p.m. He dined with her on the ninth at Imspond, her house in Bedford Village. Then, later in the year, he flew in to New York with Harden on June 9, and the following day went with Irene to Boston for Danny's graduation from Harvard. The three of them drove back to town on the thirteenth, and they lunched on the fourteenth and had dinner again on the nineteenth. In these talks, it was agreed that Danny would do a postgraduate year at Brandeis.

David wrote to Howard about the "great thrill" of the Harvard graduation. Howard was still in Asheville but living in a hotel now, under the fond care of Rose Mary Phillips. Howard was always cheerful and removed from the facts of David's life. He had written to congratulate Jennifer on getting an Oscar for *Love is a Many-Splendored Thing* (she was only nominated), and he had loved *A Farewell to Arms*.

David explained to Howard that their mother was as well as could be expected, except that she did not get around as much. He gave the best news he could of Howard's daughters, though David was involved in their broken lives more painfully and helplessly all the time, and he had to tell Howard that the institutionalized Florence was being divorced by her husband.

The letter to Howard did not mention Mary Jennifer, who would be four that summer, and was rather more in the care of her father than of her mother that year. It did not mention Jennifer, either. Yet Mary Jennifer was the marvel of David's life. This is not to say he was a good or wise father. He spoiled the child for all he was worth—and beyond. But he attended to her and played with her as he had never done with the boys. In the process, he was rejuvenated. Danny visited Tower Grove that summer of 1958, and saw a shift in the relationship between David and Jennifer:

> Mary Jennifer assumed the position of attention—number one—and Jennifer went back to number two, and couldn't get back to being the center of David's life and I think it partly destroyed *her*. . . . She gave him this child, she had this image of the three of them walking into the rainbow together. Instead of which, he was saying, "Oh, you've given me a little creature that I can really control and totally obsess over." The home movies and the Polaroids—here was somebody that he could take pictures of all day and all night long. . . . But finally I'm sure there were times when Jennifer was saying, "Remember me? I'm the one who created this with you."

Jeffrey had taken a mews flat in London, to survey his prospects. David wrote to Jeffrey in the summer of 1958, warning him about changes for the worse in the film business and proposing that his son go into finance or back to college. In fact, Jeffrey was now living well on his investments. David's letter was not encouraging or tolerant, yet the edge of aggression toward Jeff was altered. The failure of *Farewell* and the difficulties in his own marriage had made David more appreciative of forgiveness:

I am also worried by your statement that "something is bound to develop." This sounds suspiciously like Micawber. It is most definitely *not* true that something is *bound* to develop. . . .

I am working day and night, at least six days a week, and spend my Sunday making detailed notes for the succeeding six days and nights. I am fifty-six years old, and could wish that it were different. Having worked this hard for the last thirty-six years, it is time that I should be enjoying myself and relaxing more. But I made a great many mistakes, and I am paying for them.

Jennifer flew to Zurich on September 8, and David went to New York on the twenty-third. He had a busy week there conferring with Irene. Their occasion for this was the chance that Jeffrey might at last give up film for another line of work—high finance. At the same time, David gave a lengthy interview to the Columbia University Oral History Project. He was in a retrospective mood. In an effort to promote *A Farewell to Arms*, he had let *Life* publish some extracts from his memos on the film. A couple of publishers had called him, wanting to know if there were more.

On October 8, he set sail for Europe on the *Queen Elizabeth*. In fact, he had fresh projects and a new adviser to help him. This was Arnold Grant, a lawyer with offices in New York and Los Angeles, where he was a partner with Greg Bautzer. Grant was forty-nine in 1958, a self-important yet plain man, but so intellectually penetrating he attracted several glamorous women. He was ambitious to be more active in show business, and he believed he could put David's affairs in order; with this attitude, he began as a more civil, more patient Myron. Yet he would prove an executioner to many of David's illusions. That he was able to have that effect was only because he first charmed away David's regular wall of bombast, disorder, and second-guessing.

The two men made plans in the summer and early fall of 1958. David looked at the ruins of his past: *Farewell*, the tax debt, the overhead, the uncertainty of how to handle TV rights—how could he muster the willpower for new films with this deadweight behind him? Grant replied with soaring philosophy:

> There is no question that with concentration, attention to detail and the expenditure of time and energy, those men who devote themselves to abandoned mines make a solid living on working the tailings. However, those men have limited talent, no imagination, or have contented themselves with the philosophy that allows for a happy life as long as they are expending their energy and making a better than average living. . . .
>
> This is just a long-winded way of saying, David, that I am thor-

oughly conscious of the inherent values in the ultimate residuals of all of your properties, and I never intend to allow them to go by lightly or be dramatically undervalued.

However, unless I am deterred by you, or find it impossible to sell an over-all package to others, it is my intent to use all of the tailings of your past to try and come up with a completely clean slate, a new and potentially profitable contract, and from two to four million dollars in cash. If that is in the cards, I would resist as strongly as possible re-examination, re-evaluation, re-negotiation and reappraisal of the possible values in legal positions, residuals, foreign, TV, etc. I would try to get you to turn your back on these tailings.... I want that time and energy spent on driving down a new shaft in virgin territory. I see all the joy and genius in you alight when you look ahead. I see only despair, defeat and frustration when you keep sorting over those remnants of the past.

This was not rescue, it was mind reading! And the language was so metaphoric, so incantatory; it made David feel like a lost genius—being rediscovered. For something like a year, Arnold Grant was a Svengali, and David had the thrill of being a protégé.

His immediate challenge, however, was his trap: to put Jennifer back to work. He had two projects in mind; they had both been there a long time: *Tender is the Night* and the story of Mary Magdalene. The Fitzgerald novel had always intrigued him, and he had several times come close to making it. In 1951, for instance, he had wanted George Cukor to direct it, with Cary Grant as Dick Diver and Jennifer as Nicole. But Grant had been reluctant to do it with Jennifer, in part because he was a good friend to Irene.

Writing to Morgan Maree, David said the book was "the tragic story of the destruction of a man of enormous promise—by his own weakness, by great wealth, and most of all by his undying passion for and loyalty to a woman who is wrong for him. This is a story with countless counterparts in life." David was too smart not to hear what he was implying, but was he too self-dramatizing to worry? In the time when he prepared *Tender is the Night*, Jennifer was in serious analysis. Several observers thought her unhappy and disturbed. Yet David proposed to have her, fortyish, play a younger, mentally ill woman. Was that generosity—or a kind of vengeance against her for being there, too problematic to dislodge?

Many writers were considered for *Tender is the Night*—Lillian Hellman, S. N. Behrman, Romain Gary, John Cheever—before David settled on Ivan Moffat, who had worked on *Giant* and *Bhowani Junction*. David and Moffat conferred in Los Angeles in the summer of 1958 on a script.

The two men became good friends and enjoyed working together. Yet

Moffat observed how at Tower Grove, "David and Jennifer lived a life of considerable unreality, each giving the other the illusion of what they wanted themselves to be—he a great producer still, and she a great movie star. Each nourishing this for the other."

David ordered in scripts from studio heads. Jennifer did not read them, but she saw them come and go. David did read them and assured her they weren't right. It was a little reminiscent of the situation in *Sunset Boulevard*. As the script for *Tender is the Night* developed, Jennifer was often in the house, but never a party to their conferences.

Moffat was invited to Sunday parties, and as he got to see more of Jennifer he realized that, beneath the shyness, she had a strange, beguiling boldness and a sense of mischief. On one Sunday evening, she rounded up the gang and took them off to a gay nightclub in Santa Monica, changing from a blue silk suit to a pink one and nearly getting David to take his tie off.

At such times, David was the figure of fun—and he went along with it, though Jennifer became livelier as evenings went on, while David tired. Moffat noted David's way of talking as very characteristic: "pronouncements rendered quietly, as if he were sovereign—but with a slight sense of irony." Once at the dinner table a visitor asked what the word "goy" really meant. David gave Moffat a quick, private grin and said, "Somebody who is unnecessarily Gentile." The laughter welled up, and David's delight was evident.

When Jennifer flew to Zurich in September it was to begin a stay that would last, essentially, until the end of the following March, in analysis with Dr. C. A. Meier and living at the Dolder Grand Hotel. By October 13, David had joined her there. But he then installed not just Moffat at the Dolder Grand, but Edward Anhalt, too, his writer on the Mary Magdalene picture.

Anhalt had written *Not as a Stranger* and *The Young Lions*. David had a novel about Mary Magdalene, *The Scarlet Lily*, but his scheme was his own. He told Anhalt: "I want to combine Mary the sister of Lazarus, the adulteress Jesus saved from the stoning, the whore who washed His feet and the Mary Magdalene who was the first to see Him resurrected, into one character and tell the gospel story through her. And I want to tell it as a purely Jewish story, which is what it was—do you like that?"

The writer had liked it, and so he set to work. They would be politically daring. Anhalt found David open to every idea, ready to argue all night, and full of extemporaneous story lines. They believed they would shock people, for they wanted to make their Mary the lover of Barabbas who then falls in love with Jesus.

Life at the hotel lived up to these plots. Sometime in October, Jeffrey drove into town in an Alfa Romeo, with Ileana Bulova as his companion.

They were followed by a van that carried the lady's luggage. Madame Bulova was the widow of the watch manufacturer, a good deal older than Jeffrey, and ravishingly beautiful. David was flabbergasted to see his son—torn, he said, between acting thirteen and thirty—with so lustrous and sophisticated a consort. Jeff thought his father was jealous.

Ileana upstaged Jennifer and another lady at dinner, Adele Beatty, who was with Stanley Donen, her husband-to-be. Society turned tighter spirals when Lauren Bacall joined the group: she had just, briefly, been engaged to Frank Sinatra, who had had a recent affair with Adele. Neither work nor analysis stopped for gaiety. There were many lively dinners. But one guest saw something less than fun. There was an evening at a Zurich restaurant when Jennifer sent the car away. This entailed so steep a walk up the hill to the Dolder Grand that David was rapidly out of breath. Jennifer then proposed a shortcut over rough ground, and David was defeated. Someone took him back down the hill to get a cab. The onlooker felt Jennifer hated David and that she was unpredictable in her reaction to things.

By early December, Anhalt had finished a draft of *Mary Magdalene*. He gave it to David, and shortly thereafter the two men sat down to discuss it:

"What did *you* think?" asked David.

Anhalt sighed: "I think it's anti-Semitic."

David agreed. "I don't know if I want to make a picture like that. We should ask some Jews."

"They're in Israel," suggested Anhalt.

D.O.S. considered this and allowed that, since he had never been to Israel, would it be possible to get an official invitation from Prime Minister David Ben-Gurion?

Anhalt had connections. He got on the phone, and in due course a telegram arrived. David, Jennifer, Anhalt, and his wife flew to Tel Aviv December 11. The plane hit turbulence on the way. Jennifer took refuge in the bathroom. David ordered champagne and was horrified when it was served in common water glasses.

Arrangements had been made for producer and writer to pitch their Magdalene story to a special panel that included the Israeli ambassador to the United Nations, Moshe Dayan, and some Biblical scholars. The meeting was at the King David Hotel on a Saturday. Because of that, the hotel bar was closed.

"I can't get through this without a drink," said David, when he appreciated the extent of the Sabbath.

So the convened dignitaries sought a special dispensation whereby David could be supplied with martinis.

The meeting began, and David proposed that, in fairness, the writer,

Mr. Anhalt, should tell the story. The scholars approved of this respect for authorship. Anhalt began to speak, and David took a drink and lit a cigarette. But after thirty seconds, he broke in: "Excuse me, Eddie, I think you should add. . . ."

He was off. Anhalt waited to resume. David spoke. Anhalt sat down. For two hours, David acted out the entire script, chain-smoking and calling for fresh martinis. "He was brilliant," said Anhalt, elated to hear his story told so well. David ended on his knees before the panel, eyes wide, arms outstretched, like Jolson with his mother.

"Tell me," he cried. "Is *that* anti-Semitic?"

The scholars looked at the diplomats.

"Yes," they said, "it is."

Exhausted, dismayed, the group from Hollywood went back to the airport, their car being stopped for fear of terrorists after the 1956 combat.

"What are we going to do with the script?" Anhalt wondered.

David looked out at the unhelpful desert. "Sell it to the Italians," he replied.

When they got back to Zurich, on the eighteenth, they found there was a problem over Christmas at the Dolder Grand. David's entourage took up a floor and a half, but the bill was not paid. There were people clamoring for holiday bookings, so the Selznicks changed hotels and countries. They had their Christmas in Kitzbühel, where David was telling people how the Jews were the only people left on earth who lived like Christians.

2 · 1959

CHRISTMAS and the New Year were passed at Kitzbühel—David, Jennifer, and Mary Jennifer, with nurse, maid, and secretaries, and Jeffrey showed up, too. He had said he would bring Ileana Bulova, until David poured cold water on that idea. Madame Bulova was talking of marrying Jeffrey, which wasn't exactly what the young Selznick envisaged. So he terminated the relationship, went to Kitzbühel for the holiday, and paired off with one of the secretaries, Lyndal Birch. Something else occurred at Kitzbühel that alarmed Jennifer. David worked too hard and had a collapse. Whether the stress was psychological or physical is not clear; it may even have been his first heart warning.

Jennifer was to go back to Zurich, to resume residence at the Dolder Grand. The couple were closer again now, but Jennifer was asking for more rest and treatment before the turmoil of work resumed. David flew to New York with Mary Jennifer, and they moved into the St. Regis Hotel for a couple of weeks.

He used the time in New York to scout extra prospects for Jennifer. One evening was spent with the Strasberg family—Lee, Paula, and their daughter, Susan, who had made a start on a film career. David had advised her on how to proceed, and Lee Strasberg wanted to work with Jennifer, on the stage or in a TV play. He would give her private teaching in his apartment, something hitherto reserved for Marilyn Monroe. As David delighted in writing Jennifer, Strasberg "said that he was absolutely convinced that you were one of the outstanding acting talents of our time and that your potential in the theatre was completely unlimited." (Later in life, Lee Strasberg admitted having had a crush on Jennifer—"except I don't think she crushed back.")

From those talks came the idea of Jennifer doing Cocteau's *The Human Voice* on TV, live or filmed, with Lee as her director. This was a short, one-person play about a woman on the phone to a lover. He sent her the play and she told him "Barkiss is willin'" so long as it would not conflict with her "real love," *Tender is the Night*. In New York, David had been to see Christopher Plummer in the play *J.B.* and was persuaded again that he was "the best young actor in the American theatre" and better for Dick Diver than anyone else, including Fox's favorite, William Holden. (In February, Holden would stay at the Dolder Grand for a few days, and Jennifer tried to promote the Fitzgerald picture to him.)

Jennifer was lonely in Zurich. There were things of David's in the hotel still—his Benzedrine and his hard candies—"all calculated to break my heart a little every time they turn up and everywhere, everywhere phantoms of Mary J. until I think I must just sit down and cry." In response, David tried to reassure her: "our separation can be ended overnight whenever either of us feel that its purpose either no longer warrants our being apart, or would not be damaged by my coming over—and/or MJS coming over, or that you have found whatever answers you seek."

On January 24, David and Mary Jennifer flew back to Los Angeles. He turned then to the new life Arnold Grant might have in store for him, and he joined with Ivan Moffat in finalizing the script for *Tender is the Night*, which had to be delivered to Fox by the end of March. Moffat had wanted a bold, linear approach, telling the story chronologically, but stylizing it so that the film seemed like a single, deteriorating party stretching over the years. That scheme was too much for David, who preferred a narrative faithful to Fitzgerald's flashback structure—even if that had never quite convinced the novelist.

Tender is the Night was one card in the hand Grant was hoping to sort for David. By the end of February, Grant proposed that David throw in his lot, single-mindedly, with either N.T.A. or Twentieth Century-Fox. Either entity could buy up the remaining TV rights that David held and act as a production home for him. But at Fox, production meant films, while N.T.A. was better suited to some kind of television work.

David was the more unable to make up his mind about partners when they were talking sums of money he needed so badly. On March 2, in one letter to Grant, he could say of Unger and Landau at N.T.A. that they were "men of astuteness and initiative" even if not "nature's noblemen" and then, two pages later, "as I think about my conversation with these men, and about this proposal, my stomach turns."

If he went to N.T.A., it would be to produce not just dramas like *The Human Voice*, sponsored programs with corporations underwriting the shows and N.T.A. syndicating them, but a "Selznick Magazine," a forum for news and nonfiction material. What deterred David about this was its modesty of scale. He was a snob still with TV, even if some of his ideas for it were original and creative. Moreover, if he did TV, why not for NBC or CBS? Therein lay another maze. David found it hard to deal with Bill Paley because of their friendship—Paley may have used this uneasiness to ward off proposals. But if he talked to NBC executives (who knew of his ties to Paley), *they* thought they were being used as a negotiating lever in an eventual deal with CBS.

At Twentieth Century-Fox, Spyros Skouras professed himself eager to do *Tender is the Night*, and ready to talk about *Mary Magdalene*. But Fox was also the outfit with which David was falling into increasing acrimony over *A Farewell to Arms*. Somehow, he could persuade himself that the "Chinese bookkeeping" on one film would be reformed with another. Skouras was the kind of person David "knew," a Greek immigrant, sixty-six in 1959, someone who had worked his way up through the business. Yet just as David condemned men *not* raised in the business, so he could be horribly patronizing about the vulgarity of a Skouras.

There were other considerations for David. He always had Jennifer to protect and promote—and Warner Brothers had proposed a long-term contract for her. Then there were his remaining plans for *Gone With the Wind*. Ever since 1952 and his rather shaky deal with Stephens Mitchell, David had been paying $15,000 a year to protect his putative right to produce the novel on TV or radio. He had been waiting, he told himself, until the money for TV got big enough and until 1964, the year in which, he claimed, MGM's rights on *his* film would lapse. Much of this was dreaming, untested at law. But David's life was preoccupied with the recovery of *Gone With the Wind* or its fresh exploitation in another medium. So, simultaneously, he was considering a TV serialization of the novel *and* a stage musical to be called *Scarlett O'Hara.*

The musical was the wildest dream. But a musical required movie rights to be appealing, and there Metro stood in the way. It claimed that David's was the only legitimate film from the novel—and would be until 1964. In the meantime, David talked to composers—Richard Rodgers, Leroy Anderson, and Stephen Sondheim—and mulled over what he was going to do.

Grant was beginning to be depressed by the range of possibilities. David concluded his March 2 letter to Grant in a delirium of doubt:

> Maybe, with your superior objectivity about myself, you can shoot all sorts of holes in both the reasoning and the program. . . .
>
> P.S. I am aware of a seeming contradiction between my instincts of fear concerning the NTA association and my suggestions of a limited association with them. I hope it is clear that I am thinking that there may be the difference, and the protection, in the very limitation of the NTA suggestions. I feel that if we could hem them in as to what I would do for them, and have very strict legal limitations on the use of my name, maybe my fears would have no proper foundation. For this reason alone, apart from its trading advantage, I think we should continue with the NTA negotiations. . . .
>
> I am also aware that between what Skouras says and what he does there is often a big spread. I should hate to give up what may be our

Arnold Grant, 1951, with his wife and Sarah Churchill

only avenue, NTA, only to find that Skouras again hides behind his hatchet men! Then it would come down to whether we could make a deal with NTA that would overcome my fears. Or perhaps do you think these fears have no proper grounding anyway?

For the moment, Grant may have vowed to try harder. Yet the evidence was in of David's capacity for forestalling action with alternatives. Two weeks before, he had read in the papers that the government was putting Ellis Island up for sale. He was in raptures, and he nudged Grant hard: "I wonder if we should not look into this. Twenty-seven acres in New York Harbor stirs the imagination; and I cannot for the life of me understand why there is not gigantic excitement."

On March 6, David's mother died. Florence Selznick was eighty-three, and her illness had been prolonged. For years, Flossie had been around, on the edge of David's parties. By the late fifties, she still looked like someone from 1930: she wore suits of wool or silk crepe, with pearls and a hat. She would take root in a chair and play a little cards with anyone prepared to talk to her. If people asked how she was, she would answer in a singsong way, "Oh, I don't know. One day is like the next. If David's here, I'm happy." Yet Danny thought his father felt embarrassed by Flossie and guilty about her—"guilt that she would milk for all it was worth."

Flossie spoke to Jennifer when she arrived and when she left. Otherwise, as Danny observed, Flossie had a baleful glance, the hint of disapproval, that was enough to make Jennifer rush back to her room to change her clothes. Beauma was an old lady, stately, severe, settled, and just growing older. "June, July, August, the summer's gone," she'd say every year.

Berman Swarttz went to visit her near the end, recalling how she always said she would be ready to go when the time came. "Don't believe it," she said now. "You always want another hour." There was for David not the grief or loss he had felt at the deaths of Myron or his father. He was not his mother's favorite, and that was something a tolerant kid had to bear with. He was struck that his old friend Merian Cooper's mother died on the same day. He wrote to Coop to say, "It is very strange to be 'little boy lost' at my age."

Jennifer responded generously from Zurich. Flossie had never been kind to Jennifer, but her daughter-in-law could fit that old lady into her half-mystical, half-Jungian view of existence. If only David had felt the force of such reassurance: "Mother Selznick really was symbolic of the 'Earth Mother,'" said Jennifer, "... because she *had* to survive and *did*, many tragedies in her life. As she said, the 'Lord' or 'God' or whoever, whatever, created us knows when it is time to go back into oblivion, or as Jung says into the 'collective unconscious' that we may in giving up our life fortify all life."

Jennifer returned to America at the end of March, a little earlier than she had planned. The Dolder Grand stay had been expensive: the hotel concierge had simply forwarded the bills to Earl Beaman, and Jennifer kept a $500-a-week allowance in hand. She asked Beaman not to tell David, in case he wanted to borrow the funds.

The death of David's mother had some financial consequences. For as long as she lived, Flossie received 40 percent of Myron's trust income. That was not just her main support; it helped pay for Howard in Asheville. But at her death, the 40 percent reverted to Joan Grill. In her lifetime, foreseeing the problem, Flossie had set up a trust for Howard. There was an insurance policy on her life, in David's benefit, but he added that to the trust fund. Now he saw that if Howard were to live a long time, the trust might run out. There was also no provision for unusual medical attention. Joan Grill had been her grandmother's darling, but Joan's family contacts were now made through lawyers. She would not help with Howard, nor did she attend the funeral.

In May, there was more work with Ivan Moffat on the *Tender* screenplay. May Romm wrote several pages of notes based on the novel. At the same time, she and David's lawyer, Barry Brannen, were asked to replace Jeffrey and Dan O'Shea as trustees for the Howard Selznick fund.

The wrestling with Fox continued. Skouras claimed he liked the *Tender* script, but there were murmurs over budgeting ceilings on so gloomy a story and uncertainty as to whether William Holden could be obtained. In the hiatus, Fox had not actually paid David for delivery of the script. The Spyros Skouras he believed he liked and understood now proved the Skouras he mistrusted. "Bon voyage and kindest regards," said Skouras on June 23, aware that David would shortly be off to Europe, and actually more focused on Grant's efforts to get Fox to repay David's overage participation on *A Farewell to Arms*. That sum had rankled David: he was still derelict in paying the last part of Charles Vidor's salary. Bill Paley had argued with Skouras about it on David's behalf, and Skouras had told him not to worry: David would not go out of pocket on the picture.

David, Jennifer, Mary Jennifer, and Shirley Harden flew to Paris on June 24. Four days later they were in Biarritz. Early in July, the family went to Lourdes, so Jennifer could see the real site of Bernadette's life. They were rewarded. It was not quite a miracle, but on July 10 Arnold Grant was able to send a copy of the agreement whereby Fox would pay David $850,000 for complete ownership of *A Farewell to Arms*. For Grant, this seemed like a small step, yet it would be his greatest achievement for David. At the same time, he concluded what seemed a lesser deal, selling off some Selznick pictures for British television. The money was not much, but the consequences would be serious.

That July 10 David and Jennifer were in Pamplona for the running of the bulls. Whom should they run into but the "author" of Pamplona, Ernest Hemingway, with Slim Hayward. Hemingway had hated the Selznick *Farewell to Arms*, and when he saw the producer and the actress he lost his temper. "I'm going to kill him," he shouted. "Son of a bitch! He ruined my book!" Slim did all she could to calm him down. Then she defied his orders and went over to talk to the Selznicks. For their part, they tried to look sheepish under the collective weight of author's scorn and $850,000 more for the "piece of crap." Producers cannot win—or so they tell themselves.

Fathers are very like producers, especially if the children have become young adults. David was feeling better about Jeff. The indefatigable Arnold Grant had introduced the son to the banking house of S. G. Warburg. In turn, Warburg had been sufficiently impressed to offer him an opening: it was a new world, and David was never unhappy having contacts of his own in superior financial networks.

Danny was now more worrisome. At Brandeis, his "lassitude" seemed to be increasing, and his studies suffered as he directed plays. David felt bound to warn Irene: "am afraid he will increasingly slip into lack of self-discipline and will develop habit of taking on additional things in order to avoid fulfilling commitments that he finds undesirable. He is one of most wonderful human beings alive, but in my opinion we should discourage him from wallowing in fog."

There was another vexation, for David had just been presented with the bill for Danny's psychiatrist—at $2,415 the fog was not cheap.

By July 21, the Selznicks were in London. The next day they were received by the American ambassador to London, Jock Whitney. David and Jock had not seen each other for several years, but there was an intermittent correspondence and a lasting affection. A year before, David had written to Jock as an amateur politician: he said he had talked to John F. Kennedy, who had told him he would not accept the vice-presidential nomination in 1960, "and I personally don't believe that he can get the top spot."

As Arnold Grant struggled to make sense of an arrangement at Fox, so David was ready to jump sideways. In the spring and summer of 1959, another enticing alignment appeared out of the smoke: Jerry Wald, an independent producer at Fox, whose contract there was running out, sought to involve David in a deal to be funded by Lou Chesler, Tex McCrary, and a Texas oilman, Frank B. Waters. There are many fat files on what was

known as the Chesler group, and David could work himself into a passion
of speculation about what it offered—or about the ways in which its offer
could be used in bargaining with other forces. Here is David, reporting to
Grant, on May 22, 1959:

> Thirdly, and most importantly, I asked Chesler, as a financier, how he
> could visualize any possibility of my making enough out of this
> enterprise to offset or equal, much less surpass, what I could make out
> of a single film. I pointed out to Chesler that the work involved on
> my part would be infinitely greater. Chesler immediately replied that,
> quite frankly, he thought it impossible for me to make enough out of
> this enterprise to equal what I could make elsewhere, or perhaps
> through a single film. He said that the only reason he thought this
> would be preferable was that he could not conceive of any tax setup
> that I could have that would made [*sic*] it possible for me to keep
> important money made out of a single enterprise. I readily convinced
> him, with an extremely brief and superficial notion of our operations,
> that such income could flow into my company, which we would keep
> alive, and thus build up an equity in it that could eventually be hugely
> profitable to me, in terms of the sale of my stock, or in terms of a
> merger or in terms of liquidation. (I did not mention at all our loss
> carry-back, and I do not think we should do so since we contemplate
> handling this out of the sale of the assets and out of other income; and
> I think psychologically it would be too difficult to explain to him why
> we have a loss record.)

The year slipped away. In the fall, it seemed possible that everything could be rewritten with "Columbia" instead of "Fox." David did not
let this wondering detract from the great idea of what *Tender is the Night*
should be. With Fox questioning its cost, David planned *more* showmanship,
not less. As well as Jennifer, he wanted Kirk Douglas, Lee Remick, Louis
Jourdan, Margaret Sullavan, and Joseph Cotten. To sustain this cast, it
needed grander scale. "I have a lot of ideas as to how to make it a more
definitive portrait of the period—including, for instance, the gay and glamorous trans-Atlantic shipboard life of the times, with the masked ball that
was characteristic of those crossings; the polo games in which the rich
indulged; the Folies Bergere of the time—on which we can go as far as our
courage permits; etc. Those will increase the costs, but not by all that
much."

By the end of the year, David had a director in mind—John Frankenheimer, one of the new generation, trained in TV. Frankenheimer was
twenty-nine, and he had directed one film, *The Young Stranger*. He shared
David's latest idea, that Montgomery Clift was an ideal Dick Diver. The

script had been with Fox nine months, yet nothing had advanced. Another man might have concluded Fox was not overly excited. But David supposed the failings of the studio were part of a greater malaise that left the whole ramshackle enterprise ready for . . . new management? In all the deals and delays, David nursed some secret wish to be put in charge of one of those studios. He was cautious with the wish, for he knew it was not exactly the proper ambition for an honest independent.

But on December 5, 1959, trying to rally Arnold Grant for another year, David did let it slip:

> I'm now absolutely determined that we are not going to get caught with this lousy alternative deal, that we are going to delivery [*sic*] Clift, and that we are going to get the picture made under the original deal. I am even more determined to load it with such showmanship that the people at 20th will get another lesson in what makes good and big pictures. I know I have imposed upon your patience greatly, but just stick with me on this, Arnold, and we'll show the picture business within the next year or so a new enterprise that is attuned to the time, and within a few years, we will be taking over 20th Century! That is, if we want to.

For moments, at least, David could believe he was still a kingmaker. That same December, he had another boost. Irene came to him for advice. She believed that Warners was underreporting income from the movie of *A Streetcar Named Desire*. She had had an audit, but could hardly understand it—in her knowledge, no one had had more experience of such reports than David. Would he take "five or ten minutes with it"?

David sighed. "I have pushed everything aside," he claimed, "because actually there is not much of value that would not take many days!" So he employed his Christmas break, in New York, on an eight-page analysis of the theory of audits and of Irene's in particular. He managed to be gloomy about the way the business cheated, yet optimistic about the fruits to be won still. But he had one fear:

> I do hope you will not get me involved in those discussions. I have dealings with Warners right now that could be seriously prejudiced. If Jess Morgan, or the auditor, or Tennessee Williams, or MCA on behalf of Tennessee Williams, or anybody else told Warners that these questions originated with me, it would reinforce them in their conviction that they do not like to deal with me because of my "concern with the small type," and I could lose a hundred times as much as is involved in this.

3 · 1 9 6 0

THE ''LITTLE BOY'' in David was not quite lost, even if at fifty-seven he had reproached Danny for not sending him condolences when Flossie died. He had a girl child to play with, who was five in August 1959. This was belated bounty for a man addicted to play: pretending, charades and board games, roulette or story conferences. As Louis Jourdan saw it:

> He was a child, in Nietzsche's sense—that a man's maturity consists of finding again the seriousness that one had as a child. He was always at play, whatever game it was *or* discussing a script with a man that he had to convince.

In September, David held Mary Jennifer's hand and took her to her first day of school at El Rodeo—Jennifer was in New York. But then, after a week of school, David lifted her out and flew with her to New York. School filled empty days only. Mary Jennifer was his creation, in a way that had proved overpowering for full-grown actresses. She was his all the time, not just in the screen's rapture. Mary Jennifer had brown hair, her father's eyes, and her mother's cheeks, and she was spoiled.

What does it mean to say a child is "spoiled"? The word sounds less drastic than "ruined" or "destroyed"; when we hear a child is "spoiled" we often smile, imagining foolish parents and immature vanity in the indulged child. Do spoiled children recover? Surely we could meet a young person and hear him say, "I was terribly spoiled as a kid," so that we believe he is over it now and wiser because of it. But doesn't "spoiling" sound like a clue? Henry James sometimes speaks of his children being "spoiled," and some moral damage is implied, for which there is no treatment.

Do spoiled children grow up to be the parents of spoiled children? Or does indulgence make a mirror for itself so that children learn self-regard? Do we really mean intolerable selfishness when we say "spoiled"? And if David was intolerably selfish, then what was the nature of his charm?—so many people treasured the charm. Was it a desire to entertain, meant to divert others from the spoilage? Or was the show designed to distract David himself?

On January 1, Margaret Sullavan died, another parent in the business; she probably killed herself in a hotel room, locked from the inside. She was trying out in a play, *Sweet Love Remember'd*, and it was going badly. She was forty-eight.

The actress had been a part of David's circle of friends. Her marriage to Leland Hayward had produced three children, Brooke, William, and Bridget. When that marriage ended, Hayward had married Slim Hawks, the ex-wife of Howard Hawks who had been married to Norma Shearer's sister, Athole, who ended in an asylum. But by the time of Margaret Sullavan's death, the Leland-Slim marriage was ending; Hayward was in love again, with Pamela Churchill.

There was a funeral for Margaret Sullavan on January 4, and David and Jennifer were among those who went to Greenwich, Connecticut, for it. Then, in October 1960, one of the Hayward children, Bridget, killed herself. Those two funerals in a year had been too much for Brooke Hayward: "The only funeral I'd relented about going to after that was David O. Selznick's, because he was almost like my own father." On that evening, when she heard about her mother's death, she was about to go onstage, off-Broadway, in her first play. Even after she heard the news, she made ready to act. But her father intervened. When he ordered the theater closed for that night she felt more anger than relief. The show must go on? Especially when life falters?

Mary Jennifer Selznick surely eased her father's last years and moderated the disappointment her parents felt professionally and personally. She knew little other life than extravagance and show, and she joined in with a will. She adored her father—for he was ready to concentrate on the rescue she offered him. So she was indulged, and she unwittingly allowed him to go on being spoiled. David would not subscribe to reality so long as there was any audience in his life. And in that last decade, Mary Jennifer commanded his performance.

David with Mary Jennifer

They had their own line in private theatricals. One day, when Anita Colby was staying with the Selznicks at Tower Grove, she and Jennifer returned from shopping to find David and Mary Jennifer in the middle of a story. Mary Jennifer was wearing a tutu and a tiara, while David was in white tie and tails and bare feet. Jennifer asked why he was dressed like that, and Mary Jennifer said they were in Rome on their way to a ball.

Not everyone who witnessed such incidents felt as enchanted as Colby. Nancy Stern once arranged for the actress and teacher Uta Hagen to work with Jennifer on some scenes. When Ms. Hagen returned, she told Nancy, "That child doesn't have a chance." Mary Jennifer had wandered in eating a piece of bacon, and in a childish way she had got grease in her hair. Jennifer had overreacted and insisted that the child have her hair completely washed, straightaway. Jennifer herself was notorious for her prolonged occupation of the bathroom.

Some friends felt Jennifer was the parent trying to discipline their daughter. She saw the spoiling and sometimes made comparisons with the way her father had spoiled her. But there was a rivalry between mother and daughter. Leonora and Arthur Hornblow called on the Selznicks for cocktails at the Waldorf. Mary Jennifer was nowhere to be seen, but David said she was going to serve the drinks. She was six—this was 1960. David opened the door and said, "Here's my darling!"

"Jennifer turned ashen," said Mrs. Hornblow. "Because Mary Jennifer was in the doorway in a trashy dressing gown, pink with ostrich feathers."

"It's awful, it's vulgar," said Jennifer.

"She *wanted* it," David explained.

Jennifer told her daughter to take the clothes off. And Mary Jennifer said, "I won't. It's beautiful, and Daddy gave it to me."

"He was like a grandfather with her," said Quique Jourdan. "He just couldn't refuse anything to her."

On another occasion, Anita Colby was present when Mary Jennifer had gone shopping with the nanny for Valentine cards. When she returned, David and Jennifer were with Colby on facing couches. The nanny retired. Mary Jennifer watched her go and then said, "She wouldn't let me get the card that I wanted for my husband. I told her I've got to have it for my husband, and she said I couldn't do that because you're my father."

Colby saw David "grinning all over the place, happy as a clam."

Danny formed a close relationship with Mary Jennifer, yet he was in awe of the little girl's control of their father. Mary Jennifer browbeat David into spending less time at the studio and making an office out of the garden house built for Bobby and Michael. Then, when she wanted her lunch, she would visit him there and say, "You have to stop dictating now, Daddy."

> He could not say no to her [said Danny]. She was enchanting and outrageous. My father turned into a marionette. . . . Jennifer could be calculating, but you always felt the wheels turning. Mary Jennifer never calculated anything. She just did it spontaneously and with a guilelessness and charm that I'm sure Jennifer not only resented, she envied. Jennifer would watch and she'd say, "David, I can't get you to do that." And he loved it! Like a child with parents competing to make a fuss of you.

Jennifer would play with her daughter. They were girls together crawling in and out of a big playhouse. But Jennifer could not quite place herself with the child compared with the adoration that existed between father and daughter. "Your father got Irene to be bad cop," she told Danny. "And I don't know how to be bad cop. I want to be good cop some of the time. It's not fair."

David's only disciplining of Mary Jennifer was teaching her how to argue, politely. Danny saw this as the start of negotiation. Mary Jennifer learned to ask for things in a very studied way—"May I impose on you, Daddy. . . ." It was a kind of theater, and David loved her precociousness. Bedtime got stretched out by elaborate debates over which book should be read.

Spoiling one day did not exclude neglect on the next. Robert Walker, Jr.'s wife, Ellie, noted that Mary Jennifer spent a lot of time alone in her room, monitored by remote cameras. Another visitor recalled that Jennifer's insecurity went so far "she wouldn't let Mary Jennifer near her until she'd had her hair and makeup done."

Such stories are far from sinister—but they were recalled years later when there was tragic reason to weigh the effect on Mary Jennifer. At the time, most people who knew David rejoiced in his happiness, the more so if they knew how badly his business was going. David was always very good at finding the silver lining. He had a child to play with, an imagination to encourage, a fellow dreamer. He was so happy, he wanted the other pride of his life to *see* the happiness. In August, he wrote to Danny:

> Mary Jennifer raced in madly the other day, screaming that her brother Danny's birthday gift had arrived. She pulled up short, proudly and gratefully holding up one shoe in each hand, proclaiming their beauty. You chose well and wisely and she could not have been more pleased. As she received two new "evening dresses" for our nightly balls, the enchanting slippers were particularly appropriate.

Gifts were not just David's way of showing love—and loving show; they were civilization for him. They verified emotional wealth in a world where all might be rich. He loved Danny the more for having inherited his grace and style at giving. Jeffrey suffered in comparison. Earlier that year, on David's fifty-eighth birthday, he had received from Jeffrey "some magnetic playing cards, sans wrapping, sans card." There had been no call from Jeff, either. "It saddens me," David told Irene, "but I feel it best that a contact with me be at his own time and choosing."

There were other gifts David gave Danny, chiefly lavish emotional support of the kind Jeffrey always felt lacking. It was David's guess by 1960 that Danny was headed for the theater. Yet in the father's boasting was there not also a pressure for success so intense it was vicarious, another of David's dreams?

> I think you are brilliantly gifted for it; I think you have the personality for it; I think you have had, by osmosis and by association and by training during your adolescence and since, an experience in it that already has been equalled by very few young men of your age. I think you have taste and discretion. I think you handle people extremely well; I think, in short, that you have all the qualifications to become a really important figure in the theatre. . . .

Danny had only to indicate a modest inclination or talent and a long carpet of career and importance rolled out in David's mind. That was spoiling, too, in a way: real creativity should be left alone, even by a parent burstingly proud of it. David could already see evidence of a lack of stamina or drive in Danny, and he did not realize how he might have affected it. For although Danny was in some ways David's surrogate, David did not digest the nature of the transference. Danny had directed a summer stock production of *Pygmalion* and fallen in love with lead actress Brita Brown. David now sounded oddly objective and wise:

> You have learned, through this experience, that because a young lady appeals to you personally, and/or because she talks a good show, does not necessarily mean that she is Duse. This was a good lesson to be learned, because it might have happened much later in your career, possibly on Broadway, with a far more damaging result. And on the other side, you must realize that it was probably awfully difficult for her, too. . . . It is always awfully hard—a mixture of personal relationships with business relationships or career relationships, but more especially in the theatrical professions.

This was made apparent in the course of 1960, as David endeavored to push ahead with *Tender is the Night* while pursuing every other possibility.

The Chesler talks continued: on February 12, David waited all day while Lou Chesler underwent dental work. They didn't sit down to dinner at "21" until midnight, and then Chesler had friends and relatives with him. Swallowing with a numb mouth, Chesler sketched futures in the Grand Bahamas. David came back agog and ablaze, telling Arnold Grant about "the opportunity of a lifetime in what, according to his computations, will be a billion dollar— literally that: 'billion dollar'—enterprise, within a matter of years."

In the same month, David auditioned Stephen Sondheim for the musical version of *Gone With the Wind* and had renewed meetings with the Duke of Windsor. "We know that the Windsors need money," David told Grant, "and I believe we could make alternate deals with them for either the picture rights, or for the TV rights." There was some misunderstanding over whether such a project would be based on the Duke's memoirs or the Duchess's; that aside, the Duchess was still taken with the idea of being played by Jennifer, while the Duke wanted Rex Harrison for himself. Then Walter Wanger had suggested that Jennifer play Justine in the Lawrence Durrell novels set in Alexandria.

By March, Jennifer had returned to Zurich. On March 11, David went into the hospital for a minor operation; he was there only two hours. He dined with Irene a couple of times, and he became increasingly agitated over *Tender is the Night*.

William Holden could not be obtained to play Dick Diver. That made Fox more fearful about a budget of $2.5 million. As David saw it, Skouras at Fox wanted the picture, while production head Buddy Adler was against it. Fox was setting the budget no higher than $1.5 million; David claimed that was impossible. But Fox was not carried away with the idea of Jennifer in the role, especially not if David was the producer. For his part, David was always using the picture in the cloud castle of alternative, large plans, with Windsors, musicals, and Grand Bahamas billions.

In March, Arnold Grant's patience broke. He had observed David very closely; he had moved from warmth and exhortation through tact and wonder to dismay. Now he wrote David a letter that is among the greatest the chronic memoist ever received. Grant understood David; he got him; he leveled him:

> In everything one undertakes, plans can be made for success or for failure. It is sheer waste of time to plan for the latter. The beauty of failure and death is that everything is done for you, tidied up, and you are soon forgotten. Either the receiver or the undertaker moves in promptly, the corpus, financial or human, is given the last rites, a few post mortems are held as to the reason for the end result and then people move on to constructive things. This is sad. Moral: stop

planning for failure. If the project in hand or any other project turns out badly, at the appropriate time it will be liquidated or buried, and whatever is realized will be realized. Preoccupation with potential failure and how to salvage remnants befogs all issues, creates an unsolved atmosphere, kills most deals before they can get started by planting in the mind of the buyer, or even the creators, a lack of confidence or hope. . . .

. . . your memos are just replete with sensitiveness, with distrust and with preoccupation of failure to the point of anticipation of failure. This in turn, without your realizing it, brings on fabulous suspicion and doubt of your new associate, which in turn leads you to all sorts of sensitivities and the ultimate "you know what you can do with your jack." These current memos bring into sharp focus constant undulations as regular as a cardiograph of a good heart; first, the hope for a deal; second, the meeting and anticipation; third, crisis of suspicion— shall we not make compromise after compromise in order to end suspicions; then a general meeting of the minds; immediately thereafter, aggressiveness, suspicions, doubt, despair, protection against failure; then a blown-up deal and, finally, efforts to revive the deal on the original basis, usually ending in another merry-go-round and another failure.

Larded in with this is a personal change in you from the exciting, confident creator into a very subjective negotiator, into a lawyer, tax accountant, statesman and one anticipating hope of a future merchandising or liquidating company. God, David, stay the exciting creator with belief and hope that you will create successfully.

David said he was embarrassed and impressed by what Grant was saying. But nothing changed. The vacillator could not settle. Later in March, Fox gave up on *Tender is the Night,* and the property reverted to David. For a moment he was full of prospects, of doing it with Billy Wilder at Columbia or through Hal Wallis or Sol Siegel. He tried to get George Cukor again to direct it, and through Cukor he went after Glenn Ford for the role of Diver. But Ford couldn't understand the end of the script, and Cukor couldn't explain it. Cukor declined, and David lamented that his old friend was ready to do "junk" when "a masterpiece like Fitzgerald's . . . is available to you." David flew from one coast to another eleven times that year in search of a deal.

Buddy Adler died. The contract with Fox was reactivated. At one time, David had John Frankenheimer lined up to direct and Christopher Plummer to play Diver. But Fox was not impressed. Many other actors were considered—Peter Finch, Dirk Bogarde, Paul Newman (six years younger than Jennifer). The arguments went on over terms: David's money and role and budget. Fox was also talking to Elizabeth Taylor about the part of Nicole. As he considered actresses for Rosemary, David found one at least—Jane Fonda—who might have made a fine Nicole.

Jennifer's age was something Ivan Moffat had never mentioned. But with Elizabeth Taylor in the offing (with Richard Burton as Diver), he did say, "That wouldn't be so bad."

David didn't respond, so Moffat knocked again: "What would be so bad about that?"

Whereupon Selznick took a deep breath and explained his sticking point. "I've made *Gone With the Wind*—and so on. I've done what I'm going to do. My only reason for *Tender is the Night* is for Jennifer to be in it. I love her, and I don't know I've done all I could for her. It's Jennifer's film—that's why I'm making it."

Moffat then allowed that some people felt she was too old.

"How old is Nicole?" asked David.

"Eighteen to twenty-eight."

"She can play twenty-eight—it's a question of being an actress who can play a beautiful, neurotic woman. And Jennifer can do that."

There was no more talk.

It was never just *Tender*, though, and to all the other chances David added another: the movie of *My Fair Lady*, over which CBS and Bill Paley had a decisive voice. CBS owned 40 percent of the show, and thus the movie rights were in its control. David got William Wyler to say he was interested, and he tried to fix a meeting with Paley:

> We have the finances all lined up, and I am sure can make you an offer that not only compares favorably with what you can get elsewhere, but may quite possibly be even better ... and it seems to me that it is obvious that the makers of *Gone With the Wind*, and *Ben Hur*, respectively, are in a position to get not only the best picture but also the biggest gross possible out of the property.

It never came to a meeting: Paley could be as cool as he was generous. David admitted to Irene, "Things with me are very dreary on the professional and business fronts, but I expect that to change shortly. If not, I will apply for the role of Micawber in my old age."

They got worse. In making that sale of some films for television in Britain, David had provoked a boycott there. This justified Fox in saying *Tender is the Night* could not be made with David's name on it. He was dropped; he would be paid off. Fox reneged on the agreements with Frankenheimer and Plummer. Henry King would be the director. The studio brought in a new producer, Henry Weinstein, a novice, without prior movie experience, from New York television. No one could stop David talking to Weinstein or sending him memos. Weinstein did his best. He read every memo and answered most of them politely. David saw only ambition and treachery in Weinstein; he said he was a worm training to be a snake. Jason Robards would be the compromise Diver.

When Danny heard that, he burst out, "Dad, you can't let them do that."

"He's a wonderful actor," said David.

"But he has no romantic quality."

Then David sighed, and said, "Well, Dick Diver doesn't have to be that handsome."

There was something in the voice that made Danny shut up: resignation at powers too great for David, but something more—the insight, the experience that Divers sometimes were as homely as D.O.S.

In all of this loss and humiliation, David was helpless—but beyond restraint. In September, he had been determined to throw a big party for Leonard Bernstein (there *might* be a project in the offing); then he was horrified to find it had cost $2,553. David was seriously broke, and Fox was taking away rights and provisions for the film before it would give David his money. The Skouras he had once liked was now the worst of wretches. Bill Paley came forward, without prompting. On November 7, he sent David a check for $100,000 so that there need be no caving in to Fox. It was a loan, but without date. David thought it "all the more wonderful because it was voluntary." He fought back at the studio, and so it paid him. On November 25, David repaid Paley, with $105.56 interest. He told Bill, "Your warm and generous friendship did a great deal to make it possible for us to cling to our faith in human nature. . . ."

David did realize that the patient and industrious Arnold Grant had never billed him. He wrote to Grant, "Jennifer and I have been through such a horrendous time with those beasts at Twentieth that I think you should know that the only thing that kept us from despairing of the decency of the human race was the generous behavior of two people, Bill Paley and yourself. Also, I have a new objective in life which is to try to contribute to the rescue of this wonderful medium from the reptiles that are now wrapped around it."

But in 1961, Arnold Grant would go over from the column of stalwarts to join the reptiles.

4 · 1961

DURING 1960, David had felt tightness in the chest. In the fall, he consulted with Dr. Prinzmetal in Los Angeles about the use of nitroglycerine. Doctors disagreed as to whether or not he had a heart problem, but they all urged rest and care. Whenever Henry Weinstein went up to Tower Grove for discussions, he was amazed at David's energy. Weinstein liked to walk while he talked and thought, but David had the same habit. Once or twice they bumped into each other—discussing how Weinstein could deliver David's opinions to Henry King. They agreed to divide the room into two walking strips.

Weinstein saw a brilliant, impromptu thinker, wonderfully read, engaging, and entertaining—an "authentic genius." But he could never reconcile David's openness in person, his readiness to exchange ideas without fear of lost advantage, with the paranoid tone of the memos. David may never have trusted Weinstein: he felt the young man was part of his betrayal by Fox. Sometimes now he conceded that Jennifer was too old for Nicole, but insisted the film *had* to be done. Here was a labor of old love and the pressing need for $350,000 from Fox for the project. As Weinstein saw it:

> I would talk to him about the script. He would agree, and then the next day he would change his mind . . . brilliantly informed, very, very aware of everything, but he had lost that central drive. . . . He was thrashing about, trying to hold on to something in himself. . . . I got the sense that David had invented himself and was unhappy with the invention. That he determined to make this highly cultured man and in so doing went so far from his own roots, whatever they were, that he found himself isolated.

There were other projects in the air during their walks, notably the Scarlett O'Hara musical. But Weinstein thought the schemes to play it in two theaters simultaneously and to have it done on closed circuit television were fanciful. The project he liked most was John Hersey's *The Wall*, about the Holocaust. Weinstein believed this meant something important to David. Maybe the bizarre trip to Israel had started new thoughts.

For years, David had distanced himself from Jewish causes or alignments. It was the one topic over which he and Ben Hecht ever clashed and the one situation in which Hecht abandoned his cynicism. In the early 1940s, when Hecht had been working to help set up a state of Israel in Palestine, David had been very wary. "I am an American first, a Jew secondarily," he declared. "As an American, I have the right to interfere or to protest only in American affairs. The fact that my antecedents were of the Jewish race is purely incidental as far as I am concerned."

Hecht had retaliated with a famous ruse. He asked three people the question: "Would you call David O. Selznick an American or a Jew?" Leland Hayward, Nunnally Johnson, and magazine editor Martin Quigley all answered, "Jew." But that does not mean David was ever persuaded—or secure. The tumult of his indecisiveness has no one explanation. But among the contenders is the awkwardness he felt, or the lack of enthusiasm, in playing the one role that many friends felt was obvious.

On February 1, 1961, David flew to Mexico City. From there he went to Cuernavaca, where Jennifer joined him on February 11. They stayed at the home of Merle Oberon and Bruno Pagliai, and David fired off a wire to Sam Goldwyn wondering if he could do a remake of Stella Dallas, with Jennifer as the mother. There was no end of new ideas, and no undue dismay when Goldwyn said it was impossible. On the thirteenth, they moved to Acapulco, at the Las Brisas Hotel, and four days later Jennifer flew to Dallas to see her parents. With Shirley Harden, David went back to Mexico City on the twenty-second, and there he had what was unquestionably a heart attack. He nearly fainted from the pain in his chest. A local doctor told him to get to a lower altitude. On the twenty-fifth, they flew back to Los Angeles.

He did not tell Jennifer or really alter the hectic and frustrating life he was leading. Did he know there was no other life he could be comfortable with? Was he prepared to accept the gamble of living dangerously? Did he still kid himself that he was not seriously ill?

Rather than rest at home, he next undertook an emotionally upsetting journey. But to have backed out might have been a signal of failing vitality. On March 8, he went to Atlanta for a gala showing of Gone With the Wind to mark the centenary of the Civil War. David had said at first he did not want to go: he felt the classic movie was an epitaph waiting for him. But he could no more stay away than he could stop fussing over the income Joan Grill was getting from the picture.

Danny accompanied his father, very excited and convinced that David was having a good time. There were balls and parties as well as the screening of Metro's latest reissue. But the survivors were already reduced in number. Gable had died on November 16, 1960, from a heart attack suffered one day after he finished work on The Misfits. Vivien Leigh and Olivia de Havilland went to Atlanta, and it was evident that Melanie had aged more gently than Scarlett.

David signed autographs, a cigarette in one hand and a pen in the other. Danny sat on one side of Vivien as the film began on March 10, with David on the other. The first time Gable appeared, Vivien cried out, "Oh Clark! He was so young, I can't believe he's gone." David sneaked out to the lobby several times to smoke a cigarette, but he was back in his seat for the final curtain.

"Oh David," said Vivien. "It's still so wonderful."

"So are you," he told her, with the fullest smile Danny had ever seen on his father's face. He went onstage, and in the great applause he seemed to stand more erect. Strangers were thanking him for his most natural talent—that of delivering extraordinary gifts.

Afterward, he and Danny drove to Savannah and Sea Island and flew to Nassau for a few days. He went back to New York, where Jennifer met him. But he saw Irene, too, on that visit, and had her select a piece of jewelry he could give her. There were other things to talk about. He admitted to fears about leaving too little to support Mary Jennifer. Irene suggested that Jeffrey and Danny hardly needed inheritance: they had trust funds from both Mayer grandparents, as well as the money their parents had given them. They would be Irene's heirs one day. So everything could go to Jennifer and Mary Jennifer. David had another concern—but there was hope in it, too: if Jennifer died, would Irene bring the child up? "He went on to explain," said Irene, "that if I agreed, all he then had to do was sell the idea to Jennifer. He considered this a perfectly reasonable approach."

There was a madness in David that would not have heard the edge in Irene's irony. Mary Jennifer was a gift he longed to present. He often took Mary Jennifer to see Irene and hardly noticed how the two were a little afraid of each other.

David never told Mary Jennifer he was ill—how could he warn a child who was only ten when he died? Yet he did not prepare her for any difficulty; he did not teach her to be reasonable or quiet. Indulging her helped him stay cheerful. Mary Jennifer was shown many of the Selznick movies, and she was obsessed with *Portrait of Jennie*, in which the child says to the older man, "I wish that you would wait for me to grow up—so that we could always be together."

David and Jennifer flew back to Los Angeles on March 26. On the following day, David entered Cedars of Lebanon Hospital for a four-day checkup. While there, he received a bill for services from Arnold Grant in the sum of $162,231, with a request for return receipt. There was a letter with the bill, an indictment such as only Grant could deliver. The lawyer asked to be spared any response except a check.

For a full month, David and his lawyer, Barry Brannen, experimented with answers, denials, refusals, outrage, including:

> If it possessed more charm, your letter would be worthy of Lewis Carroll. You indict me for sins which you refuse to state; you refuse to receive any answer; you condemn me, out of hand; and you pass sentence on me in terms of a gigantic "fine." What is this, the Grant School of Law? Or a new totalitarian regime that you are seeking to establish?

In his eventual reply, on April 28, David simply said he had been down with pneumonia or he would have written more promptly. The delay had not inspired him; the habitual self-defender seemed daunted by Grant's severity. So David complained, argued some items in the bill, rehashed Grant's original promise of billing only when David was solvent, and said he would do his best, as and when funds allowed.

Grant's rebuttal to this (May 19) was extreme beyond reason. It speaks to an anger repressed over two and a half years. Efficiency of Grant's kind loathed David's untidiness and could hardly prevent itself from going a little crazy in response:

> Let's look at the record. I found your conduct offensive and in a simple, calm, straightforward, unemotional letter terminated our friendship. As friendship is purely a personal thing, termination is an undeniable personal privilege. Simultaneously I rendered a bill for my professional services. . . .
>
> To this letter and bill you responded with a communication filled with venom, distortions, vicious accusations, blatant falsehoods and endless contradictions. To what purpose? Your letter answers this question with utmost clarity. Every line tells that you resorted to this denunciation solely to avoid, evade or reduce your just debt. . . . Your ability to see in yourself the embodiment of all that is able, worthy, fair and virtuous has long been known to me as has been your capacity for invective and false accusation against all who at any time either see in you less than your own self-image or call you to account.

As spring turned to summer, the correspondence became uglier, yet all it said, really, was that the lawyer was taking his client to court. The fee was not outlandish by the standards of show business or the amount of work done—when Shirley Harden prepared a digest of Grant's work for D.O.S., it ran twenty-two pages. But the bill was more than David could pay. Grant claimed his efforts had secured over $1 million for Selznick. Still, David was running on empty and agonizing over tax debts and overhead.

On May 9, one day before his fifty-ninth birthday, Jennifer flew to Paris to begin the location shooting for *Tender is the Night*. He was in New York still, at the St. Regis, perplexed that Jennifer sent birthday greetings to Los Angeles in error: "Have a nice day. Have a nice life. With love from your Nicole." On his birthday, David had dinner with Danny and Irene, and the following Sunday he went to the country with his former wife. He flew back to Los Angeles on the nineteenth, and Mary Jennifer baked him a chocolate cake, observing to the kitchen staff at Tower Grove, "My daddy will love any cake I bake."

The shooting of *Tender is the Night* was a pleasure for no one. Much of it was done in Zurich, not the easiest place for Jennifer. Joan Fontaine, who was playing Baby, observed that Jennifer was frequently on the phone to David, yet in no way reassured. Paula Strasberg was also at Jennifer's side, advising her. Henry King treated this consultation with scorn. He was a veteran, he had no great sympathy for the book, and he disapproved of psychiatry. As Ivan Moffat saw it, King had no idea of European café society life. The picture was a job for him, something to be completed with as little trouble as possible. Which left Jennifer—playing a disturbed girl—having to digest the calls and terse memos from David:

> I know King feels strongly that ending and indeed entire story must concentrate on Nicole Dick and you can hammer away the fact that story between them goes right out window if it is resolved by Tommy in barbershop scene instead of between Dick Nicole in workroom scene. Also I know he has been bitterly opposed to affair and I think you can attack swimming scene on basis it is either exact equivalent or entirely innocent in which case ludicrous contradiction at end of boat scene and that therefore either way it should be eliminated. He will accurately tell you it was I who argued for swimming scene but you can use this to prove you are arguing your own points not mine also you can say I completely changed my own mind about this in consequence of solution of Dick's sacrificial pretended hardness in workroom scene but with lines indicating Nicole believes he has turned on her because of her going off with Tommy whereas if scene played properly with Dick's words belied by his face which Nicole does not see then audience is aware of what Nicole does not know concerning overhearing scene on boat leading to his sacrificial decisions to clear out. Main thing is for you to be pleasantly firm.

Moffat was on the set, and he got cables, too: one, of sixty pages, was delivered in a box. "He said, 'Maintain this . . . maintain that.' But it was higgledy-piggledy. Didn't give effect to anything. It was to relieve him of his burden. Henry King said, 'I just can't read it.' "

Jennifer was home by June 13, but two weeks later David flew with Shirley Harden to Berlin for the Golden Laurel Awards at the film festival. Jeffrey by then was living in Geneva and working in the financial world. David invited his son to join him at the festival and then go on a trip down the Rhine. In Berlin, the two Selznicks were taken to lunch by the new head of UFA, at his villa. Jeffrey felt he was asked along to alleviate his father's loneliness. The UFA boss was baiting David, trying to outbid him in stories of success. "Well, Mr. Selznick," he asked D.O.S. "How much do you make a year?"

Jeffrey's ears perked up at this, and yet again David was obliged to put on a show to maintain the belief of others.

"There hasn't been a year in the last twenty or more," he told the German, "that I haven't made at least a million dollars."

On their way back to the hotel, Jeffrey said it had been quite a question and quite an answer.

"Oh, you get used to crap like that," said David. "You just handle it that way."

In fact, the combined earnings of David and Jennifer in recent years had been as follows:

1957	$207,749
1958	177,637
1959	331,800
1960	56,504
1961	137,485

David returned to Los Angeles on July 24. With the family together again, they divided their time between Tower Grove and a beach house at Malibu. As *Tender is the Night* was being cut, Henry Weinstein admitted Henry King's pacing was as slow as David had warned. Perhaps it could be saved in the editing? David doubted it: King filmed in a standard, static way; his shots had to be used for what they were. Once upon a time, David would have lived in the cutting room until it worked. Now, he was forbidden to be there.

On October 19, David and Shirley Harden were invited to a preview of the film: it happened to be at Riverside again, the town where *Gone With the Wind* had first met its public. This time, nothing was said. "I didn't think he liked it at all," said Weinstein.

David had talked about the other opportunities for Jennifer that would follow *Tender is the Night*. But he had less energy for convincing himself.

He wrote to Beaman and Brannen, "For some reason I can't seem to be able to impress upon either of you the urgency and seriousness of the crisis that we face. I imagine this is because we have faced these before, overcome them, and perhaps you both take it for granted that somehow or other I will pull some rabbit out of the hat that will accomplish this again."

There was a new picture idea, *Heart of a Nation*, a large, inspirational movie about the soul of America, something that needed a young producer whose foolishness was still unabashed. The musical of *Wind* dragged on. There might be a TV pilot for *The Farmer's Daughter*. But the deadly equation of income and overhead had to be balanced, so David thought of selling Tower Grove, getting out of California altogether, and going back east. He worried about the London office, headed by Doug Brunger but bringing in foreign earnings that amounted to only 15 percent of the company's needs.

All this time, David had ignored the Arnold Grant suit. Then, in November, Grant won a default judgment against Selznick in New York for $159,727. There was nothing to do but hire another lawyer, Ambrose Doskow, to challenge the judgment. Doskow warned David to remove any properties in New York that might be attached. This made it a little less likely that David could move there. David was worried the Grant judgment would jeopardize other deals. As he stepped out of the St. Regis on the evening of November 24 to go to the theater, agents served a summons and complaint on him for not paying the Grant fee.

Nineteen sixty-one was a year in which nothing had been accomplished. *Tender is the Night* had been made in defiance of David. He had seen his dreams for it ruined. Urged to rest, he had put in close to 50,000 miles of travel, in pursuit of prospects. In November, too, he heard that Jeffrey was about to become a financial free-lancer—"simply a promoter," David called it. "The whole world, and especially Europe, is too full of promoters and entrepreneurs who drift around with no goals other than to make a fast buck, or maybe a fast million bucks."

5 · 1 9 6 2

TENDER IS THE NIGHT opened on January 19, 1962. In the days beforehand, David tried to steel himself and Jennifer for its reception. He had no illusions about how the picture would play. His pride was hurt; his own judgment was at fault in the film: the script had been in his making, and Nicole was his Nicole. But David's vision of Hollywood in the early sixties was blunt and accurate: "Studio administration cannot be calloused and cynical toward the ambitions of, and the promises made to, the creators, without paying dearly for so hard-shelled an attitude. . . . I think this is where the bus stops."

He regretted that someone like Richard Burton or Peter O'Toole had not been Diver, that Jane Fonda had been ruled out as Rosemary, and that Louis Jourdan or Marcello Mastroianni had not been cast as Tommy. The film did badly. At 146 minutes, it was very slow; the seventy-four-year-old Henry King would not direct again. The reviews were damning, yet Jennifer came away better than anyone. If no one could get over her age, several critics thought her more fully involved than she had been in recent work. She showed evidence of this in an interview with Hedda Hopper: "*Tender* is a wonderful love story, with a most unusual relationship between Nicole and her husband. He is her lover as well as her psychiatrist, and it doesn't work out. She is healed, but, in the process, he is utterly destroyed."

David went to New York alone at the end of January. He had dinner with Irene on February 6 and 23. He was aroused by reports of the new television deal for college football: it had been $6 million for the package of games the year before, and now CBS had bid $10.2 million. In another year . . . $12 or $15 million? His dwindling energies picked up with the beat of some show still going on. For a moment, he could believe the rights to a TV version of *Gone With the Wind* were "by a wide margin the biggest thing we have ever owned, bigger even than the film GWTW from a profit standpoint." Moreover, his contract to those rights with Stephens Mitchell depended on David's continued "best efforts" to make a production deal. But when he thought of what would be entailed in a weekly series, or twelve ninety-minute shows, his heart sank.

So he tried to sell the show: he reckoned he would cajole the networks into an auction. NBC said they needed to see the original movie to make up their minds; David told them he had a print of his own, which they could see without having to alert MGM. CBS was not interested: over lunch, Bill Paley let David know he did not believe in it. By the middle of February, David was telling Ambrose Doskow that "my doctor has told me that I am very badly in need of a rest of at least a couple of weeks." This was Connie Guion in New York, who said his chest pain was due to a circulatory problem. David told Doskow that he expected "a breather, financially, for at least a little while," in which case he was off to Japan, Tahiti, or maybe just Palm Springs.

He had to settle for returning to Los Angeles, and it was not until April 24 that he was back in New York, once more on his own, to be deposed for the Grant case. As if to tweak David's nose, early in May, the fifty-three-year-old Grant took a bride: Bess Myerson, Miss America in 1945 and a panelist on "I've Got a Secret" on TV. David spent two days giving deposition on May 7 and May 10, his sixtieth birthday. He dined with Irene, and he went to the country with her for the weekend. The following week he was deposed yet again, and on the eighteenth he had a dinner party with Irene and Danny for Danny's birthday.

David's life was preoccupied with such family occasions and the requirements of the law. There is a further sign of his wish to attend to things in that he called Asheville to ask whether Howard could be brought up to New York to see him. Rose Mary Phillips replied that Howard was not well enough to travel—she said nothing about her own health. David fretted. If he made the trip, by way of Charlotte, it entailed five planes. But on May 19, he went to Asheville, and he gave Howard a raincoat. "It was certainly nice seeing you again after all these years," Howard wrote to him. (As far as I can tell the brothers had not met in fourteen years.) "I will write again in a few days and hope that you will get more rest. Love always, Howard."

The summer was spent in Los Angeles, with Jennifer and Mary Jennifer. There were people trying to get David a proper position back in the business. For ten days in June, at the request of Ray Stark, he went to the offices of Seven Arts to examine its properties and see "how I could best fit in." David was bewildered: "They have the delusion that making deals, and raising more money, and constantly reorganizing their financial setup, is going to make their stock and their stock options worth gigantic fortunes." He wrote to Morgan Maree about the experience, and the letter was a jumble of contradictions: "I certainly don't need a job. I have demonstrated for a great many years that I am perfectly competent, one way or another, of making what money I need" on one page and then on the next, "I need income—*big* income."

Seven Arts came to nothing. But the television version of *Gone With the Wind* was developing. Pat Weaver, once president of NBC, believed that major sponsors could be found—Coca-Cola or General Motors—for thirty one-hour shows. Selznick would get $40,000 per episode in rights and $200,000 per episode as a production fee. For a month or more, David was optimistic over the deal. He called Weaver "the only man I have met in television with the imagination and showmanship, and willingness to break precedent." But this glow faded: David's "rights" were not certain, MGM was making competitive moves, and Weaver found sponsors worried "about the effect of the series upon the negro question."

There were still movie projects being talked about. On August 10, David met with his old SIP aide William Wright (who was now at Warners) in hopes of new pictures for Jennifer. He suggested a story about Isadora Duncan, an adaptation of Vita Sackville-West's *No Signposts in the Sea*, and even a remake of *The Letter* in which the murdered lover was black.

It was Jennifer's wish to spend more time in Zurich in the coming winter, but David and Mary Jennifer would go along, too, and David would try to tempt Jennifer into some more traveling. Tower Grove was closed up; David had left instructions with Beaman and Shirley Harden to sell it if they could. He felt no great urge to come back.

Jennifer flew ahead of him, and David had a few more days in New York. There was yet more deposing to do for the Grant case. David was agitated because the process of disclosure meant Grant had access to Selznick files and might pass on the private fury David had expressed against such as Spyros Skouras. He became angrier with Grant when the lawyer was hired by Twentieth Century-Fox in the drastic changes that overtook the studio that year. Skouras was ousted as Darryl Zanuck returned from Europe, compelled, he decided, to rescue first *Cleopatra* and then the entire studio. Arnold Grant was made chairman of the executive committee.

Therefore, David planned to fight meaner. He did whatever he could to round up discreditable details about Grant, and he suggested that the lawyer had tried to conceal his Jewish origins—without seeming to realize that Grant was a noted contributor to several Jewish causes. David browbeat Ambrose Doskow: "I am now absolutely convinced that Grant sent me that letter with his bill for one reason, and one reason only—that he was mortally offended from a status standpoint, that I had stopped using him." At the same time, David reckoned that a $75,000 settlement was not just fair, but to be expected.

Barry Brannen suggested gently that maybe David was already giving Doskow too much advice—and Doskow one day would have his own bill to present. But David could not take the hint: "I have never understood," he told Brannen, "why a lawyer should resent getting advice from the person most concerned—his client." Brannen might have responded that no one ever won rest or ease by second-guessing his own lawyer. David had an answer—"you forget that I am the Dean of the Selznick School of Law."

Even the Dean had to face facts. By the end of the year a settlement was reached, a compromise that could have been worked out over lunch: Grant's bill was cut in half. David paid $72,000, and the strange chess match was at an end.

In New York, on September 6, David and Irene dined together as worried parents. Jeffrey had fallen in love, and there was talk of marriage. The woman was Janine Durand-Ruel, the young widow of one of Paris's most famous art dealers. She had been in the south of France in the summer of 1962, said Jeffrey, "and I was sitting in Geneva nursing a market condition where I was short of the market, with a profit, but waiting for the right time to close up the positions. She put a lot of pressure on me to get going on the holiday, which I finally did. The market turned on me when I was out of touch and I lost a lot of money."

Later that summer, Irene was in Europe asking to meet Janine. The rendezvous was arranged in Biarritz, but it was a disaster. "My mother never liked French ladies generally, and she disliked this one in particular and on sight. The behavior between the two women was something so awful, each of them fighting over me, as it were."

Irene had heard rumors, and she did not find Janine honest in every answer about her background. When Irene returned to Paris, she began to investigate. As her father had been accustomed to do, she engaged a private detective. In early September, at about the time of the New York dinner with David, Irene had telephoned Jeffrey and reported what she called "scandalous" findings. Jeffrey was outraged. "How dare you?" he shouted. "I don't want to hear, now or ever, and I don't want to speak to you ever again." There was a breach between mother and son that lasted years. David was left trying to be peacemaker. He would do what he could, he promised Irene, when he got to Europe.

David was reunited with Jennifer and Mary Jennifer in Venice, and by the fifteenth they were once more installed in the Dolder Grand Hotel in Zurich. Two days later, David was in Paris and invited to call on Jeffrey and Janine in their lavish apartment on Avenue Foch. David and Janine shared no language and Jeffrey believed the meeting went quite well. As ever, he reckoned his father was both impressed by and a little envious of the son's conquest and showy life-style: there was a Gauguin on the wall and a Monet *Lilies*, paintings Janine had inherited from her first husband.

But David insisted on talking about the problem. Jeffrey said he didn't want to hear the enquiry reports.

"Well, you're wrong," said David. "You're being very stupid. Your mother only wants the best for you."

"No," said Jeff. "I think she's done something that is absolutely despicable. And I'm ashamed of you for taking her side in this."

David then conducted his own investigation, misunderstood the reports, but described what he had found in a letter to Janine:

> I told Jeff, there is no rational reason for lying about one's birthplace, unless one has something to hide. I thereupon told Jeff that I myself was going to check on your birthplace. I did so; I found that you were not born either in Greece or on the outskirts of Paris, but in a small

town in France. I sent Jeff a copy of your birth certificate, together with details of your family background, which were enormously different from what he told me you had told him. There was nothing reprehensible in any of this. That you came of poor and humble stock was, if anything, in your favor as far as I was concerned, and certainly as far as his mother was concerned. But I emphasized to Jeff that these strange falsehoods were certainly worrisome, and indicated that there might be truth to the other gossip about you. . . . For Jeff, let me say that he stood by you, and that he said he was sure he knew the explanations for your untruthful statements. I mention this in the hope that the shocks you may receive from this letter will not restrain you from a feeling of reciprocal loyalty towards him.

There are moments when one wonders how any outsider would wish to contrive a way into this family. David and Jeffrey were rivals over who should best play the role of big shot standing on an abyss of grand dreams and overdrawn credit. But no one could ever surpass David at convoluted self-righteousness. And no son could surmount the lifelong struggle between father and mother. Whatever David thought of Jeff, or Janine, he could not escape the intimidating direction of his coparent; he was not resolute with Irene—he was an actor in her productions. In New York, Danny was reeling on the edges of the battle. But in letters to Jeffrey that fall he made clear who had to be the center of the drama:

> I refer, of course, to notre mere, and the problems that she, her existence, her behavior, her temperament and problems bring with her. I cannot say that I have learned to "live and let live" with it, but I am trying slowly, over a long period of time . . . to forge the basis of some sort of mature relationship. . . . What a hell of a week-end this has been. First Mother tells me that she hired detectives to do background work on Janine and gets a terrible blast from me that sends her into tears, and then Dad tells me that I have to be gentle towards Mother, because she can't stand having two sons dislike her at the same time. . . . What bullshit. I am tired and angry and only slightly wiser.

In the fall of 1962, David played with the idea of a consortium of top filmmakers that he would assemble as a kind of studio. Billy Wilder and Otto Preminger declared an interest. Zanuck heard about it and called David, hoping the group would find shelter at Fox.

The plans never materialized, but David still had the flair and the reputation to keep company with great filmmakers. He was not always right in his opinions—times were changing—but that never deterred him from speaking. In the late 1950s, David had heard Billy Wilder's plans for the innovative *Some Like It Hot*. He was wary of comedy coming out of brutal reality—but comedy was never David's forte. David Lean's *Lawrence of Arabia* was his kind of picture, and in the winter of 1962 he saw a preview of Lean's cut and told the director: "David, tomorrow they're going to come and see you and ask you to cut the movie. *Gone With the Wind* was about the same length, and when we'd finished it they asked us to cut it. We didn't. Just remember it was the biggest success of all time. Don't let them get their hands on your movie."

He was in London, Paris, and Zurich. But in October, he had to go back to America. Rose Mary Phillips, the woman who had looked after Howard, died of cancer. It was unclear whether Howard could cope without some companion, and David began to consider bringing his brother to a retirement home in California.

By November 24, he was back in Zurich. Jeffrey and Janine were to be married in December: David had been invited, and he planned to attend, even though Irene was barred. But then Jeffrey and Janine arrived at the Dolder Grand, and Jeff asked Jennifer to tell David he was no longer invited because of *his* research activities.

David was further offended that Jeffrey nevertheless sought a wedding present, preferably money, that Janine was indifferent to Mary Jennifer, and that Janine was wearing not just Jeff's engagement ring, but one from an earlier engagement, broken off. He told Janine:

> I therefore realized that whereas I had desired to start you off as a married couple with a conventional gift, this was far outside the realm of a romantic marriage, and was instead based in large degree on materialistic possessiveness, as was also indicated by the contracts specifying the complete separation of the funds of the couple—which is a very far cry from the American and Jewish tradition in which Jeff was brought up.

David didn't understand the French laws, but he may have wished that some "separation" could have protected him from Irene.

Jeffrey and Janine were married in Paris on December 7, 1962, without another Selznick present. A few days later, in St. Moritz, where David had taken Jennifer and Mary Jennifer for the New Year, he had constricting pain in the chest. He was short of breath, and he could scarcely walk. It was a warning attack, and nitroglycerine tablets eased the pressure. But there was no escaping the self-imposed melodrama of character.

6 · 1963

IN ST. MORITZ, as he recovered from the heart attack—yet concealed it from his immediate family—David did make changes. He gradually gave up cigarettes for a pipe and small cigars; he tried not to inhale. He cut fat out of his diet, and he concentrated on bread, fruit, and vegetables. His weight came down to just below 200 pounds. But he did not have the lung capacity for serious exercise.

Late in 1962, he had hoped there was a purchaser for the Tower Grove house. Howard Hughes had said he might be interested, and David had asked Shirley Harden to make sure the house was spruced up for Hughes's visit—the tycoon would only look at the property at night—with flowers: "nothing costly like roses, but the daisies and wild flowers that are customary." He had hopes of getting $1 million for the house. But no one was sure whether Hughes ever made the visit. In 1963, that shy man was found in default over his TWA holdings, and shortly thereafter he began to live in hotels.

There were other things likely to make David think of Europe from now on. In November 1962, just before leaving New York, he had had lunch with Joe Vogel, the president of MGM, and Bennett Cerf, who was on the Metro board. The ostensible purpose had been the ongoing argument over rights in *Gone With the Wind*. But the talks had broadened in scope. David said Hollywood was over—the most interesting pictures were coming from Europe. Suddenly, Vogel said, "Nothing would please him more than for me to become 'MGM' in Europe." As David recovered in St. Moritz, he considered the merits of that idea as opposed to his other major alternative—creative leadership in a consortium to advance closed circuit and cable television. This is the last hurrah of David's enthusiasm, boosted by the likelihood that 1963 would see the retirement of the tax debt and might bring a lucrative deal with MGM. He sounded out the choice to Barry Brannen, unaware that Vogel's offer had been just lunch-table talk or that the closed-circuit dream was years away. But the weakening man could launch himself on airwaves of international communication:

> I think, however pretentious it may seem to you, that I can enormously expedite the cause of medical research, and perhaps step up by

years the solution of the problems of cancer, heart research, etc.—by closed circuit—of research and of operations and of experiments, once weekly throughout the year, worldwide, with audiences of doctors and research workers, simultaneously in thousands of cities. I believe that I can enormously step up American education, and indeed world education, with classrooms literally numbering millions of pupils, with the great brains of the world lecturing to classes of thousands in every one of hundreds of cities simultaneously, instead of to small classrooms. I believe we can start a university of the air that will revolutionize education. I believe that we can do the same in primary and secondary education. I believe that we can have a medium for the advancement of democracy that will be a weapon against Communism that will be beyond compare. I believe, in short, that I can justify my life with this medium.

The urge to rescue or lift up strangers was boundless. But relatives gave him a harder time; they abided, they had real, ineducable difficulties, and they knew him too well to be blind admirers.

On January 21, leaving Jennifer in Zurich, David and Mary Jennifer flew back to New York. He dined with Irene that night, and for the next few days he and his daughter inspected likely schools for her in the city.

In California, Shirley Harden was trying to find somewhere for Howard to live. She looked at senior citizens' homes in Seal Beach and Goleta. Howard, still in Asheville, was pleased that this was a move David wanted and was organizing. In fact, David was against the trouble of a visit all the way across country if the arrangements were not satisfactory. He thought Berman and Ruth Swarttz should do some of the research, and he wondered about ways of getting a free plane ticket for Howard. In the spring of 1963, Howard was brought west, to Santa Barbara, to look at the New Horizons home at Goleta. But he was unhappy there, and he became angry with the disappointment. By April he had gone back to North Carolina to resume residence at Appalachian Hall.

Jennifer returned from Zurich on February 20, and in the next month David pursued discussion with MGM for some European deal. Terms were never spelled out, but there was at least talk about how overhead would be calculated. David had two pictures in mind: *Heart of a Nation* and an adaptation of Eugene O'Neill's *Strange Interlude*, with Jennifer in the role of Nina Leeds (played by Lynn Fontanne onstage and by Norma Shearer in the disastrous 1932 movie), who ages from eighteen to sixty-eight.

Then again, family intruded. David got a telephone call from Jeffrey, who had written over $6,000 in bad checks because of the financial crisis that had begun in the summer before his marriage. The call was "frantic," according to David, asking for the wedding present now, in cash. David wired $3,000 to his son. Days later, the problem had grown worse: Jeffrey was now deeper in the hole. He had taken a loan and used Danny's inheritance from Margaret Mayer as a guarantee. Now the loan was being called, and Jeff was short. He risked criminal proceedings because of the bad checks, and yet—David felt—he was conducting himself still in a big-shot manner. David believed Janine was only aggravating Jeffrey's grandeur, and he told her:

> I cabled him that he should come over at once, at my expense, tourist, and I would pay both his trip and his bill at a modest hotel (for by this time I was outraged that Jeff was living in luxury hotels all over the world on other people's money). I made two conditions. The first was that he bring with him all the figures so that I would have the actual truth, instead of a distorted or incomplete version thereof. The second was that I received assurances that you had the full facts, for I felt that it was inconceivable that you should go on living as you were and that you would permit this, if you knew the full truth about Jeff's condition.

Jeffrey took umbrage and refused the trip. Whereupon David learned that the Madison Hotel in New York also had bad checks his son had issued on a recent visit. David and Irene covered these debts to avoid prosecution and "because we are a family that has always been scrupulous about our obligations." David told his daughter-in-law he would not talk to Jeffrey again until he apologized:

> As to his contemptible beliefs that I was worried about my own position at the Bankers Trust . . . and as to his even more disgraceful belief that I got him out of his bad check charge because of my fear of the notoriety, I tell you now, and firmly, that I am quite prepared to see him become a notorious character, even to seeing him go to gaol, where he is headed if he doesn't *completely* change his entire thinking.

In April, David went with wife and daughter to Jamaica for ten days. He had another birthday coming up, and it prompted one of his poems. As a versifier, he had not advanced in forty years. Nearly every claim he made for himself in this 1963 effort could be refuted. Yet that does not detract from the naive, self-idealizing sincerity of the poem. David believed in himself as a created character, a kindly old gent in a Christmas story by Dickens. The clash this figure made with his own author is central to the comedy and the disaster of being David O. Selznick.

Now my Sixtieth has passed
(My Sixty-first, to be precise)
The change I find in me is vast;
Indeed, I think I'm rather nice.

No more I yearn for far-flung fame
That glows so for the new,
Nor do I press to win the game;
I'm slightly shocked you do.

My love is lovely, lasting, deep,
The distant fields I need not now
The chase is o'er. I do not weep:
My libido is sweet and slow.

I do not hate: it's much too late
And such a waste of time.
I'm not green-eyed, I hope not snide.
Perhaps I'm in my prime.

By May 30, they were back in California, where they spent the summer, apart from Jennifer's next trip to Zurich, from July 14 to August 8. David was searching into fresh things for Jennifer to do: a play by Lillian Hellman—a François Truffaut film—or even the Eva Perón story? (He called the latter *"Viva Villa* with sex.") It is less clear whether Jennifer now attended to these prospects. The production deal with MGM slipped away, there was no deal on the *Gone With the Wind* rights, and the overhead—at Tower Grove, Culver City, and in England—ate into David's confidence. He told Beaman, "I lay awake at night worrying about the condition of our affairs in the event of anything happening to you and/or myself." He was borrowing more heavily on the remaining insurance policies—if he was not careful, he might die without benefit.

But on September 27, the original lien filed for a tax default of $1,662,942 was withdrawn. He had paid off the debt and the interest, amounting to $434,610. Still, for the year 1963, the only income the Selznicks had was the $125,000 salary that David paid himself, as well as proceeds from the sale of a diamond and emerald ring that David had bought Jennifer in 1949. He had also had to pay $76,929 in state income taxes for those default years. The rate of taxation in California was another reason to make him consider living elsewhere.

Extra sources of income had been harder hit because of the illness of Douglas Brunger, head of the London office and the man charged with collecting foreign earnings. Brunger was devoted to David, but the pressure for better performance had undermined his health. Ruefully, David supposed that Doug was suffering from "memo-itis": "He says he is unrecognizable, that his face is all swollen up, and that he spends the largest part of the day in a dark room. I certainly felt like a villain." Even at this late stage, most foreign earnings came from reruns of *Duel in the Sun.*

As the summer ended, David took up his New York campaigning again, and now he surrendered on *Gone With the Wind.* During the fall, a deal was worked out. David would give up all his disputed rights to a radio or television dramatization of the Margaret Mitchell novel. In return, he received $475,000 immediately, another $200,000 as and when the original movie played on television, and half the profits from any TV adaptation.

It was a deal made for cash now and a generous one in view of his uneasy claim to rights. Yet David felt he was forced to be the same old chump. There would never be another chance. On the eve of signing the MGM contract, he begged Bill Paley to make a better offer on behalf of CBS. "I cannot get over the very strong feeling that this is *basically* wrong," he argued. The musical *Scarlett O'Hara* was lost. The profits were hardly likely to accrue in David's lifetime. Above all, David could see what would happen one day, when *Gone With the Wind* the movie—*his* movie—played on TV:

> In my opinion it is utterly inevitable that even within the next year or so MGM will receive offers of one million dollars—and it will not be surprising if this comes from CBS—for just the rights for only one use, as you yourself have estimated; and that it will refuse this offer, inevitably (and despite the fact that its future use will be worth millions more, here and abroad) simply confirmation of the absurdity of the present deal.

But Paley would not make a competing offer. On December 13, the contract was signed. The movie did not make its way to the television screen until 1976, when NBC showed it on two evenings. They paid $5 million for that one screening and reported an audience of 162 million. Then, in 1978, with Paley still in charge, CBS did buy the TV rights, for the two nights for twenty years, for $35 million. In 1986, theatrical rights to the movie passed to Turner Broadcasting when Ted Turner paid over $1 billion for the MGM library of films. A year later he prevailed upon CBS to sell him the TV rights to *Wind*: in return, the network was able to renew its license to screen *The Wizard of Oz*; it also received a large but undisclosed sum of money.

Sometime in the fall, there was a small dinner party at Tower Grove: Brooke Hayward and her husband, the actor Dennis Hopper; Dominick Dunne and his wife; an English socialite, Mrs. Susan Ward, and a Spanish count. When Hayward became ill during the evening, Dr. Myron Prinzmetal was called to the house to attend her. But as the group waited, David himself showed the signs of what Dominick Dunne believed was a heart attack—he was also sure that Jennifer appreciated the nature of the problem. When the doctor arrived, it was not Prinzmetal, but a young assistant. The doctor saw David and Jennifer privately and then told everyone there was nothing to worry about: it was only indigestion. The next day Jennifer called people, asking that the incident not be talked about.

The final doubts and deliberations over *Wind* coincided with the assassination of John Kennedy: David was at Tower Grove when that news came. In his shock, he did not send a letter he had dictated and typed to Bill Paley's wife, Babe. It had been "one of the most extraordinarily difficult letters" he had ever had to write, for it asked if—in the event of his death and Jennifer's—Babe would look after Mary Jennifer.

He said in the letter that this was not a financial burden: there was insurance for Mary Jennifer and for her education. He also said that the chance of both parents dying before Mary Jennifer came of age was "extremely remote." But "I have waking nightmares." He went on to talk about his upbringing—"I have been from my youth an extremely bad Jew"—and he described how that September, at Jennifer's suggestion, he had taken Mary Jennifer to synagogue for the first time. The child was half Jewish, half Gentile, and David was perpetually open-minded. He did wonder if, in, say, a Protestant baptism, Babe Paley would stand as her godmother. But the letter was not sent. (In what proved his last will—dated May 27, 1964— David nominated Danny as Mary Jennifer's guardian if Jennifer died, too, and if Danny was unable or willing, then he nominated Babe Paley.)

In December, there was some reconciliation with Jeffrey. Janine had been ill, and Jeff needed a loan to pay the medical bills. David said, of course—this was written the day before signing the *Gone With the Wind* contract, but he had to make clear to Jeffrey how very tough the times were. Nearly all the *Wind* money was booked for old debts:

> Our economies have come right down to the smallest items, both at the studio and at home. We have even let the messenger go at the studio, even though we need substitute messenger service, and therefore this saves only a relatively few dollars per week—but I mention this solely to give you an indication. We have abandoned a vacation trip which I very badly need, because we simply cannot afford it. . . . You might as well know that I have borrowed up to the hilt on every bit of life insurance I have. Naturally of course, all of this is very confidential, and I will appreciate it if you will tear this memo up—and confirm to me that you have done so—as soon as you have read it.

7 · 1964

AROUND CHRISTMAS 1963, David and Ben Hecht got into another idea together. Hecht was seventy, still a free-lance, listening to every offer and sneering at most of his assignments. There was no other friend with whom David had so much history. That December, Hecht conceived the notion of a play about Sinclair Lewis and Dorothy Thompson. "The basic conflict in the play," he told David, "would be between a phony political expert and an artist. Dorothy was a combination nymphomaniac and sadist. Louis [*sic*] found her unbearable from their first night together. He spent some twelve years of his life daydreaming of living it without Dorothy."

David was "terribly excited," foreseeing a superb role for Jennifer so long as the version of Dorothy Thompson could be given "compensating attractiveness and charm, as the man will seem like an utter idiot to have fallen for her in the first place and to have married her."

Then Hecht cooled. He had to follow the immediate dollar, and Charlie Feldman had asked him to work on the script of *Casino Royale*, "in which James Bond single-handedly shuts down a score of brothels and stamps vice out of the whole of Europe." Ben was also beginning to think that Lewis, the boozing genius, was a rather hackneyed figure. He was drawn instead to the story of a celebrated English medium, a woman (whose name he had forgotten) who had made psychic communication respectable in English society. David was undaunted: "Jennifer has long been fascinated with the field, and has often suggested a play or movie on the subject."

He was spending time at Palm Springs and La Quinta, doing his best to rest, playing a little golf, but hating the cold that set in around three in the afternoon. By February, Hecht was back on Sinclair Lewis, and David tried to persuade him to come to the desert: "Knowing your speed, I actually think you could do the play in record-breaking time, at least a first draft . . . it would be a joy for me to once again be collaborating with you, or editing you, or whatever you want to call it." But Hecht could not manage a trip, so David played golf with screenwriter Harry Kurnitz and a young play-wright, Sidney Michaels.

David flew to New York for a week in early March for another family crisis. Daniel had met a pretty, dark-haired woman who was a pianist and who was taking acting classes. They had fallen in love and had been living together. David was nervous on Danny's behalf. He felt the couple were too young, and he said he'd had his own infatuations as a youth; he compared this woman with Jean Arthur. Irene was much more hostile. But a date was set for the marriage, and there was talk of having it at Tower Grove.

Then Irene and David called Danny to see them at Apartment 1007 of the Pierre. They assailed him and said he risked throwing his life away. He weakened and said he would back off. When he went home, the woman was writing wedding invitations.

"My mother says I don't love you," he told her.

"Is that true?"

"I don't know."

So the woman quit.

As Danny looked back on it: "My parents were just partners with me in the investment house of Daniel Selznick. The question is whether I had fifty percent and they each had twenty-five percent, or whether we were one-third, one-third, one-third—which would have made me a minority partner."

While in New York, David was also trying to find some producing deals for himself. There was never any alternative to fresh income if he could not control his expenses. He had a couple of days in Las Vegas in the middle of the month with Bill Paley and Walter Thayer (a lawyer and Jock Whitney's associate). Then on April 12, he went back to New York to see Connie Guion.

He saw Irene. On April 14, they went to a preview of the World's Fair. On the seventeenth, David called on a new lawyer, Arnold Weissberger. And on Saturday, April 18, Ben Hecht had a fatal heart attack in his apartment on West Sixty-seventh Street. On the Sunday, David went to see Irene in the country, and in the evening he entered the hospital for a checkup.

He was let out of the hospital on the twenty-first to attend Hecht's funeral at Temple Rodeph Sholom on West Eighty-third Street. One of the eulogists was Menachem Begin. He was back in the hospital the same evening, as Dr. Guion found elevated blood glucose and uric acid levels. She told him the pain he was feeling came from gout. By April 24, David moved into the Waldorf. Three days later he returned to the World's Fair with Danny and Irene. April 29 would have been their thirty-fourth wedding anniversary.

David flew back to Los Angeles on May 4. He was at Tower Grove when at 1:00 a.m. on May 10—his sixty-second birthday—he was woken by chest pain. Nitroglycerine relieved it, but he called Dr. William Molle to the house. An electrocardiogram was taken, showing abnormalities. Dr. Molle diagnosed myocardial ischemia. In addition to nitroglycerine, he proposed rest, Nitroglyn, and Percodan.

A few days later, David was seen by his specialist, Dr. George Griffith, who confirmed mild coronary artery insufficiency with myocardial ischemia, as well as diabetes and gout. Griffith urged that the low-fat diet be continued, that David walk a couple of miles every day on the flat, and "he should keep the nitroglycerin always within hand reach and use it promptly at the very slightest onset of any constricting pain in the chest. He should not confuse the sharp, stabbing pain from the chest deformity that he has had for years with the coronary insufficiency pain." In addition, Griffith suggested "long, complete rest," preferably a sea voyage. David was now on colchicine and Orinase daily, and he kept a bottle of nitroglycerine tablets in his pocket.

If any voyage was undertaken, David was equipped with a list of cardiologists in every port. He also carried a letter from Griffith and his file of electrocardiograms. As far as can be gathered, he told no one of his condition except Earl Beaman, to focus Beaman's mind on the problems. What this came down to was a weekly expenditure of about $8,500— comprised of insurance premiums, interest on the loan taken out on the insurance, the Culver City office, running the Tower Grove house and interest on a new mortgage on the property, secretaries, the office in London, and hotels or other living arrangements that David might choose to make, to say nothing of federal and California taxes.

No one at a loss to explain how he was spending $8,500 a week—or how he might raise that money—was likely to find complete rest. But David could wear himself out in its pursuit. He did try to live up to the doctor's expectations. On May 27, having signed his will with a secretary, Margaret Hodgson, he flew to New York and the next day set sail for France.

David had gone to France conscientious about his need for rest. A few days before setting out, he warned Barry Brannen that he intended "only an occasional letter or memo." Brannen was to restrict himself to passing on bare summaries and any good news, and he should be prepared to hear nothing back from David. That dream! The one topic on which David was ready to correspond was what to do with Howard. He surveyed his family and saw that he was left with the responsibility. But he did not want his children to have to assume it one day. Near the end of a letter to Brannen, he was overtaken by a brain wave about Howard: "Curiously, the one that I think I am likely to turn to, and the one that I think would be the best qualified to undertake it and would undertake it as a favor to me is my former wife, Irene." But in this case, David did spare Irene a blind copy of the letter.

By June 6, David and Margaret Hodgson were installed at the Carlton Hotel, in Cannes, which was about $1,000 a week for the two of them. Mrs. Hodgson was responsible to Beaman for money; she had traveler's checks that she issued to her boss. Yet she had no inside information about his heart, and she merely observed he got tired from getting in and out of cars and inspecting villas the family might move into when Jennifer and Mary Jennifer arrived. That was his morning routine. Then he rested in the afternoon and began dictation at 8:00 p.m. David also went on a short cruise on Sam Spiegel's yacht. This alarmed Mrs. Hodgson, for it likely meant losses at gin rummy. Gambling was much reduced in David's last decade, but he could not resist Monte Carlo. So Mrs. Hodgson went along, too, and stayed in charge of the chips. When David had a win, she put those chips aside and refused to give them back, "at the cost of making a scene." They showed a profit. If only David had had a keeper at the casinos long before—or could have kept hold of a Mrs. Hodgson. Unfortunately, she resigned: the hours were too long and the sunshine too tempting.

Thus, early in July, with wife and daughter now arrived, David found himself without a secretary. The circumstances at the Carlton were not restful enough, so the Selznicks moved to the Hôtel du Cap, at Antibes, which was more expensive than the Carlton. David knew this was "ridiculous," yet he believed they could live more cheaply there than at Tower Grove. Though far removed from New York and allegedly resting, David was now seeking a deal at Columbia whereby he would get $50,000 for executive-producing a small picture and $100,000 for one that he produced personally—"Knowing myself, there would not be that much difference!"

News was coming slowly from Beaman. But David could calculate that with the job and income from London, they might muster as much as $5,000 a week. The sums were pitiless. Insurance was the huge burden. Yet, simultaneously, David was desperate to protect wife and child *and* considering dropping more of his policies to balance the books. So he told Beaman to close down the Culver City office and move into the smaller house in the garden at Tower Grove.

On July 18, David had another attack, "the worst to date" he told Beaman. He saw Dr. A. J. Meyer of Cannes, who reported pain and arrhythmia not alleviated by the usual tablets. The French doctor prescribed Sintron, an anticoagulant, as well as injections of heparin. Accordingly, David's electrocardiograms showed some improvement. But rest became a mockery.

David was forever on the phone back to America, chasing ideas, while, on the Riviera, he bumped into many European picture people. In America, on the other end of the phone, Ivan Moffat dreamed up a perfect project for the moment:

> It would be called The Film—about a D.O.S. character on his last legs as far as Hollywood was concerned, but famous in Europe still. He's holding court to make an unspecified film on an uncertain subject, and people flock to him with ideas which sometimes even harden into reality, then fade into evanescence. But in the course of this all sorts of people's lives are changed, liaisons are made, marriages broken, hopes raised and dashed. And all the time the D.O.S. character knows perfectly well that The Film will never be made. But at least the sojourn in the south of France will be tax-deductible.

On July 20, he handwrote a thirty-three-page letter to Beaman that is equivalent to the mounting worries of a man who cannot sleep. It is as terrible a letter to read as it must have been to write. What else could Beaman do but remain "there" at the other end, a wall to beat on, a witness to his boss's collapse? David had never in his life been able to employ true lieutenants, people he trusted, whose decisions left him time for his most vital work. He demanded figures from Beaman and then said they couldn't be true. Beyond self-defense, he lashed out, trying to find someone responsible for his own inability to manage.

> It has been obvious for a very long time that I can't make $442,000 a year—even if it's all tax-free—which is $8,500 wkly. *What is the actual figure that it is all the more impossible to pay??!!* I can't pay $8500 wkly. Far more so even, I can't go on meeting greater needs that we not only are unable to project, but that we deceive ourselves do not exist. . . .
>
> It's only seven months ago that I was happy to accept the *GWTW* sacrifice because it made me clear of debt. Now, despite a lot of income (how much?) in the interim, it is all gone and I am again and increasingly mortgaging my insurance and my home! I should be locked up!

Quique and Louis Jourdan were also staying at the Hôtel du Cap that summer. They were unaware of the heart condition. They saw that David was often breathless and had difficulty with stairs, but they believed this was "asthma." Still, when he sat up late with Quique, playing cards, David was back to smoking cigarettes. He was in a reminiscing mood: "He talked only about when he met Irene and L. B. Mayer didn't want her to get married because he wanted the other daughter to get married first. Edie. Then he had to wait. All the things he was saying, it was like Jennifer didn't exist. He only was talking about his early life with Irene."

Jeffrey visited David at the Hôtel du Cap that summer. He thought his father had aged. "Are you all right?" he asked.

"I have to be a little careful," said David.

The next day they were going on a boat ride and David slipped on the dock. "It didn't look bad to me," said Jeffrey, "but there was a terrible overreaction. He had to be helped up and he went ashen."

"I guess I'd better tell you the truth," said David. "I have a heart problem." They talked more seriously, and Jeffrey noticed that his father—for the first time—seemed to have no plans. Every thought was to make his affairs as secure as possible.

Then on August 16, David slipped again and chipped the bone in his right ankle. He had to go to bed for three days. While laid up, he wrote by hand a twenty-six-page letter to Douglas Brunger in London, at the same time lashing him for being slack or critical in the past while urging him on to greater efforts. Brunger, who had only lately recovered from his own illness, a malady of stress and overdevotion, had been driven to remonstrate with David over the confusion and second-guessing. But David could now tolerate only obedience and loyalty:

> I cannot and will not be restrained or even inhibited in the making of decisions or the expression of my viewpoints concerning either the future or our best guide, the lengthy list of our errors of the past by either a stubborn insistence that we have been right when we have so obviously and repeatedly been far from right, or by the alternatives of either continuing the more Dickensian characteristics of our operations or of suffering your threats of resignation, or even of living under the sword of your fear of another break-down.

At the Hôtel du Cap, David had met a Dutch businessman—not in pictures. He had shown him Brunger's report of income from Holland and the man had said casually that the figure seemed low. It was enough to spur David to take over the Dutch market himself immediately! Again, how could a Brunger read this letter, let alone deal with it? Brunger had done his best and had steadily brought in money. But he could not escape the role of whipping boy. In bed at the French hotel, David was remorseless:

> Finally, Doug, let me point out, *please*, once more, that I am not an amateur in any branch of this business. I am your senior in it by at least a quarter of a century. I was a distribution executive, and I managed theatres, *more than forty years ago*—and have been in every branch of it ever since. . . . When people, including yourself, tell me the "facts" about what can and cannot be done, is it unnatural that I lose patience? So *listen to me, Doug*: don't buy what some obscure buyer

tells you as being "facts", and superior to what I—one of the most famous experts in the history of the motion picture business, and your boss to boot—tells you! It is true, God knows, that I have made less out of my pictures than has been made by others out of a quarter of the number of less successful films. This has been due—*as the figures prove*—to our stupidity—my stupidity, if you will.

The next day, David wrote to Beaman that he was coming back and that he would have to make his base in New York. He had been endeavoring from Antibes to get Mary Jennifer into the Dalton School in New York (while maintaining her place at Buckley in Los Angeles, in case they went back to California). The letter was also obsessed with the proper care of Mary Jennifer's pets back at Tower Grove. There was never one note of real restraint—even in the pit of melancholic scrimping he wondered whether to go to Santa Barbara or the Caribbean for his next vacation.

I am of course aware that the costs of this holiday have run several thousand above what I estimated—and the costs of the doctors will be high! I know what this has done to your already difficult budgetary problems—and hope that you will have been able to complete which-ever of the loan arrangements have seemed most advantageous. . . . Brunger may quit, but I doubt it—and I resolved that I must either kill him or cure him. I know now that we can do *very* much better in foreign, but I realize it may involve me in much work in either a further education of Doug or in training a new man. I see now what was the British doggedness, character and thick-headedness, courage but incurable myopia, that led to Dunquerque, Gallipoli, Suez! . . . I am sanguine about the future of both the old assets and new enter-prises; the "holiday"—despite what was done to me by Margaret, Brunger and my foot!—has been worth whatever it cost, and I do see things much more clearly, I think.

He asked Beaman to find him a secretary from New York. In Los Angeles, Marjorie McDougall, the bookkeeper, told Beaman, "Just try to get someone who will work from 9:30 a.m. to 9:30 at night, without lunch or dinner."

On September 1, the Selznicks flew from Nice to Paris, and on the next day they boarded the *United States* at Le Havre. At 2:05 a.m. on the fifth, the ship's doctor, A. S. Ludwig, was called to David's cabin. Two nitro-glycerine tablets had failed to ease the pain. Ludwig gave him Lanoxin, and after ten hours the heart returned to a normal rhythm.

The *United States* arrived in New York on the seventh, and Jennifer and Mary Jennifer flew immediately to California. David stayed in the city, at the Waldorf. Very shortly after his return he went to see Irene and told her he was dying.

8 · 1965

IN SEPTEMBER 1964, David took up residence at the Waldorf Hotel. The broken ankle was not healing, largely because David was so restless. He admitted to an orthopedic specialist, "My foot seems to be considerably worse. I believe this is due, at least in part, to the tortuous position I had to assume for that series of six X rays. However, you might say, with justice, that it is due more to my inability—temperamentally, physically, and professionally—to carry out your prescribed course of treatment."

He saw Irene on several occasions—she must have noticed the limp and the discomfort. Yet years later, when she wrote her book, Irene felt certain the "ankle" had been a ruse to cover his fear of undue exertion or activity. There was no doubt about the fracture; David had X rays to prove it. Still, Irene had come away with the memory of a pact between them, a secret that told her how unique their understanding was. Mary Jennifer returned to New York for the school term at Dalton. But Jennifer stayed in Los Angeles for a while.

David found other company in a series of bright, attractive young women for whom he was something like a mentor. One was Pat Newcomb, a publicist in the movie business. Another was the film critic and novelist Renata Adler. As Danny observed it, Renata was like a young, rather more intellectual Irene. "He mentioned not once," said Danny, "but five times, how this would be a wonderful wife for *me*. Every time he had one evening with her, he wanted another. He couldn't get enough of her mind, her companionship. But he kept saying, 'She should be going out with you, not me.' "

The third friendship was the most touching and important, and the one in which the producer believed he had a real unknown to conjure with. Yvette Curran was in her midtwenties, living in Queens with her husband and two young children. She was half French, half Hungarian, and she had been born and raised in Egypt before coming to America with her soldier husband. She was dark, beautiful, and she had a mysterious accent.

She was a fan. Beginning with *Gone With the Wind*, she had made fifty albums of stills, pictures, and cuttings from the career of David Selznick. She had written to his office in Los Angeles earlier, saying she had the

*Yvette Curran—photo by
D.O.S.*

albums and that she proposed leaving them to Selznick in her will. The
letter reached Danny while David was in France in the summer of 1964.

When David returned to New York, Danny mentioned this fan in
Queens. The mention of her will gave David the impression she must be
elderly. He was also nervous of meeting such devotion, in case he proved a
disappointment. But one day in September 1964 he called the telephone
number in Queens that Danny had given him, and he invited Mrs. Curran
to the Waldorf.

The young woman knocked at the door and fell in love: "He was
wearing a canary-yellow silk shirt and brown shoes. With white hair and
rosy cheeks. He was gorgeous, a god! He spoke in stereophonic sound."

They got on—it was not hard. He told her things the way a stranger
can be told: he had a year to live; Jennifer was not there; he was lonely; there
was his ex-wife, a few blocks away—he did enjoy seeing her. Yvette came
over to the hotel whenever she could. They went to the World's Fair,
though she felt he was wary of being seen. For her birthday, in November,
he gave her a gold charm bracelet in the form of a paged book. It had
engravings of Rhett and Scarlett and, on one page, "Produced by David O.
Selznick." But Yvette's husband grew uneasy at all the visits, and by the end
of the year, the relationship broke up.

David also made short trips to Atlantic City and Chicago, with Mary
Jennifer living like Eloise at the Waldorf. David was going through the
motions of looking for projects for Jennifer, but he was more concerned to
rationalize the terrible weekly deficit. For the year 1964, the Selznicks earned
$113,221. But their expenses against income were over $150,000, of which
nearly $99,000 went on interest or state taxes and loans taken out on the
insurance.

Mary Jennifer at the
St. Regis Hotel

Christmas was spent at the Waldorf, and on the twenty-sixth, David, Jennifer, and Mary Jennifer returned to Los Angeles. On January 6, David and his daughter flew back to New York and moved into the Waldorf once more. He telephoned Yvette, and again she took the subway into the city to see him. He was weak, and he slept for six hours while she sat beside him. She hated Jennifer for not being there. When David woke he said, "I wanted to wake up and see you."

Irene came to see David at the hotel on January 14 as he was still not well enough to go out. Because the father was not now always able to take Mary Jennifer out on weekends, Danny was enlisted as an "uncle." But Danny's own life was being interfered with, so Irene decided he should be told the truth. David chose this time to ask Irene to help him get a new cardiologist—Dr. Isadore Rosenfeld—in case any word of his condition should get back by way of Connie Guion to the Paleys. He did not want Bill depressed—Irene believed—but David was also eager to preserve whatever professional prospects there might be left.

He had found a play for Jennifer: *The Goddess on the Couch*, by Patricia Joudry, about a psychiatrist and his wife. He had been working on it for several months with the author. At the outset, he was sure it would make it all the way to New York so that they could be "heavy participants in the profits."

Irene called Danny and said, "He's got this cockamamie thing he's doing with Jennifer. If you really want to help him—he *did* have this attack; well, it was a little more serious than you've been told. I told him he should let somebody take it over, and he says he doesn't trust anybody, unless it's you."

Danny was amazed: "*You* want me to do this?" he asked his mother. "Take up this play for Jennifer?"

She said, "It's for your father—not for her."

Danny agreed on the condition that David would not interfere; it was for the son to get a director, do the casting, see to the rewrites, and handle the actress. David said, of course, but he had always said of course.

Danny hired Windsor Lewis to direct and Barry Morse for the male lead. He worked on the text with Patricia Joudry, and he had the title changed to *The Man with the Perfect Wife*. The rehearsals were to be in New York, and the play had a couple of engagements in Florida for March.

David and Mary Jennifer flew back to Los Angeles on February 19 and a few days later the young actor and photographer Dennis Hopper took pictures of Mary Jennifer on the beach. Mother and daughter flew to New York on February 28 for the play rehearsals.

Danny enjoyed the work and believed it was going well. But his stepmother was on the phone to his father every night, and soon the telegrams to Danny began to arrive, building her remarks into onslaughts. They were the same old telegrams, and they grew worse and worse. Danny went to Jennifer and begged her to stop talking to David. She could only say, "He gets things out of me. I don't even know that I'm feeling them until I tell him."

By March 15 Jennifer was in Florida for the play. David remained in Los Angeles, and on March 7 he attended a banquet given by the Screen Producers Guild for Alfred Hitchcock. As one of the hosts of the tribute, he made a speech at the Beverly Hilton Hotel that began as a lively attack on Hollywood's current methods. But he wandered and repeated himself, and some felt he was old and exhausted when he sat down.

He flew to New York on March 23, and a few days later he went down to Miami to see the play at the Royal Poinciana Playhouse. Danny took the occasion to sit down with David. "I'm going to ask you to read something," he told his father.

Danny gave him one of the worst cables from the rehearsal period. It was three pages, single-spaced. "Read that," he asked. "I'm sure you haven't read it before."

David read and realized, "Boy, it's really rough!"

"Can you imagine being at the receiving end?" asked Danny.

"Honestly," said David, "I should have reread it before I sent it. Because it was my son—"

"No," Danny interrupted. "It's terrible for anyone."

"Well, I'm really sorry," said David. "I just didn't know what this read like."

Then again on April 9, David flew back to Florida with Mary Jennifer to see the close of the production at the Coconut Grove Playhouse. The local reviews were cheery, but there was no question of the play going on to New York. Jennifer had been paid $3,277 for the production—but $6,403 had been spent on her hairdresser.

After the play, on April 12, David, Jennifer, Mary Jennifer, and Danny went to Nassau and Jamaica for a few days. Danny had several long talks with his father. They went all the way back to Jean Arthur and forward to the insurance arrangements he had made for Jennifer and Mary Jennifer. But he admitted he had had to cash in the policies that had Danny and Jeffrey as beneficiaries. In Danny's estimate, Jennifer still had little sense of how ill David was. Danny believed his father was ready to go, though he was cheerful still and often funny. As David went back over his life, Danny thought he saw a pattern:

> First you were under your mother's control, then you were under Irene's control, then Jennifer, and now Mary Jennifer has you tied up.

"It's true," said David. "It's true." Rueful and ecstatic, and ready for more if he had the chance.

On May 2, Jennifer flew back to L.A., leaving David and Mary Jennifer at the Waldorf. Yvette reappeared: she gave him a cashmere sweater for his sixty-third birthday. David dined with Irene on May 5, five days before the birthday. But he had a problem to raise with her. For the coming weekend he had been invited by the Paleys to Kiluna. He wanted to go, but he knew "his" room there was on the third floor and he was not sure he could handle all the stairs without having Bill see his condition. Irene worked out a plan whereby he could cunningly find diversions on the landings and so arrange his weekend that he had to go upstairs only the one time, to bed on the Saturday night. It worked. Paley never found out.

The business situation was just as grim and just as much in need of cunning show. David kept talking to people: he was airing out projects for Jennifer with Ross Hunter at Universal, especially the life of Sarah Bernhardt. And he was always trying to grasp the hectic figures of his own business:

> I suppose I am the only individual in the world [he told Beaman], certainly the only one who spends this amount of money, who does not know what he is spending weekly. . . . There can be little question but that my illness, and the unfortunate possible permanent effects on my health, have been occasioned by tensions growing out of financial worry.

On May 17, 21, and 23, David had dinner with Irene and Danny. Also, in May, he went with Irene to a dinner party given by Arthur and Leonora

Hornblow. During the course of the meal, he had to leave the table and go to a bedroom to lie down. Irene called the cardiologist, and Mrs. Hornblow sat with David. "It's all right, Bub," he told her when he saw her distress, "it's not so much fun anymore." The attack passed.

On May 25, from the Waldorf, David wrote to Howard. His brother was again talking about moving: Arizona had been mentioned, but that was too hot in summer, and thus Howard's thoughts had turned to Los Angeles. So David wrote in weary reproach:

> Dear Howie, I am not feeling too well these days (although you should not worry about it) and I am extraordinarily deluged with problems. Therefore, I must ask you to please, please not put me through all this again there is just not the money available to have you move about at will and at whim. . . . Keep your fingers crossed, not only for yourself, but for me, since I am going through rather a rugged period. Please know always that I have your best interests at heart, and that I want you to be well and happy.

Jennifer came to New York from May 27 to June 7.

On June 8, David and Irene had dinner together: he was flying back to Los Angeles the next day with Mary Jennifer. After dinner, they talked and then David stretched the evening out by hiring a horse and carriage.

David

"We rode through the park a few times and then endlessly up and down Fifth Avenue. Our conversation was as aimless as our route. It got very late. There was a certain poignancy in his inability to say goodbye. I'm not sure I could have managed it if he had said it."

David and Mary Jennifer flew west on June 9. Danny drove out to the airport with them, and David said, "We should really go and see Howard sometime."

David kept up the pattern of calls. On Monday, June 14, he had lunch with Beaman, and that evening at the house he saw *The Yellow Rolls-Royce.* On the fifteenth, he was making calls for a school for Mary Jennifer. The Jourdans came to the house for dinner. On the sixteenth he saw the French musical *The Umbrellas of Cherbourg,* and he ran *Zebra in the Kitchen* for Mary Jennifer. But he was too tired to stay up for *The Pumpkin Eater.* On the seventeenth he called Howard in Asheville and he was reading Betty Friedan's *The Feminine Mystique.* He saw Sam Goldwyn and began to consider a book of his memos. On the eighteenth, the Friday, he called a doctor about having Mary Jennifer's tonsils out, and he went to Barry Brannen's office at 3:00 p.m. to be deposed again in another coming case over foreign assets.

The weekend was long; he did nothing on the Monday. That evening, David and Jennifer had a quiet dinner at home with Robert Walker, Jr.'s wife, Ellie, and a friend of hers, Saul Rifkin, a young actor who had been welcomed into the Selznick circle. Saul interested David especially because he was a devout Orthodox Jew.

After dinner, David had a creme de menthe frappe and he began dozing. There was a simmering, snoring noise. Jennifer told Saul she loved the sound, for it made her feel comfortable and secure.

Then David stirred, and he asked Saul to come into his study for a talk. They sat down together beneath the Brackman "Portrait of Jennie." David said he had been wondering about Judaism and he asked Saul if he could perhaps talk to Mary Jennifer. The young man felt that David was awkward or ignorant on the subject. "There was not much energy in him," said Rifkin, "but he was so intelligent, very elegant and gentle, sweet and loving. I was to do what I could to let Mary Jennifer know what it was to be a Jew."

At noon on Tuesday, June 22, he was back in Brannen's office to continue the deposition and to deal with a possible sale of movies to Metromedia. He was talking, on his feet, and then he stopped and said, "Mind if I sit down?"

The fatal heart attack struck at about 12:30 p.m. Brannen sent for an ambulance and telephoned Jennifer. She was at Cedars-Sinai Hospital at 1:00 when the ambulance arrived. At 2:22 p.m. David Selznick died.

At the Pierre Hotel, the phone rang in Irene's apartment. It was Jock, at the *Herald-Tribune* office. There was something coming over the wire about David being in the hospital. Then Jock called again to say it was official.

"Do I go to the funeral?" he wanted to know.

"Why are you asking me?"

"Who should I ask?"

"There's only one person to ask. Yourself."

Jock wanted Irene to go with him and Bill. But she was against it.

Danny came to the Pierre, and together they called Jeffrey in France.

Then Paley called. "It's been overdue," Irene told him, and he was startled, put out, for he had never guessed. There was a party at "21" that evening, a birthday party for Babe Paley's daughter. Bill said Irene should go.

When he came to collect her he said he'd called Jennifer and she had not known about the heart problem.

"Who knows better?" he'd challenged her. "You or his widow?"

"Let it go," said Irene.

But Paley was irked and so upset he needed some diversion. Connie Guion was at the party, and she said this had been David's first heart attack. Irene replied that the doctor was covering for Jennifer. So all night at "21" Paley sat next to her but would not talk to her. Knowledge was the final power and intimacy.

The Hornblows were elsewhere in town, at the opening of *Kismet*. They met Olivia de Havilland there, and she said, "Isn't it awful about David?" So the Hornblows went straight to the Pierre and were taken aback to find that Irene knew and had gone out anyway.

Twenty-five years later, Irene said, "I went to the party because I didn't want to stay at home and blow my brains out."

When she got back to the Pierre it was one in the morning and *The New York Times* was out. David had got it right. There he was on the front page, in a recent picture, white-haired and grinning: "David O. Selznick, 63, Producer of 'Gone With the Wind' Dies." In the immediately adjacent story there was word that the House of Representatives had passed legislation requiring that cigarette packets carry a warning that smoking may be hazardous to health.

On the night of the twenty-second, Danny flew to Los Angeles. By the time he reached Tower Grove, it was dawn on the twenty-third and Jennifer was asleep on the couch. They talked about the funeral.

"Your mother must come."

"Jennifer, I don't think she's intending to."

"Oh no, she's as important a part of his life as I was. The two Mrs. Selznicks should be there together. Let's call her."

They got through to the Pierre, and Danny was on the other extension. Jennifer made her request, and Irene said, "It's very kind of you, Jennifer, but I really think I am best represented by my sons."

Danny was there when Mary Jennifer woke up. He was ready to talk to her. But the little girl said, "Would you mind if I don't really feel like talking now." Danny said that was fine. He spent several hours on the phone before he saw Mary Jennifer again.

"Can we talk now?" he wondered.

"Sure, what do you want to talk about?"

"Is there anything you want to say?"

"No."

He felt his half sister was closed off. "I knew it would be devastating because she'd seen him morning, noon, and night. He'd never prepared her for living without him. And I knew that the worst was ahead for her."

The marionette was gone, but the women who had worked the strings for so long—the manipulators?—were left, and every one of them felt cut adrift.

THE FUNERAL of David O. Selznick was held in the Church of the Recessional at Forest Lawn in Los Angeles on Friday, June 25. It took place in the Christian church because the 200 people present were too many for the Jewish temple. Rabbi Max N. Nussbaum led the service, and there were four speakers. In his will, David had ordered no ceremony, but no one believed he meant it.

Joseph Cotten read a piece he had composed himself. Cary Grant read a tribute written by Bill Paley. It said, "The one word that fits David Selznick better than any other is extravagance. He was extravagant in every way in his generosity, friendship, attention to those who sought him out for advice and guidance and his love for those he loved." George Cukor read a piece contributed by Truman Capote. And Katharine Hepburn read from Rudyard Kipling's "If." No one remarked on it, but Hepburn had never been close to David. She was speaking because Irene had asked her.

Among the letters Jennifer received there was one from Jock Whitney, who said:

> He and I have found our lives lately to be in rather different directions, but my affection and admiration travelled with him always. Our earlier lives together were full of fun—some fury, too—but all of it resulting in an unbreakable weld.
>
> I have never loved any man more—nor ever will.

Jock wrote to Irene, too, as he set out for the funeral: "I will be thinking of you—the whole time of this sad journey—of the fantastic, unselfish love you have offered dear David all these many years. If he truly did have two wives you were the helpmeet—without you he would have always been lost. I too, my one friend."

Not long thereafter, there was a meeting in Morgan Maree's office attended by Jennifer, Jeffrey, and Danny, as well as Barry Brannen. The will was explained: Jennifer was the chief heir. Jeffrey and Danny received a few mementos and the great collection of their father's archive—papers, scripts, designs, screen tests, bills, poems, and memos. Irene was to have the landscape painting by George Bellows, the one that had started their collection. There were six life insurance policies paid up that realized $129,438. But Maree then pointed out that no one had much to hope for immediately: the estate was in the red by about three quarters of a million dollars.

Those debts and more that developed were eventually settled when Maree and Brannen sold off all rights in twenty-four pictures to ABC for $1.75 million. When everything was done and liquidated, Jennifer had a little under a million dollars from the estate of David O. Selznick.

JENNIFER MADE a bad film, *The Idol*, that was released in 1966. Under the direction of Lee Strasberg, she played at last in *The Country Girl* on stage in New York. The reviews for both shows were dismal.

On November 9, 1967, the actor Charles Bickford died in Los Angeles. He had played with Jennifer in *The Song of Bernadette* and *Duel in the Sun*; he had worked for David, earlier, in *No Other Woman*, and he had played Oliver Niles in George Cukor's *A Star is Born*. On the same day, Jennifer was found unconscious in the surf at Point Dume in Malibu. This was after a telephone call to her doctor in which she said she had taken some sleeping pills and was going to take more.

She recovered, and at some time in the next few years she made a bonfire of all the letters she had had from David. In 1971, she met the industrialist Norton Simon. They were married a little over three weeks later, on a boat off the coast of England. Mary Jennifer Selznick, who was then sixteen, learned of the marriage in the newspapers.

In 1974, Jennifer appeared in *The Towering Inferno*, in which her character dies in a fall from the burning building.

Mary Jennifer took acting lessons with Uta Hagen and underwent extensive psychoanalysis. She had an abortion, she attempted suicide, and she was in the locked facility of a psychiatric ward. She went to live in Pasadena, and members of her family were ordered not to see her. Her psychotherapist went away for a month, and on May 11, 1976 (two days after Mother's Day and one day after what would have been David's seventy-fourth birthday), Mary Jennifer threw herself from the twenty-second floor of 10701 Wilshire Boulevard, the tallest building in Westwood and a land-mark visible from her therapist's office.

HOWARD SELZNICK lived fifteen years longer than David. He died in 1980, at the age of eighty-two. He lived then in Los Angeles under financial care organized by Berman Swarttz and Danny.

By then, Howard's older daughter, Ruth, was dead. She committed suicide in 1968, soon after the plane crash in which her son, Steven Swarttz, died. Steven and his cousin Myron had been flying over the Sierras in a small plane on the way to Las Vegas. In the same crash, Myron lost a leg. Myron's mother, and Ruth's younger sister, Florence, was by then, and is still, in an institution in Pasadena.

ON MARCH 28, 1989, Myron Selznick's daughter, Joan, was found dead in her small house on top of the cliffs at Laguna Beach in California. She was fifty-eight, she lived alone, and it was believed that she had not been out of the house in over a decade. On the ground floor of the house there was trash so deep it came up to thigh level: it consisted of papers, books, unopened mail, diaries, checks, clothes, old food, vodka bottles, pictures, photographs, and childhood toys. In an upstairs room she kept the still tidy files of the Myron Selznick Agency.

This seeming derelict died with an estate of which the most significant items were:

> two houses in Laguna Beach
>
> a farm in Michigan
>
> a ranch, a house, and two beach lots in Hawaii
>
> Hill Haven, Myron's old house at Lake Arrowhead
>
> the plot on Wilshire Boulevard where Myron's office had once stood, now leased to Neiman Marcus
>
> and her father's interest—6.77 percent—in *Gone With the Wind*

JEFFREY AND JANINE SELZNICK were divorced in 1969. By then, Jeffrey had produced one film in France, *La Longue marche*, in 1966, directed by Alexandre Astruc.

Danny was associate producer on *Targets*, the first film directed by Peter Bogdanovich, in 1968.

Jeffrey was married again, to Anne Wace, in 1971. He lived for some time in England and Jamaica while working in agriculture and the clothes business. He and Anne were divorced in 1978, and Jeffrey returned to live in America. Danny married Joan Keller in 1972. He made several films for television and was executive director of the Louis B. Mayer Foundation from 1980 to 1984. In 1988, Jeffrey became president of the Foundation.

In 1981, Jeffrey and Danny dealt their father's archive to the Harry Ransom Humanities Research Center at the University of Texas in Austin.

In 1989, together they produced a two-hour documentary, *The Making of a Legend: Gone With the Wind*, which played on Ted Turner's new television channel, TNT. In the same year, its fiftieth anniversary, *Gone With the Wind* was rereleased in a restored print. At that time, A. D. Murphy of *Variety* estimated that the film had achieved rentals of $841 million (in 1987 dollars).

Danny and Joan Keller were divorced in 1985. In 1989, Danny married Susan Dryfoos. In 1987, Jeffrey had married Barbara Smalley. Neither Jeffrey nor Danny has had children.

IRENE did not marry again. She no longer produced for the stage after a disappointing production of Graham Greene's *The Complaisant Lover* in 1961. She lived in her apartment at the Pierre Hotel—1007—with the Matisse, the Vuillard, the Bellows, and the other pictures. She grew lonely and sometimes bitter—yet she could be brilliant, beguiling, stealthy, and manipulative

*Irene Mayer Selznick,
early 1980s*

company still, in person or over the phone. Her feelings about David, till the end, were as helplessly mixed as his had always been about anything important. She died soon after dawn on October 10, 1990, in 1007; she was eighty-three.

The meetings I had with Irene occurred when she was in the age range of seventy-eight to eighty-three—so none of them, allowing for meals, diversions, and alarums, lasted longer than twelve hours. No matter her age and infirmities, she was one of the strongest, most compelling, tyrannical, theatrical, and entertaining people I have ever known. "Of course," she said, always alert to grievance, "I won't be there to read the damn book."

AND DAVID? Near the end, he had admitted to other people that being him wasn't the same old fun anymore. He was ready to get off and not too afraid to die. Thank God it was quick—he would have been an invalid who sent schools of nurses to their graves. But he was sad and angry to think the picture business was dying, too. For he never saw that his kind of movie was just a moment in our weather, and he did not appreciate how far his moment had changed the climate.

He cringed at his obvious obituary, yet he guessed he was saved by it, and I suspect that till the end *Gone With the Wind*, or the thought of it, moved him to tears. For it was with that film that his unique turmoil had been vindicated. The picture shows no sign of fading. As years pass, it comes to represent the spirit of a time and its culture. *GWTW* stands for Hollywood and for a large part of being American.

The Selznicks were larger than life . . . or an alternative to it? David O. vibrated, like a thrilled violin note, somewhere between the urge to escape and the hope of rescue. He was always hurrying on in his search for liberty, the pursuit of happiness, and the dream of retained childhood. He was, at times, a fool, a coward, a liar, a scoundrel, and a bore—he was just like us. Yet he was able to amaze people, to move them, to stir them up. He was moist with the readiness to love and be loved, even if there was much confusion as to whether he sought fulfillment in life or in his show. And in that respect, I think, he was as we would all want to be—at least for some of the time. He was a character, and he might have been better off in a book. I have done my best to put him there.

In the attempt, I came to love him and some of those he loved. But I would be afraid to be them. For these were fearful people—terrorists and terrified—swept along by show business, so seldom able to take hold of life. They were their own creation, figments of their own imaginations. How tempting it would be to think that delusion is gone, along with the old Hollywood. But show business is a light of our life now, and David was a pioneer of that enthralled doubt no longer sure whether it is alive or a story being told.

Still, Hollywood is not the same. It is no longer as romantic about itself: there is nothing as golden in America as the first age; perhaps that is why we are so drawn to starting again. A book on David that has the records risks showing the many, untidy betrayals of romance. David's life may seem sad. But he seldom saw it that way, and when there were moments of sadness, or worse, he made them highlights in a story. He was of an emotional, daydreaming size that does not fit in today's meaner, crouched Hollywood.

At his death, some saw how great the loss was. Katharine Hepburn wrote to Irene about her status as survivor and the world's chance to see what an age had passed: "the big individual driving forces—extraordinary people—in this age they seem a kind of fairy tale—& yet you knew it all—but you—somehow—were grown up enough to grow up—you felt the romance but were not entirely swept in with it—like a curious town crier."

Bill Paley's eulogy looked forward, to heaven, where David was probably already running the show—"and if I know my man, I am sure he will manage to get some of us in who wouldn't make it otherwise—and he will be grinning, and he will be full of joy and laughter, and he will tell us what to do, and he will be David."

Should heaven be so vulnerable to dictators? Could any well-run establishment endure David's changes of mind? Yet what hotel would not want to hire his smile and its encouragement? He had such hope. In *Beat the Devil*, amid mounting disorder, Humphrey Bogart's Billy Dannreuther says, "It's my expectations that hold me together." David lacked the irony and the insight—he *was* artfully excluded from *Beat the Devil*. But he was kept alive by the things he longed to see, and that is a key to showmanship. For anyone with serious and inspired designs on an audience must begin with himself.

ACKNOWLEDGMENTS

When Daniel Selznick first approached me about writing this book, in February 1986, his one large proviso was that I had to meet, and be approved by, his brother, Jeffrey. As time passed, I developed a remarkable relationship with the two brothers. We became good friends; they claimed at various times that I was almost part of the family, knowing how mixed a blessing that could be. As they coproduced a full-length documentary film, *The Making of a Legend: Gone With the Wind*, for Turner Entertainment, they asked me to write its script. We worked together on the film. They introduced me to the David O. Selznick Archive at the University of Texas at Austin and gave me privileged access to its materials. They talked to me over the years about their father and their family: the transcript of our formal interviews runs to over 400 single-spaced pages. But there were so many other occasions when the talk was more casual or intimate, over the phone, at dinner, in a car, or while doing something else. In addition, they opened every door they could in their parents' world, suggesting interviews, making introductions, and generally supporting the project.

We had an early agreement that gave them no rights or interest in the book and no say in its opinions or conclusions. Their only requirement was to see the text before it was published and to comment on matters of fact. They have done that, conscientiously and to the book's great advantage. The book was often painful or surprising for them; it sometimes conflicted with what they had been raised to believe. Still, they have never sought to influence me unfairly, and they have always insisted that the point of view be mine—or the reader's.

Yet they are both Selznick and Mayer enough to feel involved, proprietorial, and *right*. So I am the more grateful to them for honoring our agreement so faithfully. In return, I hope I have been of some use to them in recounting a story that was frequently beset by myth, denial, and evasion as they grew up. For in large part they gave me not just their father's life to write, but their own.

Their mother, Irene Mayer Selznick, was someone I had known a little since 1983. When I mentioned the possibility of the book to her, her first response was that it was impossible. She talked at length about this, and as she went on more and more came out about the past. Then she decided it was really not up to her, that she would neither approve nor disapprove the book, but that she did have some confidence in the care I would take. For four years, this debate went on: she made amazing confessions, yet never quite admitted what she was doing. She introduced me to several of her oldest friends and gave them the nod to talk. She also gave me many papers that she had kept from the past. These were to use in the book and to be added to the Austin collection when that work was done. And we talked—at the Pierre, on sudden dinner excursions, over the phone. Hours and years of it, unrecorded, for she was alarmed at the thought of others hearing what she said. So I took notes.

Irene was not quite like her sons. Her umbrella of saying neither yes nor no was a shadow in which every possible influence could be exerted. I think it was that game which gave her most pleasure. Irene's memory was not as good as she believed—neither was her candor as complete. She could say very little without freeing the actress and spellbinder that nature had made of her. There are many matters still unanswered in my mind—which was what she intended. I may have been seduced. I know I loved her, and miss her. But the reader must judge how she appears and how reliable she was. Whatever the reader's conclusion, Irene was vital in shaping my enquiry.

This needs all the more to be stressed in that Jennifer Jones, David's second wife, declined to be a part of the process. Daniel asked her on my behalf. Then I made repeated requests. I regret that the answer was always no, and I still do not understand why. I hope that one day Jennifer Jones will find a way to tell her side of the story. And I hope that, despite her decision, this book has been fair to her.

David Selznick's business and personal papers went to the Harry Ransom Humanities Research Center at the University of Texas in Austin in 1981. Jeffrey Selznick was with me the first time I faced the collection—three million items, 57,000 pounds of paper, some 6,000 Hollinger boxes—and he still teases me about my mixed look of delight and terror. The collection is vast, sprawling, and neurotic: it is a mirror of David Selznick. Dr. Decherd Turner, director of the Ransom Center, could not have been more hospitable or friendly to my project. When he was succeeded by Dr. Thomas Staley, I enjoyed the same great benefits of access and service from his staff. In the last few years, Tom Staley has begun the challenging task of cataloguing the collection. At present, this work is not yet complete. But I would encourage other writers and scholars to go to the Selznick Archive. It is so rich and so detailed that nearly every aspect of Hollywood history can be pursued there. Above all, the archive is a unique record of a company's business history. This is laid out as obsessively as the details of David's gambling and the disastrous profusion of his memos. Rudy Behlmer's wonderful selection, published as *Memo from David O. Selznick* in 1972, employed only a tiny selection. Moreover, it emphasized the trait of decisiveness in David, whereas the full weight of the memos reveals a less certain and more beleaguered man, compelled sometimes to take decisions. I have used David's words wherever possible, while trying to do the one thing in life no one managed—keep him brief. I can only say that much, much more remains. After five years with David, I still find it hard to believe that one man dictated so much.

My most valued ally at Austin has been Dr. Charles Bell, for several years now the person in charge of the Ransom Center's film collection. No one could have been more resourceful, encouraging, amusing, or so consistent a supporter of my venture. I owe him more than these thanks can begin to suggest. The Ransom Center is fortunate in having him.

There are other people at the center who deserve my warmest thanks: Roy Flukinger, Roberta Cox, Ray Daum, Prentiss Moore, Jamie Duke, Beverly Deutsch, and Pat Bassinger. In addition, a group of students at the University of Texas were hired through the agency of Turner Entertainment to do research work on *Gone With the Wind*. Their work was of such a high order as reflects well on the Radio-Television-Film department at Austin. They were Steve Lee, Jeff Sconce, Shannon Kelly, Eric Schaefer, and Mary Mallory, and I thank them all.

As my own work advanced, Mary Mallory became an essential help to my son Mathew, who spent six months in Austin doing research for me. Mathew did pioneering work in mapping out the range of the collection and examining the personal material. No part of this entire project was more valuable to this author than the chance to work with his son. When Mathew moved on, to Oxford and his Ph.D., Mary Mallory took over the work in Austin. This overlapped usefully with her own M.A. thesis on Myron Selznick (research of great value). Mary has been an indefatigable assistant in this work. No one has ever known the Austin collection better, and no one has a greater appetite for any detail of Selznick history. I could not have done this book without her and Mathew.

There are other archives and collections that have helped. Mrs. Betsey Whitney allowed me to see some of her late husband's business papers, which were then in storage at Morgan's of Manhattan. Dr. Howard Gotlieb and his staff helped me with the Irene Selznick papers at the Mugar Library, Boston University. I was able to examine the George Cukor papers and other materials at the Academy of Motion Picture Arts and Sciences Library in Los Angeles, and I am especially grateful to Howard Prouty. The Turner organization allowed me to see the Metro-Goldwyn-Mayer papers that it has. I was able to use the Sidney Howard papers at the Bancroft Library, University of California at Berkeley. And I was given very special access to the papers of Myron Selznick, which were part of the disputed estate of his daughter, Joan. That permission was granted by the several heirs to the estate and made possible by the Trustee Department of the Bank of California at Newport Beach, where I was especially helped by Kathy Knight and Roxanne Haddon.

Next, I want to thank the people who agreed to be interviewed for this book. A few of the conversations were conducted by correspondence or over the phone, but the great majority were done in person, and many called for several sessions. It is a tribute to David Selznick that so many of these witnesses prepared so carefully. Nearly all of them were struck that David *deserved* to be talked about. It is hard to raise one group of witnesses above another, for everyone contributed in so many different ways. Still, there were a few whose recollections were indispensable.

Niven Busch was not just my first interview; he went farther back with David than nearly anyone, he was my neighbor in San Francisco, and a friend who urged me on in so many ways. I would also give special thanks to Leonora Hornblow; Marcella Rabwin, who was close to David in his great days and is still so alert and cheerful that one knows the closeness helped those days; Kay Brown; Anita Colby, who trusted me with so much and who loaned me her own Selznick files; Lady Nancy Keith; Jenia Reissar; Dorothy Hirshon; Louis and Quique Jourdan; Fay Wray; Katharine Hepburn, not just for her own talk, but for taking me to see Laura Harding.

In addition, my thanks go to Edward Anhalt, Charles Bennett, Max Bercutt, Mary Brian, Douglas Brunger, Dorothy Colodny, Stanley Cortez, Yvette Curran, Cyril Cusack, Frank Davis, Rena Davis, Olivia de Havilland, Peter De Rome, Dominick Dunne, William Erickson, Arthur Fellows, Rhonda Fleming, Joan Fontaine, Maxine Graybill, Nancy Green, Anne Greenberg, Anne "Cookie" Grossman, Lois Hamby, Aljean Harmetz, Mary Rechner Hawk, Al Hirschfeld, Victor Hoare, John Houseman, Josephine Hutchinson, Frances Inglis, Sam Jaffe, Bruce Jeffer, Evelyn Keyes, Ring Lardner, Jr., Silvia Lardner, Sunny Lash, Petter Lindstrom, Anne MacNamara, Guy Madison, Joseph L. Mankiewicz, Sam Marx, Marjorie McDougall, Dorothy McGuire, Butterfly McQueen, Winston Miller, Ivan Moffat, Jess Morgan, Oswald Morris, Elsa Neuberger, Melissa Oshier, William S. Paley, Tina

Pine, Michael Powell, Aileen Pringle, Stephen Randall, Maurice Rapf, Ron Rifkin, Wells Root, Ann Rutherford, Arthur Sachs, Budd Schulberg, Milton Selznick, Stephen Selznick, Judy Shepherd, Allan Shumofsky, Lionel Stander, Berman Swartz, Daniel Taradash, James Toback, Ann Todd, Ben Unger, Ellie Wood Walker, Henry Weinstein, Barbara Windom, Jerry Young, Loretta Young.

I owe special thanks to Ron Haver, who loaned me several tapes of interviews he had made for his 1980 book, *David O. Selznick's Hollywood*—so beautiful a work that the qualities of its text are sometimes unfairly overlooked. Leonard Leff passed on material he had gathered in researching his excellent *Hitchcock & Selznick*. That book helped me in another way: it is so good on the films the two men made that I felt able to save a little space.

There were other writers in the area of Hollywood biography, all devoted to research, who were kind enough to share some thoughts: Matthew Bernstein (who is doing Walter Wanger), David Stenn (Jean Harlow), Todd McCarthy (Howard Hawks), Charles Higham (Louis B. Mayer), Steven Aronson (Leland Hayward), and, above all, Pat McGilligan (George Cukor) and Steven Bach (Marlene Dietrich).

I am grateful to Mary Ann DiNapoli for research in Brooklyn and New York; to Keith Besonen for Los Angeles; to Antonette Burroughs for Cleveland; to David Sleasman of the Curtis Theatre Collection, University of Pittsburgh; to Dr. Paul McHugh and Nancy McCall of the Medical Archives Committee at the Johns Hopkins Medical Institutions. Peter Smith and Abigail Franklin helped me with enquiries at Columbia University. I am also grateful to the staff of the Columbia Oral History Project.

Bob Gottlieb was always a good friend to this project, nursing my friendship with Irene Selznick, drawing my attention to some valuable things in her papers and then reading the typescript with special care and insight. Over the years I was fortunate to receive, variously, hospitality, help, and advice from the following: George Trescher, Tom Luddy, Harry and Mary Jane Ufland, Thelma Schoonmaker, Pat McGilligan, Charles Combs, Shelley Wanger, Barbara Kohn, Judy Cameron, Richard and Mary Corliss, Richard Jameson and Kathleen Murphy, Virginia Campbell, Lee Goerner, Melanie Jackson, and Ken Conner, whose reading of the work in progress was invaluable.

Tom Rosenthal of André Deutsch was the publisher who did most to set this book up. He handled the contract with the Selznick brothers and then brought Alfred A. Knopf in as American publisher. Throughout, he was a wise, strong friend, enormously generous in his response to the book itself and very skilled in his dealings. Laura Morris, also at Deutsch, read the book with great insight and offered many helpful suggestions. She was a loyal friend always. In America, Sonny Mehta's belief in the book was such that he and his wife, Gita, offered superb hospitality and company whenever I was in New York. Jonathan Segal edited the book at Knopf and has my lasting admiration and respect. I could go on but, as he says, the book is long already. His assistant, Ida Giragossian, and the excellent copy editor, Jeffrey Smith, also have my gratitude.

There are two people left: Lorraine Latorraca typed the book many times, swiftly, correctly, and often with piercing ingenuity, for the author's handwriting is never good and often gestural. Lorraine also did a great deal of research, library checking, transcribing, and newspaper hunting. I came to rely on her so much, I hope I didn't take her for granted.

My wife, Lucy, entered into the Selznick family with me and responded with humor, stoicism, love, forgiveness, and—at just the right times—belief, skepticism, disbelief, and enthusiasm. She was the book's first and best reader. She also—at just the right time— enlarged our own family, with Nicholas, nicely offsetting the influence of the Selznicks.

Agee, James. *Agee on Film.* Boston: Beacon Press, 1958.

Aherne, Brian. *A Proper Job.* Boston: Houghton Mifflin, 1969.

Allen, Jane. *I Lost My Girlish Laughter.* New York: Random House, 1938.

Bagnold, Enid. *Autobiography.* Boston: Little, Brown, 1969.

Balio, Tino. *United Artists.* Madison, Wis.: University of Wisconsin Press, 1976.

Beaton, Cecil. *The Wandering Years: Diaries: 1922–1939.* Boston: Little, Brown, 1961.

Behlmer, Rudy, ed. *Memo from David O. Selznick.* New York: Viking, 1972.

————. *Inside Warner Bros. (1935–1951).* New York: Viking, 1985.

Berg, A. Scott. *Goldwyn.* New York: Alfred A. Knopf, 1989.

Bergman, Ingrid, and Burgess, Alan. *Ingrid Bergman: My Story.* New York: Delacorte, 1980.

Bishop, Jim. *The Mark Hellinger Story.* New York: Appleton-Century-Crofts, 1952.

Black, Shirley Temple. *Child Star.* New York: McGraw Hill, 1988.

Bosworth, Patricia. *Montgomery Clift.* New York: Harcourt Brace Jovanovich, 1978.

Brownlow, Kevin. *Behind the Mask of Innocence.* New York: Alfred A. Knopf, 1990.

Busch, Niven. *Duel in the Sun.* New York: Morrow, 1944.

Callow, Simon. *Charles Laughton: A Difficult Actor.* New York: Grove Press, 1987.

Cameron, Judy, and Christman, Paul J. *The Art of Gone With the Wind.* New York: Prentice-Hall, 1989.

Capra, Frank. *The Name Above the Title.* New York: Macmillan, 1971.

Cotten, Joseph. *Vanity Will Get You Somewhere.* San Francisco: Mercury House, 1987.

Crowther, Bosley. *Hollywood Rajah: The Life and Times of Louis B. Mayer.* New York: Holt, Rinehart and Winston, 1960.

Davis, Bette. *The Lonely Life.* New York: Putnam, 1962.

Du Maurier, Daphne. *Rebecca.* New York: Doubleday, 1938.

Durgnat, Raymond, and Simmon, Scott. *King Vidor, American.* Berkeley, Cal.: University of California Press, 1988.

Edwards, Anne. *Shirley Temple: American Princess.* New York: Morrow, 1988.

Eisner, Lotte. *Fritz Lang.* London: Secker & Warburg, 1976.

Farber, Stephen, and Green, Marc. *Hollywood Dynasties.* New York: Putnam, 1984.

Flamini, Roland. *Scarlett, Rhett and a Cast of Thousands.* New York: Macmillan, 1975.

Fontaine, Joan. *No Bed of Roses.* New York: Morrow, 1978.

Gaberscek, Carlo, and Jacob, Livio. *Hollywood in Friuli. Sul set di Addio alle armi.* Pordenone: Cineteca del Friuli, 1991.

Gabler, Neal. *An Empire of Their Own.* New York: Crown, 1988.

Geist, Kenneth L. *Pictures Will Talk: The Life and Films of Joseph L. Mankiewicz.* New York: Scribner's, 1978.

Grafton, David. *The Sisters: The Lives and Times of the Fabulous Cushing Sisters.* New York: Villard, 1992.

Greene, Graham. *The Pleasure Dome: The Collected Film Criticism 1935–40.* Edited by John Russell Taylor. London: Secker & Warburg, 1972.

Grobel, Lawrence. *The Hustons.* New York: Scribner's, 1989.

Hadleigh, Boze. *Conversations with My Elders.* New York: St. Martin's Press, 1986.

Harmetz, Aljean. *The Making of the Wizard of Oz.* New York: Alfred A. Knopf, 1977.

Hart-Davis, Rupert. *Hugh Walpole.* London: Macmillan, 1952.

Harwell, Richard, ed. "The Hollywood Journals of Wilbur G. Kurtz," *Atlanta Historical Journal,* summer 1978.

———, ed. *Margaret Mitchell's Gone With the Wind Letters: 1936–1949.* New York: Macmillan, 1976.

———, ed. *Gone With the Wind as Book and Film.* Columbia, S.C.: University of South Carolina Press, 1983.

Haver, Ronald. *David O. Selznick's Hollywood.* New York: Alfred A. Knopf, 1980.

———. *A Star is Born.* New York: Alfred A. Knopf, 1988.

Hays, Will. *The Memoirs of Will H. Hays.* New York: Doubleday, 1955.

Hayward, Brooke. *Haywire.* New York: Alfred A. Knopf, 1977.

Hecht, Ben. *A Child of the Century.* New York: Simon & Schuster, 1954.

Hepburn, Katharine. *Me.* New York: Alfred A. Knopf, 1991.

Houseman, John. *Front and Center.* New York: Simon & Schuster, 1979.

Huston, John. *An Open Book.* New York: Alfred A. Knopf, 1980.

Jackson, Carlton. *Hattie: The Life of Hattie McDaniel.* Lanham: Madison Books, 1990.

Johnson, Nunnally. *The Letters of Nunnally Johnson.* Edited by Dorris Johnson and Ellen Leventhal. New York: Alfred A. Knopf, 1981.

Johnston, Alva. "Russell Birdwell." *The New Yorker,* August 19 and 26, September 2 and 9, 1944.

Kahn, E. J., Jr. *Jock: The Life and Times of John Hay Whitney.* New York: Doubleday, 1981.

Kazan, Elia. *Elia Kazan: A Life.* New York: Alfred A. Knopf, 1988.

Keith, Slim, with Tapert, Annette. *Slim.* New York: Simon & Schuster, 1990.

Keyes, Evelyn. *Scarlett O'Hara's Younger Sister.* Secaucus, N.J.: Lyle Stuart, 1977.

Knef, Hildegard. *The Gift Horse.* New York: McGraw-Hill, 1971.

Korda, Michael. *Charmed Lives.* New York: Random House, 1979.

Koszarski, Richard. *An Evening's Entertainment: The Age of the Silent Feature Picture, 1915–1928.* New York: Scribner's, 1990.

Kotsilibas-Davis, James, and Loy, Myrna. *Myrna Loy: Being and Becoming.* New York: Alfred A. Knopf, 1987.

Lambert, Gavin. *On Cukor.* New York: Putnam, 1972.

———. *GWTW: The Making of Gone With the Wind.* Boston: Atlantic–Little, Brown, 1973.

Lasky, Betty. *RKO: The Biggest Little Major of Them All.* Englewood Cliffs, N.J.: Prentice-Hall, 1984.

Lasky, Jesse, Jr., and Silver, Pat. *Love Scene: The Story of Laurence Olivier and Vivien Leigh.* New York: Crowell, 1978.

Leamer, Laurence. *As Time Goes By: The Life of Ingrid Bergman.* New York: Harper & Row, 1986.

Leff, Leonard J. *Hitchcock & Selznick.* New York: Weidenfeld & Nicolson, 1987.

Lindfors, Viveca. *Viveka . . . Viveca.* New York: Everest House, 1980.

Linet, Beverly. *Star-Crossed: The Story of Robert Walker and Jennifer Jones.* New York: Putnam, 1986.

Logan, Joshua. *Josh.* New York: Delacorte, 1976.

MacAdams, William. *Ben Hecht: The Man Behind the Legend.* New York: Scribner's, 1990.

Mallory, Mary. "Agent Provocateur: The Tradition and Influence of Myron Selznick on the Motion Picture Talent Agency Business." *Master's thesis, University of Texas at Austin, 1990.*

Marion, Frances. *Off With Their Heads!* New York: Macmillan, 1972.

Marx, Samuel. *Mayer and Thalberg.* New York: Random House, 1975.

McBride, Joseph, ed. *Hawks on Hawks.* Berkeley, Cal.: University of California Press, 1982.

———. *Frank Capra: The Catastrophe of Success.* New York: Simon & Schuster, 1992.

McGilligan, Partrick, ed. *Backstory: Interviews with Screenwriters of Hollywood's Golden Age.* Berkeley, Cal.: University of California Press, 1986.

———., ed. *Backstory 2: Interviews with Screenwriters of the 1940s and 1950s.* Berkeley, Cal.: University of California Press, 1991.

———. *George Cukor: A Double Life.* New York: St. Martin's Press, 1991.

Montagu, Ivor. *With Eisenstein in Hollywood.* New York: International Publishers, 1969.

Myrick, Susan. *White Columns in Hollywood.* Edited by Richard Harwell. Macon, Ga.: Mercer University Press, 1982.

Neal, Patricia. *As I Am.* Boston: G. K. Hall, 1988.

Negulesco, Jean. *Things I Did . . . and Things I Think I Did.* New York: Simon & Schuster, 1984.

Niven, David. *Bring On the Empty Horses.* New York: Putnam, 1975.

Olivier, Laurence. *Confessions of an Actor.* New York: Simon & Schuster, 1982.

Pierce, Arthur, and Swarthout, Douglas. *Jean Arthur: A Bio-Bibliography.* New York: Greenwood, 1990.

Powell, Michael. *A Life in Movies.* New York: Alfred A. Knopf, 1987.

Ramsaye, Terry. *A Million and One Nights.* New York: Simon & Schuster, 1926.

Samuels, Charles. *The King: A Biography of Clark Gable.* New York: Coward-McCann, 1961.

Schary, Dore. *Heyday.* Boston: Little, Brown, 1979.

Schatz, Thomas. *The Genius of the System.* New York: Pantheon, 1988.

Schickel, Richard. *The Men Who Made The Movies.* New York: Atheneum, 1975.

Schulberg, Budd. *What Makes Sammy Run?* New York: Random House, 1941.

———. *Moving Pictures.* New York: Stein & Day, 1981.

Selznick, Irene Mayer. *A Private View.* New York: Alfred A. Knopf, 1983.

Smith, Sally Bedell. *In All His Glory: The Life of William S. Paley.* New York: Simon & Schuster, 1990.

Spoto, Donald. *The Dark Side of Genius: The Life of Alfred Hitchcock.* Boston: Little, Brown, 1983.

Swanson, H. N. *Sprinkled With Ruby Dust.* New York: Warner Books, 1989.

Thomas, Bob. *Selznick.* New York: Doubleday, 1970.

Trager, James. *Park Avenue.* New York: Atheneum, 1990.

Truffaut, François. *Hitchcock.* New York: Simon & Schuster, 1966.

Vickers, Hugo. *Cecil Beaton.* Boston: Little, Brown, 1985.

Vidor, King. *A Tree is a Tree.* New York: Harcourt, Brace, 1953.

Walker, Alexander. *Vivien: The Life of Vivien Leigh.* New York: Weidenfeld & Nicolson, 1987.

Wallis, Hal, and Higham, Charles. *Starmaker.* New York: Macmillan, 1980.

Wapshott, Nicholas. *The Man Between: A Biography of Carol Reed.* London: Chatto & Windus, 1990.

Wellman, William. *A Short Time for Insanity.* New York: Hawthorn, 1974.

Wilder, Margaret Buell. *Since You Went Away.* New York: McGraw-Hill, 1943.

Wray, Fay. *On the Other Hand.* New York: St. Martin's Press, 1989.

Yoch, James J. *Landscaping the American Dream: The Gardens and Film Sets of Florence Yoch, 1890–1972.* New York: Abrams, 1989.

Zierold, Norman. *The Moguls.* New York: Coward-McCann, 1969.

Zolotow, Maurice. *Billy Wilder in Hollywood.* New York: Putnam, 1977.

SOURCE NOTES

Abbreviations

A   Academy of Motion Picture Arts and Sciences, Library
DMS   Daniel Mayer Selznick
DOS   David O. Selznick
DT   David Thomson
DTO'S   Dan O'Shea
FAS   Flossie Selznick
H   Sidney Howard papers, Bancroft Library, University of California at
                Berkeley
HRC   Harry Ransom Humanities Research Center, University of Texas in Aus-
                tin (home of the David O. Selznick Archive)
IGM   Irene Gladys Mayer (1907–1930)
IMS   Irene Mayer Selznick (1930–1990)
IMS/B   the collection of Irene Mayer Selznick papers in the Mugar Library, Bos-
                ton University
IMS/DT   papers given by IMS to DT for this book, then to be placed at HRC
JHW   John Hay Whitney
JW   the papers of Joan Selznick Grill Williams, in care of Bank of Califor-
                nia, Newport Beach, California
KB   Kay Brown
LBM   Louis B. Mayer
LJS   Lewis Jeffrey Selznick
Memo   *Memo from David O. Selznick*, ed. Rudy Behlmer (1972)
MS   Myron Selznick
MS/F   the office files of the Myron Selznick Agency, part of the estate of Joan
                Selznick Grill Williams

PROLOGUE: SEPTEMBER 9, 1939

p. ix   Composed from Los Angeles *Times*, September 9 and 19, 1939; interview with LJS (March
        31, 1991) on the car route; IMS, *A Private View*, pp. 218–20; interviews with Hal Kern, James
        Newcom, William Ericson.

PART ONE

p. 2 "Yeah, I knew Lewis J." and following: Interview with Sam Jaffe, February 25, 1991.

3 a net worth of over $11 million: Barry Brannen to MS, March 31, 1942, and 1921 prospectus for shares, issued by H. V. Greene Company (HRC).

"the only gentleman in the business": DOS, Columbia Oral History, September 1958, p. 1.

"I only remember him": Ibid., pp. 1–2.

Lewis J. Selznik: *The National Cyclopedia of American Biography*; Frances De Curtis to DOS, March 27, 1941 (HRC); application for marriage license, October 15, 1896, Court of Common Pleas, Allegheny County, Pennsylvania.

5 Joseph Seleznik: Application for citizenship, March 25, 1893, Court of Common Pleas, Cuyahoga County, Ohio.

Lewis's naturalization papers: Court of Common Pleas, September 29, 1894, Court of Common Pleas, Allegheny County, Pennsylvania.

on later marriages and children of Joseph Seleznik, see various records of Cuyahoga County, Ohio, and 1900 Census for Cleveland, Ohio.

6 The Sachs family: Interviews with Arthur Sachs, August 21, 1991, and Rena Davis, August 22, 1991.

Florence Selznick: Application for marriage license, October 15, 1896, Court of Common Pleas, Allegheny County, Pennsylvania.

8 "denied reality": IMS, *A Private View*, p. 107.

Myron: Court of Common Pleas, Allegheny County, Pennsylvania.

9 "One relative in a place": DOS to FAS, May 8, 1949 (HRC).

Bay Ridge: New York City Telephone Directory; Upington's General Directory of the Borough of Brooklyn; Trow's New York City Directory; 1905 New York City Census (Brooklyn).

10 "a little boy": May Cushing Walsh to DOS, February 3, 1940 (HRC).

"His tendency to become": DOS to Howard Dietz, June 20, 1934 (HRC).

11 "my father was": *Memo*, p. 3.

David's room: Apartment appraisal (270 Park Avenue), October 30, 1923 (HRC).

12 "David was brighter": Interview with Al Hirschfeld, September 17, 1990.

14 a "jester": Ramsaye, *Million*, p. 761.

"less brains": Ibid.

15 "dragged down": *Memo*, p. 5.

World Film Company: Kevin Lewis, "A World Across from Broadway: The Shuberts and the Movies," *Film History*, no. 1, 1987.

"They tell me": Lewis J. Selznick, *The Moving Picture World*, January 23, 1915.

16 "a good, solid": Interview with Sam Marx, March 7, 1989.

"a nice doddering fellow": Ibid.

"a fake": Ibid.

school records: Hamilton Institute for Boys; Columbia University entrance examination; Archibald Shaw to whom it may concern, September 22, 1922 (HRC).

17 "a group": Interview with Niven Busch, June 2, 1983; also in Patrick McGilligan, ed., *Backstory*.

18 "discussing the picture business": *Memo*, p. 4.

Clara Kimball Young: Ramsaye, *Million*, pp. 762–63; transcript, *Clara Kimball Young v. Lewis J. Selznick and Select*, U.S. District Court of New York, October 28, 1920.

One day: Interview with Rena Davis, August 22, 1991.

19 "Dear Sir": DOS to Lewis J. Selznick, November 15, 1916 (HRC).

p. 19 "In response to yours": DOS to Lewis J. Selznick, October 30, 1916 (HRC).
20 "first, she has": DOS to Lewis J. Selznick, November 23, 1916 (HRC).
"Dear Miss Koch": DOS to Edith Koch, March 15, 1917 (HRC).
"A sound sleep": *The Brain Exchange*, October 14, 1922, p. 2.
21 "Don't let anyone": *The Brain Exchange*, November 11, 1922, p. 7.
"Ten Commandments of Selling": *The Brain Exchange*, October 14, 1922, p. 2.
22 "Dear Mr. Moses": DOS to Vivian Moses, February 15, 1917 (HRC).
23 "I congratulate you": Ramsaye, *Million*, p. 766.
"L.J.'s gall": Budd Schulberg, *Moving Pictures*, p. 6.
24 "TO NICHOLAS ROMANOFF": Ramsaye, *Million*, p. 766.
"I will enter": Lewis J. Selznick to Famous Players–Lasky Corporation, August 6, 1917, pp. 2–3 (HRC).
25 "Watch what I say": IMS, *A Private View*, p. 96.
26 "He was broken": DOS to Howard Dietz, June 20, 1934, p. 1 (HRC).
"to devise and produce": Ibid.
27 "both poet and promoter": IMS, *A Private View*, p. 108.
"was so generally": DOS to Howard Dietz, June 20, 1934, p. 2 (HRC).
"She was so intrigued": Ibid.
Legend had it: Ramsaye, *Million*, p. 765; DOS, Columbia Oral History, p. 3.
28 But in 1920: *New York Times*, September 8, 10, 11, 12, 14, 22, 25, 29, October 5, November 23, December 10, 1920; *Variety*, September 17, 24, October 1, 15, 1920.
29 Corinne Griffith: Vitagraph to Lewis J. Selznick, December 15, 1919 (HRC).
Long Beach on Long Island: Interview with Rena Davis, August 22, 1991.
30 Marguery Building: James Trager, *Park Avenue*, p. 89; Trager to DT, October 31, 1990.
"Mother Selznick": Interview with Niven Busch, June 2, 1983.
"This was in 1919": Interview with Maurice Rapf, November 5, 1987.
31 seeing girls: Interview with IMS, March 18, 1989; interview with Yvette Curran, July 23, 1991.
"David Selznick": *The Brain Exchange*, October 30, 1920, p. 9.
32 "A young eagle": *The Brain Exchange*, May 19, 1920, p. 1.
"Business before pleasure": *The Brain Exchange*, June 30, 1920, p. 10.
33 "I asked Howard": Randolph Maller deposition, September 8, 1943 (HRC).
"Howard never did anything": Ibid.
34 "I go to see": IMS, *A Private View*, p. 107.
"It has often been": *The Brain Exchange*, January 18, 1921, p. 5.
35 "He was a mass": IMS, *A Private View*, p. 108.
"The Man Who Was Nobody": Early writings (HRC).
"But there is no": Randolph Bartlett, May 7, n.d., in early writings (HRC).
36 balance sheet: Barry Brannen to MS, July 8, 1940 (HRC).
"to consolidate": H. V. Greene Company prospectus (HRC).
37 "To provide": Ibid.
38 Cecelia and Leonard Morris: FBI report, December 5, 1935 (copy sent to DOS) (HRC).
Motion Picture Producers and Distributors of America: Will Hays, *The Memoirs of Will H. Hays*, pp. 323–30.
Sam E. Morris: *The Brain Exchange*, October 14, 1922, p. 4.
Columbia: Peter Smith to DT, August 23, 1991; *Memo*, p. 5.
39 "I am eighteen": DOS to Yale Board of Admissions, March 16, 1921 (HRC).
Yale: Yale Board of Admissions to DOS, December 16, 1921 (HRC).
"They maintain": Orville Petty to DOS, September 21, 1922 (HRC).

p. 39   "David O. Selznick": *The Brain Exchange*, November 11, 1922, p. 1.
   40   "our very best picture": Edward Montagne to DOS, n.d. (HRC).
           "Give you a thrill?": *The Brain Exchange*, November 11, 1922, p. 1.
           One Week of Love: Ibid.
   41   "Lots of conversation": Ibid.
   42   William Rosenfeld: Lewis J. Selznick files, October 1922 (HRC).
           270 Park Avenue: Apartment appraisal, October 30, 1923 (HRC).
   43   "Production activity suspended": MS to DOS, January 26, 1923 (HRC).
           Three days later: Minutes of special board meeting, Selznick Pictures Corporation, January
           29, 1923 (HRC).
   44   "a remarkable man": Interview with Al Hirschfeld, September 1, 1990.
           "and stated that": Minutes of special board meeting, op. cit.
           "Many things have transpired": Nick Carter to DOS, February 10, 1923 (HRC).
           "He controls a Chinese valet": Early writings (HRC).
   45   "Hollywood is": *Time*, March 3, 1923.

PART TWO

   48   "unfortunate way": DOS to Charles Sachs, October 5, 1944 (HRC).
   49   "of pending litigation": Konta & Kirchwey to E. M. Willis, February 8, 1923 (HRC).
           "Everything we owned": *Memo*, p. 5.
           "we were living": Ibid., p. 6.
           Hyman Winik: *New York Times*, January 14, 1930.
           Samuel Falk: Mortgage agreement, February 1, 1923 (MS/F).
   50   "He then proceeded": Joe Toplitzky to MS, June 4, 1935 (HRC).
           involuntary bankruptcy: *New York Times*, March 7, 1923.
           committee: Ibid.
           Myron: *New York Times*, October 23, 1924.
           "he had knowledge": *New York Times*, July 16, 1925.
   51   "a Long Island": DOS to A. C. Blumenthal, February 22, 1923 (HRC).
           "because my entire": DOS to William J. Connery, February 28, 1923 (HRC).
   52   Dempsey vs. Firpo: Production costs (HRC); *Memo*, p. 6; *New York Times*, various issues in
           August–September 1923.
           "We ran Firpo's": *Memo*, p. 6.
   53   "I cannot endure": Quoted in Alexander Walker, *Rudolph Valentino* (London: 1976), p. 74.
           "Based on the experience": Lewis J. Selznick, June 11, 1923 (HRC).
   54   *Roulette*: W. C. J. Doolittle to DOS, May 3, 1924, and DOS, memo, October 31, 1924
           (HRC).
           "I am in the radio": Lewis J. Selznick, April 28, 1924 (HRC).
   55   "He had a great laugh": Interview with Aileen Pringle, May 8, 1988.
   56   *Mignonette*: Early creative writings (HRC).
           "*I think it must be nice*": Ibid.
   57   "*I kissed her*": Ibid.
           "I do not see": DOS to Reginald Ford, June 26, 1924 (HRC).
           "stealthily carrying on": Ibid.
           "appearing now under": DOS to Louella Parsons, November 25, 1924 (HRC).
           "The Idiot's Gazette": Early writings (HRC).
   58   "Sellsnix and Chump": May 8, 1924, early writings (HRC).
           "A little fat": Quoted in Kevin Brownlow, *Behind the Mask of Innocence*, p. 308.

p. 58 "Fifteen Reasons": Early writings (HRC).

59 "I understood": Ben Hecht, *A Child of the Century*, p. 381.

60 "no high purpose": Early writings (HRC).
"The picture man": Ibid.
"And now": Ibid.

61 "His Semitic instincts": Early writings (HRC).
"leaving one despondent": DOS to ?, n.d. (HRC).

62 "Hecht, by the bye": Ibid.
"where winter spends the summer": Early writings (HRC).

63 "Democracy overtaken": Ibid.
"I urge you": DOS to Ben Hecht, n.d. (HRC).
"selling scenarios": Ben Hecht to DOS, August 10, 1925.
"its a peach": Ben Hecht to DOS, August 23, 1925.
"flat broke": DOS to Barry Brannen, June 19, 1940 (HRC).
"anybody with a good memory": Hecht, *Child of the Century*, p. 446.
"I am about to meet": Ibid.

64 "Everybody was trying": Ibid., p. 447.
Gomez Grant: DOS to David Scholtz, August 29, 1925 (HRC).
Lake Worth: Earl J. Reed to Equitable Finance and Securities, February 8, 1926 (HRC).
Briton Busch: Memo, February 8, 1926 (HRC); Briton Busch to DOS, October 31, 1936 (HRC); interview with Niven Busch, March 3, 1989.

65 "the little Gods": Violet Chapman to DOS, June 1940 (HRC).
"I don't believe": DOS to Barry Brannen, June 19, 1940 (HRC).
Charles Apfel: Charles Apfel to DOS, November 11, 1941 (HRC).
"I am enclosing herewith": DOS to Ben Hecht, February 2, 1926 (HRC).

66 "One day": Interview with Samuel Marx, March 7, 1989.

67 "To able independent": *Manpower*, July 20, 1926 (MS/F).
Utica Holding Company: *New York Times*, July 24, 1926.
"Don't start selling": *Manpower*, September 7, 1926 (MS/F).

68 "a masterpiece": DOS to Wilhelmina Morris, n.d. (HRC).
"I'll have to try again": Ibid.
"I've developed": Ibid.

69 Nick Schenck: *Memo*, p. 7; IMS, *A Private View*, pp. 105–6.

72 "I do not know": DOS to Harry Rapf, October 5, 1926 (HRC).
"I know beyond doubt": DOS to Harry Rapf, October 5, 1926 (HRC).
"The one picture": Ibid.
"The idea of the title": DOS to Harry Rapf, October 11, 1926 (HRC).

73 "inside stuff": DOS to Harry Rapf, October 11, 1926 (HRC).
"I shall not": DOS to Harry Rapf, October 11, 1926 (HRC).
"This one got saved": IMS, *A Private View*, p. 96.

74 "the Biltmore boobery": DOS to Ruth Feld, n.d. (HRC).
"Not drunk enough": IMS, *A Private View*, p. 97.

75 Gertrude Regina: Interview with IMS, May 9, 1988.

76 "Jacob beat my father": Ibid.
"He was as good-looking": Ibid.

77 "My father": IMS, *A Private View*, pp. 20–21.
"He would call Edie": Interview with IMS, May 9, 1988.
"Edie was": Ibid.

p. 78   "Revenge": Ibid.

79   "She would take": Ibid.
"She thought I was": Interview with IMS, May 6, 1988.
"A Rodin bronze": Early writings, August 1928 (HRC).

80   "Let them develop": Quoted in Samuel Marx, *Mayer and Thalberg,* p. 100.
Villa Carlotta: Interview with IMS, November 4, 1987.

81   "Trying to kiss me!": IMS, *A Private View,* p. 97.
"They played serious": Ibid., p. 98.
"Myron was compact": Ibid.
"as suspicious": Ibid., p. 117.

83   "I'm doing my best": IGM to DOS, October 12, 1927 (HRC).
"Have you heard": IMS, *A Private View,* pp. 102–3.
"virility and the": Hunt Stromberg to DOS, October 13, 1927 (HRC).

84   "If you don't apologize": Marx, *Mayer and Thalberg,* p. 104; *Memo,* p. 15.

85   "I devised": *Memo,* p. 16.
"The terms you spoke of": DOS to B. P. Schulberg, May 21, 1928 (HRC).
"I've heard lots": Jean Arthur to DOS, n.d. (HRC).

86   "I have your touching": B. P. Schulberg to DOS, September 7, 1928 (HRC).
"I desperately": IMS, *A Private View,* p. 117; interview with Sam Jaffe, February 25, 1991; interview with IMS, September 15, 1988.

87   Julian Anker: Arthur Pierce and Douglas Swarthout, *Jean Arthur: A Bio-Bibliography,* pp. 12–13.
"She was not one": IMS, *A Private View,* p. 117.
"How can two opposites": Ibid., p. 110.

88   "How amazed": IGM to DOS, September 19, 1928 (HRC).
"When you're nearly": IGM to DOS, September 21, 1928 (HRC).
"Also you have not as yet": IGM to DOS, October 21, 1928 (HRC).

89   "I see your friend": Ibid.
"And how is": IGM to DOS, September 30, 1928 (HRC).
"I am not asking": IGM to DOS, October 21, 1928 (HRC).
"My dear vacillating idealist": Ibid.
"the transitional period": B. P. Schulberg to supervisors, November 8, 1928 (HRC).

90   "Are your nipples": Interview with IMS, November 4, 1987.
"Oh, I'd follow him": Interview with IMS, May 6, 1988.
"He looked at": Interview with IMS, September 15, 1988, and April 14, 1989.
"Then he brought her": Interview with IMS, May 6, 1988.

92   "I feel confident": DOS to Ernest Schoedsack, April 2, 1929 (HRC).
"I think your": Merian C. Cooper to DOS, n.d. (HRC).
"Young David Selznick": Budd Schulberg, *Moving Pictures,* p. 306.

94   "For my father": Interview with IMS, May 9, 1988.
Russian Eagle: Letter on menu, August 31, 1929 (IMS/DT).

95   "seemed very, very solo": Fay Wray, *On the Other Hand,* p. 97.
"Oh, lost ecstasy": Interview with Fay Wray, July 21, 1989.
"I was the sort of person": Interview with IMS, May 9, 1988.
"If that's you": Interview with IMS, September 17, 1988.

96   "Standing in their": IMS, *A Private View,* p. 121.
"We found those rides": Ibid., pp. 121–22.

97   "With Ben gone": DOS to Jesse Lasky, October 8, 1929 (HRC).

p. 97 "Despite my feelings": Ibid.

98 "tragic, unhappy ending": Jesse Lasky to DOS, October 22, 1929 (HRC).
"The proposed statement": DOS to M. C. Levee, November 11, 1929 (HRC).

99 "Up to this point": DOS to B. P. Schulberg, January 23, 1930 (HRC).
"I have taken the liberty": DOS to B. P. Schulberg, December 19, 1929 (HRC).

101 "Train empty": DOS to IGM, January 11, 1930 (IMS/DT).
"oh! please rush": Ibid.
"It's cold and gray": DOS to IGM, January 12, 1930 (IMS/DT).
"Darling as though": IGM to DOS, January 13, 1930 (IMS/DT).
"standing still": IGM to DOS, January 13, 1930 (HRC).
"All this morning": DOS to IGM, January 22, 1930 (IMS/DT).
"your respect for": Ibid.

102 "the only one": DOS to IGM, n.d. (IMS/DT).
"comes the astounding": Ibid.
"two silly girl-chasing": Ibid.
"Five thousand dollars": Ibid.
Mr. Meyer: Ibid.

103 "Irene darling": DOS to IGM, January 27, 1930 (IMS/DT).
"I'll see you": DOS to IGM, February 1, 1930 (IMS/DT).
"Morpheus has begun": IGM to DOS, February 1, 1930 (IMS/DT).
"My arms are": DOS to IGM, February 3, 1930 (IMS/DT).
"I wish that": IGM to DOS, February 3, 1930 (IMS/DT).

104 Edie's wedding: IMS, *A Private View*, pp. 130–31; Los Angeles *Times*, March 20, 1930.
"L.B. can't control": IMS, *A Private View*, p. 128.

105 "Up the whole": DOS to IGM, March 11, 1930 (IMS/DT).

106 "What date": IMS, *A Private View*, pp. 131–35.

107 "I seemed to myself": Ibid., p. 136.
April 29: Ibid., pp. 136–37; Los Angeles *Times*, April 30, 1930.

PART THREE

110 "The poor man": Interview with IMS, September 29, 1990.

111 "After chasing from": MS to DOS, May 2, 1930 (IMS/DT).

112 "We were typical": Interview with IMS, September 29, 1990.
"He said": Ibid.
"If you'd removed": Ibid.
"He said he had": IMS, *A Private View*, p. 141.

113 "a wonderful staff": Lewis J. Selznick to Morris Safier, September 9, 1930 (MS/F).
"an impossible man": Lewis J. Selznick to Morris Safier, November 13, 1930 (MS/F).
"learn to be extravagant": IMS, *A Private View*, p. 148.

114 "unspoiled as to money": DOS to B. P. Schulberg, July 18, 1930 (HRC).
"positively torturing": DOS to B. P. Schulberg, October 8, 1930 (HRC).

115 "Isn't Mr. Schulberg": Ivor Montagu, *With Eisenstein in Hollywood*, p. 140.
Sarnoff offer: David Sarnoff to Adolph Zukor, September 18, 1930; Zukor to Sarnoff, October 19, 1930 (HRC).
"a really great": *Memo*, p. 19.
"Schulberg list: n.d. (HRC).

116 "repeatedly bemoaned": DOS to B. P. Schulberg, February 2, 1931 (HRC).
"I think I have": DOS to B. P. Schulberg, June 15, 1931 (HRC).

p. 117 Santa Monica Social: George Cukor to DOS, July 14, 1931 (HRC).
       "This young production": *Hollywood Reporter*, July 17, 1931.
   118 "Enjoying Myron": DOS to IMS, July 24, 1931 (IMS/DT).
       "Pie-Face Monument": Ibid.
       "Say, what is this": IMS to DOS, July 27, 1931 (HRC).
       "Darling, please hide": Ibid.
       "Keep kissable": DOS to IMS, July 31, 1931 (IMS/DT).
       "I long to be": IMS to DOS, August 1, 1931 (HRC).
   119 "To Swopes": DOS to IMS, July 31, 1931 (IMS/DT).
       "Yesterday": DOS to IMS, July 31, 1931 (letter) (IMS/DT).
       "formerly Ollie": Ibid.
       "Have been": Ibid.
   120 "Warning": IMS to DOS, August 2, 1931 (HRC).
       Cooper: DOS to IMS, July 31, 1931 (letter) (IMS/DT); Merian Cooper to Richard
       Goldwater, July 19, 1963 (HRC).
   121 "too important": DOS to Joe Schenck, October 20, 1931 (HRC).
       Milestone: IMS, *A Private View*, p. 152; *Memo*, pp. 44–45; DOS to RKO Radio Pictures,
       September 5, 1931 (HRC).
   122 "Of course, David": IMS, *A Private View*, p. 153.
       "There is only one word": Howard Selznick to DOS, October 30, 1931 (HRC).
   123 "He would wait": Interview with Niven Busch, February 20, 1989.
       "He was insulting": Mildred Selznick deposition, Superior Court of California, *Mildred
       Selznick v. Florence, Myron and David Selznick*, March 1943, p. 93.
       Sam Dubrow: Interview with Jack Dubrow, September 7, 1943 (HRC).
       "I can't blame you": Mildred Selznick deposition, p. 93.
   124 Leo Kessel: Leo Kessel to Sam Hirschfeld, August 28, 1931 (MS/F).
       "thought it was": Merian Cooper to Richard Goldwater, July 19, 1963 (HRC).
       Cooper and Lewis J. Selznick: Ibid.
       "He seemed": Ibid.
   125 "would come in": Pandro Berman in Ron Haver, *David O. Selznick's Hollywood*, p. 70.
   128 "My dear Jimmy": Lewis J. Selznick to James Metzenbaum, June 10, 1932 (HRC).
   129 "Movies were like": IMS, *A Private View*, p. 154.
       "Second years": DOS to IMS, April 29, 1932 (IMS/DT).
       "Finally I came out": Interview with Marcella Rabwin, November 12, 1987.
   130 "Connie was": Interview with IMS, March 10, 1989.
       "He was very": Interview with Marcella Rabwin, November 12, 1987.
       "a stern, agentlike": Ibid.
   131 "I haven't read it either": King Vidor, *A Tree is a Tree*, p. 193.
   133 "She was quite unlike": Gavin Lambert, *On Cukor*, p. 60.
       "Well, there I was": Laurence Olivier, *Confessions of an Actor*, pp. 90–91.
       Katharine Hepburn contract: DOS to Mr. Richards, July 6, 1932 (HRC).
   134 "the only reason": DOS to Jenia Reissar, November 9, 1944 (HRC).
   135 "Largely through": *On Cukor*, p. 46.
   137 gambling: Monthly records (HRC).
   139 Clover Club: Interview with IMS, May 5, 1989.
       "Promise me": IMS, *A Private View*, p. 172.
       "You will note": Ben Kahane to DOS, June 4, 1932 (HRC).
       "the gloom is": Ibid.

p. 140   "chaotic studio condition": DOS to Ben Kahane, August 22, 1932 (HRC).
         A son was born: Cedars of Lebanon Hospital baby card (105359); IMS, *A Private View*,
         pp. 173–74.
         "Pop was resplendent": IMS, *A Private View*, p. 173.
         "Give him to me": Interview with IMS, January 1, 1989.

141   "Can't you tell": IMS, *A Private View*, p. 174.
         "So we are three": Ibid.
         "There were more": Ibid., p. 175.
         "Dear little mother": LBM to IMS, August 11, 1932 (IMS/B).
         "kissed his youth": Interview with IMS, January 1, 1989.

142   "Pop's eternity": Ibid.
         "utterly impossible": DOS to Ben Kahane, October 24, 1933 (HRC).
         "The world knows": *Memo*, p. 45.
         "He was most": Interview with IMS, November 21, 1987.

143   "He was like": Interview with Katharine Hepburn, November 2, 1990.
         "I really loved him": Interview with Laura Harding, November 2, 1990.
         Marcella Bannett: Interview with Marcella Rabwin, November 12, 1987.
         "cold and": Interview with Katharine Hepburn, November 2, 1990.

145   in October: DOS, Statement of Receipts and Disbursements, October 1932 (HRC).
         family home: Title Insurance (March 24, 1932, and October 24, 1932) (HRC); IMS, *A
         Private View*, pp. 195–96.

146   "That you may know": DOS to LBM, November 12, 1932 (HRC).
         "His record is too": Ibid.
         "R.K.O. had an": Ibid.
         "Moreover, I believe": Ibid.

147   "would refuse": DOS to David Sarnoff, December 16, 1932 (HRC).
         "total propositions": DOS to David Bruce, December 16, 1932 (HRC).
         "If you want": DOS to Henry Luce, December 17, 1932 (HRC).

148   "I ask you to reflect": David Sarnoff to DOS, December 19, 1932 (HRC).
         "definite offer": DOS to C. V. Whitney, December 31, 1932 (HRC).
         "afraid we will have": Ibid.
         "Pop would not want": IMS, *A Private View*, p. 186.
         "tremendously optimistic": DOS to MS, January 13, 1933 (HRC).
         "Suddenly": IMS, *A Private View*, p. 187.
         "Pop, it's David": Ibid.; interview with IMS, May 6, 1987.

149   "Take care": IMS, *A Private View*, p. 187.
         "Where have you": Ibid., p. 188.
         "I have never": Interview with Marcella Rabwin, November 12, 1987.
         "Hours toward the dawn": DOS early writings (HRC).

150   negotiations: Personal contract notes (HRC).
         "sudden": Los Angeles *Times*, February 3, 1933.

151   "That by consenting": Nick Schenck and LBM to Irving Thalberg, February 4, 1933
         (HRC).

152   "There are, however": Irving Thalberg to LBM, February 25, 1933, in Crowther, *Hollywood
         Rajah*, p. 170.
         "to spare Irving": Frances Marion, *Off With Their Heads!*, p. 256.

153   "suddenly the entire": Merian Cooper in Haver, *Selznick's Hollywood*, p. 122.
         An earthquake: Los Angeles *Times*, March 11, 1933.

p. 153   "Hurry up": IMS, *A Private View*, p. 191.

154   "I've only the hope": DOS to IMS, March 16, 1933 (HRC).
"I write you": DOS to LBM, June 14, 1933 (HRC).

155   "I want to get out": Ibid.
"All past accomplishment": Ibid.
"Eddie is doing": DOS to Nick Schenck, May 15, 1933 (HRC).
"My grief": DOS to LBM, June 14, 1933 (HRC).

157   "Darling George": IMS to George Cukor, October 14, 1933 (A).
"I'll be rather": Quoted in Haver, *Selznick's Hollywood*, p. 130.
"Rhythm of the Day": Haver, *Selznick's Hollywood*, pp. 141–42.

158   "so David throws": Ibid., p. 141.
"Nobody had a long": Interview with Joseph L. Mankiewicz, May 9, 1989.
"I am tremendously enthused": DOS to Louis Brock, January 13, 1933 (HRC).
"enormous ears": DOS to Phil Siff, January 26, 1933 (HRC).

159   bank balance: DOS, Statement of Receipts and Disbursements, 1933 (HRC).
Twentieth Century stock: IMS, *A Private View*, pp. 192–95; William Goetz to IMS, July 5, 1934 (HRC); Goetz to DOS, October 19, 1934 (HRC); DOS/IMS, annual financial statements (HRC).
"When I want": Interview with Samuel Marx, March 7, 1989.

160   "in the end": IMS, *A Private View*, p. 193.

161   "dog-fight": Ben Kahane to J. R. McDonough, October 7, 1933 (HRC).
"possibly my closest friend": DOS to Ben Kahane, October 24, 1933.
"Darling": DOS to IMS, n.d. (IMS/DT).

162   telephone: Draft of article for *Look*, n.d. (HRC).

163   "I just got a haircut": DOS to IMS, October 16, 1930 (IMS/DT).
"Not only was I": DOS to Howard Dietz, June 20, 1934 (HRC).
coup: Mary E. Mallory, "Agent Provocateur," p. 31.

164   10%: DOS to Howard Dietz, June 20, 1934 (HRC).
office routine: Interview with Maxine Graybill, April 9, 1988.
"I think he adored": Ibid.
"Insignificant": Interview with IMS, April 14, 1988.
"Marjorie didn't seem": Interview with Josephine Hutchinson, February 5, 1988.

165   "Carrots!": Ibid.
cologne: Interview with Loretta Young, January 21, 1989.
"makes great effort": Draft of article for *Look*, n.d. (HRC).
"One night": Interview with Loretta Young, January 21, 1989.

166   "a whore and a bum": Mildred Selznick deposition, Supreme Court of California, March 1943, p. 51.
"I think that as soon": DOS to MS, November 6, 1933 (HRC).

167   "get him out of town": Mildred Selznick deposition, p. 220.
Hollywood and Bronson: Memo, October 16, 1934 (HRC); Howard to Christina [*sic*] McCoy, October 12, 1934 (HRC); Mildred Selznick deposition, p. 414.
"I talked with her": Mildred Selznick deposition, p. 414.
"never a menace": Interview with Marcella Rabwin, November 12, 1987.
"Then we'd go down": Ibid.

169   "Jock was up": Quoted in E. J. Kahn, Jr., *Jock: The Life and Times of John Hay Whitney*, p. 67.
Prince of Wales: Interview with Ring Lardner, Jr., February 5, 1988.

170   Liz Whitney: E. J. Kahn, Jr., *Jock*; interview with IMS, January 22, 1988.

p. 170 "David was Jock's Jew": Interview with Dorothy Hirshon, March 14, 1989.

"Look at him": Interview with IMS, May 12, 1989.

171 "David was crazy": Interview with Dorothy Hirshon, March 14, 1989.

172 "Bill and David": Ibid.

"She was very bright": Interview with IMS, February 26, 1989.

"David was the only": Interview with Dorothy Hirshon, March 14, 1989.

173 "so as not to be": Interview with IMS, May 12, 1989.

"He lied so dreadfully": Interview with Joseph L. Mankiewicz, May 9, 1989.

174 "a very involved bunch": Jerry Sackheim to DOS, February 1934 (HRC).

"I cannot get": DOS to Samuel Marx and Kate Corbaley, March 19, 1934 (HRC).

175 Ben Hecht: DOS to LBM, September 6, 1933 (HRC); William MacAdams, *Ben Hecht*, pp. 157–59.

176 Howard Hawks: Joseph McBride, *Hawks on Hawks*, pp. 60–63.

"The crowds in the street": Don Eddy, quoted in Haver, *Selznick's Hollywood*, p. 151.

Fay Wray: Interview with Fay Wray, July 21, 1989.

177 "It really could": Quoted in MacAdams, *Hecht*, p. 159.

"Cost high": DOS to Nick Schenck, n.d., not sent (HRC).

178 "He was *fantastic*": Interview with Maurice Rapf, November 5, 1987.

"He said, 'You know' ": Ibid.

179 "I've learned a little": Merian C. Cooper to DOS, n.d. (HRC).

180 Walpole: Rupert Hart-Davis, *Hugh Walpole*, pp. 348–51.

England trip: W. K. Craig to DOS, August 16, 1934 (HRC).

181 "We photographed": Lambert, *On Cukor*, pp. 83–84.

Max Bercutt: Interview with Max Bercutt, June 15, 1990.

Fritz Lang: Lotte Eisner, *Fritz Lang*, p. 160; Kenneth L. Geist, *Pictures Will Talk*, p. 77; DOS to LBM, January 2, 1935 (HRC).

"charming personality": DOS to Sam Eckman, n.d. (HRC).

Laughton: Lambert, *On Cukor*, p. 86; Simon Callow, *Charles Laughton*, pp. 85–86.

182 drop Steerforth!: Hart-Davis, *Walpole*, p. 350.

"the highly ingenious": Callow, *Charles Laughton*, p. 86.

"It was a difficult": Lambert, *On Cukor*, pp. 83, 87.

184 gambling: Monthly records (HRC).

"My judgment is": Merian C. Cooper to DOS, June 3, 1934 (HRC).

"I think he's right": IMS, handwritten notes on cable.

Sarnoff: David Sarnoff to DOS, November 16, 1934 (HRC).

185 "During the past": DOS to Nick Schenck, n.d. (HRC).

"But the hours": Ibid.

"was being pulled like taffy": Marion, *Off With Their Heads!*, p. 257.

186 "We talk to that boy": IMS, *A Private View*, pp. 200–201.

bank balance: DOS, Statement of Receipts and Disbursements, 1935 (HRC).

187 "I, personally, feel": DOS to Greta Garbo, January 7, 1935 (HRC).

188 "I know what you feel": DOS to Kate Corbaley, June 3, 1935 (HRC).

189 "Estimate your position": Nick Schenck to DOS, October 15, 1935 (HRC).

Nick Schenck: IMS, *A Private View*, pp. 200–201.

"I'll get even": Marion, *Off With Their Heads!*, p. 257.

190 "I have matured": DOS to Nick Schenck, n.d. (1935).

191 "I imagine you have": Ibid.

"Appreciate your willingness": DOS to JHW, November 20, 1934 (HRC).

p. 192   "He listened sympathetically": Phil Siff to DOS, December 28, 1934 (HRC).
         Thalberg: *Memo*, p. 97.
         "extremely annoyed": DOS to A. C. Blumenthal, June 21, 1935 (HRC).
         cocktail party: Details of bill (HRC).
   193   "I frankly want": DOS to Harold Talbott, Jr., July 30, 1935 (HRC); interview with IMS,
         March 13, 1990.
         SIP: Corporate History, August 3, 1940 (HRC).

PART FOUR

   196   "never sent it": Margaret Mitchell to Julian Harris, April 21, 1936, *Margaret Mitchell's Gone With
         the Wind Letters*, Richard Harwell, ed., p. 1.
   197   titles: Ibid., p. xxxiv.
         "in the country": IMS, *A Private View*, pp. 195–96.
         house: IMS, *A Private View*, pp. 195–99; *Architectural Digest*, April 1990, pp. 156–59, 286.
   198   "My mother's": Interview with DMS, October 31, 1987.
         Anna Karenina preview: IMS, *A Private View*, p. 197.
   199   "we agreed that": DOS to Tommy Douglas, September 28, 1938 (HRC).
         "Irene is hearing": Ibid.
         Luce and paintings: DOS to Henry Luce, June 26 1936 (HRC).
   200   "Selznick had a": Interview with KB, February 3, 1988.
   201   "Checks should be signed": DOS to John Wharton, October 18, 1935 (HRC).
         Cukor contract: August 31, 1935 (HRC).
   202   "Jeff is developing": DOS to Margaret Mayer, December 9, 1935 (HRC).
         Bellows painting: IMS, *A Private View*, pp. 199–200; interview with IMS, March 13, 1989.
   203   five "great novels": Richard Harwell, ed., *Gone With the Wind as Book and Film*, p. 13.
   205   "We're starting": Interview with Ring Lardner, Jr., February 5, 1988.
         Birdwell: Alva Johnston, "Russell Birdwell," *The New Yorker*, August 19, 26, September 2, 9,
         1944.
         "Would we have": JHW to DOS, February 20, 1936 (HRC).
   206   "I've been working": Johnston, "Russell Birdwell," September 9, 1944, p. 30.
         "the most successful": DOS to Whitney Bolton, December 17, 1941 (HRC).
         Fauntleroy's final costs: SIP statement, December 20, 1939 (HRC).
         "Logan": Joshua Logan, *Josh*, p. 87.
   207   "By the time": DOS to MS, May 13, 1936 (HRC).
         "Why do they": Howard Selznick to Christine McCoy, October 12, 1934 (HRC).
   208   "kissing the baby": Mildred Selznick deposition, pp. 405–6.
         "James Roberts": DOS to Dr. Henry Fox, June 23, 1936 (HRC).
         "brain operation": Charles Sachs to DOS, October 17, 1936 (HRC).
         "there would be no chance": Ibid.
         "Further institutional care": Dr. Henry Fox to DOS, October 30, 1936 (HRC).
         payment: Charles Sachs to DOS, October 17, 1936 (HRC).
         "fat, placid": IMS, *A Private View*, p. 208.
         "I remember my parents": Interview with LJS, December 6, 1988.
   209   "You'd better turn": Interview with IMS, January 1, 1989.
         "she is no longer": DOS to Gregory Ratoff, August 27, 1935 (HRC).
   210   "Rumor has it": Russell Birdwell to DOS, March 27, 1936 (HRC).
         "Now, Logan": Logan, *Josh*, p. 88.
   211   "We really didn't": Interview with Arthur Fellows, January 17, 1989.

p. 211   "I am getting": DOS to Richard Boleslavsky, April 28, 1936 (HRC).
"Surely a *little*": DOS to Richard Boleslavsky, June 17, 1936 (HRC).
"At the time": Corynn Kiehl to DOS, July 18, 1936 (HRC).

212   "magnificent possibility": KB to DOS, May 20, 1936 (HRC).
"ponderous trash": Interview with Marcella Rabwin, November 12, 1987.
"And I'm saying": Interview with Silvia Lardner, March 8, 1988.
"This is an": KB to DOS, May 21, 1936 (HRC).
"the more I think": DOS to KB, May 25, 1936 (HRC).
"Were I with M-G-M": DOS to KB, May 26, 1936 (HRC).

213   "seemed very interested": DOS to KB, May 28, 1936 (HRC).
"*Gone With the Wind* is": Ronald Colman to DOS, August 28, 1936 (HRC).
"if Metro deal falls thru": DOS to KB, May 28, 1936 (HRC).
"Forget it, Louis": In Roland Flamini, *Scarlett, Rhett and a Cast of Thousands*, p. 4.

214   "He flew New York": DOS to MS, June 24, 1936 (HRC).
"I am wreck": DOS to JHW, June 26, 1936 (HRC).
"She has not heard": KB to DOS, July 7, 1936 (HRC).
"She just called": KB to Silvia Schulman, July 7, 1936 (HRC).
"I bet Annie": Silvia Schulman to KB, July 7, 1936 (HRC).

215   "If you can close": Silvia Schulman to KB, July 7, 1936 (HRC).
"Is Sylvia there": KB to Silvia Schulman, July 7, 1936 (HRC).
"You are sure": KB to Silvia Schulman, July 7, 1936 (HRC).
"Absolutely certain": Silvia Schulman to KB, July 7, 1936 (HRC).
agreement: July 30, 1936 (HRC).

216   "the best Civil War": J. Donald Adams, *New York Times Book Review*, July 5, 1936.
"It is dramatic": Henry Steele Commager, New York *Herald-Tribune Books*, July 5, 1936.
"I can recall": Herschel Brickell, New York *Post*, June 30, 1936.
"The narrative pace": Isabel Paterson, New York *Herald-Tribune*, June 30, 1936.
"I would be upset": Margaret Mitchell to Stark Young, September 29, 1936.
It Happened in Hollywood: Haver, *Selznick's Hollywood*, p. 191.

217   "a concept of my own": *Memo*, p. 98.
"He never told me": Interview with IMS, May 6, 1990; Haver, *Selznick's Hollywood*, p. 192.

218   "Suggest looking": DOS to William Wellman and Robert Carson, July 30, 1936 (HRC).
"there—it wouldn't": Interview with IMS, May 6, 1990.

219   Lardner and Schulberg: Interview with Ring Lardner, Jr., February 5, 1988.
"that . . . is the only way": DOS to KB, August 31, 1936 (HRC).
"It will be impossible": Margaret Mitchell to KB, September 23, 1936 (HRC).
"the next best thing": DOS to KB, September 5, 1936 (HRC).
"Life has been awful": Margaret Mitchell to KB, October 6, 1936 (HRC).
Hepburn: Interview with Katharine Hepburn, November 2, 1990.

220   Lamar Trotti: Margaret Mitchell to KB, October 6, 1936 (HRC).
"probably the two best": DOS to KB, September 25, 1936 (HRC).
"I have never had": DOS to KB, October 8, 1936 (HRC).

221   "I have been re-reading": Sidney Howard to DOS, November 1, 1936 (H).
"When I sold the book": Margaret Mitchell to Sidney Howard, November 21, 1936 (H).

222   *The Garden of Allah*: Report of finished production (HRC).
Ray Klune: Interview with Ray Klune, July 30, 1987.
"The tests are": DOS to Tallulah Bankhead, December 24, 1936 (HRC).
"They bought groceries": Interview with IMS, May 5, 1989.

p. 222 "It will wreck": Interview with Ring Lardner, Jr., February 5, 1988.
  223 "This treatment": Sidney Howard to DOS, December 14, 1936 (H).
        Vivien Leigh: Alexander Walker, *Vivien*, p. 83.
        calendar: December 16–17, 1936 (HRC).
  226 "very happy indeed": DOS to Sidney Howard, January 6, 1937 (HRC).
        "It would be difficult": Ibid.
        "I feel, too": Ibid.
  227 "The book is written": Sidney Howard to DOS, January 11, 1937 (HRC).
        "After I looked": John Lee Mahin in Haver, *Selznick's Hollywood*, p. 201.
  228 "This is Vicki Lester": DOS to William Wellman, January 25, 1937 (HRC).
        Charles Morrison: Charles Morrison to KB, February 2, 1937; Charles Morrison to DOS,
        February 2, 1937; KB to Charles Morrison, February 3, 1937 (HRC).
        "You will have": Lowell Calvert to DOS, February 1, 1937 (HRC).
        "I have no enthusiasm": DOS to KB, February 3, 1937 (HRC).
        first item: Memo, November 3, 1936 (MS/F).
        "he looks fifty-seven": *The Bystander*, August 12, 1936.
        "The first time": Interview with Arthur Fellows, January 17, 1989.
  229 "We had been up there": Interview with Loretta Young, January 21, 1989.
        "He would explore": Interview with IMS, March 13, 1989.
  230 "As far as Fairbeam": MS to Nat Deverich, August 21, 1937 (HRC).
        DOS income: Statement of Receipts and Disbursements, 1936 (HRC).
  231 "I am aware": DOS to John Wharton, January 13, 1937 (HRC).
        "La Cava would": DOS to John Wharton, April 16, 1937 (HRC).
        Benzedrine: IMS, *A Private View*, pp. 162, 217; interview with IMS, May 6, 1988; *Journal of the
        American Medical Association*, December 18, 1937, pp. 2064–69; Lester Grinspoon and Peter
        Hedblom, *The Speed Culture* (Cambridge, Mass.: Harvard University Press, 1975), pp. 45–49,
        70–71, 87, 141.
        "I think the Benzedrine": Interview with IMS, May 5, 1989.
  233 "to get definite": DOS to Merian Cooper, February 23, 1937 (HRC).
        "If, however": Ibid.
        Root: Interview with Wells Root, December 3, 1987.
        "a terribly overbearing": Interview with Donald Ogden Stewart, in McGilligan, ed., *Back-
        story*, p. 341.
        "Bad but better": Sidney Howard, diary, April 7, 1937 (H).
        "Sure . . . how do": Sidney Howard to Polly Howard, April 14, 1937 (H).
  234 "he would sign-language": IMS, *A Private View*, p. 211.
        "I am winning": DOS to IMS, April 13, 1937 (IMS/DT).
        "I am home": DOS to IMS, April 14, 1937 (IMS/DT).
        "Bad day with thinking": Sidney Howard, diary, April 19, 1937 (H).
        "Selznick hates color": Sidney Howard to Polly Howard, April 17, 1937 (H).
  235 "This was really": *Memo*, p. 98.
        "the trouble with": Ibid.
        A Star is Born figures: SIP report, December 20, 1939 (HRC).
  238 "If there is anybody": LBM in Crowther, *Hollywood Rajah*, pp. 220–21.
        gambling: Monthly records (HRC).
  239 Lardner-Schulman marriage: Interviews with Ring Lardner, Jr., February 5, 1988, and Silvia
        Lardner, March 8, 1988.
        "Mr. Brand rises": Jane Allen, *I Lost My Girlish Laughter*, pp. 51–52.

p. 240 "an all-day discussion": Sidney Howard to Polly Howard, April 21, 1937 (H).
"Selznick, a very nice": Sidney Howard to Polly Howard, April 22, 1937 (H).
"This fellow Selznick": Sidney Howard to Harold Freedman, April 29, 1937 (H).
"In connection": DOS to William Wright, April 12, 1937 (HRC).
241 "For example": John Wharton to DOS and JHW, April 15, 1937 (HRC).
242 "In my opinion": Ibid.
"I should like": Ibid.
"After all": DOS to George Schafer, June 9, 1936 (HRC).
243 United Artists: Balio, *United Artists*, pp. 142–53.
"would always sooner": Interview with IMS, January 22, 1989.
"I believe I told you": DOS to John Wharton, May 23, 1937 (HRC).
244 "the United Artists crowd": Ibid.
"Nicholas Schenck": Calendar, May 17, 1937 (HRC).
"I read in the paper": DOS to John Wharton, May 23, 1937 (HRC).
246 "Contrary to": DOS to John Wharton, May 23, 1937 (HRC).
248 "My entire approach": KB to DOS, November 25, 1936 (HRC).
"that this expedition": KB to DOS, November 29, 1936 (HRC).
"the madhouse": KB to DOS, December 5, 1936 (HRC).
"How's you-all": Ibid.
"We arrived yesterday": George Cukor to DOS, March 29, 1937 (HRC).
249 "Honorable Gentlemen": Anon. to SIP, February 1938 (HRC).
"I'm Scarlett O'Hara": Ibid.
"As to my being": Tallulah Bankhead to DOS, December 25, 1936 (HRC).
"You wanted comedy": DOS to JHW, June 12, 1937 (HRC).
251 "keeps screaming": Sidney Howard to Polly Howard, July 31, 1937 (H).
"Last night I dined": Sidney Howard to Polly Howard, August 5, 1937 (H).
Fellows: Interview with Arthur Fellows, January 17, 1989.
"for the good": Johnston, "Russell Birdwell," *The New Yorker*, September 9, 1944.
252 *Nothing Sacred* costs: SIP statement, December 20, 1939 (HRC).
"Dear Leland": Ben Hecht to Leland Hayward, July 1, 1937 (HRC).
"Don't be so generous": DOS to MS, November 24, 1937 (HRC).
253 "there will be no war": John Wharton to JHW and DOS, January 22, 1937 (HRC).
254 "A European war": DOS to John Wharton, August 16, 1937 (HRC).
"unless the picture": Lowell Calvert to DOS, March 27, 1937 (HRC).
255 "My father had been": Interview with IMS, May 9, 1988.
George Schaefer: Lowell Calvert to DOS, March 30, 1937; George Schaefer to DOS, July 6, 1937 (HRC).
"if the big deal": DOS to John Wharton, July 8, 1937 (HRC).
256 "As you know": DOS to Lowell Calvert, August 9, 1937 (HRC).
"I do not want": DOS to Merian Cooper, n.d. (HRC).
257 "into spasms of excitement": DOS to John Wharton, September 2, 1937 (HRC).
David's earnings: SIP statement, December 20, 1939 (HRC).
258 "did not seem": IMS, *A Private View*, pp. 210–11.
"Dear David": Ben Hecht to DOS, December 21, 1937 (HRC).
259 "Inasmuch as you": Lowell Calvert to Francis Altstock, January 21, 1938 (HRC).
260 "The suggested policy": John Wharton to JHW, February 19, 1938 (HRC).
"to leave the Company": Ibid.

p. 260 "Cholly asks": Cecil Beaton drawing, *Vogue*, February 1938.
"if there is any": Cecil Beaton, diary, January 1938, quoted in Hugo Vickers, *Cecil Beaton*, p. 208.

261 "horrible, disgusting": Interview with Katharine Hepburn, November 2, 1990.

262 "How can you listen?": Interview with IMS, May 12, 1990.
"David just wanted": Interview with Joseph L. Mankiewicz, May 9, 1989.
"psychology and experience": DOS to JHW, January 19, 1938 (HRC).
"There is, in fact": Ibid.

263 "colour is now": Sidney Howard to Polly Howard, January 16, 1938 (H).
" 'Oh, Farr' ": Sidney Howard to Polly Howard, January 20, 1938 (H).
"I would come": Interview with Charles Bennett, January 20, 1988.
"With any other agent": DOS to MS, June 30, 1938 (HRC).

264 Ingrid Bergman: Interviews with Elsa Neuberger, November 5, 1987; Kay Brown, February 3, 1988; Jenia Reissar, June 1, 1988; Ingrid Bergman and Alan Burgess, *Ingrid Bergman: My Story*; Jenia Reissar to KB, October 4, 1938.
"It could have been written": Bette Davis, *The Lonely Life*, p. 174.
"unpleasant": Interview with Katharine Hepburn, November 2, 1990.

265 *"Hurry, Miss Mitchell"*: Phyllis McGinley, *Redbook*, April 1938.
"damned as an imitation": DOS to Jack Warner, March 8, 1938 (HRC).
"splendid interest": Jack Warner to DOS, March 8, 1938 (HRC).
"building up our list": DOS to DTO'S, June 3, 1938 (HRC).
"make clear to Mr. Goldwyn": DOS to JHW, March 14, 1938 (HRC).

266 "It breaks my heart": DOS to JHW, June 10, 1938 (HRC).
"If the picture": Ibid.
"Most of all": Ibid.

267 chart: n.d. (HRC).

268 "It has been obvious": JHW statement, August 9, 1938 (HRC).
"Scarlett O'Hara was not": Margaret Mitchell, *Gone with the Wind*, p. 3.

269 Scarlett votes: Dorothy Carter to DOS, July 28, 1938 (HRC).
"It might interest": George Cukor to DOS, February 11, 1938 (HRC).
Paulette Goddard: Paulette Goddard to DOS, June 21, 1938; Russell Birdwell to DOS, December 20, 21, 1938 (HRC).
"At first": IMS, *A Private View*, p. 214.

270 Cukor salary: DOS to Marcella Rabwin, January 25, 1938 (HRC).
"Incidentally, this": George Cukor to DOS, May 9, 1938 (HRC).
"I am frankly": DOS to JHW, May 9, 1938 (HRC).
"I think this may": Ibid.

271 " a swift pain": DTO'S to DOS, November 30, 1938 (HRC).
"I could have done it": Interview with Katharine Hepburn, November 2, 1990.
"It may be that Garrett": DOS to DTO'S, November 20, 1938 (HRC).

272 "in a rather obligatory": Evelyn Keyes, *Scarlett O'Hara's Younger Sister*, p. 31; interview with Evelyn Keyes, December 2, 1987.
"While it is": DOS to Marcella Rabwin, November 12, 1938 (HRC).
"David loved the ladies": Interview with Loretta Young, January 21, 1989.

273 Joan Fontaine: Joan Fontaine, *No Bed of Roses*, p. 99; Joan Fontaine to DT, June 12, 1990.
Myron and production: Douglas Churchill, "The Great Myron Selznick Mystery," *New York Times*, December 4, 1938; *Variety*, July 27, August 3, 10, 17, 24, November 6, 1938; DOS to Henry Ginsberg, August 10, 1938 (HRC).

p. 274   "be careful": DOS to Henry Ginsberg, August 10, 1938 (HRC).
"one of the most startling": *New York Times*, December 4, 1938.

275   "Open Letter": MS to Joe Schenck, LBM, Darryl Zanuck, October 5, 1938 (HRC).
"In all fairness": Ibid.
"And the best Scarlett": DOS to Ed Sullivan, September 20, 1938 (HRC).

276   "You want to play": Walker, *Vivien*, p. 104.
"Forgive me": Vivien Leigh to William Wyler, August 31, 1938 (MS/F).
"pure, driving": Olivier, *Confessions*, p. 107.
Beaumont: Interview with IMS, November 4, 1987.
"Mrs. V. M. Hollman": Vivien Leigh file (MS/F).

277   "I have honestly": IMS to DOS, n.d. (HRC).
"You may judge": DOS to IMS, December 3, 1938 (IMS/DT).

278   "As for the findings": IMS to DOS, December 7, 1938 (HRC).
"crouched in the back": Olivier, *Confessions*, p. 107.
"there was someone": Ibid.
"I said innocently": Ibid.
"It was around 6 p.m.": Interview with Maxine Graybill, April 9, 1988.

279   O'Shea: Walker, *Vivien*, pp. 11–12; DTO'S to DOS (daily report), December 8, 1938 (HRC).
"meet Scarlett O'Hara": Olivier, *Confessions*, p. 108; Walker, *Vivien*, p. 113.
"You used to start": IMS to DOS, December 11, 1938 (HRC).
"Please tell Miss Fontaine": IMS to DOS, December 13, 1938 (HRC).

280   December 10: Daily production report, call sheet, budget reconciliation (HRC).

281   "During the same": DOS to IMS, December 14, 1938 (IMS/DT).

282   "refuses under any": DOS to George Cukor, December 8, 1938 (HRC).
"Sound the trumpets": DOS to IMS, December 10, 1938 (HRC).
"You have missed": DOS to JHW, December 10, 1938 (HRC).
"Shhhhh: she's the": DOS to IMS, December 12, 1938 (IMS/DT).
"That it was going": IMS to DOS, December 12, 1938 (HRC).
"Your long tale": DOS to IMS, December 14, 1938 (IMS/DT).
"all kinds of cheery": IMS to DOS, December 16, 1938 (HRC).
"How is your romance": IMS to DOS, December 16, 1938 (HRC).

283   "Irene was something": John Huston, *An Open Book*, p. 300.
"And please": IMS to DOS, December 16, 1938 (HRC).
"I look at her": DOS to IMS, December 17, 1938 (IMS/DT).

284   Sunny Alexander: Interview with Sunny Alexander Lash, March 10, 1988.
"I'd be the": Olivier, *Confessions*, p. 109.
"all manner of trouble": DOS to Jenia Reissar, November 9, 1944 (HRC).

285   "She's a honey!": Wilbur Kurtz in "Technical Advisor," *Atlanta Historical Journal*, summer 1978, p. 108.
"Vivien is a bawdy": Susan Myrick, diary, March 3, 1939.
"out of millions": Hedda Hopper, Los Angeles *Times*, January 16, 1939.
"She certainly is": Margaret Mitchell in notes from Russell Birdwell to DOS, January 17, 1939 (HRC).

286   "an astonishing percentage": Ibid.
Leslie Howard: DOS to DTO'S, October 14, 1937 (HRC); interview with Marcella Rabwin, November 12, 1987.

287   "to have a reading": Fontaine, *No Bed*, pp. 113–14; Kurtz, "Technical Advisor," p. 103.

p. 287   Olivia: Olivia de Havilland to LJS, August 10, 1987.

288   "As for Tara": Kurtz, "Technical Advisor," p. 62.

"If anyone had told me": Margaret Mitchell to Susan Myrick, February 10, 1939.

"However": F. Scott Fitzgerald to DOS, January 23, 1939 (HRC).

"Scott, I want": Interview with James Toback, March 2, 1991.

289   "Don't get panicky": DOS to JHW, January 25, 1939 (HRC).

"the next couple of months": Ibid.

"As a result": Statement by DOS and George Cukor, February 13, 1939 (HRC).

290   "ignominious tale": Publisher's blurb, Patrick McGilligan, *George Cukor: A Double Life*.

"In reality, Gable": Boze Hadleigh, interview with George Cukor in *Conversations with My Elders*, p. 133.

"As stars went": Ibid., p. 146.

Flamini: Flamini, *Scarlett, Rhett*, p. 232.

291   "Clark never opened": DOS, interviewed by Charles Samuels, March 25, 1961; Charles Samuels, *The King*, pp. 221–33.

"I don't want Cukor": Samuels interview with DOS, March 25, 1961.

"ace in the hole": Haver, *Selznick's Hollywood*, p. 267; "Rhett by Clark Gable," *Gone With the Wind* program, 1939.

"the worst possible selection": "Rhett by Clark Gable."

292   "You are wrong": Susan Myrick to Margaret Mitchell, February 14, 1939.

"had been damned patient": Ibid.

293   "I therefore": DOS to George Cukor, February 8, 1939 (HRC).

"I saved him his job": Interview with IMS, May 29, 1989.

Butterfly McQueen: Interview with Butterfly McQueen, June 1, 1987.

Cukor's contract: George Cukor to DOS, February 11, 1939; DTO'S to Ernest Scanlon, February 11, 1939; termination agreement, March 2, 1939 (HRC).

"So George": Susan Myrick to Margaret Mitchell, February 14, 1939.

294   Vidor: Aljean Harmetz, *The Making of the Wizard of Oz*, p. 164; Raymond Durgnat and Scott Simmon, *King Vidor, American*, p. 173.

"David . . . you haven't": Interview with Marcella Rabwin, November 12, 1987.

"George would have done": Quoted by John Lee Mahin, in McGilligan, ed., *Backstory*, p. 256.

295   "As far as I can": Transcript of conversation (HRC).

Ben Hecht: Columbia University, Oral History, June 1959.

296   "David had done": Ibid.

"They tell me": Reggie Callow, interviewed by Rudy Behlmer (A).

297   "With George and Victor": Olivia de Havilland to LJS, August 10, 1987.

"contemplate any allowance": Ray Klune to Henry Ginsberg, April 5, 1939 (HRC).

Ann Rutherford: Interview with Ann Rutherford (BBC).

298   "I thought the stuff": Sidney Howard to Polly Howard, April 5, 1939 (H).

"How really astonishing": Sidney Howard to Polly Howard, April 8, 1939 (H).

"Rewrite it for me": Ibid.

"The whole thing": Ibid.

"My own private weariness": Sidney Howard to Polly Howard, April 18, 1939 (H).

299   Ways to Kill a Baby: Flamini, *Scarlett, Rhett*, p. 293.

"Larry met me": Ibid., p. 294.

"It was a case of": Interview with Marcella Rabwin, November 12, 1987.

300   Bank of America: Agreement, May 26, 1939 (HRC).

301   "Sound the siren": DOS to JHW, June 27, 1939 (HRC).

p. 301 "of great good luck": IMS, *A Private View*, p. 216.

"After shooting began": Ibid., p. 217.

302 Sunny Alexander: Interview with Sunny Alexander Lash, March 10, 1988.

"How do you do": Ingrid Bergman and Alan Burgess, *Ingrid Bergman*, p. 63.

"Is Mr. Selznick": Bergman and Burgess, *Ingrid Bergman*, Ibid.; interview with Jenia Reissar, June 1, 1988; interview with KB, February 3, 1988.

"I waited for": Interview with Jenia Reissar, June 1, 1988.

Kay Brown: Interview with Kay Brown, February 3, 1988.

303 "and there was this man": Bergman and Burgess, *Ingrid Bergman*, p. 65.

304 "where I saw her wince": Fontaine, *No Bed*, p. 149.

"He was especially": Bergman and Burgess, *Ingrid Bergman*, p. 73.

Intermezzo: Interview with Arthur Fellows, January 17, 1989.

305 Alfred Hitchcock: Leonard Leff, *Hitchcock & Selznick*.

Fontaine: Fontaine, *No Bed*, p. 149; DOS daily calendar, June–July 1938 (HRC); Joan Fontaine to DT, June 12, 1990.

"Darling—I feel": DOS to IMS, n.d. (IMS/DT).

306 "As I outlined": Alfred Hitchcock to DOS, May 4, 1939 (HRC).

307 "He surely has": Hal Kern to DOS, May 5, 1939 (HRC).

"disappointed beyond words": DOS to Alfred Hitchcock, June 12, 1939 (HRC).

309 "she doesn't seem": DOS to JHW, August 18, 1939 (HRC).

"the only one": Ibid.

"Almost on impulse": Brian Aherne, *A Proper Job*, p. 286.

"The last test": JHW to DOS, August 21, 1939 (HRC).

310 "How long": Aherne, *A Proper Job*, p. 315.

"the picture is turning": DOS to Howard Dietz, May 2, 1939 (HRC).

"in his opinion": DOS to JHW, June 7, 1939 (HRC).

311 "I suppose it is": JHW to DOS, June 9, 1939 (HRC).

"I am afraid": DOS to JHW, June 10, 1939 (HRC).

"whom I invited": DOS to Lowell Calvert, July 17, 1939 (HRC).

"the greatest picture": Ibid.

Blumenthal: DOS to A. C. Blumenthal, August 2, 1939 (HRC).

312 "Angel—I took": DOS to IMS, August 9, 1939 (IMS/DT).

313 "This is against": Hal Kern interview, quoted in Haver, *Selznick's Hollywood*, p. 293.

William Erickson: Interview with William Erickson, December 1, 1987.

"There were a lot": IMS, *A Private View*, p. 219.

314 "When Margaret Mitchell's": Hal Kern interview (RM Haver).

"It was as though": IMS, *A Private View*, p. 219.

315 "I realize it": DOS to Ben Hecht, October 11, 1939 (HRC).

316 "whether he would like": DOS to Frank Capra, January 22, 1940 (HRC).

"You do whatever": Quoted in Haver, *Selznick's Hollywood*, p. 298.

"When I mentioned": DOS to DTO'S, October 9, 1939 (HRC).

318 "The part of each": DOS to KB, September 20, 1939 (HRC).

319 costs: Budget reconciliation, December 23, 1939 (HRC).

"This picture has done": DOS to Nick Schenck, September 23, 1939 (HRC).

320 "He and Birdwell": DOS to KB, November 28, 1939 (HRC).

321 "I was awfully distressed": Vivien Leigh to IMS, October 21, 1939 (IMS/DT).

322 lay-offs: KB to JHW, Francis Altstock, and Ernest Scanlon, March 11, 1941 (HRC).

Hattie McDaniel: DOS to Howard Dietz, November 29, 1939 (HRC).

p. 322 press screening: Daily memo, December 6, 1939; DOS to Russell Birdwell, December 6, 1939 (HRC).

"The greatest motion mural": Frank Nugent, *New York Times*, December 20, 1939.

"the world's greatest": *Hollywood Reporter*, December 23, 1939.

323 "Dear David": Abe Berman to DOS, December 15, 1939 (HRC).

"Dearest Irene and David": George Cukor to DOS and IMS, December 14, 1939 (HRC).

324 "There was a hush": Interview with Evelyn Keyes, December 2, 1987.

"I think all of you": Margaret Mitchell, WSM coverage, December 15, 1939.

326 "For years": Interview with IMS, May 29, 1990.

"The meeting place": Ibid.

328 "And what was desperate": Ibid.

330 "As for Manderley": DOS to Alfred Hitchcock, June 12, 1939 (HRC).

331 "Well, in the": François Truffaut, *Hitchcock*, p. 163.

Olivier: Fontaine, *No Bed*, p. 116.

"It is just": DOS to Alfred Hitchcock, September 19, 1939 (HRC).

332 "Cutting your film": Ibid.

"When the picture": IMS, *A Private View*, p. 223; interview with IMS, November 4, 1987.

"stately": Leff, *Hitchcock & Selznick*, p. 79.

333 "How alive was her": Daphne du Maurier, *Rebecca*, Chapter 6.

"I refer to": DOS to Alfred Hitchcock, October 17, 1939 (HRC).

334 afraid Daphne du Maurier: DOS to KB, February 27, 1939 (HRC).

"The whole story": DOS to JHW, September 6, 1939 (HRC).

PART FIVE

338 "Jock is now": DOS to IMS, n.d. (IMS/DT).

339 "I procured the right doctor": IMS, *A Private View*, p. 233.

"He made clear": Ibid.

340 "he wanted me to know": Interview with Berman Swarttz, November 30, 1989.

341 "The entire election": DOS to Russell Davenport, n.d. (HRC).

"After some loud-voiced": Ibid.

342 "I've had enough now": Interview with LJS, December 4, 1988.

"I am afraid": DOS to Vivien Leigh, July 13, 1940 (HRC).

343 "Stony Batter was hardly": Interview with IMS, June 26, 1989.

"Myron would listen": Interview with LJS, December 3, 1988.

344 "Dear Joan": DOS to Joan Fontaine, August 15, 1940 (HRC).

345 "very ambitious": Interview with Katharine Hepburn, November 2, 1990.

net worth: DOS and IMS tax records, 1939, 1940 (HRC).

346 "Any plan for the future": Francis Altstock to JHW, January 29, 1940 (HRC).

"As he termed it": Ibid.

347 "The only way I could see": *Memo*, p. 301.

"I didn't approve": IMS, *A Private View*, p. 227.

"that it was Mr. Selznick": Francis Altstock to JHW, June 12, 1940 (HRC).

348 "I should like to observe": DOS to JHW, June 27, 1940 (HRC).

349 "I am sure": DOS to Leo Spitz, December 2, 1940 (HRC).

"We have all along": DOS to JHW, June 30, 1941 (HRC).

350 "violent personal animus": JHW to DOS, July 22, 1941 (HRC).

"believes in doing business": Ibid.

p. 350   "has come to the conclusion": DOS to Marjorie Daw Selznick, May 31, 1939 (HRC).
351   "Myron is, as we all know": DOS to Maxine Graybill, June 22, 1940 (HRC).
"You must know": Marjorie Daw Selznick to MS, February 3, 1940 (MS/F).
352   *"One day and I remember":* Joan Selznick, n.d. (JW).
"In our discussion": Barry Brannen to DOS, July 30, 1940 (HRC).
"He didn't like the Jews": Ibid.
Ishii: Eataro Ishii file, War Relocation Authority, 71.113 (Washington, D.C.: National Archives).
"If this means": Barry Brannen to DOS, July 30, 1940 (HRC).
353   "Beyond this": DOS, to whom it may concern, November 24, 1940 (HRC).
"The horse and mule": MS to DOS, May 22, 1941 (HRC).
354   "When the institution": IMS, *A Private View*, p. 255.
"Last week Myron": Howard Selznick to Charles Sachs, April 21, 1941 (HRC).
Howard . . . tests: Hartford Retreat to DOS, January 29, 1941, and February 21, 1941; Dr. A. A. Brill to Selective Service Board, October 29, 1942 (HRC).
355   "He likes to attract": Report, Hartford Retreat, March 29, 1941 (HRC).
"You are right, Eleanor": Howard Selznick to Eleanor B., March 27, 1942 (HRC).
356   "He couldn't have been nicer": Interview with John Houseman, April 13, 1988.
"John and David": Interview with IMS, April 14, 1988.
357   "Have you tried": DOS to JHW, January 4, 1939 (HRC).
"pretty deeply immersed": DOS to Orson Welles, August 2, 1939 (HRC).
"is almost certainly": Orson Welles to DOS, August 5, 1939 (HRC).
"Put D.O.S. and John Houseman": Interview with IMS, April 14, 1988.
"We finished it": John Houseman, *Run-through*, p. 478.
358   "riled David all the time": Interview with John Houseman, April 13, 1988.
"Only today I received": DOS to Alexander Korda, June 5, 1941 (HRC).
359   "Dear Charlie": DOS to Charlie Chaplin, February 27, 1940 (HRC).
360   "her refusal to return": Jenia Reissar to DOS, January 19, 1942 (HRC).
"since you did not consider": Ibid.
"Olivier really hated": Interview with Jenia Reissar, June 1, 1988.
361   "You are totally wrong": Petter Lindstrom to IMS, January 7, 1985 (Lindstrom).
362   "4. I announced Joan": DOS to Frank Vincent, June 23, 1942 (HRC).
363   "stirred . . . to revolt": Houseman, *Run-through*, p. 482.
"When I informed": Ibid., p. 486.
364   "Psychological stories": Val Lewton journal, February 11, 1941 (HRC).
"He began by announcing": Ibid., November 14, 1941 (HRC).
"may have been a better": MS to DOS, September 24, 1942 (MS/F).
366   "Right in the middle": Draft script for *Hollywood Comes A' Visiting*, n.d.; LM to Whitney Bolton, March 24, 1942 (HRC).
"the little girl": DOS calendar, July 16, 1941 (HRC).
"Regarding Phyllis Thaxter": DOS to KB, July 22, 1941 (HRC).
"Lovely big-eyed girl": KB to DOS, July 23, 1941 (HRC).
"You have really": DOS to KB, July 29, 1941 (HRC).
"but I didn't dare": KB to DOS, July 23, 1941 (HRC).
"please don't think me": KB to DTO'S, July 31, 1941 (HRC).
368   "She has the 'cutes' ": DOS to KB, June 4, 1941 (HRC).
"I don't know": DOS to Whitney Bolton, August 2, 1941 (HRC).
"I was so amazed": Interview with Frances Inglis, April 12, 1988.

p. 368 "and I should not": DOS to KB, August 19, 1941 (HRC).

"It was within": Interview with Frances Inglis, April 12, 1988.

369 "We must face": DOS to John Houseman and Alfred de Liagre, August 21, 1941 (HRC).

"damned good": Interview with John Houseman, April 13, 1988.

"Give me that": Ibid.

"It was not until": Ibid.

370 "bitter disappointment": DOS to KB, DTO'S, and Ray Klune, September 9, 1941 (HRC).

371 "Sorry you were out": Phylis Walker to DOS, September 14, 1941 (HRC).

"After opening night": Phylis Walker to DOS, September 19, 1941 (HRC).

"Of course, Franken": KB to DOS, September 5, 1941 (HRC).

"She has undoubted talent": Rose Franken to DOS, September 26, 1941 (HRC).

372 "of being a daughter": DOS to Leland Hayward, October 17, 1941 (HRC).

"whether she does *Claudia*": DOS to Rose Franken, September 30, 1941 (HRC).

"How could it?": Interview with Dorothy McGuire, July 19, 1989.

"jumping for joy": KB to DOS, October 3, 1941 (HRC).

"My present impression": DOS to DTO'S, October 14, 1941 (HRC).

"The girl is inclined": DOS to DTO'S, October 24, 1941 (HRC).

373 "Chloe O'Shea": Whitney Bolton to DOS, December 22, 1941 (HRC).

"Delly has spent": DOS to KB, December 27, 1941 (HRC).

"I still like": DOS to Whitney Bolton, December 22, 1941 (HRC).

"JENNIFER JONES IS OKAY": Jennifer Jones to KB, February 4, 1942 (HRC).

374 "Stella Unger": LM to Whitney Bolton, March 24, 1942 (HRC).

375 "Most Wonderful of Women": DOS to IMS, August 13, 1942 (IMS/DT).

376 "She didn't seem to react": DOS to DTO'S, August 22, 1942 (HRC).

"The time had come": IMS, *A Private View*, p. 225.

377 incomes: DOS and IMS, tax records 1940 (HRC).

378 "20th Century proved": IMS, *A Private View*, p. 193.

Twentieth stock: IMS, tax records, 1942 (HRC).

"and she didn't like": Interview with IMS, August 8, 1989.

379 "David cursed Betsey": Interview with IMS, March 19, 1989.

"Something's happening": Interview with William S. Paley, May 11, 1989.

"they said that either": *Memo*, p. 301.

Wind was sold: Ernest Scanlon to DOS, August 3, 1945 (HRC).

380 1987 dollars: Roger L. Mayer to LJS, January 22, 1988 (reporting the estimates of A. D. Murphy of *Variety* and the Turner Finance Department).

"a fortune for him": DOS to DTO'S, September 17, 1943 (HRC).

Whitney sale to MGM: Ernest Scanlon to DOS, September 17, 1943 (HRC).

381 income: DOS and IMS, tax records, 1942, 1943 (HRC).

"From and after": Property agreement, December 30, 1942 (HRC).

"After all, it was": DOS to Maynard Toll, May 4, 1948 (HRC).

"It was unfeeling of me": IMS, *A Private View*, p. 226.

382 "There wasn't a difficulty": Interview with IMS, June 26, 1989.

"never advised me": Ibid.

Lindstrom: Interview with Petter Lindstrom, November 15, 1987.

"His spirit was fine": IMS, *A Private View*, p. 241.

383 "David talked about": Interview with William S. Paley, May 11, 1989.

"The one thing": DOS to Sol Rosenblatt, November 23, 1940 (HRC).

384 "I would like to get": Merian Cooper to DOS, July 18, 1941 (HRC).

p. 384 "A few thyroid": DOS to Merian Cooper, January 21, 1942 (HRC).
"I cannot tell you": Merian Cooper to DOS, January 8, 1942 (HRC).

385 "I will thank you": DOS to William S. Paley, December 27, 1940 (HRC).
"I had thought": DOS to James Forrestal, September 16, 1942 (HRC).

386 "Telling him": DOS to Merian Cooper, December 22, 1942 (HRC).
"either be compulsory": DOS to James Forrestal, March 9, 1943 (HRC).
"We are glad to": James Forrestal to DOS, March 27, 1943 (HRC).

387 Houseman: Interview with John Houseman, April 13, 1988.

388 "Miss Pringle": DOS to Joseph Steele and Ray Klune, March 19, 1943 (HRC).
"Have asked Cagney": Barbara Keon to DOS, March 31, 1943 (HRC).

389 "So Irene": Interview with Aileen Pringle, May 8, 1988.
April 4: Official program (HRC); Los Angeles *Times*, April 5, 1943.
"I don't see the harm": DOS to Joseph Steele and Ray Klune, March 19, 1943 (HRC).
"China: A Symphonic Narrative": Narrative script, March 30, 1943 (HRC).
"We shall not abrade": Los Angeles *Times*, April 5, 1943.

390 "particularly in showing": DOS to John Grierson, June 21, 1943 (HRC).
"Hollywood Bowl": John Grierson to DOS, July 21, 1943 (HRC).
"Dear Davido": Aileen Pringle to DOS, n.d. (HRC).
"182,500 multivitamin": DOS to Madame Chiang Kai-shek, December 11, 1943 (HRC).

391 "You could just tell": Interview with Frances Inglis, April 12, 1988.
"All the others *looked*": Quoted in Beverly Linet, *Star-Crossed*, p. 86.

392 "I didn't know": DOS to William Goetz, October 14, 1942 (HRC).
"I just differ": William Goetz to DOS, October 12, 1942 (HRC).
"Jennifer was very": DOS to Joseph Steele, January 4, 1943 (HRC).

393 "Joe tried": Frances Inglis to DTO'S, February 5, 1943 (HRC).
"This was Nancy Kelly": Interview with Dorothy Hirshon, March 14, 1989.

394 "If you hold out": Shirley Temple Black, *Child Star*, p. 380.

395 "Despite his amazing": Joseph Steele release (not sent), September 8, 1943 (HRC).
"Also I'd like to urge": DOS to DTO'S and Ernest Scanlon, July 23, 1943 (HRC).

396 *Since You Went Away*: Production reports and budget reconciliation (HRC).
"There was always": Interview with Stanley Cortez, July 21, 1989.
"If you haven't heard": Joseph Cotten, *Vanity Will Get You Somewhere*, p. 59.
"Have you ever seen": Ibid., p. 60.

397 "Personally, I detected": Black, *Child Star*, p. 357.
"Irene used to call": Interview with Lois Hamby, December 1, 1987.

399 "to be struck": Cotten, *Vanity*, p. 60.
"blend of serious talent": James Agee, *Agee on Film*, pp. 106–8.

400 "Mr. Selznick's": Ibid., p. 108.

401 "combined marquee audit": DOS to PL, February 19, 1944 (HRC).
"Unfortunately": Ibid.

402 "He said that": Don King to DOS, September 8, 1944 (HRC).
"My chief memory": Ben Hecht to DOS, January 20, 1944 (HRC).
"Dickens": Don King to Kay Mulvey, April 22, 1944 (HRC).

403 "a strangely contrived": Terry Ramsaye, *Motion Picture Herald*, July 21, 1944.
"The picture seems": Ibid.
"Myron Selznick": *Hollywood Reporter*, March 24, 1944.

404 "He was very insecure": Interview with Loretta Young, January 21, 1989.

405 Joan Bennett: Interview with IMS, March 13, 1989.

p. 405 "He was very envious": Interview with Joseph L. Mankiewicz, May 9, 1989.

406 "Did he notice?": Interview with IMS, April 14, 1988.

"There were days": Mary Rechner Hawk to DT, June 5, 1988.

407 "He was in a scruffy": Interview with LJS, December 3, 1988.

"I think you would": DOS to MS, August 22, 1942 (HRC).

"I will give it": MS to DOS, August 29, 1942 (HRC).

"Just so there will be": DOS to MS, November 11, 1942 (HRC).

408 "I should say": Ibid.

"Myron has not yet": Francis Chambers to Dr. Edward Strecker, November 25, 1942 (HRC).

"Frankenstein, as it": DOS to Dr. Edward Strecker, November 30, 1942 (HRC).

"Let me say in passing": Ibid.

409 liquor inventory: Hill Haven, August 8, 1943 (MS/F).

Lester Roth: Roth to MS, March 4, 1943 (MS/F).

"in the last few years": George Cukor to MS, January 28, 1944 (MS/F).

"a terrific disappointment": MS to George Cukor, February 11, 1944 (MS/F).

410 "so hurt himself": Francis Chambers to DOS, March 24, 1944 (HRC).

"But perhaps": DOS to Francis Chambers, April 18, 1944 (HRC).

estate: Final Account of Estate, Superior Court, County of Los Angeles, September 29, 1953.

"As I have told you": DOS to Jennifer Jones, November 8, 1943 (HRC).

411 "It rings a bell": Interview with IMS, July 25, 1989.

"to seek my help": DOS to Margaret McDonell, May 18, 1944 (HRC).

412 "I also assume": Ibid.

413 "the actress was busy": New York Times, May 6, 1944.

414 "We in publicity": Don King to DOS, July 3, 1944 (HRC).

"She looked like": Interview with Anita Colby, February 6, 1988.

"As Catholic mother": Ann Whalen Perfect Sodality to Jennifer Jones, January 26, 1944 (HRC).

"that our Phylis": Sister Ursula to DOS, March 1944 (HRC).

415 "I am thinking particularly": John Harkins to DOS, July 18, 1944 (HRC).

"Will you help": DOS to Harriett Flagg, December 12, 1944 (HRC).

"I'm not a very deep": DOS to Jennifer Jones, gift card (HRC).

gifts: DOS to Harriett Flagg, December 12, 1944 (HRC); personal files of Anita Colby.

"I didn't like her looks": Interview with IMS, August 9, 1990.

416 "it was terrible": Interview with Leonora Hornblow, November 6, 1987.

417 "My only answer": IMS, A Private View, p. 263.

"Indeed, he was completely": DOS to Loyd Wright, January 26, 1944 (HRC).

"I cannot see myself": Ibid.

419 "A big, toothy grin": Dore Schary, Heyday, p. 133.

"would approve of the basic idea": Ibid.

"It was long": Ibid., p. 136.

"You applied the lash": Dore Schary to DOS, February 21, 1944 (HRC).

420 "Were I more sensitive": DOS to DTO'S, March 4, 1944 (HRC).

"Whether you like the script": Schary, Heyday, p. 136.

"I am swamped": DOS to Dore Schary, September 10, 1944 (HRC).

421 "Just as it is apparent": DOS to Dore Schary, September 28, 1944 (HRC).

"just nothing": Ibid.

"create a whole new story": Ibid.

p. 422   "he was actually going insane": IMS, *A Private View*, p. 235.

423   May Romm: Interviews with Dr. Dorothy Colodny, July 21, 1989, and September 8, 1989.
"Dr. Romm was": IMS, *A Private View*, p. 236.

424   "She was impressed": Interview with Dr. Dorothy Colodny, July 21, 1989.
"He knew more": IMS, *A Private View*, p. 236.
"Why don't *you* come?": Interview with Anita Colby, February 6, 1988.
"Take it up with May": Ibid.

425   "David was making the film": Interview with IMS, February 18, 1989.
"a well constructed": DOS to DTO'S, November 26, 1943 (HRC).
"Page 28. Scene 77": Eileen Johnston to DOS, Ben Hecht, and Alfred Hitchcock, June 16, 1944 (HRC).

426   "I am paying": DOS to May Romm, June 8, 1944 (HRC).
"Not only does Doctor Romm": Eileen Johnston to DOS, July 6, 1944 (HRC).
"which includes a sequence": DOS to Karl Menninger, September 22, 1944 (HRC).

427   "many very unfortunate": Karl Menninger to DOS, October 2, 1944 (HRC).
"I spent a considerable time": May Romm to Karl Menninger, September 25, 1944 (Dr. Dorothy Colodny).

428   "You'll understand this": Interview with Petter Lindstrom, November 15, 1987.

429   "You have made a lot": Harry Rapf to DOS, July 31, 1944 (HRC).

PART SIX

432   1941 gifts: IMS, index of Christmas gifts, 1941 (HRC).

433   Interviews with DMS, October 31, 1987, and LJS, December 3–4, 1988.

440   "Well, she had a secretary": Interview with LJS, December 3, 1988.
"With her I": IMS, *A Private View*, p. 249.

441   "Darling, it is so": Ibid.
"I couldn't absorb": Ibid., p. 252.
"I hadn't known the thought": Ibid., p. 265.

444   "He was then": Ibid., p. 110.
"I must leave you": Ibid., p. 266.
"David lost Irene": Interview with William S. Paley, May 11, 1989.
"If you're married": Interview with Dorothy Hirshon, March 14, 1989.

445   "She was the only person": Interview with Leonora Hornblow, March 15, 1989.
"Jennifer hadn't caused": IMS, *A Private View*, p. 267.

446   gambling figures: Monthly records (HRC).
"Then he did give her up": IMS, *A Private View*, p. 267.
"Don't leave me": Interview with LJS, December 4, 1988.
"There was a good deal": Interview with Dorothy Hirshon, March 14, 1989.

447   "In addition, Miss Jones": DOS to H. L. Ducker, June 9, 1944 (HRC).
"I would that the check": DOS to Jennifer Jones, Christmas 1944 (HRC).

448   "You want to make a bet": Interview with John Houseman, April 13, 1988.
"he has represented": DOS to Charles Koerner, September 1, 1944 (HRC).
"I have nothing": Ibid.

449   "No, if it were my picture": Ibid.
"He tells me": Interview with Niven Busch, June 2, 1983.
Duel script: Production files (HRC).

450   "I want Jennifer to have": Interview with Anita Colby, February 6, 1988.

451   "I'll never forget it": Ibid.

p. 452   "Vidor says to me": Interview with Niven Busch, June 2, 1983.
          "I went out to location": DOS to George Volck, November 10, 1945 (HRC).
    454   "Terribly excited about": DOS to Colonel William Paley, April 5, 1945 (HRC).
          "and still regarded": Huston, *An Open Book*, p. 109.
    455   "I instantly liked": Paul MacNamara, "David O. Selznick's Yellow Peril," *Los Angeles*, June
          1986, p. 152.
          "Enough, enough": IMS, *A Private View*, p. 270.
          "The terrible day": Ibid., p. 271.
    456   "It was four-thirty": Interview with LJS, December 4, 1988.
          "I think Dad was": Interview with DMS, October 31, 1987.
    457   "it must have been": Interview with IMS, March 13, 1989.
          "He said no": Interview with LJS, December 4, 1988.
          "I cannot accept": JHW to DOS and IMS, August 19, 1945 (HRC).
          "Make what you will": IMS, *A Private View*, p. 273.
          "We haven't been getting": Louella Parsons, Los Angeles *Examiner*, August 24, 1945.
    458   gambling: Monthly records (HRC).
          "She's a Catholic convert": Interview with Anita Colby, February 6, 1988.
          "padded about the room": Schary, *Heyday*, p. 149.
    459   "Dear Daddy": Quoted in DOS to IMS, September 25, 1945 (HRC).
    460   "Jock was the most": Interview with Dorothy Hirshon, March 14, 1989.
          "At the risk": IMS to DOS, September 25, 1945 (HRC).
          "The bracelet . . . looks": IMS to DOS, October 10, 1945 (HRC).
          "found her": DOS to Ernest Scanlon, November 8, 1945 (HRC).
    461   "I am certainly": Paul MacNamara to DOS, February 20, 1946 (HRC).
          "I must frankly": DOS to Sister Ursula, November 15, 1945 (HRC).
    462   "self-consciousness and nervousness": DOS to Ernst Lubitsch, October 6, 1945 (HRC).
          "So that Selznick": New York *Post*, December 15, 1945.
    463   "because he thought": Interview with IMS, September 16, 1988.
          "I don't know why": Interview with Anita Colby, February 6, 1988.
          "in this case": DOS to Dolly Thackrey, December 17, 1945 (HRC).
    464   "the main thing": DOS to Milton Kramer, December 17, 1945 (HRC).
          "No actress in the history": DOS to Paul MacNamara and Anita Colby, September 16, 1946
          (HRC).
          "it is questionable": Ibid.
    465   "It isn't orgasm music": Quoted in Bob Thomas, *Selznick*, pp. 232–35.
    466   "In the whole long": William Dieterle to DOS, March 28, 1946 (HRC).
    467   "the best I ever": Interview with Allan Scott in McGilligan, ed., *Backstory*, p. 329.
          "Oh, yes, I was": Interview with Leonora Hornblow, November 6, 1987.
          "Far be it from": Arthur Hornblow to DOS, January 9, 1947 (HRC).
          "She never believed": Interview with Leonora Hornblow, November 6, 1987.
          "He got very drunk": Patricia Neal, *As I Am*, p. 77.
    468   "to get away from": Joseph Breen to DOS, February 27, 1945 (A).
    469   "*Duel in the Sun* is": Hedda Hopper, Los Angeles *Times*, December 30, 1946.
          "might go off": Joseph Breen to Eric Johnston, February 4, 1947 (A).
          "The duel in the sun climax": William Gordon memo, January 16, 1947 (A).
    470   "If the public's": Bosley Crowther, *New York Times*, May 8, 1947.
          "I took my daughter": John Rankin, House of Representatives, *Congressional Record*, June 19,
          1947.
          "This production": Ibid.

p. 470 "will unquestionably be": DOS to Henry Luce, January 9, 1947 (HRC).

471 "I have formed": Ibid.

The Best Years: A. Scott Berg, *Goldwyn*, pp. 409–20.

472 March 23, 1946: Production reports (HRC).

474 Scanlon: Ernest Scanlon to DOS, March 20, 1948 (HRC).

"I was able": *Memo*, p. 303.

"very candidly he thought": DOS to Selvin, February 17, 1947 (HRC).

"I intend to go further": DOS to Charles Skouras, October 26, 1944 (HRC).

475 "At the time Chaplin": DOS to Selvin, February 17, 1947 (HRC).

476 "I repeat, and please": DOS to Leonard Case, July 13, 1950 (HRC).

477 "I wanted plays": IMS, *A Private View*, p. 290.

"a few first flash": DOS to IMS, September 17, 1946 (HRC).

478 "She was not crazy": Interview with IMS, May 5, 1989.

"he claimed his life": IMS, *A Private View*, p. 292.

"David was always afraid": Interview with IMS, May 5, 1989.

479 "I can't believe": Jenia Reissar to DOS, October 26, 1944 (HRC).

480 "If Larry delays": DOS to Jenia Reissar, December 3, 1946 (HRC).

"With further reference": DOS to Jenia Reissar, December 9, 1946 (HRC).

481 Bergman letter: DOS to Ingrid Bergman, January 13, 1947 (HRC).

"People here also agreed": Jenia Reissar to DTO'S, January 13, 1948 (HRC).

"In addition": DOS to Jenia Reissar, June 29, 1948 (HRC).

482 "A glove-fitting role": Franclien Macconnell to DOS, June 19, 1933 (HRC).

484 Valli: DOS to DTO'S, September 3 and 18, 1946 (HRC); Valli to Jenia Reissar, n.d. (HRC).

485 "a silly society woman": Jenia Reissar to DTO'S, August 11, 1946 (HRC).

"I met David": Interview with Louis Jourdan, July 20, 1989.

"I did go": Ibid.

"with horny hands": Truffaut, *Hitchcock*, p. 214.

"with an enormous amount": DOS to DTO'S, December 6, 1946 (HRC).

486 "I am on the verge": Ibid.

"Even though I": Ibid.

"The old alibi": DOS to DTO'S and Ernest Scanlon, December 28, 1946 (HRC).

"I will take full blame": DOS to DTO'S and Ernest Scanlon, January 25, 1947 (HRC).

487 "since the camera": Geraldine Deardoff to Geoffrey Shurlock, February 25, 1947 (A).

twenty minutes: Interview with Arthur Fellows, January 17, 1989.

income: Statement of distribution results, June 30, 1950 (HRC).

488 Quebec: Oliver & Co., financial statement, December 31, 1948 (HRC).

"on a prolonged": Interview with DMS, October 26, 1990.

"Myron is gone": Interview with IMS, April 14, 1989.

489 "This is going": Interview with IMS, September 17, 1989.

490 Washington: Interview with LJS, December 4, 1988.

Hemingway: Slim Keith, *Slim*, p. 113.

"Slimbo": Interview with IMS, February 5, 1988.

Louella Parsons: Broadcast, May 5, 1946, transcript (HRC).

491 Firth Avenue: DOS to Ernest Scanlon, April 4, 1947 (HRC).

"I would suggest": Ibid.

"He had the worst Christmas": Interview with LJS, December 6, 1988.

492 gambling losses: Monthly reports (HRC).

"The thing that's so remarkable": Interview with LJS, December 3, 1988.

p. 492 "You disgust me!": Interview with IMS, September 15, 1988.

493 "Goddamn you": Interview with IMS, September 17, 1988.

"He just carried": Interview with DMS, January 19, 1989.

Matisse: IMS, *A Private View*, pp. 231–33; DOS to Paul Rosenberg, November 19, 1948 (HRC).

495 "It is more difficult": DOS to Paul MacNamara and Anita Colby, January 15, 1947 (HRC).

"Perhaps also you could": Ibid.

"so that she is not": DOS to Mervin Houser, February 7, 1947 (HRC).

"Dearest Darling": DOS to Jennifer Jones, February 7, 1947 (HRC).

496 "It is now clear": Jed Harris to DOS, September 2, 1947 (HRC).

497 "I don't understand": DOS to David Hempstead, November 25, 1946 (HRC).

"The minute that": DOS to David Hempstead, William Dieterle, and Peter Berneis, January 20, 1947 (HRC).

498 "If this child is": DOS notes on Jed Harris notes, May 3, 1947 (HRC).

"Another thing": DOS story conference notes, May 3, 1947 (HRC).

Hempstead: Interview with Arthur Fellows, January 17, 1989; DOS to Richard Hungate and DTO'S, December 18, 1948 (HRC).

499 "wretched beyond words": DOS to David Hempstead, February 26, 1947 (HRC).

"looks about seventeen": Ibid.

"Everything about it": DOS to DTO'S, March 12, 1947 (HRC).

500 "He said": Interview with Arthur Fellows, January 17, 1989.

"Accordingly, what they": DOS to DTO'S, April 3, 1947 (HRC).

"What is the difference": Ibid.

501 "Can't commence to tell": DOS to DTO'S, May 13, 1947 (HRC).

"I hope to get": DOS to Ernest Scanlon, May 17, 1947 (HRC).

"and it is a little": DOS to Argyle Nelson and David Hempstead, July 22, 1947 (HRC).

502 *Portrait of Jennie*: Statement of distribution results, June 30, 1950 (HRC).

call girls: Interview with Lois Hamby, December 1, 1987.

"The staff that made": DOS to DTO'S, July 6, 1948 (HRC).

Custody and Property Settlement: Custody, August 30, 1947; property, December 30, 1947 (HRC).

503 "Why do you think": IMS, *A Private View*, p. 282.

"He finally said": Ibid.

"it would be unwise": Morgan Maree to IMS, May 6, 1946 (HRC).

504 "the intruder from Hollywood": Elia Kazan, *Elia Kazan: A Life*, p. 327.

"the Parties have confidence": Custody agreement, August 30, 1947 (HRC).

505 "As it is": DOS to John Huston and William Wyler, October 24, 1947 (HRC).

506 "A sickness permeated": Huston, *An Open Book*, p. 152.

"I read it instantly": DOS to IMS, October 15, 1947 (HRC).

"which I thought": DOS to IMS, November 22, 1947 (HRC).

"There was too much respect": IMS, *A Private View*, p. 308.

507 "Don't deprive me": Ibid., p. 312.

"as though he were folded up": Ibid., p. 313.

"fell in a heap": Ibid.

"get into a straight": DOS to Morgan Maree, December 8, 1947 (HRC).

Irene's company's profits: IMS Co. accounts (IMS/B).

508 "She was obviously trembling": DOS to Ernest Scanlon and DTO'S, December 23, 1947.

"of such irresistible appeal": IMS, *A Private View*, pp. 232–33.

"What I didn't understand": Ibid.

p. 509 "There's a one-set success": Billy Rose, San Francisco *Chronicle*, January 27, 1948.

"hearing your voice": DOS to Phylis Walker, January 17, 1948 (HRC).

"Then there was a message": Interview with Loretta Young, January 21, 1989.

510 "since the next time": DOS to Phylis Walker, January 21, 1948 (HRC).

"how much is to be": Leonard Case to DOS, October 21, 1948 (HRC).

"He slapped her hard": Interview with Anita Colby, February 6, 1988.

"the unhappiest woman in love": Interview with Anne MacNamara, October 17, 1991.

511 gambling, 1945–48: Monthly records (HRC).

"DOS says": Ernest Scanlon memo, March 8, 1948 (HRC).

512 "were the worst coupling": Interview with Nancy Keith, May 6, 1989.

"I then had a long": DOS to DTO'S, March 16, 1948 (HRC).

513 "I know you are not": DOS to Sam Spiegel, August 19, 1948 (HRC).

"It wasn't a very good": Huston, *An Open Book*, p. 184.

"Jennifer Jones has been": *Life*, December 6, 1948; Paul MacNamara to DOS, December 20, 1948 (HRC).

515 net worth: Price Waterhouse, reports and accounts, December 31, 1944, 1945, 1946 (HRC).

"Then he offered": IMS, *A Private View*, p. 305.

516 "I suppose it would be": IMS to Morgan Maree, n.d. (HRC).

517 IMS dividends: Canceled checks (HRC).

518 "certainly since we started": DOS to Ernest Scanlon, October 16, 1945 (HRC).

"In the event": DOS to Ernest Scanlon, Earl Beaman, and DTO'S, March 17, 1949 (HRC).

519 "He was honest, square": Interview with IMS, May 9, 1988; interview with Jess Morgan, November 27, 1989.

520 bank loans: Security–First National Bank to Vanguard, August 29, 1947 (HRC); Earl Beaman to DOS, August 12, 1949 (HRC).

"going like the hammers": Interview with Lois Hamby, December 1, 1987.

"I was told DOS": Ibid.

521 to buy out Irene: Joseph Willard, memo, October 10, 1947 (HRC); Willard to Ernest Scanlon, March 24, 1948 (HRC).

"I am typing": DOS to Maynard Toll, May 4, 1948 (HRC).

523 "I don't even know": Interview with DMS, January 19, 1989.

"Congratulations for your": Roberto Rossellini to Jennifer Jones, August 23, 1948 (HRC).

524 "become some kind of": DOS to Marjorie Daw Selznick, September 4, 1948 (HRC).

"I took the liberty": Ibid.

525 "Tell me about yourself": Hildegard Knef, *The Gift Horse*, pp. 199–201.

526 auction: Interview with Arthur Sachs, August 21, 1991; DOS to DTO'S and Arthur Sachs, May 8, 1949 (HRC).

527 "David didn't want": Interview with Quique Jourdan, July 20, 1989.

"tiny men bubbling about": Interview with Nancy Keith, May 6, 1989.

"And her kind": Interview with LJS, December 4, 1988.

"DAVID": IMS, *A Private View*, p. 305 (this telegram cannot be found in the Selznick Archive or in the papers of IMS).

528 *"My wife is"*: DOS, n.d. (HRC).

PART SEVEN

534 "is like trying": MS to DOS, November 5, 1941 (HRC).

"when charm failed": Michael Korda, *Charmed Lives*, p. 173.

535 Cary Grant: Contract, London Film Productions and SRO, May 4, 1948 (HRC); DOS to Jenia Reissar, June 10, 1948 (HRC).

p. 535 "You can do better": Graham Greene, *The Pleasure Dome*, p. 3.

536 "I spent countless hours": DOS to Betty Goldsmith, October 16, 1948 (HRC).

537 "It would be little short": Ibid.

"feel he would be": DOS to Jenia Reissar, September 20, 1948 (HRC).

"Jenia visited me today": Alexander Korda to DOS, October 7, 1948 (HRC).

538 "Carol . . . give me": Interview with Jenia Reissar, June 1, 1988.

"For your confidential information": DOS to Jenia Reissar, October 6, 1948 (HRC).

539 "Miss Reissar is mistaken": Alexander Korda to Rosemary Clifford, December 3, 1948 (HRC).

"nothing that contributed": *Memo*, p. 398.

541 "Jennifer hasn't slept": Interview with Jenia Reissar, June 1, 1988.

542 "It was a shame": Interview with Michael Powell, April 13, 1985.

"about as far removed": DOS to Michael Powell and Emeric Pressburger, July 21, 1949 (HRC).

"Be assured that": DOS to Jennifer Jones, July 27, 1949 (HRC).

543 "a crick in his foot": DOS to IMS, August 14, 1949 (HRC).

"The doctors explained": Ibid.

"The whole tone": DOS to Louella Parsons, September 12, 1949 (HRC).

544 "I think she was": Interview with Jenia Reissar, June 1, 1988.

"I shall find the time": DOS to Michael Powell and Emeric Pressburger, August 30, 1949 (HRC).

545 "I hate to say this": Ibid.

"In the scenes": Ibid.

546 "Mickey, you simply": DOS to Michael Powell, August 31, 1949 (HRC).

"Me still Tarzan": DOS to Jennifer Jones, September 14, 1949 (HRC).

547 "never had the guts": Michael Powell, *A Life in Movies*, p. 521.

548 "I gave myself": DOS to Michael Powell and Emeric Pressburger, October 6, 1949 (HRC).

549 "After long discussions": Alexander Korda to DOS, October 28, 1949 (HRC).

"Now, because of": Ibid.

"I have always maintained": DOS to Alexander Korda, November 2, 1949 (HRC).

550 "an old English cold": Michael Powell and Emeric Pressburger to DOS, November 3, 1949 (HRC).

"rights against yourself": Alexander Korda to Jennifer Jones, November 24, 1949 (HRC).

Frank Davis: Interview with Frank Davis, January 21, 1989.

551 "The tragedy of the thing": Lancelot Joynson-Hicks to DTO'S, April 4, 1950 (HRC).

arbitration: Award of Arbitrator, U.S. Southern District of New York (55.139), May 24, 1950 (HRC).

sixpence: Lancelot Joynson-Hicks to Alexander Korda, October 18, 1950; Korda to Joynson-Hicks, October 19, 1950 (HRC).

552 "Just before leaving": DOS to IMS, September 20, 1949 (IMS/DT).

553 "Breathing good will": IMS, *A Private View*, p. 327.

"wasn't his wealth": Ibid.

"Kazan volunteered": DOS to Charles Feldman, March 1, 1950 (HRC).

"annoying and embarrassing": DOS to DTO'S, April 25, 1950 (HRC).

"my own production plans": Ibid.

"get the almost fantastically": DOS to Elia Kazan and Tennessee Williams, April 27, 1950 (HRC).

554 "He looked better": Elia Kazan to Jennifer Jones, May 19, 1950 (HRC).

p. 554 "I think *Gone to Earth*": DOS to DTO'S, May 4, 1950 (HRC).

Paley: DOS to William S. Paley, January 15, 1954 (HRC).

555 "You know what you": DOS to DTO'S, April 14, 1950 (HRC).

556 "Believe me, Dan": DOS to DTO'S, April 16, 1950 (HRC).

"I just cannot imagine": DOS to William Wyler, June 22, 1950 (HRC).

557 "As for the age": Ibid.

Brideshead: Louis Talcott Stone to Evelyn Waugh, July 28, 1950; Waugh to Stone, August 1, 1950; Stone to Waugh, September 6, 1950 (HRC).

558 "I can scarcely think": DOS to Miss Poole, December 30, 1949 (HRC).

"Also, and very important": DOS to Morgan Maree, December 28, 1950 (HRC).

income: Income tax returns, 1948, 1949 (HRC).

559 "some gent in the": DOS to IMS, February 9, 1950 (HRC).

"It is clear": DOS to Earl Beaman, July 17, 1951 (HRC).

560 "spurious elegance": DOS to William Wyler, November 11, 1949 (HRC).

"An ambitious girl": Ibid.

561 "Oh, David": Interview with Anne MacNamara, October 17, 1991.

"As I think": DOS to LJS, December 6, 1950 (HRC).

"European film academy": DOS to Victor Hoare and Jenia Reissar, September 5, 1950 (HRC).

562 "She is going on 17": Ibid.

"but it was more": Interview with LJS, December 6, 1988.

"delighted beyond my": DOS to Jennifer Jones, September 3, 1950 (HRC).

563 "I have sent": Jennifer Jones to DOS, September 4, 1950 (HRC).

"God, how hungry": DOS to Jennifer Jones, September 14, 1950 (HRC).

"flat on her back": DOS to LJS, December 6, 1950 (HRC).

"I didn't know": Interview with LJS, December 4, 1988.

564 "My father wanted": DOS to LJS, December 6, 1950 (HRC).

566 *The Third Man*: Financial report, June 9, 1951 (HRC).

"Henceforth, I am ceasing": DOS to Morgan Maree, July 26, 1950 (HRC).

568 Selznick Studio: Bill of Sale and Assignment, August 28, 1950 (HRC).

"I didn't like the climate": Interview with IMS, August 24, 1990.

liquidation: Earl Beaman statement on tax situation, 1951–54, June 6, 1958 (HRC).

569 bankruptcy: Interview with Frank Davis, January 21, 1989.

570 Mayer and MGM: Crowther, *Hollywood Rajah*, pp. 274–88; interview with Leonora Hornblow, November 6, 1987.

Goetz daughters: Interview with Barbara Windom, August 6, 1991.

"When he said": IMS, *A Private View*, p. 359.

571 "Dad, that's terrible": Interview with DMS, January 19, 1989.

"He's getting increasingly": Ibid.

"There was an unspoken": Ibid.

572 "If there was": Ibid.

"My dearest Jennifer": Quoted in DOS to DTO'S, August 18, 1950 (HRC).

573 "one terrible row": DOS to IMS, May 4, 1951 (HRC).

"The battle began": Viveca Lindfors, *Viveka . . . Viveca*, p. 167.

"I was just simply": Interview with LJS, December 4, 1988.

"develop a comradeship": DOS to LJS, June 7, 1951.

574 "Thus, if": Ibid.

"You don't understand": Interview with LJS, December 5, 1988.

p. 574   "He thought it was": Ibid.

575   Walker: Linet, *Star-Crossed*, pp. 268–76.

"in every decision": DOS to Dore Schary, September 1, 1951 (HRC).

"the doctors and the": Ibid.

"portrayed a startling": Ibid.

576   "Well . . . to cut": DOS to IMS, October 21, 1952 (HRC).

"fake meningitis": Ibid.

577   De Sica: Jenia Reissar to DOS, March 12, 1948 (HRC).

"I'm through": Interview with Jenia Reissar, June 1, 1988.

"at one of the nice": Interview with Frank Davis, January 21, 1989.

"In Jamaica": Interview with William S. Paley, May 11, 1989.

578   "honeymoon plus his": DOS to Morgan Maree and Jess Morgan, May 17, 1952 (HRC).

579   "There is something": DOS to Margaret Nilsson, January 5, 1952 (HRC).

Ruby Gentry: Raymond Durgnat and Scott Simmon, *King Vidor, American*, pp. 285–95.

"Reliance upon the": DOS to Joseph Bernhard, April 23, 1952 (HRC).

580   "I have just finished": DOS to Al Lichtman, September 26, 1952 (HRC).

"I remember that when": Interview with DMS, January 19, 1989.

582   *The Bad and the Beautiful*: John Houseman, *Front and Center*, p. 373.

583   "It was made absolutely clear": Oswald Morris to DT, August 28, 1989.

584   "Jennifer is madly": Quoted in Patricia Bosworth, *Montgomery Clift*, p. 245.

Jennifer ran: Interview with Peter De Rome, October 31, 1990.

"The man has to have": DOS to Vittorio De Sica and Marcello Girosi, November 13, 1952 (not sent) (HRC).

585   "the distortion of Jennifer's face": DOS to Vittorio De Sica, February 23, 1953 (HRC).

Davis: Interview with Frank Davis, January 21, 1989.

"the cure is more sleep": DOS to IMS, March 13, 1953 (HRC).

"there just is no comparison": DOS to John Huston, January 27, 1953 (HRC).

"he is easy": DOS to John Huston, January 30, 1953 (HRC).

586   "difficult even determine": DOS to John Huston and Humphrey Bogart, February 12, 1953 (HRC).

"I do not believe": Oswald Morris to DT, August 28, 1989.

587   "devoted so much time": DOS to Vittorio De Sica, October 21, 1953.

"There is no reason": Ibid.

Tudor City: Interview with Arthur Fellows, January 17, 1989; interview with LJS, December 4, 1988.

"I have taken very much": DOS to Morgan Maree, December 17, 1953 (HRC).

588   "I can't tell": Ibid.

"terribly damaging photography": DOS to Morgan Maree, January 25, 1954 (HRC).

"shirking all unexciting": DOS to IMS, September 10, 1953 (HRC).

589   Ruth: Dr. Frederick Hacker to DOS, January 28, 1956 (HRC); DOS to Ruth Selznick Swarttz, February 3, 1956 (HRC).

"pretty much like": Interview with Berman Swarttz, November 30, 1989.

"it distresses me": DOS to LBM, February 22, 1952 (HRC).

590   "probably too consistently": DOS to LBM, October 1, 1953 (HRC).

"My reason for sending": DOS to IMS, October 2, 1953 (HRC).

591   "Do, please, L.B.": DOS to LBM, October 1, 1953 (HRC).

"Isn't there a far": Ibid.

p. 591   "two dreadful oversights": Schary, *Heyday*, p. 274.
"and this pose": DOS talking to Hedda Hopper, February 16, 1954 (A).
"I think it's the most": Ibid.

592   "Nothing can disturb": DOS to LBM, October 1, 1953 (HRC).
"You know I *really*": DOS talking to Hedda Hopper, March 1954 (A).
"We're being plenty tough": Ibid.

593   "There is something *drastically*": DOS to Joan Grill, August 19, 1955 (HRC).
"Lest I subject myself": DOS to LBM, October 1, 1953 (HRC).

595   "it was *the manner*": DOS to William S. Paley, January 15, 1954 (HRC).

596   "Entire project is": DOS to Frank Davis, April 6, 1954 (HRC).

597   "I don't recall": DOS to Rose Hecht, January 15, 1954 (HRC).
"Walking at dawn": Hecht, *A Child of the Century*, p. 467.
"I simply cannot": DOS to Frank Davis, July 21, 1954 (HRC).

598   "His admiration was 100%": Dwight Van Meter notes, September 27, 1954 (HRC).

599   "While viewing the disappointing": Tommy Reynolds to DOS, October 25, 1954 (HRC).
"just like everyone else": Interview by Robert Cunniff, *Television Magazine*, February 1955.

600   "We must rule out": DOS to Betty Goldsmith and Nancy Stern, August 30, 1954 (HRC).
"so that I can perhaps": Ibid.

601   "a terribly morbid": DOS to Sam Jaffe, March 1, 1953 (HRC).
"a particularly strong hunch": Ibid.
"I have learned": Sam Jaffe to DOS, February 9, 1953 (HRC).

602   "Selznick insists": Draft for letter, Sam Jaffe to Joseph L. Mankiewicz (not sent), n.d. (HRC).

603   "It was like a surgeon": Interview with Sam Jaffe, February 25, 1991.
Rock Hudson: DOS to Sam Jaffe, April 14, 1954 (HRC).
"He forgets that I had": Interview with Nancy Stern, February 8, 1988.

604   "I can truthfully say": Sam Jaffe to DOS, May 7, 1954 (HRC).

605   "a decorous but": Brooks Atkinson, *New York Times*, December 22, 1954.
"beautiful and grave": Wolcott Gibbs, *The New Yorker*, January 1, 1955.
Jourdan: Interview with Louis Jourdan, July 20, 1989.
"She had a strange": Interview with Nancy Stern, February 8, 1988.
"She never wrote": Enid Bagnold, *Autobiography*, p. 295.

606   "Irene!": Ibid., p. 307.
"It contains many": DOS statement, June 1954 (HRC).

607   MGM deal: Deal memo, November 26, 1954 (HRC).
"We stayed at the": Interview with Frank Davis, January 21, 1989.

608   "I want freely": DOS to Eddie Mannix, May 2, 1955 (HRC).
"If this makes her": DOS to Buddy Adler, March 12, 1955 (HRC).

609   tax arrears: Tax returns, 1951–57 (HRC).

610   "These are the thoughts": DOS to Frank Davis, Victor Hoare, and Earl Beaman, April 26, 1955 (HRC).
"Nor is it only": Ibid.
"His habits are not": Dr. Robert Hotchkiss to Connie Guion, May 17, 1950 (HRC).
"the great importance": Connie Guion to DOS, May 23, 1950 (HRC).

611   "You spoke of having": Connie Guion to DOS, June 27, 1953 (HRC).
"weighing perhaps": DOS to Connie Guion, May 28, 1956 (HRC).
"I had the feeling": Interview with Frank Davis, January 21, 1989.

p. 612 "You simply must realize": DOS to DTO'S, September 2, 1955 (HRC).
        "I am trying": DOS to DTO'S, November 22, 1955 (HRC).
  613   "It looks to me": DOS to William S. Paley, January 20, 1956 (HRC).
        "although if I had": DOS to IMS, March 13, 1953 (HRC).
        "I am arriving": DOS to IMS, June 10, 1955 (HRC).
  614   "Would like after first": DOS to LJS, April 26, 1956 (HRC).
        "The notion that 50%": DOS to LJS, September 17, 1956 (HRC).
  615   "He is such a": DOS to IMS, August 2, 1956 (HRC).
        "In case your wife": *The Letters of Nunnally Johnson*, p. 126.
        "over the idea of": DOS to the Duke of Windsor, November 16, 1956 (HRC).
  617   "David never did anything": Huston, *An Open Book*, p. 301.
  618   "and also because": DOS to John Huston, October 25, 1956 (HRC).
        "I wish you would": DOS to Ben Hecht, December 19, 1956 (HRC).
  619   "had simply become": Huston, *An Open Book*, p. 303.
  620   "You simply must": DOS to Arthur Fellows, January 9, 1957 (HRC).
        "It's difficult at this": DOS to Arthur Fellows, January 10, 1957 (HRC).
        "I should be less": DOS to John Huston, March 19, 1957 (HRC).
  621   "Because every hour counts": Ibid.
        "I can't tell you": Interview with Arthur Fellows, January 17, 1989.
        "you and I alone": Ben Hecht to DOS, March 3, 1957 (HRC).
  622   "Copycat": DOS to IMS, March 27, 1957 (HRC).
        "I am confronted": Pier Paolo Pasolini, notes, March 18, 1957 (HRC).
  623   "You are harping": Charles Vidor to DOS, April 27, 1957 (HRC).
  624   Morris: Oswald Morris to DT, August 28, 1989; interview with Morris by Markku Salmi
        in Carlo Gaberscek and Livio Jacob, *Hollywood in Friuli*, pp. 193–209.
        "Because I feel": DOS to Ben Hecht, May 22, 1957 (HRC).
  625   "I don't know": DOS to Arthur Fellows, May 15, 1957 (HRC).
        "He said, 'You're obviously' ": Interview with LJS, December 5, 1988.
        "vaguely disturbed": DOS to Charles Vidor, July 30, 1957 (HRC).
        "It would be tough": Ibid.
  626   Lake Maggiore: Interview with Arthur Fellows, January 17, 1989.
  627   LBM's illness: IMS, *A Private View*, pp. 359–65; Crowther, *Hollywood Rajah*, pp. 325–27.
        funeral: Crowther, *Hollywood Rajah*, pp. 1–4, 327–28; interview with LJS, February 16, 1991.
        will: IMS, *A Private View*, p. 367; interview with LJS, February 16, 1991.
  628   "You can buy a brothel": Interview with LJS, February 16, 1991.
        "Dad behaved so terribly": Interview with DMS, January 19, 1989.
        "Dad had built it": Ibid.
  629   "Dear Irene": DOS to IMS, "Afterwards" (IMS/DT).

        PART EIGHT

  632   "short, sharp stabs": Dr. George Griffith, report, September 19, 1957 (HRC).
        "probably travels as much": Ibid.
  633   "It's very difficult": Interview with LJS, June 8, 1991.
        "very tense, grey": Dr. Connie Guion to DOS, January 9, 1958 (HRC).
        "On the whole": Ibid.
        Farewell: Distribution report, Earl Beaman to DOS, January 26, 1959, and April 21, 1959
        (HRC).
  634   IRS: David O. and Phylis Selznick, statement, June 30, 1958 (HRC).

p. 635   expenditures: Ibid.

"continuing to exploit": Ibid.

"And at 9:30": Interview with Leonora Hornblow, November 6, 1987.

"Well, Irene": *The New Yorker*, December 7, 1957.

636   "great thrill": DOS to Howard Selznick, July 14, 1958 (HRC).

"Mary Jennifer assumed": Interview with DMS, January 19, 1989.

637   "I am also worried": DOS to LJS, May 27, 1958 (HRC).

"There is no question": Arnold Grant to DOS, November 21, 1958 (HRC).

638   "the tragic story": DOS to Morgan Maree, September 14, 1959 (HRC).

639   "David and Jennifer": Interview with Ivan Moffat, February 25, 1991.

"pronouncements rendered": Ibid.

He told Anhalt: Interview with Edward Anhalt, March 7, 1989.

640   Madame Bulova: Interview with LJS, December 5, 1988.

King David Hotel: Interview with Edward Anhalt, March 7, 1989.

642   "said that he was": DOS to Jennifer Jones, January 22, 1959 (HRC).

"except I don't think": Cindy Adams, *Lee Strasberg* (New York: Doubleday, 1980), p. 260.

"Barkiss is willin' ": Jennifer Jones to DOS, January 20, 1959 (HRC).

"the best young actor": DOS to Jennifer Jones, January 22, 1959 (HRC).

"all calculated to break": Jennifer Jones to DOS, January 20, 1959 (HRC).

"our separation": DOS to Jennifer Jones, January 22, 1959 (HRC).

Moffat: Interview with Ivan Moffat, February 25, 1991.

643   "men of astuteness": DOS to Arnold Grant, March 2, 1959 (HRC).

Stephens Mitchell: Agreement between Mitchell and SRO, September 23, 1952, and between Mitchell and DOS, December 1, 1956 (HRC).

644   "Maybe, with your": DOS to Arnold Grant, March 2, 1959 (HRC).

645   "I wonder if we": DOS to Arnold Grant, February 19, 1959 (HRC).

"Oh, I don't know": Interview with DMS, October 26, 1990.

"Don't believe it": Interview with Berman Swarttz, November 30, 1989.

"It is very strange": DOS to Merian Cooper, March 11, 1959 (HRC).

"Mother Selznick": Jennifer Jones to DOS, March 12, 1959 (HRC).

646   "Bon voyage and": Spyros Skouras to DOS, June 23, 1959 (HRC).

647   "I'm going to kill": Keith, *Slim*, p. 260.

"am afraid he will": DOS to IMS, March 14, 1959 (HRC).

"and I personally": DOS to JHW, August 7, 1958 (HRC).

648   "Thirdly, and most": DOS to Arnold Grant, May 22, 1959 (HRC).

"I have a lot": DOS to Arnold Grant, September 30, 1959 (HRC).

649   "I'm now absolutely": DOS to Arnold Grant, December 5, 1959 (HRC).

"I have pushed everything": DOS to IMS, December 31, 1959 (IMS/B).

650   "He was a child": Interview with Louis Jourdan, July 20, 1989.

Sullavan: Brooke Hayward, *Haywire*, pp. 15–16.

651   "The only funeral": Ibid., p. 302

652   "That child doesn't": Interview with Nancy Stern, February 8, 1988.

"Jennifer turned ashen": Interview with Leonora Hornblow, November 6, 1987.

"She wouldn't let me": Interview with Anita Colby, February 6, 1988.

653   "He could not say": Interview with DMS, October 26, 1990.

Ellie: Interview with Ellie Wood Walker, March 1, 1992.

"Mary Jennifer raced": DOS to DMS, August 24, 1960 (HRC).

654   "It saddens me": DOS to IMS, May 10, 1960 (HRC).

p. 654 "I think you are": DOS to DMS, August 24, 1960 (HRC).
"You have learned": Ibid.

655 "the opportunity of a": DOS to Arnold Grant, February 13, 1960 (HRC).
"We know that": DOS to Arnold Grant, February 10, 1960 (HRC).
"In everything one undertakes": Arnold Grant to DOS, March 4, 1960 (HRC).

656 "a masterpiece like": DOS to George Cukor, May 4, 1960 (A).

657 "That wouldn't be so bad": Interview with Ivan Moffat, February 25, 1991.
"We have the finances": DOS to William S. Paley, August 1, 1960 (HRC).
"Things with me": DOS to IMS, May 10, 1960 (HRC).

658 "Dad, you can't let": Interview with DMS, October 26, 1990.
Bernstein: Marjorie McDougall to DOS, October 14, 1960 (HRC).
"all the more wonderful": DOS to William S. Paley, November 7, 1960 (HRC).
"Jennifer and I": DOS to Arnold Grant, November 7, 1960 (HRC).

659 "I would talk to him": Interview with Henry Weinstein, April 11, 1989.

660 "I am an American": Quoted in Thomas, Selznick, p. 77.
"Would you call": Ibid.; see also DOS to Ben Hecht, February 26, 1942 (HRC).
Stella Dallas: DOS to Sam Goldwyn, February 10, 1961; Sam Goldwyn to DOS, February 11, 1961 (HRC).
Atlanta: DMS, Introduction, in Judy Cameron and Paul J. Christman, The Art of Gone With the Wind, pp. 18–19.

661 "He went on to explain": IMS, A Private View, p. 379.

662 "If it possessed": DOS to Arnold Grant, April 3, 1961, not sent (HRC).
"Let's look at": Arnold Grant to DOS, May 19, 1961 (HRC).

663 "Have a nice day": Shirley Harden to DOS, May 10, 1961 (HRC).
"My daddy will love": Shirley Harden to Jennifer Jones, May 19, 1961 (HRC).
Fontaine: Fontaine, No Bed, pp. 265–66.
"I know King": DOS to Jennifer Jones, May 13, 1961 (HRC).
"He said, 'Maintain this' ": Interview with Ivan Moffat, February 25, 1991.

664 "Well, Mr. Selznick": Interview with LJS, December 5, 1988.
earnings: Income tax statements, 1957–61 (HRC).
"I didn't think": Interview with Henry Weinstein, April 11, 1989.

665 "For some reason": DOS to Earl Beaman and Barry Brannen, November 20, 1961 (HRC).
"simply a promoter": DOS to LJS, November 6, 1961 (HRC).

666 "Studio administration cannot": DOS to Spyros Skouras, December 8, 1961 (HRC).
"Tender is a": Quoted in Linet, Star-Crossed, p. 297.
"by a wide margin": DOS to Barry Brannen, February 17, 1962 (HRC).
"my doctor has told me": DOS to Ambrose Doskow, February 15, 1962 (HRC).
"a breather, financially": Ibid.

667 "It was certainly nice": Howard Selznick to DOS, May 24, 1962 (HRC).
"how I could best": DOS to Morgan Maree, June 21, 1962 (HRC).
"I certainly don't need": Ibid.
"the only man I have": DOS to Barry Brannen, July 16, 1962 (HRC).
"about the effect": DOS to Barry Brannen, October 9, 1962 (HRC).
Wright: William H. Wright Collection (A).

668 "whether his name": DOS to Ambrose Doskow, August 23, 1962 (HRC).
"is an eager": Ibid.
"I have never understood": DOS to Barry Brannen, July 25, 1962 (HRC).

669 "and I was sitting": Interview with LJS, December 5, 1988.

p. 669 "My mother never liked": Ibid.

"How dare you?": Ibid.

"Well, you're wrong": Ibid.

"I told Jeff": DOS to Janine Durand-Ruel, April 2, 1963 (HRC).

670 "I refer, of course": DMS to LJS, October 23, 1962 (LJS).

671 "David, tomorrow": Interview with David Lean, *Le Monde*, May 4, 1989.

"I therefore realized": DOS to Janine Durand-Ruel, April 2, 1963 (HRC).

672 "nothing costly like roses": DOS to Earl Beaman, Robert Hagstrom, and Shirley Harden, November 11, 1962 (HRC).

"Nothing would please him": DOS to Barry Brannen, January 3, 1963 (HRC).

"I think, however pretentious": Ibid.

674 "I cabled him": DOS to Janine Durand-Ruel, April 2, 1963 (HRC).

"because we are": Ibid.

"As to his contemptible": Ibid.

675 *"Now my Sixtieth"*: Creative writings (HRC).

"Viva Villa with sex": William H. Wright, notes on meeting, August 10, 1962 (A).

"I lay awake at night": DOS to Earl Beaman, n.d. (HRC).

taxes: Income tax returns, 1962, 1963 (HRC).

676 "He says he is": DOS to Earl Beaman, May 13, 1963 (HRC).

"I cannot get over": DOS to William S. Paley, October 2, 1963 (HRC).

"In my opinion": Ibid.

small dinner party: Interview with Dominick Dunne, February 3, 1992.

677 "one of the most": DOS to Babe Paley, November 19, 1963 (HRC).

"Our economies have": DOS to LJS, December 12, 1963 (HRC).

678 "The basic conflict": Ben Hecht to DOS, December 17, 1963 (HRC).

"terribly excited": DOS to Ben Hecht, December 30, 1963 (HRC).

"in which James Bond": Ben Hecht to DOS, February 11, 1964 (HRC).

"Jennifer has long been": DOS to Ben Hecht, January 23, 1964 (HRC).

"Knowing your speed": DOS to Ben Hecht, February 14, 1964 (HRC).

679 "My parents were just": Interview with DMS, October 26, 1990 (HRC).

Dr. Molle: Notes, May 12, and 19, 1964 (HRC).

680 Dr. Griffith: Notes, May 20, 1964 (HRC).

"only an occasional letter": DOS to Barry Brannen, May 22, 1964 (HRC).

"Curiously, the one": Ibid.

681 "at the cost": Margaret Hodgson to Earl Beaman, June 10, 1964 (HRC).

"Knowing myself": DOS to Earl Beaman, July 8, 1964 (HRC).

Dr. Meyer: Notes, n.d. (HRC).

682 "It would be called": Interview with Ivan Moffat, February 25, 1991.

"It has been obvious": DOS to Earl Beaman, July 20, 1964 (HRC).

"He talked only about": Interview with Quique Jourdan, July 20, 1989.

683 "Are you all right?": Interview with LJS, December 5, 1988.

"I cannot and will not": DOS to Douglas Brunger, August 17, 1964 (HRC).

"Finally, Doug": Ibid.

684 "I am of course": DOS to Earl Beaman, August 18, 1964 (HRC).

"Just try to get": Marjorie McDougall to Earl Beaman, August 23, 1964 (HRC).

Dr. Ludwig: Notes, September 7, 1964 (HRC).

685 "My foot seems": DOS to Dr. John Stump, September 14, 1964 (HRC).

"He mentioned not once": Interview with DMS, October 26, 1990.

p. 685 Yvette Curran: Interview with Yvette Curran, October 31, 1990.

687 "He's got this cockamamie": Interview with DMS, October 26, 1990.

688 "He gets things": Ibid.

"I'm going to ask you": Ibid.

689 "First you were under": Ibid.

Kiluna: Interview with IMS, January 22, 1989; IMS, *A Private View*, p. 381.

"I suppose I am the only": DOS to Earl Beaman, February 1, 1965 (HRC).

690 "It's all right, Bub": Interview with Leonora Hornblow, November 6, 1987.

"Dear Howie": DOS to Howard Selznick, May 25, 1965 (HRC).

691 "We rode through": IMS, *A Private View*, p. 382.

"We should really": Interview with DMS, October 26, 1990.

"There was not much energy": Interview with Ron Rifkin, February 4, 1992.

692 "Do I go to": Interview with IMS, January 22, 1989.

"It's been overdue": Ibid.

"Isn't it awful": Interview with Leonora Hornblow, November 6, 1987.

"I went to the party": Interview with IMS, January 22, 1989.

"David O. Selznick, 63": *New York Times*, June 23, 1963.

"Your mother must come": Interview with DMS, October 26, 1990.

693 "Would you mind": Ibid.

EPILOGUE

695 "The one word": William S. Paley tribute, June 25, 1965 (HRC).

"He and I": JHW to Jennifer Jones, June 30, 1965 (HRC).

"I will be thinking": JHW to IMS, n.d. (IMS/B).

700 "the big individual": Katharine Hepburn to IMS, June 24, 1965 (IMS/B).

"and if I know": William S. Paley tribute, June 25, 1965 (HRC).

This list is intended for reference and clarity and does not provide full credits or details of release date. Such information can be found in Ronald Haver's *David O. Selznick's Hollywood*. However, this list includes more than just the pictures on which DOS is credited as producer or executive producer.

EARLY WORKS

1923   *Will He Conquer Dempsey?*
        Rudolph Valentino and His 88 American Beauties

1924   *Roulette* (Aetna Pictures, released by Selznick Distributing)
        directed by S. E. V. Taylor; screenplay by Gerald C. Duffy, from story by William Briggs McHarg
        with Edith Roberts, Norman Trevor, Maurice Costello, Mary Carr, Walter Booth, Effie Shannon, Montagu Love

1928   *Spoilers of the West* (MGM)
        directed by W. S. Van Dyke; screenplay by Madeleine Ruthven and Ross B. Wills, from story by John Thomas Neville
        with Tim McCoy, Marjorie Daw, William Fairbanks, Chief Big Tree

        Wyoming (MGM)
        directed by W. S. Van Dyke; screenplay by Madeleine Ruthven and Ross B. Wills
        with Tim McCoy, Dorothy Sebastian, Charles Bell, William Fairbanks, Chief Big Tree

PARAMOUNT

1928   *Forgotten Faces*
        directed by Victor Schertzinger; screenplay by Howard Estabrook, from a story by Richard W. Child; adaptation by Oliver H. P. Garrett
        with Clive Brook, Mary Brian, Olga Baclanova, William Powell

1929   *Chinatown Nights*
        directed by William Wellman; screenplay by Ben Grauman Kohn and Oliver H. P. Garrett
        with Wallace Beery, Florence Vidor, Warner Oland, Jack McHugh, Jack Oakie

The Man I Love
directed by William Wellman; screenplay by Herman Mankiewicz
with Richard Arlen, Mary Brian, Olga Baclanova, Harry Green, Jack Oakie

The Four Feathers
directed by Merian C. Cooper, Ernest B. Schoedsack and Lothar Mendes; screenplay by Howard Estabrook and Hope Loring, from the novel by A. E. W. Mason
with Richard Arlen, Fay Wray, Clive Brook, William Powell, Noah Beery

The Dance of Life
directed by John Cromwell and Edward Sutherland; screenplay by Benjamin Glazer, from the play *Burlesque* by George Manker Watters
with Nancy Carroll, Hal Skelly, Ralph Theodore, Charles Brown, Dorothy Revier, Al St. John, May Boley, Oscar Levant

1930   *Street of Chance*
directed by John Cromwell; screenplay by Howard Estabrook
with William Powell, Jean Arthur, Kay Francis, Regis Toomey, Stanley Fields, Brooks Benedict

Sarah and Son
directed by Dorothy Arzner; screenplay by Zoë Akins, from the novel by Timothy Shea
with Ruth Chatterton, Fredric March, Fuller Mellish, Jr., Gilbert Emery, Doris Lloyd, William Stack, Philippe De Lacy

Honey
directed by Wesley Ruggles; screenplay by Herman J. Mankiewicz, from the novel and play *Come Out of the Kitchen!* by Alice Duer Miller and A. E. Thomas
with Nancy Carroll, Stanley Smith, Skeets Gallagher, Lillian Roth, Harry Green, Zasu Pitts

The Texan
directed by John Cromwell; screenplay by Daniel Nathan Rubin, from the story "The Double-dyed Deceiver" by O. Henry
with Gary Cooper, Fay Wray, Emma Dunn, Oscar Apfel

For the Defense
directed by John Cromwell; screenplay by Oliver H. P. Garrett
with William Powell, Kay Francis, Scott Kolk, William B. Davidson

Manslaughter
directed by George Abbott; adapted by Abbott from the film by Cecil B. DeMille (1922)
with Claudette Colbert, Fredric March, Emma Dunn, Natalie Moorhead

Laughter
directed by Harry d'Abbadie d'Arrast; screenplay by Donald Ogden Stewart, from a story by d'Arrast and Douglas Doty
with Nancy Carroll, Fredric March, Diane Ellis, Leonard Carey, Ollie Burgoyne

RKO

1932   *The Lost Squadron*
directed by George Archainbaud; screenplay by Wallace Smith, with additional dialogue by Herman J. Mankiewicz and Robert S. Presnell
with Richard Dix, Mary Astor, Erich von Stroheim, Dorothy Jordan, Joel McCrea, Robert Armstrong, Hugh Herbert, Ralph Ince

Symphony of Six Million
directed by Gregory La Cava; screenplay by Bernard Schubert and J. Walter Ruben, from the short story by Fannie Hurst
with Ricardo Cortez, Irene Dunne, Anna Appel, Gregory Ratoff, Lita Chevret, Noel Madison, Helen Freeman

State's Attorney
directed by George Archainbaud; screenplay by Gene Fowler and Rowland Brown, from a story by Louis Stevens
with John Barrymore, Helen Twelvetrees, William Boyd, Jill Esmond, Mary Duncan, Oscar Apfel, Raul Roulien, Ralph Ince

Westward Passage
directed by Robert Milton; screenplay by Bradley King, with dialogue by Humphrey Pearson, from the novel by Margaret Ayer Barnes
with Ann Harding, Laurence Olivier, Irving Pichel, Juliette Compton, Zasu Pitts, Bonita Granville

What Price Hollywood?
directed by George Cukor; screenplay by Jane Murfin, Ben Markson, Gene Fowler and Rowland Brown, from a story by Adela Rogers St. Johns
with Constance Bennett, Lowell Sherman, Neil Hamilton, Gregory Ratoff, Louise Beavers, Eddie Anderson

Roar of the Dragon
directed by Wesley Ruggles; screenplay by Howard Estabrook, from the novella *A Passage to Hong Kong* by George Kibbe Turner
with Richard Dix, Gwili Andre, Edward Everett Horton, Arline Judge, Zasu Pitts

The Age of Consent
directed by Gregory La Cava; screenplay by Sarah Y. Mason and Francis Cockrell, from the play *Cross Roads* by Martin Flavin
with Dorothy Wilson, Richard Cromwell, Eric Linden, Arline Judge, Aileen Pringle

Bird of Paradise
directed by King Vidor; screenplay by Wells Root, Wanda Tuchock and Leonard Praskins, from the play by Richard Walton Tully
with Dolores Del Rio, Joel McCrea, John Halliday, Creighton Chaney, Richard Gallagher, Bert Roach, Napoleon Pukui

A Bill of Divorcement
directed by George Cukor; screenplay by Howard Estabrook and Harry Wagstaff Gribble, from the play by Clemence Dane
with John Barrymore, Billie Burke, Katharine Hepburn, David Manners, Bramwell Fletcher, Henry Stephenson, Paul Cavanagh

The Conquerors
directed by William Wellman; screenplay by Robert Lord, from a story by Howard Estabrook
with Richard Dix, Ann Harding, Edna May Oliver, Guy Kibbee, Julie Haydon, Donald Cook, Harry Holman, Richard Gallagher

Rockabye
directed by George Cukor; screenplay by Jane Murfin and Kubec Glasmon, from the play by Lucia Bronder

with Constance Bennett, Joel McCrea, Paul Lukas, Walter Pidgeon, Sterling Holloway, Jobyna Howland, Walter Catlett

The Animal Kingdom
directed by Edward H. Griffith; screenplay by Horace Jackson, from the play by Philip Barry
with Leslie Howard, Ann Harding, Myrna Loy, Neil Hamilton, William Gargan, Henry Stephenson, Ilka Chase

The Half-Naked Truth
directed by Gregory La Cava; screenplay by La Cava, Corey Ford, Ben Markson and H. N. Swanson, from the stories of Harry Reichenbach
with Lupe Velez, Lee Tracy, Eugene Pallette, Frank Morgan

Roadhouse Murder
directed by J. Walter Ruben; screenplay by Ruben, adapted by Laszo Bus Fekeete
with Eric Linden, Dorothy Jordan, Bruce Cabot, Phyllis Clare, Roscoe Ates, Purnell Pratt, Gustav von Seyffertitz, David Landau, Roscoe Karns

Young Bride
directed by William Seiter; screenplay by Hugh Stanislaus Stange
with Helen Twelvetrees, Eric Linden, Arline Judge, Roscoe Ates

Little Orphan Annie
directed by John Robertson; screenplay by Wanda Tuchock and Tom McNamara, adapted by Harold Grey and Al Lowenthal
with Mitzi Green, Buster Phelps, May Robson, Kate Lawson, Matt Moore, Sidney Bracey, Edgar Kennedy

Hold 'em Jail
directed by Norman Taurog; screenplay by S. J. Perelman, Walter De Leon, Mark Sandrich and Albert Ray, adapted by Tim Whelan and Lew Lipton
with Bert Wheeler, Robert Woolsey, Edna May Oliver, Roscoe Ates, Edgar Kennedy, Betty Grable, Paul Hurst, Warren Hymer, Robert Armstrong

The Phantom of Crestwood
directed by J. Walter Ruben; screenplay by Bartlett Cormack, from a story by Cormack and Ruben
with Ricardo Cortez, Karen Morley, Anita Louise, Pauline Frederick, H. B. Warner, Sam Hardy, Mary Duncan, Skeets Gallagher

The Penguin Pool Murder
directed by George Archainbaud; screenplay by Willis Goldbeck, from the novel by Stuart Palmer and a story by Lowell Brentano
with Edna May Oliver, James Gleason, Robert Armstrong, Mae Clarke, Donald Cook, Edgar Kennedy, Gustav von Seyffertitz

Hell's Highway
directed by Rowland Brown; screenplay by Brown, Samuel Ornitz and Robert Trasker
with Richard Dix, Tom Brown, Rochelle Hudson, Louise Carter, C. Henry Gordon, Oscar Apfel, Warner Richmond

Renegades of the West
directed by Casey Robinson; screenplay by Albert Shelby La Vino, from a story by Frank Richardson Pierce
with Tom Keene, Betty Furness, Roscoe Ates

Thirteen Women
directed by George Archainbaud; screenplay by Bartlett Cormack, from a story by Tiffany Thayer
with Ricardo Cortez, Irene Dunne, Myrna Loy, Jill Esmond, Florence Eldridge, Kay Johnson, Julie Haydon, Harriet Hegman, Mary Duncan, Peg Entwhistle

Men of America
directed by Ralph Ince; screenplay by Samuel Ornitz and Jack Jungmeyer, from a story by Humphrey Pearson and Henry McCarty
with Bill Boyd, Charles Sale, Dorothy Wilson, Ralph Ince

1933   *Topaze*
directed by Harry d'Abbadie d'Arrast; screenplay by Ben Hecht, from the play by Marcel Pagnol
with John Barrymore, Myrna Loy, Albert Conti, Luis Alberni, Reginald Mason, Jobyna Howland, Jackie Serle, Frank Reicher

The Great Jasper
directed by J. Walter Ruben; screenplay by H. W. Hanemann and Robert Tasker, from the novel by Fulton Oursler
with Richard Dix, Florence Eldridge, Werna Engels, Edna May Oliver, Bruce Cabot

Our Betters
directed by George Cukor; screenplay by Jane Murfin and Harry Wagstaff Gribble, from the play by W. Somerset Maugham
with Constance Bennett, Gilbert Roland, Charles Starrett, Anita Louise, Grant Mitchell, Violet Kemble-Cooper

King Kong
directed by Ernest B. Schoedsack and Merian C. Cooper, screenplay by James Ashmore Creelman and Ruth Rose, from a story by Cooper and Edgar Wallace
with Fay Wray, Robert Armstrong, Bruce Cabot, Frank Reicher, Sam Hardy, Noble Johnson, James Flavin, Steve Clemento, Victor Wong

Christopher Strong
directed by Dorothy Arzner; screenplay by Zoë Akins, from the novel by Gilbert Frankau
with Katharine Hepburn, Colin Clive, Billie Burke, Helen Chandler, Ralph Forbes, Jack LaRue

Sweepings
directed by John Cromwell; screenplay by Lester Cohen, Howard Estabrook and H. W. Hanemann, from the novel by Cohen
with Lionel Barrymore, Allan Dinehart, Eric Linden, William Gargan, Gloria Stuart

The Monkey's Paw
directed by Wesley Ruggles; screenplay by Louise M. Parker and Graham John, from the story by W. W. Jacobs
with C. Aubrey Smith, Ivan Simpson, Louise Carter, Bramwell Fletcher, Betty Lawford

No Other Woman
directed by J. Walter Ruben; screenplay by Ruben, from a story by Eugene Walter and Owen Francis

with Irene Dunne, Charles Bickford, Gwili Andre, Eric Linden, Buster Miles, Leila Bennett, J. Carroll Naish

Little Women
directed by George Cukor; screenplay by Sarah Y. Mason and Victor Heerman, from the novel by Louisa May Alcott
with Katharine Hepburn, Joan Bennett, Paul Lukas, Edna May Oliver, Jean Parker, Frances Dee, Henry Stephenson, Douglass Montgomery, Spring Byington

The Silver Cord
directed by John Cromwell; screenplay by Jane Murfin, from the play by Sidney Howard
with Laura Hope Crews, Irene Dunne, Joel McCrea

MGM

1933   *Dinner at Eight*
directed by George Cukor; screenplay by Herman J. Mankiewicz and Frances Marion, from the play by George S. Kaufman and Edna Ferber
with Marie Dressler, John Barrymore, Wallace Beery, Jean Harlow, Lionel Barrymore, Lee Tracy, Edmund Lowe, Billie Burke, Madge Evans, Jean Hersholt, Karen Morley

Night Flight
directed by Clarence Brown; screenplay by Oliver H. P. Garrett, from the novel by Antoine de Saint-Exupéry
with John Barrymore, Helen Hayes, Clark Gable, Lionel Barrymore, Robert Montgomery, William Gargan, Myrna Loy, C. Henry Gordon

Meet the Baron
directed by Walter Lang; screenplay by Allen Rivkin and P. J. Wolfson, from a story by Herman J. Mankiewicz and Norman Krasna
with Jack Pearl, Jimmy Durante, Zasu Pitts, Ted Healy, Edna May Oliver

Dancing Lady
directed by Robert Z. Leonard; screenplay by Allen Rivkin and P. J. Wolfson, from the novel by James Warner Bellah
with Joan Crawford, Clark Gable, Franchot Tone, May Robson, Fred Astaire, Robert Benchley, Nelson Eddy, Ted Healy, the Three Stooges

1934   *Viva Villa!*
directed by Jack Conway; screenplay by Ben Hecht, from the book by Edgcumb Pinchon and O. B. Stade
with Wallace Beery, Leo Carrillo, Fay Wray, Donald Cook, Stuart Erwin, George E. Stone, Henry B. Walthall, Joseph Schildkraut, Katherine DeMille

Manhattan Melodrama
directed by W. S. Van Dyke; screenplay by Oliver H. P. Garrett and Joseph L. Mankiewicz, from a story by Arthur Caesar
with Clark Gable, William Powell, Myrna Loy, Leo Carrillo, Nat Pendleton, George Sidney, Isabel Jewell, Muriel Evans, Thomas Jackson, Noel Madison, Mickey Rooney

1935   *David Copperfield*
directed by George Cukor; screenplay by Howard Estabrook and Hugh Walpole, from the novel by Charles Dickens

with Freddie Bartholomew, W. C. Fields, Lionel Barrymore, Maureen O'Sullivan, Madge Evans, Edna May Oliver, Lewis Stone, Frank Lawton, Elizabeth Allan, Roland Young, Basil Rathbone, Elsa Lanchester, Jean Cadell, Jessie Ralph, Lennox Pawle, Violet Kemble-Cooper, Una O'Connor, Hugh Williams

Vanessa: Her Love Story
directed by William K. Howard; screenplay by Hugh Walpole and Lenore Coffee, from the novel by Walpole
with Helen Hayes, Robert Montgomery, Otto Kruger, May Robson, Lewis Stone

Reckless
directed by Victor Fleming; screenplay by P. J. Wolfson, from a story by Oliver Jeffries (DOS)
with Jean Harlow, William Powell, Franchot Tone, May Robson, Ted Healy, Nat Pendleton, Rosalind Russell, Henry Stephenson

Anna Karenina
directed by Clarence Brown; screenplay by Clemence Dane and Salka Viertel, from the novel by Leo Tolstoy
with Greta Garbo, Fredric March, Basil Rathbone, Freddie Bartholomew, Maureen O'Sullivan, May Robson, Reginald Owen, Reginald Denny, Phoebe Foster, Gyles Isham

A Tale of Two Cities
directed by Jack Conway; screenplay by W. P. Lipscomb and S. N. Behrman, from the novel by Charles Dickens
with Ronald Colman, Elizabeth Allan, Edna May Oliver, Reginald Owen, Basil Rathbone, Blanche Yurka, Henry B. Walthall, Donald Woods

SELZNICK INTERNATIONAL PICTURES

1936   *Little Lord Fauntleroy* (SIP/United Artists)
directed by John Cromwell; screenplay by Hugh Walpole, from the novel by Frances Hodgson Burnett
with Freddie Bartholomew, C. Aubrey Smith, Dolores Costello, Henry Stephenson, Guy Kibbee, Mickey Rooney, Eric Alden, Jackie Searl, Reginald Barlow, Ivan Simpson, E. E. Clive, Constance Collier, Una O'Connor, May Beatty, Joan Standing, Jessie Ralph, Lionel Belmore

The Garden of Allah (SIP/United Artists)
directed by Richard Boleslavsky; screenplay by W. P. Lipscomb and Lynn Riggs, from the novel by Robert Hichens
with Marlene Dietrich, Charles Boyer, Basil Rathbone, C. Aubrey Smith, Tilly Losch, Joseph Schildkraut, John Carradine, Alan Marshal, Lucille Watson, Henry Brandon

1937   *A Star is Born* (SIP/United Artists)
directed by William Wellman; screenplay by Dorothy Parker, Alan Campbell and Robert Carson, from a story by Wellman and Carson
with Janet Gaynor, Fredric March, Adolphe Menjou, May Robson, Andy Devine, Lionel Stander, Elizabeth Jenns, Edgar Kennedy, Owen Moore

The Prisoner of Zenda (SIP/United Artists)
directed by John Cromwell; screenplay by John L. Balderston, adapted by Wells Root from the novel by Anthony Hope

with Ronald Colman, Madeleine Carroll, Douglas Fairbanks, Jr., Mary Astor, C. Aubrey Smith, Raymond Massey, David Niven, Eleanor Wesselhoeft, Byron Foulger, Montagu Love

Nothing Sacred (SIP/United Artists)
directed by William Wellman; screenplay by Ben Hecht, from the short story by James H. Street
with Fredric March, Carole Lombard, Charles Winninger, Walter Connolly, Sig Rumann, Frank Fay, Maxie Rosenbloom, Aileen Pringle, Margaret Hamilton, Hedda Hopper, John Qualen, Hattie McDaniel

1938   *The Adventures of Tom Sawyer* (SIP/United Artists)
directed by Norman Taurog; screenplay by John V. A. Weaver, from the novel by Mark Twain
with Tommy Kelly, May Robson, Jackie Moran, Walter Brennan, Victor Jory, Marcia Mae Jones, Victor Kilian, Nana Bryant, Ann Gillis, Mickey Rentschler, Cora Sue Collins, Charles Richman, Spring Byington, Margaret Hamilton

The Young in Heart (SIP/United Artists)
directed by Richard Wallace; screenplay by Paul Osborn and Charles Bennett, from the novel *The Gay Banditti* by I. A. R. Wylie
with Janet Gaynor, Douglas Fairbanks, Jr., Paulette Goddard, Roland Young, Billie Burke, Richard Carlson, Minnie Dupree

1939   *Made for Each Other* (SIP/United Artists)
directed by John Cromwell; screenplay by Jo Swerling
with Carole Lombard, James Stewart, Charles Coburn, Lucille Watson, Eddie Quinlan, Alma Kruger, Ruth Weston, Donald Briggs, Harry Davenport, Esther Dale, Russell Hopton, Ward Bond, Olin Howland, Louise Beavers

Intermezzo: A Love Story (SIP/United Artists)
directed by Gregory Ratoff; screenplay by George O'Neil, from the original Swedish film by Gosta Stevens and Gustaf Molander
with Leslie Howard, Ingrid Bergman, Edna Best, John Halliday, Cecil Kellaway, Enid Bennett, Ann Todd, Douglas Scott

Gone With the Wind (SIP/MGM)
directed by Victor Fleming; screenplay by Sidney Howard, from the novel by Margaret Mitchell
with Clark Gable, Vivien Leigh, Leslie Howard, Olivia de Havilland, Hattie McDaniel, Butterfly McQueen, Thomas Mitchell, Victor Jory, Ann Rutherford, Evelyn Keyes, Barbara O'Neil, Alicia Rhett, Ona Munson, Jane Darwell, Oscar Polk, Laura Hope Crews, Rand Brooks, Mary Anderson, George Reeves, Fred Crane, Cammie King, Violet Kemble-Cooper, Ward Bond

1940   *Rebecca* (SIP/United Artists)
directed by Alfred Hitchcock; screenplay by Robert E. Sherwood and Joan Harrison, from the novel by Daphne du Maurier
with Laurence Olivier, Joan Fontaine, Judith Anderson, George Sanders, Nigel Bruce, Reginald Denny, C. Aubrey Smith, Gladys Cooper, Florence Bates, Melville Cooper, Leo G. Carroll, Leonard Carey, Lumsden Hare, Edward Fielding, Philip Winter, Forrester Harvey

1944 *Since You Went Away* (SIP/United Artists)
directed by John Cromwell; screenplay by D.O.S., from the book by Margaret Buell Wilder
with Claudette Colbert, Jennifer Jones, Joseph Cotten, Shirley Temple, Monty Woolley, Lionel Barrymore, Robert Walker, Hattie McDaniel, Agnes Moore-head, Alla Nazimova, Guy Madison

I'll Be Seeing You (SIP/United Artists)
produced by Dore Schary; directed by William Dieterle; screenplay by Marion Parsonnet, from the novel *Double Furlough* by Charles Martin
with Ginger Rogers, Joseph Cotten, Shirley Temple, Spring Byington, Tom Tully, Chil Wills, John Derek

1945 *Spellbound* (SIP/United Artists)
directed by Alfred Hitchcock; screenplay by Ben Hecht, from the novel *The House of Doctor Edwardes* by Francis Beeding
with Gregory Peck, Ingrid Bergman, Michael Chekhov, Leo G. Carroll, Rhonda Fleming, Jean Acker, Donald Curtiss, John Emery, Norman Lloyd, Steven Geray, Paul Harvey, Erskine Sanford, Victor Kilian, Wallace Ford, Regis Toomey

1946 *Duel in the Sun* (SRO)
directed by King Vidor; screenplay by D.O.S., from the adaptation by Oliver H. P. Garrett of the novel by Niven Busch
with Gregory Peck, Jennifer Jones, Joseph Cotten, Lionel Barrymore, Lillian Gish, Charles Bickford, Butterfly McQueen, Walter Huston, Herbert Marshall, Tilly Losch, Joan Tetzel, Harry Carey, Otto Kruger

1947 *The Paradine Case* (SRO)
directed by Alfred Hitchcock; screenplay by D.O.S., from the adaptation by Alma Reville and James Bridie of the novel by Robert Hichens
with Gregory Peck, Valli, Ann Todd, Louis Jourdan, Charles Laughton, Ethel Barrymore, Charles Coburn, Joan Tetzel, Leo G. Carroll, Isobel Elsom

1948 *Portrait of Jennie* (SRO)
directed by William Dieterle; screenplay by Paul Osborn and Peter Berneis, from the adaptation by Leonardo Bercovici of the novel by Robert Nathan
with Jennifer Jones, Joseph Cotten, Ethel Barrymore, Lillian Gish, Cecil Kellaway, David Wayne, Albert Sharpe, Florence Bates, Maude Simmons, Felix Bressart, Henry Hull, Clem Bevans, Maude Simmons

EUROPE, ETC.

1949 *The Third Man* (London Films/SRO)
produced by Alexander Korda and D.O.S.; directed by Carol Reed; screenplay by Graham Greene
with Joseph Cotten, Orson Welles, Valli, Trevor Howard, Bernard Lee, Ernest Deutsch, Erich Ponto, Sigfried Breuer, Wilfred Hyde-White, Paul Hoerbiger, Hedwig Bleibtreu, Geoffrey Keen
(not released in the U.S. until 1950, with small changes—e.g., the original narration is by Carol Reed, but in the American release it is done by Joseph Cotten)

1950 *Gone to Earth* (London Films/Vanguard)
presented by Alexander Korda and D.O.S.; produced by D.O.S.; directed and

screenplay by Michael Powell and Emeric Pressburger, from the novel by Mary Webb

with Jennifer Jones, David Farrar, Cyril Cusack, Sybil Thorndike, Edward Chapman, Esmond Knight, Hugh Griffith, George Cole, Beatrice Varley, Frances Clare (*Gone to Earth* ran 110 minutes; the U.S. version, reedited and with some reshooting, was released by RKO in 1952, at 82 minutes as *The Wild Heart*)

1954   *Indiscretion of an American Wife* (Columbia)
produced by Vittorio De Sica and D.O.S.; directed by De Sica; screenplay by Cesare Zavattini, Luigi Chiarini and Giorgio Prosperi, with Truman Capote (dialogue)
with Jennifer Jones, Montgomery Clift, Gino Cervi, Dick Beymer
(released in the U.S. at 63 minutes; the Italian version, *Stazione Termini*, ran 85 minutes)

"Light's Diamond Jubilee"
directed by King Vidor, Norman Taurog, Roy Rowland, Christian Nyby and William Wellman; written by Ben Hecht, John Steinbeck, Arthur Gordon, Max Schulman and Burton Benjamin
with Joseph Cotten, Judith Anderson, David Niven, Lauren Bacall, Kim Novak, Guy Madison, Walter Brennan, Helen Hayes, George Gobel, Dorothy Dandridge, Eddie Fisher, Robert Benchley, Erin O'Brien Moore, Harry Morgan, Debbie Reynolds and President Dwight D. Eisenhower

1957   *A Farewell to Arms* (Twentieth Century-Fox)
directed by Charles Vidor; screenplay by Ben Hecht, from the novel by Ernest Hemingway and the play by Laurence Stallings
with Rock Hudson, Jennifer Jones, Vittorio De Sica, Alberto Sordi, Kurt Kasznar, Mercedes McCambridge, Oscar Homolka, Elaine Stritch

JENNIFER JONES (INCLUDES THE FILMS ON WHICH D.O.S. HAD, OR TRIED TO HAVE, A LARGE INFLUENCE)

1943   *The Song of Bernadette* (Twentieth Century-Fox)
produced by William Perlberg; directed by Henry King; screenplay by George Seaton, from the novel by Franz Werfel
with Jennifer Jones, William Eythe, Charles Bickford, Vincent Price, Lee J. Cobb, Gladys Cooper, Anne Revere, Roman Bohnen, Mary Anderson, Patricia Morison, Edith Barrett, Blanche Yurka, Marcel Dalio, Jerome Cowan, Tala Birell, Ian Wolfe, Dickie Moore, Linda Darnell

1945   *Love Letters* (Paramount)
produced by Hal Wallis; directed by William Dieterle; screenplay by Ayn Rand, from the novel by Chris Massie
with Jennifer Jones, Joseph Cotten, Ann Richards, Anita Louise, Cecil Kellaway, Gladys Cooper, Byron Barr, Robert Sully, Reginald Denny, Ernest Cossart, James Millican, Lumsden Hare

1946   *Cluny Brown* (Twentieth Century-Fox)
produced and directed by Ernst Lubitsch; written by Samuel Hoffenstein and Elizabeth Reinhardt, from the novel by Margery Sharp
with Jennifer Jones, Charles Boyer, Peter Lawford, Helen Walker, Reginald

Gardiner, Reginald Owen, C. Aubrey Smith, Richard Haydn, Sara Allgood, Florence Bates, Una O'Connor

1949   *We Were Strangers* (Columbia)
produced by Sam Spiegel; directed by John Huston; screenplay by Huston and Peter Viertel
with Jennifer Jones, John Garfield, Pedro Armendariz, Gilbert Roland, Jose Perez, Morris Ankrum, Tito Renaldo, Paul Monte, Leonard Strong, Roberta Haynes, Lelia Goldoni

Madame Bovary (MGM)
produced by Pandro S. Berman; directed by Vincente Minnelli; screenplay by Robert Ardrey, from the novel by Gustave Flaubert
with Jennifer Jones, Van Heflin, Louis Jourdan, James Mason, Christopher Kent, Gladys Cooper, Gene Lockhart, Frank Allenby, John Abbott, Harry Morgan, George Zucco, Ellen Corby, Eduard Franz, Paul Cavanagh

1952   *Carrie* (Paramount)
produced and directed by William Wyler; screenplay by Ruth and Augustus Goetz, from the novel by Theodore Dreiser
with Jennifer Jones, Laurence Olivier, Eddie Albert, Miriam Hopkins, Basil Ruysdael, Ray Teal, Barry Kelley, Sara Berner, William Regnolds, Mary Murphy, Jacqueline DeWitt, Harry Hayden, Walter Baldwin, Dorothy Adams, Royal Dano, James Flavin, Margaret Field

Ruby Gentry (Twentieth Century-Fox)
produced by Joseph Bernhard and King Vidor; directed by Vidor; screenplay by Sylvia Richards, from a story by Arthur Fitz-Richard
with Jennifer Jones, Charlton Heston, Karl Malden, Tom Tully, Bernard Phillips, James Anderson, Josephine Hutchinson, Phyllis Avery, Herbert Heyes, Myra Marsh, Charles Cane, Sam Flint, Frank Wilcox

1954   *Beat the Devil* (Santana-Romulus/United Artists)
produced by the Woolf Brothers and John Huston; directed by Huston; screenplay by Truman Capote and Huston, from the novel by James Helvick
with Jennifer Jones, Humphrey Bogart, Gina Lollobrigida, Robert Morley, Peter Lorre, Edward Underdown, Ivor Barnard, Bernard Lee

1962   *Tender is the Night* (Twentieth Century-Fox)
produced by Henry T. Weinstein; directed by Henry King; screenplay by Ivan Moffat, from the novel by F. Scott Fitzgerald
with Jennifer Jones, Jason Robards, Jr., Joan Fontaine, Tom Ewell, Cesare Danova, Jill St. John, Paul Lukas, Bea Benaderet, Charles Fredericks, Sanford Meisner, Carole Mathews, Alan Napier

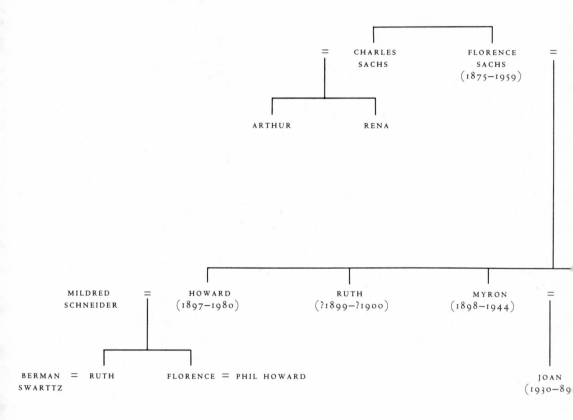

FAMILY TREE: SELZNICKS AND MAYERS

(Note: This tree is by no means complete. It does not include the second and third marriages of Joseph Seleznik.)

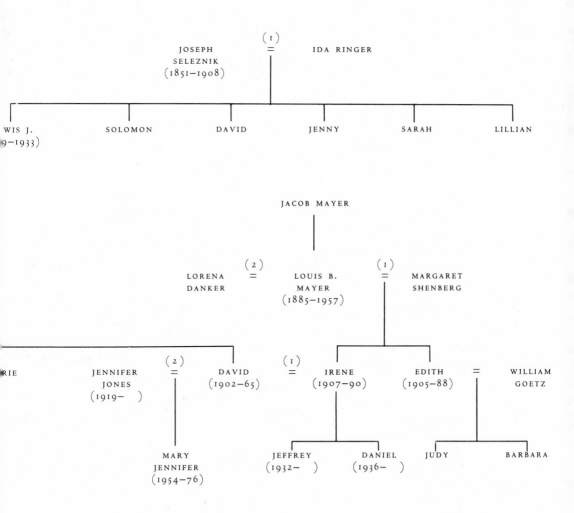

JOSEPH
SELEZNIK
(1851–1908)

(1)
=

IDA RINGER

WIS J.
9–1933)

SOLOMON

DAVID

JENNY

SARAH

LILLIAN

JACOB MAYER

LORENA
DANKER

(2)
=

LOUIS B.
MAYER
(1885–1957)

(1)
=

MARGARET
SHENBERG

RIE

JENNIFER
JONES
(1919–   )

(2)
=

DAVID
(1902–65)

(1)
=

IRENE
(1907–90)

EDITH
(1905–88)

=

WILLIAM
GOETZ

MARY
JENNIFER
(1954–76)

JEFFREY
(1932–   )

DANIEL
(1936–   )

JUDY

BARBARA

INDEX

PHOTOGRAPHIC CREDITS

The author and publisher are grateful to the following for providing photographs and for giving permission for them to be printed:

Selznick Properties and the David O. Selznick Archive, Harry Ransom Humanities Research Center, University of Texas at Austin, for pictures on pages 1, 7, 9, 10, 18, 26, 47, 55, 84, 105, 152, 193, 195, 204, 217, 259, 280, 300, 351, 355, 397, 399, 404, 411, 412, 431, 451, 452, 462, 465, 468, 489, 525, 531, 534, 536, 538, 541, 547, 548, 560, 562, 583, 604, 616, 626, 631, 687
Museum of Modern Art Film Stills Collection, 30, 61, 86, 126, 136, 183, 200, 236, 333, 393, 428, 443, 484, 522
Lewis Jeffrey Selznick, 68, 74, 78, 111, 138, 144, 171, 180, 186, 232, 261, 273, 286, 308, 325, 406, 514, 528, 540, 634, 698
Clarence Sinclair Bull, 109, 130
Yvette Curran, 327, 686
Bettmann Archive, 644
Judy Cameron, 318
Herbert Gehr and Time-Life, ii
Campbell Studios, New York, 28
Al Hirschfeld—drawing reproduced by special arrangement with Hirschfeld's exclusive representative, the Margo Feiden Galleries Ltd New York © Al Hirschfeld, 37
Abbe, 42
Ed Sweeney of Van Rossem Studio, 166
Louise Dahl-Wolfe, 261
Dallinger Photo of Hollywood, 337
Rivkin Studio, Tulsa, 365
Dick MacQuiddy, 370
Johnny Florea, 388
Dr. Dorothy Colodny, 422
Peter A. Juley & Son, New York, 497
Estudios Camara, Mexico City, 567
Regal Photos, Brooklyn, 578
La Cineteca del Friuli, 623
Ken Heyman, 651

Henri Cartier–Bresson and Magnum Picture Agency, 690
Jarry Lang, 698
Peter Stackpole and Time-Life, 344
Sotheby's, New York, 494

A NOTE ABOUT THE AUTHOR

David Thomson was born in London, has taught film studies at Dartmouth College, and now lives in San Francisco. He is the author of several other books, including the acclaimed *A Biographical Dictionary of Film*, the novels *Silver Light* and *Suspects*, and *Warren Beatty and Desert Eyes*. He also wrote the screenplay for the documentary film *The Making of a Legend: Gone With the Wind*.

A NOTE ON THE TYPE

The text of this book was set in a digitized version of Centaur, the only type face designed by Bruce Rogers, the well-known American book designer. A celebrated penman, Rogers based his design on the roman face cut by Nicolas Jensen in 1470 for his Eusebius. Jensen's roman surpassed all of its forerunners and even today, in modern recuttings, remains one of the most popular and attractive of all type faces.

Composed by American–Stratford Graphic Services, Inc., Brattleboro, Vermont

Printed and bound by Halliday Lithographers, Inc., West Hanover, Massachusetts

Designed by Iris Weinstein

WESTERN UNION

1930 OCT 16 PM 4 16

S178 14=HOLLYWOOD CALIF 16 409P

MRS DAVID SELZNICK=

601 NORTH CAMDEN DRIVE BEVERLYHILLS CALIF=

I JUST GOT A HAIR CUT AND YOUVE NO IDEA HOW HANDSOME I LOOK=

DAVID.

SELZNICK INTERNAT

CULVER CITY

INTER

John Hay Whitney

Afterwards.

Irene,

Strange, this vacuum he has left.
Is not love that has been lost,
tenderness, nor even paternal protection.
Her it is as though we had
lived fearfully in the shadow
of a magnificent, forbidding Vesuvius,
which is now sudde...
more the little ark...
its slopes, no m...
lava... You, abov...
That I never ate...
sured the eruptions. Yet I...
stand in awe. And I can...
that the world this day...
different than all the days of...
our lives before....

for the unsung
heroine — and victim —
of "Gone With the Wind"
with the devotion
of her aged husband.

heroine — and victim —
of "Gone With the Wind"
with the devotion
of her aged husband.

Darling

the mom...
miserable
the first
and I s...

of money —
the loss of
upset me :
I have brok...
to you, and
the torture...
I feel. At
first time,
... of remo...
face myse...

share my opi...
I don't thin...
kily friendl...
other thing...
ld have tru...

... All that's inv...
ere it my picture
but since it isn'
n't be difficult...

... the following:

it seems...
d fortunat...
e the char...
worse, sig...
here are...

dition of...

...ubly with the cr...
t we just hadn't...
uth which you will recall is t...
e Valli was even considered fo...

...izing of Bergman...
...er as a consequence of the use...

Thus, Jennifer would be the innocent
error on our parts; and since is...

Dr. Burlingame
Hartford Retreat
Hartford, Connecticut

Dear Dr. Burlingame:

... sorry that I missed